CLARENDON L

CLARENDON LAW SERIES

Introduction to Roman Law
By BARRY NICHOLAS

Natural Law and Natural Rights
By JOHN G. FINNIS

Public Law and Democracy
By P. P. CRAIG

Precedent in English Law (4th edition)
By SIR RUPERT CROSS AND J. W. HARRIS

Playing by the Rules
By FREDERICK SCHAUER

Legal Reasoning and Legal Theory
By NEIL MACCORMICK

The Concept of Law (2nd edition)
By H. L. A. HART

An Introduction to Constitutional Law
By ERIC BARENDT

Discrimination Law
By SANDRA FREDMAN

The Conflict of Laws
By ADRIAN BRIGGS

The Law of Property (3rd edition)
By F. H. LAWSON AND BERNARD RUDDEN

Introduction to Company Law
By PAUL I. DAVIES

Personal Property Law (3rd edition)
By MICHAEL BRIDGE

An Introduction to the Law of Trusts
By SIMON GARDNER

Employment Law
By HUGH COLLINS

Public Law
By ADAM TOMKINS

Contract Theory
By STEPHEN A. SMITH

Administrative Law (4th edition)
By PETER CANE

Criminal Justice
By LUCIA ZEDNER

An Introduction to Family Law (2nd edition)
By GILLIAN DOUGLAS

Unjust Enrichment (2nd edition)
By PETER BIRKS

Atiyah's Introduction to Contract Law (6th edition)
By STEPHEN A. SMITH

Equity (2nd edition)
By SARAH WORTHINGTON

An Introduction to Tort Law (2nd edition)
By TONY WEIR

Land Law
By ELIZABETH COOKE

Law in Modern Society
By D.J. GALLIGAN

PHILOSOPHY OF PRIVATE LAW

WILLIAM LUCY

School of Law, University of Manchester

OXFORD
UNIVERSITY PRESS

Great Clarendon Street, Oxford OX2 6DP

Oxford University Press is a department of the University of Oxford.
It furthers the University's objective of excellence in research, scholarship,
and education by publishing worldwide in

Oxford New York

Auckland Cape Town Dar es Salaam Hong Kong Karachi
Kuala Lumpur Madrid Melbourne Mexico City Nairobi
New Delhi Shanghai Taipei Toronto

With offices in

Argentina Austria Brazil Chile Czech Republic France Greece
Guatemala Hungary Italy Japan Poland Portugal Singapore
South Korea Switzerland Thailand Turkey Ukraine Vietnam

Oxford is a registered trade mark of Oxford University Press
in the UK and in certain other countries

Published in the United States
by Oxford University Press Inc., New York

First published 2007

British Library Cataloguing in Publication Data
Data available

Library of Congress Cataloging in Publication Data
Data available

Typeset in Ehrhardt
by RefineCatch Limited, Bungay, Suffolk
Printed in Great Britain
on acid-free paper by
Biddles Ltd., King's Lynn, Norfolk

ISBN 978–0–19–870068–5 0–19–870068–7

1 3 5 7 9 10 8 6 4 2

Acknowledgements

While there are sure to be missteps and slips in what follows, it is a pleasure to thank those who have tried (and likely failed) to save me from particularly egregious errors. Roger Brownsword, Peter Cane, Eleanor Curran, James Davey, Neil Duxbury, Tony Honoré, Gerry Johnstone, Richard Mullender, Ken Oliphant, Mark Reiff, Jane Stapleton and Stuart Toddington have all read portions of the book and I'm grateful for their feedback and corrections. Rather than thank these kind souls for each and every correction and suggestion which I've incorporated in the text I do it here, where it should be done: up front. I know they will recognize their suggestions and improvements when they see them. Portions of the book were also presented as papers at a number of institutions and conferences. I must thank all who sat through such presentations for both their patience and their thoughts, but particularly those at the Universities of Keele and Leicester and the audiences at the SLS Annual Conference at Strathclyde in 2005 and the Australian Legal and Social Philosophy Conference in Auckland in 2006. Thanks are also owed to Melanie Jackson of OUP for her efficient and supportive work.

I owe a debt of gratitude to three fine institutions. I had the pleasure to teach a course on philosophy of private law at the Law Faculty at McGill University in winter 2005 and I'm grateful for the help I received from everyone there. However, I owe specific thanks to the Dean, Nicholas Kasirer and Stephen Smith for their hospitality and help. Also, two of my students at McGill – Lucas Stanczyk and Sara Nadéau-Seguin – were particularly helpful and diligent; they helped to make teaching, thinking and writing the kind of co-operative endeavour it should always be. Some of the chapters were completed during my brief stay at Cardiff Law School and I'm grateful to former colleagues there and the institution for support. Just about all of the chapters of this book were either initiated, worked on, or completed in the libraries of the University of Manchester, which have rarely let me down over twenty years of use. Since I am now also employed by that University, I can spend even more time rummaging around and troubling the always helpful library staff.

Finally, some folks – friends, family and the zealots of L4 – who didn't help with this book in any way, save to remind me that there are, of course, many, many things more important than work. For that they deserve thanks, especially Wendy, the world's most reluctant cyclist.

Contents

I

Introduction

This book is about philosophy of private law: it aims to provide an overview of the principal issues that constitute the subject. At numerous points, however, it intervenes in arguments about some of those issues, taking up the cudgels in specific disputes. The book therefore aims, in addition, to be an instance of philosophy of private law. Given these two aims, two questions require immediate attention: what is private law and what is philosophy? These questions seem difficult enough to answer in isolation since a vast literature, developed over centuries, generates diverse answers to each. When the questions are conjoined and we ask both 'what is philosophy of private law?' and 'why philosophize about private law?', the job of finding plausible answers appears even more awkward. Fortunately, our task here is not that of generating exhaustive and compelling answers to each question. Rather, we concentrate upon the question about the nature of Anglo-American private law, consider in the main only contemporary, legal-philosophical efforts to answer it, and highlight some of the distinctive features and problems those answers generate. Doing this does not mean that questions about the nature of philosophy and about the impulse toward philosophical reflection in private law can be ignored altogether. But it does mean that we can afford to be brief with these issues while, hopefully, not underestimating their importance and complexity. This chapter aims to situate the question about the nature of private law and the philosophical responses to it by doing two things. First, and somewhat predictably, by attempting to define key terms. To that end, the section below clarifies what is meant by 'philosophy' while the second section (p.12) elucidates what is meant by 'private law'. The third section on p.21 sketches the contours of contemporary philosophy of private law and the fourth (p.44) sketches the structure of the book. Second, the attempt to define key terms and situate our question is wide-ranging, at some points going considerably beyond the disciplinary boundaries of 'philosophy' and 'private law'.

PHILOSOPHY

At least two tendencies or 'styles' dominated philosophy during much of the twentieth century and still exercise a grip today. The precise contours and conditions of each, and their alleged manifold incompatibilities, are much disputed. Sometimes the two tendencies are described geographically, in terms of a divide between Anglo-American and European (or Continental) traditions. A problem with this demarcation is that the philosophers included in each camp do not always have conveniently appropriate nationalities, there being, for example, German philosophers among the leading lights of the Anglo-American strand, and British and North American philosophers with distinctively 'European' interests. On other occasions a slightly more promising attempt is made to capture the divide in terms of method or style. On one side stands the analytical tradition, marked by a preoccupation with language and a commitment to the philosophical 'analysis' of words, concepts and propositions. On the other side is the Continental tradition in which a number of different but ostensibly comprehensive philosophical doctrines – usually said to begin with phenomenology, include both Marxism and existentialism and run up to present-day deconstruction and critical theory – have dominated.[1] The different philosophical schemas invoked in this tradition are nevertheless in some sense similar and provide a vivid contrast with analytical philosophy's apparently mundane concern with language and the meaning and use of concepts. This is because the schemas invoked usually either embody a bold view of the nature of the human condition or an ambitious account of the conditions under which knowledge, reality and experience are possible, and derive from them a range of philosophical problems and solutions.[2] By contrast, such apparently grand philosophical schemas are almost completely absent from analytical philosophy, which instead abounds with discussions of particular concepts, their meaning and limits. However significant this distinction might be, it

[1] Helpful guides to this philosophical terrain include T. Baldwin, *Contemporary Philosophy* (Oxford: Clarendon Press, 2001), H.-J. Glock (ed.), *The Rise of Analytic Philosophy* (Oxford: Blackwell, 1997), R. Bubner, *Modern German Philosophy* (Cambridge: Cambridge University Press, 1981) and V. Descombes, *Modern French Philosophy* (Cambridge: Cambridge University Press, 1980).

[2] Schemas of both kinds are embodied in much of the most notable French and German philosophy of the last century: see, for example, G. Gutting, *French Philosophy in the Twentieth Century* (Cambridge: Cambridge University Press, 2001), Part II; Bubner, ch. 1; and P. Gorner, *Twentieth Century German Philosophy* (Oxford: Clarendon Press, 2000), chs 2–5.

cannot properly be captured by the 'Continental' geographical modifier, since it is as objectionable here as in the previous categorization. Perhaps the safest way to proceed is to distinguish analytical and non-analytical traditions, recognizing that most proponents of the former were and are English-speaking philosophers while most proponents of the latter were and are not, and to affirm that what divides them is a commitment to, or eschewal of, philosophical schemas.

The predominant style of philosophy brought to bear upon Anglo-American private law in the last three or so decades is analytical. More specifically, it derives from that strand of analytical philosophy, dominant from the late 1940s until the late 1960s, that aimed to resolve traditional philosophical problems and to break new philosophical terrain by attending to ordinary language. These 'linguistic' or 'ordinary language' philosophers assumed that many standard philosophical problems arose from philosophers' lack of attention to the way in which the words and concepts in question were used in everyday speech.[3] The distinctions and nuances of everyday speech, it was held, gave clues as to the source of philosophical difficulty and illuminated a path to reliable common sense judgments. The latter were certainly not regarded with suspicion by philosophers of this stripe: they did not, for example, see common sense as so much misleading or ideological surface froth that philosophers had to either penetrate or set aside. Rather, they often held, once common sense and the distinctions and nuances of everyday speech which provided access to it were heeded, that many of the problems that had dogged philosophy for centuries would be 'dissolved'. So, for example, J. L. Austin sought to throw light on age-old philosophical problems like how knowledge of other minds is possible, and the dispute between free will and determinism, by reference to ordinary language. His conclusion on the latter dispute was typical: '[d]eterminism, whatever it may be, may yet be the case, but at least it appears not consistent with what we ordinarily say and think'.[4]

This deflationary task was conjoined with a positive programme that had at least two aspects. One claimed to yield philosophical advances by also attending to ordinary language, for a 'sharpened awareness of words [may] . . . sharpen our perception of the phenomena'.[5] For Austin, a

[3] Two classic contributions to the genre are J. L. Austin, *Philosophical Papers* (Oxford: Clarendon Press, 1961) and L. Wittgenstein, *Philosophical Investigations* (Oxford: Blackwell, 1958).

[4] *Philosophical Papers*, p. 179.

[5] *Philosophical Papers*, note 3, p. 130 (cited approvingly but laxly in H. L. A. Hart, *The Concept of Law* (Oxford: Clarendon Press, 2nd edn, 1994) p. v.).

sharpened awareness of words made possible a better appreciation of what they were used to do, illustrating some phenomena that philosophers had traditionally missed.[6] One such was that some utterances function in neither only a purely descriptive way nor are solely nonsense, but instead 'do' something, and Austin's account of what they can do was undoubtedly philosophically original and significant. For H. L. A. Hart, a heightened awareness of words allowed a better understanding of the idea of obligation in law than previous jurists, including both Jeremy Bentham and John Austin, had offered. Indeed, an appreciation of how the language of obligation was used showed that two quite different notions – 'being obliged' and 'having an obligation' – were in play and that only the latter properly characterizes the claim law makes upon us.[7] The second aspect of the positive programme is plain from the fact that these philosophers, for all their emphasis upon the philosophical power and resources of ordinary language, were not beyond recommending changes or additions to that language. This was because, occasionally, a sharpened awareness of words actually dulled our perception of phenomena and new words or meanings were required for elucidation.[8]

Overall, the common sense tone of ordinary language philosophy and the clarity and briskness of the writing and thinking of its principal proponents added to its intuitive appeal, which derived from an apparently simple truth. It is that our access to and knowledge of the world was only possible through language and that the well-entrenched distinctions and discriminations of that language have some presumptive epistemological significance. That being so, it seems obviously correct for language to become the primary object of philosophical interest and easy to move from that position to one which concentrated only upon *ordinary* language. Furthermore, it seems reasonable to speculate that the tone, clarity and intuitive appeal of ordinary language philosophy, combined with the fact that it had an almost completely unrestricted view of its subject matter, explain its influence in disciplines – like law and sociology – often beyond the philosophical pale.[9]

[6] J. L Austin, *How to do Things with Words* (Cambridge, Mass.: Harvard University Press, 2nd edn, 1975), p. 3.

[7] *The Concept of Law*, note 5, pp. 82–91.

[8] See Austin, note 6, lecture XII, for a vivid illustration. The claim that this strand of analytical philosophy had no positive programme is therefore an exaggeration, but nevertheless common: an example, by no means unique, is E. Gellner, *Words and Things* (London: Victor Gollancz, 1959), p. 19.

[9] See H. L. A. Hart, *Essays in Jurisprudence and Philosophy* (Oxford: Clarendon Press, 1983), p. 3.

Since the ordinary language strand of analytical philosophy served as the intellectual milieu into which contemporary philosophy of private law was born, much of the latter is therefore marked by close attention to the meaning and use of key words and concepts in both private law and ordinary language. The analysis of the meaning of ideas like 'responsibility', 'causation', 'conduct', 'wrongfulness', 'justice' and many more is therefore the fulcrum of contemporary philosophy of private law and, furthermore, the analyses offered are often entirely unprogrammatic. This does not mean that the work done is chaotic, although bad examples of it might be, but that it rarely if ever brings to bear upon private law a comprehensive philosophical schema, such as those supposedly embraced by generations of non-analytical philosophers. Rather, the only schema most often in play in philosophy of private law is our non-philosophical, non-legal common sense, against which not only jurists' but also courts' analyses and arguments are usually tested. Since the actual lack of and generalized suspicion towards comprehensive philosophical schemas is a hallmark of analytical philosophy in general, and was certainly a hallmark of its ordinary language branch, it is unsurprising to find it carried through into contemporary philosophy of private law.[10] Hence private law is rarely approached by contemporary philosophers and jurists through the lens of phenomenology, existentialism, or deconstruction, although some self-consciously critical jurists have sought to invoke such 'fancy theory'.[11]

Talk about different styles and strands of philosophy does not, of course, illuminate the core of the philosophical task. And, while proponents of different philosophical styles will undoubtedly approach their task differently, there is probably a single recognizable task in which all are engaged. At its simplest, it can be characterized as the attempt to

[10] There are, however, some indications that North American jurists are keen to hitch their wagon to burgeoning philosophical schemas. One, often dubbed 'naturalism', is ably discussed in B. Leiter, 'Naturalism and Naturalised Jurisprudence', ch. 4 of B. Bix (ed.), *Analyzing Law* (Oxford: Clarendon Press, 1998). Another, philosophical pragmatism, is invoked by J. Coleman: see his *The Practice of Principle* (Oxford: Clarendon Press, 2001). Both schemas are far more modest than those that mark out much non-analytical philosophy but might, if they remove any presumptive weight from judgments of common sense and ordinary language, make a difference to the way in which philosophy of private law is done.

[11] D. Kennedy, 'Distributive and Paternalist Motives in Contract and Tort Law, with Special Reference to Compulsory Terms and Unequal Bargaining Power' (1982) 41 *Maryland L R* 563–658, p. 564. This self-deprecatory language should not detract from the fact that the invocation of such bodies of thought can challenge the complacence that often accompanies a dominant intellectual framework.

become reflective about some aspect of human life or the human condition. As between analytical and non-analytical philosophers, this shared task manifests itself in a number of different ways, with various starting points and end products. The impetus is, however, always reflection upon some matter or other and this self-conscious thinking through and questioning, sometimes grandiosely called 'wonder', is a hallmark of any 'philosophical' approach.[12] It need not, of course, be the hallmark of the discipline of philosophy as it currently exists in universities and, even when it is, it is certainly not unique to that academic discipline. In this sense, one can be philosophical without being a professional philosopher.[13]

Reflection might seem a disappointingly modest goal to the philosophically inclined but it nevertheless takes us some considerable way along a philosophical path. Take, for example, a topic much debated by analytical political philosophers over the last thirty years, namely, justice. Reflection upon our current beliefs about justice and the ways in which that notion is used in our language may lead, in the first place, to some degree of systemization of those beliefs and, as a result, some modification in our use of the concept. Note that in attempting to organize our beliefs about justice we are engaged in an effort to either impose or discover their latent unity and that the systematizing or unifying of our beliefs can bring at least two other steps in its wake. First, because unity in this context is primarily a matter of consistency, some existing beliefs about justice might be rejected because they conflict with other more important beliefs. Second, to be fully reflective, this process must involve another step, namely, the articulation and evaluation of the reasons for rejecting some existing beliefs about justice and maintaining others. This is a matter of commending our newly systematized set of beliefs about justice as being in some respect better than our previous set. A standard way in which analytical philosophers recommend the products of their reflection is by highlighting how the new way of understanding and thinking avoids problems that the previous less reflective view engendered. The problems avoided are usually of a limited sort: our previous way of thinking about justice, for example, may have generated contradictions or paradoxes, may have been in tension with other (non-justice) beliefs or,

[12] Many contemporary professional philosophers would be embarrassed to speak in such terms but, for a beautiful exception, see M. Hollis, *Invitation to Philosophy* (Oxford: Blackwell, 1985), ch.1.

[13] And professional philosophers are sometimes philosophical in an altogether different sense: see A. J. Ayer, *More of My Life* (London: Collins, 1984), p. 53.

more modestly, may have had counter-intuitive consequences in particular cases.

Reflection need not always lead us to jettison beliefs about – and thus change the way we use – some concept or other. Reflection about some concept – the nature of causation, for example – might instead lead to a better, more complex understanding of existing beliefs. Our beliefs about causation might be thought confused because they provoke contradictory reactions to the same situation. Suppose that Farmer A's crops are destroyed by fire caused by sparks from Entrepreneur B's trains. There are at least two initial reactions to this, neither of which is obviously wrong. It might be thought that A is just as much a cause of his own damage as B, since without A there would be no damage: if A did not farm there, there would be no crops to burn. But it might also be maintained that, since the sparks came from B's trains, B is the cause of the damage. If our judgment in this matter must be of the either/or kind, requiring us to decide who, either A or B, caused the damage, then we face a problem. One way to resolve it is by jettisoning one or other initial reaction, but reasons must be offered for this and, if those reactions were both plausible, compelling reasons one way or another will be hard to find.

Both reactions could be consistent if it were true that each is appropriate in a different context. On this view the conceptions of causation embodied in each create difficulty only when applied beyond their natural habitat. Within the context of appraising human conduct, only that conduct which is both unusual in a particular context and one of the causes of the outcome in question is normally singled out as being causally significant. If A has farmed for many years and has never lost crops to fire until immediately after B's spark-emitting trains began to run upon the railway built close by, then we are likely to conclude that B's trains caused the damage. This is so even when it is realized that a vast range of conditions, over and beyond B's spark-emitting trains running nearby, are necessary in order for A's crops to be damaged by fire. There must be, at the very least, oxygen in the air, combustible materials (A's crops) present, and some means of bringing sparks into contact with those materials. These conditions, viewed from a general scientific causal perspective, are every bit as causally significant to the destruction of A's crops as the recent construction and operation of the railway. Had there been no oxygen (!), no wind, or no crops in the field, then there would have been no damage to A.

The intuitive appeal of both conclusions – that B caused A's damage and that A, by growing crops, caused his own damage – need not be contradictory. For this to be so, we must accept that the two conceptions of causation in play, the appraisive conception used when examining human conduct and the scientific conception operating when we examine the natural world, are both acceptable in their place. Their respective places are the world of human conduct and the natural world, and difficulty arises from applying the scientific conception to the realm of human conduct. That is not to say this should never be done. That would be implausible since we can, without too much strain, regard human beings, their conduct, practices and institutions, as part of the natural world. Rather, it is to observe that the utilization of the scientific conception of causation in the realm of human conduct will almost always run up against the causal judgments made in that realm. Since that conception is not generally used by the human agents whose conduct constitutes that realm, there will be some degree of dissonance between the two. Recognizing this commits one neither to a view of the relative merits of each conception of causation, nor to a view as to the possibility of making such an assessment.

The product of philosophical reflection in the analytical tradition could be characterized thus: greater systematicity or unity in our beliefs on some matter as well as a better – less confused, more consistent – understanding and use of the object of those beliefs (the concept or idea in question). Reflection upon our beliefs about and the meaning of justice or causation may lead to a clearer view of the form, variety and function of those concepts, ensuring that familiar confusions are avoided as well as raising new questions and issues. Yet the reflection in which philosophers of private law are engaged is rather mundane in comparison to some issues that have traditionally occupied philosophers. Philosophy of private law is reflection about a specific set of issues generated by a specific institution and its constitutive practices, the institution being private law and the constitutive practices being the roles, procedures and routines that serve to distinguish that institution from other social institutions.[14] Some philosophers have questioned whether philosophy's task should ever be constrained by the details of particular practices and institutions.

[14] In more general terms, an 'institution' for our purposes: (i) has a set of functions, either explicitly laid down or which have evolved over time; (ii) embodies distinctive roles; (iii) has a clear set of discernible features and (iv) is the locus for the exercise of power, either private or public or both. Hence on this view, 'private law', 'schools' and 'the family' are undoubtedly institutions. 'Practices' is simply an expansive way of referring to the usually distinctive set of traditions, routines, roles and 'moves' within particular institutions. For a more expansive but not unproblematic view of practices, see B. Tamanaha, *Realistic Socio-Legal Theory* (Oxford: Clarendon Press, 1997), pp. 168–172.

This question illuminates a tension within both styles of philosophy already noted. For some analytical and non-analytical philosophers alike, philosophy's reflective task is geared towards one principal goal, namely, the discovery of truth. The elucidation of the conditions under which propositions with any subject matter are true and false (epistemology), as well as the attempt to unearth the fundamental constituents of reality (metaphysics and ontology), have been thought by many philosophers to give philosophy a significant priority over the other disciplines in the social and, sometimes, the natural sciences. Accepting that the claims of the social sciences do indeed depend upon the existence of certain things in our world, and also involve the affirmation or denial of claims about those things (how they are best understood, how they relate to or influence one another), appears to support this conception of philosophy's priority. Think of an imaginary but not too fanciful claim historians might make about, for example, the causes of industrial disputes in a specific economic sector during a particular epoch. Suppose historians claim such disputes resulted from the introduction of new technologies and associated new working practices, combined with the growth in trade union militancy among all workers in all economic sectors. There is a claim to truth involved here, namely, that this explanation is correct. There is also a claim about some of the constituents of social reality, many being so obvious that we are inclined to take them for granted: that there is 'militancy', that there are 'trade unions', 'technologies' and 'working practices'. There is also a claim about the relationship between these constituents. On the conception of philosophy's reflective task we are now considering, philosophers provide general accounts of fundamental concepts (the nature of truth and falsity, the constituents of reality, the nature of causation), upon which such subsidiary claims as those made by the historian ultimately depend. We can call this the over-labourer conception of philosophy and contrast it with the co-worker conception.[15]

The latter conception also has supporters among both analytical and non-analytical philosophers and it is a reaction to the unhistorical and abstract tendencies immanent in the over-labourer conception. The concern with 'truth', 'causation' and other notions only in their most general and abstract senses is often said to engender remoteness from human conduct and existing practices and institutions. On this view, such

[15] This terminology is a reaction to P. Winch, *The Idea of a Social Science and its Relation to Philosophy* (London: Routledge, 2nd edn, 1990), ch. 1. The co-worker conception occupies the ground between the over-labourer and Winch's under-labourer conceptions of philosophy.

remoteness causes either philosophy's marginalization from the other disciplines and life itself, or yields philosophical misrepresentations of much human conduct and many of our practices and institutions. The co-worker conception regards philosophy as an equal working alongside other disciplines, tackling the specific problems they throw up at specific historical junctures. On this view, the problems of philosophy are not always and ever the same (the nature of truth, causation, etc.,), but differ according to different historical conditions. The problems tackled by the ancient philosophers are unlikely, despite the superficial similarity brought about by translation into our language, to be precisely the same as those exercising philosophers and proponents of the human sciences today, primarily because the communities which gave rise to them are so radically different. On the co-worker conception, philosophy is also more closely engaged than the over-labourer conception would permit with the details of actual human conduct, since it works from within the context of existing practices and institutions. It could be characterized as philosophy 'from below', its questions being generated by problems within 'ground-level' existing practices and institutions, rather than 'from above', its questions and problems arising within the Olympian perspective of a general 'theory' of truth or of what there is. Interestingly, while this characterization invites the over-labourer's rebuke that the co-worker conception loses philosophy in the trees of contingent detail constitutive of existing practices and institutions, thereby obscuring the genuine philosophical wood, it would receive plaudits from ordinary language philosophers. Their interest in the manifold uses of language in various contexts ensured that their conception of their role was that of co-workers rather than over-labourers.[16]

The dispute between these two conceptions of philosophy's reflective task is not one that needs be resolved here, if that is indeed possible. Philosophy of private law, as its name implies, begins from an appreciation of the contours of, and the issues and difficulties within, the institution and practices of private law here and now. This much is obvious, since to reflect upon practices or institutions at least requires a degree of familiarly with them. Notice that this starting point does not assume that the co-worker conception of philosophy is the only viable conception: it claims only that the details of the practice or institution in question should be the point of departure. This claim is thus quite compatible with the claim that both over-labourer and co-worker conceptions of

[16] See also Hart, note 9.

philosophy's task are viable and, indeed, with the claim that a degree of ascent and descent between each conception is possible. Beginning the process of reflection from within a specific set of practices or institutions and their problems therefore implies nothing about the possibility or desirability of transcending the limits of those practices or institutions.

Those limits might be transcended if, for example, it is established that some concepts in play in some practices and institutions are irredeemably problematic. In that case, the philosopher is entitled to either denounce the practice or institution in question for its recourse to them, or to offer better analyses of those concepts and the practice or institution that embodies them. The latter task could be characterized as a matter of reflective ascent, moving from reflection within the confines and details of some specific practice or institution to a more general perspective constrained only by certain epistemic standards and requirements of argumentative consistency and validity. The insights generated from that perspective could then be used to revisionary effect upon the beliefs, practices and institutions that provoked reflection in the first place. When this move from the insights of a general perspective to the details of existing practices or existing beliefs is made, not as a means of testing the general perspective, but rather as a recommendation for the abandonment or revision of existing views, it is an instance of reflective descent. Both moves have often been made by moral philosophers.[17] Usually a 'theory' of morality is offered that systematizes ordinary moral beliefs, thereby avoiding the snags and clarifying the puzzles to which those beliefs are allegedly prone. In addition, the more general but less problematic moral theory is commended because it generates the same solutions non-philosophers normally offer to specific moral problems. There is a process of reflective ascent here – from allegedly problematic ordinary moral beliefs to a more general perspective constrained by, in the main, epistemic standards and argumentation requirements – and descent, since the general and supposedly more consistent moral theory reforms the basis of ordinary non-philosophical moral beliefs. The weight attached to the ukases of non-philosophical moral sense, and the readiness to depart that realm for one supposedly more consistent and general, is a function of the particular philosopher's view of philosophy's reflective task. Those inclined to the over-labourer conception will be quicker to

[17] For J. O. Urmson, utilitarian moral philosophers are usually proponents of reflective descent, Aristotle being an exemplary instance of reflective ascent: see his *Aristotle's Ethics* (Oxford: Blackwell, 1988), p. 17.

depart the realm of ordinary beliefs, practices and institutions than those propounding the co-worker conception.

In summary, philosophy is a matter of reflection and, in the linguistic strand of the analytical tradition, that process is conducted through the analysis of the meaning of words and concepts. The words and concepts in play here are those embodied in the institution and practices of private law, it being they that set the initial problems for the philosopher in this field. This, of course, is not to say that the philosopher cannot offer analyses of the key words and concepts of private law that depart from the understandings of those words and concepts held by participants in the practice. Nor is it to say that the philosopher cannot bring to bear upon the practice an analysis of words and concepts formulated independently of the practice but apparently also in play within it. In each case, though, the institution and its practices exercise a gravitational pull over the philosophical analysis, either at its inception or its conclusion.[18] The strength of this pull – whether it completely determines the shape and substance of the philosophical analysis, or only highlights a few features that any acceptable analysis must accommodate – is a difficult and contested matter that surfaces intermittently in the remainder of the book. Our immediate task is, however, to clarify what might be meant by the term 'private law'.

PRIVATE LAW

PRIVATE LAW AND COMMON LAW

For present purposes 'private law' is a shorthand reference for those ostensibly discrete legal doctrinal categories of tort law, contract law, the law of unjust enrichment or restitution, and the law of real and personal property. Other doctrinal categories could well be added to this list, but only if the rationale for so doing is clear. Furthermore, knowing the rationale for adding to this list assumes a rationale for the existing entries on the list. The articulation of such a rationale is an important task for private lawyers, although it is not at all clear that they have discharged it successfully. Take, for example, a once standard response to the request for a rationale. It holds that the doctrinal categories just subsumed under the rubric of private law are so subsumed because they are *common law*

[18] The image echoes a particularly helpful description of one way in which precedents function: R. Dworkin, *Taking Rights Seriously* (Cambridge, Mass.: Harvard University Press, 1978), p. 111.

products.[19] That is, those doctrinal categories were (i) created by many judges over a long period of time in the course of deciding particular cases and (ii) were derived from, or are part and parcel of, customary practice.[20] The two conditions are not alternatives, since it is conceivable that some – perhaps all – common law doctrines might satisfy both. The second condition has long been shrouded in ambiguity because the nature of 'custom' or 'customary practice' has never been clearly specified. The terms have at various times been used to refer to 'the normal practices of the realm', supposedly known by all citizens; more specifically, they have signified either the standard practices and assumptions of courts and lawyers or the ordinary expectations of members of a particular, usually commercial, practice.[21] A fourth meaning, never explicitly articulated by judges or lawyers, is that custom and customary practice is what judges think (or, perhaps more accurately, guess) those involved in particular practices think or expect.

Accepting these two features as hallmarks of the common law serves to distinguish it from the other main type of law by reference to its method of creation and genealogical roots. The other principal type of law is, of course, statute law which, by contrast, is a product of the political process and need have no connection at all with custom, however understood. Unfortunately, while this distinction between common law and statute law is helpful for some purposes, it does not generate a plausible account of what makes private law private, of why we should lump together the doctrinal categories already mentioned under one label. For, although it is undoubtedly true that contract law, the law of unjust enrichment, tort and property law were created by judges, it is also true that large parts of these bodies of law now take statutory form. Contract law, for example, cannot be understood without reference to the many statutes that constitute it, including *inter alia*, the Misrepresentation Act 1967, the Unfair Contract Terms Act 1977, the Sale of Goods Act 1979, the Limitation Act 1980, the Supply of Goods and Services Act 1982, the Consumer Protection Act 1987, the Contracts (Rights of Third Parties) Act 1999, the Unfair Terms in Consumer Contracts Regulations 1999 and the

[19] I've made this mistake myself: see 'Rethinking the Common Law' (1994) 14 *Oxford Journal of Legal Studies*, 539–564.

[20] We should not assume that the fact that the common law is judge made entails a system of precedent: the latter is a relatively recent feature of the common law. See G. Postema, 'Philosophy of the Common Law', ch. 11 of J. Coleman and S. Shapiro (eds.), *The Oxford Handbook of Jurisprudence and Philosophy of Law* (Oxford: Clarendon Press, 2002), p. 589.

[21] See Postema, p. 592.

swathe of domestic and European statute law governing contracts of employment. Statue law is also important within tort law and constitutes almost the whole of the law of real property and sizeable chunks of the law of personal property. From our list, only the law of unjust enrichment is almost entirely a common law product.

To maintain, then, that the categories on our list are linked because they are common law products is misleading, blinding us to the fact that those doctrines are today as much products of statute law as of judicial decisions reflecting custom. Moreover, even if these categories were entirely common law products, with no statute law components at all, a problem would still arise with the suggested rationale for our list. If the rationale for inclusion under the rubric private law is something like 'the doctrines must be common law products', then we must include many more than those already mentioned. In particular, the list must include much from the realm of public law, such as the doctrines of ultra vires and natural justice, the problem being that this realm is often thought to be significantly different from private law. If many of the doctrines of public law are, like private law doctrines, common law products, then we are without a rationale for the entries on our private law list.

PRIVATE LAW IN ITS OWN RIGHT

Where else might we look for an account of what links the various doctrinal categories on our list? This question informs much of the remainder of the book; it cannot therefore be satisfactorily answered in this chapter. However, three other conceivable answers to this question – the remedies argument, the state argument and the normative argument – are briefly noted here.[22] The remedies argument, which has two steps, is not quite as unhelpful as that just considered, but it is too problematic to warrant adoption without amendment. Furthermore, the amendment necessary ensures that this argument actually collapses into the normative argument, which, properly speaking, is not a single argument but a family of similar arguments. Most plausible versions of the state argument are also ultimately reliant upon some or other version of the normative argument, the latter providing the foundation for the former.

The first step of the remedies argument holds that the feature all categories on our private law list have in common is their distinctive

[22] 'Conceivable' because two of the three, although commonly stated in discussion, are rarely if ever stated in print. I have therefore constructed them in what seems to me the most plausible form.

remedies. That is, the remedies for the wrongs those areas of law define and proscribe (torts, breach of contract, etc.,) constitute a family quite different from the remedies available in other areas of law such as public law. The crucial question, then, is: in what does the difference consist? It could be argued that judicial remedies in private law are primarily compensatory.[23] The standard remedy for a private law wrong is an award of damages and, in most instances, the purpose of such an award is to compensate one party for the wrong done by the other. An award of compensatory damages is not the only remedy for private law wrongs, since the courts also have a range of other remedies available, including injunctions. These other remedies, though, have a subsidiary status within private law, the award of damages usually being regarded as the remedy available as of right to an innocent party. The subsidiary remedies, such as injunctions and orders of specific performance, are available only when special conditions are met, the most common being a demonstration that an award of damages would not remedy or abate the wrong.

This argument must be extended by the claim that judicial remedies in public law are qualitatively different from private law remedies because, whereas the latter are primarily compensatory, the former are directive. That is, public law remedies are in the main orders, in the form of the writs of certiorari, prohibition and mandamus, commanding an agent or body to do what should be done or to desist from what ought not to be done. There are, of course, other remedies available in public law, including the declaratory judgment and, in some instances, an award of damages. However, the primary function of the principal remedies and these subsidiary alternatives is not to compensate for wrongs done, but to prevent them being done or from continuing. An award of damages is usually only made in public law to compensate for a standard private law wrong (such as a tort or breach of contract) committed by a public or quasi-public body. This does not subvert the distinction offered, since it amounts only to a recognition that public and quasi-public bodies are legal persons for the purposes of private law.

The second step of the argument, which simply adds depth to the first, notes not only the difference in the substance of private and public law remedies, but also a difference between both their availability and procedural requirements. Provided one can establish all the ingredients of a

[23] The qualifier 'judicial' is necessary because there is a range of self-help remedies available: see A. Burrows, 'Judicial Remedies', ch. 18, Vol. II, of P. Birks (ed.), *English Private Law* (Oxford: Clarendon Press, 2000).

private law wrong, the courts will in almost all instances then award a remedy. This is not the case in public law, since the available remedies are subject to conditions (of *locus standi*, justiciability and ripeness) over and beyond those a claimant must establish to bring an action in the first instance. A claimant must establish a wrong of some kind – maladministration, for example – and then satisfy the additional requirements for the award of a remedy. Additionally, special procedures must be followed in the pursuit of a public law remedy, these being part of the application for judicial review, which itself is considered by a special panel of judges. No equivalent panel, and no such special procedure, exists in private law.[24]

These two steps do indeed serve to distinguish public and private law remedies. A discriminating grasp of the details and variety of private and public law remedies may require that these distinctions are qualified to some extent, but there still remains a discernible set of differences. Yet even if this is so, the remedies argument invites the following sceptical response. It is undoubtedly true that there are differences between public and private law remedies, some of which are rightly identified by the argument under consideration. But it may also be true that these differences are simply the product of historical contingency, historical accidents that lack any deeper significance. That being so, the highlighted distinctions count for little. Once the remedies argument is amended so as to deal with this objection, it simply becomes a version of the normative argument. For, in requiring a demonstration that the distinctions the remedies argument highlights are not simply historical accidents, the sceptical response demands a normative proof of their general significance such that, were those distinctions not present in the law, or were they imperilled, then there would be strong reasons to invent or protect them. And unless proponents of the remedies argument have recourse to claims, traditionally favoured by philosophers of the common law, invoking the wisdom of history, the most likely source for such a proof will be a moral or political or otherwise normative account of the public law/private law distinction.

The principal version of the state argument also ends up at exactly this

[24] See P. Craig, *Administrative Law* (London: Sweet and Maxwell, 4th edn, 1999), chs. 21–23. Although there are distinctions between public and private law, we must not let them mislead us into thinking that the public/private distinction is securely founded in English law. For an argument – from the perspective of administrative law – that it is not, see J. Allinson, *A Continental Distinction in the Common Law* (Oxford: Clarendon Press, 1996).

point. Its initial claim is that public law is the legal realm in which the state – the political apparatus of government in all its forms – is most directly involved. Furthermore, the task of public law is to regulate the relationship between the state and the citizen, to provide protection for the latter against the excesses of the former while allowing legitimate state aims and governmental policies to be pursued. The fact that fundamental human or citizenship rights are often in play in public law cases, these rights allegedly being threatened or ignored by some branch of government or other public body, makes the two claims of the state argument appear undeniable. But it seems that both claims can be accepted without yielding a completely clear distinction between public and private law.

Consider the first claim. While it is undeniably true that the state is directly involved in public law litigation, it is also true that the state in one of its many forms can just as easily be involved in private law litigation as either claimant or defendant. Of course, the state is not directly present in each and every private law case as claimant or defendant, while this might be true of each and every public law case, but of what significance is that? Moreover, there is a clear sense in which the state is present in every aspect of the legal system, public or private, since it, or some manifestation of it, attempts to uphold the law prior to breach and enforces the court judgments that usually follow breach. Indeed, the whole system of justice in most countries is dependent upon state funding in order to function and that, surely, vouchsafes the omnipresence of the state in the legal system.

The claim that the state is present in public law in ways in which it is not in private law therefore stands in need of modification. This presence, it might be maintained, is not a matter of quantification, so the argument is not one that insists the state is in some way 'more' present in public law than private law, but rather qualitative. It is the nature of the relationship between the state and citizens in public law that is significant and, it might be affirmed, that relationship is what distinguishes public law from private law. What, then, is the nature of this relationship and how is it significantly different from the relationship between claimant and defendant in private law? An answer to this question could be derived from one of the theories of the normative foundations of public law and constitutionalism, but in almost all instances this derivation cannot be direct. This is because these theories are concerned *only* with the normative foundations of public law and *not* with the ways in which, if at all, those foundations are different from the normative foundations of private law.[25] But if there is indeed such a normative difference or set of differences between public law and private law, then this version of the state argument obviously becomes a normative argument: its key claim is that these two areas of law embody different types of moral, political or normative concern. Exactly this claim is, however, denied by one resolutely non-normative version of the state argument, its principal motive being to save public law from just the kind of normative, philosophical theorizing into which the version of the state argument just considered clearly delivers it. On this alternative version of the state argument, the relationship between citizen and state in public law is significant because it is adjudicated through the medium of 'reason of state'. This medium, it is argued, embodies considerations quite different from those in play in private law and therefore gives public law both a distinctive content and method, neither of which need to nor can properly be understood by, recourse to accounts of the normative foundations of public law.[26]

The relative merits of these two versions of the state argument cannot be considered here. If the second is powerful, then it may indeed serve to distinguish public law from private law in non-normative terms. If it is not, then it seems that all the remaining efforts to distinguish public from private law rest at some point upon one or other version of the normative argument. Arguments of this type differ considerably in the way in which they answer the question of what links the doctrinal categories on our private law list and, by extension, of what distinguishes them from the categories on a public law list. What they have in common, though, is an argument showing why the distinction between private and public law either ought to be brought into being or should be maintained, and the reasons animating the 'ought' and 'should' here are usually moral or political reasons. Take, for example, Nigel Simmonds's claim that there is a deep tension in our political aspirations:

> On the one hand is the value we place upon individual project pursuit: the freedom of the individual to formulate and execute his or her own plans and projects without regard to the value or disvalue placed upon the content of those plans and projects by others. On the other hand is our recognition of the

[25] See, for example, T. R. S. Allan, *Law, Liberty and Justice* (Oxford: Clarendon Press, 1993) and *Constitutional Justice* (Oxford: Clarendon Press, 2001). Other interesting contributions to this debate are P. Craig, *Public Law and Democracy in the United Kingdom and the United States of America* (Oxford: Clarendon Press, 1990) and, more recently, A. Brudner, *Constitutional Goods* (Oxford: Clarendon Press, 2004).

[26] This is a brutally short summary of the complex and rich argument in M. Loughlin, *The Idea of Public Law* (Oxford: Clarendon Press, 2003).

> contingency of social formations and the impossibility of wholly abdicating responsibility for the overall character of our society. Such recognition leads us to the value of our collective project pursuit: our collective freedom and responsibility to determine, through appropriate political mechanisms, the broad structural features of our own society.[27]

This tension can be accommodated within public and private law if they are assigned different roles, the former being the legal realm of collective project pursuit whereas the latter is the legal realm of individual project pursuit. That is not to say the two do not condition one another: the collective projects a polity pursues undoubtedly set the background framework against which individuals' private goals can be realized. Furthermore, that background framework can make some such private goals either impossible or almost so – think, for example, of a legal ban, supported by a referendum, on smoking in public places combined with a legally mandated system of supply that delivered cigarettes only to private abodes. The realm of individual project pursuit can similarly impact upon and perhaps even undermine collective projects, provided free-riding behaviour is possible in the latter.[28] It must not be overlooked that the realm private *law* demarcates as the sphere of individual project pursuit is a *legal* sphere. It is a domain in which one can pursue one's individual goals only so far as is consistent with the prohibitions and constraints of 'the general scheme of legal rules and rights'.[29] Nor is public law any different in this respect, except insofar as it can be regarded as upholding that general scheme of legal rules and rights through instruments like Bills of Rights or Charters of Rights and Fundamental Freedoms. Although not all public law doctrines and cases involve such instruments, it is nevertheless appropriate to regard those doctrines and cases as also subject to the same general scheme, albeit implicitly so, since such schemes often dominate all other law. Such schemes could therefore be regarded as 'higher law' and they exist, in various forms, in most modern democratic states, even those in which constitutional rhetoric is dominated by the notion of sovereignty.

This normative answer holds that the distinction between public law and private law should exist and ought to be maintained because it

[27] 'The Possibility of Private Law', ch. 6 of J. Tasioulas (ed.), *Law, Values and Social Practices* (Aldershot: Dartmouth, 1997), p. 144.

[28] A free-rider obtains a benefit without paying all or any of its cost. Free-riding can undermine collective endeavours where the goals of such endeavours will be achieved without everyone contributing and, knowing this, too many refrain from contributing so that the goals are not achieved.

[29] Simmonds, note 27, p. 145.

embodies and accommodates a tension between competing aspirations and their cognate values, both of which we accept. The distinction between public and private law is a means of giving both spheres the autonomy and respect they need to flourish, while protecting each from the possibly imperialistic tendencies of the other. Each set of values is appropriate in its place, yet each becomes degraded or otherwise objectionable beyond its domain. Although this is a pleasingly neat picture, if it is to succeed as an answer to the question about the distinctiveness of private law, at least three other things must be true. First, it must be the case that we succumb to the tension Simmonds highlights and that there is a genuine difference between the points in tension. Second, each point in tension must be every bit as significant and deserving of support as the other, there being no easy and obvious way of ranking them in relation to one another. Third, it must be possible to accommodate this tension within the law. With regard to private law, this means that the doctrinal categories on the private law list can plausibly be understood as on the whole permitting, protecting and facilitating private project pursuit. Moreover, those doctrinal categories must do this in such a way as to insulate private project pursuit against the injunctions of collective project pursuit, forming a *prima facie* barrier against prospective collective projects that would reduce the realm of private project pursuit. Even if these three requirements are met (and it seems that the first two are the least, and the third the most, problematic), there remains a question about the degree to which such a normative account of the public/private law distinction must accommodate the details of legal doctrine.

This question embodies an issue – that of the degree of gravitational pull actual actions, practices and institutions have upon philosophical accounts of them – already noted. It is especially pressing within the context of an institution and set of practices as complex and detailed as private law, because this detail and complexity is a fertile source of dispute about what is crucial and what is trivial within the institution and its cognate practices. Disagreement on this matter is an obvious cause of controversy about the descriptive adequacy of different accounts of private law, of what makes private law distinctive. The issue of gravitational pull also highlights another closely related matter. Our expectations of an account of private law may include not only an account of what links all the doctrinal categories on the private law list, but also an analysis of the variety of private law obligations and their various bases. The doctrinal categories on the list embody a range of obligations: for example, to compensate for breach of contract or breach of duty of care, or to return benefits unjustly received. It is an important and interesting task to give an account of the bases of these various obligations over and beyond simply holding that they are imposed by law. While undeniably true, this is uninformative, since it is still interesting and sensible to ask 'upon what grounds does or should the law impose such obligations?'[30]

At this point private lawyers might object that questions about the nature and basis of obligations are the territory of *philosophy* and so, indeed, they are. But it is not just the topic of obligations that opens up philosophical territory; private lawyers are already in the philosophical domain (as we have defined it) once they raise the question of what, if anything, makes private law private. While this question of the distinctiveness of private law has been only of fitful interest to legal scholars and judges,[31] it really should be one of the central questions of contemporary philosophy of private law. Oddly, it is not. This is perhaps because, since this is certainly not the *only* important philosophical question that can be asked of private law, it has been starved of attention. Two other philosophical questions have indeed received a huge amount of attention, and they are noted in the next section. Moreover, the answers to these two questions occupy the remainder of the book. That is not to say that the question of what makes private law private is henceforth ignored, although it does remain in the background until the concluding chapter. For, among the issues considered there, is whether or not the answers offered to the two popular philosophical questions about private law can be utilized so as to answer the less fashionable question. The elucidation of these two questions in the following section is conducted through a brief outline of the history and contours of *self-consciously* philosophical thought about private law and preceded by a sketch of the site of philosophy of private law.

PHILOSOPHY OF PRIVATE LAW

THE TERRAIN

The starting point of any philosophical account of an institution and its constitutive practices must be what the participants take to be the *core*

[30] Recently a good deal of attention has been fruitfully brought to bear on this question. This work is marred only by inattention to what, if anything, might distinguish private law obligations from other legal obligations. See, for example, the essays in P. Birks (ed.), *The Classification of Obligations* (Oxford: Clarendon Press, 1997).

[31] See The Rt. Hon. Sir Harry Woolf, 'Public Law – Private Law: Why the Divide? A Personal View' (1986) *Public Law* 220–238.

concepts of the practice or institution, the ideas and beliefs that might give its various features some underlying coherence. These concepts must be recognized by participants in the institution, for only then can the philosopher be sure she has identified the right institution. Indeed, it is usually these very concepts that give the institution most of the distinctive features that set it apart from other, related institutions. Furthermore, the philosopher is well advised to begin with core concepts, namely those that participants regard as particularly important, in order to distinguish wood from trees. Almost any complex institution and its constitutive practices will have many, many features, and its participants are surely the most promising initial source of information about which features are more and which are less fundamental. Philosophers must be tentative here, for there is no guarantee that the core concepts of any particular practice or institution do indeed give it coherence. At least part of the philosophical task is to determine whether that is the case. Since private law (and law in general) is a highly self-reflective institution and set of practices, incorporating a tradition of written self-reflection by both practitioners and scholars, it is not difficult to determine which are the most important concepts participants think inform and underpin it. This can be determined by an examination of the doctrines elucidated in the standard textbooks and discussed in leading cases and the commentaries thereon. Of course, the core concepts of private law are unlikely to be explicitly and neatly labelled in these sources. They are, after all, core concepts in a *double* sense. Not only are they regarded as the *most important*, they are also at the *centre* of private law and are thus likely to be assumed or taken for granted in such discussions, operating as implicit unifying principles of the institution and its practices. The core concepts of private law can be divided into two classes, *structural* and *substantive*. Although the membership of each class is almost identical, the distinction is nevertheless worth making.

The core *structural* concepts of private law are those that set the parameters within which private law litigation takes place and which give it its shape. These concepts must therefore unify or underpin the evidential, procedural and doctrinal rules that give the private law relation its traditional form, namely, that of a dispute between two particular parties only, claimant and defendant. The claimant, the party who claims to have been wronged, brings an action only against the party she alleges is responsible for that wrong, the defendant. If the court agrees that the defendant is indeed responsible for wronging the claimant, the defendant is compelled to make good the claimant's damage and this is usually done via monetary compensation. In private law the claimant is not able to bring an action against anyone other than the defendant, nor is the claimant able to claim compensation from anyone other than the defendant or others similarly situated. (By 'similarly situated' we mean those others who might also be legally responsible for the claimant's harm and who are thus eligible to join the defendant as co-defendants.) A claimant in a breach of contract case cannot, having established to a court's satisfaction that the defendant has indeed wronged her by breaching their contract, then claim compensation from the defendant's wealthier friend or relative or from a wealthy stranger. Nor can the defendant suggest that the claimant either sue or be compensated by another, richer party if that richer party is not legally responsible for the claimant's harm. Additionally, neither claimant nor defendant can claim that compensation for harm be paid, on grounds of public welfare or efficiency, from general taxation or some other source.

That private law binds claimants and defendants together through the medium of compensation is not the only interesting feature of its structure. Another feature, just as obvious and, in fact, logically prior to the compensatory link, is that private law connects claimant and defendant only through the nexus of one having allegedly wronged the other. It makes no difference whether claimant and defendant are two private citizens or two vast commercial conglomerates: the dispute must be formulated and executed as between these two. Only these two parties (or their agents) have to affirm or deny wrongdoing and only they (or their agents) might be compensated or have to pay because of wrongdoing. Another significant and obvious feature of the private law relationship, implicit in the discussion so far, is that it connects claimant and defendant through some event, some wrongdoing, in the past. The structure of private law litigation is thus backward-looking, forcing claimant, defendant and judge to account for a relevant past event, to demonstrate that it certainly is, or is clearly not, a legal wrong. It is on the basis of a dispute about a past event, and an assessment of its legal significance, that a court either makes or refuses an order for compensation as between claimant and defendant.

The core structural concepts of the private law of contract and tort, the only areas of doctrine with which we will henceforth be concerned, are therefore notions like responsibility, conduct, causation and wrongfulness. Without recourse to these notions, the normal features of decisions about liability in these areas of private law cannot be maintained. The point can in fact be put in stronger terms, since the usual ways in which private law (by which we mean, henceforth, contract and tort) binds claimants and defendants together are neither possible nor intelligible without invoking these concepts. These concepts therefore have a claim upon our attention and deserve the label 'core', since they provide the fulcrum upon which much else depends. The fact that private law binds only claimant and defendant in these fairly restrictive ways, and the fact the courts are usually only concerned with what has occurred in their relationship, has lead some to describe the form or structure of private law and its core concepts as 'bilateral'.[32] This term is useful as a compressed way to refer to both the core structural concepts and the features of private law those concepts make possible and intelligible, the only caveat being that this single term covers a range of different but related issues. With this caveat in mind, it will be adopted henceforth.

The nature of the alleged wrong or harm in private law disputes is determined by legal doctrine, the law in the textbooks, judicial decisions and statutes. The substance of the various branches of private law, such as contract and tort, delineate the constituents of legally actionable wrongs. The substance of private law simply is the various doctrines that, for example, describe what a contract is and the remedies for breach, or those that specify to whom and when we owe a duty of care and the consequences of breach of that duty. The *substantive* concepts of these areas of private law are therefore simply those that make up these doctrines: concepts like 'foreseeability', 'breach', 'duty of care', 'consideration', etc. These are not, however, properly regarded as the *core substantive concepts* of private law as a whole, since many are unique to particular segments of private law: the doctrine of consideration, for example, has no or little application beyond the confines of contract law. However, almost all of the substantive concepts of particular areas of private law doctrine rest upon or at some point invoke general notions of responsibility, conduct, causation and wrongfulness. Indeed, many of the substantive concepts of private law elaborate, extend or restrict some or other of these general notions within particular legal contexts. The decision as to whether or not damages are owed in negligence is, for example, simply a decision that the claimant was 'responsible' for the 'harm' in question, that he 'caused'

[32] This term and idea was originally formulated by J. Coleman, 'The Structure of Tort Law' (1988) 97 *Yale Law Journal* 1233–1253. It has been developed further by, *inter alios*, E. Weinrib, *The Idea of Private Law* (Cambridge, Mass.: Harvard University Press, 1995), chs. 1 and 2; and J. Coleman, *The Practice of Principle* (Oxford: Clarendon Press, 2001), pp. 13–24. The account in the text emphasizes the overlap between structural and substantive core concepts and therefore differs from Coleman's.

it and that it was indeed a legal 'wrong'. It is a decision which, admittedly, is arrived at through consideration, interpretation and application of the substantive concepts of the law of negligence, but we should not allow that to obscure the general notions that those substantive concepts rest upon. Since almost all substantive private law doctrines and their key concepts invoke or elaborate the notions of responsibility, conduct, causation and wrongfulness, these latter are most appropriately described as *core substantive concepts* of private law as a whole. As such, they inform, are applied and elaborated in the *substantive doctrines and concepts* of particular areas of private law. Henceforth, the former are usually referred to as 'core concepts', the latter as either 'substantive concepts or doctrines'.

Is there a problem with the fact that the *core substantive concepts* of private law which inform the substantive doctrines and concepts of particular areas of private law, are exactly the same as the *core structural concepts* that give private law its bilateral structure? It would seem so, since it is surely pointless to distinguish two lists that contain exactly the same entries. If the first guest list we composed for our party contained exactly the same list of people as our second, third and fourth lists, then the latter would indeed be open to the charge of redundancy. However, matters are not exactly the same with regard to the core structural and substantive concepts since, although the two lists have the same entries, the lists themselves do not have the same function. The first, the list of core structural concepts, serves in the broadest terms to distinguish private law from other social institutions by highlighting some of its distinctive features. The second list, the core substantive concepts, serves by contrast to situate its entries by reference to other components of the institution, showing how those other components – the substantive doctrines and concepts of the various areas of private law – both invoke and elaborate core substantive concepts. The second list in fact gives its entries much more depth, showing how they are understood in a number of particular contexts: it provides not just a snapshot of the core substantive concepts, but also sketches their various habitats and the company they keep. The first list, by contrast, provides nothing but a snapshot, there being either no need for context; or, perhaps, the context is provided by other institutions – such as public law or social insurance – rather than private law itself. Having distinguished the functions of these two identical lists, that difference will be more or less ignored in what follows. Henceforth, core structural and core substantive concepts of private law are usually dubbed 'core concepts'.

PHILOSOPHY OF PRIVATE LAW: THEN AND NOW

At least three historically distinct bodies of work might be thought to cast some philosophical light upon the core concepts of private law, although only two actually do so. The first sustained but brief source of philosophical reflection upon core private law concepts is Aristotle's. The second body of work is that of the classical theorists of the common law, while the third is the work done over the last three or four decades by contemporary analytical philosophers of private law. Although our concern is with the latter body of thought, it is important to clarify its links with, and differences from, earlier work.

The strongest links exist between contemporary philosophy of private law and the work of Aristotle. This may seem a little surprising, since the historical gulf between the two bodies of work is immense. However, it is true that many of the main concerns of contemporary philosophy of private law are found in Aristotle's brief, insightful and occasionally difficult discussion in the *Nicomachean Ethics*.[33] A vivid example is Aristotle's analysis of voluntariness and (liability-) responsibility, which is an obvious precursor to contemporary philosophy of private law's concern with the intelligibility of core private law concepts. At an abstract level these core concepts, which delineate when those called to account in private law are responsible and therefore usually blameable for their (or others) conduct and its consequences, are the same as those that interested Aristotle. For, although the range of legal, moral and other responsibilities differs across societies and time, it is unlikely that the structure of the notion of what it is to be responsible has changed. Equally, while our list of what can be a causal force in the world has clearly changed over time (for Aristotle and the ancients, the gods were a crucial determinant of one's life chances, whereas this seems silly to modern secularists), the underlying concepts of causation have remained roughly similar.[34]

That is obviously not to say that either the core concepts or substantive

[33] J. Barnes (ed.), *The Complete Works of Aristotle* (Princeton, New Jersey: Princeton University Press, 1984), Vol. II. Some particularly helpful discussions are R. Sorabji, *Necessity, Cause and Blame* (London: Duckworth, 1980), part V; W. Hardie, *Aristotle's Ethical Theory* (Oxford: Clarendon Press, 1968), chs. VIII, IX and X; J. O. Urmston, supra, note 17; S. Meyer, *Aristotle on Moral Responsibility* (Oxford: Blackwell, 1993).

[34] R. Sorabji, supra, parts I and III, is a good account of such similarities and differences. For an illuminating account of what might be truly different in Ancient Greek conceptions of responsibility and cognate notions, see B. Williams, *Shame and Necessity* (Berkeley: University of California Press, 1993).

doctrines of contemporary private law are the same as those of the legal system of ancient Athens. A high level of doctrinal similarity would be unlikely simply because these legal systems exist in such vastly different cultural and economic contexts. There are, furthermore, some obvious and significant differences. An example, vivid from both Aristotle's discussion and from the limited accounts we have of Athenian law, is that the divide between criminal law and private law was nowhere near as pronounced for the ancients as it is for contemporary lawyers.[35] However, although detailed doctrinal formulations of responsibility might differ between legal systems of different epochs – and do indeed differ between legal systems of the same epoch – those formulations nevertheless often draw upon general, shared notions of responsibility, harm and causation. The underlying similarity might be like that between different styles of piano playing: jazz piano is quite different from classical piano, yet both rely upon a shared understanding of chords, polyphony and harmony.

Beyond its interest in making the core concepts of private law intelligible, contemporary philosophy of private law is also preoccupied with the normative basis of both those core concepts and the substantive doctrines of private law. It is interested, that is, in the moral, political and other values that might be embodied in – and provide normative justification for – the core concepts, substantive doctrines and overall structure of private law. This, too, is a discussion that Aristotle can be said to have initiated. A great deal of the contemporary philosophical discussion about the normative basis of private law revolves around the relation between, and proper analysis of, the notions of corrective and distributive justice. These notions and their relation was one of Aristotle's central concerns in book V of the *Nicomachean Ethics*. Almost all the issues and difficulties he confronts there are present in contemporary debate. It is therefore not too great an exaggeration to claim that 'Aristotle's account of corrective justice is the earliest – and in many respects, still definitive – description of the form of the private law relationship'.[36]

There is no such clear correspondence between the concerns of the classical common lawyers and contemporary philosophers of private law. Classical common law thought differs from both contemporary and ancient philosophy of private law in one main respect: it rarely attended

[35] It is doubtful that our distinction between criminal and private law has any resonance at all in Athenian law: see S. C. Todd, *The Shape of Athenian Law* (Oxford: Clarendon Press, 1995), pp. 262–284. Chs. 1–5 of this fine book are a scrupulous guide to the sources of knowledge about Athenian law and their difficulties.

[36] E. Weinrib, supra, note 32, p. 56 (footnote omitted).

to the intelligibility of private law's core concepts or their value. Rather, the primary interest of the classical common lawyers lay with the nature of that type of law, of which the whole of private law was then part. The type of law was common law – customary, judge-made law – and many English jurists and philosophers of the seventeenth and eighteenth centuries were deeply concerned about the legitimacy, rationality and historical pedigree of this type of law.[37] They asked questions such as, for example, is common law but part of statute law, the origins of which have been forgotten? Or is it, by contrast, *sui generis*, and, if so, from whence does its legitimacy come? If this body of law is customary and judge-made what, exactly, is its relationship to actual customs? Furthermore, if judges do have power to fashion the development of this type of law, how can it be systematic and coherent?

It is a mistake to say there are no similarities between classical common law thought and contemporary philosophy of private law. It is obviously true that, in a sense, the subject matter of both is the same: the core concepts and substantive doctrines of private law are, broadly speaking, common law products. This similarity does not, however, ensure that the concerns of philosophers of private law and of common law are significantly similar. For, while it could be said that both groups share a concern with intelligibility, with examining the coherence and clarity of their respective subject matters, those subject matters are quite different. Clarifying and examining private law's core concepts is a different exercise to that which the classical common law thinkers undertook. They saw their job as that of clarifying and examining the nature of the common law, a judge-made and therefore developing system of law supposedly resting upon ancient custom of one kind or another. Although one could seek insights into the nature of the common law by studying the ways in which judges have formulated and developed the core concepts and substantive doctrines of private law, classical common lawyers hardly ever did this. Certainly, they never did this with an eye to elucidating, defending and perhaps commending these concepts. Whatever work of this kind they did was done solely in order to decide particular cases or to aid those who might argue or decide future cases. The classical common law thinkers were, first and foremost, judges and practitioners.

The two principal concerns or questions that occupied Aristotle –

[37] The principal influences were Sir Edward Coke and Sir Matthew Hale; for a superb treatment of their thought, the responses to and elaborations of it, see G. Postema, *Bentham and the Common Law Tradition* (Oxford: Clarendon Press, 1986), part I.

hereinafter the question of 'intelligibility' and the question of 'normative basis' – are also key questions for contemporary philosophy of private law. Both Aristotle and contemporary philosophers of private law attempt to clarify the nature and, where possible, offer some argument in defence of the core concepts and substantive doctrines of private law. Distinctively contemporary, though, is the heavy emphasis upon the second question, for much contemporary philosophy of private law is relentlessly normative. That is, many contemporary philosophers of private law see their prime task as that of articulating the moral and political value of private law (as a whole or parts thereof).[38] So, for example, they chart the connection between contract law and moral-cum-political values like autonomy and freedom and then attack or defend that relation; they often do likewise with the relationship between areas of private law and different conceptions of justice and efficiency. That this is the dominant approach of contemporary philosophy of private law of the last three or so decades raises two points. First, it is worth remembering that this was not always so. Second, we must consider, albeit very briefly, why it is so.

That the question of the normative basis of private law (or 'the normative question') has not always been dominant is obvious from a glance at any jurisprudence textbook of the first half of the 20th century. Large parts of these texts were devoted to analyzing important private law concepts, like responsibility, liability, possession, and ownership.[39] These texts therefore share the concern of both Aristotle and contemporary philosophers of private law with the intelligibility of some of the core concepts of private law. It would, of course, be foolish to regard these jurisprudence texts as self-conscious contributions to 'philosophy of private law'. They were works of 'analytical jurisprudence' which, while certainly not coextensive in either its interest or history with analytical philosophy, nevertheless shared with the latter an interest in delineating and clarifying concepts.[40] What these texts illustrate is that

[38] Some private lawyers certainly do not see things this way. See the pungent remarks of T. Weir, *Tort Law* (Oxford: Clarendon Press, 2002), p. ix.

[39] See, for example, J. Salmond, *On Jurisprudence* (London: Sweet and Maxwell, 1st edn, 1902; 12th edn, by P. J. Fitzgerald, 1966) or F. Pollock, *A First Book of Jurisprudence* (London: Macmillan, 1st edn, 1896; 6th edn, 1929).

[40] In England, analytical jurisprudence predates analytical philosophy by a number of decades. The latter is usually said to have come into being with the work of B. Russell and G. E. Moore in the first half of the twentieth century (see the essays by P. Hacker and R. Monk in H.-J. Glock, supra, note 1, for discussion). The former is regarded as a product of J. Bentham and John Austin. Austin's principal work was first published in 1832, while much of Bentham's work was unpublished during his lifetime (1748–1832). Much turns upon whether Bentham should be regarded as an early analytical philosopher.

the intelligibility question can be pursued to the exclusion of the normative question, since few if any of them ever broached the issue of the moral, political or other justification of core private law concepts. The almost exclusive concern with intelligibility goes some way towards explaining why some early key philosophy of private (and criminal) law texts, written during the twilight years of jurisprudence textbooks, also devoted relatively little attention to the normative question.[41]

As to why contemporary philosophy of private law is predominantly normative, three related but speculative suggestions can be made. No suggestion alone, nor when all taken together, constitute a completely compelling case. The first suggestion points to the spectre of democracy. Although we have severed the dubious connection between private law and common law (in which the two are assumed to be synonyms), doubts about the legitimacy of the latter still haunt the former. The common law was judge-made law and large chunks of private law are derived from it. Indeed, it is still the case that judges develop and thus change private law, often quite radically. How do we know that their changes are beneficial? And, perhaps more importantly, is it legitimate for judges to change the law in this way? Both questions raise what might be called the spectre of democracy. It is embodied in two common assumptions. In public affairs we tend to assume, first, that some type of democratic procedure is a good means of determining whether or not a legal development or policy change is for the good of all, or a contribution to the 'public good'. Second, we assume a democratic procedure *ipso facto* confers legitimacy on any such change. Judge-made law grinds against both assumptions and therefore appears *prima facie* objectionable.

Much contemporary philosophy of private law can be understood as attempting to quell this objection by showing not the legitimacy of judge-made law in the abstract, but the legitimacy of judges continuing to develop and change private law in accordance with some set of normative principles. The legitimacy of this process derives not from some democratic mandate as to the underpinning normative principles of private law, but from the plausibility or rational power of these principles. Philosophers attempt to show that these principles – whatever they might be – are either normatively necessary and true or, at least, plausible. The point of these arguments is this: it surely cannot be wrong for judges to do what

[41] See, for example, the first edition of H. L. A. Hart and T. Honoré, *Causation in the Law* (Oxford: Clarendon Press, 1959) and chs. II, IV and VI of H. L. A. Hart, *Punishment and Responsibility* (Oxford: Clarendon Press, 1968). The original publication dates for these essays were, respectively, 1958, 1960 and 1961.

is normatively required or permissible, to decide cases on the basis of the normative principles that underpin or are implied by legal doctrine. In addition, proponents of these arguments may assume that democracy is neither an incorrigible nor perhaps even a suitable method for determining normative right and wrong.

That contemporary philosophy of private law unwittingly responds to a difficulty which preoccupied classical common law thought raises a question. Have the arguments of the classical theorists of the common law, purportedly showing the legitimacy, rationality, longevity and venerability of this type of law, been refuted or simply forgotten? While those arguments were not formulated as a response to the democratic objection to common law, they were intended to weaken a logically equivalent argument. The argument was most famously offered by King James in the *Case of Prohibitions Del Roy*.[42] James maintained that his reason and faculties were every bit as effective and reliable as those of the judges and, therefore, he was every bit as well equipped to adjudicate disputes as they were. More so, perhaps, since although James and the judges were at least equivalent in their cognitive powers, he was, by virtue of his role as divinely ordained monarch, surely entitled if not duty-bound to take part in the administration of justice and the resolution of disputes in his kingdom. Although this argument is quite different in substance from the democratic objection to the common law – it relies upon a conception of the absolute power of monarchs that is anathema to the democrat – its structure is the same. For it, just like the democratic objection, questions the legitimacy of judicial law-making: why do judges resolve disputes and determine what justice requires, when I (the absolute monarch) or we (the people) can do the same? Sir Edward Coke's diplomatic response to James's objection has, it seems, proved either forgettable or unsatisfactory. Most likely the latter, since each move in Coke's reply was and remains richly problematic.

The second consideration which might explain the predominantly normative character of contemporary philosophy of private law is the idea of de-traditionalization or modernization. This complex idea and process has been explored in the main by sociologists but it also echoes, perhaps faintly, in legal philosophy. At the most elementary level, the process of de-traditionalization entails a collapse of faith in historically well-established sources and structures of authority, such as the 'Church',

[42] Edward Coke, *The Reports of Sir Edward Coke, Knt.* (Dublin, 1792–3), v. 12, 64.

our social 'betters' or simply tradition itself.[43] In societies undergoing this process the fact that something has 'always' been done in one manner rather than another, or that some social practice or institution has existed for as long as can be remembered, is not in itself sufficient to justify that action, practice or institution. Nor will recourse to the supposed superiority of those who act so, or who uphold and promote certain institutions and practices be sufficient. The collapse of faith in well-established structures of authority goes hand in hand with the rejection of any individual's or social group's claim to 'natural' superiority. The only grounds that can support anything like a claim to superiority in modernized societies are those that invoke special expertise or training. Professional groups like lawyers or doctors, for example, claim (limited) superiority on this basis.

The legal-philosophical echo of de-traditionalization exists in Ronald Dworkin's notion of the interpretive attitude.[44] This takes hold in communities in which citizens expect their practices and institutions to have a point or purpose and to be sensitive to that point or purpose, perhaps changing so as to accommodate it better. In this situation, the point, purpose or value of particular practices and institutions can become a contested matter and, when that is so, recourse to normative argument is just as often a result as a cause of contestation. When societies are modernized or non-traditional, most of their institutions and practices are prone to normative contestation, primarily because appeals to the past or natural superiority are unavailable. Normative argument often fills the void. If law in general, and private law in particular, exist in societies that are either de-traditionalized or undergoing that process, then this might count as part of an explanation for the predominantly normative character of some areas of legal scholarship.

The third factor that might explain the pronounced normative character of contemporary philosophy of private law holds that it is a reaction to the economic analysis of law (hereinafter *EAL*). This very popular and sophisticated approach to law in general, and private law in particular, has dominated North American legal scholarship for the last thirty or so years. Yet it is not just the normative tenor of contemporary philosophy of private law that is a reaction to *EAL*. Contemporary philosophy of private law's concern with method and with the intelligibility of core private law concepts is also part of an attempt, at the very least, to

[43] The essays in P. Heelas, S. Lash and P. Morris (eds.), *Detraditionalization* (Oxford: Blackwell, 1996) provide a good conspectus.

[44] R. Dworkin, *Law's Empire* (Oxford: Hart Publishing, 1998), pp. 47–48.

supplement and, at the most, to completely discredit *EAL*. Contemporary philosophy of private law's reaction to *EAL* is therefore wide-ranging, complex and deserving of attention. In what follows that reaction is sketched but not evaluated; the various ripostes that *EAL* may make are also ignored.

CONTEMPORARY PHILOSOPHY OF PRIVATE LAW: THE REACTION TO *EAL*

The story of the development of *EAL* is an interesting one, having at least three stages.[45] The earliest forms of *EAL* as we recognize it today were concerned with the operation and effectiveness of the legal regulation of economic competition. Some of the insights of that first phase of *EAL* were then taken up and extended to law in general. Chief proponent and evangelist of this second phase of *EAL* was Richard Posner, whose work has examined almost every area of law and public policy through the prism of economic analysis. The third phase of *EAL* is currently unfolding and has at least two strands. One involves developing and defending some of the underlying normative values that inform *EAL*, while the second is an attempt to deflate the apparently imperialistic tendency of second phase *EAL*. This tendency has been curbed by exploring areas of compatibility between *EAL* and non-economic approaches and between efficiency and other values.

Our only concern here is second phase *EAL*. It made at least three radical claims about law.[46] First, it held that legal doctrine does not have a particularly important role in explaining the way in which the law develops. Despite the effort non-economically inclined lawyers expend upon clarifying particular legal doctrines and their implications; and despite the fact that appellate judges attempt to justify their decisions by reference to a defensible understanding of the details and value of the relevant legal doctrines, legal doctrine neither drives nor explains legal change. That, at least, was once Posner's view. He regarded the doctrinal arguments judges use to justify their decisions as mere 'surface froth', as a layer of considerations that actually disguise the true underlying logic

[45] A wide-ranging and much more thorough account of this story is found in ch. 5 of N. Duxbury, *Patterns of American Jurisprudence* (Oxford: Clarendon Press, 1995), especially pp. 381–416.

[46] The claims are found in R. Posner, *Economic Analysis of Law* (New York: Aspen, 5th edn, 1998), chs. 1, 2 (especially pp. 27–29), 8 and *The Economics of Justice* (Cambridge, Mass.: Harvard University Press, 1981). Posner's views have not remained static: see *The Problems of Jurisprudence* (Cambridge, Mass.: Harvard University Press, 1990), ch. 13 and *Frontiers of Legal Theory* (Cambridge, Mass.: Harvard University Press, 2001), ch. 3.

informing judicial decisions. The second claim is about this logic: it is, for Posner, neither a matter of pure reason nor unrefined experience, but efficiency. The notion of efficiency, however understood, is therefore both guiding thread and driving force of legal development. Just as M. Jourdain had been speaking prose for decades without knowing it, so judges have, on the whole, unwittingly adhered to the ukases of efficiency in doctrinal fields as diverse as contract, criminal and tax law.[47] The third claim consists of a series of arguments, initially somewhat hesitantly articulated, purporting to show that efficiency is a normatively respectable foundation for the law in general and most of its particular branches.

At the level of general legal philosophy and within the more specific context of private law, *EAL*'s three claims met two principal, related objections. One objection aimed to undermine efficiency's normative appeal, while the other attacked its explanatory role. Efforts to undermine the normative appeal of efficiency began by noting the ambiguity of the notion in *EAL*. It could embrace at least three different ideas with rather different normative implications and standing. 'Efficiency' in *EAL* might be understood, first, to refer to Pareto-optimality or Pareto-superiority, second, to the Kaldor-Hicks conception of efficiency and, third, to the idea of wealth-maximization.[48] While each version of efficiency meets with some normative objections, the third is perhaps the most morally troubling simply because it is hard indeed to conceive of wealth-maximization as an independent and significant value.[49] Consider the question 'is increasing wealth in a community morally good in its own right?' By 'in its own right' is meant good regardless of whatever other values an increase in wealth promotes or makes possible. An increase in wealth might, for example, improve the quality of life of a community's citizens by allowing more to be spent on health care, food or housing. But once the good consequences of wealth-maximization are ignored, then it seems that the answer to our question must be 'no'. If so, the search must begin for the other values that wealth-maximization invariably advances, since it is only valuable as an instrument for promoting them. If

[47] Not all judges were blind to the economic rationale of the law. The formula used by the American Judge Learned Hand to decide a negligence case is almost always cited by proponents of *EAL*: see R. Posner, *Economic Analysis*, supra, ch. 6.

[48] For helpful elaboration see J. Coleman, *Markets, Morals and the Law* (Cambridge: Cambridge University Press, 1988), chs. 3 and 4.

[49] The classic version of the argument is found in R. Dworkin, *A Matter of Principle* (Oxford: Clarendon Press, 1986), ch. 12 at pp. 237–249.

wealth-maximization does not invariably advance those other values, then its appeal is illusory.

The general argument about the value and significance of efficiency is one reason why contemporary philosophy of private law is predominantly normative. Persuaded that efficiency is of little independent (moral) value, yet also troubled by the apparent simplicity and explanatory power of *EAL*, many non-economically inclined philosophers of private law began to search for other moral and political values that private law might embody. This search, combined with the related task of weighing and delineating these respective values, has been the fulcrum of much of their work. So, for example, philosophers of private law have argued that the principal doctrines of contract law are an elaboration of the values of individual autonomy and freedom rather than efficiency; and that tort law is not simply – or not at all – a means for the efficient reduction of accident costs but a manifestation of the value of corrective justice. Arguments such as these are not solely *normative*, for they claim not only that the non-economic values supposedly embodied in private law are better or more important than the (alleged) value of efficiency. They often also claim that *EAL* in general and the notion of efficiency in particular does not provide a satisfactory *explanation* of either the structure or substance of private law. This claim requires elaboration.

First, a reminder of the structure/substance distinction. The structure of private law is found in the distinctive shape of private law disputes: a claimant sues a defendant, claiming both that the defendant has perpetrated a legal wrong against him and that the defendant is therefore legally obliged to compensate him. The core structural concepts of private law, like responsibility, conduct, causation and wrongfulness are the glue that bind claimant and defendant together. The substance of private law simply is the doctrines of private law, those chunks of law that specify the various standards of liability, the exact nature of the many private law wrongs and the large number of defences to, and remedies for, such wrongs. The substance of private law is premised upon the core concepts of responsibility, causation, conduct and wrongfulness, but includes, in addition, the distinctive shape these general concepts are given by particular legal doctrines. What it is to be responsible under the doctrine of negligence in the law of tort is different from, because a detailed elaboration of, what it is to be responsible in the most general sense.

The claim that *EAL* cannot adequately explain the *structure* of private law is easily summarized. It holds that there is no plausible, efficiency-based account of why private law binds claimant and defendant together.

With regard to tort law, this argument has three principal steps. The first takes for granted the *EAL* claim that the purpose of much of tort law is to reduce the costs of accidents. This is done by deterring those who might cause accidents, deterring those who might take inefficient precautions against accidents and by placing liability on the party who can avoid accidents at the lowest cost. The *EAL* account of the function of tort law therefore combines efficiency and deterrence. The second step notes that the requirement of efficiency in this context – impose liability on the cheapest cost avoider – provides no principled reason why claimants should sue defendants. This is because there is no necessary connection between the class of defendants and the class of cheapest cost avoiders: someone other than the defendant in a particular case could well have taken more efficient (cheaper) precautions to avoid the accident between claimant and defendant. Surely, in that situation, efficiency demands that the claimant sue this other party? And that, of course, is certainly not the law. *EAL* allegedly has only an ad hoc response to the question of why claimants should sue defendants, namely, that this should be done when the costs of determining who is the cheapest cost avoider are too high. It follows from this that, when those costs are either low or non-existent, claimants should sue the cheapest cost avoider, not the defendant.[50] Again, this is certainly not the law.

The third step raises a question. Why, from the perspective of efficiency, should the defendant compensate the claimant even if he has caused her harm? Since the claimant's harm has already occurred, questions about whether or not its infliction was efficient seem redundant. There is no obvious efficiency gain from redistributing the cost of the harm from the claimant to the defendant. The difficulty here is that efficiency in particular and *EAL* in general is forward- and not backward-looking. The only obvious question the defendant's past infliction of harm upon the claimant raises, from the perspective of efficiency, is how similar inefficient events could be most efficiently avoided in the future. At this point deterrence can come into play: imposing liability on the defendant might reduce the costs of accidents in the future by deterring this particular defendant from expensive, harmful activity. But even if this particular defendant is deterred, that does not entail that the *overall* costs of accidents will thereby be reduced if other potential harm-causers, situated similarly to the defendant, are not also deterred. And, if our goal is to deter every member, or the vast majority, of the class of potential

[50] This argument belongs to J. Coleman, 'Structure' and 'Practice', supra, note 32.

inefficient harm-causers, the imposition of a duty on this particular defendant to compensate this particular claimant is neither a necessary nor even obvious means of achieving that. Furthermore, efficiency considerations might tell not only against a particular claimant receiving damages from a particular defendant but also against the very idea of claimants being compensated by defendants. If the administrative costs of existing legal systems are high, then it may be more efficient for claimants to be compensated from a social fund or general system of insurance. The force of the third step is the same as the second: the notion of efficiency provides an implausible account of why private law binds particular claimants and defendants together.

This argument is not immediately applicable to contract law. This is because of an asymmetry between *EAL*'s account of the structure of contract law, on the one hand, and its account of the structure of tort law, on the other. While it is claimed that *EAL* provides no plausible account of what it is that binds together claimants and defendants in tort law, it supplies an initially plausible account of the connection between claimants and defendants in contract law. *EAL* holds that contract law's function is to allow parties to enter into efficiency-increasing transactions; the tie that therefore binds claimant and defendant in a contract law dispute is their effort to create just such a transaction. They have in some respect failed, otherwise there would be no legal dispute, and the job of the judges and the doctrines of contract law they apply is, wherever possible, to resolve the dispute in whatever way 'mimics the market'. By that, proponents of *EAL* mean that contract disputes should be resolved in whatever way the parties would have specified had they been contracting in an ideally competitive market with no transaction costs or other impediments. This is a goal worth pursuing on the assumption that, first, fully informed agents transacting in ideally competitive markets do what is in their own best interests and, second, that, in so doing, they thereby bring about increases in efficiency (however understood).

As to the question 'why must claimants sue defendants?' in contract law disputes, the answer *EAL* provides is clear: the defendant is the party with whom the claimant attempted to enter into an efficiency increasing exchange. As to the related question – 'why must the defendant, if found by the court to be in breach of contract, compensate the claimant?' – *EAL's* answer is equally clear: the defendant thwarted this effort at efficient exchange. These answers therefore appear to accommodate quite felicitously the structure of contract law disputes. The situation is not, however, as rosy as it seems.

The problem is that efficiency again raises its forward-looking head. Since breach has already occurred, the effort to determine whether or not it was efficient appears wasteful. The costs of this event have already been expended and reallocating them is not obviously more efficient than leaving them where they fall. This is certainly true when the dispute is examined only from the perspective of what is efficient as between the two disputants. In resolving the dispute, the courts might, however, take up the perspective of what will be most efficient overall, now and in the future. The courts will therefore be uninterested in the specific dispute in question except as a token of a general class of potential disputes. Suppose, for example, that the dispute concerns who, defendant or claimant, is responsible for maintaining shared areas in rented premises. When contracts are silent or ambiguous on such matters, a court aiming to bring about an efficient resolution for a similar class of future disputes should choose the option which will be cheapest and most obvious for future contractors (who may not, as a result of transaction costs, explicitly address the issue). A decision on this basis minimizes the significance of the particular dispute in question. What is currently the overall most efficient resolution, or what will be most efficient for future contractors, may not be efficient for either party to the dispute here and now. It is therefore claimed that the structural feature of contract law that *EAL* does not satisfactorily explain is its backward-looking nature, its apparent obsession with what the parties did in the past and the legal evaluation thereof.

The claim that *EAL* provides an unsatisfactory explanation of the *substance* of private law is simple. It maintains that efficiency does not adequately account for some important private law doctrines. We will note only two specific instances of this general argument, one involving the law of contract, the other concerning tort law. Many of the doctrines dealing with the formation of contracts (offer, acceptance, consideration and intention to create legal relations) seem obviously to embody some notion of consent. Other contract doctrines, too, seemingly embody and elaborate that notion – think, for example, of the defences of duress or undue influence, or of the doctrine of incapacity. Furthermore, the notion of consent in play here is distinctive: it is promissory. The relevant notion of consent is that which exists in either the making of and assenting to a promise, or in the mutual exchange of promises. One criticism of *EAL* is that it cannot adequately capture the significance contract law places on promissory consent.[51] This is said to be because, if the goal of

[51] C. Fried, *Contract as Promise* (Cambridge, Mass.: Harvard University Press, 1981), p. 5.

contract law is nothing other than the promotion of efficient exchange, then that goal can often be achieved whether or not the parties to a transaction consent. Forcible, non-consensual exchanges might promote efficiency every bit as well as, possibly even better than, the kind of consensual exchanges the law of contract regards as vital.

The argument on this issue becomes considerably more complicated. Some economists, such as James Buchanan, espouse a conception of efficiency that is premised upon consent.[52] They thereby either completely avoid the problem just noted (if consent and promissory consent are not significantly different) or minimize it (by leaving themselves the task of showing how, although significantly different, consent and promissory consent are indeed related). Some proponents of *EAL* try to combine consent and efficiency in a different way but, in so doing, face a problem. It is that of establishing a plausible and strict ranking of these respective values consistent with both the central claims of *EAL* and the substantive doctrines of contract law. The view of the critics is that *EAL* cannot achieve both of these aims. If efficiency outweighs consent, then *EAL* cannot explain large parts of contract doctrine; if consent outweighs efficiency, then *EAL* is false to one of its guiding insights.

A conceivable complaint against economic analysis of tort law is that the notion of efficiency either makes no sense of some principal tort doctrines, or makes insufficient sense of them when compared to other notions like, for example, corrective justice. The first element of this complaint cannot, however, be sustained in the face of much economic analysis of tort law, since that work undoubtedly achieves or exceeds a *prima facie* hurdle of explanatory intelligibility. Economic analyses of substantive tort law doctrines undoubtedly make some sense of those doctrines.[53] The second, weaker element of the complaint is also somewhat flawed, since it is usually underdeveloped. That is, a complete statement of the objection requires a direct comparison of the economic and non-economic accounts of some or other tort law doctrine, yet this is hardly ever provided. The classic early works in this area simply show how corrective justice provides a basis for some principal tort law doctrines. Their authors either wrongly assume that this is enough to discredit *EAL* or, having acknowledged the role of *EAL* in provoking their

[52] A brief and helpful treatment of Buchanan's position is provided by J. Coleman, *Risks and Wrongs* (Cambridge: Cambridge University Press, 1992), ch. 4.

[53] See, for example, S. Shavell, *Economic Analysis of Accident Law* (Cambridge, Mass.: Harvard University Press, 1987) and W. Landes and R. Posner, *The Economic Structure of Tort Law* (Cambridge, Mass.: Harvard University Press, 1987).

work, subsequently ignore it in favour of corrective justice.[54] Articulating an alternative to *EAL* is, of course, only a first step in the effort to discredit it. A plausible second step would demonstrate the ways in which the alternative account improves upon *EAL*.

The different standards of liability in tort law have figured most prominently in corrective justice analyses. Proponents of corrective justice have thought it important to show that the notion explains why and when liability in tort law requires negligence and when and why it rests upon strict liability. If the intended implication is that *EAL* cannot do this, then this is a mistake: it can. At this point, though, we are in danger of underestimating the importance of this strand in the reaction to *EAL*. For, when taken alone, the argument that corrective justice can make sense of some important *substantive* doctrines of tort law is not particularly powerful but, when conjoined with the various arguments showing that *EAL* cannot adequately explain the *structure* of tort law, the cumulative effect is impressive. It is that *EAL* can neither account for the bilateral nature of tort law nor is efficiency the only possible value to make sense of tort law. In this company, the argument that corrective justice makes sense of a large number of substantive tort law doctrines takes on a significance it lacks on its own.

The various arguments supposedly showing that *EAL* cannot adequately explain either the structure or substance of private law have had two important consequences. One was that these arguments quite naturally spurred reflection upon, and a search for, the values that might better explain that structure and those doctrines. At this point, the attack upon the explanatory power of efficiency and *EAL* blends into the normative attack previously noted. A second consequence of these arguments was that they provoked reflection upon another issue already touched upon, namely, that of method in philosophy of private law. The guiding thought of many philosophers of private law here was that *EAL*'s apparent insensitivity to the structure and substance of private law flowed from the method employed to explain and understand this complex institution and its constitutive practices. This issue is awkward and requires some elucidation.

The method *EAL* deploys to explain the social institutions and practices that constitute the distinctive social form that is 'the law' has never

[54] See G. Fletcher, 'Fairness and Utility in Tort Theory' (1972) 85 *Harvard L R* 537–573; J. Coleman, 'Moral Theories of Torts: Their Scope and Limits: Part I' and 'Moral Theories of Torts: Their Scope and Limits: Part II' in M. Bayles and B. Chapman (eds.), *Justice, Rights and Tort Law* (Dordrecht: D. Reidel, 1983).

been explicitly labelled and delineated.[55] Nevertheless, it is clear that *EAL*'s method pays little attention to the views of participants in the practices and institutions it seeks to explain as to the contours, value and purpose of those practices and institutions. This must be so, if Posner's dismissive attitude to judges' own explanations of their decisions – they are, remember, merely 'surface froth'[56] – is taken seriously. The fact that it has been taken seriously explains, for some philosophers, why *EAL* is blind to the structural contours of private law. Any participant in the institution would recognize that the bilateral structure of private law is one of its most significant features; equally, it might be said, participants in the tort law aspect of the institution would maintain that corrective justice plays an important role in explaining and unifying its various doctrines. Ignoring the views of participants ensures that these supposedly obvious features of private law are either overlooked or misrepresented.

Within general legal philosophy, the divide between methodological approaches that are sensitive and those that are dismissive towards the views of the participants whose conduct constitutes the practices and institutions in question has been characterized, not without ambiguity, as one between 'internal' and 'external' approaches. This, in turn, echoes a wider distinction employed within discussions about method in the social or human sciences: that between purely reason-based and purely cause-based explanations of human action, social practices and institutions.[57] There are at least three related suppositions that animate reason-based, 'internal' approaches to the explanation of social action, practices and institutions. One is that human actions, practices and institutions are (obviously) the products of human agency. Another holds that, generally speaking, human agents act for reasons and interpret each other's actions, and the practices and institutions those actions often constitute, as reason-based. And a third insists, in light of the first two suppositions, that those seeking to explain and understand human actions, practices and institutions at a theoretical level – sociologists, anthropologists, psychologists, philosophers and other citizens – must begin by taking seriously the views of those whose actions, practices and institutions are in question.

[55] An exception to this general rule is J. Kraus, 'Philosophy of Contract Law', ch. 18 of J. Coleman and S. Shapiro, supra, note 20.

[56] R. Posner, *Economic Analysis*, supra, note 46, p. 27. Now a judge, there is no record of Posner's view of his own judicial pronouncements.

[57] See my *Understanding and Explaining Adjudication* (Oxford: Clarendon Press, 1999), chs. 1, 2 and 5.

By contrast, cause-based, 'external' approaches to the explanation of social action, practices and institutions reject one or more of these suppositions. Doing so means that participants' views as to the nature or value of the action, practice or institution under investigation are of relatively little importance to proponents of this approach.

Most contemporary philosophers of private law think the external, purely cause-based approach mistaken. At a very general level it is this that animates their disagreement with *EAL*. It also explains why much contemporary philosophy of private law strives to take seriously, and makes regular recourse to, the views of those whose conduct constitutes that practice and institution. The views of the participants exercise a powerful gravitational pull over philosophical accounts of the institution and its constitutive practices. Contemporary philosophers of private law are, however, quite often vague as to who counts as a participant in the practices and institution of private law. They also frequently equivocate on the question of how closely their philosophical accounts of the institution and its practices must resemble participants' understandings of the institution and its practices. This latter question is particularly vexed, since some contemporary philosophers of private law wish to convict *EAL* of ignoring features of private law that participants think important, while themselves offering philosophical accounts of private law in a theoretical language that participants would neither use nor understand.[58]

Unfortunately, the many interesting difficulties that arise from the methodological consensus within contemporary philosophy of private law cannot be further explored here. Rather, a summary and some indication of our future direction is necessary. The discussion so far, if well founded, warrants one conclusion: that contemporary philosophy of private law's agenda contains at least three pressing issues. These are, first, the question of the intelligibility of the core concepts of private law; second, the question of the normative foundation, if any, that these concepts and the substantive legal doctrines founded upon them have; and third, the question of the distinctiveness of private law. The first two questions are undoubtedly taken seriously by contemporary philosophers of private law while the third, as already noted, is rarely explicitly addressed.

It might be assumed that the responses to these three questions need not be linked. It seems natural, for many of us, to regard the responses as

[58] See E. Weinrib, supra, note 32; A. Brudner, *The Unity of the Common Law* (Berkeley: University of California Press, 1995) and my 'The Crises of Private Law', ch. 7 of T. Wilhelmsson and S. Hurri (eds.), *From Dissonance to Sense: Welfare State Expectations, Privatisation and Private Law* (Aldershot: Ashgate, 1999).

quite discrete, so that an answer to one question does not necessarily provide an answer to one or all of the others. Thus, showing that the core concepts of private law are intelligible does not in itself appear to say anything about whether or not those concepts and the legal framework arising upon them are normatively respectable. Equally, providing an account of the intelligibility or normative appeal of those concepts apparently does not ensure that those concepts and their superstructure of legal doctrine are distinct from the core concepts of other areas of law. Yet the view that there is no necessary connection between the answers to these questions is, as will be seen below, sometimes contested. For some philosophers, the task of making the core concepts of private law intelligible is only possible against a normative background: moral, political and other values, they claim, determine the meaning and range – or the intelligibility – of those concepts. If that is so, then our response to the first question is determined by our response to the second question. It might be maintained, in the same vein, that the response to the second question also determines the response to the third. We will return to this issue later in the book.

The significance of claiming that there are *at least* three issues on the agenda of contemporary philosophy of private law must not be overlooked. There are many other issues deserving our attention, some of which have been hinted at – the question of method or the current state of *EAL*, for example – and some which have not, yet all of which must be set aside here because of constraints of space. There are also entirely different approaches to private law in general and philosophy of private law in particular that are not tackled here, but which have some claim to our attention. Approaches rooted in what, at the outset, was labelled the non-analytical philosophical tradition have said much about private law and its problems. Contemporary legal scholarship drawing upon this tradition is self-consciously critical in a way that the work examined in what follows is not, although this difference is often exaggerated. At the level of legal philosophy, at least, the differences between self-consciously critical and supposedly non-critical approaches are neither numerous nor very great, although the clouds of hyperbole enveloping the disputants often obscure this.[59] These critical approaches, for all their interest and vigour, cannot be accommodated here.

[59] For more on this theme, see *Understanding and Explaining*, supra, note 57, ch. 8.

OUTLINE

The remainder of the book is divided into two parts and a conclusion. Part I addresses the question 'who did what?' It grapples with the issue of the *intelligibility of the core concepts of private law* that lay down the preconditions for legal-liability responsibility. The notions with which we will be concerned are responsibility, conduct, causation and wrongfulness. These notions, remember, are the core concepts of the law of contract and tort and, although they undoubtedly function in other areas of private law also, a more expansive study might have to add to this list. There are no principled reasons for refusing to do so, only pragmatic ones: considerations of time and space limit the list of core concepts with which we will be concerned. And that, of course, is to make no judgment about the merit of an examination of other potential core concepts of private law like ownership, possession and title. Part II tackles the question 'who pays and why?' The general issue that preoccupies us here is that of *the normative basis or foundation of private law*. As already noted, private law remedies are primarily aimed at compensating the victim of a wrong. The question this raises is simple: why should private law wrongdoers compensate those they wrong? What, if anything, could be the normative basis of this legal obligation to make reparation? Attempts to answer this question promptly raise another: if the legal obligation to make reparation is well founded, can the normative arguments that support it also serve to distinguish private law from public law? This, obviously, returns us to the issue of *the distinctiveness of private law*. This question is tackled in the conclusion which also briefly draws together the principal threads of the discussion in Parts I and II.

Part I

Who Did What?

2

Legal Liability-Responsibility

The following four chapters tackle what many jurists and philosophers call 'legal liability-responsibility'.[1] This compendious phrase refers to all the general components usually necessary to incur legal blame and, in private law, to be compelled to comply with a court order to pay damages or otherwise remedy the harm done. There are other kinds of liability-responsibility, the most significant being 'moral liability-responsibility'. This lays down the requirements for legitimately praising and blaming those whose conduct is either morally wrong or morally commendable. Both moral and legal liability-responsibility have a similar function, namely, attributing conduct and its outcomes to agents. However, whereas legal liability-responsibility usually concerns itself only with the attribution of conduct and outcomes that are baleful, moral liability-responsibility deals with both good and bad conduct and its outcomes. This is but one of a number of differences between the two types of liability-responsibility and between law and morality. In general terms, law is a more formal and detailed body of standards for conduct than morality, dealing with bad outcomes rather than good and which, broadly speaking, maintains minimal rather than aspirational standards for conduct. Given such differences between law and morality, it would be folly to assume that legal and moral liability-responsibility are synonymous, yet equally wrong to think that they never overlap.[2] Our general knowledge of both law and morality suggests that many legal wrongs (theft, deception, damaging others' property or persons) are also moral wrongs. That being so, we might expect the components for ascribing these wrongs to wrongdoers to be in some respects similar.

[1] H. L. A. Hart, *Punishment and Responsibility* (Oxford: Clarendon Press, 1968), pp. 211–222.

[2] Good treatments of the overlaps and differences between law and morality that avoid the scholastic complexities of the contemporary jurisprudential debate about legal positivism and legal idealism (or natural law) are: T. Honoré, 'The Dependence of Morality on Law' (1993) 13 *Oxford Journal of Legal Studies* 1–17 and his 'The Necessary Connection between Law and Morality' (2002) 22 *Oxford Journal of Legal Studies* 489–495; P. Cane, *Responsibility in Law and Morality* (Oxford: Hart Publishing, 2002), pp. 6–15.

Furthermore, a standard way in which to judge the acceptability of any part of the law and, therefore, the acceptability of components of legal liability-responsibility, is by reference to areas of non-legal thought. Morality is one such area, and it is common for lawyers, jurists and philosophers to compare and contrast legal liability-responsibility with moral liability-responsibility. There is room for dispute here, however, about the way in which the comparison should be conducted. For many philosophers and jurists, it is the law that should be examined and, if necessary, refined or restructured in light of morality and, more specifically, in the light of philosophical accounts of morality. Yet prioritizing philosophical accounts of morality in this way has been criticized by some jurists. They suggest that, since the law has to resolve questions of liability-responsibility in a huge variety of cases, and since many legal analyses of such cases are collated in law reports and textbooks and used as the basis for both legal training and the analysis of subsequent cases, it is as good a source of wisdom about responsibility as the moral arguments of philosophers.[3] The interplay between legal and moral liability-responsibility, and between moral-philosophical and legal or juristic treatments of the two, is explicit or implicit in most of the chapters in this part of the book.

What are the components of legal liability-responsibility in private law? There are at least four: basic responsibility, conduct, causation and wrongfulness. These components are, of course, the very same as those that were dubbed, in the previous chapter, the core concepts of the law of contract and tort. The point of referring to these same concepts as the components of (private law) legal liability-responsibility is not to create confusion, although it may seem so. Rather, it is necessary in order to show in a more vivid way that, taken together, these core concepts embody a distinctive model or conception of responsibility, which will be elucidated in the third section (p.53) below. While the claim here is only that this model characterizes legal liability-responsibility in private law, it has been argued that it characterizes legal liability-responsibility *tout court* and, moreover, is the most fundamental conception of responsibility we have, underlying moral, legal and all other conceptions of responsibility. Those further claims are not on our agenda. The core concepts of private law – or the components of legal liability-responsibility – are; they are examined in Chapters 3–6 below, in the following order. Chapters 3 and 4 tackle the two most important aspects

[3] See P. Cane, ibid, pp. 2–3 and, for a helpful caution, J. Feinberg, *Doing and Deserving* (Princeton, New Jersey: Princeton University Press, 1970), pp. 39–41.

of the notion of responsibility as it is used in discussions, both legal-doctrinal and philosophical, of liability-responsibility in private law and, because there is often a good deal of overlap, criminal law. The overall argument of these two chapters is that, of the two aspects of responsibility thought to be crucial to assessments of legal liability-responsibility, only one actually is; the other is more or less redundant. Chapter 5 addresses the closely related components of conduct and causation, and argues that the former is nowhere near as problematic a component as is often thought and, in addition, defends a classic 'ordinary language' account of the latter. Chapter 6 examines the issue of wrongfulness in private law. While maintaining that wrongfulness is a crucial component of liability-responsibility in private law, this chapter delineates its two dimensions and considers whether private law wrongs are anything more than 'merely legal' wrongs.

Five preliminary points must now be made before turning to the substantive matters in the following chapters. The first point is a qualification. It is that the discussion in the remainder of the book assumes that those in the frame for legal liability-responsibility are human beings: it assumes that legal persons – those capable of initiating and being called to account in legal action – are always natural persons.[4] This, of course, is untrue, since some legal persons (corporations, for example) are certainly not natural persons or human beings. The slight risk of confusion is justified because human beings are the central case of legal persons. Indeed, the problems the law often faces with non-human legal beings (can corporations be convicted of murder?) are explicable almost entirely by reference to its assumption that human beings are paradigmatic legal persons. While not denying that this assumption can be problematic, it nevertheless informs all of what follows. The second point, tackled in the section below, is about the nature and purpose of our fourfold division of the components of legal liability-responsibility in private law. The third, which is the fulcrum of the third section on p.53, elucidates the general conception of responsibility that these four components of private law liability-responsibility embody. The claim made and elucidated is that legal liability-responsibility is a species of outcome responsibility; the argument justifying this conception of responsibility is also outlined but is not properly evaluated until Part II of the book. The fourth and fifth points concern, respectively, the limited scope of the discussion in

[4] An excellent treatment of the issue is R. Tur, 'The "Person" in Law', in A. Peacocke and G. Gillett (eds.), *Persons and Personality: A Contemporary Inquiry* (Oxford: Blackwell, 1987).

this part of the book and some matters of terminology. They are dealt with in section four on p. 61.

COMPONENTS AND CORE CONCEPTS

The number of components of legal liability-responsibility in private law, or the number of core concepts, depends upon the classification used and its rationale. The classification employed here has only three guiding principles: economy, clarity and descriptive accuracy. The four components identified are discernibly different, although they undoubtedly overlap, which is not surprising. Each component, after all, relates to similar aspects of the same area of human conduct, namely, the ascription of responsibility. Each component could possibly be subdivided, for they are complex and might benefit from being further atomized. However, since each component has, as subsequent chapters show, rather different functions, this further subdivision might merely blur salient differences. We can note tensions within each component and overlaps between them without denying their significant differences.

One such significant difference is that not every component of legal liability-responsibility is necessary for every type of liability in private law. Some, like basic responsibility, are virtually omnipresent while others are not: which components are necessary and when is a question answered by the substantive doctrines of private law. So, for example, the components of legal liability-responsibility in play for vicarious liability in the tort of negligence are not the same as those in play in the tort of trespass. And the components of legal liability-responsibility necessary for liability for breach of contract are not exactly the same as those required for liability in tort under *Rylands v Fletcher*.[5] Moreover, it is not only true that the substantive doctrines of private law determine which components, from the list of four components of legal liability-responsibility, count for each cause of action; it is also true that the substantive law often offers distinctive *interpretations* of the components that are in play. The basic responsibility component, for example, is not understood in exactly the same way in the property torts as it is in contract law. This makes the philosopher of private law's task complicated. For, while aiming to elucidate the general core concepts of private

[5] (1886) LR 3 HL 330. A fascinating account of the case and its background is provided by A. W. B. Simpson, *Leading Cases in the Common Law* (Oxford: Clarendon Press, 1995), ch.8.

law, the philosopher must also ensure that, for example, her general account of responsibility is sensitive to the specific varieties of that notion found in private law. This complication brings another in its wake: the question of whether or not all the components of legal liability-responsibility *should* be in play in each and every type of liability in private law. This normative question is difficult and raises issues different from those that dog the effort to make the components of legal liability-responsibility intelligible.

That the four components of legal liability-responsibility in private law are or should be descriptively accurate raises the question of what, exactly, these components purport to describe. We might be tempted by a brisk answer: the law. This is surely correct, but it must be expanded in at least two ways. First, by briefly recapping some points made in the previous chapter. One point was that these components describe private law in the sense that they illuminate its distinctive structure: they allow us to distinguish this institution from others. That is how these components, in their guise as the core *structural* concepts of private law, function. But it is not just the fact that they illuminate the structure of private law that allows us to regard these components as descriptively accurate. It must also be true that participants in the institution and its constitutive practices regard these components as playing a pivotal role in the institution and its practices. Indeed, theorists – those seeking to explain and understand some aspect of social life – can only be sure that they have correctly identified the institution or practice in question if it is true that their descriptive language overlaps with the descriptive language used by participants. If those whose behaviour, actions, routines and practices constitute the institution 'private law' would reject every entry on our list of core concepts, then it seems likely that we have misdescribed and misunderstood the institution.[6]

The second way in which the brisk answer must be expanded is by addressing a difficulty. It arises from the fact that some components of legal liability-responsibility are explicitly identified and discussed in the law (basic responsibility and causation, for example), while others (wrongfulness and conduct) are either taken for granted or rarely explicitly tackled. For most lawyers and judges, it goes without saying that legally actionable causes embody obvious instances of wrongfulness

[6] 'Likely' but not certain if ideology or false consciousness is possible. For an introductory statement of this idea, see my *Understanding and Explaining Adjudication* (Oxford: Clarendon Press, 1999), pp. 224–248.

and that, for wrongs to come about, conduct is necessary. While all the textbooks of private law certainly discuss the notions of capacity and causation, they rarely concern themselves with, for example, analysis of the exact constituents of 'conduct' or of why it is wrong to breach contracts. Nevertheless, while the components of conduct and wrongfulness are certainly but often implicitly in play in private law, the fact that they are less frequently discussed means there is less doctrine or law with which the philosopher's general account of these components must comport. This might, but need not, make the philosopher's analysis of these implicit concepts more rather than less contestable.

Ensuring that the components of legal liability-responsibility discussed in subsequent chapters are descriptively accurate involves guaranteeing that the analyses offered fit most *explicit* treatments of those components in legal doctrine and makes sense of what is *implicit* within much legal doctrine. In addition to 'fitting' the institution and practices of private law, the analyses of the core private law concepts provided by philosophers must also attempt to make good sense of those concepts. The analyses offered must, wherever possible, make those concepts and the practices and institution in which they are embedded both intelligible and coherent.[7] Moreover, on each dimension of fit and intelligibility there is room for dispute. Since few accounts of the components of legal liability-responsibility will be consistent with every bit of legal doctrine and every judicial decision that embodies or discusses those components, there can be argument about whether or not the conflicts between philosophers' analyses and the law itself are regrettable or commendable. This argument is likely to be complicated by the fact that the disputants might have different theories of legal mistakes. Since few if any lawyers, jurists and philosophers think that all legal doctrines and all judicial decisions are correct, they must therefore have an account of what makes some right and some wrong. If their accounts of what makes decisions and doctrines right and wrong differ, then they can easily disagree over particular cases and, therefore, over the contours of the concepts that supposedly fit with or make sense of those cases.

[7] This view of the philosopher's or jurist's task is related to, but clearly not the same as, the judge's task specified in R. Dworkin, *Law's Empire* (Oxford: Hart Publishing, 1998), pp. 254–258.

LEGAL LIABILITY-REPONSIBILITY IS OUTCOME RESPONSIBILITY

The components of legal liability-responsibility in private law embody a particular conception of responsibility. What is meant by this is not that these components provide accounts of, for example, basic responsibility, causation, conduct or wrongfulness that are radically different from the way in which those notions are understood in other areas of the law or in our non-legal lives. Rather, while employing these notions in fairly standard ways, legal liability-responsibility in private law takes as crucial a feature of our conduct that other conceptions of liability-responsibility allegedly ignore or regard as relatively unimportant. This feature is the outcomes of our conduct. This is why the conception of responsibility legal liability-responsibility embodies is best characterized as outcome responsibility.[8]

That legal liability-responsibility takes the outcomes of our conduct as crucial might not seem the least bit newsworthy. Indeed, it might be thought absolutely obvious. But this attitude of bored familiarity may be shaken once it is understood exactly how legal liability-responsibility regards outcomes as crucial and how this supposedly differs from other conceptions of liability-responsibility. We will take the latter point first. Consider the ways in which we might want our conduct and its outcomes to be judged and, by extension, the ways we might want to be judged as persons, since judgments upon our conduct often inform judgments about the kind of person we are. The different ways of being judged could be arranged on a spectrum, judgment solely on the basis of our intentions being placed at one end, judgment solely according to the outcomes of our conduct occupying the other. Intermediate points between the two can be occupied by various permutations: judgment according to intentions and conduct, judgment on the basis of intentions, conduct and its outcomes, and judgment on the basis of conduct and outcomes.

Outside heaven and the embrace of our loved ones, we are rarely judged solely according to our intentions. For, while our intentions might always be good, this does not guarantee that our conduct and its outcomes are always good. One reason why this is so is because our efforts at good

[8] The original and classic statement of the idea is found in T. Honoré, *Responsibility and Fault* (Oxford: Hart Publishing, 1999), ch. 2.

conduct, based on good intentions, can often either fail or have unforeseen bad outcomes. Indeed, it is surely an undeniable feature of the human condition that chance and unforeseen events, as well as simple human fallibility and misjudgment, ensure that acting with good intentions does not necessarily result in either good conduct or good outcomes. (How often has 'I had no idea X would react in that way/be hurt by my deed' or cognate phrases been said by well-intentioned people?[9]) It is also true that many of us intuitively resist being judged solely according to the outcomes of our conduct, since the role of chance and other factors in determining the results or consequences of what we do, or try to do, seemingly makes such judgment unfair. A natural and common response to an adverse judgment arrived at solely by reference to the outcomes of our conduct is 'I didn't intend it'. Whatever exculpatory power this response has derives from the common gap between intentions, on the one hand, and conduct and its outcomes, on the other. Yet it is equally natural and common to mitigate the exculpatory power of this claim by another: 'intended or not, there is a bad outcome here that was undoubtedly the result of your conduct'. Both murderers and clumsy people bring about the deaths of others and, while the latter can justifiably claim that they are not murderers because they did not intend to kill, that almost never operates as a complete excuse or justification for the outcome. The outcome is baleful and serious whether or not it was intended.

As a general matter, it is probably the case that common sense resists, as do many moral philosophers, both judgment solely on the basis of intentions and judgment solely on the basis of the outcomes of conduct.[10] What is significant about legal liability-responsibility in private law is that it is often a matter of judgment on the basis of outcomes: one's intentions and one's conduct are less often rarely directly in issue. It is the outcomes of what one does that matter in most significant cases of liability for private law wrongs.[11] So, for example, one need not intend to breach a contract into which one has entered in order to be liable for breach, nor need one intend to trespass on the person or property of another, or

[9] See P. G. Wodehouse, *Joy in the Morning* (London: Herbert Jenkins, 1947), chs. 9 and 10 for an arresting account of one of the many calamities brought about by Edwin, the well-intentioned boy scout.

[10] Peter Cane is more certain than I that there are many philosophers who endorse judgment solely on the basis of intentions; he names some suspects in Cane, supra, note 2, at pp. 94–110.

[11] 'Most' because I have in mind liability for breach of contract and negligence which, as a purely quantitative matter, surely constitute the largest tranche of private law litigation in the areas with which we are concerned.

intend to breach a duty of care, to be liable in tort. If one has simply brought these events about, then that is enough for liability, provided some of the conditions outlined in Chapters 3 and 5 are satisfied. At this point, we may be less bored and rather more troubled by the claim that legal liability-responsibility often regards outcomes as crucial.

Furthermore, that worry may increase once the private law position of 'shortcomers' is noted.[12] In contract law, a shortcomer is the tradesman or -woman whose work is always shoddy, the surgeon who often makes mistakes, the supplier who is usually late delivering. In tort law the shortcomer is the driver – plain bad or a learner – who is just more accident-prone than other drivers; the doctor who, through nerves, is inattentive to her patients' symptoms; or the auditor who is just hasty at work and in life. These people function in this way as a result of a range of factors: they might be poorly trained, or simply bad at their jobs, or some feature of their characters, personalities or physiques may make them unsuitable for what they do. The result is that they never perform particularly well and are always at risk of running up against and being found wanting by the objective standards of the law. The surgeon may simply be one of those constantly clumsy human beings, but the fact that he finds it hard to achieve the standard of a reasonable surgeon is no defence to liability in negligence. Similarly, the mechanic who finds concentration and application difficult cannot use that as a defence to an action for breach of contract: the law judges him against the standard of a reasonably competent mechanic, not the standard of a bad one. Shortcomers, then, are those at constant risk of incompetence as a result of some feature of themselves or their circumstances or a combination of both.

Is it appropriate to judge shortcomers by reference to the outcomes of their conduct, even when, as seems to be almost always the case, it is actually or virtually impossible for them to conduct themselves in accord with the law? Can it be right for the law to ignore shortcomers' near complete inability to reach the standard required and to focus only on what they brought about and not upon what they could have done or hoped or intended to achieve? A negative answer to these questions seems natural if the view that blame should attach only to agents whose conduct

[12] The phrase is Honoré's, supra, note 8, pp. 16–17. For a brief but dispiriting legal catalogue of shortcomings see, *inter multos alia*, *McFarlane v Tayside Health Board* [2000] 2 AC 59 (HL) (failed sterilization operation); *Victoria Laundry v Newman* [1949] 2 KB 528 (late delivery of boiler); *Ashington Piggeries Ltd v Christopher Hill Ltd* [1972] AC 441 (supply of contaminated animal feed); *Century Insurance Co Ltd v Northern Ireland Road Transport Board* [1942] AC 509 (smoking while pumping petrol, with predictable result).

intentionally or recklessly brings about a harmful outcome is ubiquitous. Indeed, this view surely explains the shock that many feel on reading decisions like *Nettleship v Weston*[13] in tort or *Rainieri v Miles*[14] in contract. In these cases the defendant undoubtedly neither intended nor was reckless as to the harm caused to the claimant. From this, the judgment that the defendant was not at fault seems inexorably to follow and so, too, does a severe moral indictment of private law. Tony Honoré challenges this view and instead answers these two questions with a qualified 'yes'. He notes that the position of shortcomers is much the same as those caught by strict liability in private law. Objective standards in law, he argues, are the same as strict liability because they bind those subject to them (i) whether or not they could actually adhere to the standard; and (ii) regardless of whether they brought about the wrong in question either intentionally or recklessly. He therefore holds that a justification for outcome responsibility will have much the same content as a justification for strict liability. Honoré's justification has three principal steps, but they must be preceded by two preliminary observations.

First, we must in fairness take some of the heat from the just noted moral indictment of private law. For, while our initial reaction might be that it is wrong to hold defendants liable in cases like *Nettleship* and *Rainieri*, we must appreciate one implication of this. It is that the harmful outcome in these cases, which undoubtedly results from the defendant's conduct, has little or no moral or legal significance. This judgment seems hasty when we appreciate the defendant's causal role in bringing it about, for the defendant clearly caused the claimant's harm. With this in mind, the moral iniquity now appears more evenly distributed. For it is morally troubling simply to ignore the harm defendant caused claimant and also morally worrisome to hold defendant liable for it, whether or not she could have avoided it and whether or not she brought it about intentionally or recklessly.

It is the latter moral worry that Honoré aims to dissipate. The way he does so is our second observation, and it seems a particularly unpromising move on his part. It consists of accepting that liability regardless of whether one could have done otherwise, and regardless of one's intentions or knowledge, is akin to being liable for bad luck. At first glance, this seems to exacerbate rather than reduce the moral worry about outcome responsibility. But Honoré claims that being legally liable for one's bad

[13] [1971] 2 QB 691. [14] [1981] AC 1050 (HL).

luck is less objectionable if one also receives the benefits that flow from one's good luck. Our conduct can have both good and bad outcomes and these outcomes are often beyond our control. It is rare to regard the benefits many receive in life that stem from good fortune – the good luck of being born into a particular family or at a particular time, or with particular character traits or physical attributes – as not 'really' theirs and therefore illegitimate. While we accept that these advantages are indeed a matter of luck, we do not also accept that those advantages should, for that reason, be neutralized or redistributed.[15] Similarly, the footballer who scores a fortunate goal, the ball bobbling in off his knee, does not for that reason have the goal removed from his season's tally nor is his team 'therefore' disadvantaged or the opposition compensated for his good luck. And when he misses as a result of bad luck – the wind blows the ball off course or his team-mate unwittingly blocks a goal-bound shot – the opposition are not as a result disadvantaged nor his team advantaged. What Honoré initially thought underpinned this series of perfectly commonplace judgments about how we live with the consequences of our good and bad luck, and thus what underpins the broader notion of outcome responsibility, is something like the idea of a wager:

> Imagine that when we reach a decision to do X rather than Y – let us say to attempt a U-turn rather than to go on to the next roundabout – we are choosing to put our money on X and its outcome rather than Y and its outcome. When we opt for the U-turn rather than the roundabout, we implicitly bet that we will get to our destination quicker by making the U-turn. Our decision for U-turn rather than roundabout will be like a decision to put money on L'Escargot rather than Red Rum to win the Grand National. . . . [W]hen we choose X (. . . the U-turn), the bet we make is to be analysed as follows. We bet we can do X (the U-turn) and that X will have the more favourable outcome (getting there quicker). In calculating the odds for achieving the favourable outcome we have to discount the chance that we may not be able to do X or that the outcome of X, if we do it, will not be what we predict. Thus, we may not manage the U-turn; we may instead cause an accident. Or, we may manage it but find we were misinformed about the route, so that is would have been quicker to go on to the roundabout anyhow.[16]

This is only 'something like' and not 'the same as' an ordinary wager because in the latter we usually know both the likelihood of success and

[15] By contrast, some theorists of distributive justice *do* accept this second point: see, for example, John Rawls's response to these kinds of natural and social contingency in his *A Theory of Justice* (Oxford: Clarendon Press, revised edn, 1999), pp. 11–13 and 87–88.

[16] Honoré, supra, note 8, p. 25.

failure and the exact benefits and losses that will result. By contrast, such information about outcomes is rarely available to us when we act in everyday life. Moreover, when we wager, we do so explicitly: it is hard to bet 'impliedly' or 'accidentally' on a football team to win a game or on a horse to win the Grand National. Considerations such as this, combined with the elucidation of some other complexities lead Honoré to retract the betting analogy. Its replacement is the idea 'that everything we do can be thought of as taking [or creating] certain risks and accepting others. When we take or accept risks, in our own minds or in law, we normally have in mind potential benefits that appear to outweigh the risks. . . . To translate this pervasive feature of human life into a series of bets (with whom? for what stake? at what odds?) is probably to distort it'.[17] This idea does exactly the same work as the betting analogy with none or fewer of the attendant difficulties.

The idea that our conduct, by virtue of being an intervention or refraining in an already functioning and causally complex world, *creates* risks and that, by the same token, we must *accept* risks already immanent in the world resulting *inter alia* from the conduct of others, is difficult to deny. That, at least, is true for all except those who view the world as a static, Newtonian system. Furthermore, it is an eminently plausible candidate for the animating idea of outcome responsibility and, at the same time, gives depth to a series of ordinary judgments. It makes sense of our practice, in everyday life and in law, of praising and blaming others *solely* on basis of the outcomes of their conduct, praising and blaming, that is, whether or not those outcomes were intended or foreseen and whether or not they could have been avoided. It is also the basis upon which Honoré takes the three steps that constitute his justification for outcome responsibility. Such a system of allocation according to outcomes is fair if, first, it applies 'impartially to all those who possess a minimum capacity for reasoned choice and action'.[18] Second, it is also 'reciprocal in that each such person is entitled to apply it to others and they to him'; and, third, it is beneficial, entitling each person 'to potential benefits that are likely on the whole to outweigh the detriments to which it subjects him'.[19]

The first step in this argument, the idea of capacity, will be examined

[17] T. Honoré, 'Appreciations and Responses', ch. 9 of P. Cane and J. Gardner (eds.), *Relating to Responsibility* (Oxford: Hart Publishing, 2001), pp. 225–226. For the additional complexities to which the betting analogy gave rise, see the essays by A. Ripstein and S. Perry (respectively chapters 3 and 4) in the same volume.

[18] Honoré, supra, note 8, p. 26. [19] Ibid.

in – and is in fact the fulcrum of – Chapter 3. It is referred to there as either capacity or basic responsibility, the two terms being regarded as synonyms. The second step of the argument requires little attention, provided it is understood solely as illuminating a general feature of moral standards, be they rules or principles or some other kind, namely, that they are equally binding on all subject to them. This step of the argument could, however, be taken more broadly and regarded as referring to some of the factors touched on by the third. Since this interpretation is neither charitable nor forced upon us by this particular segment of Honoré's text, it is eschewed here.[20] The third step of the argument is potentially the most significant and difficult. One difficulty concerns the calculation envisaged by Honoré: is the weighing of benefits and burdens under the system of outcome responsibility made across a life, a segment thereof or limited only to the point in time at which a question of outcome responsibility arises? Furthermore, must it be the case that, in order for weighing to be possible, all benefits and burdens yielded by the system of outcome responsibility must be commensurable? And, if not, how is weighing possible without a single metric or scale? Another problem here is how this particular benefit and detriment test for the system of outcome responsibility relates to the similar but not identical principle that Honoré maintains underpins liability in tort law. This principle 'places on every member of the community the burden of bearing the risk that his conduct may turn out to be harmful to others, in return for the benefit to himself that will accrue should his conduct turn out as he plans'.[21] And this principle, quite obviously, has no requirement that overall benefits must outweigh detriments.

While the justificatory argument for the system of outcome responsibility is important, it is not our current concern. It will be tackled in Part II of the book where three competing accounts of the normative foundations of private law are examined. The current task is to highlight the fact that legal liability-responsibility in private law is best understood as a specific form of a more general conception of responsibility, namely, outcome responsibility. Furthermore, being a *conception* of responsibility

[20] It might be argued that this interpretation is forced upon us by the text cited in note 21, below. While this may or may not be true, the issue is hardly an important one for the simple reason that the thought expressed therein is deserving of attention in its own right, whether it casts light on the second step or not.

[21] Honoré, supra, note 8, p. 80. For good treatment of this 'principle of risk' or 'risk distributive justice', see the essays by Perry and Ripstein, supra, note 17, at pp. 65–70 and pp. 42–50 respectively.

means that outcome responsibility is but one type of responsibility among other types. To say that it is a *conception* of responsibility is to hold that it is in at least one crucial respect similar to, and in other aspects very different from, other conceptions.[22] What these various conceptions have in common is the *concept* of responsibility. How does this concept hold together outcome responsibility and those other moral and legal conceptions of responsibility that emphasize the importance of intentions and awareness to praise and blame? In this way: each conception supposes that those in the frame for praise or blame are able to account for themselves, are responsible in what has been called 'the basic sense'. Different conceptions of responsibility all accept that to be responsible one must have 'the ability to explain oneself, to give an intelligible account of oneself, to answer for oneself, as a rational being. In short it is exactly what it sounds like: response-ability, an ability to respond.'[23] Where conceptions of responsibility differ is principally on the matter of what, in addition to basic responsibility, is necessary and appropriate before agents can rightly be praised and blamed, rewarded and punished, for either their conduct or its outcomes. And what is distinctive about outcome responsibility is, of course, that it requires very little more than basic responsibility for an agent to be in the frame for blame or praise for the outcomes of their conduct.

Finally, a warning. The claim that legal liability-responsibility in private law is a specific form of the more general notion of outcome responsibility might give rise to confusion. It will arise from eliding the distinction just drawn: legal liability-responsibility is *a form of and not the same as* outcome responsibility. This mistake creates an expectation that a justification for the latter should directly and immediately justify all features of the former. This expectation would be perfectly reasonable were they identical, but since they are not it should in the first instance be resisted. Since the specific form of outcome responsibility that is legal liability-responsibility occurs within a particular institution and its constitutive practices, which are undoubtedly informed by a diverse range of concerns, its justification might in some respects differ from that supporting the general conception.

[22] A classic statement of the concept/conception distinction, see R. Dworkin, supra, note 7, pp. 70–72.

[23] J. Gardner, 'The Mark of Responsibility' (2003) 23 *Oxford Journal of Legal Studies* 157–171, p. 161.

SCOPE AND TERMINOLOGY

The scope of the discussion in this part of the book is limited. It concentrates upon what was called, in Chapter 1, 'the intelligibility question' and only occasionally becomes involved in the normative evaluation of one or other component of legal liability-responsibility. The principal task is therefore to illuminate the nature of these components, while also establishing that most of them do indeed fit and make sense of some of the substantive doctrines of private law. This task is not the same as that of determining whether or not these core concepts and doctrines of private law are normatively respectable. That is a matter of, *inter alia*, determining the moral, political or other value of those concepts and doctrines, and of showing that they have a claim to our support, or even obedience, over and beyond the simple fact that they are part of the law. The law undoubtedly claims our obedience, but can it do so on moral, political or other normative grounds? Moreover, are there moral, political or other normative grounds that support private law, its doctrines and core concepts, and which generate an obligation to obey or at least behave in accordance with private law? This, of course, is part of what in the previous chapter was called 'the normative question', and it is the fulcrum of Part II of the book. Although both questions are therefore treated in different parts of the book, it must be recognized that they are related in significant ways. Indeed, one point of treating them separately is to show how common it is to shuttle back and forth across the border between them. The deeper matter of their proper relation arises in both Chapter 6 and Chapter 7.

Finally, terminology. The chapters that follow often speak of 'private law', 'the law', 'the substantive law', 'legal doctrine' or 'doctrine'. Nothing technical is meant by these phrases: they refer to the law of contract and tort as we find it stated in textbooks, statutes and judgments. The law as so stated is one fundamental aspect of the institution of private law and its constitutive practices, but the latter also embrace the specific structures of private law (like courts) and their operative personnel (such as judges). Another set of terms – 'juristic' and 'jurisprudential', 'jurist' and 'philosopher' and a variety of cognates – also looms large in what follows. Again, nothing technical is intended by these terms, save that they have in common the aim to designate a body of thought, and the cadre of thinkers that generates it, that goes beyond simple chronicling of the law. While undoubtedly useful, such simple chronicling, which would take the form of a listing of cases and statutes and the ways in which they impact upon existing law, is certainly not the limit of the scholar's task, nor has it been the limit of the practitioner's task. While it seems infuriatingly vague to refer to work beyond this limit as 'jurisprudential' or 'philosophical', this vagueness has an advantage: it is protestant, since it does not exclude very much, and provocative, inviting further reflection upon the issue of what jurists should do, if anything, beyond chronicling the law.[24]

[24] For some thoughts on this issue, see my 'Private Law: Between Visionaries and Bricoleurs', ch. 8 of P. Cane and J. Gardner, supra, note 17. A fascinating account of legal doctrinal scholarship is A. W. B. Simpson, 'The Rise and Fall of the Legal Treatise: Legal Principles and the Forms of Legal Literature' (1981) 48 *U Chicago LR* 632–679.

3

Responsibility I: Basic Responsibility

> [W]hen we read of people dressing up a pig in human clothes and hanging it as a human criminal, it does seem to indicate that they were in some kind of a conceptual muddle.
>
> N. Humphrey, Foreword, E. P. Evans, *The Criminal Prosecution and Capital Punishment of Animals* (London: Faber and Faber, 1987), p. xix.

The specific notion of responsibility in play in legal liability-responsibility is often thought to have two dimensions: basic responsibility and ability or opportunity to do otherwise. Basic responsibility – which is also sometimes called capacity, thus maximizing the chances of confusing the two dimensions – is the idea that those in the frame for legal sanctions must have the cognitive and other capacities necessary to enable them to give an account of their conduct.[1] These capacities revolve around the idea of having and giving reasons for conduct and, in a sense, they are correctly regarded as setting the threshold for what it is to be a responsible being, both in law and in life. To have these capacities is to be responsible in its most foundational sense; thus, the terms 'capacity' and 'basic responsibility' are synonyms. However, in what follows the latter phrase is preferred, the reason being that it is useful to have a compendious phrase to refer to both the range of quite specific capacities that might be referred to by 'capacity' talk and to the general idea of being a responsible being. Use of the single term 'capacity' in this context is a recipe for confusion.

Those who do not satisfy the basic responsibility requirement, who cannot have or give reasons for their conduct, are usually absolved from liability. Thus in the tort of negligence it is the case that tortfeasors who bring about harmful outcomes as a result of insanity, automatism or

[1] See J. Gardner, 'The Mark of Responsibility' (2003) 23 *Oxford Journal of Legal Studies* 157–171. For a related version of this requirement, where the emphasis is on the very similar ability to deliberate and to inform one's conduct with one's deliberations, see: B. Williams, 'Voluntary Acts and Responsible Agents' (1990) 10 *Oxford Journal of Legal Studies* 1–10. Both have much in common with R. J. Wallace's idea of responsibility as reflective self-control: see his *Responsibility and the Moral Sentiments* (Cambridge, Mass.: Harvard University Press, 1996), chs. 1, 5 and 6.

unknown hypoglycaemia are relieved of liability.[2] A similar requirement that defendants be capable of giving an account of their conduct exists in the property torts, even those that do not require fault, for if defendants cannot act intentionally they cannot commit the tort.[3] It is also the case that minors, the intoxicated and the severely mentally disturbed are rarely held to the contracts they enter into or to the deeds they execute.[4] In each instance where basic responsibility is lacking, the moment at which it is absent is important, albeit for different reasons. Lack of basic responsibility at the time of the conduct that brings about a harmful outcome almost always negates legal liability-responsibility and does so, even though, at the time of trial, the defendant no longer suffers this lack. Lack of basic responsibility at the time of the trial, however, negates only the defendant's ability to answer the specific charge against him and the trial is set aside. The trial will be resumed, subject to some procedural requirements, if and when basic responsibility returns. That basic responsibility can come and go, as these two possibilities suggest, is obvious; that it is a matter of degree is no less obvious. Who, after all, does not know agents who are better, either as a result of greater self-reflection or awareness or education, at accounting for themselves and their conduct than others are at accounting for theirs?

In addition to basic responsibility, the notion of responsibility in legal liability-responsibility is said to include a requirement that defendants had the ability or opportunity (or both) to do otherwise at the time of their conduct.[5] This requirement relates to basic responsibility thus: in addition to the capacity to give an account of their conduct before or at the time they engaged in it, defendants are assumed to be able to refrain or have had the opportunity to refrain from that conduct. If this

[2] Some of the cases treat the issue as a duty of care question, which is distinctly odd. For discussion, see R. Mullender, 'Negligence, the Personal Equation of Defendants and Distributive Justice' (2000) 3 *Tort Law Review* 211–227.

[3] See B. Markesinis and S. Deakin, *Tort Law* (Oxford: Clarendon Press, 5th edn, 2003), pp. 436–437 and 439; see also p. 174 (negligence).

[4] R. Brownsword *et al.*, *The Law of Contract* (London: Butterworths, 1999), pp. 549–565.

[5] Ascribing a commitment to this principle is dangerous without first specifying what exactly it entails. *If* it entails that in order to be liable defendants must have been able to conform their behaviour to the law, even though they did not actually so conform, then the principle has many supporters. See H. L. A. Hart, *Punishment and Responsibility* (Oxford: Clarendon Press, 1970), pp. 39, 174, 181, 201, 218 and 227; S. Perry, 'Responsibility for Outcomes, Risk, and the Law of Torts', ch. 3 of G. Postema (ed.), *Philosophy and the Law of Torts* (Cambridge: Cambridge University Press, 2001), p. 91; P. Cane, *Responsibility in Law and Morality* (Oxford: Hart Publishing, 2002), pp. 65 and 114; and R. Bigwood, *Exploitative Contracts* (Oxford: Clarendon Press, 2003), pp. 114–116.

assumption is displaced, if the defendant could not have done otherwise, because of either lack of ability or opportunity, then it is thought in some sense improper (unfair, immoral, unjust) to impose liability. Something like this assumption and the notions of fairness and propriety on which it rests *seems* to underlie some of the various vitiating factors in contract law, such as duress and undue influence, and the defence of necessity in tort. Clearly, this requirement is not the same as the idea of basic responsibility and, in fact, does not even follow from it in the way normally assumed. A defendant may, for example, be perfectly able to give a robustly rational account of his conduct either at the time, just before or just after he engaged in it – 'I entered into the contract because, if I'd refused, the other party would have shot me' – that apparently denies any opportunity to refrain. Hence, although it is common to tie both basic responsibility and the notion of ability or opportunity to do otherwise together, they are quite independent, and this is true even though the idea of capacity – to give an account of one's conduct and to do otherwise – plays a role in both. So as to keep these two requirements separate, they are henceforth labelled 'the basic responsibility requirement' and 'the alternate possibilities requirement'. The former is examined in the remainder of this chapter, while the latter is considered in Chapter 4.

THE BASIC RESPONSIBILITY REQUIREMENT

FOUR CASES AND TWO QUESTIONS

Mansfield v Weetabix Ltd[6] was a negligence action. The claimant sued the defendant company because one of the defendant's employees drove a truck into the claimant's property which was, as a result, badly damaged. The driver, Mr. Tarleton, had crashed into the claimant's property because his judgment and ability to drive had been seriously impaired as a result of a hypoglycaemic episode brought on by malignant insulinoma; he 'had an impaired degree of consciousness because of the malfunction in his brain caused by the deficiency in glucose'.[7] Mr. Tarleton was unaware of this condition and had no reason to believe he suffered from it until after the accident.

For a judge with the basic responsibility requirement in mind, it might seem that *Mansfield* would be a relatively easy case to decide, particularly if it had been established that Mr. Tarleton was unconscious.[8] For,

[6] [1998] 1 WLR 1263 (CA). [7] Ibid, p. 1266, para. E (per Leggatt LJ).
[8] See *Roberts v Ramsbottom* [1980] 1 All ER 7.

whatever the basic responsibility requirement might mean in detail, it must at least mean something like this: that at the time or just before the conduct that caused the harmful outcome, the defendant was able to give an account of what he was doing. At the very least, 'what he was doing' includes the conduct or deed in question (in this case, driving a truck) but need not, as a general matter, include the particular outcomes of that conduct (in this case, a badly damaged building). Furthermore, to be able to give an account of what one did surely requires, as a bare minimum, consciousness or awareness: how can one, in normal circumstances, *account for* one's deeds without being *aware* of doing them? However, on the facts in *Mansfield* it was not clear that Mr. Tarleton had indeed lost consciousness and this caused some initial difficulty. The court overcame the difficulty by simply refusing to accept a bright-line distinction between complete and sudden loss of consciousness or awareness, on the one hand, and gradual and incomplete loss of consciousness or awareness, on the other.[9] It was accepted that Mr. Tarleton's medical condition was so severe as to radically impair his judgment. Although he might well have been conscious, the idea of him being able to give anything like a coherent account of his conduct at the time was implausible.[10] Thus the court could have easily concluded that Mr. Tarleton lacked basic responsibility.[11]

Mansfield and cases like it raise at least two questions about basic responsibility. First, is actual awareness even necessary for liability in private law? Second, if either actual awareness or something closely related to it is usually necessary for liability in private law, what else, if anything, is also required?

As to the first question, the somewhat surprising answer is 'no'. This seems odd since basic responsibility is a matter of being able to account for one's conduct and one cannot, in normal circumstances, give an account of one's conduct without being aware of it. But this is not to say that one can never give an account of conduct of which one was unaware. In some obvious instances of conduct done without awareness, the normal contemporaneous cognitive connection between an agent and her deeds is

[9] Supra, note 6, p. 1267, para. H (per Leggatt LJ).

[10] Normally a good driver, he had been involved in three accidents just before the one that gave rise to this legal dispute; a police officer called to the scene of one thought Mr. Tarleton was 'behaving strangely' (ibid, p. 1265, para. G) which, given his condition, was unsurprising.

[11] This is not how the court actually decided the case, though: see ibid p. 1268, para. E (per Leggatt LJ).

severed. Such is the case when, for example, an agent does something while sleepwalking. Here it is true that the agent could not, at the time of the conduct, have accounted for it, which is not to say that an account of the conduct cannot subsequently be given, both by the agent and others. However, such *ex post facto* accounts lack a feature usually taken for granted in both agents' accounts of their conduct and in the accounts of onlookers. To see this, consider how the sleepwalker and others will usually account for that conduct: all will accept that whatever was done while sleepwalking, and the sleepwalking itself, was done by the agent. It is accepted that the agent was undoubtedly a causal force in the world. But while the deed is regarded as the agent's in a causal sense, it is also accepted that it was not something the agent could account for in the sense of having reasons for it, either at the time or beforehand. The normal circumstances in which agents and others account for their conduct, then, include a connection, assumed until explicitly denied, between the agent, their conduct and the agent's reasons for it. Abnormal circumstances include those in which this connection is lacking.

Accounts of conduct that do not relate it to any reasons the agent actually had for acting apparently deny basic responsibility. Such accounts show that the conduct was neither part of anything the agent had reason to do, nor was it merely an habitual component of some more general, reason-based course of conduct such as, for example, my habitual racket-twirling when awaiting a serve. If, in *Mansfield*, Mr. Tarleton had been unconscious, he would, obviously, have been unaware of what he was doing, provided we define his 'doing' as driving his vehicle into the claimant's property. In a very obvious sense, he therefore could not have had reasons to do what he did. However, he undeniably caused the damage that the claimant suffered and there was undoubtedly a causal reason or explanation why it came about (Mr. Tarleton's medical condition). But this reason was not, nor in the circumstances could it have been, his reason for doing as he did.

How, in the light of these considerations, can it be maintained that awareness is *not* necessary for liability in private law? Quite easily, once a distinction between *actual* awareness and the *capacity for awareness* is drawn. For, while a defendant's actual awareness of the conduct which brings about a private law wrong will undoubtedly do for liability, it is usually enough if a defendant merely had the capacity to be aware of that conduct. Hence if we assume that Mr. Tarleton was unconscious at the time of the accident he caused, that would not have automatically lead to an exculpatory judgment. For the court would then have been most interested in why and how Mr. Tarleton came to be in that state. Why? In order to determine whether or not he had contributed to bringing about his own unconsciousness and, in so doing, had undermined his own basic responsibility.

If, for example, it had been established that, although unconscious at the time of the accident, Mr. Tarleton had actually been aware of his medical condition and its attendant risks, the decision in the case would undoubtedly have been different. For, provided he had the ordinary cognitive *capacity* to foresee, Mr. Tarleton would have been able to foresee circumstances in which he could well cause an accident. Moreover, were he taking medication for his condition, he would or could know (again assuming the ordinary cognitive capacity to foresee) that similar bad consequences would follow his forgetting to take medication. Therefore, he could, both before and after the event in question, have given an account of why it came about that was based in circumstances he knew or could have known, understood or could have understood, and could therefore to some extent control. This is also true of a healthy driver who simply falls asleep at the wheel. She could, assuming the ordinary cognitive capacities to foresee, give an account, both before and after the accident caused by her falling asleep, of ways in which it could come about based upon circumstances she knew or could easily know (driving when tired is dangerous), understand and could control. While unaware of the deed (defined as driving her car into another) at the moment it occurred, our sleeping driver nevertheless has the general cognitive capacity to foresee how this event could come about and, in many instances, that is enough for liability in private law.

Hence, if a driver causes an accident while unconscious, but having actually been aware, or having had the capacity to be aware, of the circumstances in which he might become unconscious, he is, all other things being equal, unlikely to escape liability. In law those circumstances become his responsibility, by virtue of his actual knowledge, or his capacity to know, that they could arise and his actual understanding of, or capacity to understand, how they could be circumvented. Holding agents liable for their conduct and/or its outcomes in these circumstances is to hold them liable for maintaining their own basic responsibility. If agents undermine or fail to maintain their own basic responsibility – their own capacity to answer for and hence be aware of their conduct – then they often take the legal consequences of that. The answer to the first question raised by *Mansfield* is, then, a qualified one: while actual awareness is certainly enough for liability, only the capacity for awareness seems to be *necessary* for liability.

The answer to the second question is that something more than actual awareness or the capacity for awareness is indeed usually required for liability. Thus, although *Mansfield* and related cases support the claim that either actual awareness or the capacity for awareness is *necessary* for basic responsibility, it is not the case that either kind of awareness is always itself *sufficient* to ground liability in private law. What this 'something more' may be can be seen if we think again of Mr. Tarleton. If he could not have controlled his truck because of some mechanical failure, then there would be no question of either him being personally liable or of the defendant company being liable, supposing that the failure was nothing to do with them. Mr. Tarleton would, of course, have been aware of what was happening (an accident), but that was certainly not something he was *doing*. It was, rather, something that was *happening* to him despite his endeavours or wishes. The driver's position here is exactly the same as that of the defendant in the old trespass case of *Smith v Stone*.[12] In this case the defendant was charged with trespassing on the claimant's land and that cause of action, then as now, is strict in that it requires neither that the defendant intended to enter upon another's land without permission nor even that the defendant was aware of so doing. It is enough simply that the defendant did indeed enter upon the land of another without permission and that she was, at some point in that process, acting intentionally. Therefore, a defendant will not be liable if, as was true in *Smith*, he is carried upon the land of another against his will. By contrast, where a defendant enters upon the land of another to escape threats, there is liability, since the act of entering upon the land was intentional: *Gilbert v Stone*.[13] In *Smith* the defendant was aware of what was happening, but the happening was not his deed. In *Gilbert*, the defendant's deed – entering upon the land of another – was undoubtedly his, an action he had reason to do and did, and was plainly not an event in which he was simply swept up.

Taken together, *Mansfield, Smith* and *Gilbert* tell us that liability in private law requires that defendants be aware or have the capacity for awareness *and* that their awareness be directed to a particular deed or set

[12] (1647) Style 65, 82 ER 533. This decision should be contrasted with *Stanley v Powell* [1891] 1 QB 86 which some think implies that the intentional element in trespass to person is more extensive than in trepass to land. This is not, however, the only plausible reading of the case.

[13] (1647) Style 72, 82 ER 902. It is not clear from the report that this is the same Mr Stone who was involved in *Smith v Stone*. If so, he was undoubtedly having a bad day. See also *Morriss v Marsden* [1952] 1 All ER 925 (QB) on the importance of intentional conduct to liability in trespass to the person cases.

of deeds. But must a defendant's awareness extend to all the outcomes of that deed or those deeds? A contract case, *Re Park's Estate*, suggests an answer. Here it was held that the claimant was bound by a contract of marriage because, although not perfect, his mental condition at the time of the agreement was sufficiently robust to allow him to understand the nature of the transaction. The court held, as have many others, that for the purposes of liability in contract law an agent must not only be aware of acting, but also appreciate, albeit in quite general terms, the nature of the transaction into which they have entered. In *Re Park's Estate* LJ Singleton said that '[i]n order to ascertain the nature of the contract of marriage a man [or woman] must be mentally capable of appreciating that it involves the responsibilities normally attaching to marriage. Without that degree of mentality, it cannot be said that he understands the nature of the contract'.[14] Taking *Re Park's Estate* in conjunction with *Mansfield, Smith* and *Gilbert* we might conclude that liability in private law requires some conduct of which the defendant was both *aware* (or was capable of being aware) and *had reason to do*, which is usually but not necessarily combined with an *awareness of some of its outcomes or circumstances.*

Two points must be noted about the last element of this conclusion. First, its qualified nature. That awareness of some consequences is *usually but not necessarily* required highlights the fact that some forms of liability in private law do not require the defendant to have any actual awareness of the circumstances or outcomes of his conduct. It would, for example, make no difference to liability in cases like *Gilbert* that the defendant was unaware that the land upon which he had entered belonged to another. No knowledge of that circumstance is necessary. Second, this element would be misleading were we to assume that it requires only *actual* awareness on behalf of the defendant of some particular circumstance or consequence. That, of course, will do for liability but it is not always necessary: rather, the *capacity* for such awareness of consequences as opposed to *actual* awareness itself is often enough. This is most obvious from negligence cases in which questions of the existence of a duty of care and foreseeability of damage are determined by the reasonable person standard. The effect is that the courts are almost always uninterested in whether or not the particular defendant (i) did or did not actually foresee that this particular claimant or class of claimants would be effected by the particular harm that occurred; and (ii) did or did not actually foresee the type of harm that actually occurred. It is enough

[14] [1953] 2 All ER 1411 (CA), p. 1430.

if it is established that the defendant had the *general capacity to foresee* such harm to such victims; where that general capacity is lacking, the defendant either escapes liability or the duty and foreseeability standards are mitigated.[15] Similarly, a defendant who breaches her contract need not *actually* foresee the extent or even the type of damage that the claimant incurred, provided she has the general capacity to foresee some damage.[16] If that general capacity is lacking, then it is also unlikely that she could understand the general nature of the transaction into which she entered.

Our answers to the two questions have generated three related claims about what basic responsibility requires of those in the frame for liability in private law. They are that those in the frame for liability (i) must either be aware of their conduct, or have had the capacity to be aware of it; (ii) that some aspect of their conduct must be 'theirs' in the sense that they did it and had reason to do it; and (iii) they must usually either be aware of, or be capable of being aware of, some of the circumstances or outcomes of that conduct. Needless to say, these claims require close attention. Four issues in particular merit examination. First, the possible weakness of the foundation upon which these claims are built; second, some terminological complexities; third, the proper description of conduct, its outcomes and the role of 'intentionality'; and, fourth, the idea of general capacity. The first two issues are tackled in the subsection below, while the third is dealt with in the first subsection of section two (p.74). The second subsection (p.82) deals with an issue – rationality – arising from those discussed in the previous subsection, while the third subsection (p.90) examines general capacity. One further issue – the general status and rationale of basic responsibility in private law – is tackled in the section four (p.99). Finally, note that our effort to elucidate the three claims and their various ramifications will draw upon not just the work of philosophers of private law, but also upon that of philosophers of criminal law. Although there are many substantive differences between these areas of law both draw upon a family of related core concepts.

FOUNDATIONS AND TERMINOLOGY

The three claims about the basic responsibility requirement in private law rest on four cases. While there are undoubtedly other cases that also support these claims, it could nevertheless be argued that the support

[15] See *McHale v Watson* (1966) 115 CLR 199 (HCA) and *Mullin v Richards and another* [1998] 1 All ER 920 (CA).

[16] This much is clear from *Hadley v Baxendale* (1854) 9 Exch 341 and *Victoria Laundry (Windsor) v Newman Industries Ltd* [1949] 2 KB528.

provided by the cases cited is equivocal. Of those cases, it is not wildly implausible to hold that, far from showing that there is indeed a general basic responsibility requirement in private law, they in fact show that no such general requirement exists. Rather, they show that whatever basic responsibility requirement does exist actually differs not only as between contract and tort but also within these two doctrinal fields. And if this is true of these four exemplary cases, surely it is true *a fortiori* of whatever other cases could be called upon? Moreover, a closer look at the cases may confirm this doubt. For example, *Mansfield* and *Smith* tell us that liability in tort requires only that the defendant has knowingly acted or refrained or, perhaps better, has intentionally acted or refrained, whereas *Re Park's Estate* shows that in contract more than this is required. In contract the defendant must also have had some understanding of some outcomes of his deeds. Furthermore, within tort law there are some causes of action – negligence, for example – which require not only that defendants do something intentionally *but* also that they understand or were capable of understanding some of the outcomes of that deed. If a defendant lacks this capacity because, for example, of her youth, then she is not generally speaking liable.

This objection is not, however, as powerful as might initially appear. Focusing upon particular cases will certainly generate a slightly disjointed picture. This is unsurprising, since private law cases rarely explicitly tackle the question of basic responsibility in general terms. What is said about this matter is said in relation to the specific circumstances of particular cases. Moreover, there is no *a priori* reason to think that, except at the most minimal level, basic responsibility should be and is the same for all types of liability in private law. Since the different branches of private law have different functions and embody either different values, or embody the same values but in different degree or ranking, we should not be shocked by some variability in basic responsibility in these different areas. Yet this should not blind us to the minimum but general requirement of basic responsibility in private law. This requirement insists that a *necessary* condition for much, possibly all, liability in private law is a combination of actual awareness or the capacity for awareness *and* an intentional doing or refraining (conduct). That conduct must have as one of its outcomes a private law wrong, the exact nature of the wrong necessary for liability being determined by the relevant substantive branches of private law, which also determine whether the defendant actually must be aware – or must simply be capable of being aware – of *any, some* or *all* of the outcomes of their conduct.

The status of and rationale for this minimal but general basic responsibility requirement in private law is the topic of section three (p. 99). For now, some matters of terminology need be addressed. In this area it is easy to be overwhelmed by a plethora of terms such as 'conduct', 'action', 'deed(s)', 'outcome(s)', 'consequences' and 'results'. All six terms have already been used in this and preceding chapters, it having been taken for granted that we have a clear idea of the differences and similarities between them. That assumption can be dangerous, especially if ordinary usage does not provide bright-line distinctions between these cognate terms. Assuming rather than demonstrating that ordinary usage is not univocal, the most economical and appropriate way in which to set down a marker for our usage of these terms is to stipulate.[17] For our purposes, therefore, the terms 'conduct', 'action(s)' and 'deed(s)' are closely related, which is also surely the case when they are used in ordinary language. However, the former is broader than the latter two in our schema, since it will be used to refer to both actions and omissions, while the two terms 'action(s)' and 'deed(s)' will be treated as synonyms only appropriately used to describe positive doings (or attempts at such doings). In what follows, the terms 'action(s)' and 'deed(s)' are contrasted with 'omission(s)' or 'refraining(s)', synonyms for negative doings (or attempts at such doings). The term 'conduct' is henceforth an umbrella term, referring to either positive or negative doings as and when appropriate.

Conduct (either actions/deeds or omissions/refrainings) can set in train other events that flow from it and all such events set in play are hereinafter referred to as the 'outcomes' of conduct. This term, like conduct, is also an umbrella term, for it refers to two aspects of the events conduct can set in train which are often worth distinguishing, namely, 'results' and 'consequences'. The difference is that the

> *result* of an action [or, for our purposes, deed or segment of conduct] is an outcome *entailed* by . . . [a given] description of . . . [an] action, which must occur if the action is done: Pat's death is the result of my action of 'killing Pat', in that if I have killed her she must have died. A *consequence* of an action is an event or state of affairs distinct from, but *caused* by, the action as described: Pat's death is a consequence of my action of 'shooting Pat'; that I shoot her does not entail her death, but my shooting her causes her death.[18]

[17] For various types of definition, see R. Robinson, *Definition* (Oxford: Clarendon Press, 1954), chs. II–VI.

[18] The distinction belongs to R. A. Duff, *Intention, Agency and Criminal Liability* (Oxford: Blackwell, 1990), p. 42. It is also invoked by Perry, supra, note 5, p. 73.

Finally, note that conduct always takes place in a particular context or set of circumstances. Some of these are such that they are almost always taken for granted: on planet Earth, for example, one drives in the unavoidable presence of gravity. But when one drives it is not always the case that road and traffic conditions are bad or that one's car has a mechanical fault. Such circumstances as these vary each time one drives, but they, in conjunction with many other like circumstances, can sometimes effect one's liability. Furthermore, some circumstances are ingredients of private law wrongs, so that in trespass to land, for example, it need not be the case for liability that the defendant knows the land belongs to another but it must actually belong to another. The key feature that allows us to distinguish circumstances from outcomes is that the former are not generally caused by either the defendant's or claimant's conduct, whereas results and consequences are. In a trespass case, the defendant's conduct is moving over the land and this has no causal impact on the ownership of that land. Similarly, the defendant's conduct in killing Pat has no causal impact at all upon whether or not Pat is a policewoman.[19]

BASIC RESPONSIBILITY: A CLOSER LOOK

DESCRIPTION, AWARENESS AND INTENTION

The first and second claims about basic responsibility hold that to be in the frame for legal liability defendants (i) must be aware of their conduct, or have had the capacity to be aware of it; and (ii) that some aspect of their conduct must be theirs in the sense that they did it and had reason to do it. Each claim raises potential difficulties that are worth exploring and, where possible, resolving. Thereafter the idea of rationality, which has been a brooding omnipresence in most of what has been said so far, is examined.

The first claim raises at least two potential problems. One concerns the notion of capacity to be aware or, as we will call it, capacity awareness (as distinct from actual awareness). Since this notion is also in play in the third claim about basic responsibility, it is therefore dealt with separately in the third subsection (p.90). Another problem – what philosophers call the difficulty of individuating action or conduct[20] – is considered here. It

[19] Duff, ibid.

[20] Some philosophers speak only of 'act'-individuation and might cavil at both the definition of conduct offered in the text and the implicit claim that omissions or refrainings can be individuated. Neither cavil is worth pursuing here, for the simple reason that neither would have significant legal consequences.

is the issue of correctly describing the conduct of which the agent has to be aware or of which the agent could have been aware. If I enter a room, flip a switch, turn on the light and, unknown to me, thereby alert a prowler to my presence, how many things have I done?[21] There could well be four things here, but in normal circumstances it is certain that, if I was aware of doing any of them, I was aware of only three: entering, flipping and illuminating. And how many things have I done if, in pumping water from a well to supply a house, I operate the lever on the pump, which fills the tank and the water is then consumed, with deadly consequences, by the occupants? Or what if I enter into a complex commercial contract which, while containing a rich variety of detail, also emerged from a long and intricate process of negotiation and bargaining: have I done only one thing (entered into a contract) or many, many things (including that)?

Faced with examples such as these, most philosophers have taken up one of two incompatible positions on the correct way to individuate conduct. Coarse-grained accounts of conduct-individuation are so called because they tend to lump together what could be regarded as a whole series of micro-acts or segments of conduct. Of the water pumping example, they hold that operating the lever simply is poisoning the occupants and that, in another common example, pulling a trigger simply is shooting or killing one's victim.[22] Unsurprisingly, proponents of fine-grained accounts resist what they regard as the process of elision at the heart of coarse-grained accounts: of the examples, they maintain that operating the lever and pulling the trigger are in no sense identical with poisoning the occupants or shooting one's victim.[23] Both accounts suffer from well-worked difficulties. A principal snag for coarse-grained accounts is the fallibility of the apparent identity claim at their core – operating the lever simply *is* poisoning the occupants. By contrast, fine-grained accounts risk over-populating the world with many more acts

[21] The example is from D. Davidson, *Essays on Actions and Events* (Oxford: Clarendon Press, 2nd edn, 2001), p. 4.

[22] Leading coarse-grained theorists include G. E. M. Anscombe, *Intention* (Oxford: Blackwell, 1957); Davidson, ibid; J. Hornsby, *Actions* (London: Routledge and Kegan Paul, 1980); A. White, *Grounds of Liability* (Oxford: Clarendon Press, 1985), ch. 4; and M. Moore, *Act and Crime* (Oxford: Clarendon Press, 1993), ch. 11. Another label for coarse-grained theorists that is used in the literature is 'identifiers': see White, ibid, p. 35.

[23] Principal fine-grained theorists (also known as 'separators': see White, ibid) include A. Goldman, *A Theory of Human Action* (Princeton, New Jersey: Princeton University Press, 1970); J. Thomson, *Acts and Other Events* (Ithaca: Cornell University Press, 1977); and C. Ginet, *On Action* (Cambridge: Cambridge University Press, 1990).

or segments of conduct (operating the lever, pumping the water, poisoning the occupants, etc.) than common sense is inclined to accept.

Now suppose, despite the appearance of stalemate, that there were a clear winner in this philosophical argument. Even if that were the case, there are reasons to think that this victory would have little influence within private or criminal law doctrine. This is because, when the law specifies actionable legal wrongs, those wrongs are hardly ever tied to specific act or conduct descriptions but are instead tied only to general act or conduct descriptions. In the philosophical terminology, the law usually specifies only act-types rather than act-tokens.

> An act-type is simply an act property, a property such as mowing one's lawn, running, writing a letter, or giving a lecture [or walking on someone else's land]. . . . To perform an act is . . . to exemplify a property. To perform the act of giving a lecture is to exemplify the property of giving a lecture. A particular act, then, consists in the exemplifying of an act-property by an agent at a particular time. [We can] call such particular acts: '*act-tokens*'.[24]

Breaching one's duty of care in negligence is clearly an act-type, whereas manufacturing ginger beer in such a way that decomposing snails appear in the end product is an act-token, a particular act embodying the property 'breach of duty of care'. Since act-types are general properties, and act-tokens particular instances of such properties, the level of specificity required of a description of an act-type is much less than that of an act-token. Dealing in act-types therefore ensures that there is less scope for a multiplicity of contested descriptions to emerge, the main burden of lawyers and judges being that of determining what conduct constitutes a token of what type of legal wrong. Furthermore, since the constituents of any particular private law wrong (act-type) are themselves rarely contestable, being by now relatively well fixed by either case law, statute law or both, there is little room for an outbreak of descriptive multiplicity such as might make the dispute between coarse- and fine-grained accounts of conduct individuation salient.

Some have thought that jurisdictional and related problems in both private and criminal law make the philosophical dispute between these competing accounts salient for lawyers and judges, but this is something of an exaggeration. This is primarily because courts have never been anything other than pragmatic when deciding, for example, where the

[24] Goldman, ibid, p. 10.

actus reus of murder takes place or where a tort was committed.[25] Difficulties about the allegedly correct description of the conduct in question – for example, did the *actus reus* of murder occur when defendant shot the victim in state X, or when the victim died in state Y? – do not weigh heavily with judges who have developed a number of tests, not all of them compatible, to deal with these issues.[26] These tests are in fact more sensitive to the values and policies of the area of law in question than to what some regard as the metaphysical truth of the matter about individuation.

Moreover, two considerations suggest it is a mistake to expect matters to be otherwise. First, some philosophers are far more pragmatic about individuation than their coarse- and fine-grained brethren, holding (in a muffled echo of pragmatic judicial practice) that one's approach to the individuation and description of conduct is determined by one's purposes. Since there is a variety of such purposes – and seeking metaphysical truth is but one among them – it is said that as a result there can be a plethora of descriptions of the same segment of conduct, each presumably sensitive to its purpose.[27] It will be no surprise if philosophical and judicial purposes diverge and thus even less of a surprise if, as a consequence, philosophical and judicial responses to the individuation problem differ. Of course, the ultimate weight of this point depends upon there being independent reasons supporting both judicial and philosophical pragmatism, reasons that do not simply highlight the weaknesses of fine- and coarse-grained accounts. One such reason is our second consideration. It is that the law should be parsimonious when taking metaphysical or philosophical sides, doing so only when absolutely vital, in order to avoid unnecessary controversy. That it seems unlikely that the law will ever have to take philosophical sides on the issue of individuation

[25] In claiming that the courts respond pragmatically to this question, as they do to some others that raise large philosophical issues, I do not mean to invoke a theoretical or philosophical account of pragmatism. Rather, I use that word in its ordinary, everyday sense. For just the kind of theoretical account of pragmatism that I want to avoid, for reasons too numerous to recount here, see R. Posner, *The Problematics of Moral and Legal Theory* (Cambridge, Mass.: Harvard University Press, 1999), ch. 4.

[26] For treatments of some of the cases, see Moore, supra, note 22, pp. 293–301, and White, supra, note 22, pp. 41–43. Moore is highly critical of judges' lack of philosophical seriousness on the issue of individuation, believing that what he takes to be good metaphysics leads to good law. For a more measured view of the relationship between legal and philosophical judgments in the general area of responsibility, see J. Feinberg, *Doing and Deserving* (Princeton, New Jersey: Princeton University Press, 1970), ch. 2.

[27] See Duff, supra note 18, p. 41. Presumably, amid all the descriptions, there is some one thing that is being described? See Moore, supra, note 22, ch. 4.

is suggested by the fact that neither of the principal views appears to yield unambiguous or conclusive answers to specific doctrinal questions nor is one obviously and unambiguously correct. The former feature could, of course, be a consequence of the fact that competing approaches to the metaphysics of individuation are just as 'blunt' as general normative theories often are, setting only the general parameters within which legal doctrinal questions must be understood but not determining the answers thereto.[28] That latter feature is simply a consequence of philosophical stalemate.

Let us return to the second claim about basic responsibility. It, like the first, also poses at least two difficulties. The first raises the question of which, if any, events in the world are properly an agent's deeds as opposed to events in which an agent is engulfed. My walking downstairs to get the morning newspaper seems obviously to be my deed, but what about the trip and fall half way down? And what is it that makes lifting my leg when dancing or playing football my deed, but my leg's moving as a result of the doctor's tap on my knee something quite different? Many philosophers seek to distinguish between my deeds and events in which I am involved by invoking the related notions of intention and agency. A standard move here is to hold that for a deed to be an agent's in the strongest sense, a sense which founds the claim that she is indisputably its author, she must have both done it and intended it. And what the latter means is, at least, *that the deed in question was one of the agent's purposes and, as such, was something she had reason to do*.[29] So, if I intend (have reason) to and do lift my leg (when playing football, for example), that is my deed, but my leg moving as a result of the doctor testing my reflexes is not (assuming I am not trying to cheat the test). Invoking the notion of intention to deal with the first difficulty also appears to solve a second, namely, that of *determining the relation between doing something for reasons and doing something intentionally*. On this view, they are one and the same. While this view is not completely uncontroversial, it is sufficiently robust

[28] For insightful elaboration of this general theme, see: N. E. Simmonds, 'Bluntness and Bricolage', ch. 1 of H. Gross and R. Harrison (eds.), *Jurisprudence: Cambridge Essays* (Oxford: Clarendon Press, 1992). I extend Simmonds's notion of bluntness beyond its original contours and claim it is a feature not just of law (as he maintains) but of morality and, perhaps, general philosophical theories. For me, bluntness cuts both ways (!).

[29] Hence Davidson's view that deeds intentional under some description, although not the only deeds attributable to my agency, can certainly be ascribed to my agency: supra, note 21, ch. 3.

as to require no defence here.[30] Altogether more problematic is one of the two accounts of agency that can be built upon it.

Accounts of agency are usually either narrow or wide. A narrow view holds that agency is best understood as acting intentionally and that this is a matter of acting for reasons. The parameters of agency are restricted on this view since, although some of our conduct is intentional, much of it is not. Furthermore, what I intentionally do has many outcomes, few of which are usually intended. Yet those outcomes seem rightly attributable to me and are clearly dissimilar to mere 'events' in which I am caught up. So, although a narrow view of agency offers a clear distinction between conduct that is properly mine (my intentional conduct) and mere events (everything else), it relegates to the latter category some material that seems inappropriate there (the unintended outcomes of my intentional conduct). By contrast, a wide view of agency extends agents' conduct considerably beyond their intentional actions. Intentional conduct is, on such a view, but a subset of what agents do. The wide view attributes to agents and their agency all the outcomes of their intentional and non-intentional conduct as well as that conduct itself. This view therefore regards human beings as the authors of all that they causally bring about in the world. The event in the world that is my accidentally bumping into you is as much my deed as my intentionally slapping you; both are results of my agency. This need not, however, imply that you should respond to both manifestations of my agency in the same way. The wide view of agency is perfectly compatible with the standard differences in our reactive attitudes to intentional and other kinds of conduct. As was once famously remarked, even a dog knows the difference between being kicked and being tripped over.[31]

Private law doctrine does not take a position on which view of agency is correct, nor does it need to; it can accommodate either. Were it to adopt the narrow view, the only consequence would be the realization that liability in private law (as in criminal law) exceeds the bounds of agency. This much is obvious from the fact that in private law the dominant

[30] My linking intentional action with reason-governed action, the notion of purpose providing the linking medium, ensures that the account of intentional conduct here is broadly compatible with that offered by Duff, supra, note 18, ch. 3. Two useful critical evaluations are J. Gardner and H. Jung, 'Making Sense of *Mens Rea*: Anthony Duff's Account' (1991) 11 *Oxford Journal of Legal Studies* 559–588 and A. P. Simester, 'Paradigm Intention' (1992) 11 *Law and Philosophy* 235–263.

[31] The phrase is credited to the American judge and jurist O. W. Holmes, but where he said it and when is unclear (to me at least).

model of responsibility is outcome responsibility.[32] Alternatively, private law could adopt the wide view, a consequence being the recognition that legal liability often does not extend as far as agency. This again is obvious, since one is not always or even often liable in private law for all the causal outcomes of one's (intentional) conduct. Of course, were there a clear metaphysical truth of the matter here – suppose, for example, that the wide view of agency was obviously correct – then that would provide a reason why the law ought to embody that view. This reason is not, however, particularly weighty, since metaphysical truths must be accommodated within the existing set of values and discriminations that the law makes. It is an open question as to which set of considerations – legal or metaphysical – should dominate.

Finally, a possible confusion that flows from our conversion of the last part of second claim about basic responsibility (doing something having had reason to do it) into a claim about intentionality (doing something for reasons simply is doing that thing intentionally), must be dispelled. It can arise in this way. Because it is certainly not necessary for liability in most areas of private law for the defendant to have intended to bring about the wrong in question, or even to have intended those outcomes of their conduct which constitute that wrong, some conclude that liability here has 'no mental element'.[33] Take two examples. Liability in negligence certainly does not depend upon the defendant intending, being reckless toward, or even being practically indifferent to, the specific outcomes of their conduct; similarly, liability for breach of contract does not depend upon the defendant having intentionally, recklessly or negligently failed to perform their obligations. So is it folly to claim that basic responsibility in private law requires those in the frame for liability to have done something that they had reason to do, which is to say, to have acted intentionally?

Yes and no. Yes, if by that claim we mean that defendants must have brought about private law wrongs like a breach of duty of care or breach of contract intentionally. It is very rare indeed that defendants are required to intentionally bring about the whole or even part of a private law wrong. No, if we mean, as I do, that private law wrongs must in the normal course of events be the *outcomes* of intentional conduct. Think again of liability in negligence. The wrong here includes some conduct

[32] See Chapter 2, pp. 53–60 for a reminder.

[33] See P. Cane, '*Mens Rea* in Tort Law' (2000) 20 *Oxford Journal of Legal Studies* 533–556, p. 536.

(whatever it is that breaches the duty of care) which has some specific outcomes (among which are included foreseeable damage to the claimant). However, only the conduct that breaches the duty, or some conduct of which that breach is an outcome, need be intentional. The situation is the same when we consider liability for breach of contract. The wrong here is failure to perform one's contractual obligations and it is enough for liability that non-performance be an outcome of some intentional conduct; non-performance itself need not be intentional. Thus, assuming these examples are representative, it can be said that although it is rare that private law wrongs must be brought about intentionally, such wrongs must almost always *flow* from intentional conduct. Indeed, some intentional conduct is almost always required for liability in private law insofar as defendants must be responsible in the basic sense. To be able to account for some aspect of one's conduct is, in most instances, to be able to act for reasons; and acting for reasons is a matter of having reasons as the goals or causes of some aspects of one's conduct. Having reasons as the goals or causes of one's conduct is to engage in that conduct intentionally.

Note that if liability must flow from intentional conduct, then an important asymmetry arises between the second claim and the other two. Recall that in the first and third claims about basic responsibility the notion of capacity – capacity to have reasons and capacity to foresee outcomes – is in play. It has no such role in the second claim, which holds that to be liable defendants must *actually* have done something intentionally that has as a consequence a private law wrong. 'Mere' *capacity* for intentional conduct is not enough. Why? Because intentional conduct is the best indicator we have of basic responsibility. This is not to say it is the same as basic responsibility since, as the other two of the three claims show, basic responsibility involves more than intentional conduct. But the presence of intentional conduct – the sheer fact that the defendant's conduct was based on reasons – entails, first, that the defendant was aware of that conduct and the reasons for it and, second, that on this occasion the defendant had the capacity to act on reasons. From these entailments two less secure but common and obvious inferences can be drawn: first, that in general the defendant has the capacity to act on reasons and, second, again in general, the defendant has the capacity to foresee some of the outcomes of their conduct. Of course, these latter two inferences do not necessarily follow from the first two; the most that can be said is that they follow in the normal course of events. Moreover, it is these two inferences that are most often in play in cases in which basic responsibility is in issue. In *Mansfield*, for example, no one would have thought of denying the claim that the accident flowed from some intentional conduct on Mr. Tarleton's part, since at some point it was undoubtedly his purpose to drive his vehicle. What was contested were the inferences normally drawn about what those capable of intentional conduct are also capable of or have the capacity to do. This idea of capacity is thus very important and also potentially problematic; we will examine it once the equally problematic notion of rationality has been elucidated.

RATIONALITY

The notion of rationality is forced upon our agenda by the simple fact that it is closely related to each of the three claims made about basic responsibility. Once it is accepted that intentional conduct, which as we have seen is a matter of doing or refraining for *reasons*, is an element of basic responsibility, the topic of rationality becomes salient. It makes a further claim upon our attention when we recall that basic responsibility requires agents be aware, or have the capacity to be aware, of some segment or outcome of their conduct. This recollection prompts a question about the type of awareness necessary. And it is tempting, particularly when under the influence of second claim about basic responsibility, to answer that the type of actual or capacity awareness required is *rational* awareness. This, of course, raises yet more questions, two of the most pressing being: what is rational awareness and does it admit of degrees?

A promising and obvious way of answering the first question would be to invoke the many analyses of the general notion of rationality offered by philosophers, economists, social and game theorists. Although they differ in many respects, these analyses converge on the view that there is a general, fairly complex concept of rationality in conduct available to us and that it has at least four features or senses, some of which are closely related.[34]

The first is evident from the fact that sometimes when we speak of an agent being rational we mean that they are a good evaluator and selector of methods by which to realize their goals, whatever those goals may be. Furthermore, 'good' here means having a track record of choosing

[34] Good overviews of rationality in action are P. Moser (ed.), *Rationality in Action* (Cambridge: Cambridge University Press, 1990) and S. Hargreaves-Heap *et al.*, *The Theory of Choice* (Oxford: Blackwell, 1992). Rationality in belief, while obviously a related notion, has rather different features: a fine treatment is R. Nozick, *The Nature of Rationality* (Princeton, New Jersey: Princeton University Press, 1993), ch. III.

methods which are the cheapest or quickest or least disruptive or most effective. Conduct is either rational or irrational on this view according to how efficiently it brings about specified ends. Since rationality in this sense is a matter of determining the most efficient means to particular ends, this sense is best characterized as instrumental. The second sense in which rationality is commonly used is the substantive sense. Here a rational agent is one whose selection of long-term ends and shorter-term goals is in accord with what reason demands. So, just as the *means* of realizing particular goals and ends can be assessed as more or less rational, so too can those *ends* and *goals* themselves. On this view, there are reasons why some actions or courses of conduct – aiding those in peril, caring for one's parents and offspring – should be pursued and reasons why others – killing the innocent, torturing children – should not, and these reasons must resonate within agents' goals and ends. Ends and goals that are plainly contrary to reason should not be adopted, either directly (I am going to kill V) or as means of achieving other, ostensibly rational goals or ends (killing V and harvesting his body parts will help me and a number of others to live better lives). A substantively rational agent is therefore one whose ends, goals and conduct are all in accord with reason. While this sense of rationality is regarded as either dubious or unintelligible by some, that is not in itself enough to discredit it; the project of determining which ends and goals must rationally be pursued has been and still is a live one for many moral philosophers.

Remaining focused on ends and goals helps to illuminate a third sense that rationality often bears. For one way in which we assess agents and their conduct as either rational or irrational is by invoking the notion of consistency. An agent is often regarded as rational if their goals and ends form a consistent set: hence members of the set must not undermine one another (as the goal to eat as much chocolate as possible would undermine the goal of eating healthily) or must not be significantly jointly impossible (it is almost certainly true that one cannot eat chocolate for every meal and eat healthily). Note that goals and ends can be insignificantly jointly impossible in an obvious sense – one cannot practise the violin and swim at the same time – but both can undoubtedly be done given proper management and they need not undermine or conflict with one another. But it is not only agents' ends and goals that can be subject to a consistency test and thus assessed as either rational or irrational – exactly the same test can be applied to the set of means agents adopt to achieve their ends and goals. Indeed, this level of assessment can be fairly complicated, since the members of an agent's set of means not only have to be consistent with one another but also consistent with the agent's set of goals and ends. On this sense, then, an agent's conduct is judged rational or irrational by virtue of its consistency or inconsistency with (i) their goals and ends and (ii) the other courses of conduct (means) to which the agent is already committed.

The final sense rationality can bear is obvious. The term can be used to highlight that which is consistent or instrumentally or substantively rational in *general*, by reference to nothing but the universal rules of standard logic and epistemic canons of information-gathering and evaluation. Or, it can be used to refer to what is rational in a *particular* context of choice and action, and in light of the abilities of particular agents. This sense is most appropriate when determining the rationality of beliefs, for what it is rational to believe is often determined by the context in which one finds oneself. If one has unlimited time and large amounts of reliable information the beliefs about Q that one arrives at might well be more reliable than if one has very little time and next to no reliable information. Although the beliefs about Q arrived at in each of these situations will most likely be different, it can still be maintained that in each set of circumstances the beliefs arrived at were rational. In the first situation, it could be said that the beliefs arrived at were rational according to general standards for reliable belief formation while, in the second, rational in that particular context. Since our beliefs often determine our conduct, the point can be extended. Both agents and their conduct can thus be judged either rational or irrational at large or within some particular circumstance or context.

With the four senses of the general concept of rationality in mind, the second question can easily be answered: of course rational awareness admits of degrees, since it is surely obvious that agents can be more or less rational in each of these senses. It might thus be assumed that the only remaining task for the philosopher of private law is therefore to determine whether all or only some of the senses of rationality are important for legal liability and in what degree. But, although this is undoubtedly an important task, it is not one to which philosophers of either private or criminal law have devoted much time. Indeed, jurists' accounts of rationality are at best rather emaciated and distant relatives of the general concept just outlined. Since these accounts are, when compared to the general concept of rationality, so limited, it is wrong to regard them as competing conceptions of that general concept. This is because competing conceptions of a concept agree on the broad contours of a concept and go on to contest or elaborate some of those contours in different ways.[35] Why is it that the accounts of rationality jurists think underpin basic responsibility rarely make any mention of the general concept of rationality and, therefore, ignore which if any of its senses are in play and in what degree?

Only speculative answers are available to this question, since the jurists involved fail to provide even the slightest textual hints as to how they think it should be answered.[36] But from the fact that these jurists' accounts of rationality are so narrow it is charitable to infer a particularity of purpose, and that purpose could be something like this: these accounts aim only *to characterize rationality as a capacity that can be manifest in actual conduct by actual agents*. Even though it might be objected that this is just what general accounts of rationality also aim to do, it must be conceded that such accounts (obviously) tend toward generality and abstraction. Jurists' accounts do not or, at least, do so to a far lesser degree: their accounts of the notion of rationality that underpins basic responsibility are (obviously) limited by context and this could well explain the lack of any extrapolation to or from the general notion of rationality. What, then, do jurists say of this notion? Generally speaking, they say two rather different things, depending upon whether they embrace a maximal or minimal account of the idea of rationality that underpins basic responsibility. That jurists offer such accounts implies two things: first, that they all agree that some degree of rational awareness is usually necessary for legal liability; second, that they all agree that such awareness is a matter of degree, although they disagree as to how high or low the standard should be set.

Maximal accounts are in broad agreement on at least three issues. First, that rationality here is a matter of understanding or being able to understand the requirements of morality and law. Second, that it involves a capacity for deliberation or reasoned choice and, third, that this capacity must also be manifest in action: rational agents have the capacity to ensure that their deliberations inform their conduct.[37] Maximal accounts differ only over how one or more of these three issues is best delineated or unpacked. So, for example, Tony Honoré holds that the first issue – that

[35] R. Dworkin, *Law's Empire* (Oxford: Hart Publishing, 1998), pp. 70–73.

[36] Indeed, some invoke the notion of rationality rather too hastily, as if it were unproblematic and not in need of analysis: see M. Smith, 'Responsibility and Self-Control', ch. 1 of P. Cane and J. Gardner (eds.), *Relating to Responsibility* (Oxford: Hart Publishing, 2001), pp. 2–7.

[37] See Hart, supra, note 5, p. 227; T. Honoré, *Responsibility and Fault* (Oxford: Hart Publishing, 1999), pp. 14–15, 26–32, 36, 122, 138 and pp. 219–220 of his 'Appreciations and Responses', ch. 9 of P. Cane and J. Gardner, ibid.

of understanding or being able to understand what law and morality require – demands a general understanding on the part of those subject to the law of 'both the system of allocation according to outcomes and how in practice to use causal notions to settle what counts as the outcome of an action'.[38] By contrast, Herbert Hart, Honoré's long-time collaborator, is nowhere near so specific, being content to elucidate the requirement of knowledge of law and morality only in the most general, almost vague, terms.[39] Maximal accounts deserve their name because, as can be seen from the three issues just noted, they add more to the notion of basic responsibility than the requirement that agents engage in intentional conduct which has a private law wrong as one of its results or consequences. For, while this requirement might be subsumed under or implied from the second and third issues upon which maximal accounts agree, the first issue is clearly much wider than this requirement. Actually understanding the requirements of law and morality, for example, entails some knowledge of both, and this, obviously, goes beyond simply engaging in intentional conduct.

Minimal accounts, unsurprisingly, omit one or more of the three issues that maximal accounts include, usually offering a conception of rationality which rarely goes beyond that already implicit in the idea of acting for reasons. John Gardner's account is a good example that must, however, be treated with caution since he does not explicitly set himself to offer an account of rationality. Nevertheless, Gardner's view of basic responsibility as 'an ability to offer justifications and excuses . . . the ability to explain oneself, to give an intelligible account of oneself, to answer for oneself, as a rational being'[40] obviously incorporates such an account. Moreover, it is an account of rationality which, without more, is far less demanding than those offered by Honoré and Hart, primarily because it does not require knowledge of either law or morality. It is similar to maximal accounts only in the sense that the ability to explain oneself, to give an intelligible account of oneself, is very closely related to both the capacity for deliberation and the ability to ensure deliberation informs conduct. Peter Cane also espouses a minimal account, holding that rationality in this context is merely a matter of being able to reason practically and 'to be guided by rules'.[41] He is keen to emphasize that the

[38] Honoré, *Responsibility and Fault*, ibid, p. 32.

[39] Hart, supra, note 5, pp. 227–229.

[40] Supra, note 1, at p. 161. See also his 'The Gist of Excuses' (1998) 1 *Buffalo Criminal Law Review* 575–598, pp. 588–589.

[41] See Cane, supra note 5, p. 35 (see also p. 114).

level of rationality, which is but part of the capacity the law requires for liability, is low.[42] Cane's minimal account of rationality is similar to Gardner's in two respects: first, it does not explicitly require knowledge of the law or of moral right and wrong; second, the capacity to be both guided by rules and to reason practically (which at some point must, at the very least, overlap even if they are not one and the same capacity) are surely closely related to the ability to explain oneself.

Since basic responsibility could rest upon one or other of these two different accounts of rationality, it is worthwhile attempting to choose between them. This is not, however, a straightforward matter, primarily because the criteria by which such a choice could be determined are both contestable and evenly balanced. One surely relevant criterion is 'fit': is one account of rationality better represented in legal doctrine than the other? Cases like *Morriss v Marsden* might incline us against maximal accounts since they show that, in some areas of private law at least, provided the defendant is capable of engaging in intentional conduct, he need not also appreciate that his conduct is either morally or legally wrong.[43] But there are not a great many cases in similar vein and *Morriss*, like just about any other private law case, is not unimpeachable. Proponents of maximal accounts would, of course, need to find some legal doctrinal peg upon which to hang an argument against *Morriss*, but that is not too difficult if it is true that no single conception of rationality is dominant in private law. This possibility, however, simply compounds the difficulty of choosing between accounts. For, if the legal doctrinal picture is mixed, each account being represented in the law, the fit criterion is of little help.

Nor is it easy to choose between the two on what might be dubbed coherence grounds. That is to say, since both accounts are reasonably intellectually robust and intelligible, neither one nor the other can be dismissed as being incoherent. Since it is also true that neither one nor the other has obviously bad consequences, imperilling some of our other securely held views or committing us to other unpalatable views, it is difficult to choose between them.

The remaining criterion that might determine our decision in favour of one account or the other is that of normative acceptability. This is a matter of showing that the balance of normative reasons shows that one or other account is better. Such reasons can be drawn from within the law and based upon its internal value structure and can be either narrow,

[42] Ibid at pp. 65, 72, 76–77 and 114–115.

[43] Supra, note 13.

having force only within a particular area of legal doctrine like private law or some segment of it, or wide, having force across the legal system as a whole. Alternatively, such reasons can be drawn from outwith the law, from the framework of some general and allegedly powerful moral, political or other normative theory that acts as a standard against which the law is to be assessed. If such a moral, political or other normative theory supports one or other conception of rationality, then that acts powerfully in its favour. It might, for example, be the case that some such normative theory would support the argument that maximal accounts of rationality in basic responsibility are just too demanding, setting the threshold for liability so high as to devalue the interests of victims of wrong-doers. Yet it is equally likely that the opposite view could also be supported by some normative theory or other and this illustrates the previously noted difficulty of 'bluntness'.[44] The difficulty, remember, is double-edged in that normative theories are not only often indeterminate because they are equally rationally matched one with another, so that plausible normative theory N supports legal choice 1, while plausible normative theory N1 supports legal choice 2, but also indeterminate in the face of specific legal choices. That is the situation in which no plausible normative theory generates an answer to a specific legal choice, either at the level of doctrine – where the choice takes the form of a specific question such as 'is merely doing what one is contractually bound to do good consideration for a subsequent promise?' – or at the level relevant here, namely, that of the foundations or presuppositions of legal doctrine.

If neither the fit, coherence nor normative criterion determines a choice between the two accounts of rationality, nor can an argument combining one or more criterion be constructed which makes one conception more salient than the other, then the following suggestion might be canvassed: embrace complexity. Since one account is not obviously normatively better than the other, since one is not clearly better rooted in legal doctrine than the other, and since neither is obviously incoherent, it seems to be the case that the reasons in favour of each are closely balanced. From this it is reasonable to infer that both accounts might indeed be valuable, that it might be a good thing if both play a role in the law, although not in the same specific area of doctrine. We might then go about arguing that there are reasons why one account of

[44] Simmonds, supra, note 28. The bluntness argument must not be confused with the more general and infirm argument about the redundancy of moral philosophy offered in R. Posner, supra, note 25, chs 1 and 2.

rationality does and should play a role in one area of private law and reasons why the other does and should play a role in another area. This possibility should never be ruled out in advance, although it sometimes is by philosophers of private law who mistake complexity for either untidiness or incoherence.

Furthermore, it seems that Honoré, one of our so-called rational maximalists, embraces just this kind of complexity. For, although he often affirms a maximal account of rationality, he sometimes also affirms a minimal account.[45] The apparent inconsistency disappears once it is noted that it is only when discussing private law liability that depends on fault – taken to mean intentional or reckless wrongdoing – that Honoré is a maximalist; when liability does not so depend, then he is a minimalist. Interestingly, the main concern of another maximalist – Hart – was with responsibility and excusing conditions in the criminal law where fault is, of course, an ingredient of most serious crimes. What we have here, then, is an apparently neat way of explaining and attempting to justify the complexity or variation within private and possibly criminal law on the issue of rationality. In those relatively rare areas of private law where liability requires fault (a requirement rather more common in the criminal law) basic responsibility entails a maximal account of rationality. And in the many areas of liability in private law where liability does not require fault, basic responsibility entails only a minimal account of rationality. But even this neat argument is not absolutely convincing, for this reason. It must demonstrate that the link between fault and maximal accounts of rationality is sufficiently strong to show that those who would sever it are mistaken. Yet since a conception of fault can, without obvious incoherence, be built upon the foundation of a minimal account of rationality,[46] the nature of this mistake is unclear.

Finally, let us briefly return to the general concept of rationality. Although jurists's accounts of rationality in basic responsibility are emaciated relatives of the general concept, it is worth noting a faint resemblance between them. It is between the first and second features of the general concept of rationality, on the one hand, and the related ideas of rational deliberation – or the capacity for such deliberation – and ability to translate deliberation into conduct, that figure in the work of both maximalists and minimalists, on the other. This similarity or, perhaps

[45] Honoré, *Responsibility and Fault*, supra, note 37, at e.g., p. 26 and p. 29, where the capacity for 'reasoned choice and action' is thought enough for liability (but see p. 122 for an interesting qualification).

[46] See Gardner, supra, note 1.

more accurately, consistency suggests that the latter could indeed be used to throw light upon the former, the idea of rational deliberation being read through the prism of accounts of instrumental and substantive rationality. Whether there might be interesting and useful intellectual payoffs from this process is not a matter than can be determined here; it nevertheless seems at first glance an issue worthy of attention from philosophers of both private and criminal law.

GENERAL CAPACITY

The idea of capacity figures in the first and third claims about basic responsibility. These two claims hold, respectively, that defendants must either actually be aware of their conduct or have had the capacity to be aware of it, and be aware of some of its outcomes and circumstances or have had the capacity to have been aware of them. What, then, might capacity mean here?

There are at least two salient understandings of capacity available in this context, although one has already been nailed to our mast. For the claim that defendants are only required to have the capacity for awareness of some outcomes of their conduct, as opposed to being actually aware of those outcomes, already commits us to one understanding of capacity. This claim and its cognates (about, for example, capacity to foresee effects rather than actual foresight of effects) commit us to the view that basic responsibility in private law rests upon the idea of *general* as opposed to *particular* capacity.[47] The difference between them is this: use of the former when, for example, we say that G can sink a six foot putt, does not commit us to saying that on any particular occasion now or in the future G will indeed sink a six foot putt. We must, however, have some basis for the claim that G can sink six foot putts and this, obviously, must be provided by what G has done in the past. We can only rightly claim that G can sink six foot putts if she has indeed done so at some point and, moreover, has actually sunk more six foot putts than she has missed. That being so, we can say that G has the capacity to, or G can, sink six foot putts: what is meant is that this is something at which G normally succeeds. This clearly does not imply that G will never or has never failed to sink a six foot putt; but if, from the moment at which we claim G has the general capacity to sink six foot putts, G never again sinks such a putt,

[47] What follows is derived from Honoré's classic discussion: *Responsibility and Fault*, *supra*, note 37, 'Appendix: Can and Can't'.

our judgment must change. The most we could then say was that G lacks a general capacity she once had.

Particular capacity is a matter of what G can or is able to do on a specific occasion. Suppose G has a seven foot putt before her. Can she sink it? This will be depend not just on G's general capacity, but also on all the relevant factors operative in this specific context like, for example, the rub of the green, the climatic conditions, G's own situation and, perhaps, the reactions of her playing partner. If she does in fact sink it, even though she has never before sunk a seven foot putt, we must conclude that she was able to sink that particular putt on that particular occasion. This obviously does not warrant the claim that G normally sinks (or has the general capacity to sink) seven foot putts, since we must be assured that this putt was not a fluke or a one-off. If G misses the seven foot putt we can, on the assumption that she has never before sunk a seven foot putt, say that she lacks both the particular and general capacity to sink such putts. One success would, however, refute the former judgment, although it would take many more successes to refute the latter judgment.

Is the difference between general and particular capacity or, what is the same thing, between can (general) and can (particular), simply reducible to the difference between a majority of successes or failures and one particular success or failure? If a tennis player has won one grand slam title then it is undoubtedly the case that he had the capacity (particular) to win a grand slam. But that fact alone will not obviously license the claim that he is capable of wining any more grand slams or, what is the same thing, has the general capacity to win grand slams. Indeed, that claim could only be made if and when he has a record of grand slam success or, perhaps, near misses. It therefore seems that the difference between general and particular capacity is indeed reducible to the number of successes or failures: single instances of either undoubtedly demonstrate particular capacity or the lack of it, while they tell us nothing or very little about general capacity or incapacity. If someone has just now succeeded in doing something for the first time, then this is neutral between them either having or lacking the general capacity to do that, while if someone has only ever done something once, in a history of many attempts, then that is surely evidence of lack of general capacity.

Why is it the case that the notion of capacity in play in basic responsibility is general capacity? What, if anything, makes general capacity better or more appropriate than particular capacity in this context? General capacity is the preferred notion here because it is parsimonious, incurring fewer problematic commitments than the alternative. Particular capacity has two such problematic commitments. First, it appears committed to what is called, in the next chapter, the principle of alternate possibilities. At its simplest, this principle holds that liability in private law, and liability-responsibility in general, turns on the ability of the agent to have done otherwise at the time of wrongdoing. If the notion of capacity in play in basic responsibility is particular, the question that must be asked of any defendant in the frame for legal liability is: could she, in all the circumstances of this case, have conducted herself in accordance with the law? If the answer is negative, the principle of alternate possibilities requires no liability, since on this view it is in some sense wrong to blame, punish or impose duties of recompense on those who could not have done otherwise than they did.

The second commitment follows directly from the first: it is a commitment to anti-determinism, where that means the espousal of one of a variety of theses which hold that some instances of human conduct cannot be explained by a body of knowable and general causal laws. This commitment is incurred in the following way. Suppose the answer to the question 'could the defendant have conducted herself in accordance with the law?' is answered affirmatively. That is, we hold that although the defendant *did not* actually conduct herself in accordance with the law in those particular circumstances, she *could* (particular) have so conducted herself in those precise circumstances. This implies that the causal context – a combination of circumstances, including those 'internal' to the defendant, like her mood, levels of fatigue and concentration etc., and those 'external' to her, like the general environment in which she is operating – in which the conduct arose was such that the outcome (conduct not in accord with the law) was not completely determined. It was not completely causally determined because the defendant had the power to do otherwise in that very causal context, and so was able to bring about a different outcome, namely, conduct in accord with the law. This, of course, raises an awkward question: why is the defendant's power to do otherwise not part of the causal context of the conduct that actually occurred? Why, in other words, is it not the case that the defendant's alleged ability to do otherwise was itself causally determined and determined in such a way that it was not exercised? This is the point at which a commitment to anti-determinism arises, if it is maintained that the defendant's ability is in some sense free from the causal forces that determine every other aspect of the conduct and its context. This ability must, therefore, be counter-causal, must in some sense run against or be free from the causal forces in play elsewhere and be unpredictable or unknowable or random. And that is the very reason why this commitment is problematic: the difficulty of integrating the counter-causal potential of human agents with our ordinary, causal view of the world and its processes.

General capacity lacks these two problematic commitments. It is not committed to the view that the defendant could have done otherwise in the precise circumstances in which their conduct took place; it is not therefore committed to holding that the defendant has, or agents in general have, some mysterious counter-causal power. General capacity

> does not imply a capacity to have behaved differently on the occasion for which the agent is being criminally prosecuted [or sued in private law] or morally censured. . . . When we say that someone can do something (has the capacity to do it) we use "can" in a general, not a particular sense: we mean that the person will in general succeed in doing it if they try. To assert that someone could have acted differently on a given occasion does not mean that given the precise circumstances, including the impulses to which the agent was subject, that person could have done something different. It is rather that doing something different was not ruled out by the agent's general capacities. It is after all perfectly familiar that we fail, say, on a particular occasion to jump a six-foot ditch, though we know perfectly well that we can jump it, perhaps because we have done it before.[48]

In the first and third claims about basic responsibility, then, holding that the defendant had the capacity to be aware of her conduct or to be aware of some of its circumstances or outcomes, is not to hold that she was actually aware of that conduct or its circumstances or outcomes. Rather, it is to hold that such awareness is something she is usually or normally capable of, even though she was not so aware on this particular occasion. Now, although this general sense of capacity seems perfectly intelligible, and while it lacks the awkward commitments the particular sense has when invoked in this context, it might be thought to be infirm in at least one respect.[49] This concerns the alleged moral significance of this account of general capacity.

[48] Honoré, *Responsibility and Fault*, supra, note 37, p. 139.

[49] For analysis of some other difficulties, see the essays by P. Pettit and M. Smith in P. Cane and J. Gardner (eds.), supra, note 36. The only false step in these two pieces is Smith's dubious replica counter-example: ibid, p. 15. Smith fails to follow up the implication of a replica being not just a 'molecule for molecule duplicate' (ibid), but also trait for trait, disposition for disposition, emotion for emotion duplicate. If the replica is the latter, then it surely undoubtedly embodies, even though it does not exist for long enough to act upon, the general capacities of the original. It is the fact that the original has these capacities that licenses the judgment that the replica also has them, if it is indeed a true replica.

The doubt about the moral significance of general capacity arises in the following way. Consider two situations:

(i) the defendant did C and could not in the particular circumstances of the case do other than C (but in general the defendant has the capacity to do not-C); and

(ii) the defendant did C and could not in the particular circumstances of the case do other than C (but in general lacks the capacity to do not-C).

Now it might appear to some that there is no morally significant difference between these situations and that Honoré's view, which holds that liability is appropriate only in (i), is wrong. Since in both situations there is a sense in which the defendant could not have done otherwise, how is it that the presence of a general but unexercised capacity in (i) adds up to a significant moral and legal difference between it and (ii)? Honoré's answer invokes the idea of fairness, holding that, because of their lack of general capacity, the defendant in (ii) is likely always to be disadvantaged by any liability regime that ignores his incapacity. The fact that he can not (general) do not-C means that he can not avoid future liability for C whatever he does; he is therefore likely always to lose under the regime of outcome responsibility that characterizes liability in private law. By contrast, the defendant in (i) has a good chance of avoiding future liability for C, since he has the general capacity to do not-C, by which is meant that in the majority of instances in which he attempts not-C he succeeds in doing not-C. He is not therefore likely to be an all-time loser under a regime of outcome responsibility. The moral difference, then, is holding the defendant liable in (i) is to hold him liable for a bad outcome which he could quite conceivably have avoided on this occasion had circumstances been different and could quite conceivably avoid in the future, whereas holding the defendant liable in (ii) is to hold him liable for something he could not conceivably avoid, either on this occasion or at any point in the future. The intuition at work is that it seems improper to hold defendants liable for conduct they can not, both in general and in particular, possibly avoid.

While this argument seems powerful at first glance, there is a snag. It takes us back to the position of shortcomers and the role of strict liability in private law. In Chapter 2 it was argued that legal liability-responsibility is a species of outcome responsibility and it was noted that, when compared with some other conceptions of responsibility, outcome responsibility is distinctive because of its concern with outcomes. Outcome responsibility is a conception of responsibility that judges us first and foremost on what we bring about in the world, often ignoring both our abilities and what we intended. Outcome responsibility might, as a result, seem to treat shortcomers – those always at risk of falling below the objective standards of private law – harshly, since it seems unfair to hold them liable for breaching standards of conduct they could not achieve. Indeed, it is the case, as Honoré rightly points out, that shortcomers are treated much the same way in private law as those subject to forms of strict liability. One strand of Honoré's argument is the demonstration that, once the role of objective standards and the treatment of shortcomers in private law are appreciated, it must be accepted that there is more strict liability than often assumed. In addition to what can be called formal instances of strict liability in private law – those instances explicitly labelled as such by the statutes, cases and textbooks – there is a large realm of informal strict liability wherein objective standards are enforced regardless of the particular abilities of those bound by them.

This might seem unobjectionable if it is the case that both shortcomers and those subject to formal strict liability must have general capacity in order to be liable *and* general capacity is understood as so far delineated. For, with the golfer example weighing heavily, we have assumed an obvious and relatively unproblematic understanding of general capacity. On this view, in order for there to be liability in private law it needs be established that the defendant, even if a shortcomer and therefore unable to act in accord with the law in this specific case ('can' particular), nevertheless had the general capacity ('can' general) so to act. The position of the legal shortcomer would then be exactly analogous to that of the golfer who usually sinks six-foot putts but who, on some occasions, misses such putts. It does not seem inappropriate to criticize the golfer nor, other things being equal, to hold the shortcomer liable, if both could in general do what they failed to do on a particular occasion. Furthermore, if both golfer and shortcomer have this general capacity, neither will be an all-time loser under the system of outcome responsibility, since by virtue of that capacity both should on the whole benefit more from the system than they lose. Thinking specifically of the shortcomer, the general capacity to do what the law requires or to avoid doing what it prohibits should enable him, on the whole, to avoid its maw and to take the benefits that flow from the outcomes he brings about in the world. What, then, is the problem?

It arises from the fact that Honoré seems to equivocate between the understanding of general capacity just offered and another, more problematic understanding. Sometimes Honoré holds that the general capacity required for strict liability is 'a general capacity for decision and action' (p. 40), combined with (i) knowledge of the system of outcome responsibility and its constitutive causal concepts; and (ii) knowledge that special responsibility attaches to some socially dangerous activities.[50] The latter point suggests that Honoré has instances of formal strict liability in mind, since social dangerousness is often regarded as a hallmark of genuine strict liability torts and crimes. Whether or not that is correct is not relevant here, nor are the details of the first subsidiary claim. What is crucial is the broad claim, namely, *that general capacity is simply the capacity for decision and action*. For, if shortcomers and those subject to strict liability are bound by this understanding of capacity, their position is quite different from that of the golfer and those who have the general capacity to do what would have avoided liability or blame. And so, too, might be our judgment of the propriety of holding shortcomers liable and of strict liability in general.

If our golfer has the general capacity to do what would have avoided blame, if, that is, he can (general) sink six-foot putts, it does not seem unfair to blame him when he fails on a particular occasion because we are holding him to a standard that is, for him, usually achievable. Similarly, it does not seem unfair to hold shortcomers to legal standards that they have the general capacity to achieve, even though they fail to match those standards on particular occasions. Again, the standard is an achievable one for them. By contrast, if capacity for shortcomers is understood in the second way, then they are liable whether or not they could (general) have done whatever was necessary to avoid liability. By analogy, the golfer would be blamed for missing the six-foot putt even though he could not in general do what would avoid blame, namely, sink six-foot putts. Shortcomers and our golfer are liable, on this view, if they had the capacity for decision and action, understand the system of outcome responsibility and its constitutive concepts, and have brought about a bad outcome. Moreover, they are blamed whether or not the standard they are held to was achievable. This seems especially harsh once we are reminded that

[50] 'To be outcome responsible . . . [agents] must understand both the system of allocation according to outcomes and how in practice to use causal notions to settle what counts as the outcome of an action . . . [and] to choose to act knowing that the outcome of the action will be attributed to the agent' (Honoré, *Responsibility and Fault*, supra, note 37, p. 32); in addition, '[t]o have capacity for strict liability the person must understand that a special responsibility attaches to socially dangerous activities. The relevant choice is the decision in light of that knowledge to embark on the activity in question' (ibid).

some and quite possibly all shortcomers such as, for example, learner drivers, trainee surgeons and incompetent muleteers, lack the general capacity to do what is required to avoid liability. That is, they are not in general able to act as fully qualified drivers (of either motor vehicles or mules) or surgeons. Therefore, although they are nevertheless legally liable, their position is quite unlike that of the golfer who has the general capacity to sink six-foot putts or the defendant who can in general avoid bringing about legal wrongs. While the latter are both held to an achievable standard, shortcomers clearly are not.

Once separated, these two readings of general capacity must also be labelled. The first, which we took, in light of some of the examples Honoré used, to be obviously correct, is the 'avoidability' reading.[51] It holds that defendants must have the general capacity to do what would have avoided liability. The alternative is the 'choice' reading, which holds that defendants must have, *inter alia*, the general capacity for decision and action but not the general capacity to do what would have avoided liability. Since these readings of general capacity are not identical, it is necessary to clarify exactly how they relate to one another. It seems obvious that if any agent has the general capacity for decision and action, then that agent must also have the general capacity to decide and engage in some particular segment of conduct.[52] And, among the particular segments of conduct in which an agent with the general capacity for decision and action can engage must be included, all other things being equal, segments of conduct that avoid legal liability. Of course, it does not follow that it is always possible that an agent with general capacity for decision and action can make any particular class of decisions and engage in any particular class of conduct: this is the force of our 'other things being equal' proviso. The world might be arranged, for example, so that an agent with the general capacity for decision and action, who can therefore make many different classes of decision and engage in many different types of conduct, cannot make a specific class of decision nor engage in a particular type of conduct. If this class of decisions and conduct is the

[51] Stated as such, it clearly belongs to Stephen Perry: see his 'Honoré on Responsibility for Outcomes', ch. 4 of P. Cane and J. Gardner, supra, note 36, pp. 74–79 and 'Responsibility for Outcomes, Risk, and the Law of Torts', supra, note 5, pp. 81–97. It is unclear whether or not Honoré thinks Perry's reading correct. His comments at p. 227 of 'Appreciations and Responses', supra, note 37, are unhelpful: they warn against a mistake (believing that defendants can (particular) always do otherwise) that Perry has shown no inclination to make.

[52] Engaging in conduct does not, of course, imply that consequences or outcomes that result are as one would wish.

class 'decisions and conduct that would avoid legal liability', as is perfectly conceivable, then the agent has the general capacity for decision and action but neither the specific nor general capacity to decide and engage in conduct that avoids legal liability. So, although the general capacity for decision and action *includes* the general capacity to engage in particular segments of conduct that avoid legal liability, the former does not guarantee the *possibility* of the latter. By contrast, any instance of genuine conduct – which is to say, any outcome an agent has caused which is also rooted in their reasons – that avoids legal liability is by definition an instance of the general capacity for decision and action.

Since these two readings of general capacity are not identical, it might be maintained that a choice be made between them. The grounds upon which such a choice must be made are by now familiar. If one or other reading better captures the law, then, if all other considerations are equal, that reading should be preferred. The difficulty is that neither reading is obviously more securely embedded in the law than the other. Nor should this be a surprise, for the simple fact is that private law discussions of basic responsibility have not yet reached the level of detail found in the two readings. Of the cases mentioned here, and of the remainder that touch upon the issue of basic responsibility, none have presented an opportunity for judicial analysis of either reading of general capacity, although all accept that the basic responsibility requirement must be satisfied. The 'fit' criterion does not, therefore, determine the choice between these two readings.

Nor, for that matter, does an intelligibility or coherence criterion. That is to say, since both readings are *prima facie* intelligible and coherent, neither one nor the other nor both can be rejected on that ground. It thus seems that by far the most salient criterion in play in this choice is the normative one. While one or other reading of general capacity could be preferred on normative – usually moral or political – grounds, those grounds would have to be both specific and precise. They would have to give reason for regarding the wrong done to shortcomers by being held to a standard they could not achieve, which would occur if we adopted the choice reading of general capacity, as more important than the harm done to the victims of those shortcomers. In which case, the argument for the avoidability reading of general capacity is made out. Or they would have to give reason for valuing the harm to victims of such shortcomers as more important than the wrong such shortcomers would suffer if liable, in which case the argument for the choice reading of general capacity is made out. The development of an argument one way or the other is no means impossible, but even cursory familiarity with much contemporary moral and political philosophy suggests that it lacks the level of detail required to answer such a specific question. The job of constructing such an answer will not therefore be a matter of simply 'reading off', in the way that the answers to yesterday's crossword can be read from today's newspaper, from some moral or political theory. Rather, it will be an altogether more demanding and creative task. Whether or not the principal theories in contention for the role of normative foundation of private law have the resources for this job is not tackled here. Further consideration of the choice between these two readings of general capacity must await another occasion.

BASIC RESPONSIBILITY: STATUS AND RATIONALE

The analysis of basic responsibility offered here yielded three initial claims that were subsequently unpacked. The three claims are that, generally speaking, those in the frame for private law liability (i) must either be aware of their liability attracting conduct or have had the capacity to be aware of it; (ii) that some aspect of their conduct must be theirs in the sense that they did it and had reason to do it; and (iii) that they must usually either be aware of, or have had the capacity to be aware of, some of the circumstances or outcomes of their liability attracting conduct. Taken together, these three claims establish that, at its broadest, basic responsibility is a matter of actually giving or having the capacity to give a reason-based account of one's conduct. This includes the ability to behave intentionally – to have and act upon reasons – since private law wrongs must be the outcome of intentional conduct even if not themselves intentional. It also includes actual foresight of, or the capacity to foresee, some outcomes of one's conduct; and actual awareness, or the capacity to be aware, of some of the circumstances of one's conduct. Furthermore, it was shown that in this context capacity must be understood in terms of 'can-general' rather than 'can-particular'. At this point two remaining questions about basic responsibility must be answered: Is basic responsibility actually embodied in private law? And, whether it is or not, should it be? These are, respectively, questions about *status* and *rationale* of the basic responsibility requirement.

The first question can be quickly dispatched. Our discussion so far suggests that the basic responsibility requirement is an entrenched feature of private law. Most areas of private law insist, either explicitly or implicitly, on basic responsibility before there can be liability. We have seen that the capacity requirements in contract law, for example, ensure that only those who are responsible in the basic sense can enter into binding contracts. In addition, many of the principal forms of liability in tort, like trespass, negligence, nuisance and defamation are triggered only by the conduct of agents capable of acting intentionally, even though they need not intend to bring about the wrong in question. However, it is also true that there are some areas of liability in private law, particularly tort, where questions as to the existence of basic responsibility seem otiose. The vicarious liability of an employer, for example, seems never to turn upon the issue of the employer's basic responsibility, although the basic responsibility of the employee is sometimes an issue.[53] While the justification for this particular doctrine is somewhat oblique, it is clearly regarded as an exception to the private law norm.[54] Nevertheless, its existence means it is misleading to say basic responsibility is a necessary condition for liability in private law where what is meant is that liability is *impossible* without it. Also, since common law adjudication is an incremental process in which judges focus primarily upon the particular case before them, it is quite possible for some decisions to be inconsistent with others and for judges, over time, to change their mind on a particular issue. In this environment it would not be a great surprise to find occasional exceptions to the basic responsibility requirement.

Of course, departures from the basic responsibility requirement are not immune to criticism. Arguments are available, to both lawyers in the courtroom and jurists in the seminar room, that suggest the requirement should be a necessary condition for all but the most exceptional types of liability in private (and criminal) law.[55] What are these arguments and how strong a case do they make? There are at least four arguments available. As will be seen, while three of the four purport, without aid from the others, to show that basic responsibility should be a necessary condition for legal liability-responsibility, one (the second) has greater power when combined with another.

One argument aiming to establish the importance of basic responsibility is the efficacy argument. Hart stated it in a typically elegant way:

[53] See *Buckley and Toronto Transportation Co v Smith Transport Ltd* [1946] 4 DLR 721.

[54] A good treatment of the issue is Markesinis and Deakin, supra, note 3, pp. 532–558.

[55] See Gardner, 'Gist', supra, note 40 at p. 588 (remember that he is concerned only with the criminal law); Cane, supra, note 5, speaks of capacity (which for him includes both basic responsibility and something like the principle of alternate possibilities) as a 'precondition of legal liability': p. 72.

> Though a legal system may fail to incorporate in its rules any psychological criteria of responsibility, and so may apply its sanction to those who are not morally blameworthy, it is none the less dependent for its efficacy on the possession by a sufficient number of those whose conduct it seeks to control of the capacities of understanding and control of conduct which constitute capacity [or basic]-responsibility. For if a large portion of those concerned could not understand what the law required them to do or could not form and keep a decision to obey, no legal system could come into existence or continue to exist. The general possession of such capacities is therefore a condition of the *efficacy* of law, even though it is not made a condition of liability to legal sanctions. The same condition of efficacy attaches to all attempts to regulate or control human conduct by forms of *communication*: such as orders, commands, the invocation of moral or other rules or principles, argument and advice.[56]

In the absence of beings capable of basic responsibility, then, law cannot exist. Since law is surely an instance of regulation through written and oral communication, it is impossible or senseless without beings capable of understanding such communication. And that capability, obviously, is undoubtedly part of, but not exactly coextensive with, basic responsibility.

So obvious is the argument from efficacy that it seems utterly irrefutable. That appearance is confirmed as correct once we attempt to challenge one or other of the assumptions upon which it rests. We could, for example, deny that law is a communicative method of regulating human conduct but this denial is entirely counter-intuitive; just about any lawyer and any citizen will concede that law is a matter of words, of interpretation and counter-interpretation, of nit-picking reading and pedantic writing, of communication. Understood thus, law undoubtedly presupposes the existence of beings capable of understanding its communication. Challenging this presupposition is self-defeating, since to *argue* that human kind consists of beings unable either to communicate or to understand the law's communications is an instance of a human being communicating with other human beings in the expectation that their communication will be understood. Of course, the challenge could be more limited. It might be argued, for example, that there are fewer human beings capable of communication and thus of understanding the law's communication than we assume.[57] This might well be right, but this limited challenge does not, without more, undermine the efficacy argument. The challenge is just as much a critique of, for example, existing

[56] Supra, note 5, p. 229.

[57] See M. Moran, *Rethinking the Reasonable Person* (Oxford: Clarendon Press, 2003), ch 4.

standards of literacy in a community, as it is an attack upon the basic responsibility requirement.

Whatever weaknesses the argument from efficacy has, they do not undermine its intelligibility or coherence. Hart might, however, be criticized for misunderstanding the scope of the argument but, as will be seen, this is somewhat uncharitable. Indeed, the criticism is already hinted at within Hart's statement, in the observation that 'general possession of . . . capacities [constitutive of basic responsibility] is . . . a condition of the *efficacy* of law, even though it is not made a condition of liability to legal sanctions'. The criticism is that if basic responsibility is indeed *a condition of the efficacy* of law, then it must also be *a condition of liability* to legal sanctions arising from either criminal or private law and that to deny the latter claim while affirming the former is inconsistent. The thought here is that those considerations which show basic responsibility to be a precondition for the efficacy of law in general also show that it is a precondition for legal liability in particular. It seems more than likely that Hart laments this inconsistency, since at a number of points he criticizes the criminal law for being too niggardly in its recognition of the importance of basic responsibility. Hart arguing that basic responsibility is a precondition for the efficacy of law, while also pointing out that it is not always recognized as a precondition of legal liability, shows him highlighting an unfortunate instance in which the law fails to live up to its commitments. But is it true that if basic responsibility is a precondition for the efficacy of law in general, it must also be a precondition of legal liability in private law? It must be, insofar as the particular (in this instance, the imposition of liability in private law) is truly a manifestation of the general (the preconditions for the operation of law *tout court*).

A second argument to support the basic responsibility requirement supplements the argument from efficacy. It differs from the efficacy argument in being less directly pragmatic, since the efficacy of law is not directly in issue here, and in taking up the perspective of the subjects of the law rather than of the law itself. It can be dubbed, non-pejoratively, an argument from human nature. Gardner articulates a version while developing an account of what it is to be a responsible being. Such beings, he says, must ultimately be thought of 'in terms of a composite speech-and-reason ability of the kind Aristotle called *logos*'; this is necessary if we are 'to grasp our natures as human beings'.[58] This view certainly draws upon an ancient and powerful strand of thought about what we – human beings

[58] Supra, note 1, p. 164.

– essentially are; it captures one of our most important ideas of and aspirations for ourselves. It is also in effect the flipside of the efficacy argument. Whereas the latter emphasizes that for law to be efficacious it must be directed to beings capable of – at the very least – understanding, the argument from human nature offers an account of the principal constituents of understanding. In this context understanding clearly presupposes (again at the very least) linguistic competence which, of course, is simply an aspect of the 'composite speech-and-reason ability' Gardner takes as a hallmark of normally functioning human beings. Both the argument from efficacy and the argument from human nature resonate strongly with those views of law which insist that it is a communicative enterprise.

Despite being richly suggestive, it could be claimed that the argument from human nature is both too contestable and too abstract. It might seem to be merely one of a number of highly contestable accounts of human nature competing to be incorporated into the law which, when so incorporated, will operate as a Trojan horse for some sectarian set of moral, political or other values. If arguments from human nature do indeed operate thus when invoked within the law, then they are certainly objectionable.[59] But the argument under consideration surely does not. This becomes obvious when it is combined with the efficacy argument. For then it is clear that the conception of human nature in play here is not simply any old contestable conception that might embody a particular scheme of sectarian values; rather it is *the* conception that underpins the law itself, *understood as a communicative enterprise*. The argument from human nature therefore invokes a conception of human nature that the law itself *must* invoke. And this conception, clearly, is both thinner than other conceptions, because unlike them it is not particularly morally or politically contestable, and more general than they, in the sense that it is presupposed by all of them. As to the claim that the argument from human nature is abstract, it is surely correct. But, again, when taken in conjunction with the efficacy argument we can see that it is abstract in a very specific and helpful way. It shows us what we must assume about human beings if law is a communicative enterprise. That is undeniably a general and abstract claim but, unlike some such claims, it tells us

[59] In recent legal disputes contestable conceptions of human nature have featured as a means to prohibit or uphold some or other sexual practice. For an excellent account of one particular legal controversy of this kind, see M. Nussbaum, *Sex and Social Justice* (Oxford: New York, 1999), ch. 12.

something important and illuminating. The compliant under discussion is thus a red herring.

The remaining two arguments supporting the basic responsibility requirement are more immediately derived from important principles of political morality than the previous two. The third is clearly independent of the others, having power in its own right and requiring little or no support from them. It is the argument from liberty, an interesting version having been offered by Neil MacCormick in a gloss upon Hart. MacCormick holds that, underlying the reasons Hart offered as to why criminal punishment is appropriate only for voluntary wrongdoers, 'is a principle of justice . . . concerned with giving people a fair opportunity to plan their lives and to avoid official intervention in their affairs. The value at stake is liberty in one's actings. The distributional principle is that all people ought to have the same equality of opportunity to secure their own liberty of acting.'[60] Although articulated within the context of the criminal law, there is no obvious reason why this principle should not also have weight in private law, if it can be utilized there and is indeed compelling. As to the first point, there is no real difficulty employing the principle in the private law context, provided two slight amendments are made. The first amendment is the substitution of MacCormick's and Hart's use of 'voluntary' by either 'basic responsibility' or 'capacity'. The substitution seems unproblematic, since the former term is closely connected with the latter synonyms and, in some of Hart's discussions at least, is sometimes used exactly synonymously with them. The second amendment takes more time to elucidate.

It concerns the idea of equality of opportunity in this principle. That idea is a rich one but is probably best understood – because it avoids unnecessary confusion and keeps ostensibly different considerations distinct – as entailing equal access to particular options such as, for example, specific jobs, primary education or mental health care. In MacCormick's principle, no such specific option is in play; rather, the general idea of liberty in one's actings is said to be the object of equality of opportunity. The problem is that the idea of 'equal opportunity to secure liberty' is vague and MacCormick's concern can surely be captured in clearer language. In particular, the related ideas of maximizing liberty and equality of liberty seem more illuminating.

To see this, consider using MacCormick's principle to support the

[60] N. MacCormick, *H. L. A. Hart* (London: Edward Arnold, 1981), p. 146 (discussing the arguments in Hart, supra, note 5, at pp. 181–183).

basic responsibility requirement. Instead of arguing, as MacCormick's formulation dictates, that the requirement must be maintained in order to uphold equal opportunity to secure liberty in acting, the claim would be as follows. Regarding basic responsibility as a precondition for liability (i) upholds a larger realm of liberty than would exist if neither that requirement nor some equivalent were required; and (ii) ensures the same amount of liberty for all citizens insofar as it is general, that is, applicable to all. The first point is obvious when a system of law premised upon the basic responsibility requirement is compared with one that is not. There will be more liability in the latter, since both those who have and those who lack basic responsibility will fall within the maw of the law, and less in the former, since only those who have basic responsibility are in the frame for liability. Moreover, a basic responsibility requirement that includes the choice reading of general capacity ensures more liability than one tied to the avoidability reading because the former requires less for liability (capacity for choice and decision) than the latter (choice, decision and avoidability). If we assume a conception of negative liberty, and combine it with the claim that liberty is, on such a conception, quantifiable, then the conclusion that accepting basic responsibility as a condition for liability upholds a larger realm of liberty than a principle that rejects basic responsibility quickly follows.[61] It is also true, on the same assumptions, that basic responsibility combined with the avoidability reading of general capacity upholds a larger realm of liberty than when combined with the choice reading. Furthermore, a conception of quantifiable, negative liberty enables us to determine the effect of a universal basic responsibility requirement upon the liberty of citizens and its effect would, of course, be the same for all.

Is MacCormick's principle, as amended, compelling? A proof of the value of liberty, even if available, cannot be undertaken here. Liberty is, though, undoubtedly an important political value in our culture and, as such, should be upheld wherever possible. If our legal systems can be structured in such a way as to ensure more rather than less liberty for citizens, then that is presumptively a good thing. Since a legal system with a basic responsibility requirement will ensure (all other things being equal) greater liberty to citizens than one that lacks such a requirement, then that requirement has some presumptive weight. Whether or not its

[61] Three excellent treatments of the idea of negative liberty are H. Steiner, *An Essay on Rights* (Oxford: Blackwell, 1994); I. Carter, *A Measure of Freedom* (Oxford: Clarendon Press, 1999); and M. Kramer, *The Quality of Freedom* (Oxford: Clarendon Press, 2003).

weight overrides all other considerations depends upon the role of liberty in our scheme of political values. While liberty is often regarded as important, it is not always accepted as pre-eminent, despite some powerful arguments to that end. For present purposes, our conclusion is modest: for supporters of liberty, MacCormick's principle certainly supports the basic responsibility requirement.

The fourth argument has already been noted both in Chapter 2 and in the previous section of this chapter. It can therefore be dealt with briefly. It is the argument from unfairness and its most interesting contemporary proponent is Honoré. The argument, remember, is that if those who lack the general capacity aspect of basic responsibility are held liable, then they will end up as constant losers under a system of outcome responsibility. Thus, it is 'unfair to apply the system [of outcome responsibility] to the incapable, for whom there is no likely surplus of benefit over detriment'; '[t]he reason for allotting responsibility to people on the basis of their general capacity is that they stand to win most of the time, because it is true by definition that, when they try, they usually perform up to their ability'.[62] The argument probably has more power when basic responsibility includes the avoidability reading of general capacity as opposed to the choice reading, since application of the latter entails whatever degree of unfairness is implicit in being held to a standard one cannot (can general) achieve. This quibble does not significantly undermine the general point that liability for those that lack basic responsibility is unfair: heaping disadvantage upon disadvantage conflicts with most of our intuitions about fairness, not to mention some of our well-entrenched beliefs about justice.

Do these four arguments add up to a compelling case for basic responsibility? More precisely, do they show that basic responsibility should, generally speaking, be a necessary condition for liability in private

[62] The two statements are from Honoré, *Responsibility and Fault*, supra, note 37, pp. 26–7 and p. 38 respectively. For the same refrain, but in the context of the criminal law, see p. 141: 'If life in community is to be looked on as something like a competition, in which those with impaired capacities find it more difficult to get things right, it seems fair that they should be punished or censured less when they get them wrong. They start the race from behind or have already fallen behind, so that if they stumble, any punishment should take account of the handicap they already bear. [.] For, to the extent that they are punished, the punishment may well operate as an additional handicap, so that next time round (say when they come out of gaol) they start from still further behind. It is as if the horse carrying the heaviest weight was obliged to carry a still heavier weight. It may be that this way of looking at behaviour, in the context of fair competition, explains why, given the competitive model of society which responsibility presupposes, capacity is taken into account when punishment and censure are in issue.'

law? Taken together, the first two arguments are undoubtedly a coherent and powerful package. It is difficult to take issue with them, and thus undermine basic responsibility, without lapsing into something close to a performative contradiction: without, that is, invoking the very concepts and ideas that the two arguments claim are vital constituents of the idea of law itself. The second pair of arguments also appear powerful, drawing as they do upon general political principles and values important in our culture. These two do not, however, supplement one another as effectively as the first pair. At least, this is the case if it is true that the ideas of liberty and of equality (a conception of which must ultimately inform Honoré's argument from unfairness) are independent of one another.[63] That being so, they can pull in different directions in one and the same case. For example, an argument from liberty could pull towards a restrictive reading of basic responsibility in order to ensure a wide sphere of freedom from legal intervention, while an argument from fairness might, because of its concern with equality between wrongdoers and their victims, insist on more rather than less legal liability. This potential tension requires management and cannot simply be swept under the carpet. Nevertheless, the four arguments do succeed in highlighting the normative significance of the basic responsibility requirement and illuminate what is sacrificed when it is not insisted upon. All four resonate particularly strongly with what can be called generic rule of law values: the erosion or rejection of basic responsibility therefore seems also to threaten another political ideal that is held dear.

Does anyone deny that basic responsibility is or should be a necessary condition for almost all instances of liability in private law? Full-frontal attacks upon the requirement are hard to find; most critical arguments concern its contours or the details of some of its constituents. A family of reductionist views of basic responsibility can sometimes be mistaken for direct attacks upon the requirement but, as a matter of fact, these views actually emphasise one dimension of basic responsibility to the exclusion of all others.[64] They are therefore probably best treated as instances of

[63] For a challenging argument that one is derived from the other see: R. Dworkin, *A Matter of Principle* (Oxford: Clarendon Press, 1986), ch. 8.

[64] Two contrasting examples: R. Epstein, *A Theory of Strict Liability* (San Francisco: Cato Institute, 1980), in which causation is ostensibly the most crucial factor in legal liability-responsibility judgments, and W. Malone, 'Ruminations on Cause-in-Fact' (1956) *Stanford LR* 60–99, in which policy factors are alleged to be far more important than causal inquiries in exactly the same kind of judgments! One criminal law related discussion did, in parts at least, look like a full-frontal attack on basic responsibility: B. Wootton, *Crime and the Criminal Law* (London: Stevens, 1963).

modification rather than rejection. Perhaps the nearest to a full-frontal attack upon basic responsibility comes, surprisingly, from Honoré, one of its most interesting defenders. Its constituents are Honoré's claims (i) that agents can be responsible without general capacity and (ii) that lack of general capacity sometimes only reduces but does not eliminate legal liability or moral blame.[65] A hasty reading of these claims can generate the judgment that Honoré thinks general capacity, which we have argued is a vital component of basic responsibility, is unnecessary for legal liability responsibility. One mistake here is to assume that Honoré's first claim must commit him to the view that *legal or moral liability responsibility* without capacity (or basic responsibility) is either possible or desirable. Rather, it is clearly more in accord with Honoré's general position to regard this claim as stating an undeniable truth: that those who lack general capacity (or basic responsibility) do not by virtue of that lack cease to be causal forces in world. They are, therefore, undoubtedly *causally responsible* for the outcomes they bring about in the world, whether or not they had capacity or satisfied the basic responsibility requirement when bringing them about. Furthermore, as Honoré recognizes, what agents without capacity bring about in the world certainly contributes to their biographies and will serve to some extent to make them the people they are.[66] But because the second claim holds unambiguously that there can be moral or legal liability-responsibility in the absence of capacity, this charitable interpretation of the first claim seems implausible. It also suggests that Honoré does not take the four arguments in favour of basic responsibility as seriously as he should. What is going on?

Perhaps this. Honoré might well be reluctant, as many will be, to completely ignore the harm inflicted on victims by those lacking capacity. Were we to hold that the harms brought about by those without capacity do not attract either legal liability or moral blame we would, in effect, regard those harms as having very little or no moral significance. And that

[65] *Responsibility and Fault*, supra, note 37, pp. 9–10.

[66] Ibid. Such outcomes must contribute to the identities and characters of agents who bring them about not in the way that conduct that is genuinely theirs does, since conduct engaged in and outcomes brought out when of general capacity are clearly expressions of their agency. Rather, conduct engaged in and outcomes brought about without capacity presumably contribute to character and identity in the same way as living through an illness or momentous events or having had a particular upbringing do: they are things one has experienced rather than things one has done. The dissimilarity is, of course, that conduct and outcomes in absence of capacity are caused by agents, whereas their upbringing or their ailments, or the momentous events they have lived through, usually are not.

judgment is a hard one to make with great confidence. Although Honoré accepts that lack of capacity reduces moral blame and legal liability, sometimes to zero, his unwillingness to hold that it should always do so may manifest his discomfort with the idea of regarding the harm done by those lacking capacity as insignificant. This discomfort may persist even in the face of the four arguments in favour of the basic responsibility (or capacity) requirement. What we have here, of course, is an illustration of the range and complexity of the normative considerations possibly in play when offering a justification for just one of the core concepts of private law. Those considerations will receive further attention in the second part of the book; our immediate task, however, is to examine the second part of the responsibility component of legal liability-responsibility in private law.

4

Responsibility II: Alternate Possibilities

For many lawyers, philosophers and citizens, the idea that legal and moral liability-responsibility require that those in the frame for blame could have done otherwise is sacroscant. At its most simple, 'this principle states that a person is morally responsible for what he has done only if he could have done otherwise'.[1] In the criminal law the principle seemingly holds that 'a person is not to be blamed for what he has done if he could not help doing it'.[2] The principle is also apparently in play in the two areas of private law with which we are most concerned: many claim that to be liable in either contract or tort, an agent must have had the ability or opportunity to avoid liability.[3] This principle is henceforth labelled the principle of alternate possibilities. This chapter argues that one version of this principle is redundant: it does no significant work in our thinking and our intuitions about the conditions for legal liability-responsibility.[4] Most of our commitments about legal liability-responsibility are better explained by a more sophisticated version of the principle, which also avoids a difficult snag that besets the simple alternative. That, at least, is the argument offered here. To that end, a number of steps are taken.

The first section (p.112) clarifies exactly what the principle of alternate possibilities might entail, offering two principal interpretations of

[1] H. Frankfurt, *The Importance of What We Care About* (Cambridge: Cambridge University Press, 1988), p. 1.

[2] H. L. A. Hart, *Punishment and Responsibility* (Oxford: Clarendon Press, 1968), p. 174. See also O. W. Holmes Jr., *The Common Law* (New York: Dover, 1991 (first published in 1881)), p. 55.

[3] See S. Perry, 'Responsibility for Outcomes, Risk and the Law of Torts', ch. 3 of G. Postema (ed.), *Philosophy and the Law of Torts* (Cambridge: Cambridge University Press, 2001), p. 91 and R. Bigwood, *Exploitative Contracts* (Oxford: Clarendon Press, 2003), pp. 114–116. Also interesting is Holmes, ibid, at *inter alia* pp. 95 and 144, and P. Cane, *Responsibility in Law and Morality* (Oxford: Hart Publishing, 2002), pp. 65 and 114.

[4] The issue of moral liability-responsibility and the role of the principle of alternate possibilities within it is not directly tackled in what follows, although some of the arguments considered have equal force against the principle within both moral and legal liability contexts.

how it can be understood and arguing that only one of these interpretations is ultimately defensible. This allows, in the second section (p.121), a defence of that ('sophisticated') interpretation against some ostensibly powerful arguments. This is combined with additional commentary upon the alternative ('simple') interpretation. The two interpretations of the principle of alternate possibilities are then put to work upon two segments of legal doctrine in section three (p.135), the point again being to demonstrate the superiority of one over the other. This is done obliquely, for it is argued that, while the simple version of the principle provides a poor account of these doctrines, the sophisticated version provides no account at all. Rather, all of our defensible intuitions in these two areas are accommodated on other grounds. Thus, although the sophisticated version of the principle has nothing to say about the doctrines in question, it nevertheless performs the useful role of redirecting the search for principles that can and do explain those doctrines. Furthermore, the sophisticated version is a smooth fit with everything said in Chapter 3 about basic responsibility, so the picture that emerges of two fundamental components of liability-responsibility in private law is a coherent one.

The apparent reformatory zeal of this chapter might be thought problematic. If this part of the book aims only to make the principles of legal liability-responsibility in private law intelligible, then it seems inappropriate to reject outright a version of a principle that many regard as fundamental. While not denying that many do indeed value the simple version of the principle of alternate possibilities, the argument that it should be jettisoned changes no legal doctrine nor impacts upon any case. Doctrine and cases are *better* explained by either the sophisticated version of the principle which is itself *better* because it has fewer snags than the alternative; or by reference to other considerations that are frequently obscured. The reform recommended is, then, quite modest, affecting only how we understand some of the words we use and leaving relatively untouched their illocutionary effect.[5] We will continue to act and react in the same way – continue to do the *same things* – when the sophisticated version of the principle is adopted. Yet the grounds on which we do so become more visible and open to evaluation. Thus, although apparently

[5] By which I mean, following J. L. Austin, that what we *do* when we use either the simple or the sophisticated version of the principle remains more or less the same. For the general point, see ch. 10 of Austin's *Philosophical Papers* (Oxford: Clarendon Press, 1961) and his *How to do Things with Words* (Oxford: Clarendon Press, 1962), chs. VIII and IX. This point does not commit us to distinguishing, as Austin attempted without much success, between illocutionary and perlocutionary speech acts.

new, the sophisticated version of the principle simply provides a clearer view of the basis of existing practice.

THE ALTERNATE POSSIBILITIES REQUIREMENT

Determining the meaning of the alternate possibilities requirement, over and above that contained in the statements just reported, is difficult. This is primarily because the principle is usually taken for granted, which is not to say that reference is never made to the principle. Rather, the position is just the contrary, the problem being that the many invocations of the principle are too glib: since it is taken for granted, its exact meaning is assumed to be obvious. Showing that the principle has two primary interpretations is one burden of this section, the other being a demonstration that only one of these interpretations is ultimately defensible. In addition, the following section seeks to protect this defensible interpretation against some ostensibly powerful criticisms. The overall aim is to show that what is supposed to be obvious – the content of the principle – is actually fairly complex.

Harry Frankfurt's statement of the principle of alternate possibilities (hereinafter *PAP*), that someone is 'morally responsible for what he has done only if he could have done otherwise', has the virtues of brevity and simplicity. But these virtues have a concomitant disadvantage, namely, that much is left unsaid. One relatively trivial point that must be spelled out is that *PAP* operates only at the time at which the person in the frame for moral and, presumably, legal liability-responsibility, did or brought about that for which they might be liable. Which is to say: it must be established that at the time A did or brought about X that he could instead have refrained from X or done not-X.[6] It matters not that A could have refrained from X or done not-X prior to or after doing X: those alternative possibilities are almost always irrelevant to a judgment of liability-responsibility.

A second point is that some versions of *PAP* offered by philosophers of criminal and private law have quite different elements. For, in addition to

[6] The awkward locution 'A did or brought about X' is henceforth dropped, but the following caveat must be borne in mind. The locution is necessary because, if X is a private law wrong, it rarely must be done intentionally and the phrase 'A did X' quite naturally leads us to assume, all other things being equal, that A intended to do X. 'Brought X about' and its cognates covers the normal instance of private law liability, namely, that in which X (a private law wrong) need only be an outcome of some intentional conduct on A's part. In what follows, 'A did X' and all similar phrases does not mean only 'A intended X' but also 'A brought X about'.

claiming *PAP* entails that agents have the ability to do otherwise or, what seems to be the same thing, that they could have helped doing what they did, it is often also claimed that agents must have had *control* of their conduct at the appropriate time.[7] This additional idea adds some degree of complexity to *PAP*, especially since it is in no way identical with ability to do otherwise. Clearly, one can be in control of one's conduct without having the ability to do otherwise: this is the case when, for example, I am engaged in obsessive compulsive behaviour or when my conduct takes place in an environment controlled by Frankfurt's demon.[8] Furthermore, it seems that the idea of control over one's conduct is in fact co-extensive with basic responsibility. Chapter 3 argued that this component of legal liability-responsibility in private law has at least three features and, taken together, they surely imply that defendants must have control over some aspect of their conduct or, at least, have the general capacity to control some aspect of their conduct. This being so, the control aspect of some formulations of *PAP* and the complexity it threatens can be safely ignored. Rather than adding anything to *PAP*, talk of control simply describes an aspect of basic responsibility.

Another element often added to *PAP* is the idea of *opportunity*, understood as entailing the possibility that agents can actually exercise either the ability to control conduct so as to adhere to the law or the ability to avoid doing what the law prohibits.[9] While the latter two limbs of this addition are relatively unproblematic, since they are merely equivalents expressed in the language of doing or refraining, the first limb is not.[10] This limb is significantly different from that to which it is added, for ability to do otherwise need not imply that that ability could actually be exercised at the time of the conduct in question. This is obviously so if the ability in issue is understood in terms of general capacity (can general), for there is no implication here that saying G can – has the ability to – sink six foot putts means he can sink a particular six foot putt. All we

[7] See Cane, supra, note 3, p. 65; Hart, supra, note 2, pp. 218 and 227 (Hart also holds that there should be no liability where defendants could not help doing what they did: ibid, pp. 39 and 174). Philosophers who add this additional control requirement to *PAP* do so to rule out chance occurrences being the basis of liability. For good philosophical treatment of this version of *PAP* (dubbed 'alternate possibilities control') see: J. M. Fischer, 'Recent Work on Moral Responsibility' (1999) 110 *Ethics* 93–139, p. 99.

[8] See p. 121.

[9] Cane, supra, note 3, p. 114; Hart, supra, note 2, pp. 181 and 201; Perry, supra, note 3, p. 91.

[10] It is not always easy to translate positive statements about doings into negative statements about refrainings and vice versa, as we will see in ch. 5.

are committed to, on an account of general capacity, is this: it must be true that G succeeds in the majority of instances in which he attempts to sink six foot putts. But in its central, ordinary sense a genuine 'opportunity' surely entails more than this, namely, the actual or outright possibility of doing or refraining from that which one has the opportunity to do or refrain from at the time of the conduct in question. It implies, in other words, not the general capacity to act or refrain, but the particular capacity to actually act or refrain in some specific circumstances. On this view, we would say that if, given our knowledge of all the factors operative in the causal web, it was not actually possible for G to sink a particular six foot putt on a specific occasion, then he did not have a genuine opportunity to sink it. And this judgment, of course, is arrived at regardless of G's general capacity to sink such putts. This point has, as will soon become clear, a crucial bearing on how 'could have done otherwise' may be understood but, before turning to that, a further complication with opportunity needs be noted and set aside. It is that some jurists who emphasize the importance of opportunity to do otherwise for liability often slip between that claim and the claim that liability depends upon *fair* opportunity to do otherwise.[11] Again it must be noted that these two claims are not identical, the latter having an obvious normative component that the former lacks or, perhaps, to which the former is not obviously and explicitly committed. Some of the considerations that inform the way in which this element of fairness must be understood, and the various complexities to which it gives rise, were touched upon in the final section of Chapter 3. They are not tackled again here.

The third point about *PAP* concerns the precise meaning of 'could have done otherwise'. This point is the most important because, unlike the previous two, it serves to distinguish two significantly different interpretations or versions of *PAP*. In so doing, it also raises the question of how these two versions – earlier dubbed 'simple' and 'sophisticated' but which for obvious reasons are relabelled here – should be evaluated. So, what exactly does 'could have done otherwise' mean? Does it mean that at the time A did X he could, as a matter of fact, have refrained from X or done not-X, even if all the causally salient circumstances that prevailed when X occurred remained the same? If that is so, then in order to be satisfied *PAP* seems to require that, at the time A did X, there was an outright possibility of A refraining from X or doing not-X, that

[11] Hart, supra, note 2. See also G. Watson, *Agency and Answerability* (Oxford: Clarendon Press, 2004), p. 10 and ch. 9 for the apparently related notion of 'reasonable opportunity'.

possibility being under A's control. Alternatively, 'could have done otherwise' might be understood in less demanding terms, as simply signalling that if circumstances had been significantly different, then A would have behaved differently: in the circumstances that obtained, A did X but had those circumstances differed significantly, then A would have refrained from X or have done not-X.[12] The principal difference between these two formulations of 'could have done otherwise' is that the former is an *actual sequence* version of *PAP*, whereas the latter is a *conditional* version.[13] The former reading is appropriately called an actual sequence version because it holds that, in order for A to be responsible for X, it must be true in the actual circumstances which obtained when A did X that A could in fact have refrained from X or done not-X. Which is to say that in the actual sequence of events that occurred there was an outright possibility of A refraining from X or doing not-X. The conditional version is so named because it asks not 'could A have refrained from X or done not-X in the exact same (actual) circumstances in which he did X?' but 'could A have done other than X if conditions had been significantly different?'[14]

It is now obvious that the actual sequence version of *PAP* is the one that must be espoused by those jurists who claim that the idea of opportunity is an important element of *PAP*. This is because 'opportunity', in its central sense at least, implies more than that agents in a particular context would have acted differently if circumstances had been significantly different (which is all that the conditional version of *PAP* requires). It implies that agents had the outright possibility to do otherwise at the time of the conduct in question. Furthermore, while the substance of the conditional version of *PAP* is surely a truism about human agents in

[12] The requirement that differences be 'significant' functions so as to aid discrimination between sensible changes to circumstances and silly changes; I have nothing to say about what the criterion of significance might be in the abstract.

[13] These terms appear in S. Hurley, *Justice, Luck, and Knowledge* (Cambridge, Mass.: Harvard University Press, 2003), pp. 16–17 and are used by many other philosophers (see, for example, Fischer, supra, note 7, p. 125). However, the usage in the text differs in one very significant way from the philosophical norm: Hurley, Fischer and others usually use the 'actual sequence' terminology to refer only to versions of *PAP* that lack a conditional element. This is nothing more than a stipulation and it is not particularly well founded, unless our actual sequence version of *PAP* (which has such a conditional element yet is dubbed an 'actual sequence' version to highlight the very fact that the outright possibility to do otherwise must exist in the *actual circumstances* in which the conduct was brought about) is somehow incoherent.

[14] Henceforth the term 'not-X' is used to refer to both 'acts other than X' and 'refraining from X'. While the latter is the contrary of X, the former need not be. The elision is purely stylistic.

general, namely, that insofar as they have even the most minimal powers of rationality their behaviour changes when circumstances change significantly, the substance of the actual sequence version is not. The claim that agents always have genuine opportunities to do otherwise is simply false. The advantage in being able to say which jurists espouse which version of *PAP* is this: it becomes easier to evaluate their respective accounts of legal liability-responsibility. For, if some such accounts rely upon a version of *PAP* that is weak or in some respect dubious, that is a good reason, all other things being equal, to reject those accounts. This, of course, raises an obvious question: how are the two versions of *PAP* to be evaluated?

One standard way of defending or attacking any philosophical position is by reference to broader philosophical and non-philosophical considerations that are either indubitably true or thought likely to be true. In this context, the most salient philosophical consideration is determinism, it now being almost orthodoxy for some that determinism is either true or likely to be true. Hence it must be established that, in order to be philosophically respectable, each version of *PAP* is compatible with this philosophical doctrine. At its most general, determinism holds that all human conduct is – and all events in the natural world are – caused. The many varieties of determinism make different claims about the precise nature of the causes that determine human conduct and events in the natural world, and they also differ as to the ways in which those particular causes can or should be explained by reference to universal law-like causal generalizations. However, lurking in the background of every version of determinism about human conduct is the claim that it, like everything else in the world, is caused and its causes are in principle knowable.[15] Determinism is the default position of most philosophers of action and of many moral and political philosophers; they are therefore inclined to reject any anti-deterministic interpretation of the components of liability-responsibility. Since the actual sequence version of *PAP* requires the outright possibility of A's doing otherwise at the time and in the exact same circumstances in which he did X, it is committed to holding that A has a contra-causal or extra-causal freedom and such a freedom is prima facie incompatible with determinism.[16] Since the conditional version of

[15] This is the principle of universal causality which is thought insufficient in itself to entail determinism; for an admirably clear account of what more might be needed, see P. van Inwagen, *An Essay on Free Will* (Oxford: Clarendon Press, 1983), pp. 2–8 and ch. III.

[16] 'Extra-causal' is van Inwagen's term, coined as a result of dissatisfaction with the 'contra-causal' alternative: see ibid, pp. 14–15.

PAP, when conjoined with the idea of 'can general', is not in this way incompatible with determinism, it is preferable.

Rejecting the actual sequence version of *PAP* in this way might seem trite. Why, after all, should the truth of determinism be accepted? There is no overwhelmingly compelling answer to this question, nor can all the attempts to answer it be evaluated here: the deep waters of the free will and determinism debate will take too long to navigate and the voyage promises, for current purposes, very little direct reward.[17] There is nevertheless one consideration which is, in the current context, particularly salient, and which should incline us toward determinism.[18] It highlights not so much the plausibility of determinism but the implausibility of indeterminism. The actual sequence version of *PAP* requires that agents have a contra-causal power and this seems quite mysterious. A world in which most of our scientific, cultural and economic knowledge is only regarded as such by virtue of its causal power, and in which some causal, law-like connections seem to pay dividends, in terms of knowledge, prediction and technology, is an inhospitable place for such a power. This is so *a fortiori* when a theistic world-view is abandoned. A power that is truly beyond the web of causality and causal understanding seems more appropriately assigned to the realm of the bogus and 'supernatural' rather than to the fabric of our actual world.

Some have, however, claimed to find in the natural world something analogous not to this contra-causal power as such, but to the indeterminacy or unpredictability that it embodies. It is often said that Heisenberg's uncertainty principle, which implies that position and momentum values for two particles cannot both be determinate, since the determinacy of one value in one particle (momentum, for example) brings about indeterminacy in the other value (position) in the other particle, illustrates an analogous indeterminacy.[19] But, although most respectable physicists accept that the truth of the uncertainty principle is beyond

[17] Which is not to say the debate is uninteresting or stagnant. Some particularly interesting recent contributions are: van Inwagen, supra, note 15; D. Dennett, *Elbow Room* (Oxford: Clarendon Press, 1984); R. Kane, *The Significance of Free Will* (New York: Oxford University Press, 1996); see also the essays in R. Kane (ed.), *The Oxford Handbook of Free Will* (Oxford: Clarendon Press, 2005).

[18] I am not, of course, maintaining that this consideration is particularly salient *tout court*; in the general range of reasons pro and con determinism, it might be of relatively little weight.

[19] 'Brings about' is deliberately ambiguous between the epistemic (often thought to be favoured by Werner Heisenberg himself) and ontological (favoured by Niels Bohr) readings of the principle.

doubt, its relevance to the explanation of human conduct is nevertheless questionable. The extrapolation from the domain of quantum mechanics to human conduct is a huge one and there are no well-established reasons to think that quantum mechanics is, in general, a good source of insight into human conduct. It is certainly the case that few other truths and principles in this domain have proved useful in the human or social sciences. There is, as a result, an immediate presumption against the principle's relevance here. Furthermore, even if the extrapolation were plausible, what the principle tells us about human conduct seems every bit as unpalatable as what determinism supposedly tells us. Whereas the latter, at the very least, holds that all human conduct is caused, the former ostensibly tells us that some aspects of human conduct are entirely 'indeterminate' or unpredictable and/or random. What succour can indeterminists possibly take from this supposed truth? The alleged unpredictability or utter randomness of some aspect of human conduct is surely a reason for despair rather than celebration; embracing it thus seems an *ad hoc* move to prop up an ailing theory rather than a requirement of the cold light of reason.

Nor should the rejection of the actual sequence version of *PAP*, because of its incompatibility with determinism, be impugned on the equally dubious but sometimes seductive ground that a dalliance with determinism puts at risk all that we hold dear. This misguided thought often takes this form: determinism makes our ordinary moral, reactive attitudes either impossible or redundant. These attitudes – of resentment and indignation, or of love and appreciation, and their various cognates – are our perfectly natural and predictable responses to the deeds and, by extension, the character of others, and are thought operative only when the conduct that triggers them is in some sense undetermined or contra-causal. The truth of determinism is therefore regarded as a huge threat to a vital component of our moral lives. But sober analysis suggests this is far from being so, since the assumption that our reactive attitudes require contra-causal freedom or some other, equivalent anti-deterministic view, is unfounded. Indeed, it has been argued that whatever redundancy arises in this context actually engulfs the effect of determinism upon these very reactive attitudes: the truth or falsity of determinism leaves these attitudes and the practices that embody them almost entirely untouched.[20] If

[20] See Sir P. Strawson, 'Freedom and Resentment' (1962) xlviii *Proceedings of the British Academy* 1–25. A fruitful reworking of these Strawsonian themes is R. J. Wallace, *Responsibility and the Moral Sentiments* (Cambridge, Mass.: Harvard University Press, 1996), chs. 2 and 3.

that it so, then our inclination towards the truth of determinism here, and thus our preference for the conditional rather than actual sequence version of *PAP*, is hardly worrisome.

Our conclusion is that the actual sequence version of *PAP* should be rejected. That, of course, has no effect at all upon the conditional version of *PAP*, which is adopted henceforth. Thus talk of 'could have done otherwise' or 'ability to do otherwise' should be interpreted accordingly, unless context requires otherwise. This means that when *PAP* is in play we are interested in whether or not the defendant or agent in question had the general capacity to do otherwise and not whether the defendant could actually have done otherwise in the actual causal circumstances of the case. One reason for this has already been elucidated: our preference for the conditional version of *PAP* is in part based upon the potentially dubious metaphysical commitments of its competitor. The other reason arises from our commitment to the notion of general capacity (as outlined in Chapter 3) and requires some unpacking.

The two readings of general capacity distinguished in Chapter 3 are related in an important way. The relationship is that the choice reading is more fundamental in the sense that it entails (but does not of course guarantee the practical possibility of) the avoidability reading.[21] This claim should not, however, overshadow the second, namely, that if practically possible, then the avoidability reading certainly entails the choice reading, albeit it in a limited sense. Any actual instance of genuine conduct that avoids legal liability is by definition an instance of the capacity for decision and action, albeit not necessarily an instance of the *general* capacity for decision and action. This is because this particular conduct could conceivably be the first manifestation of the capacity for decision and action so it might, therefore, be an instance of 'can particular' rather than of 'can general'. However, both readings are equally important in another respect, namely, that each entails the conditional version of *PAP*. How?

We can focus only upon the choice reading of capacity. Since the choice reading entails the avoidability reading, then if the choice reading also entails the conditional version of *PAP*, so too must the avoidability reading entail the conditional version of *PAP*. The entailment arises because the general capacity for decision and action – the choice reading itself – operates through the medium of reason and thus embodies a minimal degree of rationality. Exactly that minimal degree of rationality

[21] See Chapter 3, pp. 96–97.

is the core of the conditional version of *PAP*. What is this minimal degree of rationality? Nothing more than the capacity to rationally modify conduct in light of significant changes in circumstances. This is undoubtedly part of what it means to be capable of decision and action, to have the general capacity to decide and to act upon one's decisions. It might be objected that the general capacity for decision and action is not actually the same as the capacity to *change* one's decisions and conduct in light of different circumstances, but the complaint is surely wrong-headed. For it implies that the capacity to decide and act is exercised regardless of relevant circumstances and thus regardless of relevant reasons. Now, while this is practically possible – while, in other words, agents can exercise this capacity badly in particular cases – the capacity is in its central sense a matter of deciding and acting in light of relevant reasons. Indeed, it is the presence of some degree of rational deliberation that allows us to distinguish conduct that is genuinely an agent's from that which simply happens to her. In this context, the general capacity for decision and action must, on the whole, run through the medium of reason for, if it does not, we are unable to say that this general capacity is one the agent genuinely has, as opposed to being one with which her conduct simply coincides.

Does either the choice or avoidability reading of capacity entail the actual sequence version of *PAP*? Given the formulation of the actual sequence version used above, this seems unlikely: this version of *PAP* can be coherently stated without any reference to rationality at all. Of course, some reference could be added, but the significant point is that it must be *added* – it is in the first instance extraneous to this version of *PAP* rather than one of its constituents. This suggests that if there is any entailment relation it must be indirect and, the more indirect such alleged connections are, the more difficult they are to establish.

The idea of general capacity is an essential component of the basic responsibility requirement. That, at least, was the argument of chapter 3, the final section of which elucidated the various normative considerations that might support the basic responsibility requirement. These same considerations are the basis of our commitment to general capacity, which commitment in part drives our preference for the conditional version of *PAP* over the actual sequence version. Furthermore, the conceptual considerations just noted suggest that the link between general capacity and the conditional version of *PAP* is not based solely upon normative factors. Rather, the link is also a matter of conceptual cartography, the conditional version of *PAP* being related to the notion of general capacity in ways in which the actual sequence version is not. Thus, having nailed our colours to the mast of the conditional version of *PAP*, that version must now be defended against two powerful and related arguments. The first, offered by Frankfurt, is generalized by the second, offered by Susan Hurley. The aim of this composite argument seems to be the rejection of all versions of *PAP* but, as is obvious, our interest lies only with the conditional version. It is argued that this version of *PAP* emerges unscathed from both Frankfurt's demon and Hurley's intuition.

FRANKFURT'S DEMON AND HURLEY'S INTUITION

There is another philosophical near-orthodoxy to accompany that about determinism: it is that *PAP* plays no significant role in our moral liability-responsibility judgments.[22] Despite first impressions, the ability or capacity to do otherwise is actually redundant. While by no means the only argument to this end, Frankfurt's early discussion of *PAP* is canonical. In it he poses the following counter-example to *PAP*, involving the somewhat demonic or otherwise fiendish Black:

> 'Suppose someone – Black, let us say – wants Jones_4 to perform a certain action. Black is prepared to go to considerable lengths to get his way, but he prefers to avoid showing his hand unnecessarily. So he waits until Jones_4 is about to make up his mind what to do, and he does nothing unless it is clear to him (Black is an excellent judge of such things) that Jones_4 is going to decide to do something *other* than what he wants him to do. If it does become clear that Jones_4 is going to decide to do something else, Black takes effective steps to ensure that Jones_4 decides to do, and that he does do, what he wants him to do [. . .]. Whatever Jones_4's initial preferences and inclinations, then, Black will have his way.
>
> . . . Given any conditions under which it will be maintained that Jones_4 cannot do otherwise, in other words, let Black bring it about that those conditions prevail . . .
>
> Now suppose that Black never has to show his hand because Jones_4, for

[22] Although the arguments of Frankfurt and Hurley are the principal focus of this chapter, they are not the only philosophers to have cast doubt on *PAP*; see, in addition, D. Dennett, 'I Could Not Have Done Otherwise – So What?' (1984) LXXXI *Journal of Philosophy* 553–565 (there is a reply by P. Van Inwagen at 565–567); J. M. Fischer and J. Ravizza, *Responsibility and Control* (Cambridge: Cambridge University Press, 1998), chs. 1–6; Fischer, supra, note 7, pp. 108–125; and D. Pereboom, 'Alternative Possibilities and Causal Histories' (2000) 14 *Philosophical Perspectives* 119–137. Excerpts from the first, third and fourth pieces appear, the latter two under different titles, in R. Kane (ed.), *Free Will* (Oxford: Blackwell, 2002).

> reasons of his own, decides to perform and does perform the very action Black wants him to perform. In that case, it seems clear, $Jones_4$ will bear precisely the same moral responsibility for what he does as he would have borne if Black had not been ready to take steps to ensure that he do it. It would be quite unreasonable to excuse $Jones_4$ for his action, or to withhold the praise to which it would normally entitle him, on the basis of the fact that he could not have done otherwise. This fact played no role at all in leading him to act as he did'.[23]

The counter-example certainly seems to do the work required of it: given the story Frankfurt tells, it does indeed seem unreasonable to excuse $Jones_4$. However, two broader claims than this are hung from the hook of the counter-example. One, which must be added for our purposes, seems trivial but turns out not to be so: that what is true of judgments of moral liability-responsibility is also true *a fortiori* of judgments of legal liability-responsibility. The other, suggested by Frankfurt himself, is that it is a mistake to think *PAP* is a requirement for moral liability-responsibility. Both claims are considered in what follows, although we begin with the second. This claim gives rise to two major issues that are tackled in the following subsections; it is during the treatment of the second issue that the first broad and seemingly trivial claim is contested.

THE EXTRAPOLATION PROBLEM

The first issue concerns the range of Frankfurt's argument that *PAP* is irrelevant to judgments of moral liability-responsibility. The problem is that the (just cited) example used to generate this claim does not support it in all respects. The most the example shows is that, in cases involving fiends like Black doing what Black does, it appears wrong to relieve $Jones_4$ or those similarly placed of responsibility. But Black, of course, plainly has the kind of incredible powers had only by a few comic-book villains. And, since the argument that *PAP* is irrelevant to judgments of liability-responsibility arises from this science fiction scenario, it can be suggested that the implications it generates should not be taken too seriously. The background thought here is equivalent to that which lawyers often espouse: just as hard cases make bad law, science fiction might make bad philosophy. Of the responses available to this attempt to minimize the effectiveness of Frankfurt examples, two are fairly obvious. One is to insist, presumably by reference to recent scientific developments, that the fictional aspect of the example does not deserve that name: it is now more or less science fact rather than science fiction and therefore incumbent

[23] Frankfurt, supra, note 1, pp. 6–7.

upon us to accommodate it in our moral thought. Another response, which is examined here, is to try to generalize the intuition – that *PAP* is irrelevant to judgments of liability-responsibility – beyond the science fiction example. This strategy is adopted by Hurley.

Hurley pursues this strategy in a disarmingly simple way: she offers two non-science fiction examples of conduct arising from agents' reasons and compares two different scenarios in each example.[24] The first example involves Wilma, who does C for reasons R and 'would not have done other than C whether or not she could have'.[25] In one scenario, Wilma does C for reasons R and it is true that, at the time Wilma did C, she could not and would not have done other than C; in the second scenario, Wilma does C for reasons R but here it is true that she could, at the time she did C, have done not-C even though she would not have. In the second scenario, then, there is an alternative sequence in which Wilma can do not-C; in the first, there is no such alternative sequence. Of this example, Hurley asks: 'Is Wilma any more responsible in the second scenario? Is what matters for her responsibility the actual causes of her act and the dispositions they involve, or the outright possibility of an alternate sequence?'.[26] Her answer is that if we take Frankfurt cases seriously, they show, just as this example shows, that the key factor in determining our responsibility judgments is not the ability to do otherwise but rather the quality of the 'mechanism' which drives one's conduct.[27] If that 'mechanism' is responsive to reasons and those reasons, regardless of their quality, determine some aspects of one's conduct, then one is responsible for those aspects. Hence, if Wilma is responsible in either of the two scenarios, then she is responsible in both, given that her conduct arises from a reason-responsive mechanism. In Hurley's judgment,

> what matters for responsibility is not the outright ability to act rightly instead of wrongly [the ability to do otherwise], all else constant, but rather the character of the operative disposition [or mechanism] . . . If . . . [Wilma] would have acted wrongly, on the same kind of mechanism and given the same

[24] Supra, note 13, pp. 66–70. She actually discusses three examples but one, a medical case, is irrelevant for our purposes.

[25] The 'would not have done otherwise whether or not she could have' formulation is important for Hurley's argument about the basis upon which agents act: supra, note 13, p. 71. It is not important for us and so the less jarring 'even if s/he could have' is adopted.

[26] Ibid, p. 67. Hereinafter, all page references in brackets in the text are to this work.

[27] 'Mechanism' is a vague term in Hurley's (and others') work, but is intended to capture the (presumably deliberative?) medium through which conduct comes about: see ibid, p. 61 for her comments on the term and its content. For worries about the notion as it occurs in another account of responsibility, see Watson, supra, note 11, pp. 296–299.

> kind of reasons, whether or not there was an alternative sequence in which she did not act wrongly, then why should the alternative sequence matter to her responsibility? (p. 67).

Hurley's second example concerns evil Ethel. Ethel has reasons to cause pain to others and desires to do so, whenever possible. '[S]uppose that this desire, along with Ethel's belief that a certain act would be hurtful, . . . provide a . . . reason for her to do it' (p. 68) and suppose, in general, that Ethel acts on her reasons to hurt others whenever possible. The reason-responsive mechanism on which she acts, then, ensures that

> when she does the wrong thing, in accordance with her evil reasons, it is true of her that she would not do as she does if she did not believe it to be hurtful . . .
>
> Ethel acts on a mechanism with these dispositions when she acts in accordance with her evil reasons, whether or not she could have done otherwise. Can it then make any difference to her responsibility for acting this way in a given situation whether there is an alternative sequence of causes such that she is able to do the right thing in that situation? Given that she would not do the right thing whether or not she could, why is it relevant whether she could? (ibid)

Unsurprisingly, Hurley's response to this question is negative: so far as she can see, the existence of an alternative scenario in which Ethel can avoid engaging in evil conduct is not significant to any judgment of responsibility we might make about her. The reason responsive mechanism is, for Hurley, the one and only factor that informs such judgments. For her, to repeat, the irrelevant alternative intuition holds that 'what matters for responsibility is . . . the character of the operative disposition' (p. 67). If that disposition is part of an operative reason responsive mechanism, then that appears to be enough for responsibility.

Hurley's examples apparently present plausible instances in which the existence of an alternative possibility is irrelevant to responsibility. But, in order to generalize successfully the intuition behind Frankfurt cases beyond the realm of science fiction, the examples need to do two additional things. First, a key element of each example – the idea that 'an agent would not have done X whether or not she could have' – must bear a great deal of argumentative weight and, if it is incoherent or otherwise problematic, then Hurley's case is compromised. And there is indeed a potential problem here, since Hurley attempts to demonstrate the power and plausibility of this element by means of a 'possible worlds' argument (pp. 72–76). While now more common than they once were, it is not entirely clear, except in a few cases, what arguments such as these actually establish; there is thus some doubt as to whether or not they are philosophically fruitful. However, since the underlying issues are complex, this potential difficulty must be set aside.[28] The second thing Hurley's examples must do is show that, even if the irrelevant alternative intuition behind the examples is correct and can be generalized, the intuition defeats both versions of *PAP*. This requirement, which concerns the general viability of the irrelevant alternative intuition and its effect upon *PAP* is the principal determinant of the power of the Frankfurt/Hurley assault upon *PAP*. In the subsection that follows, the question of clarification – which version, if any, of *PAP* does the Frankfurt/Hurley assault effect? – is treated first and the question of substance – what, if any, weight does the irrelevant alternative intuition have? – is tackled afterwards.

PAP AND THE IRRELEVANT ALTERNATIVE INTUITION

Two versions of *PAP* were elucidated in section one, although only one – the conditional version – was regarded as defensible. Before recapping the reasons for that judgment and turning our attention exclusively to the conditional version, a point about Frankfurt cases and the actual sequence version of *PAP* must be noted. That version of *PAP* requires that, in order to be responsible for C, an agent must have been able to have done otherwise than C at the time they brought C about, this being interpreted to mean that, at the time of C, there was an outright possibility of the agent doing not-C in the exact same circumstances. The causal web in which C came about must not, therefore, be so tightly woven as to make it impossible for the agent to do anything other than C; there must be elbow room which allows the agent the causal space to either do C or not. It is this space that Frankfurt cases appear to rule out, for it seems, if we return to the example stated above, that Jones_4 has no alternative but to do as Black wishes. It is just this that some philosophical proponents of the actual sequence version of *PAP* have denied.[29]

Look again at Frankfurt's example of Jones_4. What must be possible to

[28] The literature on possible worlds is large and predominantly difficult, especially for the non-specialist. A useful introduction to the general terrain is J. Divers, *Possible Worlds* (London: Routledge, 2002), chs. 1–3. For a fairly rare instance of the idea (or a version of it) being put to illuminating use, see J. Bennett, 'Morality and Consequences' in S. McMurrin (ed.), *The Tanner Lectures on Human Values* ii (Salt Lake City: University of Utah Press, 1981), pp. 56–65.

[29] The arguments of some of the principal antagonists are clearly laid out in Fischer, supra, note 7, at pp. 117–123.

trigger Black's intervention? $Jones_4$ deciding to do something other than what Black wants him to do. But what is it to have such a power which, in the circumstances of the example, will surely be satisfied by $Jones_4$'s decision not to do what Black wishes him to do, that is, to do nothing rather than something? If $Jones_4$ decides to do nothing rather than something, then that will trigger Black's intervention. It seems then, that in the very core of the example designed to show the irrelevance of *PAP* to judgments of responsibility, there is something very close to a power to do otherwise, a power which could well be contra-causal and thus entail the actual sequence version of *PAP*. And this power, $Jones_4$'s power to decide to do other than what Black wishes him to do, while it will not result in anything occurring other than what Black wishes to occur, may well be a sufficient basis for judgments of moral liability-responsibility. This, at least, is what a number of philosophers have argued and, if the argument is a good one, then Frankfurt examples are robbed of whatever power they may have. Thus the irrelevant alternative intuition does not get off the ground and presents no threat at all to *PAP*.

The main way in which this argument is evaluated is by reference to the foundation of moral responsibility. While some philosophers concede that $Jones_4$ is able to decide to do otherwise, they argue that that ability is far too flimsy a basis upon which to rest moral responsibility judgments; other philosophers have disagreed. The correct resolution to this dispute does not, however, matter for current purposes, since two other points are more pressing. First, it is clear that the power of Frankfurt examples is not as overwhelming as might initially seem, nor are their implications unambiguous. Second, the type of argumentative strategy used by these defenders of the actual sequence version of *PAP* to undermine the power of Frankfurt cases must be noted. For that exact same strategy, of showing that the position one is defending actually exists in the heart of the argument of those who attack it, is one of the principal arguments employed below to defend the conditional version of *PAP* against Hurley's irrelevant alternative intuition.

Our judgment that only the conditional version of *PAP* is defensible rests upon two arguments. One highlighted the infirmity of the alternative, actual sequence version of *PAP*, while the other was based upon the reasons supporting our invocation of the idea of general capacity in Chapter 3 and the conceptual connections between that idea and the conditional version of *PAP*. Although the idea of general capacity has two interpretations, the idea of 'can general' is a vital component of both. And that idea, of course, is not one that requires the outright possibility of doing otherwise. Since nothing in our account of capacity or basic responsibility requires that defendants can (particular) do otherwise in the specific circumstances in which their conduct came about, we are inclined to reject the actual sequence version of *PAP* because it makes can (particular) necessary to responsibility and liability. There are, then, two important links informing our argument. One is that the actual sequence version of *PAP* relies upon the idea of can (particular) and that idea is both metaphysically suspect (because it seemingly implies anti-determinism) and unnecessary for liability-responsibility in private law. The other is that the conditional version of *PAP* relies upon the idea of can (general), that this idea is not metaphysically suspect and that it is and should remain a requirement for legal liability-responsibility. Since we have thus rejected the actual sequence version of *PAP*, the first question in this subsection is narrower than initially indicated. It is not 'what is the effect of the irrelevant alternative intuition on *PAP*?' but 'what is its effect upon the conditional version of *PAP*?'

That version of *PAP*, remember, holds that one requirement for liability is that, at the time X did C, he could, if circumstances had been significantly different, have done not-C. This version certainly does not entail that in the precise circumstances as they existed when X did C there was an outright possibility of X doing not-C. Rather, it holds only that had those circumstances differed significantly, then X's conduct would have differed. So, although the causal die was cast such that X would not fail to do C in the circumstances that obtained, it is nevertheless sensible to speak of X being able to do otherwise in two intelligible and related senses. Either X has the general capacity for decision and action when he does C, even though that capacity is not actually exercised on this particular occasion; or X has the general capacity to do not-C, even though that capacity is unexercised on this occasion. The broad idea of general capacity (to do, or to avoid doing) thus makes it plausible to say that, although the causal forces in play on one particular occasion ensured that X missed a six-foot putt, he could nevertheless have done otherwise, since at the time he missed it was true of him that he generally sunk such putts. Having the general capacity to sink six-foot putts is quite compatible with that capacity being unexercised on particular occasions. The link between the conditional version of *PAP* and the notion of general capacity could not, therefore, be more vivid. What, then, is the effect of the irrelevant alternative intuition upon this version of *PAP*? Four arguments suggest that its effect is minimal.

The first argument is textual. There are a few hints that Hurley's articulation of the irrelevant alternative intuition, and thus the whole burden of her argument, is aimed not at the conditional version of *PAP* but only against the actual sequence version. So, when Hurley introduces the examples intended to illustrate the irrelevant alternative intuition, she describes this as a process of bringing 'into play alternate sequences and outright possibilities – what the agent could have done, all else constant, as opposed to what she would have done under various counterfactual conditions' (p. 65). Outright possibilities are not, of course, relevant to the conditional version of *PAP* but are crucial to the alternate sequence version. She also invokes the notion of outright possibilities in her attempt to refute Michael Otsuka's riposte to Frankfurt cases, clearly assuming that her target in attacking *PAP* is the alternate sequence and not the conditional version (p. 77 and p. 78).[30] Moreover, Hurley also suggests that her argument is narrower than Frankfurt's, since at some instances his seems to undermine conditional sequence versions of *PAP*, while she thinks her own does not (p. 75, note 17). While this evidence suggests that the conditional version of *PAP* is certainly not Hurley's principal target, it is not in itself conclusive. This is because even the most acute are prone to textual slips and also because authors are not always the best judge of the range or power of their arguments. Furthermore, there is little to stop others attempting to extend Hurley's argument beyond its intended range. Thus we proceed *ex abundanti cautela* and develop three additional arguments to show that the power of the irrelevant alternative intuition, and the considerations supporting it, do not extend to the conditional version of *PAP*.

The second argument claims that nothing in either Frankfurt cases or Hurley's two examples is inconsistent with the idea of general capacity that supports the conditional version of *PAP*. That is to say, the cases of $Jones_4$, Wilma and Ethel are ones not only in which each agent acts on a reason responsive mechanism, but also cases in which each agent has general capacity. Thus it can be said of $Jones_4$, of Wilma and of Ethel that, when each acted, each either had the general capacity to avoid doing that act or to do otherwise (the avoidability reading of general capacity), or each had the general capacity for decision and action (the choice reading of general capacity) when they acted. What are the grounds for this claim? Let us begin with a hybrid example, $Jones_5$: this is a case in which $Jones_5$'s own reason responsive mechanism ensures that he acts as he does and will not do otherwise even if he can. Assuming that $Jones_5$ has

[30] M. Otsuka, 'Incompatibilism and the Avoidability of Blame' (1998) 108 *Ethics* 685–701.

actually done something that places him in the frame for blame, the fact that he has done something (let us call it C) tells us at least two things. First, that he could (can particular) do C at the time he did it. Second, that $Jones_5$ had general capacity for decision and action and/or the general capacity to avoid C, assuming that the decision and action in question (to do whatever, or to do not-C) is a genuine segment of his conduct. The two limbs of this second claim are the most interesting for present purposes. For, if either limb is indeed satisfied by $Jones_5$ (and thus by $Jones_4$, Wilma and Ethel), then it shows he (and they) satisfy the conditional version of *PAP*.

The first limb invokes the choice reading of general capacity and this, remember, entails the conditional version of *PAP*. The choice reading holds that a vital component of private law liability-responsibility is that defendants had, at the time of the conduct that brought about the legal wrong, the general capacity for decision and action. The fact that this is a general capacity is, of course, compatible with it being unexercised on particular occasions, but it must be true that the capacity is in play in the majority of an agent's conduct. If it is not, then there is no basis for claiming that the agent has this general capacity. Is this capacity satisfied in the case of $Jones_5$ and, by extension, the cases of $Jones_4$, Wilma and Ethel? The examples need not be pored over in detail to see that this must be conceded, if it is accepted that the reason responsive mechanism that Hurley posits in the cases of Wilma and Ethel is also in play in the case of $Jones_4$. He, remember, does the deed in question for his own reasons and, in so doing, makes any intervention by Black unnecessary. Something like a reason responsive mechanism must therefore be in play. That being so, Wilma, Ethel and $Jones_4$ surely have the general capacity for decision and action: what, after all, does this capacity entail if not the ability to act on reasons? Since all the examples are instances of agents acting on reasons, they are also examples of agents exercising the capacity for decision and action. On the assumption that these examples are not the only instances of each character having acted on reasons, then they are evidence of the general capacity for decision and action.

How could the second limb possibly be satisfied? How, in other words, could we come to the conclusion that, in a situation in which $Jones_5$ has done C, he had the general capacity to avoid doing C? The fact that $Jones_5$ has the general capacity for decision and action tells us something about the capacity to avoid C, but not much: while the choice reading of general capacity undoubtedly entails the avoidability reading, it does not guarantee its practical possibility. Nor does the fact that $Jones_5$ has done C once tell us anything about his having the general capacity to do C, although it might tell us something about his capacity to avoid C or to do not-C. For, if $Jones_5$ has done C for the first time, then that provides some support for the claim that $Jones_5$ is often able to avoid doing C or able to do not-C. If $Jones_5$ could not avoid doing C, by which we mean he lacks the general capacity to do other than C or not-C, he would presumably do C much more often. But if he has only done C once the implication is that C is something he can usually avoid. Moreover, even if $Jones_5$ often does C, this will only imply that he lacks the general capacity to do other than C if, in the majority of cases in which he acts, he does C. And, if the majority of $Jones_5$'s acts are instances of C-ing, that is itself a basis for a claim questioning both his ability to do otherwise and his basic responsibility, for he appears to be in the grip of a non-rational obsession or compulsion.

Note that this argument does not hold that the fact that $Jones_5$ has done C for the first time *conclusively* shows he has the general capacity to do other than C. Rather, it is nothing more than a common, negative inductive generalization: if we know of Z that he has never been convicted of a crime, we are technically right to infer that he is not a criminal. This does not, of course, mean that Z has never committed a crime, it being neutral between two competing propositions, namely, that Z has never committed a crime and that Z has committed crimes but has never been convicted. But as a general matter, it is not unreasonable to infer from the absence of a criminal record the general capacity to avoid doing what the criminal law prohibits and/or the general capacity to avoid conviction. Similarly, it is not unreasonable to infer from a first criminal conviction that Z is, generally speaking, law-abiding and has the general capacity to avoid doing what the law prohibits. Of course, this inference can be weakened somewhat by relevant evidence: we might, for example, learn that Z *appears* to have been engaged in a great deal of criminal activity but has escaped conviction. Yet, unless the vast majority of *all* his conduct is criminal, this still does not undermine the generalization that Z has the general capacity to avoid doing what the law prohibits.

It seems, then, that the examples supporting the irrelevant alternative intuition are quite compatible with the existence of general capacity, understood as avoidability, and, therefore, with the conditional version of *PAP*. Yet this is not to say anything as bold as that the irrelevant alternative intuition is compatible with Otuska's principle of avoidable blame.[31]

[31] Ibid.

In contrast to the account of *PAP* and general capacity propounded here, Otsuka's principle is tied to an anti-determinism that insists on the outright possibility of doing otherwise at the time of the conduct in question. However, once this metaphysical commitment is set aside, the similarity between Otsuka's principle and the avoidability account of general capacity is clear. So, too, is part of the basis of their appeal, namely, the intuition that avoidability plays a role in some of our responsibility judgments. While Otsuka argues that this intuition is in play in moral liability-responsibility judgments, our only claim, as is clear from the following argument, is that the intuition is and certainly should be in play in judgments of legal liability-responsibility.

The third argument to suggest that the effect of the irrelevant alternative intuition upon the conditional version of *PAP* (and general capacity) is minimal holds that that intuition is limited. The argument supposes that, if valid, the intuition has weight only in relation to some judgments of moral responsibility and lacks weight, and should indeed be eschewed, when making legal liability-responsibility judgments. This argument constitutes a direct challenge to the first broad claim – that what is true of moral liability-responsibility is true *a fortiori* of legal liability-responsibility – often hung from the hook of Frankfurt examples. The argument consists of two claims, one highlighting the uniqueness of legal liability judgments, the other the significance of judgments of general capacity for legal liability.

The special feature of legal liability judgments that makes them unlike most other responsibility judgments is that they are conduits of state power. They conduct this power either directly, when made in the course of adjudication and thence acted upon by the forces of the justice system, or less directly, when part of lawyers' and citizens' assessments of what the law requires and thus of how agents should and should not conduct themselves. This power is undoubtedly significant and, perhaps, the most important source of power in the lives of citizens. The consequences of its exercise could not be more important since, at the least, it can financially cripple those subject to it and, at worst, can lead to imprisonment. Bearing in mind the possible consequences of an adverse judgment of private law liability-responsibility, we realize that Robert Cover's celebrated dictum – that legal interpretation takes place in a field of pain and death – is only a slight exaggeration in this context.[32] That legal liability-responsibility judgments carry this potentially awesome power provides a

[32] R. Cover, 'Violence and the Word' (1986) 95 *Yale Law Journal* 1601–1629, p. 1601.

reason why it may be appropriate to treat them differently from other judgments of liability-responsibility. And one way in which judgments of legal liability-responsibility may be treated differently is by insisting that the requirements such a judgment must satisfy are more demanding than the requirements for other liability-responsibility judgments.

There are some obvious ways in which the requirements necessary for a judgment of legal liability-responsibility are more stringent than those required by, for example, judgments of moral liability-responsibility. That such judgments are legal already means they are subject to the usual constraints of legal judgment: they must be, *inter alia*, consistent with the existing case and statute law, fall within the range of permissible judgment or 'discretion', be consonant with the available evidence and arrived at in accordance with a range of procedural safeguards. But, in addition, it is not unreasonable to insist on more by way of the substance of judgments of legal liability-responsibility than is necessary in non-legal judgments of liability-responsibility. So, for example, it might be accepted that it is enough for moral liability-responsibility that agents have basic responsibility or capacity, as outlined in Chapter 3. Provided they have the capacity to act on reasons, and their conduct is often a result of deliberation based on reasons, then that is enough. It is not necessary that the agent was able to do otherwise at the time of the conduct in question. By contrast, judgments of legal liability-responsibility might be said to require more than this in order to ensure (i) that the power they unleash is not triggered lightly; and (ii) that those subject to that power are indeed appropriate objects or addressees of the law.

As to the first point, it seems obvious why this power, if it is indeed as significant as has been claimed, should be exercised cautiously. This argument, of course, shows only that this power should be hedged with constraints; it says nothing precise about the exact contours and content of those constraints. The second point does address this issue. It holds that this power should only be brought to bear upon appropriate beings: thus we now think it silly to claim damages from dogs and to punish pigs.[33] These beings lack basic responsibility. But even beings with basic responsibility may not be appropriate addressees of the law: much depends on how the components of basic responsibility are understood. In Chapter 3 those requirements included the notion of general capacity

[33] For an engaging account of some of these now apparently silly practices see: E. P. Evans, *The Criminal Prosecution and Capital Punishment of Animals* (London: Faber and Faber, 1987 (first published 1906)).

and, of course, that notion has in this chapter been aligned with the conditional version of *PAP*. Why insist that the addressees of private law have general capacity and satisfy the conditional version of *PAP*? The answer differs slightly depending on which reading of general capacity is in play. The choice reading of general capacity is an attempt to guarantee that only those generally capable of decision and action are subject to the law: it holds, in other words, that only beings of this type should be in the frame for legal liability-responsibility. The avoidability reading holds just the same: it must do so, since it is entailed by the choice reading. Yet the avoidability reading requires even more: it is an attempt not just to ensure that those subject to the law are capable of decision and action, but also that they are held to an achievable standard. The standard is 'do not do (or avoid doing) what the law prohibits' and we know whether this is generally achievable by an agent by virtue of the number of times he has fallen short. If an agent constantly falls short of this standard, then it is likely that they lack the general capacity required for liability.

For these reasons it seems appropriate that a judgment of legal liability-responsibility satisfy more stringent conditions than a non-legal judgment of liability-responsibility. If these reasons, or considerations like them, are persuasive they can constitute a wedge between legal liability-responsibility judgments, on the one hand, and other kinds of liability judgment, on the other. We must now turn to the final argument minimizing the effect of the irrelevant alternative intuition. This argument does not attack that intuition itself but instead seeks to protect those who would reject it, or minimize its range, against an allegedly obvious source of embarrassment. The embarrassment is this: those who affirm either version of *PAP* must accept that the principle (i) has no role in explaining how conduct actually comes about; or (ii) has no role in explaining when an agent is morally responsible.[34] Isn't it silly to espouse such a redundant principle? Only if it is indeed redundant.

There is one perspective from which *PAP* is clearly irrelevant to the explanation of human conduct and its outcomes. This can be labelled the 'how perspective' and it is exclusively interested in how some segment of conduct and its outcomes came about. Think of the case of the Weak Muleteer. A muleteer lacks the necessary skill and patience to control his

[34] The second claim is assumed, *inter alios*, by Pereboom, supra, note 22, and sometimes explicitly stated (see, for example, p. 133), although nowhere it is stated as bluntly as in the excerpt of this essay published in Kane, supra, note 22, at p. 112. The first claim appears in Hurley, supra, note 13, at pp. 66, 67, 68 and 78.

mule train and, as a result, they stampede and crush someone.[35] Within the how perspective, our principal interest in this case is the precise causal genesis of this baleful outcome, much in the way contemporary accident scene investigators seek to establish how a particular aircraft accident came about. Within this perspective, human agency is assumed or taken for granted: it is important only as one among the many causal factors necessary to bring the outcome about. The fact that the Muleteer or pilot was negligent, reckless or even intended to bring about the baleful outcome is irrelevant from this perspective; and so, too, is any consideration of whether and in what sense the Muleteer or pilot could have done otherwise. For the how perspective aims only to clarify or reconstruct the causal genesis of the conduct and its outcomes; once human agency is assumed, talk of both 'mental states' and alternative possibilities becomes redundant.[36]

There is also open to us, in addition to the how perspective, a viewpoint that can be labelled the 'why perspective'.[37] The two are undoubtedly related, in that the latter is informed by the former, but they are not identical, particularly insofar as the why perspective betrays an interest in the reasons of the agent whose conduct is in question, and also insofar as that interest is but the precursor to an appraisal of the quality of that agent's conduct and character. Indeed, a substantial part of the why perspective is appraisive in these two senses. And from within the appraisive component of the why perspective, questions about mental states and, furthermore, general capacity and the conditional version of *PAP*, are usually vital. What an agent intended, what he was reckless about, and what he was indifferent to, when he brought about some baleful outcome, ordinarily make a big difference to the degree of blame or opprobrium to which he is subject. Although the causal 'how' story of the way in which this outcome came about could be the same in each instance of intentional, reckless and negligent conduct, our appraisive judgments will usually differ in each case. Those judgments rest upon a system of valuation in which bringing about baleful consequences intentionally is worse than bringing about those exact same consequences

[35] As reported in T. Honoré, *Responsibility and Fault* (Oxford: Hart Publishing, 1999), p. 21 (the example is from the Roman jurist Gaius).

[36] The term 'mental states' is employed for the sake of convenience; nothing of substance about the correct analysis or nature of those 'states' should be inferred from its use.

[37] Both perspectives were clearly delineated, albeit in narrower terms than used in the text, in H. L. A. Hart and T. Honoré, *Causation in the Law* (Oxford: Clarendon Press, 2nd edn, 1985), pp. 23–25.

either recklessly or negligently. This, of course, does not imply that outcomes brought about recklessly or negligently are not bad; rather, they are simply less bad than the same intentionally brought about outcomes.

From within the appraisive component of the why perspective, the general capacity of the agent whose conduct is in question is also usually very important. For our appraisive judgments are not only calibrated to mental states, but also to the rational or intentional status of beings with those states. If addressees of the law lack the general capacity for decision or action, or lack the general capacity to avoid doing what the law prohibits, then they are unlikely to be responsible in the basic sense. Or, in the favoured terminology of many lawyers, they lack capacity. I take it to be a truism that the presence or absence of this capacity is vital to our appraisive judgments both within and beyond the law. And, if that is so, then general capacity and the conditional version of *PAP* are equally vital. From this perspective, rather than being irrelevant, *PAP*, general capacity and the other components of basic responsibility are crucial. Those who argue otherwise either underplay the importance of the appraisive component of the why perspective in our judgments of others and their deeds, or are beguiled by and thus exaggerate the range of the how perspective.

PAP, DURESS AND NECESSITY

The doctrine of duress in contract law holds that certain forms of pressure applied by one party to the other during either formation or modification of a contract can constitute, provided some conditions are satisfied, good grounds on which to set the obligation aside. This somewhat compressed formulation raises two immediate questions. First, what kinds of pressure count as duress? Second, what other conditions must be satisfied in addition to that which requires the existence of certain types of pressure at particular times?

In English law, the kinds of pressure that can count as duress are fairly limited: the courts have established that actual physical force, or the threat of physical force, to either person or property can amount to duress, as can significant threats to prosperity (economic duress). In addition, the courts usually require that these threats are wrongful, that they are of such force as to impact upon a person of reasonable fortitude and that they actually play a role (are a causal factor in) the innocent party's decision to enter into the contract. The courts are therefore unlikely to regard a 'threat' never again to contract with the other party as wrongful, since this is a perfectly legitimate position for a contracting party to take. The courts will also usually disregard a 'threat' that has no or very few adverse consequences for the innocent party and, further, are almost certain to ignore a 'threat' that has no impact at all upon the deliberations of the innocent party. An innocent party who was aware of a threat but disregarded it, or who already had compelling, independent reasons to enter into the contract, cannot claim to have been influenced by the threat.[38]

Even as superficial a sketch of the doctrine of duress as this one can give rise to this thought: if any substantive doctrine of private law is explicable by reference to *PAP*, it is this. For what have we in a duress scenario but a situation in which the innocent party cannot do otherwise? And, that being so, *PAP* is surely directly in play. Although tempting, this thought is far too hasty and, as a result, profoundly mistaken.

Consider first the actual sequence version of *PAP*. That holds, remember, that for X to be responsible for doing C, there must actually have been an outright possibility of X doing other than C at the time she brought C about. It must therefore be the case that the causal web in which X brought about C was not so tightly drawn that it was impossible for X to do anything other than C. If it was indeed impossible for X to do anything other than C, then X is not responsible for C. Does the actual sequence version of *PAP* underpin the doctrine of duress? If in the previous two sentences 'C' is replaced by 'entered a contract', it might seem so: if a threat by the other party ensured that it was indeed impossible for X to do anything other than enter into the contract, then *PAP* requires that X be relieved of responsibility. But the problem with this argument is obvious: it is almost always literally false to say that it is genuinely physically impossible for X to do other than enter into a contract in a duress situation. The alternative in a duress situation is almost always physically possible, albeit lacking salience, since any human agent with a sane value system will usually opt for the least-worst option. Indeed, it is just this assumption that those who issue threats rely upon: their threats are efforts to manipulate the innocent party's situation such that any rational process of deliberation will lead them to do what the issuer of the threat wishes them to do. If the innocent party acts in the way the threatener wants, then that action is usually perfectly rational given the situation of choice. But saying this by no means entails the claim that this outcome

[38] For a general treatment of the doctrine in English law see, for example, J. Beatson, *Anson's Law of Contract* (Oxford: Clarendon Press, 28th edn, 2002), ch. 7.

was the only possible outcome in that choice situation: it is normally still undoubtedly possible for the innocent party to refuse to act in the most salient way. If this is true, then it is clear that the actual sequence version of *PAP* is no use at all in this context. Since in all 'ordinary' duress situations it is almost always possible for the innocent party not to act as the threatener wishes, then there is almost always an outright possibility to do otherwise. The innocent party is therefore, on this version of *PAP* at least, almost always responsible and thus liable in duress situations.

Proponents of this version of *PAP* might find this conclusion unpalatable. But the most plausible attempts to avoid this conclusion serve only to illustrate the inadequacy of *PAP* rather than to add to its explanatory power. Think, for example, of one particularly tempting response proponents of the actual sequence version of *PAP* might make here. They accept that it is always actually possible for the victim in a duress situation to do otherwise, but maintain instead that victims in such situations must be relieved of liability because it is unreasonable to expect them to do otherwise in those circumstances. While perfectly intelligible and respectable, this response does nothing to reinforce the explanatory power of *PAP* and, indeed, undermines it. For all the work is being done here, not by the components of the actual sequence version of *PAP*, but by the added extra: the idea of reasonableness. This idea is completely independent of *PAP* for, rather than highlight what is and is not actually possible in the situation in which the innocent party acted, it leads instead to consideration of the normative expectations it is reasonable to have of innocent parties in duress situations and to an account of wrongfulness against which to judge the conduct of the threatener.

It seems clear that, despite first impressions, the actual sequence version of *PAP* has nothing significant to say about the doctrine of duress. Can the conditional version of *PAP* do any better? No, it cannot, although this should not in anyway embarrass its supporters. That this version of *PAP* does not provide an explanatory basis for the doctrine of duress is obvious once we bear in mind the rational structure of a duress situation. It is, as was noted above, one in which the threatener manipulates the innocent party's situation such that one option is far more salient than any other. In manipulating things so, the threatener is simply assuming that the innocent party will act rationally when faced with this situation and, despite their other wishes, do as the threatener wants. Most sane and rational agents will indeed do as the threatener wishes in a genuine duress scenario, albeit with regret and, possibly, complaint. And one of the grounds for the innocent party's regret when they act as the threatener wishes is obvious: they would rather not do what the threatener wants them to do. Yet, in so doing, and thus adjusting their conduct to the threat, they invariably satisfy the conditional version of *PAP* which, remember, holds that it must be true of X that, when he acted, he would have done otherwise if circumstances had been significantly different. Furthermore, in so satisfying *PAP* their conduct will also embody at least one and quite possibility both readings of general capacity. At the very least, the innocent party shows herself capable of decision and action in this scenario (can particular) and, on the assumption that this is not the first time her decisions have informed her conduct, it also illustrates her general capacity (can general) to decide and act.

Since the conditional version of *PAP* is thus clearly satisfied in just about any plausible and realistic duress situation, and because the actual sequence version of *PAP* is irrelevant in any such situation, *PAP* neither explains nor articulates our worries about such situations. So why is duress a worry and what is the basis of that concern? Stephen Smith has provided one of the best recent accounts of the nature and basis of the doctrine of duress. He holds that two underlying principles explain both our common sense intuitions about such situations and a great deal of the case law. The first is the 'wrongdoing principle', the second the 'autonomy or consent principle'.[39] The principles do not operate, for Smith, in an 'either/or' way; that is, both can operate in one and the same duress situation and both can explain the same areas of legal doctrine. He thinks, however, that the first principle should be preferred.

The wrongdoing principle holds contractual obligations created as a result of a salient threat by A to B should not be enforced either because the threat is itself wrongful, judged primarily against the standards of the law, or because allowing such a contractual obligation to stand unjustly enriches A, since it allows him to benefit from his own wrong. In terms of a distinction more favoured by criminal lawyers than private lawyers, when viewed from the perspective of the wrongdoing principle duress seems more a matter of excusing B from his obligation than holding that B's non-performance is justified.[40] This seems obvious once we note that

[39] S. Smith, *Contract Theory* (Oxford: Clarendon Press, 2004), pp. 316–340. The substance of Smith's view has changed only a little since his 'Contracting Under Pressure: A Theory of Duress' (1997) 56 *Cambridge Law Journal* 343–373; the changes are not relevant for current purposes. For a different account of duress, see Bigwood, supra, note 3, ch. 3 and pp. 289–291.

[40] It should not be assumed that criminal lawyers regard the distinction as unproblematic nor that they would apply in this way. For a helpful treatment see: V. Tadros, *Criminal Responsibility* (Oxford: Clarendon Press, 2005), pp. 120–124.

the wrongdoing principle draws upon what can be dubbed private law's general schema of protected interests and its catalogue of relative culpability. The former provides an account of the protection private law accords to all citizens and thus gives some guidance on the particular issue of what threats are wrongful: a threat to kill you is undoubtedly far more serious, given the importance the law attributes to your interest in life, than a threat not to speak to you again. Private law's catalogue of relative culpability arises upon this schema of protected interests: it lays down in general terms the kind of conduct that is wrongful (for example, breaching one's contracts, unjustly enriching oneself) which usually marries up with some or other protected interest. Yet this catalogue also includes factors that can exacerbate such wrongdoing (such as, for example, intentionally harming another as opposed to accidentally harming them). Needless to say, there is little here to suggest that either version of *PAP* is implicated in the doctrine of duress.

Things might appear otherwise when the consent principle is examined. It holds 'that a court may refuse to enforce a prima facie valid contractual obligation on the ground that the defendant did not consent to that obligation'.[41] But why should consent matter in this context? It might be held that if B enters into a contract with A as a result of a salient threat made by A, then B *therefore cannot* consent to entering into the contract. And, since B enters into the contract without consent, it may be thought that, when he entered into the contract, he could not have done otherwise.[42] Thus, the basis of the duress claim under the consent principle is the actual sequence version of *PAP*. But there are at least three severe problems with this argument. The first is the alleged connection between coercion and lack of consent which in this argument appears to be an entailment: coercion always negatives consent. Now a great deal depends upon how consent is defined here, but whatever definition is invoked must surely be able to accommodate the idea of agents' unwilling actions being a product of their agency. I can act unwillingly, with regret, hesitation and/or reluctance, in a great many situations, some of them being circumstances in which I have been threatened by other agents, some being scenarios in which I am 'compelled' to act as result of natural forces or my own agency. There is undoubtedly agency here, in the sense that I know what I do and do it intentionally, yet I do so with reservations

[41] Smith, *Contract Theory*, supra, note 39, p. 323.
[42] A similar argument is sketched by Smith, *Contract Theory*, supra, note 39, p. 326.

and am clearly not wholehearted. Is this situation best characterized as one in which there is no consent to doing the deed I do unwillingly? Possibly, but only if lack of consent is taken as a synonym for acting with reservations or reluctance. If taken as an indicator of a lack of agency, akin to a denial of basic responsibility, then talk of lack of consent in such situations is surely misplaced. In a duress situation, as in many other scenarios in which I act unwillingly, the unwilling conduct is both intentional and a product of deliberation. It is thus undoubtedly my conduct. If it is in this sense mine, then why should I not be held to its consequences?

The second problem highlights a difficulty with one tempting answer to this question. The answer has already been considered and need not occupy us long: it holds that I should not be held legally liable for this instance of my agency because there was no alternative. And, of course, if taken to invoke the actual sequence version of *PAP* this is plainly false in just about any plausible, 'normal' duress situation we could imagine. It is, in all such duress situations, always physically possible to do otherwise, that is, to act contrary to the threat. This might actually require amazing courage or sheer foolhardiness, but neither of these eliminate the possibility that agents in duress situations can actually do otherwise. Rather, the absence or presence of these character features simply determines the likelihood, in a specific duress situation, of a particular agent complying with or ignoring the threat. If the actual sequence version of *PAP* does not explain why I am excused from the legal consequences of my agency in duress situations, what does? The beginning of a plausible answer is surely to be found in what it is reasonable to expect of human beings in such situations and to set aside the red herrings of *PAP* and lack of consent (understood as lack of agency).

The third problem arises with the consent principle itself, rather than anything it tells us about duress situations. If the only reason why consent matters in contract law is that it is an indicator of agency and thus basic responsibility, then, for reasons just articulated, the idea does little work in duress scenarios. Nor does lack of consent do any significant work in identifying situations in which the actual sequence version of *PAP* is in play. So what use is it? Smith's answer is that lack of consent often gives rise to unjust enrichment and, since the latter is a wrong in private law, it must also be so regarded in that particular segment we call contract law. But the problem with utilising lack of consent as an indicator of unjust enrichment is a serious one, well noted by Smith: for, although the consent principle understood in this way serves to explain large tracts of the law on duress in contract, it also explains much more besides.[43] Understood in this way, the consent principle far exceeds contract law; because of this, Smith concludes that it should not actually be utilised there. His judgment on this matter, based as it is upon considerations of clarity and disciplinary distinctiveness, is clearly not eccentric and, in the absence of counterveiling reasons, should be accepted. In contract law, then, the doctrine of duress must be understood in light of the wrongdoing principle and this, as we have noted, has little to do with any version of *PAP*.

An examination of other areas of private law doctrine throws up no other plausible doctrinal manifestations of *PAP*. Considerations similar to those that make the doctrine of duress appear as if it might embody one or other version of *PAP* can also make the defence of necessity in tort appear salient. But, just as those considerations were misguided with respect to contractual duress, so, too, are they misguided in relation to tortious necessity. The defence of necessity in tort law holds that some *prima facie* tortious conduct, like trespass to person or to property, is permitted provided certain conditions are satisfied.[44] Since the idea of necessity captures in our minds some notion of something 'having to be done', it is but a small step from that to the assumption that there is no alternative to what has to be done in situations of necessity. And it is an even smaller step from that assumption to the conclusion that those who act in a situation of necessity cannot do otherwise; thus the actual sequence version of *PAP* must be in play. The problem with this analysis is that this is not at all how the English courts, at least, understand the defence.

The conditions that trigger the defence of necessity have nothing at all to do with *PAP*. So, for example, in *Re F* the House of Lords maintained that the defence will defeat an action for trespass to the person when: (i) the interference with another's person is part of a good faith rescue attempt; (ii) that attempt was made in circumstances in which it was not practicable to seek the consent of the assisted person; and (iii) non-consensual rescue or assistance was something that any reasonable person would do in the interests of the assisted person in that situation.[45] What is

[43] See Smith, *Contract Theory*, supra, note 39, pp. 326–340.

[44] Among the standard textbooks, the best treatments are: B. Markesinis and S. Deakin, *Tort Law* (Oxford: Clarendon Press, 5th edn, 2003), pp. 771–772 and, *inter alia*, pp. 418–424; W. Rogers, *Winfield and Jolowicz on Tort* (London: Sweet and Maxwell, 17th edn, 2002), pp. 872–876.

[45] 2 AC [1990] 1 (HL). The statement in the text is an extended version of that offered by Markesinis and Deakin, ibid, p. 420 and is informed by the considerations adduced by Lord Goff at pp. 74–78 of his judgment in *Re F*.

crucial about these requirements is that none of them, either explicitly or implicitly, committed the court to any claim about either version of *PAP*. Neither the actual sequence version nor the conditional version of *PAP* plays any role here: it is simply not helpful to speak about the defendant in *Re F* or in any necessity case not being able to do otherwise. The basis of the exculpatory claim in such cases is not that the defendant could not in some sense do otherwise. Rather, the claim is that the defendant's conduct in the particular circumstances was not wrong *regardless of whether or not he could have done otherwise*. The exculpatory claim here therefore takes on the hue of a justification and, as such, both versions of *PAP* are irrelevant.[46] Undoubtedly relevant, by contrast, is private law's schema of protected interests and its catalogue of relative culpability. It is by reference to those interests of agents that private law protects, and in light of what kind of conduct it regards as culpable in particular circumstances, that a judgment upon the quality of the defendant's deed is made. So, the courts are unlikely ever to regard a defendant's *prima facie* tortious interference with the claimant as wrongful where that interference serves to save the claimant's life in circumstances in which the claimant herself can express no view on the intervention. By contrast, the courts will almost always regard a defendant's interference as wrongful when no significant interest of the claimant is in play and when the defendant acts officiously, or regardless of the claimant's view. Matters such as these, subsumed under the heading of wrongfulness, are the fulcrum of Chapter 6.

Other private law defences and requirements are similarly not well understood as manifestations of one or other version of *PAP*. Defences like insanity or the rules about minors are not obviously premised upon *PAP* but are obviously related to the basic responsibility component as outlined in Chapter 3. We must, then, raise the crucial question: is *PAP* actually a *requirement* of legal liability-responsibility in private law? The answer to this question depends upon which version of *PAP* we have in mind. The argument of this chapter is that the actual sequence version of *PAP* is of no relevance to legal liability-responsibility judgments in private law. Indeed, it has been suggested that it is of little relevance to any form of legal or moral liability-responsibility. The situation is somewhat different with regard to the conditional version of *PAP*. While this version does not in any obvious way throw light upon the particular legal doctrines examined here, it is nevertheless important in another, albeit

[46] For more on the justification/excuse distinction see note 40.

indirect way. It functions as a sub-component of basic responsibility. It is not in any significant sense independent of the basic responsibility requirement, since the notion of capacity in the latter informs the conditional version of *PAP* and the arguments adduced to support basic responsibility were also invoked to support this version of *PAP*. At most, this version of *PAP* is therefore subsidiary to – a minor but not insignificant component of – basic responsibility.

5

Conduct and Causation

Basic responsibility and the principle of alternate possibilities, the two components of legal liability-responsibility examined so far, differ in many ways from the component with which we are now concerned. One difference in particular is worth emphasizing, since it indicates a significant change in focus. The alternate possibilities and basic responsibility components focus upon the agent in the frame for legal liability and some of his or her competencies and some aspects of his or her situation. The specific questions that arise when applying these components are agent-specific in a very obvious sense. We ask, for example, was this particular agent able to give an account of what she did? Was some aspect of her conduct intentional? Or, is this the kind of thing that Y usually succeeds in doing? And: is he generally able to make choices and act on them? By contrast, the conduct and causation component concentrates upon agents' deeds and their consequences and outcomes. The first limb of this component provides an account of what an agent's deeds might include, while the second illuminates the principles we use in determining how to trace the outcomes and consequences of such deeds or conduct. The focus, when this component is in play, is therefore upon some of the effects the agent has brought about in the world rather than some features of the agent or their situation.

It might be the case that these three components of legal liability-responsibility can be ordered according to their importance. It could be insisted, for example, that one component – basic responsibility – must be satisfied before turning to the others. It might also be held that this ordering holds also of the remaining components on the list. In the context of legal determinations of liability-responsibility, it makes obvious sense to answer the question of basic responsibility first, since we need be sure that the person before the law is indeed a being capable of both conducting themselves in accord with the law and able to understand its guidance and ukases. The basic responsibility component in private law is, therefore, an account of what needs be satisfied for an agent to be regarded as an addressee of the law. Only when certain that they are faced with an addressee of the law should judges and other operators of the legal system go about applying legal standards to that addressee and his conduct. However, the application of legal standards to the addressee and his conduct usually requires that judges and others be satisfied that this agent brought about the wrong in question. It is one thing to determine that this agent is a responsible being in the eyes of the law, but quite another to determine that this being's conduct did indeed either manifest or bring about some particular private law wrong.

While this latter issue – which, of course, is the conduct and causation component at work – must be approached, within the legal context, after the issue of basic responsibility, it need not be so approached in non-legal life. There are many contexts in which the causal question – what brought this event about? – is raised regardless of questions of basic responsibility. The most obvious context is, of course, that of determining causation in the natural world. In determining the specific causes of an eruption, it makes no sense to determine whether the volcano 'was responsible' in the basic sense. Yet, while neither volcanoes nor animals are capable of being responsible in the basic sense, both are perfectly capable of causing outcomes in the world; we can thus determine their causal efficacy (or responsibility) without raising any question of basic responsibility.

For legal purposes, then, the basic responsibility component must take priority over the others, although this is clearly not to say that, as a matter of fact about private law litigation, this component either generates or requires the most attention. Rather, even the most cursory examination of the law reports and textbooks suggests basic responsibility is rarely an issue, in the sense that it is simply taken for granted.[1] Private law disputes are most likely to concern the application or scope of some particular legal doctrine (such as the circumstances in which doing what one is already contractually bound to do can constitute good consideration), rather than the presuppositions or underpinning principles upon which such doctrines rest. Those presuppositions are no less important for being taken for granted.

If the basic responsibility requirement is prior to the other legal liability components noted so far, what is the ranking of the remaining two? It is probably a mistake to regard the second component that we examined, the principle of alternate possibilities, as second in importance after basic responsibility. This is because our analysis of the principle in Chapter 4

[1] This assumption is sometimes challenged within a procedural rather than a doctrinal context: *Masterman-Lister v Brutton* [2003] 3 All ER 162.

showed that, in its most defensible form, it is best regarded as but an adjunct to or element of basic responsibility. Since it is not truly an independent component of legal liability-responsibility, it need not be ranked separately from the basic responsibility component. Second in our ranking, at this stage at least, must therefore be the conduct and causation requirement. Our view on this matter might change, however, when we turn in the next chapter to the wrongdoing component, particularly but not only if a significant number of private law wrongs can be brought about either without conduct on the perpetrator's part or without a causal link existing between some aspect of their conduct and the wrong in question. If conduct and causal connection are required for most private law wrongs, then it is not unreasonable to rank the conduct and causation component higher than the wrongdoing component, pending an analysis of the incidence of the latter.

What, exactly, does the conduct and causation component entail? In what follows, each sub-component is separated in order to answer this question as clearly as possible. Although a glib formulation like that used above – that the conduct sub-component determines what can count as an agent's deeds while the causation sub-component traces the outcomes or consequences of those deeds – gives a reasonably accurate and pleasingly brief picture of what this component involves, there are, as will be seen, numerous complexities. The discussion divides into two parts, one tackling the idea of conduct and its attendant difficulties, the other grappling with the idea of causation and its meaning in private law judgments of liability-responsibility. For reasons that will become apparent, the latter receives most of our attention.

CONDUCT

A man does not sin by commission only, but often by omission.

Marcus Aurelius, *Meditations* (London: Penguin, 1964), Book 9, 5, p. 139

So far, the term 'conduct' has been used in this book to refer to action and its supposed synonyms (deed, doing, movement), on the one hand, and inaction and its putative synonyms (omission, refraining, non-doing), on the other. As lawyers we might be dubious about lumping together action and inaction in this way, since we learn at an early stage that the private law segments of the common law often draw a distinction between misfeasance (faulty acts) and nonfeasance (inaction, omission, refraining or non-doing). Yet, *qua* lawyers, we also learn from an early stage that breaches of duty, such as a failure to perform a contract or to achieve a specific standard of care in negligence, often ground liability and that such breaches are plausibly described as omissions (or possibly refrainings or non-doings). We are thus in an uncomfortable position. We learn that the distinction between doing and non-doing is significant, but lack a clear account of why. And we also know that, however significant the distinction is, it is not so significant as to mark a rigid distinction between liability and no liability. If the distinction between doing and not doing mapped exactly onto the latter distinction, then we would be able to say that only doings attract liability, and that is plainly false. Moreover, many philosophers deny that the distinction between doing and non-doing has any significance at all and this must add to our discomfort.[2] Two questions therefore press upon us: how are we to account for the distinction and why, if at all, should it be thought significant?

EXPLAINING THE DISTINCTION

To begin answering these questions we must first clarify our terms. And we must do this in such a way as to avoid taking a position on the substantive issue of the significance of the distinction, if at all possible. Furthermore, the first step towards clarification calls into question the assumption that our two sets of alleged synonyms are indeed synonymous.

Doubts appear as soon as we focus upon the supposed synonyms that represent the varieties of inaction, for it quickly becomes clear that some of these are quite different.[3] For example, it is implausible to maintain that any particular inaction is always either an omission or a refraining. In ordinary language, an omission usually marks a blameworthy failure to adhere to a required standard of conduct. It therefore seems normal to regard my failure to feed and nurture my children or – presumably less seriously – to renew my car tax as omissions and distinctly odd so to regard my failure, contrary to habit, to call in to my local coffee shop one morning. That inaction is not always an omission in this sense is clear

[2] Some notable examples are: J. Harris, 'The Marxist Conception of Violence' (1974) 3 *Philosophy and Public Affairs* 192–220; J. Glover, *Causing Deaths and Saving Lives* (Harmondsworth: Penguin Books, 1977), ch. 7; P. Unger, *Living High and Letting Die* (New York: Oxford University Press, 1996). The philosophical traffic is not, however, all one way: see F. M. Kamm, *Morality, Mortality* ii (New York: Oxford University Press, 1996), part I and B. Williams, *Making Sense of Humanity* (Cambridge: Cambridge University Press, 1995), ch. 5 (one of the shortest yet most acute treatments of the issue).

[3] For some helpful observations see J. Bennett, 'Morality and Consequences' in S. McMurrin (ed.), *The Tanner Lectures on Human Values* ii (Salt Lake City: University of Utah Press, 1981), pp. 50–51.

from the fact that whenever I snooze in my study chair I am in some sense clearly not acting, but am hardly ever at the same time omitting to do something. Snoozing in my chair could only be an omission if, for example, I ought to have been lecturing at the time. Similarly, snoozing, regarded as a paradigmatic instance of inaction, is almost never also an instance of refraining, since the latter usually requires deliberate inaction. Assuming that I have not manipulated the onset of sleep with a dose of sleeping pills or alcohol, this instance of inaction lacks the deliberative element that refraining must normally have. To refrain, in ordinary use, is to have the opportunity to act and to decide, for whatever reason, not to; refrainings are, therefore, usually instances of intentional conduct. By contrast, to omit is simply not to do what one ought to; it matters not whether the omission was intentional, reckless or negligent. That a non-doing is not always an inaction is clear, since one can fail to do X by either doing a vast range of other things incompatible with doing X or simply by not doing anything at all. The term 'non-doing' is not a bad general term for referring to both refrainings and omissions but its generality can elide differences between these two and should be treated with caution. Since the term 'inaction' is the least helpful from our list of alleged synonyms, it is henceforth eschewed.

Action and its alleged synonyms are just as problematic a class as inaction and its supposed synonyms. Consider, for example, the relation between movement and action. That these clearly are not always or even often the same is evident once we consider twitches or other 'automatic' or 'involuntary' bodily movements. The movement of my leg when the doctor taps my knee is clearly not an action in anything like the sense that my serving in tennis is; indeed, it is probably not rightly regarded as an action at all. Actions, generally speaking, are defined by reference to intentionality and that is lacking in genuine reflex reactions which are nevertheless movements.[4] Both 'deeds' and 'doings' are closely related to actions; indeed, it is surely no exaggeration to regard 'deeds' and 'actions' as almost exact synonyms for most purposes. By contrast, to regard this book as my 'doing' is simply to say that is the product of many, many particular actions or deeds. The difference between these terms, in ordinary use, is therefore probably little more than a difference of degree: my 'doings', like my projects, seem elongated in both time and space, composed of many particular deeds or actions.

These various differences between the terms in our two sets of supposed

[4] For some general comments on intentional conduct see ch. 3, pp. 78–79.

synonyms provide a caution against assuming a clear and easy contrast between the sets. The contrast, as common lawyers understand it, is between misfeasance and nonfeasance but how does that translate into the terminology of ordinary language? When lawyers speak this way what specific contrast do they, or could they, have in mind? Perhaps the most obvious and likely is between action, on the one hand, and either omissions or refrainings, on the other (since the latter can be regarded as but an intentional subclass of the former, the term 'omission(s)' will be used henceforth). If private law does indeed draw a distinction between action, on the one hand, and omissions, on the other, it must be established that the distinction is: (i) secure; and (ii) marks a defensible and significant boundary. Establishing either point is not easy.

This might be thought an exaggeration, particularly with respect to the first point. For the distinction between actions and omissions has surely already been established: it is there, in ordinary language. While there is some truth in this, there is an obvious snag. It is that our language is subtle and flexible enough to allow most omissions to be re-described as actions and many actions to be re-described as omissions. It therefore seems mistaken to think that there is a deeply significant distinction between omissions and actions because, although our language often marks this distinction, it can just as easily elide it. A surgeon's accidental cutting of an artery can just as easily be described as an action badly done as an omission or failure to take proper care. In the same way, my breach of contract can often be just as effectively characterized as either an omission to do what I ought to have done or as the deliberate doing of something else (selling the goods to another). So, is it a mistake even to try to distinguish actions from omissions, never mind to try to argue that the distinction is significant?

Some philosophers and jurists think not. In particular, Jonathan Bennett has developed a reasonably reliable test for distinguishing actions (or, in his terms, positive instrumentality) from omissions (which are but a sub-component, for him, of negative instrumentality).[5] It holds that there are two hallmarks of positive instrumentality. First, there must be some movement on the agent's part such that it caused or increased the probability of outcome O occurring. Second, it must be true that only that movement or a limited number of other movements could have either brought about O or increased the probability of O occurring. By contrast,

[5] Originally in 'Morality and Consequences', supra, note 3, pp. 52–65 and, with some additional defence, in his *The Act Itself* (Oxford: Clarendon Press, 1995), ch. 6.

there is only one principal hallmark of negative instrumentality, namely, there being many, many movements on behalf of an agent such that they could be causally significant in bringing about, or increasing the probability, of outcome O. Consider Bennett's example of a vehicle being destroyed by rolling off a cliff. If John removes the chocks from the stationary vehicle's wheels and, having done that, it runs down hill and off the cliff, then his conduct is positive because, given just about any plausible statement of the details of this scenario, there is only a very limited number of acts on his part that could constitute removing the chocks. If, however, the vehicle is already in motion but John can quite easily slip the nearby chocks under the wheels, his not so doing is an instance of negative instrumentality if it is the case that there is a vast range of potential acts by John that could have resulted in the vehicle being destroyed. Among this vast number of acts, we could include reading the newspaper, drinking coffee, pondering nature, writing a book, remaining still, resting etc. etc., none of which could in any proper sense be regarded as being the same as removing the chocks.

At this point it might seem that there is another hallmark of negative instrumentality, namely, that the agent has performed an act, albeit one of the many, many acts that may have been significant in bringing about or increasing the probability of O. This point is an important one, in that it emphasizes that omissions are often actions in this sense: omitting to do A is often a matter of *doing* something other than A. This need not always be so, however, since we could imagine an instance of unintentional absolute stillness – being paralysed by fear, for example – which is not an action but is an omission (for example, to warn the others). But if we say that, generally speaking, an omission is a matter of *doing* something other than what was required, are we not in danger of actually collapsing the distinction we are attempting to elucidate? Yes, but only if the defining properties of actions and omissions are what could be termed 'intrinsic' to those types and their particular tokens. If we know what constitutes actions and omissions not by in some sense 'just looking' at the phenomena, but instead by determining the relationship of some piece of conduct to other possible instances of conduct and to some set of possible outcomes, then the properties 'action' and 'omission' are relational rather than intrinsic.[6] The view that the status of segments of conduct as actions or omissions is

[6] See Bennett, 'Morality and Consequences', supra, note 3, pp. 53–55 and *The Act Itself*, supra, note 5, pp. 86–87. The point is also well put by M. Kramer, *The Quality of Freedom* (Oxford: Clarendon Press, 2003), pp. 326–327.

relational is far more plausible than the alternative, but it does lead to the conclusion, which some might find difficult, that one and the same segment of conduct can be an omission in some respect and an action in another. For many, this might count as an insight rather than a problem.

Turning back to actions, it might seem that even here a large number of acts by John, to return to Bennett's example, can result in removing the chocks (kicking them away with his left foot, kicking them with his right foot, pushing them with his left hand, using a stick, shooting them away with a rifle, training his dog to move them, etc. etc.). This is undeniable, but the point does not undermine Bennett's test if it is true that this class will actually almost always be far smaller than the class of negative acts John could engage in such that the vehicle continued its progress down hill. Tony Honoré puts it succinctly: '[i]f there are a small number of related movements such that they would have ensured that the outcome came about, and the agent performed one of them, the conduct is positive[;] if a large number, it is negative'.[7]

This test for positive and negative instrumentality seems to work very well in all normal cases, although the extent to which it can handle bizarre cases is contested.[8] It is therefore more than adequate for use in the law, on the supposition that the capacity to handle bizarre cases is not a preeminent virtue of either legal or most ordinary thought. The test can be used to distinguish actions from omissions, provided it is acknowledged that, as a specific subclass of negative instrumentality, the latter are distinctive because invariably normative. That is, omissions take place within a context in which something ought to be done, although the 'ought' in question is not always moral (I ought to care for and nurture my children) or legal (as a vehicle driver, I must ensure that I am insured), but may be prudential (I should eat more vegetables) or broadly social (I should queue). Thus, although omissions are a normative instance of negative instrumentality, the test to distinguish negative from positive instrumentality is not itself normative.[9]

THE SIGNIFICANCE OF THE DISTINCTION

If Bennett's test is indeed a reliable way of distinguishing negative from positive instrumentality, and can also be employed by lawyers to distinguish acts (or misfeasance) from omissions (or nonfeasance), then the

[7] *Responsibility and Fault* (Oxford: Hart Publishing, 1999), pp. 51–52.

[8] See Kramer, supra, note 6, pp. 327–335 for a defence of Bennett in bizarre cases; for Bennett's own thoughts see *The Act Itself*, supra, note 5, pp. 96–100.

[9] Bennett, 'Morality and Consequences', supra, note 3, pp. 48–52, 69–70, 73–95.

question about the significance of the distinction becomes relevant. There are at least three responses to this question: one holds that the distinction between acts and omissions could not be more significant, another that it is completely insignificant, while a third maintains that the distinction rests upon two not insignificant general considerations. Each will be considered in turn. The first response holds that the distinction between acts and omissions could not be more significant because it marks a difference between conduct that can cause harm and can be culpable (actions) and conduct that cannot cause harm and cannot be culpable (omissions). While the first element of this claim – that acts can cause harm and can be culpable – is acceptable, provided we resist the urge to move immediately, as if it were a matter of logical necessity, from 'X caused harm' to 'X is (therefore!) culpable', each component of the second element is dubious. Taking the first component first, it is quite simply far from obvious that omissions cannot cause harm, which is but a segment of the slightly broader claim that omissions cannot be causes.[10] Consider my failure to feed and nourish my children, as a result of which they begin to suffer from malnutrition and various cognate ailments. Is it in any way plausible to maintain that this omission is not a cause of their ailments? Or assume my duties as an employee of a railway company are to close crossing gates on the highway when trains are approaching. Is there any way of maintaining that my failure to close the gates is not a cause of pedestrians and motorists being hit by a train that also accords with intuitive common sense?[11] Furthermore, is there any reason to doubt our intuitive common sense reaction to this case?

Now, if omissions in cases such as these seem to have undeniable causal consequences, the way is open to argue that omissions are in general causally efficacious. Of course, it could be maintained that the instances highlighted are special because, for example, they are cases in which the agent who had omitted to act had a special duty so to act. While this is certainly true, it is unlikely that the existence of the special duty turns an otherwise

[10] The case for the causal efficacy of omissions is most vividly made by J. Harris, supra, note 2, in *Violence and Responsibility* (London: Routledge and Kegan Paul, 1980), chs. 2–4 and in his 'Bad Samaritans Cause Harm' (1982) 32 *Philosophical Quarterly* 60–69. See also H. L. A. Hart and T. Honoré, *Causation in the Law* (Oxford: Clarendon Press, 2nd edn, 1985), pp. 2–3, 37–38, 59, 127–128, 138–141 and 370–371 and T. Honoré, *Responsibility and Fault*, supra, note 7, ch. 3.

[11] E. Mack would hold that the cause here can be described as the other acts I was doing when I should have been closing the gates: 'Bad Samaritanism and the Causation of Harm' (1980) 9 *Philosophy and Public Affairs* 230–259, pp. 242–243. This response is correct insofar as it highlights the relational aspect of omissions and incorrect insofar as it is an element of an unsustainable argument that there are no such things as omissions.

causally inert omission into a causally salient one; rather, the existence of the special duty sets the parameters within which we usually look for a causally salient omission. The fact that I have a duty to close the crossing gates means that the gaze of those seeking to explain and attribute liability for the accident is directed at my conduct in the first instance. This does not, however, make my otherwise causally inert omission causally efficacious, since even if I have a duty and have failed to perform it, my omission cannot automatically be assumed to be a cause of the accident. For example, if it is established that, even though I did indeed fail to close the gates, the victim of the accident would certainly have crashed through the gates had they been closed and would have been struck by the train, it is highly unlikely that my culpable omission will be considered a cause of the victim's injury.[12] The general point here is that the existence or non-existence of special duties does not determine the causal efficacy of omissions, but serves only to structure the process of determining liability responsibility.

At least part of the resistance to the view that omissions can be causes is attributable to what may be called sceptics' 'Newtonian' conception of the world. Their

> world contains only the setting in motion of trains of events where previously all was at rest. But the real world of action is busy with trains of events, some of which we have power to set in motion, others are already in motion (whether caused by other agents or by the brute forces of nature) and we have the power to stop them or, by operating or not operating the points, determine where they will end up and what damage they will do along the way.[13]

Once conceived as being replete with existing trains of events and processes, the world becomes a far more hospitable place for causally efficacious omissions than if envisaged as entirely static. In an entirely static world only the initiation of force brings about chains of events and processes and many omissions, of course, do not seem rightly described as such 'initiations'.[14] The crucial difficulty is how to reconcile these two

[12] On the basis of the considerations elucidated in the second section and derived from the account of causation offered in Hart and Honoré, supra, note 10. The example in the text is, of course, based on *R v Pittwood* (1902) 19 TLR 37.

[13] J. Harris, 'Bad Samaritans Cause Harm', supra, note 10, p. 64.

[14] 'Omissions, on the best conceptualization of them, are literally not things at all . . . [thus] . . . they cannot constitute any kind of cause at all': M. Moore, 'The Metaphysics of Causal Intervention' (2000) 88 *California LR* 827–877, p. 840. Needless to say, this extraordinarily bold claim runs contrary to the argument offered here. The very least of its problems are its counter-intuitiveness and its apparent reliance on a non-relational view of omissions as having some discernible 'intrinsic' properties (itself a view based upon a by no means uncontroversial or obviously necessary metaphysics).

views of the world and the forces and processes in it. Since both views have some appeal, the most promising approach is to attempt to combine them. Thus Herbert Hart and Tony Honoré hold that common sense and law embody both views, but that neither law nor common sense is therefore contradictory. This is because each view is appropriate in a slightly different context. The 'Newtonian' view is apposite to our vision of ourselves as initiators in a world apparently easily bent to our purposes and in which paradigmatic instances of human conduct are direct interventions in or changes of some aspect of that world. Alternatively, the view of the world as a complex series of ongoing, interrelated events and processes is appropriate when our conduct is conceived as but part of a wider causal context in which the normal course of events can be just as easily disrupted by direct interventions as by failures to act.[15] For Hart and Honoré, the former view is one we take when we think of ourselves as 'causers' of harm, the latter when we accept that we can also 'occasion' harm.[16]

When it is accepted that omissions do indeed have causal consequences, it becomes fairly easy to regard them as being in some circumstances culpable. *Prima facie*, the child neglect and railway crossing examples just given appear culpable, that is, as blameworthy instances of conduct. Save for the existence of certain excusing conditions or strange circumstances, it is simply very hard to imagine situations in which it is ever non-culpable to starve one's children so that they become malnourished or even die. Similarly, it is hard to imagine a situation, save for the existence of compelling excusing conditions, in which the causally salient omission to close the crossing gates could be non-culpable. It seems, then, that the second component – that omissions cannot be culpable – of the second element depends for much of its power upon the truth of the first component, namely, that omissions cannot be causes. Once it is established that omissions are causally efficacious, the power of the claim that omissions are not culpable dissolves completely if interpreted widely, as holding that omissions are never culpable. The truth is that some are culpable, while some are not. Note that this does not commit us to the view that omissions and actions are always culpable in the same degree; maintaining that the former can be culpable does not foreclose the claim that the latter are generally more culpable.

Some sceptics have suggested that, even if omissions can be causes and can be culpable, it is as a practical matter either impossible or very difficult

[15] See Hart and Honoré, supra, note 10, pp. 28–38.

[16] The distinction is unpacked at pp. 166–167 below.

to determine which omissions are causally salient and which culpable in any particular case.[17] While the details of any particular argument to this effect can be disputed, the general point made by these sceptics is correct, insofar as it emphasizes that causal judgments are often difficult and that a prime source of difficulty is the process of distinguishing causally relevant conditions from salient causes.[18] Yet this point is by no means a problem only for proponents of the view that omissions can be causes, since the difficulty identified is a general one: it is true of any account of the nature of causation, positive or negative. It is also true that most accounts of causation endeavour to provide an intelligible basis upon which the distinction between causally relevant conditions and salient causes is drawn, so this sceptical argument must be set aside pending consideration of the account of causation that features in the second section of this chapter (p. 163). As will be seen, that account accepts that omissions can be causally efficacious.

The second account of the significance of the distinction between acts and omissions arises from the attack upon the first account. For, once it is shown, contrary to the first account, that omissions can be causes and can be culpable, it is tempting to deny that there is any significant distinction between acts and omissions. This denial becomes an exercise in the demystification of both common sense and the law, each of which cling to the distinction between acts and omissions despite their causal equivalence. The point is then made by critics of the distinction that it must be an ideological construct, wilfully obscuring a full appreciation of the consequences of our conduct. In addition, critics argue that the distinction is based solely upon a series of moral and political judgments intended to limit our responsibility for the situation of others. If the causal consequences of our acts are regarded as more significant than the causal consequences of our omissions, this can in effect serve to protect us from either moral or legal liability-responsibility for omissions. And this, of course, is either tantamount to, or the same as, a judgment that the causal consequences of our omissions are less bad, morally and politically speaking, than the causal consequences of our actions. For critics of the acts/omissions distinction, this judgment is simply a licence to cause harm without being called to account.[19]

[17] See Mack, supra, note 11 at pp. 254–259 and Harris, 'Bad Samaritans Cause Harm', supra, note 10, pp. 63–64 for a critical reposte.

[18] This terminology is elucidated at pp. 167–170 below.

[19] This is an over-simple and too brief paraphrase of some of the arguments in Harris, supra, notes 2 and 10 in Glover and Unger, supra, note 2.

An important aspect of the substance of this second account can, however, be accepted while its conclusion can be deflated. This is the strategy employed by the third account of the significance of the distinction between acts and omissions. It holds, like the second account, that both acts and omissions can be causally salient and that both can be culpable in some circumstances. But it rejects the inference proponents of the second account draw from this claim, namely, that the distinction is 'therefore' indefensible. Rather, it sets out to defend the distinction on the basis of two general claims, one of which is undoubtedly a moral-cum-political concern, the other of which seeks to rehabilitate a common sense judgment we often make in this context.

The common sense judgment is that, *generally speaking*, directly causing harm is more culpable than omitting to do something that causes harm, at least when judged from the perspective of the outcomes brought about.[20] It is often said that our reactive attitudes usually track the distinction, so that we feel worse – more resentful, affronted and violated – towards X when she strikes us in the face than when she simply refrains from preventing Y striking us in the face. This is not to say that X's conduct in the latter instance will not be censured: it undoubtedly will, if she could have intervened with no or very little risk. Moreover, her refraining in such a situation will surely lead to a re-evaluation of our relationship with X. There are some duties we expect from, for example, close friends, and this looks like an instance in which X has failed in such a duty. Yet, whatever the range and basis of our reactive attitudes to X in this instance, the claim remains that our grievance towards her is less serious, and our response to her less intense, than if she directly attacked us herself or arranged for others to act in that way. Now if it is true that as a matter of common sense we are indeed inclined to react in slightly different ways to actions and omissions, we must determine whether or not there is any rational basis for the difference.

One suggestion is that, again *generally speaking*, the outcomes of actions are usually likely to be more harmful than the outcomes of omissions. If, for example, I poison the food being distributed to those in need, it will almost always be the case that those who consume the food will be harmed as a result. But if I fail to contribute to the aid effort to buy and deliver food to those in need, it is by no means certain that the needy will

[20] Factors other than the nature of the outcome brought about often condition culpability judgments such as, for example, the attitude of the agent. For the sake of simplicity, such factors are ignored in what follows.

suffer as a result. For it is quite conceivable that others might contribute more to the aid effort, so my non-contribution may have no harmful consequences at all.[21] Furthermore, it is usually the case that harmful actions are direct attacks upon what can be called our primary interests – in bodily integrity, in securing of holdings and peaceful stability – while harmful omissions usually disappoint expectations, being failures to do what should have been done. If these two claims – that acts are more likely to be more harmful than omissions, and that acts are more likely than omissions to attacks our primary interests – bear the hallmarks of adequate and well founded generalizations, then they can provide a plausible basis for the difference in our reactive attitudes.

To qualify as adequate generalizations each claim must, for example, be well supported by experience and have a reasonably adequate range, so that they are borne out in a majority of cases (these putative generalizations are not, remember, universal). Whether or not the claims display these hallmarks is an open question with regard to each instance in which they are invoked: it cannot simply be assumed that they are always present. Even if we are satisfied in some instance that the generalizations hold, so that acts of some kind are more culpable than similar omissions because more likely to be more harmful than the latter, this clearly cannot support the claim that omissions are never culpable nor never harmful. Moreover, proponents of this third account of the significance of the distinction between acts and omissions are able, perfectly consistently, to maintain that in some instances omissions that cause harm are every bit as culpable as actions that cause harm. Tony Honoré offers one such argument. He holds that in the sphere of 'distinct duties' harm-causing omissions can be just as culpable as harm-causing acts. This claim, although it requires elucidation, is one that will resonate with many lawyers.

Distinct duties, for Honoré, are those requirements our conduct must satisfy in addition to the negative duties of non-interference we owe fellow human beings. The latter include, of course, the duty to desist from attacking our fellows and from otherwise directly undermining their physical and material security. Distinct duties, however, often derive from some special relationship we have with some of our fellow beings and most often have a combined moral or legal basis. So, for example, as a parent I have a distinct duty to nurture my own children, in addition to the general negative duties I have towards them and all other children.

[21] The example belongs to Honoré, supra, note 7, p. 41.

This duty surely arises in part from the fact that my children are most immediately dependent upon me for support (although our society could be arranged otherwise). It is probably also the case that they have a distinct duty to me, simply by virtue of being my children, to offer some support and care in my decrepitude, over and beyond the general duties they owe to me as a fellow human being. Some distinct duties can arise from my simply undertaking to do a particular thing: to take the neighbour's children on a hike, for example, or from entering into a contractual relationship in which I am to guard a railway crossing. In both instances, I will be expected to do what I undertook to do and to do so in a safe and reliable manner. Other distinct duties may flow from conduct of mine that creates particular risks of harm to fellow beings. If my trade, for example, is quarrying by using dangerous explosives, the very fact that I thereby impose a supposedly unusual risk to others creates, at the very least, a distinct duty to take steps to warn them of it.[22]

It is evident from this account that the bases of our distinct duties, while to some degree diverse, can also clearly overlap. What is also clear is that, as a matter of common sense, everyday morality and law, we recognize these duties and, usually, accept them. What requires rather more attention, however, is the claim that breach of such duties – the omission to do what they require – is generally speaking just as culpable as directly acting so as bring about the harm in question. What is the basis for this claim and, moreover, is it plausible? Honoré's strategy is simply to provide three examples (one involving a position of responsibility, one an undertaking and the other a relationship of dependency) in each of which there is an act and an omission to do what is required by a distinct duty. He concludes that in each example we cannot reasonably say that the harmful omission is any less culpable than the harmful act:

> Take the case of Susan, a nurse whose duty is to give a patient a certain medicine at six o'clock. Without valid excuse she gives the wrong medicine or fails to give any medicine at all. Can her legal or moral culpability be different in the two cases, assuming that the impact on the patient's health is equally bad and that her character does not appear in a worse light in one of them . . .? Her duty is to use the means, positive or negative, which will enable the patient to be restored to health. The same will be true if for some reason no nurse is available and Adrian, a chemist who knows what he is doing, undertakes to give the patient the proper medicine. It is equally bad of him to give the wrong medicine and to fail to give any medicine, again assuming the harm

[22] See Honoré, supra, note 7, pp. 54–60 for a fuller account.

to the patient and the motivation to be similar. Suppose again that Adrian does not promise to give the medicine, but that he is the only person available to do so in an emergency. The act and omission will again be morally on a par.[23]

The fact that the conclusion in each example appears so obviously correct might make some suspicious, but it is difficult to unearth plausible grounds for such suspicion. The neatness of the examples, and the felicitous way in which they illustrate the distinction between distinct duties and acts, cannot in itself be good grounds for doubting the point made. (What conceivable grounds are there for being generally suspicious of neatness in juristic and philosophical argumentation?) Nor is it a valid complaint to claim that the examples and the argument simply reproduce common sense, since that is in part what Honoré is after. Of course, another part of his task is to articulate and evaluate the sometimes submerged considerations upon which many common sense judgments often rest. That the argument offered often turns upon common sense and its judgments, which are frequently matters of degree, and does not unearth strong conceptually necessary connections is also no criticism, since that is exactly its nature.[24] The crucial point for current purposes, then, is this: do our intuitions match Honoré's in the examples given? If so, then his argument stands.

The third account of the significance of the acts/omissions distinction also holds that the distinction is generally worth maintaining on moral and political grounds. The political ground consists of a concern for individual liberty and the moral ground, which can occupy the same space, also invokes a claim about agency and integrity. Of these two grounds, the former is perhaps the least problematic. It begins from the observation that the imposition of legal liability-responsibility undoubtedly can restrict individual liberty.[25] It also makes the additional value judgment that the fewer restrictions of individual liberty there are in a polity, the better, save for restrictions absolutely necessary for equal liberty for all. If some particular polity imposes legal liability-responsibility for both acts and omissions, then there is on this view less individual freedom therein than in a polity that imposes such liability only for either

[23] Honoré, supra, note 7, p. 61.

[24] Which is why some of the arguments offered against Honoré in A. Simester, 'Why Omissions are Special' (1995) 1 *Legal Theory* 311–335 are misdirected; see also P. Smith, 'Omission and Responsibility in Legal Theory' (2003) 9 *Legal Theory* 221–240.

[25] Provided the liability rules are accompanied by enforcement mechanisms that are actually deployed: see Kramer, supra, note 6, pp. 66–70.

acts or omissions, but not both.[26] Since individual liberty should in general be maximized, we should wherever possible, and consistent with other values, ensure that the realm of legal liability is narrower rather than wider. Proponents of this view can then argue, on the basis of the common sense assumption that, generally speaking, acts are more likely to be more harmful than omissions, that legal liability for the latter should be the exception rather than the rule. This view is a stable-mate of that noted in Chapter I which distinguished private law from public law on the grounds of a distinction between private and public project pursuit. When private law is envisaged as a domain of private project pursuit, in which the law ought to facilitate citizens in their pursuit of individual goals and remedy wrongful incursions that frustrate individuals' pursuit of their goals, then it is natural to regard that domain as worthy of both respect and protection. An obvious way in which this domain can be protected is by restricting the grounds upon which legal liability-responsibility arises. The acts/omissions distinction is a ready-made restriction with a basis not just in the law but also in common sense.[27]

Is this political argument plausible? The question is a difficult one to answer without involving ourselves in the large and difficult issue of the value of freedom itself. But if some significant value is accorded to that ideal, then the argument from it to the acts/omissions distinction is not implausible. Furthermore, the argument is neither vague, since the reason it adduces to cleave to the acts/omissions distinction could not be clearer, nor is it too general, since that reason does not purport to outweigh all other considerations. It holds, rather, that as a general matter the distinction should be respected, all other things being equal but, of course, other things are not always equal. It is thus no embarrassment to this argument that many legal systems often allow, albeit in limited instances, liability for omissions: Honoré's distinct duties account is a

[26] This view is therefore committed to a conception of individual freedom or liberty that can be quantified. For superb analysis of the general issue of measuring freedom see: H. Steiner 'Individual Liberty', *Aristotelian Society Proceedings* (1975) lxxxv 35–50; 'How Free? Computing Personal Liberty' in A. Phillips Griffiths (ed.), *Of Liberty* (Cambridge: Cambridge University Press, 1983) and his *An Essay on Rights* (Oxford: Blackwell, 1994), ch. 2; I. Carter, *A Measure of Freedom* (Oxford: Clarendon Press, 1999), part III; and Kramer, *The Quality of Freedom*, supra, note 6.

[27] The argument here derives from some suggestive hints in N. E. Simmonds, 'The Possibility of Private Law', ch. 6 of J. Tasioulas (ed.), *Law, Values and Social Practices* (Aldershot: Dartmouth, 1997), pp. 150–153 and his 'Justice, Causation and Private Law', ch. 8 of M. Passerin d'Entreves and U. Vogel (eds.), *Public and Private* (London: Routledge, 2000).

good example. Yet that account of distinct duties, and the political argument itself, can come under attack in the same way. As against the political argument, it could be maintained that liberty is not itself a value but valuable only insofar as it furthers another, or other, more important values. As against Honoré's account of distinct duties, it might be similarly be argued that such duties are only compelling insofar as they uphold or promote another or other more important values. This is, in essence, a consequentialist (and most often utilitarian) attack upon the acts/omissions distinction and the means of supporting it. This attack, and utilitarianism in general, are the usual triggers for the moral argument by which the third account defends the acts/omissions distinction.

The principal claim of this moral argument is that if there were unrestricted moral or legal liability-responsibility for omissions, then our agency and integrity would be diluted. This is particularly so if the wider theory of moral right and wrong which denies the significance of the acts/omissions distinction is utilitarianism.[28] For in many versions that moral doctrine holds that the most morally significant feature of the world is the overall amount of pleasure or pain, preference satisfaction or preference dissatisfaction (or equivalent but possibly more complex cognates). Utilitarianism's ultimate moral injunction is that we ought to strive to bring about more pleasure or preference satisfaction and less pain or preference dissatisfaction. Precisely how such pleasure or pain, preference satisfaction or dissatisfaction, comes about is not morally important for utilitarianism, so its commitment to the acts/omissions distinction is at best tentative. At worst, it might be non-existent since, on a properly utilitarian view, it is difficult indeed to envisage circumstances in which the fact of some state of affairs being brought about by either positive or negative instrumentality could effect the moral quality of that state of affairs. Similarly, it is hard on a utilitarian view to give an account of how, if at all, the fact that a state of affairs was brought about intentionally, or recklessly, or negligently

[28] See J. J. C. Smart's 'An Outline of a System of Utilitarian Ethics' in J. J. C Smart and B. Williams, *Utilitarianism: For and Against* (Cambridge: Cambridge University Press, 1973) for a good overview of utilitarianism. Also helpful is A. Sen and B. Williams (eds.), *Utilitarianism and Beyond* (Cambridge: Cambridge University Press, 1982). The reposte to utilitarianism in the text was first offered by B. Williams, 'A Critique of Utilitarianism' in Smart and Williams, ibid, pp. 108–118 and is developed further in chs. 1 and 3 of his *Moral Luck* (Cambridge: Cambridge University Press, 1981). Although this riposte is regarded as a moral argument in the text, it might also be more than that: for illuminating discussion see S. Scheffler, *Human Morality* (New York: Oxford University Press, 1992), chs. 4 and 5.

could effect its moral quality or relative culpability. All that is significant on a utilitarian view is conduct that is causally efficacious in bringing about states of affairs and whether or not those states of affairs are good or bad.

Moreover, in its calculation of what action is morally best and thus ought to be done, utilitarianism does not distinguish between those projects and actions that are mine and those that belong to others. Thus, what I should do, morally speaking, in any particular situation is not determined by reference to my own projects, interests and commitments, but by the demand to increase overall preference satisfaction or pleasure or to decrease overall preference dissatisfaction or pain. So the fact that my child is among a group of drowning people, only one of whom I can rescue, has no special moral priority for me if I determine what I should do or refrain from doing in a thoroughgoing utilitarian way. I should do or refrain from doing whatever increases preference satisfaction or pleasure, there being no guarantee, of course, that that requires that I rescue my child. It might, for example, require that I save the world famous scientist who has been developing a cure for cancer or HIV. And this, for some philosophers, is a vivid illustration of the way in which utilitarianism undermines the integrity of individual agents, since it accords no presumptive value or weight to the concerns that usually make their lives valuable. Those concerns – the values, interests and commitments that constitute our lives and make them different one from another – serve in some sense to make us the people we are. They are, contrary to utilitarianism, morally significant.

On this view, then, the acts/omissions distinction is but one means of upholding agent integrity against the demands of utilitarianism, provided it is also maintained that our acts are 'ours' in a stronger sense than are our omissions. This latter claim cannot, of course, rest on any assumption about the greater causal potency of the former as opposed to the latter. Rather, an argument must be provided to show that an agent's actions are more 'authentically' his than are his omissions and this must be but part of a more general and usually idealistic account of agency. Such an account cannot be explored here: suffice it to say that this way of defending the acts/omissions distinction requires a good deal of additional support. Nor is this its only potential weakness. The other is that this moral argument assumes that all attacks upon the acts/omissions distinction are part of a wider utilitarian position. Yet it is by no means certain that all attacks must be so located; furthermore, non-utilitarian attacks upon the acts/omissions distinction seem *prima facie* immune to the argument from integrity.[29]

We must now turn to the causation element of the current component of legal liability-responsibility. The argument of this subsection has been a limited one, in that the acts/omissions distinction has been elucidated and, in limited degree, defended. The conclusion is that, while not insignificant, the distinction is not one of the most important in private law. Nothing said here commits us to any particular view as to the propriety or otherwise of liability for specific omissions like, for example, failure to rescue.[30] Since some of the principal grounds for maintaining the distinction between acts and omissions are moral-cum-political, and since these grounds usually hold only if all other things are equal, the question of whether or not there should be liability for some particular kind of omission is not one that should be answered *a priori*. Moreover, while the distinction between positive and negative instrumentality can be drawn without recourse to normative considerations, the distinction itself only becomes significant in light of such (usually moral and political) normative considerations.

CAUSATION

From the perspective of everyday common sense, it often seems silly to belabour the idea of causation. We make causal judgments all the time – we know the 'cause' of the goal because we saw the striker heading the ball past the despairing dive of the goalkeeper, just as we know that the accident was a 'result' of the driver's lack of attention because he was using his mobile telephone. We also have a high level of confidence in these judgments. Of course, there are some problematic cases where common sense seems equivocal, but exceptional cases should not undermine the faith we have in a large swathe of causal judgments. So why labour the obvious?

It might seem surprising, but some of the most sceptical voices in the discussion of the idea of causation belong to lawyers, many of whom, like their non-lawyer fellow citizens, spend a great deal of time making causal judgments. Perhaps part of their scepticism arises from the fact that, as well as frequently making causal judgments, lawyers spend almost

[29] Such non-utilitarian attacks are conceivable rather than common. I have struggled to find an example.

[30] For an interesting comparative treatment of some of the legal issues see J. Kortmann, *Altruism in Private Law* (Oxford: Clarendon Press, 2005).

as much time disputing such judgments. Furthermore, the grounds upon which such judgments are disputed are not always obviously silly or vexatious. At the legal philosophical level, the dominant strand of scepticism about causation is still best described as 'causal minimalism'.[31] Although born of that 'mood' or body of thought conveniently labelled American Legal Realism, which flourished roughly from the 1930s until the 1960s, it has gained further vitality from two more recent, principally American, and ostensibly completely incompatible approaches to law: Economic Analysis of Law and Critical Legal Studies.[32] Most representatives of these three groups are appropriately regarded as causal minimalists because united in three beliefs: that either no or very few aspects of legal causal judgments are securely rooted in 'fact'; that those aspects which are so rooted are of little significance; and that the principal determinant of our causal judgments in particular cases is the idea of 'policy' (variously understood).[33] They therefore regard legal causal judgments that do not explicitly appeal to policy considerations as bogus, since they obscure the reality of what is going on when such judgments are made. When these three beliefs are implemented at a doctrinal level, such as the causal requirements for various torts, they yield an admirably simple two-step approach. There are, for causal minimalists and Legal

[31] Hart and Honoré, supra, note 10, p. xxxiv.

[32] N. Duxbury, *Patterns of American Jurisprudence* (Oxford: Clarendon Press, 1995), ch. 2 provides a helpful introduction to American legal realism. Two classic examples of economic analysis's fast and loose treatment of causation (in which it is a surrogate for supposedly more important values or goals) are G. Calabresi, 'Concerning Cause in the Law of Torts: An Essay for Harry Kalven Jr.' (1975) 43 *U Chicago LR* 69–108; and W. Landes and R. Posner, 'Causation in Tort Law: An Economic Approach' (1983) XII *Journal of Legal Studies* 109–134. An exemplar of Critical Legal Studies' causal scepticism is M. Kelman, 'The Necessary Myth of Objective Causation Judgements in Liberal Political Theory' (1987) 63 *Chicago-Kent LR* 579–637.

[33] For realist-influenced causal minimalists, 'policy considerations' seem to refer most often, and completely unhelpfully, to considerations judges might regard as relevant in arriving at decisions; no general statement of the properties these considerations have in common is ever forthcoming. See, for just two examples, L. Green, 'The Causal Relation Issue in Negligence Law' (1961) 60 *Michigan LR* 543–576, pp. 560–564 (the term 'policy' is bandied about as if its meaning were so obvious as not to require elucidation); and W. Malone, 'Ruminations on Cause-in-Fact' (1956) 9 *Stanford LR* 60–99, p. 61 (the term 'policy' invoked with no indication at all of its possible meaning) and 65–66 (it is simply assumed that the application of a legal rule 'is a statement of legal policy'). For proponents of Economic Analysis, the term 'policy' is usually a shorthand way of referring to whatever they take to be the goals of the area of law in question: see Calabresi, ibid, and Landes and Posner, ibid. An unusually thorough analysis of policy considerations from a proponent of Critical Legal Studies is D. Kennedy, *A Critique of Adjudication* (Cambridge, Mass.: Harvard University Press, 1997), chs 5 and 6 (where they are regarded as more or less reducible to political value choices).

Realists like Leon Green, only two questions to ask here: first, was the tortious conduct a 'but-for' cause of the damage in question? And, if so, are there any policy considerations against the imposition of liability?[34] This approach still finds favour today, even among legal scholars who are neither latter-day Realists nor proponents of either Economic Analysis or Critical Legal Studies.[35]

The remainder of this section focuses upon a powerful jurisprudential response to causal minimalism: Hart and Honoré's *Causation in the Law* (hereinafter, in both text and notes, '*CL*').[36] This book aimed not only to defend the legal understanding of the nature of causation against causal minimalism: it also sought to unearth the basis of that understanding. A related and more ambitious aim was to show both that this understanding of causation was – despite the complaints of causal minimalists and other sceptics – genuinely in play in the case law, and that it could resolve most of the tricky causal problems that had worried lawyers for centuries. For present purposes, three important issues in Hart and Honoré's account of causation in the law must be noted: the *types* of causal connection, the *nature* of causal connection and the *basis* of our causal judgments. In addition, Hart and Honoré's argument raises a fourth topic that deserves our attention and which concerns some *general matters* of criticism and defence. In the course of examining each issue an attempt is made, where necessary, to both clarify and defend Hart and Honoré's position. It should be noted, however, that where defences are offered in what follows, they are in the main responses only to fairly recent criticism. *CL* was first published in 1959 and has attracted a great deal of attention since. Honoré has defended the book against some critics on at least three occasions, including the preface to the second edition of 1985.[37] In the

[34] Green, ibid.

[35] J. Stapleton's work on causation is a remarkable recent example of a Realist approach: see, for example, her 'Unpacking Causation', ch. 7 of P. Cane and J. Gardner (eds.), *Relating to Responsibility* (Oxford: Hart Publishing, 2001) and compare it with Green, supra, note 33. While it seems likely that Stapleton would resist being tarred with this brush, the substance of her arguments ensures that it is almost inevitable. See also T. Honoré, 'Appreciations and Responses' in Cane and Gardner, ibid, at p. 233.

[36] Supra, note 10. For beginners, the best starting point is part I of the book itself, rather than the vast number of commentaries, some of which are at best idiosyncratic. Part I is best tackled slightly unconventionally, through the principal chapters (e.g., II, III and V) *followed by* the preface to the second edition.

[37] The other two occasions are: 'Causation and Remoteness of Damage', ch. 7, Vol. XI, of A. Tunc (ed.), *International Encyclopedia of Comparative Law* (Tubingen: Mohr, 1971); ch. 5 of his *Responsibility and Fault*, supra, note 7.

present context, there is neither space nor much point in revisiting such well-worn ground.

TYPES OF CAUSAL CONNECTION

Hart and Honoré claim, surely undeniably, that common sense recognizes three principal types of causal connection.[38] First is that which obtains in the relation of direct physical intervention in or manipulation of the environment, other agents or living creatures by an agent (for example, 'X hit Y'). This causal connection is also manifest in omissions, in which harm results from a failure to act. Second is the causal connection that obtains when an agent provides reasons for another agent to engage in conduct of a particular kind ('X induced Y to attack V'). Clearly this connection cannot be brought about by omission.[39] The third type exists when an agent provides opportunities for another agent to conduct themselves in a certain way ('X left Y's house unlocked which was then burgled by C'), or when an agent provides occasion for certain events to occur ('X lights a fire next to Y's property which, because of a change in wind direction, then engulfs Y's house'). This connection can be brought about just as effectively by refraining as by acting.

These three types of causal connection are certainly not the same: 'there is not a single concept of causation but a group or family of concepts. These are united not by a set of common features but by points of resemblance, some of them tenuous' (*CL*, p. 28; see also p. xxxii). Since the *inter se* relations between these types of causal connection are not straightforward, neither is the task of articulating the principles upon which the connections operate or in accord with which they are deployed. Hart and Honoré's warning on this particular matter is stark:

> many difficulties present themselves when we start to examine the common use of causal language in order to identify the "common-sense principles" which courts profess to apply. We must expect both ambiguity and vagueness as well as variations which can be explained as more or less systematic adaptations of a common notion to contexts of different kinds. These facts make it impossible to do more than select for study *standard* examples of the way in which causal expressions are constantly used in ordinary life; and even then to focus attention only on certain characteristic features which have a bearing on those aspects of causation which perplex the lawyers. As with every other empirical notion we can hope only to find a core of relatively well-settled

[38] *CL*, pp. xxxii–xxxvii and chs II, III, VI, VII, XII and XIII.

[39] Because, generally speaking, 'inducing', like 'persuading' or even 'indoctrinating', seems to require positive conduct.

> common usage amid much that is fluctuating, optional, idiosyncratic, and vague: but the study of this core, as in other cases, may be enough to shed light on at least the darkest corners. (*CL*, pp. 26–27)

Moreover, even if the principles used to apply these various causal connections can be unearthed and are coherent, there is a vital issue – perhaps the most important issue in this context – still untouched. In pointing to these three types of causal connection we have assumed what is in issue, namely, what causality looks like: it has been taken for granted that these three instances of causal connection do indeed embody that notion. But in what, exactly, does such connection consist? This issue, along with the associated question of the principles by reference to which ordinary and legal causal judgments are made, is next on our agenda. The equally pressing issue of the bases of these causal judgments – ordinary language and common sense – and their possible variability is tackled thereafter.

THE NATURE OF CAUSAL CONNECTION

For Hart and Honoré the nature of causal connection – what it means to say C caused O – depends upon the type of causal connection in question. For all instances of the first type, which can be labelled *causing harm*, the nature of the required connection is clear. It is that the conduct alleged to have caused the harm in question must (i) be a necessary member of a set of conditions sufficient to bring about that harm and (ii) must additionally accord with common sense causal principles.[40] In instances of the second type, which can be dubbed *inducing harm*, the connection is not captured by either element just mentioned. Rather, it needs be established that the reasons given actually influenced the other party's conduct and that those reasons were, in those circumstances, of a kind which would influence the conduct of ordinary human beings. The principles used to establish causal connection in this kind of instance, while also rooted in common sense, are quite different to those invoked by the second limb of the connection required for causing harm.[41] The nature of the causal connection required in the third type of case, that of *occasioning harm*, is in general captured by the first limb of the connection in cases of causing harm. That is, the conduct alleged to have provided an opportunity for another agent to do something harmful, or for other harmful events to occur, must be a necessary member of a set of conditions

[40] *CL*, p. xliv and xxlviii.

[41] *CL*, p. 23 and pp. 51–59; Honoré, *Responsibility and Fault*, supra, note 7, pp. 117–119.

sufficient to bring the consequence about.[42] The common sense principles in play here are of a different order to those covered by the second limb of the connection required for causing harm: the kind of consideration that would curtail causal connection in the latter context often actually embodies causal connection in the former.

Even this compressed statement shows why many commentators distinguish two principal elements of Hart and Honoré's account of causal connection, namely, that captured by the necessary element of a sufficient set idea (hereinafter 'NESS' or 'the NESS test') and that captured by a range of common sense causal principles (hereinafter 'common sense causal principles'). This practice is followed here, but with a caveat: this separation should not in any way be taken to imply that the NESS test is either contrary to or more technical than common sense. Rather, it is most likely that the NESS test captures or is certainly consonant with common sense. Some brief attempts to establish this are made below. The separation, although artificial and potentially misleading, has most likely taken hold because, while often ignoring the second element of Hart and Honoré's account of the nature of causal connection, philosophers have started to give the first element sustained attention. The implication seems to be that they have thus either rescued or insulated the NESS test from common sense.

A more precise statement of the NESS test than that used so far, which is henceforth taken as canonical, was offered by Richard Wright and endorsed, with a minor reservation, by Honoré.[43] It holds that 'a particular condition was a cause of (condition contributing to) a specific consequence if and only if it was a necessary element of a set of antecedent actual conditions that was sufficient for the occurrence of the consequence'.[44] However, this test often and rightly tells us that a vast number of conditions are causally significant in the production of some particular event or instance of conduct. Moreover, where the type of causal connection in

[42] *CL*, p. xlv, p. xlviii and pp. 59–61.

[43] *Responsibility and Fault*, supra, note 7, p. 98.

[44] R. Wright, 'Causation in Tort Law' (1985) 73 *California LR* 1735–1828, p. 1790 (emphasis omitted), hereinafter '*Causation*', and *CL*, p. xlviii, pp. 110–113 and chs VI and XII. See also, R. Wright, 'Causation, Responsibility, Risk, Probability, Naked Statistics, and Proof: Pruning the Bramble Bush by Clarifying the Concepts' (1988) 73 *Iowa Law Review* 1001–1077, pp. 1018–1023 (hereinafter '*Bramble Bush*') and his 'Once More into the Bramble Bush: Duty, Causal Contribution and the Extent of Legal Responsibility' (2001) 54 *Vanderbilt LR* 1071–1132, pp. 1101–1109 (hereinafter '*Bramble Bush 2*'). For a sometimes overstated critical evaluation of Wright's contribution, see R. Fumerton and K. Kress, 'Causation and the Law: Preemption, Lawful Sufficiency and Causal Sufficiency' (2001) 64 *Law and Contemporary Problems* 83–105.

question is causing harm, it is not generally enough to say that C was a NESS condition of O.[45] So, for example, on the NESS test we know that both the dropping of a lighted match in a litter bin, and the presence of oxygen in the environment, were causally significant in bringing about the destruction of a building and associated loss of life. Yet it would only be in the rarest of circumstances that we would say the presence of oxygen in the environment was the cause of the harm in question. In most normal instances, we hold that the cause of the harm is the dropping of the match. On what basis do we and can we make such claims?

By reference to a series of principles about what circumstances are normal and abnormal, as well as what conduct is voluntary (or unreasonable) and involuntary (or reasonable), in the ordinary course of human affairs.[46] In the normal everyday context, the dropping of a lighted match in a bin would undoubtedly be regarded as the cause of the fire and the losses it brought about, assuming no abnormal conduct or conditions intervened. But if, while the bin was smouldering, a passing firebug poured accelerant on the flames, our judgment would surely differ. Furthermore, if the context were one in which the presence of oxygen were unusual (a laboratory, for example, in which the flammability of materials were being tested), that NESS condition would be regarded as the cause of the harm if all other NESS conditions (the ignition of the match, dropping it in the bin, etc.) were normal features of the environment. So, in addition to the NESS test of causal connection, in some contexts we utilise a range of additional common sense principles to sort causes from NESS conditions. While the NESS test tells us what, in a broad sense, are the causes of O – talk of NESS 'conditions' is therefore potentially confusing, since these conditions are causes[47] – a range of common sense principles are utilized to make salient one or more specific causes or 'conditions' of O.[48] These common sense principles simply highlight, from the broad field of NESS conditions or causes, those or that which we regard as particularly significant.

For the three types of causal connection, then, the nature of the causal

[45] *CL*, p. xlviii; chs. VII and XIII. [46] *CL*, ch. II.

[47] Hart and Honoré use the helpful term 'causally relevant condition' to capture this idea: *CL*, p. xlviii. See also pp. lxxviii–lxxix (condition *sine qua non*).

[48] Two things should be noted about this process. First, Hart and Honoré warn that it is not in any plain sense a process of 'selection', although that terminology is appealing: see *CL*, chs I, II and p. 112 (against J. S. Mill they maintain that all causally relevant conditions need not be known prior to 'highlighting' one or holding it to be particularly salient; the process is thus not well characterized as one of selection). Second, judgments of salience are determined by context, interest or both.

connection consists of either NESS, the NESS test combined with common sense causal principles, or common sense causal principles. This, at least, is what Hart and Honoré argue. To assess the plausibility of this account of the nature of causal connection, both elements require analysis. As will be seen, the most acute contemporary critics of Hart and Honoré regard the second element as particularly problematic.

NESS

Many lawyers might rebel at the claim that to say C is a cause of O is to say C is a necessary element of a set sufficient to bring about O. The reason is obvious: the law already has a vocabulary for doing what the NESS test purports to do, and Hart and Honoré introduce unnecessary complexity into an already confused area by ignoring it. What they allegedly ignore, of course, is the 'but-for' or *sine qua non* causal test that common lawyers have used for centuries. Are these two indicators of causal connection the same or different? If the latter, on what basis, if any, can we choose between them? And must such a choice be made?

A standard, unimpeachable statement of the but-for causal test holds that it consists of one question: 'would the loss have been sustained but for the relevant act or omission of the defendant?'[49] If the answer is negative, then the act or omission in question is a but-for cause of the loss, since without it the loss would not have occurred; if the answer is affirmative, then the act or omission is not such a cause, since the loss would have occurred anyway. This test has a good deal of plausibility, primarily because it highlights an intuition we ordinarily have about causes, namely, that they must be in some sense necessary for the occurrence of a particular consequence. The sense of necessity in play in the but-for test is either the strongest sense or a reasonably strong sense. For, in requiring that for C, a putative cause, to be established as a genuine cause of O, O's existence or occurrence depends upon C's prior existence or occurrence, the but-for test must hold either: (i) that C is necessary for the occurrence of O whenever O occurs; or (ii) that C is necessary for the occurrence of O on that particular occasion in those specific circumstances.[50] The difference between these two senses of necessity is, of

[49] B. Markesinis and S Deakin, *Tort Law* (Oxford: Clarendon Press, 5th edn, 2003), p. 185.

[50] A clear statement of the different senses of necessity and sufficiency, terms that are the usual coin of philosophers in this context, see Wright, *Bramble Bush*, supra, note 44 at pp. 1020–1021. For more on the point of substance, see J. Mackie, *The Cement of the Universe* (Oxford: Clarendon Press, paperback edn, 1980), pp. 39–40 and 60–66.

course, the difference between C being always and ever required for O and C being required for O in some particular situation. It is not clear which of these two strong senses of necessity the but-for test is wedded to, nor has it ever been necessary in the case-law for judges to distinguish them. What is clear, however, is our reaction to the absence of either: where the outcome O occurs in the absence of the prior condition C, then our ordinary judgment is that that condition is not a cause of that outcome. Furthermore, the common sense basis of the but-for test is no doubt an important factor in explaining its appeal to lawyers and surely informs their adherence to it despite two obvious shortcomings. For, although consistent with our common sense assumption about the necessity of causes, the test generates outcomes that are entirely opposed to common sense in at least two standard situations: those that involve 'pre-emptive' and 'duplicative' causes.[51]

Pre-emptive causation exists in this type of instance, familiar to almost every first year tort or criminal lawyer: D shoots and kills P just as P was about to drink a cup of tea that was poisoned by C. Duplicative causation is often illustrated by an equally familiar example: C and D independently start separate fires, each of which would have been sufficient to destroy P's house. The fires converge and burn down P's house. In the former instance, the but-for test holds, counter-intuitively, that D's shot is not a cause of P's death since P would have died anyway. And in the latter instance it yields the counter-intuitive conclusion that neither C's nor D's conduct was a cause of the destruction of P's house. The reasoning is clear, although the conclusion is bizarre: would P's house have perished without C's fire? Yes, D's fire would have consumed it; C's conduct is not therefore a but-for cause. Would P's house have been destroyed without D's conduct? Yes, since C's fire would have brought this consequence about; therefore, D's conduct is not a but-for cause of the fire.

In pre-emptive and duplicative causation cases the NESS test, properly applied, yields sensible results: results, that is, which accord with both common sense and much case law.[52] Since, to be a cause on this test, a condition has to a member of *an actually existing antecedent set* of conditions sufficient to bring about the consequence in question, it holds that

[51] The terms belong to Wright, *Causation*, supra, note 44, p. 1775. The examples that follow in the text also belong to him. Wright argues, correctly, that Hart and Honoré elide this distinction which sometimes breeds confusion in their work: ibid, pp. 1796–1798.

[52] For some of the tort cases see *CL*, pp. 194–204; Wright, *Causation*, supra, note 44, pp. 1791–1798.

in the first example D's shot is a pre-emptive cause of P's death, while C's poisoning of the tea is not.[53] The former is a member of an actual set sufficient to bring about P's death, but the latter is not (assuming no tea was consumed by P prior to his death). Of course, C's poisoning P's tea *could have been* a member of an actually existing set, had things been different, but such speculative possibilities are both infinite and irrelevant. The question, after all, is 'whose conduct actually caused P's death in this case?' and not 'how could P's death have been brought about in (an almost infinite variety of) different circumstances?' Applied to instances of duplicative causation like the converging fires case, NESS holds that both C's and D's conduct are causes of P's loss: each fire is a necessary member of an actually existing antecedent set sufficient to bring about that consequence. One such set includes C's fire, and all the other necessary elements of the sufficient antecedent set; the other set includes D's fire and all the other necessary members of the sufficient antecedent set.

Duplicative causes are often regarded as problematic because we can be misled by the thought, made explicit by the application of the but-for test in these cases, that they in some sense cancel one another out. That they do not is made evident by the fact that each fire, if in itself sufficient to destroy the house, is a member of two different NESS sets, each being identical except for the fact that one includes D's fire while the other includes C's fire. But what if one fire was insufficient to destroy P's house? Surely in this instance we must conclude that the causal efficacy of this fire is cancelled out by the other? Wright thinks not:

> . . . if there were only two fires, one of which was independently sufficient and the other of which was not . . . [then] the first fire was clearly a cause, since it was independently sufficient. But the second fire also was a cause. It was necessary for the sufficiency of a set of actual antecedent conditions which included another fire (the first) that was "*at least* large enough to be sufficient for the injury if it merged with a fire the size of the second fire." The sufficiency of this set is not affected by the fact that the first fire was so large that it would have been sufficient by itself.[54]

Sensitive to the claim that his 'at least large enough' caveat is an intellectual sleight of hand, Wright holds that it is valid for the compelling reason that, if the hypothetical example were real, it would describe an actual condition that existed on that particular occasion. This is hard to

[53] The 'actually existing' set of conditions point, sometimes overlooked by Hart and Honoré, was first clarified by Wright, *Causation*, supra, note 44, p. 1795.

[54] Wright, *Causation*, supra, note 44, p. 1793.

deny, but the plausibility of the claim also depends upon our accepting that it is sensible to break the size of the first fire down into portions.[55] While this procedure might seem rather too refined for everyday thought, it is not obviously suspicious on either scientific or metaphysical grounds. Nor is there an immediately obvious reason why we should always resist refining everyday thought.

The counter-intuitive results yielded by the but-for test in duplicative and pre-emptive causation cases provide good reason to either reject it or treat it with caution. The principal proponents of the NESS test – Hart and Honoré and Wright – advocate the latter option and a number of considerations inform this approach. One, which is not explicitly stated but seems more than likely to have weight with these authors given that their approaches combine both philosophical analysis with a detailed appreciation of legal doctrine, is that the but-for test itself is, despite infirmity, so well embedded in common law legal thought. Another, which is explicitly stated, is that it is only in exceptional cases such as those involving duplicative and pre-emptive causation that the but-for test and the NESS test generate different results. This generalization has not been rigorously tested but it seems plausible. That being so, it is reasonable to regard the but-for test as a reliable surrogate for the NESS test in all but exceptional cases.[56] This is not to say that the two tests are of equal status: for Hart and Honoré and Wright the NESS test dominates.

What else can be said for the NESS test, beyond its facility in dealing with instances of causation over which the but-for test stumbles? The first thing to note is not a recommendation but a qualification. It is that NESS is not the only possible remaining test of causation, even if but-for is rejected. Indeed, lawyers in particular have developed a number of alternatives to but-for yet, since most of these are part of the causal minimalist programme, they turn out, despite initial appearances, to have little specific to say about the nature of the causal relation. Rather their main burden is to delineate that with which causal judgments should be replaced, the principal recommendations usually reducing to either a vague type of 'policy analysis' or to reliance upon unrefined and untested moral intuitions. Recommendations such as these have been ably criticized

[55] Ibid, pp. 1793–1794.

[56] *CL*, p. xlviii; Wright, ibid, p. 1792 and pp. 1802–1803; Honoré, *Responsibility and Fault*, supra, note 7, pp. 107–119.

elsewhere.[57] Contemporary philosophers, on the other hand, have in the main been less interested in the kind of causal judgments made in legal and general attributive contexts; their primary interest is in the analysis of general causal laws, their conditions and basis.[58] Of the few philosophers interested in causal judgments in attributive contexts, John Mackie has made the most telling contribution, defending a version of the but-for test and attacking aspects of the NESS test.[59] His defence of the but-for test consists of showing that it can indeed deal with problematic cases like those involving duplicative causation. While Mackie undoubtedly presents a coherent argument, it not particularly plausible, since it relies on a dose of *ad hoc* modification supplemented with a non-parsimonious 'posit'. The *ad hoc* modification is his suggestion that in duplicative causation cases the initial but-for response be set aside in favour of regarding both causes as a 'cluster'; the 'posit' is simply a matter of assuming a technical conception of causation that makes judgments the but-for test does not warrant.[60] Mackie's criticisms of the NESS test stand independently of his arguments defending but-for and have elucidated compelling replies.[61]

What, then, can be said in favour of NESS? First, besides being consistent with common sense and much case law in instances of duplicative and pre-emptive causation, the NESS test is also consonant with common sense in another way. For it, like the but-for test, and in conjunction with common sense, holds that genuine causes are in some sense necessary for the occurrence of their consequences. Yet the sense of necessity in play in the NESS test is neither of the two that could inform the but-for test. Rather, it is the weakest sense of necessity that is involved here, where the claim that C is a necessary condition of O means only that C must be one of a set of necessary conditions which, taken together, are sufficient to bring about O. This sense is so weak that the relation NESS requires between causes and outcomes could in fact be captured in terms

[57] *CL*, pp. lxvii–lxxiii and ch IV. The main body of the book (chs. VI–XV) can be read as a sustained response to this way of thinking about causation in the law. See also Wright, *Causation*, supra, note 44, pp. 1742–1745, 1761–1763 and 1774–1813; *Bramble Bush*, supra, note 44, pp. 1007–1010 and 1018–1042.

[58] See, for example, D. Lewis, *Philosophical Papers II* (New York: Oxford University Press, 1986) chs. 21 and 22 and E. Sosa, 'Varieties of Causation', ch. XV of E. Sosa and M. Tooley (eds.), *Causation* (Oxford: Clarendon Press, 1993).

[59] See Mackie, supra, note 50, chs. 2, 5 and 8.

[60] Mackie, ibid, pp. 46–48; Honoré, *Responsibility and Fault*, supra, note 7, pp. 108–110.

[61] *CL*, pp. xxxvii–xlii; Wright, *Bramble Bush*, supra, note 44, pp. 1028–1034; Honoré, *Responsibility and Fault*, supra, note 7, ch. 5.

of strong sufficiency rather than weak necessity.[62] The strongest test of sufficiency is that C must alone be sufficient for the occurrence of O, while the weakest is that C be an element in a set of existing conditions sufficient to bring O about. And the intermediate test of sufficiency is, in fact, the NESS test: that C be a necessary element of some set of existing conditions sufficient for the occurrence of O.

Second, the NESS test has a respectable philosophical lineage and is plausibly viewed as both an extension and modification of the general account of causation derived from David Hume and John Stuart Mill. Of course, the modifications required of the Hume-Mill account of causation, so that it can accommodate the singular causal judgments of law and ordinary life, are not insignificant. In particular, the substitution of invariable and unconditional sequence – this being for Mill in what causal connection consists – with the weaker notion of causal generalization, appears problematic.[63] This appearance is, however, deceptive when viewed from the terrain of common sense causal judgments. For, assuming that these judgments are indeed genuinely causal, it is a strength of the Hume-Mill account of causation that it can, albeit it with slight modification, accommodate them. If, by contrast, these judgments are regarded as bogus, modifying the general account of causation to accommodate them is pointless, serving only to weaken that account. Of course, pointing to the fact that the NESS test keeps good philosophical company is not a great recommendation of its worth, just as the fact of an individual having virtuous parents or friends is far from an incorrigible guide to her character. That is not to say that the fact of keeping good company can never be of any weight in assessing either the character of individuals or the general plausibility of philosophical positions. But when all other relevant factors – its competent handling of pre-emptive and duplicative causation, its consistency with common sense in these instances and in its general thrust about the necessity or sufficiency of causes, as well as its consonance with much case law – highlight the plausibility of NESS, it is hard not to regard its respectable philosophical lineage as yet another advantage. Were respectable lineage the only consideration in NESS's favour, it would be a mistake to accord it any weight.

A third consideration in favour of NESS has been offered by Wright. It

[62] See Wright, *Bramble Bush*, supra, note 44, p. 1020. As will be clear, the remainder of this paragraph owes a good deal to Wright's admirably clear treatment of this issue. For the classic argument intended to undermine the necessity or sufficiency of NESS, see Mackie, supra, note 50, pp. 40–43.

[63] See *CL*, pp. 44–51.

is that the NESS test 'is not just a test for causation, but is itself the meaning of causation' or, what presumably amounts to the same thing, it 'capture[s] the essence of the concept of causation'.[64] This is a difficult claim to assess, primarily because its meaning is not immediately clear. If, however, the claim is that NESS and only NESS exhausts the range of our causal language and judgments, then it is surely an exaggeration. One reason for this thought is that an open-minded analysis of our ordinary causal language suggests that NESS is but one component of our causal judgments. Other significant components are noted in the following subsection. However, Wright is inclined to disregard these other components on the ground that they are not factual and cannot 'therefore' be part of a reputable test for causal connection. Subsection three (p.183) shows why this view is mistaken. Another reason to suggest this is an exaggerated view of NESS's importance becomes apparent when the range of causal tests that have been developed by philosophers and scientists are considered.[65] To show that NESS and only NESS captures the essence of causation, these other tests and principles must each be discredited. Wright himself has not done this, nor is it clear that anyone else has. Furthermore, while in no way supporting the claim that each one of these other tests of causation is both valid and valuable, it seems likely that some at least are valuable in some contexts for some specific inquiries. That being so, the most that can be said for NESS is that it is one respectable causal test among others, particularly effective and suitable in attributive contexts, but not necessarily valuable in every context. This judgment is perfectly valid if it is true that the relationship between respectable causal tests is not that of a zero-sum game.

Finally, recall the most important limitation of the NESS test. Applied in any particular explanatory or attributive causal inquiry, the test will generate a vast range of causes: a range, that is, of causally relevant conditions all of which are necessary members of an actually existing set sufficient to bring about the consequence in question, but not all of which we would regard as causally salient. The question, then, is 'how do we distinguish between causes (those conditions regarded as particularly causally salient) and other causally relevant conditions (necessary members of a sufficient set)?' Hart and Honoré say we do this via a scheme of fairly reliable common sense causal principles. More difficult to answer is

[64] The first quotation is from *Causation*, supra, note 44, p. 1802, the second from *Bramble Bush*, supra, note 44, p. 1019.

[65] See note 58 for some examples.

the question 'why do we do this?' The most persuasive rationale is probably something like the assumption that human agency often has limits more stringent than those provided by the NESS test. Yet this is to say no more than that in the social world we accord human conduct greater significance than other causal conditions which, while true, does not go far towards providing a clear and compelling argument. It might be said that according human conduct great significance is unavoidable, since the social world – our world – is thick with reactive attitudes and thus rich in attributive judgments. It seems we cannot help regarding human agency as the principal force at work in the social world nor can we avoid regarding its limits as crucial to judgments of value and character. Again, this is not an argument but rather a statement of how things are. Nor do matters become much clearer if this series of supposedly unavoidable assumptions is linked to the idea of human identity.[66]

Common sense causal principles

The common sense causal principles by which we distinguish causes from causally relevant conditions are not, for Hart and Honoré, the least bit mysterious:

> [c]ommon sense is not a matter of inexplicable or arbitrary assertions, and the causal notions which it employs, though flexible and complex and subtly influenced by context, can be shown to rest, at least in part, on statable principles; though the ordinary man who uses them may not, without assistance, be able to make them explicit. (*CL*, p. 26)

Nor are these principles either uncommon or unusual:

> whenever we are concerned with . . . [tracing connections between human actions and events], whether for the purpose of explaining a puzzling occurrence, assessing responsibility, or giving an intelligible historical narrative, we employ a set of concepts restricting in various ways what counts as a consequence. These restrictions colour *all* out thinking in causal terms; when we find them in the law we are not finding something invented by or peculiar to the law. (*CL*, p. 70)

In the attributive context, where we have some idea of the causal genesis of some particular outcome, our interest is in whether or not it is appropriate to regard that outcome as caused by some agent's conduct. The common sense principles that, for Hart and Honoré, determine the propriety of this judgment vary according to the type of causal connection

[66] See *CL*, pp. lxxx–lxxxi and Honoré, *Responsibility and Fault*, supra, note 7, pp. 29–30.

in question. It is, however, important to note in advance that these principles are primarily concerned with only one issue, namely, identifying the *limits* of causal connection in attributive contexts. What all these principles take for granted, though, is that human conduct is almost always the key factor in the initiation of causal sequences; how could it be otherwise when the context is one of attribution, namely, the tracing of outcomes to agents? It is against a background in which human conduct is assumed to be the most causally salient factor, and in which assumptions about what is normal or usual in the course of both social life and the natural environment are also to the fore, that the common sense casual principles outlined below are deployed. Since there are three principal types of causal connection, each displaying the operation of different common sense casual principles, it is best to consider them separately.

In the case of causing harm, two reasonably complex principles – which we can label 'the principle of voluntary intervention' and 'the coincidence principle' – are at work. Here, common sense dictates that 'a voluntary act, or a conjunction of events amounting to a coincidence, operates as a limit in the sense that events subsequent to these are not attributed to the antecedent actions or event as its consequence' (*CL*, p. 71). This is so even where the consequence would not have occurred without the antecedent. All causally relevant conditions other than voluntary interventions and coincidences are factors through which we are normally happy to trace causal consequences. That this process of tracing is usually brought to an end by coincidences and voluntary conduct explains at least some of the language lawyers and citizens use when characterizing these factors: they are often called 'intervenining causes', regarded as 'stopping' or 'severing' the 'chain' of causation. For lawyers in need of a Latin maxim, they are instances of *novus actus interveniens*; for those without that need, they are simply intervening causes.

The complexity of these two limiting principles arises from the same source. It is that the principles have a number of components, some of which involve judgments of matters of degree rather than simple yes/no decisions. Two illustrations will suffice. The first is that the principle of voluntary intervention rests upon the sometimes difficult idea of voluntariness, which is almost never adequately captured by the simple question 'was the conduct in question done freely?' On a negative conception of freedom, only that conduct which is physically impossible is unfree and this, plainly, will not accommodate the concerns to which the notion of voluntariness often answers. We are, for example, almost always aware that in a case in which there are worries about the voluntariness of some conduct, there is no worry at all about the conduct being free in the negative sense. While the latter issue is almost invariably addressed with a simple yes or no answer, the question of voluntariness is almost invariably a judgment of degree. In virtually all cases in which voluntariness is an issue, the judgment required is, as Hart and Honoré show, a matter of 'more or less', of 'in some respects voluntary, in some respects not'.[67] These various respects must, of course, be accorded significance and that process implicitly involves a ranking of one such respect against others; the process of decision here is therefore not the simple application of some algorithm but a matter of judgment.

Judgments of voluntariness also often turn upon a comparison of the importance of the interests in play in a particular context. So, in a situation in which A's conduct constrains B into acting a certain way, either to harm another or to sacrifice some of his own (B's) interests, the determination of the voluntariness of B's conduct turns in part upon the 'a comparison of the importance of the respective interests sacrificed and preserved' (*CL*, pp. 76–77). If, for example, A sets fire to a house and B either incurs injury leaping from the building to escape, or is injured as a result of entering the burning building to save C, B has made a choice between evils as a result of A's conduct. Where this choice is a reasonable one, then B's injuries can be traced directly to A's conduct. But if B has incurred injury because, for example, he entered the burning building to recover his newspaper or umbrella, our judgment would differ, primarily because B's interest in either newspaper or umbrella is in no way sufficiently important to justify the risk taken and injury incurred. Not all cases, however, are as clear cut and the process of valuation involved, like the factors already noted, adds a degree of complexity to the operation of this common sense causal principle.

So, too, do three of the five criteria employed to distinguish between

[67] *CL*, pp. 74–77. Hart and Honoré could be accused of employing an over-expansive conception of voluntariness that elides a number of distinctions (between it and intentional conduct and between it and free conduct, to name two: for a brief outline of the general issue see my 'Contract as a Mechanism of Distributive Justice' (1989) 9 *Oxford Journal of Legal Studies* 132–147, pp. 136–142; for an admirably clear critique of *CL* on this specific point see A. Brudner, 'Owning Outcomes: On Intervening Causes, Thin Skulls, and Fault-undifferentiated Crimes' (1998) XI *Canadian Journal of Law and Jurisprudence* 89–114, pp. 94–97). The accusation does nothing, however, to undermine the claim that judgments about voluntariness (and/or intentionality and/or free conduct) are frequently complex and a matter of degree.

coincidences and expected or normal events in the coincidence principle.[68] This is our second illustration. One criterion used to determine whether or not an event was a coincidence is whether or not 'it is very unlikely by ordinary standards' (*CL*, p. 78); another holds that the event must be 'for some reason significant and important' (ibid). We need not pore long and hard over these two criteria to recognise that they involve matters of judgment over which it is possible to disagree. Collective judgments of what is and is not important can vary with context and they can often be in a state of flux: judgments of what was important once – taking hats off in Church, for example, or men holding doors open for women – can slowly change, thereby creating space for disagreement. Furthermore, our ordinary judgments of likelihood are almost by definition matters of degree about which we can differ; and, since such judgments are not tied to a single, correct act or conduct description, the space for different judgments is multiplied.[69]

In instances of inducing and occasioning harm the common sense principles used to distinguish causes from causally relevant conditions are and must be different from those in play when an agent causes harm. Were voluntary acts as significant here as in instances of causing harm, there would almost never be a causal link between one who induced another to act in a particular way and the outcome of that other's conduct, for the simple reason that induced conduct is often voluntary. Similarly, if voluntary conduct is a natural stopping point for tracing consequences in cases where my conduct provides an opportunity for another to do harm (I leave my neighbour's door unlocked and her house is robbed),[70] there will almost never be a causal connection between my conduct and the outcome. To insist on the same limitations on consequences here as in the case of causing harm is in fact to obliterate these other instances of causal connection. The voluntary conduct of the second party is usually the key element in the first party's bringing about a particular consequence: this much is plain if I deliberately leave my neighbour's house unlocked in the hope that it is robbed or if I cajole the local thief to steal from it. Here I attempt to bring about a result in the world through the instrument of another agent's voluntary conduct. This possibility speaks to the existence

[68] *CL*, pp. 78–80.

[69] *CL*, p. 80. The issue of act or conduct description is, of course, one we have run up against already: see Chapter 3, pp. 75–78.

[70] The classic variation on this theme is *Stansbie v Troman* [1948] 2 KB 48, yet another illustration of the fact that I. A. Richard's aphorism about history (a series of events that ought not to have happened) is also true of the law reports.

of types of causal connection in the world over and beyond that involved in directly intervening in or manipulating features of the world.

Unlike instances of causing harm, there is only one limiting principle at work when tracing the consequences of providing opportunities for others to do harm, or for harmful events to occur (occasioning harm). It has two slightly different variations that are usefully labelled as 'the principle of normal or expected interventions' and 'the principle of normal or expected events'. The first variation deals with the case of occasioning harm by other agents and, like the principles in play in cases of causing harm, its application is context sensitive. It holds that the initial conduct of the defendant in providing an opportunity for the second party's conduct is a cause of the outcome if the conduct of the second party is normal or predictable in the circumstances. The courts have therefore held that A's failure to lock B's house is indeed a cause of it being robbed by C, since C's conduct is not in the circumstances abnormal. Had C entered the house and murdered the occupants, a court might decide differently, but whether or not it does so will depend on the social environment. If it is particularly dangerous, with a high level of crime, then C's conduct could well be regarded as expected or normal for that environment and not as an intervening cause.[71] If such deeds as C's are unknown, then they are more likely to be regarded as an intervening cause. And, indeed, there are undoubtedly legal principles that will be triggered even if C's intervention – his murdering of the occupants – is not unexpected for that social environment: the fact that B has provided an opportunity for C to do this need not excuse C from liability. So, for example, in the criminal law he can easily be regarded as principal and B as secondary party. Furthermore, this case is one that also brings into sharp relief the weight of that common sense causal principle that regards voluntary conduct as a limit. If C's conduct in murdering the occupants is fully voluntary, we might hold that this is a case in which that principle outweighs the one normally in play in instances of providing opportunities. This confirms Hart and Honoré's conclusion that 'whether any given intervention is a sufficiently common exploitation of the opportunity provided to come within the risk is again a matter on which judgments many differ, though they often agree' (*CL*, p. 81).

The second variation of this principle, the principle of normal or expected events, deals with situations in which A's conduct has provided occasion not for another agent to bring about harm, but rather for some

[71] An horrific US illustration is *Hines v Garrett* (1921) 131 Va 125, 108 SE 690.

harmful event to occur that damages B. The substance of the principle is almost exactly the same as the principle of normal or expected interventions. So, for example, A's throwing a lighted match into bracken is a cause of the burning down of the forest even if the smouldering bracken only fully and completely ignited, and fire subsequently spread to the trees, by virtue of a breeze. The latter is, of course, an entirely normal and predicable event in most contexts and thus not one which 'overrides' or 'exhausts' the causal influence of A's conduct. If, however, soon after A's conduct the forest had been hit by a shower of blazing meteorites, our judgment might well differ, depending on our knowledge of the influence of both alleged causes and the regularity (presumably rare) of the latter event.

The limitations in play in instances of inducing harm, where A provides or highlights reasons B has to act in the way A wishes, are twofold, according to Hart and Honoré. A's conduct is a cause of the consequence provided it was a genuine inducement for B to act and provided that B's conduct is in accord with A's intention or plan. Clearly, '[n]ice questions may arise, which the courts have to settle, where B diverges from the detail of the plan of action put before him by A' (*CL*, p. 83). Applying this common sense causal principle is, then, just as often a matter of judgment as is application of the others.

Finally, a point about all the common sense causal principles used to trace consequences in each type of causal connection. It is that for Hart and Honoré neither these principles nor the process of applying them are *the same as or reducible to* the moral assessment of the agent and conduct in question. So, for example, with regard to causing harm, they show that the coincidence and voluntary intervention principles generate causal judgments independent of the moral quality of either the agent or their conduct. Of a coincidence case in which A batters B who, as a result of the attack, falls and is then crushed to death by a falling tree, they rightly observe that: 'A may be a robber and a murderer and B a saint guarding the place A hoped to plunder. Or B may be a murderer and A a hero who has forced his way into B's retreat. In both cases the causal judgment is the same. A had caused the minor injuries but not B's death' (*CL*, p. 78). The situation is the same with regard to instances of voluntary intervention and with respect to the causal principle deployed in instances of occasioning harm.[72]

[72] On the former, see *CL*, pp. 74–75. As to the latter, Hart and Honoré do not make the point explicitly in their treatment at pp. 81–83 but there is no reason to think that they change their position in this kind of case.

It is also obvious that Hart and Honoré think the process of applying and interpreting common sense causal principles is not *either the same as or reducible to* that involved in making legal decisions on policy grounds. Of course, much depends here on precisely what is meant by 'policy', but one factor is often salient: a policy-based decision in the legal or adjudicative context is one that invokes the explicit or implicit values or purposes of the law. While Hart and Honoré are happy to accept that such considerations do and should play a role in the interpretation and application of many areas of legal doctrine, they deny that such considerations are the same as those involved in common sense causal principles themselves. Common sense causal principles are therefore neither moral judgments of character or conduct nor legal policy decisions; they involve, as Hart and Honoré constantly emphasize, 'questions of fact' (*CL*, p. 91). Remember that it is just this claim that causal minimalists deny, albeit in slightly different ways. Moderate causal minimalists hold that there is a factual core to our causal judgments but that core, contrary to the view of Hart and Honoré, consists only of either the but-for or NESS or related tests. All other supposed 'causal' principles are actually really matters of moral assessment or legal policy. Extreme causal minimalists extend this latter claim to include every single component of our attributive causal judgments: for them the but-for test, for example, is as much a matter of legal policy or moral judgment as the voluntary intervention principle. The general issue here concerns the basis of our causal judgments; it now requires attention.

THE BASIS OF CAUSAL JUDGMENTS

For Hart and Honoré, causal judgments made in the law, and their underpinning principles, are the same as those we make in everyday life. Their basis is ordinary language and common sense, the link between the two being that what we ordinarily say is a strong indicator of what we ordinarily take to be sensible. This is not to say that the two cannot diverge from one another: we are only too aware of situations in which our thinking is bewitched by language or in the thrall of dubious everyday patterns of thought. Nor is it to hold that either ordinary usage or common sense is univocal and unequivocal: 'the language of ordinary people and of lawyers both reveal[s] and obscure[s] the truth about causal concepts' (*CL*, p. xxxiii). The task is therefore to illuminate usage that tracks common sense about causal concepts and to eschew that which leads to confusion. Because our language usually manifests the common sense principles used in the employment of causal concepts, it seems natural to follow Hart and Honoré in regarding these principles as being a matter of fact. It is the case that these are the principles we use in making causal judgments in law and everyday life. Since for Hart and Honoré the principles underpinning ordinary causal judgments in life and law do not in any obvious way invoke the kinds of consideration regarded by causal minimalists as the fulcrum of policy-based decisions, it again seems natural to label them as factual. Furthermore, because common sense causal principles also generate conclusions independent of those yielded by the moral assessment of agents and their conduct and characters, it again seems sensible to regard them as factual.

However, the claim that the common sense principles underpinning causal judgments, and those judgments themselves, are factual has proved unpalatable to many. Over the last two decades two jurists in particular – Wright, whose work has been heavily relied upon here, and Jane Stapleton – have refined and criticized many features of *CL*.[73] While there is much in the book that Wright and Stapleton admire, both agree that the factual status of common sense causal principles is an issue upon which Hart and Honoré err. In what follows, Wright's somewhat laconic statement of his doubts on this issue are briefly sketched and followed by a more detailed outline of Stapleton's reservations, which she delineates fairly extensively. The crucial point is that Stapleton and Wright have the same worry about Hart and Honoré's claim that common sense causal principles, and the judgments they warrant, are factual (hereinafter 'the factual claim'). It is argued that this worry is a mistake: it rests upon an impoverished notion of the variety of facts that populate the social world. Once we appreciate both that social facts play an important role in human life, and the properties this kind of fact has, we can see that the features of common sense causal judgments that lead Stapleton and Wright to doubt their factual status actually confirm that status. The argument, briefly put, is that common sense causal principles are social facts.

Two preliminary points

Before sketching Stapleton's and Wright's reservations about the factual claim, two matters must be clarified. First, the term 'policy' requires attention. On its own and in conjunctions like 'policy factors' and 'policy

[73] Wright, *Causation* and *Bramble Bush*, supra, note 44. Stapleton, supra, note 35 and her 'Perspectives on Causation' in J. Horder (ed.), *Oxford Essays on Jurisprudence* 4th Series (Oxford: Clarendon Press, 2000); 'Legal Cause: Cause-in-Fact and the Scope of Liability for Consequences' (2001) 54 *Vanderbilt LR* 941–1009; and 'Cause-in-Fact and the Scope of Liability for Consequences' (2003) 119 *Law QR* 388–425.

decisions' it is a shibboleth for causal minimalists but can be used to refer to at least two distinct sets of considerations. The first type of consideration can be lumped under the rubric of 'matters of institutional design/ the values and purposes of the law'. In this sense, to say that a judge has decided some case on the basis of policy is to say a number of distinct things. It might be to say, for example, that in her application of the law to the case at hand she took account of the goal or goals of the area of doctrine in question, or perhaps even some goal of the law at large. The goal of some particular legal doctrine – negligence law, for example – might be said to be something like accident reduction; taking this as given, a judge responsive to policy considerations will interpret and apply particular doctrines in particular cases so as to track or at least not undermine this goal. Other related policy considerations that could weigh heavily with judges are those that concern the efficient internal and external operation of the legal system. Judges responsive to such concerns are likely, for example, to take 'floodgates arguments' very seriously, since the courts being deluged with claims as a result of a particular interpretation of some legal doctrine will severely hamper the operation of the legal system. In addition to considerations such as this, which are internal to the operation of the legal system itself, judges responsive to policy considerations could be keen to ensure that their decisions do not have bad consequences in the world beyond the legal system. Any decision that seriously disrupts some aspect of social life would be, for such judges, *prima facie* undesirable.

While this category of policy considerations covers some diverse concerns, they are united by the fact that all of them involve the effective operation of the legal system or some aspect of it, its effectiveness being judged both internally and externally.[74] If we keep this in mind, then the use of the term policy to refer to this type of consideration need not be in any way misleading or otherwise troublesome. Unfortunately, this cannot be said of another use of the term. For some, particularly in discussions of causation in law, seem inclined to use the term to refer to the moral or evaluative appraisal of conduct, character, or both and the considerations

[74] By policy arguments, then, I have in mind both the consequentialist and some of the 'internal' considerations invoked by judges and superbly illuminated in N. MacCormick, *Legal Reasoning and Legal Theory* (Oxford: Clarendon Press, revised edn, 1993), chs. VI–VIII. Also helpful on the general issue is: J. Bell, *Policy Arguments in Judicial Decisions* (Oxford: Clarendon Press, 1983).

implicit therein.[75] To single out such considerations with the special label 'policy' is to run the risk of misrepresenting an entirely normal and indeed unavoidable feature of most developed legal systems for a remarkable or exceptional feature demanding particular attention. That feature is that the law judges us: it holds us to the standards it lays down and thus, unavoidably, evaluates our conduct and, possibly, our character.[76] This process of evaluation need not be moral, however, for the simple reason that the standards by which the law judges our conduct or our characters may not themselves be moral. But it is certainly a process of evaluation, of judgment by reference to the values of the law. Moreover, another mistake is often made when the term policy is used in this sense. Since in the causal context those who claim that causal judgments are policy judgments are most often actually claiming that such judgments are, despite appearances and the language of the judges, *moral appraisals of the conduct and character of claimant, defendant or both*, they risk obscuring the nature of their own claim. Why use the term policy to refer to a set of considerations that can be perfectly clearly and helpfully subsumed under the rubric of 'moral appraisal'? For the sake of clarity, this use of policy should be eschewed. Thus, when Hart and Honoré deny that causal judgments are policy-based decisions, they should be regarded as invoking the first sense of the term.

The second issue to be clarified before turning to the factual status of common sense causal principles concerns a lacuna. It consists of Stapleton's and Wright's *prima facie* puzzling failure to confront, directly or indirectly, the examples Hart and Honoré use to show that common sense causal judgments are neither the same as, nor reducible to, either moral judgments or policy judgments. One example, remember, holds that neither the moral status of the firebug's act of burning down the forest, nor the moral status of his character insofar as it is illuminated by such conduct, determines the judgment we make about whether or not his conduct was a cause of the blaze. Rather, as Hart and Honoré rightly affirm, insofar as the moral status of the firebug's conduct and character are judged by the outcome, that judgment presupposes some independent causal assessment attaching outcome to conduct and/or character.[77] A

[75] Both Green and Malone, supra, note 33, could be accused of this and not only because their conception of policy considerations is so inclusive as to incorporate almost any consideration judges might regard as relevant in arriving at a decision.

[76] See my 'The Possibility of Impartiality' (2005) 25 *Oxford Journal of Legal Studies* 3–31, pp. 18–19 for a ham-fisted effort to unpack this idea.

[77] *CL*, p. 74.

related example makes the point more vividly: A knocks B to the ground and, while lying there injured, B is subsequently killed by a falling tree. Our judgment, that A caused minor injuries to B but not his death, stands whether or not A was a moral imbecile and B a saint or B a murderer and A a hero.[78] Nor do Hart and Honoré accept that causal judgments such as this owe anything to a set of legal policy considerations; to think so is a 'blinding error'.[79] Rather than directly undermine these examples and thus provide a basis upon which to reject the factual claim, Stapleton and Wright cast doubt upon the factual claim from another, slightly more oblique direction. They invoke a conception of fact incompatible with the factual claim.

Some worries about the factual claim

Wright's worry about the factual claim is unambiguous. While he accepts that the causal inquiry conducted under the NESS test is undoubtedly factual, he holds that it is 'clear that the [. .] criteria [in common sense causal judgments] are neither policy neutral nor causal'.[80] But, given the care and rigour that characterizes Wright's general treatment of causation, his argument to this end is disappointingly weak. Its first step is to posit a division between three questions relevant to liability in tort law, one of which is the genuinely factual causal question embodied in the NESS test, the other two being the 'tortious liability' and 'proximate cause' questions.[81] The latter two questions are, according to Wright, both policy-laded and evaluative.[82] The second step is an attempt to show that Hart and Honoré's account of common sense causal principles ensures that the issues raised during their articulation and application are of the same kind as those that arise in the latter two questions. From this Wright infers that common sense causal principles and the judgments they warrant cannot be factual. At least two difficulties arise here.

The first is simple. Wright's argument to show that the issues raised in the articulation and application of common sense causal principles, and

[78] *CL*, p. 78. Honoré, *Responsibility and Fault*, supra, note 7, at pp. 106, 109 and 120 is keen to emphasize that causal judgments are not 'normative'. As will be seen below, in one sense this is a mistake. Common sense casual principles (just like the rules of grammar and etiquette) can indeed be normative without being matters of moral appraisal or policy judgments.

[79] *CL*, p. 3 (*inter multos alia*).

[80] *Causation*, supra, note 44, p. 1746. See also p. 1741 (on the factual status of NESS). A reprise of Wright's worries on this point is provided in *Bramble Bush*, supra, note 44, pp. 1011–1014 (in particular see note 69 on p. 1014).

[81] *Causation*, supra, note 44, p. 1745. [82] Ibid, p. 1746.

those relevant when answering the tortious liability and proximate cause questions, are identical is weak. Indeed, at one crucial point it rests upon nothing more than an asserted similarity or identity. The asserted similarity holds that many of the issues that arise in the application of common sense causal principles 'simply describe[. .] one of the principal recognized types of tortious conduct'.[83] 'Therefore', common sense causal principles raise the same issues as the tortious liability question. But is it clearly one thing to show that some issues in play when we ask question Q are similar to those in play when we ask question Q1 and another to show that question Q and question Q1 are identical. For Wright, similarity in reference leads, without further argument, to identity in substance and this is surely an exaggeration.[84] Second, in asserting this identity Wright simply assumes that questions of fact cannot also be matters of judgment, of more or less, and thus sometimes generate different answers and an accompanying degree of controversy. So, for example, he notes that the application of the limiting principle of voluntary intervention in cases of causing harm 'calls for policy judgments on matters of degree and reasonableness'.[85] Yet he does not actually show that the application of this principle is identical to the making of a number of policy based decisions. Rather he simply assumes that this must be so because the principle and its application is indeed often a matter of judgment, turning on assessments of degree, of more or less. It therefore seems that, for Wright, questions of fact and the answers to them must be as non-controversial and as rigidly determinate as the questions and answers of low-level natural science (what is the distance of the Earth from the Sun?) or arithmetic (what does 2 + 2 equal?). As we will see, Stapleton also shares this view of the nature of facts and factual questions; we will also see, in the course of unpacking and evaluating her concerns about the factual claim, why it is mistaken.

Stapleton's worry about the factual claim arises from a range of related concerns. First, she thinks that 'genuine questions of fact . . . [have] a single correct answer'.[86] This being so, she is troubled because the application of common sense causal principles is frequently a matter of

[83] Ibid, p. 1747.

[84] Wright also asserts that, as a result of eliding the difference between factual questions of causation and questions of liability-responsibility, Hart and Honoré cannot accommodate strict liability: *Bramble Bush*, supra, note 44, 1014. See Honoré, *Responsibility and Fault*, supra, note 7, pp. 102–103 for the reply.

[85] Wright, ibid, p. 1747.

[86] Stapleton, *Perspectives*, supra, note 73, p. 61. See also p. 73. Her *Unpacking Causation*, supra, note 35, p. 151–153 contains some additional thoughts about the factual claim.

judgment and such judgments can differ. Since the application of these principles can be controversial, it seems that causal questions falling to be answered by reference to them cannot have a single correct answer. If all facts and all factual questions are factual in the same sense as what some philosophers have called 'brute facts' – for example, the brute fact that the Earth is 93 million miles from the Sun – then this concern about the factual claim appears perfectly legitimate.[87] This appearance, however, becomes slightly dubious when it is noted that there was undoubtedly a time at which the answer to the question about the Earth's distance from the Sun, not to mention that of the Earth's proper relation with the Sun, was just as controversial as the answer to the question 'is there a ninth planet?' The fact of controversy about some issue may not therefore be an infallible guide to the existence of a non-factual question. Moreover, to invoke, as Stapleton does, the fact that there is controversy in forensic disputes about causal questions as evidence that there cannot be a correct, 'factual' answer to those questions is surely a mistake.[88] The fact of controversy about almost any issue in forensic disputes is perfectly compatible with there being a single correct, factual right answer. This is because it is undeniably true, by virtue of the stakes in play, that disputants to legal action have a powerful incentive to be wilful and self-interested, to cast doubt on what might otherwise be regarded as perfectly obvious and undeniable for strategic reasons. Of course, litigants are to some extent constrained in their pursuit of self-interest in the trail by the professional ethics of their legal representatives but, in a world in which even judges fear law suits more than death and taxes,[89] it is unsurprising that litigants and their legal representatives often deny the undeniable.

A second concern motivating Stapleton's doubt about the factual claim is this: the application of common sense causal principles is, for her, often a matter of 'guesswork' and dependent upon subjective matters like our experience and context.[90] This, of course, is undeniably so: Hart and Honoré make just this point, albeit in the language of what is normal and abnormal, what expectable and what unusual, in both the ordinary course of human affairs and the natural world. Where Stapleton sees guesswork,

[87] John Searle – certainly not the first philosopher to offer an account of such facts – has put the idea to informative use in *The Construction of Social Reality* (London: Penguin Press, 1995), chs 1 and 2. The example in the text is his.

[88] *Unpacking Causation*, supra, note 35, pp. 150–151.

[89] Or, more accurately, one American judge did: Learned Hand, according to R. Dworkin, *Law's Empire* (Oxford: Hart Publishing, 1998), p. 1.

[90] On guesswork, see *Perspectives*, supra, note 73, pp. 68 and 70; on subjectivity and experience, see p. 68.

others could well see 'judgment', when what is meant is something like the making of reasonably plausible and well-founded decisions in a context of incomplete information and limited time. Many, many of our ordinary decisions and thus much of our day to day practical reasoning is of this kind: I, for example, have not yet done or commissioned a full risk analysis of all the methods of transport available to me when I journey to work. On my very limited experience, it seems that the train and bus are every bit as safe as the car and I choose the former because they save time. My view of the relative safety of each mode of transport can certainly be regarded as a matter of guesswork. However, Stapleton's assumption here is surely closely related to that underlying her first concern: that matters of fact cannot be in some sense 'speculative' or incomplete ('therefore' they cannot be controversial). It seems that for Stapleton our answers to factual questions must be generated by something like an algorithm: the information used at the outset must be complete and utterly uncontroversial and an undeniable answer yielded. On this view, factual questions and their answers cannot involve matters of degree, cannot be controversial and cannot be a matter of judgment.

Nor can such questions and their answers be normative. Stapleton thinks that the application of common sense causal principles is not a process of describing facts but rather a matter of normatively evaluating facts.[91] She is therefore lead to doubt the factual claim on the basis of an unstated but undoubtedly common assumption that facts cannot be either norms or normative. And it is certain that some facts are neither normative nor norms: the fact that the Earth is 93 millions miles from the Sun seems a plausible candidate for such status. But some care must be taken with terminology here. We must, for example, strive to avoid the common slip from the claim 'C (whatever it is) is normative' to 'C is moral': standards of good scholarship and writing are, for example, surely normative but it is hard to maintain that they are, even in a peripheral sense, 'therefore' moral principles. This slippage could well explain Honoré's sometimes over strident denials that common sense causal principles and the judgments they warrant are normative.[92] Since one of his and Hart's principal aims in *CL* was to show these principles and judgments are neither the same as, nor reducible to, the moral appraisal of agents and their conduct, it might seem that a great deal was at stake in the claim that such principles and judgments are normative. If it is

[91] *Unpacking Causation*, supra, note 35, p. 153.
[92] See the references to *Responsibility and Fault* in note 78, supra.

assumed that something's being normative entails that it is also moral, then accepting that common sense causal principles are normative imperils a key tenet of *CL*. The argument offered below, that common sense causal principles are social facts, holds that many social facts are normative and that the possibility that common sense causal principles are normative should not be regarded as worrisome.

The fourth ground upon which Stapleton is lead to doubt the factual claim is a worry about what can be dubbed 'perspectivity'. In applying common sense causal principles to distinguish causally relevant conditions from causes, we are concerned to determine what factor was most causally salient in bringing about a particular outcome. Moreover, common sense causal principles tell us that, against a background of normal events and expected human conduct, the most salient causal factor is usually human conduct. Stapleton does not deny this. Rather, she holds that different instances of human conduct can become causally salient in relation to one and the same outcome depending upon the perspective we take up. Of the example of a beater being shot by a hunter, she says that an economist would give a different answer to the question of whose conduct was causally salient to this outcome than would either a lawyer or ordinary person.[93] While the latter would look to the shooter in the first instance, the economist supposedly concludes that, since everything is the cause of everything else, the presence of victims of shootings is as much a cause of shootings as is shooters shooting them.[94] This difference is apparently explicable by reference to the economist's allocative perspective, rather than his deployment of a trite and unhelpful conception of causation.

While it may or may not be true that the economist's perspective determines his causal judgments, the matter is irrelevant to the question of the status of common sense causal principles in law and life. If it is the case that no one in these latter contexts would accept the economist's causal judgment, then the fact that this perspective is open to us and warrants causal judgments different to those arrived at in law and in life is of little significance. Similarly, the fact that it can be said, on what is

[93] *Perspectives*, supra, note 73, pp. 64–66.

[94] This view is often attributed to the economist Ronald Coase, but the attribution is shaky: see, of the many to have noticed this, M. Moore, 'Causation and Responsibility' (1999) 16 *Social Philosophy and Policy* 1–51, pp. 3–4 and N. E. Simmonds, 'Justice, Causation and Private Law', supra, note 27, pp. 166–167. The claim lawyer-economists often make, that Coase somehow invented a new or different conception of causation in the course of an essay that hardly even addresses that issue, is plain silly.

alleged to be the economist's conception of cause, that Lee Harvey Oswald's great grandmother's decision to have children was the most causally salient factor in the assassination of President John F. Kennedy, is of little significance if no one in life or law would take that judgment seriously.[95] In an effort to put the issue of perspectivity squarely on to the lawyer's agenda, Stapleton suggests that different conceptions of individual responsibility are in play in the law and that these can yield different causal judgments. But there are a number of problems here. One is that Stapleton at no point unpacks these allegedly different conceptions of individual responsibility: we need to see them in detail and it must be shown: (i) that they are actually incompatible and (ii) that they do indeed determine our causal judgments. Moreover, on the latter point we must be careful to avoid a mistake that has already been noted: the fact that litigants in forensic disputes make incompatible causal judgments (or judgments about any other matter) says little about whether such claims are correct: litigants often have strong, self-interested reasons to deny the obvious. Nor is the fact that moral-evaluative and causal judgments keep close company particularly significant here: Hart and Honoré often emphasize just this point.[96] And making this point is perfectly compatible with the affirmation that causal judgments are neither the same as nor reducible to the moral appraisal of conduct or character.

Having elucidated some of the particular concerns that inform both Wright's and Stapleton's difficulty with the factual claim, it is now time to turn to the general issue. For the particular reservations Wright and Stapleton have about the factual claim share something in common. It is this: they rest on an impoverished conception of what facts can be. That conception is the brute fact conception, the view that all facts have the properties had by the fact that the Earth is 93 million miles from the Sun. However, as we will see, our conceptual schemes – the ways in which we divide up, think about and organize the natural and social worlds – have room for another conception of fact. This is the social fact conception.[97] It is a social fact that there is now a rule of etiquette which holds it is

[95] The example is Stapleton's: *Perspectives*, supra, note 73, p. 72. See also p. 74.

[96] See *CL*, pp. xlii–lv and Honoré, ch. 7 of A. Tunc (ed.), supra, note 38, pp. 3–7.

[97] Which is only remotely related to the classic treatment of social facts in E. Durkheim, *The Rules of Sociological Method* (New York: The Free Press, 1964), ch. I. As will be obvious, the account of social facts and social rules that follows owes a great deal to Searle, supra, note 86, chs. 1–6 and to H. L. A. Hart, *The Concept of Law* (Oxford: Clarendon Press, 2nd edn, 1994), chs. 2–5. The most comprehensive recent discussion of social facts, with which the argument in the text is not always consistent, is M. Gilbert, *On Social Facts* (Princeton, New Jersey: Princeton University Press, 1992).

wrong for me to eat meat with my hands at the dinner table.[98] This social fact has some properties quite different from the brute fact that the Earth is 93 million miles from the Sun.

Brute facts and social facts

In what ways do brute facts and social facts differ? One principal difference between social facts and brute facts is that the latter are not dependent for their existence upon human beliefs, whereas social facts are in part dependent upon such beliefs. The distance of Earth from Sun is and remains 93 million miles regardless of the beliefs of human beings, just as it was the case that the Earth orbited the Sun even when most of humankind believed just the opposite. By contrast, social facts are in part constituted by human beliefs, which is to say that for some social facts to exist there must be a belief about those facts shared by all (or almost all) in a social group. For example, if the printed note in my wallet is to represent value and be capable of exchange for goods and services, the concept 'money' must exist in our community and, at the very least, community members must believe, and believe that most or all other members believe, that this concept exists.[99] In addition to these beliefs, it seems equally obvious that for the community to have this concept members must have some understanding of the concept and the way it works. For a significant social fact must often be more than just a matter of belief: it must be a matter of use and use normally implies some degree of understanding. Without this range of beliefs and this kind of understanding, it would be difficult to see what could be meant by either my saying 'we have money in our community' or by an external observer claiming 'they have money in society S'.

But even more than shared inter-subjective beliefs and understandings are required before we can say that some social facts exist in a truly 'deep' sense. For this to be so, there must be some institutional manifestation of such beliefs in specific social structures and in some practices or convergences of behaviour. If the social fact of money is to be well embedded in a community it seems clear that some effort at printing and controlling

[98] It was not always so: see N. Elias, *The Civilising Process: Vol. 1, The History of Manners* (New York: Pantheon Books, 1978), p. 70.

[99] The requirement that agents believe that other agents believe and so on raises the awkward issue that philosophers call 'collective intentionality'. There are at least two different understandings of collective intentionality in the literature and the statement the text might seem, although it is intended to be neutral, to embrace only one. For a brief and clear account of the options see J. Searle, supra, note 87, pp. 25–26.

its supply, as well its generalized use, must occur; this is not to say, however, that money must have been explicitly 'invented'. Moreover, it is only when some social facts are securely embedded in the social fabric of a community that they can be said to be more fundamental than others, enabling a range of behaviours or practices previously impossible. The existence of banks lending money subject to the charging of interest, not to mention investment houses and other financial institutions doing complicated things like interest rate swaps, are only possible in a community that has a stable concept of money, with all the beliefs and practices that that implies.

If social facts are in part constituted by beliefs, and are also often embedded in institutional structures and social practices, then one possibility should come as no surprise. It is that when beliefs about some social facts change, and when institutional practices and structures that embody some social facts also change, then the social facts in question change. This is not to say either that a necessary connection exists between these variables or that the process of change, and links involved, are obvious or well understood. All that is needed for present purposes is the not implausible assumption that there is some linking (although it need not be a universal) mechanism such that change in beliefs about, or institutions or practices embodying, social facts can lead to change in social facts. Furthermore, it does not seem implausible to hold that those social facts that take institutional form – the law, perhaps, or some segment thereof – can change as a result of consideration of the institution's purpose(s) or function(s). This kind of social reflective monitoring, while not unproblematic, is certainly a common feature of complex, non-traditional societies.

Social facts far less deeply embedded in institutions, or possibly not institutionally embedded at all, but which nevertheless determine specific patterns of behaviour such as, for example, the once common rule of etiquette such that men ought to hold doors open for women, are also subject to this kind of reflective evaluation. Indeed, it is often as a result of this kind of evaluation that such rules can either change or be abandoned. The status of this particular rule of etiquette is now in doubt because of worries about its possibly objectionable or undesirable implications: does it not, for example, embody an indefensible attitude of patriarchal condescension toward women? That social facts can be subject to criticism and evaluation in this way suggests that they are to some extent malleable and subject to change. By contrast, the only way in which brute facts like the distance between earth and sun will change is if the system used to discover or measure them is changed or improved. While some such changes are perfectly conceivable, others seem inconceivable simply because the system that yields them is so deeply and fruitfully embedded in the way we see the (usually natural) world.

Bearing in mind these features of social facts, the vital question can now be posed: is it plausible to think of common sense causal judgments as social facts? There seems little critical mileage in denying that such judgments are either dependent upon beliefs shared by many members of many communities or that they are not 'deeply' social because not embedded in institutional and behavioural practices, as well as certain habits of thought. Pointing to the law courts and the law books is enough to undermine any such denial. But still the worry about the factual claim might persist, particularly because jurists like Wright and Stapleton are deeply troubled by the indeterminate and controversial aspects of common sense causal judgments. This worry, should, however, be set aside for two reasons. First, for reasons already outlined, it is not the least bit surprising for some social facts to give rise to different judgments and thus create some degree of controversy. This will almost certainly be so when social facts or their institutional and behavioural manifestations are subject to reflective evaluation. Second, some social facts are social rules and some such rules unavoidably draw upon concepts whose understanding and application calls for judgment, and those judgments are often a matter of degree. This requires some elucidation.

Are some social facts social rules? Undeniably so, and in a number of ways. Social facts are social rules if it is possible, as it surely is, that some social facts take institutional form and that those forms have a number of features. First, they can be either constitutive or facilitative or both. That is, allow something to be done that was previously impossible (the rules of chess, for example, made chess possible) and broadly define how it must be done. Or they can allow something to be done if agents have reason to do it: consider, for example, the legal rules that lay down the necessary steps for the creation of legally valid wills. This facilitative legal rule is not necessarily a constitutive rule because it may be quite possible to pass property on death without legal mandate; the rule is, however, a constitutive *legal* rule, since only it makes possible the legally binding transfer of property on death. Second, some social facts may be neither constitutive nor facilitative. The regulatory rules of morality and the criminal law, for example, do not make something possible that was previously impossible nor do they in any clear sense allow the performance of some deed if agents wish it. Rather, they aim to discourage and prevent certain kinds of conduct yet they seem just as securely factual as undeniable social facts like the facts that we have both money and a legal system in our society. Indeed, from some perspectives, the regulatory rules of morality and the criminal law can seem far more brutally 'factual' than the distance of Earth from Sun.

Having asserted that there are social rules, it is necessary to give an account of what they look like. In one sense, this cannot be done except by pointing to examples, since there is a vast array of social rules: we have so far mentioned rules of law, etiquette and chess but almost any social institution or practice is constituted by or has a body of more or less explicit rules. Yet there is another sense in which an account of social rules can be given, for it must be possible to lay down some features of such aspects of the social landscape that distinguish them from other aspects. One such feature is that social rules must to some extent be shared in a group or community; this, after all, is what distinguishes such rules from personal rules or precepts, like my 'rule' to walk three miles every weekday. Furthermore, a social rule must also be shared in the sense that it is observed by many in the community: it is difficult to say community C truly has social rule R only if they profess R without ever acting upon it. Social rules can also be distinguished from merely convergent or habitual behaviour on the grounds that social rules are regarded as laying down a standard for oneself and others to follow and give rise to what those who accept them regard as justified criticism of rule-breakers.[100] By contrast, habitual behaviour does not set a standard for oneself and others to follow, nor does a change in or rejection of a particular habit merit criticism. The fact that I drink several gimlets at my local cocktail bar every afternoon for a year does not mean that you (or anyone else) should do likewise; nor does it provide a basis for criticizing me if I subsequently give up hard liquor and take up yoga instead.

The fact that social rules have a dimension of 'oughtness', embodying standards that should be adhered to, can be captured reasonably well by saying that they are normative, provided we are clear what this means. If social rules are normative it means they embody standards that are taken as binding on some or other group of agents, although saying that those standards are binding does not, of course, guarantee that all the agents bound can or will adhere to them. There can, agents being what they are,

[100] This, of course, is drawn directly from H. L. A. Hart's account of the internal aspect of rules: supra, note 97, pp. 51–58. A helpful guide on this issue is N. MacCormick, *H. L. A. Hart* (London: Edward Arnold, 1981), ch. 3.

be failures and transgressions that give rise to criticism or correction. That is what it means to say social rules are normative; and saying this is clearly not to say that all social rules are moral rules. Those who make grammatical mistakes when speaking a language, or those who make errors of etiquette, clearly break normative rules. Yet very few, if any, breaches of the rules of grammar or etiquette are also moral mistakes.

What advantages or insights, however minimal, are yielded by the plausible claim that some social facts are social rules? Perhaps the most important is this. Once we open our mind to the existence of social rules we cannot fail to be impressed by their variety and complexity as well as their sometimes open-ended nature and, of course, by the fact that their application and interpretation is often a matter of judgment. Examples of the latter abound. Consider law 11 of the FIFA laws of the game for association football (the offside rule).[101] In applying this rule to determine whether or not to penalize a player in a *prima facie* offside position, a referee or assistant referee must decide, among other things, whether or not that player is interfering with play or gaining an advantage from being in that position. It seems obvious that applying this rule in the context of a game is certainly not like consulting an algorithm table; it is surely a matter of judgment, of more or less, and it is quite conceivable for different referees to make different decisions in one and the same case. Alternatively, we could say, using Stapleton's terms, that the application of this rule in the context of a game is often a matter of guesswork, determined by the referee's experience. The vital point for current purposes is that it is unlikely that this social rule is unique in depending in its application upon the judgment of those it binds. One need only think of the rules of etiquette and of other games, not to mention rules of law, to come up with myriad instances. Why does this matter?

It is important if common sense causal principles are best regarded as being among that subset of social facts we call social rules. As a distinct set of social rules, the function of common sense causal principles is obvious: they are, *inter alia*, the means by which we attribute outcomes in the world to human conduct and thus, in sense, determine the contours of individual identity.[102] But, *qua* social rules, common sense causal principles must also display some or most of the general features of social rules. It turns out to be these very features, which are explicitly displayed by common sense causal principles in both formulation and application,

[101] The laws are available online at *www.thefa.com* or www.fifa.com.

[102] See Honoré, *Responsibility and Fault*, supra, note 7 at pp. 29–30.

that Wright and Stapleton find most troublesome. Yet what Wright and Stapleton regard as problematic features of such principles instead illustrate their nature. If common sense causal principles are social facts and social rules, then we should expect their interpretation and application to be a matter of judgment, of more or less and, thus, to be in some instances controversial. And it is just this, of course, that Hart and Honoré often point out. If there is only one clear and unambiguous message in *CL* it is that the use of common sense causal principles is often a matter of judgment. The argument just offered is an effort to show that this message in no way imperils the factual status of those common sense causal principles.

A final point. We noted Honoré's denial of the claim that common sense causal principles are normative and suggested, possibly uncharitably, that this denial is actually a misdirected effort at rejecting the claim that these principles are reducible to, or are the same as, the moral appraisal of character, conduct or both.[103] The argument just offered – that common sense causal principles are social facts and such facts, especially when social rules, are normative – illustrates why this interpretation of Honoré's denial is particularly significant. Furthermore, common sense causal principles, while normative in the general sense that all or most social rules lay down standards, are also normative in a more specific sense. They are normative in the same way that rules of grammar are normative: they lay down guidance as to what we would and should say in certain circumstances, or when faced with certain situations. Honoré should not worry about normativity, if his true concern is to defend the claim that causal judgments are not moral appraisals, since it is simply a mistake to think that saying 'Y is normative' is always and also to say that 'Y is moral'.[104] In fact this connection only rarely holds, unless we have an incredibly expansive conception of the range of the 'moral'. Of course, it might be that there is a slippery slope from the claim that social rules are normative to the claim that they are moral, but this seems *prima facie* unlikely. Such a slope would have to take us, in a plausible and compelling

[103] That the interpretation is not so uncharitable as to be ruled out is evidenced by the fact that Honoré slips between denying causal principles are normative and denying that they are moral on other occasions: see 'Appreciations and Reponses', supra, note 35, p. 235.

[104] He articulates another worry *en passant*: 'there is something odd about calling an inescapable feature of human society "normative" ' (Appreciations and Responses, ibid). If you hold that the normative fabric of the social world is both extensive and runs deep, it is not odd but quite natural to say this. Only if the normative fabric of the social world is in some sense an 'optional' feature, and can thus be eliminated or suspended, would this claim appear odd.

manner, from the unobjectionable claim that, for example, 'the FIFA laws of association football are normative' to the very surprising claim that 'the FIFA laws of association football are moral rules or principles'. While some normative social rules are certainly moral, it seems unlikely that all are.

SOME REMAINING ISSUES

The analysis of causation offered so far has yielded three conclusions: that causal connection in law and ordinary life is best understood in terms of the NESS test and common sense principles;[105] that both the latter and the former are plausibly regarded as factual; and that, therefore, the analysis offered by Hart and Honoré in *CL* is generally correct. In the course of arriving at these conclusions, two general manoeuvres were made. One was that Wright's defence of NESS was incorporated into our analysis as if it were part of Hart and Honoré's original, on the grounds that it is both compelling and broadly compatible. This is a rare instance of the work of a commentator being the equal of the original. Another was the defence of the factual claim as against Wright and Stapleton who, on this issue at least, are undoubtedly critics of *CL*. The argument developed above was intended to show that causal principles and the judgments they license are factual in a complex and interesting way, but they are not unique in this. Two issues remain to be addressed, albeit briefly. The first concerns one possible line of attack on the account of causation offered in *CL*,[106] while the second raises a normative argument supporting that account which few critics ever seriously address. The argument is powerful and should not be ignored.

The as yet unmentioned line of attack on *CL* can be labelled 'the argument from shallowness'. There are two quite different versions of this argument but they nevertheless share a general claim: that the account of causation offered by Hart and Honoré is built upon weak and

[105] For the extent to which the English courts currently agree with this judgment, see the House of Lords decisions in *Fairchild v Glenhaven Funeral Services Ltd* [2002] UKHL 22 and *Chester v Affshar* [2004] UKHL 41 (both available from www.parliament.the-stationery-office.co.uk).

[106] It might be thought that another fertile line of attack concerns Hart and Honoré's inability to deal with certain counter-examples. That this is actually something of a dead-end is borne out by Wright's defence of NESS in *Causation, Bramble Bush* and *Bramble Bush 2*, supra, note 44 and by Honoré's belated change of mind about the proper analysis of 'the desert traveller case': see *CL*, pp. 239–241 and compare *Responsibility and Fault*, supra, note 7, pp. 111–112. For Stapleton's take on this example, see *Unpacking Causation*, supra, note 35, pp. 178–181.

unreliable foundations. One version holds that the empirical basis of *CL* is so shallow as to provide no or little support to the causal judgments arrived at by Hart and Honoré. In contrast, the other version holds that Hart and Honoré's arguments in *CL* are shaky because they lack metaphysical depth. Both versions of the argument hold, albeit for quite different reasons, that common sense and ordinary language are an insecure basis for an account of causation. However, as we will see, neither version of the argument is particularly powerful.

The empirical version of the argument from shallowness is not particularly common but did feature in David Howarth's review of the second edition of *CL* and has since been taken up by Stapleton.[107] The argument holds that Hart and Honoré's assessments of what common sense and ordinary language tell us about causation are not properly empirically supported. The evidence, it is said, is weak or speculative: Hart and Honoré tell us what common sense holds without ever conducting the kind of empirical research – going out asking citizens what they think and usually say – presumed necessary to support such claims.[108] The difficulty with this criticism is obvious. Its import is to confer legitimacy on statements about common sense and ordinary language use by insisting that those statements only be made and arrived at by one employing standard methods of empirical social science. Yet why think this? Why, in other words, assume that only empirical sociologists can provide insight into common sense and language use? And why assume that actual users of the language cannot have such insight and cannot recognize common sense? Indeed, it would seem that any competent user of the language is well equipped to make judgments about ordinary use and common sense. If Hart and Honoré qualify as such, then their views are surely worthy of consideration.

Of course the point of this version of the argument from shallowness might be intended to run deeper: what is actually being contested is not the intellectual legitimacy of Hart and Honoré's claims, but the general thrust of those claims. And the general thrust of most of the specific claims about common sense and ordinary use in *CL* is this: there is a good deal of stability and a fair degree of agreement in common sense causal judgments. But without 'proper' empirical findings with which to attack this claim, critics are left with the only manoeuvre open to Hart and

[107] D. Howarth, Book Review (1987) 96 *Yale LJ* 1389–1424 and Stapleton, *Unpacking Causation*, supra, note 35, pp. 148–155.

[108] Howarth, ibid, pp. 1402–1404.

Honoré in support of their claim: pointing to examples and to what we would find it natural to say in particular situations. Examples which show the incoherence of common sense causal judgments about the nature of causal connection in instances of causing, occasioning or inducing harm are simply not forthcoming from critics. The most they show is that there are some areas of difficulty, uncertainty and judgment. Who would disagree? Certainly not Hart and Honoré.

Micheal Moore is the leading proponent of the metaphysical version of the argument from shallowness. In a thorough but puzzling essay, one half of which is in almost complete agreement with the substance of Hart and Honoré's argument about the content of our causal judgments, Moore devotes the other half to arguing that *CL* lacks a robust metaphysical basis and this, he thinks, is baleful.[109] The puzzle, of course, is why anyone should regard it so. Since Hart and Honoré did not aim to offer a metaphysically 'deep' account of causation and, indeed, since two of their principal philosophical influences – ordinary language philosophy and the 'empiricist' tradition of David Hume and J. S. Mill – would mitigate against any such attempt, the fact that their account lacks metaphysical depth seems irrelevant. Of course, it could be argued that it is a mistake for Hart and Honoré to take the metaphysically shallow path, but this does not seem to undermine, in Moore's eyes at least, the substance of their account. So if this is a mistake, what if any are its baleful consequences? Generally speaking, judges seem relatively adept at avoiding metaphysical muddles, if and when they present themselves in legal doctrine. Without a compelling demonstration either way, it seems no more likely that judges deciding cases under the influence of *CL* will make significant metaphysical mistakes than those used to a more metaphysically rigorous regime.

Although Moore does offer some considerations to suggest that metaphysical shallowness is a vice, these seem far less powerful to those not already committed to metaphysical depth. So, for instance, the fact that some philosophers have offered semantic accounts of meaning which suggest that meaning may exist beyond our ordinary language, is surely interesting.[110] The point, however, is of limited weight until it is shown: (i) that such accounts are correct; and (ii) that they undoubtedly apply to the concept of causation. And even then we must still answer this question: why should the law embody this particular metaphysically deep account of causation? Equally, it is perfectly valid to gripe in general

[109] M. Moore, supra, note 14. [110] Ibid, pp. 854–855.

terms about 'the paradigm case argument' as it appears in ordinary language philosophy, but it is something of an exaggeration to assume it must undermine every judgment it is used to support.[111] Perhaps the key issue, though, is Moore's assumption that the law's reliance on common sense always and immediately stands in need of justification: '[o]nce we see that the nature of causation may differ significantly from the ordinary usage of "cause" by the ordinary person, the need for justification for relying on the common sense concept looms large'.[112] Yet why is it wrong for the burden of proof here to be exactly the other way around? Why, in other words, is it a mistake to expect the law to incorporate common sense understandings of concepts like causation as opposed to the understandings offered by metaphysically ambitious philosophers or natural scientists? Moore does not consider this question, but it is considered now. For our second point consists exactly of an argument as to why the law should, whenever possible, track common sense.

'Why should we care whether the speech of lawyers accords with the speech of other people? So what if the law cannot be squared with common sense?'[113] The reply to both questions derives from some of the elements of the rule of law ideal. There is a presumption in favour of the law in general incorporating common sense and ordinary language whenever possible if: (i) by incorporating these elements the law is more likely to be intelligible to its addressees than it otherwise would be; and (ii) there are reasons why the law should or must be intelligible to those it addresses and regulates. Consider the second issue first. Recall, as was noted in Chapter 3, the blatantly obvious point that as a mode of regulation law operates primarily through the medium of language. It therefore assumes that the beings to which it is addressed are capable of understanding, and are in fact to some extent constituted by, language. As Hart noted, if a large number of beings regulated by law 'could not understand what the law required them to do . . ., then no legal system could come into being or continue to exist'.[114] Yet it is one thing to hold that as a mode of regulation law operates through language and a slightly different thing to say law should utilize much of the ordinary language and many of the concepts of those it aims to regulate. It might, for example, be easier (cheaper, or in some other respect more 'efficient') for the law to regulate its addressees through a richly technical language that, while based upon the natural language of its addressees, is nonetheless understood by

[111] Ibid, pp. 856–858. [112] Ibid, p. 855. [113] Howarth, supra, note 107, p. 1402.
[114] H. L. A. Hart, *Punishment and Reponsibility* (Oxford: Clarendon Press, 1970), p. 229.

very few of them. A partially analogous situation might be that of some scientists or economists in our own community. The language of these subgroups seems broadly similar to the natural language of the community but how many in it actually understand the myriad technical terms of scientist or economist?

Is there anything *prima facie* objectionable with the law being communicated to its addressees in a richly technical, difficult to understand language? The obvious reply is that law formulated thus will be difficult for its addressees to understand or, more accurately, will be more difficult to understand than law formulated predominantly in their own non-technical common sense language. But why worry about this? At this point we stumble into the territory of the large background ideals that constitute the rule of law idea.[115] These ideals are usually important political ideals, one of which is an amalgam of individual liberty and political freedom. Again, the point is a familiar one: Chapter 3 noted Neil MacCormick's claim that citizen's should have a fair opportunity to plan their lives and that this must, in part at least, include the ability to avoid official legal intervention in their lives. And being able to avoid the law, again in part, assumes that the law is knowable and intelligible. It is impossible for me to avoid hazards I know nothing of or those that are unintelligible (consider a purely verbal warning 'the ice over there is very thin' given in a language I do not know: it is absolutely useless).

This is certainly not the only ideal informing the rule of law, but it is the one that does most work in upholding a link between legal language and concepts and ordinary language and concepts. Moreover, the link it establishes is clearly defeasible, in the sense that it does not show that the law must always and ever be formulated in ordinary language and embody common sense. Since the argument at most licenses only a general presumption in favour of the law tracking ordinary language and common sense, it must allow exceptions. And an obvious ground for making an exception to the presumption is that ordinary language and common sense lack the resources to tackle the issue in question. The issue in question could, for example, be that of the nature of causal connection in private and criminal law: but for the exception to be properly made, or for the presumption to be accorded its proper weight, it must be established that common sense and ordinary language truly cannot cope. It is just this

[115] A brief but sensitive account of what this idea might entail is provided by D. Lyons, *Ethics and the Rule of Law* (Cambridge: Cambridge University Press, 1984), pp. 194–208. See also L. Fuller, *The Morality of Law* (New Haven: Yale University Press, revised edn 1969), ch. II and J. Raz, *The Authority of Law* (Oxford: Clarendon Press, 1979), ch. 11.

claim that *CL* serves to undermine: the arguments of the book testify to the rich resources of common sense and, while they do not show that it is utterly unproblematic, they provide a reasonably clear and apparently reliable basis for legal causal judgments.[116]

[116] Stapleton, *Unpacking Causation*, supra, note 35, pp. 160–161 is one of the few to note the argument from the rule of law outlined in the text. She does not reject it but argues, on grounds we have already contested, that since Hart and Honoré's claim that causal judgments are factual is confusing, their account cannot be buttressed by recourse to such rule of law considerations. If the factual claim is nowhere near as confusing as Stapleton thinks, then such recourse might well be permissible.

6

Wrongfulness

The term 'wrongfulness' might, for the same reason, strike some as both jarring and unnecessary. The reason is that the allegedly more natural and obvious term 'wrongdoing' can surely do all the required work in this context. It cannot. Or, more accurately, some of the work it does creates a partial and misleading picture of the nature of this component of legal liability-responsibility in private law. This is because talk of wrongdoing tends to put only one aspect of private law wrongs in the picture, namely, that constituted by the conduct of the alleged wrongdoer. But private law wrongs are rarely constituted solely by the defendant's conduct; more often, that conduct must also have affected one or other of the claimant's legally protected interests, sometimes in a quite specific manner. 'Wrongfulness' has no such one-sided implication: the term is adopted henceforth so that we may appreciate better the two dimensions of this component of legal liability-responsibility. Even if this usage is somewhat stipulative – and it is not obviously so[1] – the tactic is justified in the name of clarity, for it is better to appreciate the true nature of the notion of wrongfulness in private law than to accommodate a misleading term.

It was noted in the previous chapter that the conduct and causation component of legal liability-responsibility might be regarded as more important than the wrongfulness component. This thought rested on the ground that most private law wrongs require conduct of some kind. It must therefore often be established that the defendant acted or refrained, which was itself a private law wrong in the circumstances, or that their acting or refraining brought about a situation or outcome which, in those circumstances, was a private law wrong. That this fails to show that the conduct and causation component should be ranked as more important than the wrongfulness component is obvious. This is because it is possible (perhaps even common) that the conduct in the conduct and causation component constitutes, either entirely or in part, the wrong required to trigger private law liability. The conduct and causation component and

[1] See the examples in *The Oxford English Dictionary*.

the wrongfulness component can therefore overlap. If there is indeed such an overlap, then any claim that one component is more important than the other becomes *prima facie* dubious. One step toward determining whether or not this judgment is correct is obvious: the nature of this component must be further specified. This is undertaken in the first section below. The process of specifying in detail the contours of this component raises a number of awkward issues, some of which are subject to further analysis in the second section (pp. 227–244). One of those issues is also taken up in the final subsection of section two (p.236), which provides a brief case study of an illuminating treatment of wrongfulness in private law and morality.

WRONGFULNESS

The claim that there is indeed a discrete component of private law legal liability-responsibility well described by the term 'wrongfulness' brings a number of commitments in its wake. The primary commitment is to unpack the component, determining whether or not it is coherent, genuinely discrete and philosophically interesting. The process of unpacking can proceed from two different perspectives, that of the defendant and that of claimant.[2] From the former perspective the pertinent questions revolve around what conduct of the defendant will trigger liability in private law and what, if anything, is required in addition to conduct. When examined from the viewpoint of a claimant, the issue of wrongdoing in private law raises questions about the types and range of interests protected by private law as well as the various means of protection. Each perspective is taken up separately in what follows, primarily in an effort to ensure maximum clarity. Separate treatment does not warrant a conclusion about the respective importance of each perspective over and beyond the claim, affirmed here and hopefully borne out by what follows, that both are equally important. Wrongdoing in private law is therefore a combination of a defendant's conduct and its impact upon the claimant's protected interests.

Even an account of private law wrongfulness which accepts that this component is a combination of conduct and its impact upon some or other protected interests is not, however, complete. There are numerous questions about the component that still call for attention. One question raises the matter of the coherence of private law's catalogue of protected interests

[2] I am by no means the first to notice this: see P. Cane, *Tort Law and Economic Interests* (Oxford: Clarendon Press, 2nd edn, 1996), pp. 10–11.

and is quickly followed by another, about how well or badly private law's conception of wrongdoing maps onto some morally or politically respectable account of wrongdoing. The first question is tackled in the remainder of this section; the second is the fulcrum of the second section (p.227).

THE DEFENDANT'S CONDUCT

That the conduct and causation component might be ranked higher in importance than the wrongfulness component arises from this thought: some private law wrongs require that the defendant's conduct cause harm to the claimant, that harm being at least one element of a private law wrong. Since conduct is required to bring about that harm, it is not unreasonable to regard the conduct component as more important than the wrongfulness component, since the required harm can only come about as a result of conduct. Without conduct there is no harm and thus no wrong. However, the alleged priority of conduct over wrongfulness is less obvious when we note that not all conduct brings about private law wrongs, usually because the conduct in question is not appropriately (usually causally) related to the wrong or harm suffered. In these instances there is conduct but no private law wrong. Thus without wrongfulness conduct appears to be of no interest to private law. We must say 'appears to be' rather than 'is' of no interest because the picture of private law wrongs assumed so far, in which defendant's conduct causes harm to claimant, that harm being a constituent of a private law wrong, may not fit all instances of liability.

Some private law wrongs like, for example, breach of duty of care in negligence obviously fit this picture: it requires conduct of the defendant that was a cause of some recognizable and foreseeable harm to the claimant. Without some causally significant conduct of the defendant's the duty does not arise and the claimant's harm will go uncompensated. But there are other private law wrongs in which defendant's conduct is itself the wrong and which do not require that that conduct cause some distinctive and separable harm to the claimant (or, for that matter, any other party). Two obvious examples are trespass to land and to person; less obvious, perhaps, is breach of contract. These are wrongs whether or not there is some specific tangible harm to the claimant.[3] The harm in such

[3] It might be thought that an action for breach of contract cannot succeed without pecuniary loss. The English courts have been grappling with this issue for some time: see *Jarvis v Swans Tours Ltd* [1973] QB 233; *Wrotham Park Estate Co Ltd v Parkside Homes Ltd* [1974] 1 WLR 798; *Surrey County Council v Bredero Homes Ltd* [1993] 1 WLR 1361; *Ruxley Electronics and Construction Ltd v Forsyth* [1995] 3 WLR 118; and *Attorney-General v Blake* [2001] 1 AC 268.

cases is harm in the sense of infringement of the claimant's legitimate interest in contractual performance or in his holdings or bodily integrity; it makes no difference that the claimant suffered neither physically nor economically.[4] By contrast, heads of liability like negligence require tangible economic or physical harm to the claimant over and beyond bare interference with legitimate interests.

Wrongfulness in private law might, then, take two different general forms. A private law wrong may simply be conduct that falls within a legally prohibited category, like trespass to the person or breach of contract, which constitutes a bare interference with some or other protected interest of the claimant. Or a private law wrong may be conduct that brings about specific, legally recognized types of harm to one or more of the claimant's protected interests. It is important not to be misled by these two claims. For example, that some private law wrongs are constituted by conduct falling within a legally prohibited category and which consists of bare interference with a protected interest, implies nothing about the number of possible segments of conduct that can bring about such wrongs. Nor does it imply anything about the number of instances of conduct that can bring about the other form of private law wrong. Trespass to land is a private law wrong in which a wide range of possible segments of conduct can constitute the wrong, yet all that it requires for liability is some conduct amounting to bare interference. The wrong is that conduct of the defendant's which can be appropriately re-described in the legal terminology of non-consensual entry upon the land of another. That conduct is not a closed class or, if it is, its constituents can be described in almost infinitely many ways. Thus entry upon land can be of multiple kinds including walking (in all its different forms), dancing (in all its manifold styles), running (ditto), jogging (ditto), flying (in all its different forms), travelling in a vehicle (ditto) etc. etc. The crucial point is that the defendant's conduct need not bring about anything else in order to be a legal wrong, whereas for other private law wrongs this is exactly what is required. Liability for negligence requires much more than bare interference with another's protected interest: the defendant's conduct must not only fall within the legal category of breach of duty of care, that breach must also bring about some legally recognized and foreseeable harm to the claimant. Again, the conduct that constitutes 'breach of duty

[4] Except in the sense that if there is additional physical or economic harm the level of damages awarded will be higher. That is not to say that there must be such additional harm in order to get damages.

of care' is not a closed class: many, many conceivable instances of conduct (like jogging, running, manufacturing ginger beer containing snails) can amount to breach of duty of care in the right circumstances. But whatever conduct does actually fall into that category must have a particular kind of outcome or consequence, namely, actual tangible harm to the claimant. The manufacture of ginger beer containing snails will never be tortious if no one ever drinks and is harmed by it.

It is unlikely that the two possible ways in which the defendant's conduct can constitute a private law wrong will overlap in the sense that the *same* segment of conduct can actually be and can lead to *the same* private law wrong. This is because it is hard to envisage a single segment of conduct that can at the same time be private law wrong X and bring about private law wrong X. These two claims are inconsistent if made by one who has understood our ordinary causal language, in which we take 'doing X' to be a more direct and immediate causal relation than 'bringing X about'.[5] The natural assumption when faced with these options is that the choice is an either/or one. For this assumption to be well founded there must, of course, be a way of individuating conduct such that in some circumstances and for some purposes it makes sense to speak of an event or situation being 'the same' segment of conduct.[6] If it is in some circumstances appropriate to speak in this way then the assumption that the two possibilities are alternatives is not eccentric. It is not similarly difficult to imagine the *same* segment of conduct being or bringing about different private law wrongs. Nor is it hard to conceive of *different* segments of conduct either being or bringing about the same private law wrong. The first possibility is commonplace in private law: one and the same segment of conduct can give rise to, for example, both a breach of contract and a breach of duty of care in negligence or can be both fraudulent deceit and negligent misrepresentation. As to the second possibility, it makes perfect sense to hold that a wrong can be either conduct that falls within legal category Y or conduct that in some appropriate way brings about tangible harm or outcome Y. Imposing liability for bringing about a legal wrong in both ways serves to maximize the range of liability: more conduct will be subsumed under this version of the wrong than under narrower versions. Those versions – they would hold either that the wrong is conduct of type Y *only* or that it is *only* conduct that brings Y about – are obviously triggered by fewer instances of conduct.

[5] See H. L. A. Hart and T. Honoré, *Causation in the Law* (Oxford: Clarendon Press, 2nd edn, 1985), pp. 28–32.

[6] The issue here is, of course, the same as that discussed in Chapter 3, pp. 75–78.

It might be said that the abstract formulation of the role of the defendant's conduct in private law wrongdoing – her conduct must be a private law wrong either in the sense of bare interference or in the sense of conduct that has brought about legally recognized harm – is doubly problematic. One supposed problem is this: holding that private law wrongs can occur in these two different ways is chronically reductive, overlooking the great variety of private law wrongs and their manifold requirements for liability. It might be added that it is of no benefit whatever for practising lawyers to be told that private law wrongs can come about in these two abstract ways. But this objection is clearly misplaced. It ignores the fact that this formulation is *abstract* – the claim is that this formulation makes sense of or underlies just about all the specific forms of liability in the areas of private law with which we concerned. It does not replace them. Furthermore, there might indeed be some practical pay-off from this formulation, if only the modest one of ensuring that, for example, the nature and extent of causal requirements in various heads of private law liability are not confused. It is clear that such requirements are more likely to be in play when specific harms must be brought about by the defendant's conduct and are otiose in those where the defendant's conduct simply is the wrong in question. This might be overlooked if no heed is paid to the abstract formulation.

The second alleged problem is that the abstract formulation supposedly overlooks a significant feature of some private law wrongs, namely, that they must be of a particular cognitive type. What is meant here is *not* that the wrong in question is in some way made up by what the defendant knows or thinks. Rather, the idea is that sometimes the wrong brought about or actually constituted by the defendant's conduct must be intended by the defendant, or he must be reckless or negligent with respect to it.[7] In the criminal law jurists often express this idea in the terminology of 'mental states'. So, for example, the claim is often made that murder is conduct that kills another living human being within a year and day, accompanied by the mental state of intending to kill or seriously injure that human being, or being reckless as to whether or not death or serious injury is caused. Such talk is, however, somewhat problematic, primarily but not solely because it suggests that so-called 'mental states' are in some way detachable from, perhaps even independent of, conduct. Thus lawyers are sometimes tempted to think that such 'states' reside in a mysterious place – the mind – access to which is by no means guaranteed.

[7] Or he must intend, be reckless or negligent with regard to some aspect of it.

Yet as a common sense matter we rarely have too much difficulty in determining whether some segment of conduct was either intentional or reckless or negligent, even when the agent's own view is unavailable or ignored. Reasons for action are usually inferred from the conduct in question and its surrounding context. On the supposition that the agent whose conduct is in question is in most respects the same as his fellow human beings in terms of deliberative capacity and general knowledge, then it is not too hard to determine whether, for example, some act of his was intentional or not. If he was indeed similar to his fellow beings in these respects, would we have any difficulty in saying what his intention was when he pointed and discharged a loaded gun at the victim's head? Further, would we struggle to say what his 'mental state' was if he had not bothered to ensure that the gun was unloaded?

Although the abstract formulation says nothing explicit about such matters, it is certainly not incompatible with them. The formulation can be made less abstract by asking, albeit at the risk of transferring some of the confusions of the criminal law into private law, whether and, if so, which private law wrongs require *mens rea*.[8] This question is perfectly compatible with the claim that private law wrongs are either constituted by conduct of the defendant or are brought about such by conduct, since it simply adds to that claim a concern with the deliberative state embodied by the conduct in question. A potential confusion must be avoided here, however. It was noted in Chapter 3 that some aspect of the defendant's conduct that either is or which brings about a private law wrong must be intentional. This is one of the ways of guaranteeing that the conduct in question is the property of – belongs to – a responsible being. One cannot be such a being if unable to act for reasons and thus incapable of intentional conduct.

That general claim should not be mistaken for the more specific claim that some private law wrongs require, as part of their definition, that some result or outcome or situation be brought about intentionally. In the latter instances the intention – the requisite 'mental state' – must be directed to some or all of the aspects of the private law wrong, whereas in the former case it need not. There must be intentional conduct in the former case, but the agent's intention need not extend to all or even any of the features of the wrong. So although the defendant who trespasses on another's land must act intentionally in the sense that he must, for

[8] A slightly narrower version of this question is the fulcrum of P. Cane, '*Mens Rea* in Tort Law' (2000) 20 *Oxford Journal of Legal Studies* 533–556.

example, have acted or been capable of acting for a reason, it need not also be established that his reason (intention) was to walk upon or damage the land of another. By contrast, some torts (defamation, for example) require not only that the agent's conduct be intentional in the sense of being based on reason(s), but also that he intended to bring about, or was reckless with regard to, some or other feature of the legally defined wrong itself. One way to avoid confusion here is to distinguish between *general* and *particular* intention. The meaning of intention is the same in each case, but the former refers to an aspect of basic responsibility, while the latter refers to a specific '*mens rea*' requirement for some private law wrongs.

Peter Cane's admirably clear discussion of '*Mens Rea* in Tort Law' accords in many respects with the analysis offered so far.[9] He thinks that what was just called general intention is a mark of basic responsibility and that many torts require little more than this of the defendant for liability, except some conduct. He also illuminates the way in which some torts require intention as to the outcomes or consequences of conduct and shows that in this context the distinction as drawn in the criminal law between intention and recklessness is blurred. He rightly observes that recklessness is often sufficient for (so-called) intentional torts.[10] There are, however, three points on which Cane's analysis and that offered here differ. One is probably only terminological: he thinks that the term 'deliberate' and its cognates best describe general intention.[11] One reason for this stipulation is perfectly legitimate: Cane may well wish to avoid confusion between what we have called general intention, on the one hand, and particular intention, on the other. But, although driven by the entirely commendable aim of clarity, Cane's suggestion actually runs the risk of creating confusion. For the adoption of different terms for what is in substance the same thing might be taken to suggest, quite wrongly, that there is a substantial difference here. The same 'thing' is intention, the central meaning of the term being the same in both instances of general and particular intention. The difference between the two is what is or must be intended, not the meaning of intention itself.

The second point of difference is also relatively minor. Cane is content to continue to call the intentional torts intentional even when the courts only require that they be brought about recklessly (as that term is understood in the criminal law). The objection to this is the same as that just aired: it risks confusion that can be easily avoided, since it attributes a

[9] Ibid. [10] Ibid, p. 538. [11] Ibid, p. 536 and fn. 10.

meaning to the term 'intention' that is incompatible with that adopted in the criminal law. Furthermore, there is no good reason for this difference in meaning – the only reason is that the courts have adopted it. If the virtue of coherence in a legal system is understood broadly, then this is unsatisfactory. Wherever possible, concepts and terms in play in one area of the law ought to bear the same meaning when used in other areas, in the absence of strong reasons to the contrary.[12] Such coherence is not only helpful to judges and legal advisers; it is also helpful to citizens insofar as they attempt to ensure that their conduct accords with the law.

Third, Cane does not regard negligence as in any sense a state of mind and would thus cavil at the suggestion made above that it can be regarded as such. That suggestion, of course, was accompanied by the caveat that juristic talk of 'states of mind' is probably best avoided; it should therefore be indulged in only as a last resort. For Cane, by contrast, negligence is simply conduct falling below a required standard.[13] He is partially right here and completely right on an associated point. The associated point is that it is undeniably true, as Cane affirms, that 'the plaintiff in a tort action for negligence does not have to prove inattention or inadvertence on the part of the defendant'.[14] But it is also undeniable that every central case of negligence – one, that is, in which non-intentional or non-reckless conduct is in question – is one in which the defendant's conduct manifests an attitude of 'practical indifference' to the interests of others.[15] That is the state of mind that negligence embodies and, of course, while it is certain that that state of mind need not be explicitly proven by the claimant, what must be proved is the embodiment in conduct of that state of mind. This, of course, is that the defendant failed to do as a reasonable person would have done. His conduct must have fallen below this standard and, in doing so, it assuredly manifests practical indifference.

It is possible to continue the move, implicit in the discussion so far, from more to less abstract statements of what the wrongdoing component requires of the defendant for liability. At its least abstract, we can say that the wrongdoing component requires that the defendant's conduct either

[12] An illuminating discussion of coherence – the idea 'that the multitudinous rules of a developed legal system should "make sense" when taken together' – in adjudication is N. MacCormick, *Legal Reasoning and Legal Theory* (Oxford: Clarendon Press, revised edn, 1994), ch. VII (the quotation is from p. 152).

[13] Supra, note 8, p. 537. [14] Ibid, p. 536.

[15] See R. A. Duff, *Intention, Agency and Criminal Liability* (Oxford: Blackwell, 1990), pp. 155–163. This idea underpins both recklessness and negligence for Duff.

is or brings about a private law wrong, the precise content of such wrongs being specified in our textbooks. Although perfectly correct, this response is unhelpful if our aim is to construct a deeper and more general picture of private law than the one provided by our textbooks. Because, as will be noted in the following subsection, private law is subject to some entropic forces, the detailed picture of private law wrongs in the textbooks may not be completely satisfactory. Such pictures also often rest upon a current time-slice picture of doctrine (hence the common prefatory remark in textbooks that 'the law is stated as of [whatever date]') that overlooks doctrine's historical genesis and underlying principles. While many textbooks display a constant tension between the need to describe current developments and the effort to elucidate the general principles that might underpin them, the tension is often resolved in only one way. Presumably because there is no greater sin for contemporary textbooks than a failure to be 'current', the urge to capture recent developments overrides the search for principle.

At this point jurists and philosophers can and should take centre stage. So, what is it they say about the defendant's conduct that is more specific than what we have already noted? One thing often done is an effort towards systematization of the specific types of private law wrong into broader categories or families.[16] This process is really one of pruning and tidying, for the legal growth of centuries and decades can often become unwieldy and messy.[17] Quite obviously, this process cannot begin without a 'tidy' picture in mind. Just as one cannot tidy and organize a garden without some prior idea of the appropriate place for borders and lawns, trees and bushes, so it seems that one cannot prune and reorganize private law without some conception of what it should look like. While to some extent such a picture is passed on among generations of lawyers through their education and training, it is by no means static. New areas of growth are cultivated and some old areas separated and re-grafted

[16] Perhaps the first effort was W. Blackstone, *Commentaries on the Laws of England* (Oxford: Clarendon Press, 1765), Vol. 1, Book 1, p. 118. For more recent examples, see the essays in P. Birks (ed.), *The Classification of Obligations* (Oxford: Clarendon Press, 1997) and P. Birks (ed.), *English Private Law* (Oxford: Clarendon Press, 2000).

[17] Some think this messiness an unavoidable feature of the common law and that moves towards tidiness are therefore mistaken and foredoomed: S. Waddams, *Dimensions of Private Law: Categories and Concepts in Anglo-American Legal Reasoning* (Cambridge: Cambridge University Press, 2003). For a thoughtful engagement with Waddams's various arguments see S. Smith, 'A Map of the Common Law?' (2004) 40 *Canadian Business Law Journal* 364–383.

elsewhere.[18] But which elements of this picture remain the same, binding future generations' development of private law and its catalogue of wrongs?[19] One important static element is this: private law's catalogue of wrongs has always in part consisted of a catalogue of protected interests. These interests are those of the claimant rather than the defendant and the catalogue has, as a historical matter, changed considerably. Indeed, it is no great exaggeration to say that the extension of the range of protected interests within private law is one of the main determinants of legal change. Thus, a less abstract yet still general and interesting statement about what the wrongdoing component requires of the defendant's conduct is this: it requires that the defendant's conduct undermine one or other of the claimant's protected private law interests. Although more detailed than what we have so far said about the defendant's conduct, this statement is clearly not the same as a 'mere' restatement of the doctrinal requirements for some particular private law wrong.

Three points must be noted about the claim that defendant's conduct must affect claimant's protected interest (hereinafter 'the interest claim'). First, there are defences open to defendants in private law, some of which serve to show that their conduct was either justified or excused.[20] It is therefore true that in some situations it is either not wrong or it is permissible to bring about a private law 'wrong'. Some such defences also seem to turn upon the knowledge or intentions of the defendant and thus require that defendant's conduct embody a particular cognitive state.[21] This point should not be confused with the question of which private law wrongs require '*mens rea*', although the substance of the issue is undoubtedly similar. Second, the interest claim suggests that a complete picture of wrongfulness in private law must supplement the perspective of the

[18] The birth of the law of restitution in English law is a notable instance. For discussion of some of the initial scholarly steps in its genesis see P. Birks, *Introduction to the Law of Restitution* (Oxford: Clarendon Press, revised edn, 1989) and his *Unjust Enrichment* (Oxford: Clarendon Press, 2nd edn, 2005).

[19] The term should really be 'catalogue of wrongfulness' but this is too jarring to be acceptable. Use of the term 'catalogue of wrongs' is stylistic and does not therefore imply anything inconsistent with the claims in the first paragraph in favour of 'wrongfulness' as the best term to describe this component of legal liability-responsibility.

[20] Such as the general tort defences of private defence and necessity and the specific defence of reasonable belief that the victim is guilty of an offence in false imprisonment; and proof of reasonable grounds for belief in contract under s 2 (1) of the Misrepresentation Act 1967.

[21] Such as the defence of fair comment in the tort of defamation (which requires an absence of malice); a claim of duress made in response to an action for breach of contract (which requires both knowledge of the threat and that it was a salient factor in the defendant's deliberations); and the defence under s 2 (1), ibid.

wrongdoer and his conduct with that of the victim. This is undeniably true if private law wrongs are in part a catalogue of protected interests. There are many questions we can ask of this catalogue, some of which are taken up in the following subsection. Third, the suggestion that wrongfulness in private law can only be understood if reference is made to both the defendant's conduct and its affect upon the claimant's interests is controversial for some philosophers. This issue is tackled in the final subsection of this section (p.224).

THE CLAIMANT'S PROTECTED INTERESTS

At one level the interests private law protects are easily determined. They are in part disclosed by the various heads of liability elucidated in our textbooks like, to take a few examples, breach of contract, breach of trust, trespass to person and property, and failure to take reasonable care. However, a list such as this – or even a genuinely exhaustive one – is not in itself sufficient to ensure a good grasp of the type and range of interests protected by private law for the following reason. In the common law world the different heads of private law liability, and thus the range of interests protected, did not come into being at a single time and as a neatly organized and pre-ordained catalogue.[22] Rather, some of those heads of liability predate others by a century or more and almost all were created by judges making decisions in particular cases rather than by all judges (or legislators) acting together in something like a law-making assembly. The catalogue of protected interests in the private law of the common law world is therefore the work of many (mainly judicial) hands and minds, over a long period of time. The product of their deliberations and decisions is therefore quite understandably less coherent than would be expected of the product of a single well-disciplined mind.

Furthermore, the discursive common law system of judicial decision-making, in which each judge sitting in an appeal is entitled to give a judgment articulating their reasons for deciding the case one way, and rejecting the reasons for deciding it the other way, increases the already available space for interpretation of what the law requires. The common law's system of precedent further increases this space in two ways. First, because there is no uncontroversial account of what it is that constitutes the *ratio decidendi* of a case, there can be disagreement about what are

[22] For a magisterial view of the development of private law in the civil law systems, with particular emphasis on Germany, see F. Weiacker, *A History of Private Law in Europe* (Oxford: Clarendon Press, 1995).

the crucial elements of some or other judicial decision.[23] Second, the system of precedent ensures that particular judicial mistakes can remain entrenched in the law for a great deal of time, requiring much discussion and re-interpretation in subsequent cases in order to be dislodged.[24]

This context, in which forces of entropy – decision-making by many judges over a long period of time, combined with a discursive style of legal judgment and a system of precedent – impel private law towards incoherence, cries out for some effort towards systematization. And while both judges and textbook writers are keen to assess the coherence of particular private law decisions one with another, they rarely tackle the broader issue of the coherence or otherwise of the scheme of interests protected by private law.[25] This is both a legal-doctrinal and a legal-philosophical task. Viewed as the former, it is a means of gaining purchase on the trend of legal developments and range of controversies in private law, assuming that at least some hard cases spring from difficulties in the way some interests are either protected or valued.[26] Viewed as the latter, this task plainly extends our understanding of the nature of private law and serves as preamble to a philosophical and normative task more attuned to contemporary jurisprudential taste.[27]

The discussion of claimants' protected interests here follows the movement, from higher to lower levels of abstraction, of the previous subsection. Thus, at a very general level of abstraction, claimants' protected interests can be divided into those that are 'thick' and those that are 'thin'. The difference is that the former occupy more normative space in the sense that bare interference with them is a wrong; the latter, by contrast, occupy less normative space because bare interference with them is not sufficient to trigger liability. Rather, there is usually liability for interference with thin interests only when interference causes tangible pecuniary or physical harm to the claimant. It is an interesting question why private law regards some interests as thick and some as thin; so, too, is the question of whether or not this system of valuation can be

[23] The standard English law treatment is R. Cross and J. Harris, *Precedent in English Law* (Oxford: Clarendon Press, 4th edn, 1991), ch. II.

[24] A good example is provided by the decision in *Candler v Crane, Christmas & Co* [1951] 2 KB 164. The dissent in this case is now often regarded as a better statement of the law than the majority judgment. See *Hedley Bryne & Co Ltd v Heller & Partners* [1964] AC 465 and, for example, *Henderson v Merritt Syndicates Ltd* [1995] 2 AC 145 for a current statement of the law.

[25] For a path-breaking effort see Cane, supra, note 2, parts I and II.

[26] See, for example, the breach of contract without loss cases, supra, note 3.

[27] Ch 1, pp. 28–31 offers some reflections as to the basis of this current taste.

normatively justified. Since regarding some interests as thick gives them more legal protection than those that are thin, it might be assumed that thick interests are morally more important than thin interests. This assumption is dubious.

For, although private law regards some interests as thick which are also morally very important – such as, for example, the protection of the interest in physical integrity and autonomy provided by the tort of trespass to the person – that same interest is treated as thin for the purposes of other heads of liability such as negligence. This is curious if the interest in physical integrity and autonomy is genuinely very important in moral terms: if it is so, then how can the level of protection accorded to this interest vary according to the head of liability in question? Part of the answer, of course, is obvious and found in the historical contingency of legal development, in particular the development of 'actions on the case'.[28] That this answer carries no or very little moral weight is equally obvious and serves to highlight one way in which private law's catalogue of wrongs is and should be subject to moral and political criticism. Such criticism is best made when leavened with a scintilla of historical understanding.

Some jurists and philosophers choose to mark the difference between thick and thin interests in an unsatisfactory way, holding that private law wrongs which do not require claimants suffer tangible physical, pecuniary or other loss protect 'rights'.[29] Private law wrongs that do require such loss presumably protect something other than rights. The idea behind this thought is not silly: it is that rights protect very, very important interests which should almost never be interfered with without consent. Since 'bare' interference is the wrong here, tangible loss or harm is not required for liability. But there is a twofold difficulty with this view. First, it is unlikely that some of the interests private law regards as thick are, morally speaking, of supreme importance. Think, for example, of the interest in property protected by trespass to land and compare it with the interests in physical integrity and health often (but not exclusively) protected by negligence. At the level of simple moral intuitions it seems that the named interests protected by the latter are always more important than those protected by the former. Second, an implication of this way of

[28] See D. Ibbetson, *A Historical Introduction to the Law of Obligations* (Oxford: Clarendon Press, 1999), chs. 3, 6 and 8 for expert commentary.

[29] J. Coleman, *Risks and Wrongs* (Cambridge: Cambridge University Press, 1992), p. 332 ('[w]rongs are actions contrary to rights'); P. Cane, *Responsibility in Law and Morality* (Oxford: Hart Publishing, 2002), p. 197.

marking the thick and thin distinction is that thin interests are not rights and that private law therefore spends a great deal of time protecting something less important than rights. One odd consequence of this is that we cannot regard *all* private law adjudication as a matter of weighing competing rights or as a process of making abstract rights concrete.[30] Only that segment of private law adjudication that deals with thick interests is properly regarded as being about rights. It is, however, both common and in no obvious sense strange (i) to regard both private and public law adjudication to be a matter of determining rights; and (ii) to see both private and public law as systems of rights, duties and entitlements. This common and obvious way of understanding the law should not be jettisoned on the flimsy ground of its lack of fit with a questionable categorization of thick interests. Cart is here assuredly before horse.

A commendable and less abstract effort towards systematizing the scheme of interests private law protects has been made by Cane. Taken *only* as a listing of interests protected by private law, Cane's catalogue is seven strong: breach of promise and undertakings, interference with rights, uttering untruths, breach of trust, doing harm, creating risks of harm, and making gains.[31] This might seem a very odd list of protected interests, since not all the entries are obviously interests. The reason is that Cane runs together both protected interests and types of wrongful conduct, his aim being to show the importance of both to an adequate understanding of private law. Although sharing this aim, which is discussed further in the subsection on p.224, there is no need to fully endorse Cane's potentially confusing list. In order to avoid confusion some of the entries on Cane's list are recast in terms of the interests they protect. That this can be done with little loss of sense or disagreement shows the main issue here is terminological rather than substantive.

It is obvious that private law protects our interest in others doing what they have legally undertaken to do and, on this basis, entries one and four in Cane's catalogue can be combined. The principal means of legally undertaking to do something are, of course, contracting and entering into some kind of fiduciary or trust relationship. Trustees must act as the trust and general principles of equity require, just as promisors must act in accord with the contract they created and the applicable general principles of contract law. While there are many related and more complicated

[30] This, of course, is R. Dworkin's view of adjudication: see *Taking Rights Seriously* (London: Duckworth, 1978), ch. 4 and *Law's Empire* (Oxford: Hart Publishing, 1998), chs. 7 and 8.

[31] Supra, note 29, ch. 6. Cane also discusses the criminal law in this chapter.

sub-headings of liability here – like those dealing with agency and the employment relationship – this complexity does not undermine the claim that private law upholds an interest, albeit manifest in a number of different contexts and forms, in others discharging their legal undertakings. The importance of defendant having 'undertaken' a duty is, of course, that it singles them out (as trustee, promissor or fiduciary) as one who owes a specific duty to a particular claimant or group of claimants. The duty in question is thus not just a general legal duty owed to all who may be affected by its exercise, although it could well overlap with such a duty. The duty exists only because something specific was done to bring it into being: we do not become trustees, or promisors or fiduciaries simply by virtue of being human. Something more is required to bring these duties into being.

An entry on Cane's list that must be rejected, by virtue of the argument just used against the unsatisfactory way of distinguishing thick and thin interests, is interference with rights. Little of substance follows from this, however, because the interests protected under this ground of liability (like ownership of tangible property)[32] are easily subsumable under other categories Cane uses. Two such categories – doing harm and creating risks of harm – can do some useful work here, depending upon the interests protected. Cane is surely right in thinking that the tort of negligence is the most common form of private law liability to protect against harm and notes that the tort of defamation is an instance of liability which compensates for the creation of a risk of harm.[33] The interests in play here are clear. Tort law undeniably protects interests in bodily integrity and autonomy; upholds an interest in security of holdings and in a reasonable level of protection from the conduct of others; and protects an interest in reputation. Some of these interests the law regards as thick (hence the harm necessary for liability is 'bare' interference), some as thin (in which case tangible pecuniary loss or physical or other harm is required). Moreover, these interests are protected by a range of very different doctrines (negligence, trespass to person and land, conversion are just a few examples) and this may be problematic, primarily because such a diverse range of heads of liability might create inconsistency in the level of protection the law affords to some interests. Although this might be unavoidable in a non-codified legal system in which different legal wrongs came into being at different times and in very different contexts,

[32] Ibid, p. 197.

[33] Ibid, p. 203 and p. 206 respectively (the latter is but 'one view' of defamation).

this is not an argument in its favour. It can, rather, be taken to weigh in just the opposite direction.

The third entry on Cane's list highlights, with little modification, another interest or set of interests protected by private law. This is an interest, protected in a limited number of contexts, in reliable and non-physically harmful information.[34] As to unreliable information, the utterance of deliberate untruths can, in the right circumstances, trigger at least two vitiating factors in contract law, while negligent statements can also lead to contracts being set aside and to liability in the tort of negligence. The interest in reliable information protected by private law is not in any sense a direct manifestation of morality's injunction against lying; for this to be so the level of protection private law confers would have to be far more extensive than that currently available. Thus while private law is clearly open to the criticism that it's catalogue of wrongs does not but should mirror morality's, this criticism is rarely made because the general view from which it derives, which could be dubbed extreme legal moralism, is hardly ever seriously espoused.[35]

The final entry on Cane's list – making gains – falls within the category of doing harm where A's gain, which is made at B's expense and correlates exactly with B's loss, results from A's conduct. However, 'where A's gain and B's corresponding loss cannot be traced to any conduct of A (as where A is the passive beneficiary of a mistaken payment), any liability on A to return the gain and repair the loss needs to be explained in terms of the giving and receipt of the gain'.[36] That private law, in the form of restitution or unjust enrichment, recognizes such a liability and the associated protected interest is beyond doubt. Characterizing the protected interest is a little more difficult, because some tempting formulations are too general (an interest in rectitude or an interest that others take care of one's mistakenly directed goods and money), while others are too specific (an interest in the repayment of overpaid taxes, for example). The duty here could be seen, alternatively, as one of limited altruism arising only in limited circumstances. The difficulty of articulating the interest protected might be reflected in the awkward and hesitant

[34] Ibid, p. 198; physically harmful information was provided in *Wilkinson v Downton* [1897] 2 QB 57 and could well be subsumed under the interest in physical integrity.

[35] The strongest version of legal moralism in print is not this extreme: P. Devlin, *The Enforcement of Morals* (Oxford: Clarendon Press, 1965), chs. II and III. Devlin's precursor, J. F. Stephens, *Liberty, Equality, Fraternity* (Indianapolis: Liberty Fund, 1st edn, 1992; 1873), ch. 4 is closer in his views on the criminal law but has little to say about private law.

[36] Cane, supra, note 29, p. 208.

struggle of the English courts to recognize unjust enrichment as a discrete type of legal liability.[37] Moral philosophers, being free of the difficulty of doctrinal coherence, will presumably have little difficulty in showing either the normative significance of the interest protected or the stringency of the correlative duty.

It seems that in broad terms the interests protected by private law are these: an interest in bodily integrity and autonomy; an interest in protection from the conduct of others; an interest in other's completing or performing their undertakings; an interest in protection of one's legitimate holdings and in others returning one's legitimate holdings; and an interest in maintaining one's good reputation and in reliable information. The exact contours of each interest and the duties to which they give rise are elucidated by the details of private law doctrine. Doctrine also tells us the precise ways in which defendants must interfere with those interests and the circumstances in which claimants' conduct can either reduce or completely remove defendants' duties (as, for example, by consent to interference or contributory negligence). There is no doubt that most and possibly all of these protected interests are morally significant; there is thus little doubt that many philosophical accounts of the content of morality will accommodate most of them.[38] More problematic, however, is the way in which private law protects these interests – some are accorded more protection, because regarded as thick, and some less, because classified as thin. The law is rightly open to moral criticism here if and when it gives greater protection to some interests that are not as morally important as others.

It is likely that any more precise statement of the interests private law protects will come too close to repeating the details of doctrine found in our textbooks. This is to denigrate neither doctrine nor its explication. The latter task is, in fact, an absolutely crucial precondition to the jurists' and philosophers' general task of evaluating the consistency of private law's catalogue of wrongs. But can anything else be added to the abstract account of protected interests provided here that is not simply an echo of our textbooks? The most obvious addition is, perhaps, a general account of 'harm', since this notion usually appears in conjunction with an account of interests. To claim something as an interest in this context is, of course, to say more than that it is something which is of value. The

[37] For a helpful account of some of the juristic territory, see H. Dagan, *The Law and Ethics of Restitution* (Cambridge: Cambridge University Press, 2004), ch. 2.

[38] The notion of a critical morality and its counterpoint is elucidated in the section on p. 224, below.

interests protected by private law differ from the 'interest' we have in pursuing our hobbies or pastimes, even though the latter are no doubt of value and also rightly regarded as 'interests'. Yet the interests protected by the law need not actually be 'of interest' to those that have them all the time. While we would have to say of one who no longer pursues some or other hobby that it is not now one of her 'interests', one does not lose the interests protected by private law either as a result of non-use or lack of interest in them. One has these interests regardless of whether one is interested in them. This is probably because these interests are especially valuable, but not in the sense of, for example, representing the highest or best form of ethical or moral life. Rather, the interests protected by the law are especially valuable because fundamental means of achieving most conceptions of a good life. Almost any such conception relies upon bodily integrity, autonomy, some security of holdings and protection from the conduct of others. These interests may not be 'of interest' to particular agents simply because they are taken for granted, part of the assumed context in which life is lived. Yet without these interests being protected to some degree not even Samurai warriors could pursue their conception of a good life. Thus the fact that these interests can be set back is especially troubling and the exact ways in which they can be set back is, of course, illuminated by an account of the nature of harm.

It is not obvious that the issue of harm can be subject to interesting philosophical treatment in this context. One reason is that the way interests protected by private law can be harmed is determined by the law itself and, while legal conceptions of harm should be intelligible, consistent and coherent, they are not immediately answerable to philosophical accounts. There are nevertheless interesting doctrinal questions here about the recognition of new types of harm in the law, but these are usually the result of new interests being protected by the law or of already recognised interests receiving greater protection. Furthermore, the philosophical accounts of harm that exist are themselves reliant upon a prior account of interests, thus illustrating the truism that it is only against an account of interests that harm can be determined.[39] The slightly different philosophical question of how well or badly the law's conception of harm matches up with an account of harm provided by a respectable moral or political theory is also surely interesting. But the principal task in the remainder of this chapter is both more general than

[39] See, for example, J. Feinberg, *The Moral Limits of the Criminal Law, Vol 1: Harm to Others* (New York: Oxford University Press, 1987), chs 1–3.

this and more general than the prior task of determining the ways in which private law's catalogue of interests matches up with a morally or politically respectable account of interests. The aim is to examine the ways in which private law's catalogue of *wrongs* matches up with and diverges from moral-cum-political catalogues of *wrongs*. If there is an overlap at this level, then there must be overlap, under threat of incoherence, at the slightly less abstract levels of protected interests and conceptions of harm.

TWO REMAINING ISSUES

Cane thinks that some may find a two-dimensional account of wrongfulness of the type offered here objectionable. Such an account covers what Cane calls 'the grounds and bounds of responsibility'[40] and he thinks philosophers who espouse 'agency' accounts of legal liability-responsibility and, to a lesser extent, Ernest Weinrib, will object to it.[41] 'Agent-focussed accounts of . . . [liability] responsibility typically ground it in the free exercise of human will as expressed by conduct'.[42] Whether or not there are many such accounts, and whether and to what degree Weinrib's account fits this description, are issues left unexplored here. Our interest is, rather, in the validity of the objection itself, which holds that a plausible account of wrongdoing need not contain any reference to the interests protected by private law. This is the first issue tackled here. The second, which is simply highlighted prior to a more detailed treatment, concerns the relation between private law's catalogue of wrongs and various moral-cum-political catalogues of wrongs.

The idea that an account of private law wrongfulness can be built solely from the implications of an account of the free exercise of will as expressed by conduct has the virtue of parsimony. Generally speaking, it is an intellectual virtue to offer explanations of anything – some or other feature of the natural world, or conduct, institutions, practices and ideas in the social world – using fewer rather than more concepts. However, pursuit of this virtue can become a vice, particularly where the desire for parsimony leads to the misrepresentation of the thing to be explained (*explanandum*). Features of the *explanandum* can suffer, like Procrustes' victims, from being cut to fit the *explanans*, explanatory neatness and parsimony taking priority over the true nature of the thing to be

[40] Supra, note 29, p. 181.
[41] In *The Idea of Private Law* (Cambridge, Mass.: Harvard University Press, 1995).
[42] Cane, supra, note 29, p. 182.

explained. This is exactly the risk agency accounts of legal liability-responsibility run. Any open-minded view of private law's substantive doctrines shows they not only often characterize the wrong that must be done to the claimant's interest (sometimes in a quite precise way), but that they also detail how the wrong must or can be brought about by the defendant (by either act or omission or both simpliciter, or negligently, intentionally, or recklessly). Wrongfulness, in private law is, therefore, a combination of the defendant's conduct and its affect on claimant's legally protected interests.

An account of wrongfulness that ignores one of these two elements is misleading. As Cane notes, agency accounts of responsibility, insofar as they ignore the catalogue of interests private law protects, are '[f]rom the legal point of view . . . radically incomplete'; they do not offer a 'full explanation of the grounds and bounds of . . . legal responsibility'.[43] Agency accounts therefore fail to capture a significant feature of the institution which they purport to explain and understand. And, if they cannot capture that which they purport to give an account of, then they are clearly bad accounts (in the same way as an account of Association Football that characterized the game as '22 people trying to get muddy'). At this point a familiar objection can be anticipated, best put by two related questions: what's so important about 'the legal point of view'? And: why must an account of an institution, practice or segment of conduct illuminate all aspects of said institution, practice or conduct? Questions of this type and the answers to them were the fulcrum of the methodological reflections in Chapter 1. Without duplicating the discussion there, we can observe that a *prima facie* commitment of any effort to understand and explain some aspect of social life is to take that aspect, in all its particularity, seriously or to offer some argument as to why some of its particulars can be ignored. Cane, for one, seems sure that agency accounts offer no such argument.[44]

Another reason for thinking a two-dimensional account of wrongfulness indispensable arises from quite different considerations. These are the considerations that inform accounts of the normative foundations of private law examined in Chapters 8–10. Insofar as such accounts attempt to elucidate the normative basis of the defendant's private law duty to

[43] Ibid, pp. 182 and 184. Further, '[w]e cannot fully understand the grounds and bounds of . . . legal responsibility without reference to the full range of interests protected by . . . legal liability concepts' (p. 184).

[44] Determining for sure whether or not they do so demands consideration of particular agency accounts, a task eschewed here.

correct or repair what she has done, then they are committed to showing how and why the defendant's conduct is wrong. The very idea of a duty to *correct* or *repair* the outcome or consequence of conduct is pregnant with the idea that the conduct was in some sense *wrong*: why else would it need to be repaired or otherwise put right? And conduct is surely only rarely wrong in the abstract, by which is meant wrong without having adversely affected another's interests in anyway. More usual, of course, is that conduct is wrong (in part) precisely because it adversely affects the interests of another. Furthermore, it is no great exaggeration to claim that this kind of judgment is the norm in both legal and non-legal thinking about wrongs and wrongfulness. If a judgment about the wrongness of some segment of conduct almost always requires an assessment of the impact of that conduct upon someone's interests, then that is something both conceptual-cum-explanatory and normative accounts of private law must accommodate. There certainly seems to be no immediate and compelling reason to think that this general way of determining wrongfulness is inappropriate for accounts of the normative foundations of private law.

The second issue, which raises the question of the way in which private law's catalogue of wrongs relates to respectable moral-cum-political accounts of wrongs, is complex. Not only does this raise the related issue of whether or not normative questions can indeed be kept separate from intelligibility questions, it also highlights the matter of what might be meant by 'morality' here. Both issues are tackled in the first three subsections of the following section. Furthermore, in the course of charting the relation between intelligibility questions and normative questions, and between private law wrongs and moral-cum-political wrongs,[45] a problem that besets efforts to integrate private law wrongs with normatively respectable accounts of wrongs is noted. The argument is that this, the problem of bluntness, is genuine only when a prior albeit common mistake is made. When that mistake is avoided, the bluntness problem is not a problem at all: it serves, rather, to highlight an obvious constraint or limitation upon normatively respectable accounts of wrongfulness. The subsection on p. 236 examines an interesting effort to show both overlaps and disjunctions between a specific kind of legal wrongdoing and its moral analogue. This effort also attempts, commendably, to accommodate

[45] No effort is made in this chapter to distinguish moral from political considerations, wrongs, rights or obligations (hence the frequent use in what follows of the term 'moral-cum-political'). This slackness is in part explicable, but not excusable, in light of the fairly indiscriminate usage in the literature with which the chapter is concerned. Some steps towards discrimination are taken in Chapter 8.

bluntness while illustrating another related difficulty faced by efforts to provide private law's catalogue of wrongs with a normatively respectable basis.

INTELLIGIBILITY QUESTIONS AND NORMATIVE QUESTIONS

AGAINST THE DIVIDE

It was maintained in Chapter 1 that there are at least two distinct types of question which philosophers of private law can address. One type concerns matters of intelligibility: what sense, if any, can be made of the various claims the law makes about responsibility, agency and causation? It was held that questions of this kind are not the same as, and certainly not reducible to, normative questions, that is, questions about the moral, political or other value of some concepts, doctrines or rules of private law. Affirming that these two types of question are not reducible to one another is to deny that they are identical but not, of course, to deny that they can sometimes overlap. The core claim about these two types of question is that they are different and that it is beneficial, because it reduces the risk of confusion, to keep this in mind. This core claim is, furthermore, fully compatible with the additional claim that intelligibility questions lead quite naturally or serve as preface to normative questions.

The discussion of wrongfulness to this point does not undermine the core claim because the task of clarifying the two aspects of the wrongfulness component is not, of course, in any sense a process of moral or political evaluation. Yet although not normative in those senses, that task is normative in another sense: it attempts to embody standards of good analysis and argument accepted by both jurists and philosophers. On that basis, some arguments were offered about how the two aspects of the wrongfulness component are best understood, but this claim has no obvious moral and political implications. At least, it has no such implications if giving an account of the wrongfulness component that purports to make the 'best sense' of that component does not entail 'best moral and political sense'. The movement (some would say elision) from the former claim to the latter is easy if Ronald Dworkin's view, that jurisprudential and related disputes are matters of 'constructive interpretation', is accepted.[46] Dworkin holds that to offer an account of an artistic object, like a poem or a play, or of a concept like law or justice, or to defend a

[46] *Law's Empire*, supra, note 30, chs. 2 and 3.

proposition of law in a hard case, is to do two things. It is, first, to give an argument about that object, concept or proposition that fits the way in which it is usually understood in its normal context; and second, it is to portray said object, concept or proposition in its best light. Moreover, when the concept in question is 'law' or the contested proposition is a proposition of law, then giving an account of it in its best possible light is a matter of showing it in its best moral or political light.[47]

So, is the process of making private law's core concepts intelligible also the process of portraying those concepts in the best possible moral and political light? If this were so, then the distinction between intelligibility and normative questions would seem bound to collapse. It is not obvious, however, that we should be tempted along with Dworkin to take the interpretative turn. This is principally because there is no compelling reason why we should accept, as Dworkin does, that disputes about the contours of some concepts, or the validity of some propositions must be either interpretative (and thus a matter of constructive interpretation) or semantic (in which case they are often akin to empty or pointless disputes about the meaning of words).[48] Some have sought to draw and neutralize Dworkin's semantic sting by suggesting that, for example, Herbert Hart's *The Concept of Law* does not suffer from it.[49] These seemingly parochial jurisprudential disputes might have a deeper resonance, especially if efforts to undermine or resist the semantic sting serve to create conceptual space between the two options Dworkin lays down. The space between constructive interpretation and semantic disputes could well be occupied by intelligibility and similar questions, which raise issues that are neither purely semantic nor clearly interpretative.[50] Of course, merely highlighting this possibility does nothing to show that it could be realized: much work is necessary for that to be demonstrated.

Such a demonstration may not ultimately be necessary. For even if it were established that Dworkin's interpretative turn was the only plausible option, it is still not absolutely certain that this path leads to the collapse of the distinction between intelligibility questions and normative questions. The reason is that Dworkin himself, in distinguishing between

[47] Ibid, ch. 2 at pp. 52–53 and pp. 254–258.

[48] Ibid, pp. 31–46.

[49] See T. Endicott, 'Herbert Hart and the Semantic Sting', ch. 2 of J. Coleman (ed.), *Hart's Postscript* (Oxford: Clarendon Press, 2001) and J. Coleman, *The Practice of Principle* (Oxford: Clarendon Press, 2001), pp. 155–159. Contrast N. Stavropoulos, 'Hart's Semantics', ch. 3 of *Hart's Postscript*, ibid.

[50] Coleman, *Practice*, ibid, Lecture One, sketches an approach that is surely a plausible (but not the only) candidate to occupy this space.

dimensions of fit and dimensions of justification in constructive interpretation, thereby invokes a somewhat similar distinction. That is, he assumes at some points that questions of fit are neither the same as nor reducible to questions of justification. In the juristic context the former are questions about the 'brute facts of legal history',[51] whereas the latter are about which interpretation shows the law 'in a better light from the standpoint of political morality'.[52] Since Dworkin regards issues of justification as different from issues of fit, he therefore leaves space in which an argument by analogy can be made. The pertinent analogy, of course, is between questions of intelligibility and issues of fit. If the latter are clearly distinguishable from issues of justification, why can not intelligibility questions (their nearest analogue) be clearly distinguished from normative questions?

If constructive interpretation is not the only plausible intellectual path open to us, then we lack a reason why intelligibility questions and normative questions should *generally* be regarded as indistinguishable. What must therefore be shown is that these questions are indistinguishable in particular cases and much will depend on the nature of the particular case. The notion of 'essential contestability' might serve to show that in some instances intelligibility and normative questions cannot be kept distinct. W. B. Gallie was one of the first to develop the idea that some of our concepts are essentially contestable, a hallmark being that they 'involve endless disputes about their proper uses on the part of their users'.[53] In part, such disputation was, for Gallie, a consequence of those concepts having open-ended, factual and evaluative criteria for their application.[54] Overall, Gallie thought essentially contested concepts displayed five features which he sought to illuminate first by reference to an imaginary example and then by examining five 'live' disputes about the nature of a religion, of art, of science, of democracy and of social justice.

Gallie's notion of essential contestability has proved very attractive but neither the idea itself nor the vast secondary literature to which it gave rise is evaluated here.[55] It is sufficient to note that much must be done in

[51] Supra, note 30, p. 255. [52] Supra, note 30, p. 256.

[53] W. B. Gallie, *Philosophy and the Historical Understanding* (London: Chatto and Windus, 1964), p. 158.

[54] Gallie actually speaks of essentially contested concepts being 'appraisive' rather than evaluative (ibid, p. 161), but the terms are surely very close in meaning.

[55] For two of the many discussions, see A. Mason, *Explaining Political Disagreement* (Cambridge: Cambridge University Press, 1993), chs. 1 and 2 and, for a ham-fisted effort at application, see W. Lucy, 'Rights, Values and Controversy' (1992) V *Canadian Journal of Law and Jurisprudence* 195–213.

order to show that a particular concept is essentially contested – simply invoking the idea not enough. With regard to the core concepts of private law, it needs therefore be shown that they manifest the five features of essential contestability and, of course, that they give rise to endless disputes about their proper use. Neither step seems particularly easy to establish. While there is undoubtedly some intermittent controversy in private law about aspects or the application of some core concepts, it is not apparently or even actually (!) endless. These disputes lack the longevity, passion or complexity of disputes about, for example, the nature of social justice or democracy. It is also far from clear that *all* the core concepts of private law display the five features of essential contestability. While they are certainly reasonably complex, undoubtedly play vital roles in a process of attribution and appraisal and are used – because the context is litigation – aggressively and defensively, they lack the remaining two features.[56] Thus the core concepts do not appear to refer to anything that could accurately be characterized as an 'accredited achievement' and nor do they embody the openness such achievements display.[57] This is especially so in light of the fact that the notion of agency basic responsibility embodies is so minimal. While some accounts of agency are undoubtedly aspirational, containing in part a conception of what it is to live a good life, the notion of agency in basic responsibility does little more than allow us to distinguish human agents from non-human agents.[58] Basic responsibility cannot therefore be regarded as characterizing an accredited achievement. Since these reservations weigh against the claim that the core concepts of private law are essentially contestable, the presumption henceforth is that they are not. This presumption is the basis of an admittedly tentative claim which informs all that follows, namely, that the distinction between intelligibility questions and normative questions remains robust.

It is time to examine some normative questions that can and should be raised of the wrongfulness component. Two closely related normative questions are: how well, if at all, does the catalogue of interests protected by private law map onto a morally and politically respectable map of protected interests? And: what, if anything, makes private law wrongs wrong over and beyond the fact that they are contrary to the law? The significance of these questions lies in the fact that an overlap between

[56] See supra, note 53, pp. 158–163. [57] Supra, note 53, p. 161.

[58] For a fine general discussion of agency see C. Taylor, *Human Agency and Language: Philosophical Papers 1* (Cambridge: Cambridge University Press, 1985), chs. 1 and 4.

legal wrongs and moral-cum-political wrongs generates additional reason to value the law. For if private law maps onto a morally and politically significant map of protected interests, so that private law wrongs are also moral-cum-political wrongs, then the reasons we have for maintaining the institution and practices of private law are clearly not just 'bare' legal reasons. Such bare legal reasons are joined by whatever reasons there are against the forms of moral-cum-political wrongdoing that private law protects us from and aims to discourage. This is not say that the 'bare' claim – that what makes private law wrongs wrong is that they are contrary to the law – is either uninteresting or trivial. It is to observe only that the weight of the bare claim can be supplemented.

PRIVATE LAW AND POSITIVE MORALITY

What reasons are there to think there is a significant overlap between private law wrongs and a respectable catalogue of moral-cum-political wrongs? Moreover, are there reasons that weigh against such an overlap? The problem here is that there are ostensibly good reasons pulling in both directions. One reason for thinking that there is a significant overlap between private law wrongs and moral-cum-political wrongs is obvious. It is that there is, as a general matter, a broad overlap between most legal systems' general catalogue of wrongs, among which private law wrongs are included, and the wrongs and interests recognized by the positive morality of most societies. By positive morality we mean 'the morality actually accepted and shared by a given social group'.[59] It seems that the overlap between law and positive morality was even more marked in the common law than in the civilian legal systems, for the simple reason that custom apparently played a more pronounced role in the former. Thus at one point in the common law's development it was commonplace for leading judges and jurists to emphasize the proximity between the law's standards of conduct and reasoning and those of the community (principally its men folk) of which it was part.[60] Moreover, it seems that there was no clear demarcation for some of these jurists between the common law and the customary practices and standards of the community. Although the overlap between the content of the common law and customary community standards is less pronounced now, it is still

[59] H. L. A. Hart, *Law, Liberty and Morality* (Oxford: Clarendon Press, 1963), p. 20.

[60] See G. Postema, *Bentham and the Common Law Tradition* (Oxford: Clarendon Press, 1986), ch. 1 for a fine conspectus of such views. Whether or not such claims were routine or even ever made in the early years of the common law's development is unclear: see P. Brand, *The Making of the Common Law* (London: Hambleton Press, 1992), ch. 4.

unlikely that the law's content and principles stray too far from positive morality and common sense. Furthermore, the legal standards of a particular community should be close, in both content and stringency, to that community's non-legal standards if the law is (i) to be in some sense 'of' that community; and (ii) if it is to be broadly intelligible to the community's members.

The overlap between the content of a particular community's law and its positive morality may not take us far toward illuminating the relation between private law wrongs and a respectable catalogue of moral-cum-political wrongs. This is because the overlap envisaged probably exists only at a very general level. As a matter of positive morality it is surely true that in our society we regard failure to keep promises as in most instances a bad thing; it also true that breach of contract is a private law wrong in our legal system. Similarly, as a matter of positive morality, we generally think that care should be taken to ensure that our conduct does not accidentally harm others and – lo and behold! – there is a wrong of negligent breach of duty of care in our private law. But at the level of detail – is it wrong to ask for extra payment to do that which one is already contractually bound to do? – it is unlikely there will be much overlap.

There are two possible reasons for this, only one of which is compelling. The first holds that because the questions private law has to tackle are so specific, then neither positive morality nor common sense can provide much or even any guidance in answering them. Positive morality is a matter of general principles and rules of thumb: it is rarely necessary for it to provide an answer to every question raised about its content or the way in which it should be applied. Private law, by contrast, must answer the questions litigants put before judges and these are rarely either broad or vague. They are detailed and precise: think, for example, of the questions raised in *Ruxley* or *Henderson*.[61] Even if principles of positive morality reached as far as questions such as these (which is by no means certain), those principles are most likely too broad and too unrefined to yield answers. They are 'blunt' as between the options on offer in particular private law disputes.[62]

[61] See note 3 and note 24.

[62] A version of this idea was first expressed by N. E. Simmonds in 'Bluntness and Bricolage', ch. 1 of H. Gross and R. Harrison (eds.), *Jurisprudence: Cambridge Essays* (Oxford: Clarendon Press, 1992). For Simmonds bluntness was solely a feature of legal doctrine ('rules and doctrines are blunt when, and to the extent that, they do not precisely embody any moral principle': p. 12). I claim it is also a feature of morality insofar as it does not precisely determine specific legal questions.

There is another, perhaps deeper dimension to the idea of bluntness. The sheer contingency that the principles of positive morality lack the specificity and refinement necessary to generate answers to many private law problems may illustrate a broader concern. This can be articulated in the notion that the principles of positive morality are not necessarily all-purpose tools, with unlimited range and application. The first dimension of bluntness holds, in effect, that moral principles lack a cutting edge that can be used to resolve specific legal problems; this broader dimension, by contrast, claims that there is no reason to think these moral principles can and should work in all domains. This is particularly so if the relationship between the normative domains of law and morality is not one of identity. If they are different, then principles and considerations powerful in one are not necessarily powerful in the other. A more specific manifestation of this thought is that some conduct being a moral wrong does not, without more, show that it is or should be a legal wrong. Many moral wrongs – lying, for example, or failure to be a good, loving parent – are not *ipso facto* legal wrongs and we usually assume that this is perfectly proper. But this assumption clearly rests upon a conception of the way in which the normative domains of law and morality ought to be related and this raises a key question of political morality. Setting aside that large issue, we need note a more mundane point about this second dimension of bluntness: it can either derive from or inform the first dimension. There is no necessary connection between the two; the first can be accepted without the second and vice versa.

The second reason why an overlap is unlikely, at the level of detail, between the catalogues of wrongs provided by positive morality and private law highlights a particular possibility. It is this: might it be possible for many or some private law wrongs to be wrongs in a sense quite different from that in play in positive morality? Wrong in the latter context means, obviously, 'morally wrong'. In the private law context, by contrast, wrong need not always mean 'morally wrong'. This is because some private law wrongs may be wrong only in a 'conventional' sense. That is to say, some social and legal rules are only necessary in the sense that they are responses to the need for a rule of some kind or another, there being no obviously single 'right' rule in that situation.[63] Standard examples are, of course, rules used for weights and measures and rules of the road. In both instances it is desirable to have an agreed rule: everyone benefits, in terms of convenience, efficiency, transparency and safety from

[63] See Chapter 8, fn 53 for sources.

there being a single rule about which side of the street vehicles travelling in each direction use, or from there being a standard measure of a 'litre'. Driving the wrong way down a street, without having an accident, or selling short measures of petrol, no one being physically harmed as result, are in one sense only wrong because contrary to the rule in question. In such cases it is hard to find any deeper, more significant moral-cum-political wrong than that the conduct is against a well-founded rule. In cases of promise breaking, or failing to take due care of the interests of others, however, such a deeper moral-cum-political wrong is just what we think the private law wrongs of breach of contract and of duty of care mark. In these instances we may in fact go further and claim that there is a wrong here whether or not incorporated in the law. But if this is correct – and if the claim can be extended to include the additional claim that there are few or no examples of private law wrongs that are obviously 'merely conventional' wrongs – then we are in danger of undermining this second reason. A glance at any private law textbook confirms the view that most private law wrongs are also *prima facie* moral wrongs, with the possible exceptions of some instances of breach of contract and some of the economic torts. Of course, were a great number of private law wrongs merely 'conventional' wrongs, then the smaller would be the overlap between the categories of 'private law wrong' and 'wrong in positive morality'.

These two reasons actually refine rather than refute the claim that there is an overlap between private law's catalogue of wrongs and the wrongs marked in positive morality. They show that the overlap is unlikely to be complete and exists at the level of broad categories and principles rather than at the level of detail. It might be the case that any overlap between private law's catalogue of wrongs and the wrongs generated by critical moralities is of the same degree, although much will depend upon the critical morality in question.

PRIVATE LAW AND CRITICAL MORALITY

A critical morality is a body of 'general moral principles used in the criticism of actual social institutions including positive morality'.[64] Moral and political philosophers are the most productive peddlers of critical moralities in the academy, although they are almost certainly outdone in the wider world by theists, visionaries and 'seers' of every stripe. The

[64] Supra, note 59, p. 20.

principal task that most philosophical moralists undertake is that of interrogating, refining and systematizing principles of positive morality.

Interrogating positive morality is simply the task of subjecting it to critical evaluation, both in terms of its substance and its structure. Modest philosophical moralists rarely think that positive morality is completely unacceptable, either in terms of the judgments it warrants or in terms of the coherence of its principles. The process of refinement is, for modest philosophical moralists, often a matter of reconciling tensions between various judgments and principles of positive morality, while the task of systematization can be twofold. One dimension of the task is that of developing new, more consistent substantive principles for positive morality or of developing ranking or conflict management principles, so that tensions within positive morality can be overcome. Another dimension, that does not often touch the substantive judgments of positive morality, is the effort to provide positive and critical morality with a rationally defensible basis, so that the status of moral propositions in our intellectual landscape is clear, their weight and basis, when compared with non-moral propositions, transparent.

Ambitious philosophical moralists are less quiescent in their view of positive morality and thus more radical in their prescriptions as to how it might be improved. The least quiescent view of positive morality is one that rejects it wholesale and is followed by the most radical prescription: complete replacement. While there are more or less quiescent reactions to positive morality and more or less radical responses to its alleged failings among ambitious philosophical moralists, all share the same refrain. It is that positive morality stands in need of considerable improvement and that the philosophical moralist's task is to ameliorate its baleful condition.

The degree of overlap between private law's catalogue of wrongs and the list of wrongs offered by any particular critical morality depends upon the attitude of the critical morality in question toward positive morality. A modest critical morality will likely preserve the overlap that exists between private law and positive morality, while the most ambitious critical moralities will sever it as a result of their inclination to reject positive morality *tout court*.[65] While it is not inconceivable to imagine critical moralities constructing a catalogue of wrongs independent of, and supposedly with a radically different content to, those embodied in both

[65] Friedrich Nietzsche is often assumed to be the Western World's most radical philosophical moralist and he certainly had little time for conventional morality. A nuanced assessment of Nietzsche's moral thought and its implications is provided in S. May, *Nietzsche's Ethics and his War on 'Morality'* (Oxford: Clarendon Press, 1999), part I.

private law and positive morality, that task will be neither brief nor easy. Furthermore, there is no guarantee that the new moral code espoused by an ambitious critical morality will be any more determinate, or any less blunt, than positive morality is in the face of the questions raised in private law cases. This will almost certainly be so if the reformatory impact of the new critical morality does not extend to private law. Ambitious critical moralities are not alone in this, for modest critical moralities may fail to extend this far.

There is undoubtedly overlap between the law's catalogue of wrongs and that embedded in positive morality, and a scale of declining overlap that runs from modest critical moralities at one end, where the degree of overlap is greatest, to ambitious critical moralities at the other, where it is least. Yet in the midst of this, bluntness in both its dimensions is ubiquitous. This problem affects both positive and critical moralities, its essence being (i) that such moralities are insufficiently detailed and refined to generate answers to many private law problems; and (ii) that that's a good thing, too, since there is no reason to assume moral considerations dominate all domains. This problem is examined again in the following subsection. It examines what one particular modest critical morality says about an instance of moral and legal wrongdoing, namely, promise and contract breaking. The discussion takes a modest critical morality as its example on the supposition that the account of wrongdoing such moralities offer are much closer to the catalogues embodied in both private law and positive morality. The task of establishing whether a particular private law wrong is also a moral-cum-political wrong is thereby made a little easier. Furthermore, the example is used in order to show that philosophers and jurists can live with the problem of bluntness, that it is not truly a problem. The true problem is, rather, the failure to appreciate the possibility of bluntness, manifest in the mistaken assumption that moral principles can generate answers to every question, or that such considerations are by far the most important in all realms of deliberation and conduct. As we will see, progress can still be made on the task of delineating the ways in which legal wrongs are also moral-cum-political wrongs, without ignoring the possibility of bluntness.

WRONGDOING, PROMISE AND CONTRACT: A CASE STUDY

The bluntness 'problem' is not an *a priori* truth. Whether or not it arises must be established on a case by case basis, in relation to each and every critical morality that offers a catalogue of wrongs intended to inform that found in private law. That task is not tackled here: it is the work of another book, if not a lifetime. What is attempted instead is, first, a demonstration of the way in which a particularly interesting, philosophically respectable critical morality – that offered by Thomas Scanlon in his book *What We Owe to Each Other* and exemplified in his essay 'Promises and Contracts' – accommodates bluntness and illustrates another related problem.[66] Second, a general evaluation of Scanlon's argument about the morality of promise- and contract-breaking is also undertaken. Both tasks are clearly warranted given the importance and quality of Scanlon's work, which is marked by an admirable philosophical scrupulousness. His work eschews overstatement, notes almost all the problems and limitations faced by the arguments it commends and is, furthermore, a genuinely philosophical engagement with the issue of the morality of promising and contracting. As such, it is in one respect far from unique, since many of the philosophical 'greats' have tackled the question of the normative status of promises and promise-keeping.[67] In another respect, however, it merits a triple claim to distinctiveness. First, Scanlon, unlike many philosophers before him, explicitly engages with the law and, second, unlike some of the jurists who have tackled this issue before, he leaves the water clearer than when he started.[68] Finally, 'Promises and Contracts' is an exemplary instance of what can be called a unitary and external account of contract law. 'Unitary' because it aims to derive the substance and legitimacy of contract law from a general account of the morality of promising-keeping; 'external' because, obviously, the primary conditions for the intelligibility and legitimacy of contract law are found outside contract law, in the domain of morality.

Scanlon has two main goals in 'Promises and Contracts'. First, he hopes to provide an alternative to an influential account of the morality of promise-keeping which founds promissory obligation upon conventions

[66] Cambridge, Mass.: Harvard University Press, 1998 and ch. 3 of P. Benson (ed.), *The Theory of Contract Law: New Essays* (Cambridge: Cambridge University Press, 2001). The discussion of Scanlon's essay in the pages that follow draws from my review essay 'Philosophy and Contract Law' (2004) 54 *University of Toronto Law Journal* 75–108, pp. 84–89.

[67] Two classic treatments are D. Hume, *A Treatise of Human Nature* (Oxford: Clarendon Press, 2nd edn, 1978), Book III, part II, sc. V; and I. Kant, *Groundwork of The Metaphysics of Morals* paras 402–403 and 422–440 in I. Kant, *Practical Philosophy*, translated and edited by M. J. Gregor (Cambridge: Cambridge University Press, 1996).

[68] For an account that muddies the waters, see P. Atiyah, *Promises, Morals, and the Law* (Oxford: Clarendon Press, 1981) and his *Essays on Contract* (Oxford: Clarendon Press, 1986), ch. 2. A clearer but very different account is offered in C. Fried, *Contract as Promise* (Cambridge, Mass.: Harvard University Press, 1981). A helpful discussion is D. Kimel, *From Promise to Contract* (Oxford: Hart Publishing, 2003), ch. 1.

or practices of agreement-making. Scanlon's account of the morality of promising is one in which such conventions or 'practices play no essential role' (p. 87).[69] This argument recapitulates some of Scanlon's earlier work.[70] Scanlon's second goal is twofold: to warn us that even a compelling account of the morality of promising should not be assumed to provide an argument for the legal enforcement of promises through contract law; and to articulate principles upon which the legal enforcement of some promises could be based. His principal targets are therefore: (i) accounts of promissory obligation that may be labelled 'Humean';[71] (ii) theories of the basis of contract law which hastily extrapolate from an allegedly coherent and defensible account of the morality of promising to the substance and legitimacy of contract law; and (iii) arguments denying that contractual remedies have a principled basis. Do not assume that Scanlon's attack on the second target undermines his ambition to provide a unitary and external account of contract law. He simply warns against hasty extrapolation; he does not claim that the extrapolation is always inappropriate (pp. 99–100).

Scanlon's account of the wrongness of promise-breaking begins by locating the wrong involved in making a lying promise in a general prohibition upon manipulative conduct. The underlying principle ('Principle *M*') does not depend for its plausibility upon any convention or practice of agreement-making (p. 90). Rather, its power is derived entirely from the method employed by Scanlon in his earliest work. That is, the principle's plausibility arises from the fact no person could reasonably reject it, being motivated 'to find principles for the general regulation of behavior that others, similarly motivated, also could not reasonably reject' (p. 89). Considerations similar to those that reasonable, properly motivated people take to support Principle *M* also support Principle *D*, a requirement that one take due care not to lead others to reasonably form false expectations about what one will do, and Principle *L*, a requirement to take reasonable steps to prevent loss occasioned by breach of Principle *D*. Reasonable steps, under Principle *L*, include actually doing what others have assumed one will do, warning them that one will not be acting

[69] Page references in parentheses in the text are to 'Promises and Contracts', ch. 3 of Benson, supra, note 66.

[70] See 'Promises and Practices' (1990) 19 *Philosophy and Public Affairs* 199–226 and *What We Owe to Each Other*, supra, note 66, ch. 7.

[71] By this I mean to refer primarily to the account in Hume, supra, note 67 and one or two of its recent defenders such as J. Deigh, 'Promises under Fire' (2002) 112 *Ethics* 483–506. I therefore hope the appellation is nowhere near as slippery as its contemporary moral-philosophical relative, 'Kantian'.

in the way they have assumed, or compensating them if they have suffered losses as a result of relying upon one's words or conduct. So far, perhaps, so good. But where do (non-lying) promises fit in to this framework?

Promises, for Scanlon, are primarily undertakings to do what is promised, not simply undertakings to either do what is promised or compensate the promisee (p. 92). Promises function to give assurance that one will do as one says and there are reasons for wishing for such assurance, and for wanting to give it, that go beyond the requirements in Principles *M*, *D* and *L* (pp. 94–95). These reasons lead Scanlon to the conclusion that properly motivated, reasonable people have good grounds for endorsing Principle *F*. This holds that one who acts so as to create an expectation in another that they will act in a specific way unless that other allows them not to, knowing the other wants and then knowingly giving assurance that they will so act, must act in the way indicated. Principle *F* 'goes beyond Principle *L* in requiring performance rather than compensation or warning' (p. 96). Furthermore, Principle *F*, just like Principles *M*, *D* and *L*, does not depend for its validity upon the existence of a background practice or conventions of promise-making and keeping: '[t]he moral force of undertakings of the kind described by Principle *F* depend only on the expectations, intentions and knowledge of the parties involved, and these can be created *ad hoc*, without the help of standing background expectations of the kind that would constitute an institution' (p. 98).

Almost all the difficulties for this part of Scanlon's argument concern the distance he manages to put between convention-based, Humean accounts of promise-keeping and his own. It must be noted that Scanlon does not dismiss background conventions and practices entirely, holding that their existence provides an opportunity in which the wrongs identified by Principles *M*, *D*, *L* and *F* can be brought about. His point is that reference to such conventions and practices is not essential to identify the wrong in question. Yet there is a risk, which can be noted but not explored here, that conventions and practices of promising might well intrude into Scanlon's argument despite his best endeavours. The guise under which they might enter is that of reasonableness and similar standards which play a role in all of the principles Scanlon articulates. In Principle *M*, the loss has to be 'reasonably' foreseeable and in Principle *F* reference is made to 'objectionable constraint', 'special justification' and, presumably, the expectations agents entertain must be reasonable. Now, one very tempting way in which to fill out these notions of what is reasonable, special or objectionable is by reference to the conventions and practices in which they are already at work: our conventions and practices of agreement- and promise-making. Of course, to say this is a *tempting* strategy is not to say it is *essential*; what is surely essential, though, is that notions such as reasonableness are inter-subjective, necessarily based on shared standards and expectations. And this, perhaps, is the territory in which conventions and practices are found.

Focusing specifically on Principle *F* and the relation between promises and the notion of assurance raises an additional question of Scanlon's account. For Scanlon, promises are a means of creating assurances and it is assurance that provides the basis of the obligation.[72] Why should I do as I promised? Because, by promising, I knowingly provided an assurance to the promisee that I would act in a certain way, knowing the promisee wanted such an assurance, and knowing also that the promisee will rely and formulate expectations on the basis of my assurance. If I now fail to act in accordance with my assurance (promise), I deny all the reasons which, as a reasonable and properly motivated person, I accept support Principle *F*. On something like a Humean account, by contrast, promises also provide assurance, but they do so only by virtue of being in accord with some set of background conventions or practices. The existence of such conventions or practices provide the ground upon which promises are recognised as a means of creating obligations, the basis of the obligation to act in accordance with one's promise being, in part, those very conventions. Once a promisor has used these signs, and thus shown himself willing to undertake an obligation, the promisee can be assured of the promisor's seriousness and *bona fides*. The question, then, is this: since both Scanlon's and the Humean account accommodate all the notions we take to be significant in this domain, but arrange them slightly differently, how are we to choose between them? There is no easy answer to this. There are well-known difficulties with Humean accounts of promising, the primary one being the justificatory gap between the argument establishing the value of the general convention or practice of promising and the claim that it is wrong in specific circumstances C, at time T, for X to break his promise to Y. Yet it also seems that there are instances of promissory conduct that Scanlon's account cannot handle,[73] so the balance of advantage does not obviously favour one account over the other.

This point illustrates a more general issue that faces many efforts to

[72] The point is well put by J. Deigh, supra, p. 503.

[73] Deigh, supra, pp. 504–505.

provide private law with a morally respectable catalogue of wrongs derived from a more general, critical moral or political philosophy. The issue is that just about every general and modest critical morality provides some normative support for private law taken in the broadest terms. If the morality of promising and promise breaking does indeed underpin contract law then, as the discussion has just shown, different critical moralities (in this case Scanlon's and Hume's must be supplemented with, *inter alios*, Kant's) push in the same direction. All offer some reason to think that this aspect of private law is morally or politically significant. Moreover, this pattern may well be replicated across many of the principal substantive doctrines of private law, most general and modest critical moralities providing some normative support to most or many doctrines. This situation is probably best described as one of normative 'over-determination' and it becomes a problem only when jurists and philosophers think that only one critical morality has the wherewithal to provide normative support for private law. This supposes, wrongly, that the process of offering critical moralities as normative props for private law is a zero sum game in which, if one critical morality succeeds in providing normative support, then others must fail. There is no suggestion that Scanlon falls victim to this mistake, but the mistake does seem to explain some of the zeal that informs many efforts to provide private law with a normative foundation.[74]

Only a slight quibble arises over Scanlon's attempt to achieve his second goal. His argument appears to succeed in providing an account of the circumstances in which promissory obligations can be legally enforced that avoids full-blown legal moralism. Furthermore, he also provides a principled basis for the measures of damages traditionally used in contract law. In this context, legal moralism might espouse at least two related tenets. The first holds that moral requirements are also *prima facie* legal requirements, the second that the moral grounds for acting in accord with one's promises translate directly into the law: where promises ought morally to be honoured, then they should also be legally enforced. Scanlon's initial riposte to the first tenet is that 'the fact that some action is morally required is not, in general, a sufficient justification for legal intervention to force people to do it' (p. 99). This, of course, is Scanlon's version of the second dimension of bluntness and, while he does not give the issue much attention, the underlying thought is clear. His

[74] This theme is explored in my 'Private Law: Between Visionaries and Bricoleurs', ch. 8 of P. Cane and J. Gardner (eds.), *Relating to Responsibility* (Oxford: Hart Publishing, 2001).

appreciation of the second dimension of bluntness does not, however, prevent him from offering some reasons in favour of the legal enforcement of some promises in some circumstances. Legal enforcement is justified, he argues, through the same deliberative method that yielded Principles *M*, *D*, *L* and *F*. Thus, while rejecting the first tenet of legal moralism, Scanlon embraces something like its second tenet. Properly motivated reasonable people will, Scanlon thinks, have no reasonable grounds for rejecting Principles *EL* and *EF*.

EL holds

> that if a person has led another to form expectations in the way *L* describes, and has neither warned this person nor performed as expected, and the person has suffered significant loss as a result of relying upon the performance, then the coercive power of the state may be used to force him or her to compensate the other person for this loss, provided that a law authorizing this is established and applied in a system of law that is tolerably fair and efficient. (p. 100)

Principle *EF* is by far the most complex Scanlon develops and, since it does lend itself to abbreviation, is stated here almost in full. It holds that

> [i]t is permissible legally to enforce remedies for breach of contract that go beyond compensation for reliance losses, provided these remedies are not excessive and [satisfy these] . . . conditions . . .: (1) A, the party against whom the remedy is enforced, has, in the absence of objectionable constraint and with adequate understanding (or the ability to acquire such understanding) of his . . . situation, intentionally led B to expect that A would do X unless B consented to A's not doing so; (2) A had reason to believe that B wanted to be assured of this; (3) A acted with the aim of providing this assurance, by indicating to B that he . . . was undertaking a legal obligation to do X; (4) B indicated that . . . she understood A to have undertaken such an obligation; (5) A and B knew, or could easily determine, what kind of remedy B would be legally entitled to if A breached this obligation; and (6) A failed to do X without being released from this obligation by B, and without special justification for doing so. (p. 105)

While there is some truth in the view that principles *EL* and *EF* are just legal analogues of the moral principles *L* and *F*, there is also much that is misleading. The primary difference, of course, is that the factors in play in *EL* and *EF* themselves, and also the considerations that animate the deliberative process that generates them, are in no sense identical to those informing and supporting principles *L* and *F*. It therefore seems obvious that Scanlon and the notional reasonable people deliberating on this issue take seriously the considerations that underpin the second dimension of bluntness. There is a question mark, however, over how well Scanlon's effort to accommodate bluntness fits with the substance of some of his other arguments or commitments.

Scanlon's argument in favour of *EL* and *EF* seemingly avoids legal moralism's first tenet because it does not entail 'a general conclusion about the legal enforcement of morality' (p. 102). It takes no position, for example, on the question of whether victimless moral wrongs should be legally prohibited (ibid). He is right about this, but the point is not terribly interesting. The more pressing question concerns the difference between legal moralism's position on the enforcement of promises (the second tenet) and Scanlon's position. And, of course, being able to sustain this distinction is the only way in which Scanlon will be able successfully to accommodate bluntness. The difference might be located in the fact that the kinds of consideration that weigh with agents when considering whether Principles *EL* and *EF* are reasonably rejectable include what legal moralists would regard as impermissible factors. Rather than simply affirming that the moral requirement about promise-keeping should be promptly embodied in the law, Scanlon allows considerations about the compliance and error costs of legal enforcement (p. 101; p. 108) to feature in the decision about the permissibility of enforcement. Now, Scanlon might think that legal moralists should disregard such considerations but it is not clear why: there is no obvious reason why legal moralists should be blind to questions about the efficacy and enforcement of the law. That being so, a legal moralist might find no difficulty in calling for the law to embody Principle *EL* and *EF* and on exactly the same grounds as do Scanlon's properly motivated, reasonable people. The point here is two-fold: (i) that the second tenet of legal moralism, or something very close to it, is perhaps the only viable position for one offering a unitary and external account of contract law; and (ii) that Scanlon cannot therefore accommodate the second dimension of bluntness after all.

The considerations that lead to the adoption of Principles *EL* and *EF* also provide a starting point for rebutting arguments, the most famous of which belongs to Lon Fuller and William Perdue, aiming to undermine the rationale of the expectation measure in contract damages.[75] The factors Scanlon rightly thinks are in play in deliberations about the standing of *EL* and *EF* identify different but significant interests and concerns.

[75] 'The Reliance Interest in Contract Damages: I' (1936) 46 *Yale LJ* 52–96; and 'The Reliance Interest in Contract Damages: II', ibid, at 373–420. For an effort to undermine this essay's almost canonical status, see R. Crasswell, 'Against Fuller and Perdue' (2000) 67 *University of Chicago LR* 99–161.

The losses covered by *EF*, which supports the expectation measure, are clearly no less real and of no less concern than the reliance losses covered by *EL*. The argument to the contrary attains much of its plausibility by relying on an initially intuitive but imprecise assumption about property.[76] By contrast, the considerations Scanlon invokes to support *EF* do not depend on any such assumption and are, overall, far weightier than previously adduced arguments denying the propriety of the expectation measure.

Scanlon's final move in 'Promises and Contracts' is a defence of a particular conception of the moral significance of choice. The notion of voluntariness is vital to Scanlon since it apparently underpins a number of the principles he develops and, in particular, principles *F* and *EF*. He does not directly offer an account of voluntariness though,[77] opting instead to delineate the value of choice. The basic idea here is 'the value for an agent of having what happens (including what obligations are incurred) depend on how he or she responds when presented with a set of alternatives under certain conditions' (p. 112). How does this throw light on the notion of voluntariness? Only obliquely for, as Scanlon points out, a choice is voluntary under, for example, principles *F* and *EF* 'just in case the circumstances under which it was made are ones such that no one could reasonably reject a principle that took choices made under those conditions to create binding (or enforceable) obligations' (p. 114). Thus voluntariness, for Scanlon's purposes, is entirely a product of the argument for the principles in question and not, therefore, an independent notion. This is an intriguing and original suggestion which, if successfully carried out, would replace the standard but problematic procedure here. That involves developing a general conception of voluntariness that embodies as parsimonious a range of normative commitments as possible and which is then put to work in a number of different contexts. The problem is that the more contexts differ the greater the pressure on the generality of the conception of voluntariness. Scanlon's approach allows us to escape this difficulty, which is certainly a point in its favour. Whether it creates other difficulties in its stead cannot be determined here.

[76] Thoroughly examined by P. Benson in ch. 4 of Benson, supra, note 66.

[77] He does and he doesn't: readers of p. 112 might expect him to ('[t]he account . . . I am offering . . . of choice and voluntariness'), but p. 113 clears matters up: '[t]he value of choice is not a conception of voluntariness'.

CONCLUSION

The arguments offered and to some degree defended here can be easily recapped. The first was that wrongfulness in private law has two dimensions or aspects, namely, that constituted by the defendant's conduct and that constituted by the effect that conduct has upon one or more of the claimant's protected interests. It was argued that this way of understanding wrongfulness best reflects the substantive doctrines of private law and, although somewhat abstract, is not obviously objectionable. It was also maintained that there are some overlaps and disjunctions between private law's catalogue of wrongs and those found in both positive morality and modest critical moralities. Two problems that beset efforts to found private law's catalogue of wrongs upon modest critical moralities were also highlighted. There remains one item of unfinished business.

A slightly refined version of the question raised at the beginning of the chapter is this: is the conduct and causation component of legal liability-responsibility more, less, or as important as the wrongfulness component? We are now in a position to offer a clearer account of what the wrongfulness component means in private law and of the ways in which it overlaps with, and may be informed by, considerations of both positive and critical morality. But that clearly does not equip us with an answer to the initial question. Rather, we are now able to pursue an answer to that question, since having a clear idea of what we are looking for (the conduct and causation component, on the one hand, and the wrongfulness component, on the other) makes a meaningful search possible. Furthermore, that search can only be fruitfully conducted beyond the confines of this book, in the cases and texts of private law. Only there will we find the two components at work; only there will we be able to determine for sure which of the two dominates. My hunch, for what it is worth, is that neither does.

Part II

Who Pays and Why?

7

Normative Foundations

The principal chapters in this part of the book address three closely related issues. The issues are not always tackled in the same degree of detail in each chapter, nor are they all given equal prominence in every chapter. Nevertheless, all three are almost always in play. The first issue is raised by the deceptively simple question which constitutes the title of this part: who pays and why? As well as being simple, the question might be thought redundant, since an answer to its first limb has already been provided: the defendant pays. Which is to say: once legal action against the defendant is successful, he is judged the perpetrator of a private law wrong that caused legally recognizable harm to the claimant and, for that reason, he must 'make good' the harm. While undoubtedly tritely uttered and quickly written by private lawyers, a sentence such as this is pregnant with some of the most interesting topics in philosophy of private law. One, which was noted in the first chapter, is private law's bilateral structure. This is the idea that claimant can sue and recover damages only from the party or parties who caused their harm and, correlatively, that the perpetrator of the harm must, if liable, pay only the victim in order to correct the harm done. Another topic is latent in the second part of this deceptively simple question: the trite sentence assumes that, if liable, defendants have an obligation to make good the wrong and/or the harm to which it gives rise. But what is the nature and basis of this obligation? Is it nothing more than a 'bare' legal obligation, binding in the same way and for the same reasons as general legal requirements? Or is the obligation to make recompense in private law supported by additional considerations that flow from, for example, its specific normative nature? It might be argued, for instance, that this obligation derives from a distinctive set of normative considerations, different from those that inform other areas of law, and broader than those from which the general (non-private) law derives its authority over us. In this case, the 'bare' legal obligation to make recompense in private law could be said to derive its power from, and perhaps map onto, a more general moral or political obligation of some kind. If so, then that more general moral or political obligation deserves scrutiny.

This issue of the nature and basis of the putative obligation to make recompense in private law is tackled alongside a second issue that is its elder and much larger sibling: the question about the normative basis of private law in general. This second issue has attracted a number of treatments, just about all of which take the structure and substance of private law more or less for granted.[1] They then attempt to illuminate the moral and political considerations which give that structure and substance normative significance. These considerations allegedly give reason to maintain the substance and structure of private law in something like its present form and would give reason to bring into being a system of private law with similar structural and substantive properties, were it not already part of the social world. The considerations most commonly adduced by jurists to fulfil the role of normative basis of private law form a very limited class: they consist of one or other of the two 'forms' of justice. The two forms are corrective and distributive justice; their general contours are sketched in the second section below (p.256) while some of their details will occupy Chapters 8 and 9. By contrast, Chapter 10 examines what can be called 'mixed' accounts of the normative basis of private law. In these accounts the salient normative considerations can include the two forms of justice as well as other political and moral values.

It might seem that the act of casting particular moral and political values in the role of normative basis of private law is completely unproblematic. These values simply inform or give an account of the overall point of this area of law and social life. But the idea of some notion or other 'informing' or 'providing the point of' some social institution and its constitutive practices is not as obvious and as unproblematic as often assumed. The same is true of yet another, possibly more common usage in this context, namely, that of casting certain moral or political values in the role of 'basis' or 'normative foundation' of private law.[2] The latter image, suggestive but potentially troublesome, has been used already in this book and is adopted in what follows, although only after its potential meanings are elucidated and an alternative to it considered. This is tackled in the first section below (p. 252), while Chapters 8, 9 and 10 consider how some candidates perform in the role of normative foundation.

[1] 'More or less' because any account of the law – doctrinal, philosophical or both – must accommodate a theory (or just the possibility) of doctrinal mistakes.

[2] It comes naturally to, for example, S. Perry in 'On the Relationship between Corrective and Distributive Justice', ch. 12 of J. Horder (ed.), *Oxford Essays in Jurisprudence: Fourth Series* (Oxford: Clarendon Press, 2000), p. 238.

The third issue explored in the chapters that follow is even more specific than the question about the nature and basis of the obligation to correct a private law wrong, or the harm it caused, or both. It can be put bluntly: why money? Which is to ask: why, assuming there is a compelling obligation to put right a private law wrong and the harm it brings about, must it be corrected by monetary compensation? Monetary compensation is, of course, the dominant form of remedy in the areas of private law with which we have been concerned and, while this undeniable feature of the law is deeply entrenched, it seems less obvious that it is or should be a deeply entrenched feature of the normative foundations of private law. Take, as an example, those foundational accounts that invoke the idea of corrective justice. In these accounts corrective justice provides the reservoir of considerations from which the obligation to make good a private law wrong is derived. But why assume that this moral-cum-political idea contains an argument supporting one particular feature of contemporary private law, namely the obligation to make *monetary* recompense, rather than an argument culminating in the conclusion that the perpetrator of a private law wrong must do something about it? Moreover, might it not be the case that for the purposes of corrective justice an apology, or the doing of some other deed designed to make good the wrong or harm – a week of walking your children to school or six months of driving you to work – would be sufficient, even though such alternatives are eschewed by the law?

This issue concerns the specificity of accounts of the normative foundations of private law or, for that matter, any other reasonably complex institution and its constitutive practices. The capacity of accounts of the normative basis of private law to answer specific questions like that about the obligation to make monetary recompense is a significant issue, provided an assumption is made. The assumption, which is surely reasonable, is that this specific question and others like it are not *sui generis*. Of course, this is only an assumption and can, therefore, be rebutted; a rebuttal must be assessed on its merits and within the context of the normative account in which it occurs. But until such a rebuttal is adduced, the capacity of particular accounts of the normative foundations of private law to answer specific questions about structural or doctrinal features of the law remains a live issue. It is also yet another manifestation of a more general difficulty already noted, namely, that of the degree to which 'accounts' or 'explanations' or 'understandings' of the law or other institutions must accommodate or fit the institution. If such accounts must fit each and every significant feature of the institution in question, then corrective justice accounts of the normative foundations of private law are inadequate if they do not provide a justification for the obligation to make monetary recompense. If, however, such accounts need only fit the broad contours of the institution and its constitutive practices, then this need not be considered a significant failing. The choice made on this issue obviously takes us back to an issue raised in Chapter 1: it necessitates some account of what it is to offer an account of the foundations, normative or otherwise, of an institution. It is to that issue that we must now turn. For, before examining the details of the three broadly different accounts of the normative foundations of private law in subsequent chapters, we must briefly consider how such 'foundational' accounts might function and what, exactly, is their content.

FOUNDATIONS: HOW?

What is it to give an account of the foundations, normative or otherwise, of some institution or practice? One way in which the 'foundation' image can be understood is *architecturally*. On this view the normative foundations of private law operate in just the same way as the foundations of a building, serving to underpin and support what arises upon it. While the relation between foundations and superstructure[3] is direct and one-way, the superstructure being entirely dependent upon the foundations for its existence, that existence can take a number of forms. In its most constrained form, almost all the dimensions of the superstructure – be it a building or private law – are determined by its foundations. The length, breadth and weight of the superstructure are thus limited by the length, breadth and depth of the foundation upon which it arises and cannot go beyond them, except perhaps in height. On this view, there is some sense in speaking of the superstructure as little more than a refection of the foundation, where what is meant is that the overall shape of the building or legal edifice is determined by the shape of its structural or normative foundation.

There are, however, at least three other ways in which superstructures can exist in relation to their foundations. In one, the foundation does not completely determine the contours of the superstructure, since superstructures can undoubtedly be imagined and are actually built that exceed

[3] Although it seems more natural to speak of 'structures' rather than 'superstructures' in this context, I eschew the former so as to avoid confusion arising between the discussion here and discussions elsewhere (primarily in Chapter 1) of the bilateral 'structure' of private law.

the confines of their foundations. The superstructure arises upon its foundation but is greater than them, and not only in height: while parts of the superstructure may be entirely based upon the foundation, other parts could exceed the range of the foundation in a variety of overhangs, rather as the branches of a tree exceed the circumference of its trunk. When a superstructure relates to its foundation in this way, it is inappropriate to claim that it is only a reflection of the foundation, for the simple reason that it is both dependent upon yet also exceeds its foundation.[4] If private law related to its normative foundation in this way, some but certainly not all of its content and structure would be determined by its foundation.

A second view holds that a superstructure could to some degree be autonomous of its foundation, in the sense that while it derives some support from its foundation, it also derives support from other sources, such as adjacent structures. Here the influence of the normative foundation of private law upon the content and structure of the law itself would be even more subscribed than on the previous view. A third view holds that the relationship between foundation and superstructure is one of interdependence, the superstructure possibly stabilizing its foundation in the way that a lid could stabilize struts driven into sand. Alone, the latter lack the stability that the former can provide, while the former, obviously, depends on the latter for support.[5] While there is no denying that the superstructure here is dependent on foundation and foundation on superstructure, it cannot be said that one completely determines the other. On this complex view, the normative foundation would determine some of the principal doctrines and features of the law, while the law itself will in some way determine the nature and content of its normative foundation.

The architectural understanding of the 'foundation' image is not the only one available. The image can also be understood in something like an *epistemic* sense. On this understanding, saying that a set of moral or political or other considerations provides the normative foundation of private law is to make two possible claims. One holds that those considerations make sense of the law over and beyond the sense it already has for

[4] There is a clear and intended echo between the account in the text and the idea of the 'relative autonomy' of base and superstructure in Francophone Western Marxism: see L. Althusser: *Essays on Ideology* (London: Verso, 1984), pp. 8–10; *For Marx* (Harmondsworth: Penguin, 1969), part three; and L. Althusser and E. Balibar, *Reading Capital* (London: Verso, 1997), pp. 97–100.

[5] This image belongs to G. A. Cohen. See his *Karl Marx's Theory of History: A Defence* (Oxford: Clarendon, expanded edn, 2001), p. 231.

participants; the other, that those considerations illuminate some sense or meaning immanent within the law but barely or unappreciated by participants. Furthermore, these two claims both have stronger and weaker versions, thus yielding four possibilities. The strength of each claim can differ in relation to the element all have in common, namely, the assertion that private law's normative foundations *make sense of or give meaning* to the law. At its strongest, this assertion might hold *that it is impossible to properly understand private law* without examining it in light of its normative foundation; any picture of private law that does not have recourse to this foundation is simply misleading. Holding that any genuinely adequate understanding of the constitutive practices of private law *must* include an account of its normative foundation may, however, have one problematic implication. It is that we must say of those participants who can successfully move within the practices of private law *without* an account of its normative foundation that they nevertheless have an inadequate understanding of the institution. But would we say of Sachin Tendulkar (a batsman in cricket) or Mark MacGwire (a retired hitter in baseball) that he really must have a normative theory of cricket or baseball before he plays a shot or hits a home run?

The weaker way in which the epistemic understanding may be interpreted has no such apparently problematic implication. This sense holds that attending to the normative foundation of private law *provides a deeper, more fruitful and informative picture of private law* than would otherwise be attained. The structure and substance of private law should, according to one common phrase, 'be read in light of' the normative foundation of the law; alternatively, attending to its normative foundation illuminates how private law 'hangs together in a coherent and mutually supportive structure'.[6] That, of course, is not to make the bold but questionable claim that private law is impossible to fully understand without recourse to its normative foundation. It is to claim only that a better understanding could be achieved by casting our intellectual net wider. The contrast between the stronger and weaker versions of the epistemic understanding might be well captured by an analogy from a different context: suppose we wish to understand Shakespeare's play *King Lear*. The strong version of the epistemic understanding might in this context hold that an adequate account of the play is impossible without knowledge of the political and cultural context in which it was written. The

[6] J. Coleman, *The Practice of Principle* (Oxford: Clarendon Press, 2001), p. 62; hereinafter '*PoP*'.

latter provides the intellectual foundation necessary to understand the play. By contrast, the weak version of the epistemic understanding holds that knowledge of the political and cultural context provides an intellectually deeper account, but that without it the play is nevertheless intelligible. The play can, on this view, be understood in both ways.

It is conceivable that some who offer normative accounts of private law will find any interpretation of the 'foundation' image unacceptable. It might be objected, for example, that all of the ways so far suggested in which that image might be understood convey an overly simplistic view of the relationship between the doctrines and structural principles of private law, on the one hand, and their normative basis, on the other. It could, for example, be maintained that talk of the normative 'foundation' or 'basis' of private law drives too great a wedge between the doctrines and principles of private law and their normative content, as if the latter were in some way independent of the former. This might be a mistake if the normative content of private law is 'internal' to – 'immanent' or 'embodied' within – the law, a thoroughly integrated part of it.[7] On this view, private law's normative content is not best envisaged as a separate albeit load bearing level in a taller structure; it is, rather, already intermixed within the body of the structure itself. The guiding analogy should not therefore be that of a foundation but something akin to the distribution of different colours or types of stone in a building. Imagine a structure in which stones of different types or colours occur throughout the structure. We can easily see the different types and colours and thus meaningfully maintain that they are quite different, without thereby being forced to hold that some are in any sense more important or foundational in relation to others. On this view it could be said of a particular type of stone, for example, that it is immanent in, and an important part of, the structure. Is this inappropriate or mistaken?

It might seem so, when judged against an intuitive or common sense assumption about the nature of justification (of whatever kind) and explanation. In normative justifications, we tend to assume that a justification for X, just like a good explanation of X, must have recourse to something other than X (which we can label 'Y'). But the claim that the normative basis of private law is immanent within private law, and not

[7] E. Weinrib, *The Idea of Private Law* (Cambridge, Mass.: Harvard University Press, 1995) often speaks of the 'internal structure' of the law (see p. 5 for an example). Talk of 'embodiment' and its variations comes easily to J. Coleman: see his *Risks and Wrongs* (New York: Cambridge University Press, 1992), p. 304 and *PoP*, p. xiii, xv and 62 ('explanation by embodiment').

a separable component thereof, seems dubious because it attempts to justify and quite possibly explain X (private law) in terms of X (private law). In legal scholarship suspicion towards such an approach is reinforced by the dominance of what some call 'functionalism', namely, the view '[t]hat one comprehends law through its goals'.[8] The latter are assumed to be distinct from and perhaps completely independent of the law they explain and justify. As such, they are obviously external to, rather than immanent within, the law. As will be seen in Chapter 8, Ernest Weinrib seeks to eradicate the suspicion we often have when faced with justifications and explanations of a non-functionalist type. We must, therefore, avoid portraying his account of the normative content of private law in these terms. Besides elucidating the content of three broadly different accounts of the normative basis of private law, another task is tackled in what follows. It is to determine whether and which of these normative accounts should be regarded as foundational and, if so, in what sense. This issue could well be awkward, since there is no prohibition upon these accounts being foundational in more than one of the senses used above. Furthermore, there is no guarantee that such accounts must be foundational in any one or more of these senses.

FOUNDATIONS: WHAT?

CORRECTIVE JUSTICE

> Corrective justice has usually been thought of as those principles that directly govern private transactions between individuals. . . . By contrast, the concept of distributive justice has been viewed as including those principles that ought to regulate the fair distribution of common burdens and benefits among individuals or groups of individuals.[9]

This crisp and clear statement illustrates the primary problem in attempting to offer a definition of corrective justice: it is almost impossible without invoking the spectre of that with which it competes or to which it is allegedly opposed, namely, distributive justice. The relationship between the two is explored in more depth in the next chapter, although it must be noted here that most jurists entertain only two possibilities: one can be

[8] Weinrib, supra, note 7, p. 3. This kind of functionalism in legal scholarship is not directly related to, and should not be confused with, functionalism and functional explanations in the social sciences. See A. Giddens, *Studies in Social and Political Theory* (London: Hutchinson, 1979), ch. 2 and Cohen, supra, note 5, chs. IX and X.

[9] P. Benson, 'The Basis of Corrective Justice and Its Relation to Distributive Justice' (1991–1992) 77 *Iowa LR* 515–624, p. 515.

dubbed 'the separation thesis', the other the 'the co-existence thesis'. The latter holds that both corrective and distributive justice considerations can legitimately operate in private law, while the former insists that private law is the exclusive domain of corrective justice.[10] The separation thesis regards corrective justice and distributive justice as chalk and cheese, while the co-existence thesis sees them as two different types of cheese (or chalk).

While the relationship between corrective and distributive justice appears important, it is simply an irrelevance if the two cannot actually be distinguished. Hence we must ask: is the way in which corrective justice governs private transactions between individuals significantly different from other ways in which such transactions might be regulated? In response, jurists emphasize at least two features that are allegedly hallmarks of a corrective justice approach to transactions between individuals. First, the corrective justice relation is conceived as a duty to repair between a party wronged and the party responsible for that wrong.[11] It thus only arises as a result of some significant wrongdoing by one to another: corrective justice must therefore presuppose or actually provide a catalogue of wrongs by reference to which that duty arises. It must also specify why it is objectionable to allow such wrongs to go uncorrected. This is usually done by invoking a conception of equality or some distribution of welfare and resources that predates and is disturbed by the wrongdoing in question. Part of what is wrong with conduct that triggers a corrective justice duty is, therefore, that it represents a particular kind of disturbance of a background distribution of either equality or bundles of welfare, resources or interests. Thus, before an instance of corrective injustice between X and Y, it must be the case that X's and Y's holdings were in some relevant and intelligible sense appropriate or that X and Y were in some relevant and intelligible sense equal. In order to fall within the realm of corrective justice, Y's wrongdoing must not only effect X: it must effect X in such a way as to disturb an existing relation of equality or propriety with Y. Furthermore, the fact that Y has disturbed this relation is in itself presumably insufficient to trigger the duty to repair;

[10] The separation thesis is pursued by Weinrib, supra, note 7, pp. 68–75; the co-existence thesis seems to be a fleeting background presence in Coleman's recent work: see *PoP*, pp. 57–63.

[11] One leading corrective justice jurist did not always conceive the relation in this way: see J. Coleman, 'Tort Law and the Demands of Corrective Justice' (1992) 67 *Indiana LJ* 349–379 and his 'Second Thoughts and Other First Impressions', ch. 13 of B. Bix (ed.), *Analysing Law* (Oxford: Clarendon Press, 1998), pp. 306–316.

the conduct that disturbed the relation must be in some additional sense wrong. It must, in other words, be a wrong for reasons over and beyond the fact that it disturbs some specific background relation: it must, for example, be an intentional or negligent disturbance, or bring about a precise type of damage.

The second hallmark of a corrective justice approach to private transactions is the way in which the nature and range of the duty to repair is conceived. There are two aspects to this. First, corrective justice accounts set the contours of the obligation in the sense of specifying exactly what it is that must be done by the wrongdoer. This is determined exactly by the contours of her wrong: what must be repaired is either precisely what the wrongdoer has done to the innocent party, no more and no less, or the wrongful losses to the innocent party that flow from that wrong.[12] Second, corrective justice accounts specify the parties to the obligation to repair and, again, the contours of the duty are clearly set: only wrongdoer and wrong-sufferer are directly involved. It is the alleged wrongdoer and only her to whom the wrong-sufferer must look for repair and it is the wrong-sufferer and only she to whom the wrongdoer must make recompense. Of course, there might be a third party present in the form of an arbitrator or adjudicator and, if so, corrective justice holds that the only considerations relevant when determining whether or not corrective justice has been breached are those internal to the relationship between wrongdoer and wrong-sufferer. Considerations of the overall welfare or good of the community, or other 'extraneous' factors, are either completely irrelevant or *prima facie* irrelevant.[13] A useful way in which to capture the specificity of corrective justice duties is this: they rest upon 'agent-relative' as opposed to 'agent-general' reasons.[14] That is, the reasons they provide for action are reasons for particular persons and arise from particular situations: Y must compensate X because of what has occurred between them. Y's duty here is not a general duty that we might say binds all humanity such as, for example, a duty to alleviate the

[12] Coleman, at least, sees a difference between the wrong done and the wrongful losses that flow from it; he thinks Weinrib's account of corrective justice is concerned with the former, while his own account emphasizes the latter. See J. Coleman, 'The Practice of Corrective Justice', ch. 2 of D. Owen (ed.), *Philosophical Foundations of Tort Law* (Oxford: Clarendon Press, 1995), p. 66 (hereinafter '*PCJ*').

[13] In part, which of these two options is preferred will depend upon whether the jurist in question endorses the separation thesis or the coexistence thesis (see the text accompanying note 10, supra).

[14] This distinction is invoked by Perry, supra, note 2, pp. 238–239; a *similar* distinction (agent-specific v. agent-general) is also utilized by Coleman, *PCJ*, *supra*, note 12, p. 55.

suffering of those in mortal need. A duty such as this generates reasons that bind us regardless of anything we may or may not have done to, or suffered at the hands of, another.[15]

An important aspect of theories of corrective justice is how closely their principal features reflect the content of various parts of private law. The two mirror one another most closely with regard to the bilateral structure of private law. This feature of the law holds that only those who have done specific wrongs can be sued by victims of those wrongs and only the latter must be compensated by the former. Victims of private law wrongs cannot sue whoever has the deepest pockets, nor can perpetrators of such wrongs hold that someone else compensate their victims. As we will see, accounts of corrective justice are distinct from accounts of distributive justice because they embody this structural feature of private law and endow it with moral or political significance (or both). When jurists say that corrective justice 'governs private transactions between individuals' they usually mean that it takes this structural feature of private law as a given. The fact that accounts of corrective justice so closely reflect some features of the law such as this leads to the methodological difficulties already noted about the 'distance' between explanation or justification, on the one hand, and that which is explained or justified, on the other. These snags are explored in greater depth in the next chapter.

Finally, the normative status or pedigree of corrective justice must be noted. Is it a political principle, a moral principle, neither or both? Moreover, why does it matter? To answer the first question: one of the three most interesting and significant proponents of corrective justice undoubtedly regards it as a moral principle, another apparently holds that it constitutes a 'special morality', while the third regards it as a political-cum-moral principle independent of other closely related moral principles.[16] This might matter when the explanatory and justificatory

[15] The sketch of corrective justice in this and the previous paragraph paraphrases, while ignoring some areas of dispute, the principal features of the accounts found in: Aristotle, *Nicomachean Ethics* in J. Barnes (ed.), *The Complete Works of Aristotle* (Princeton, New Jersey: Princeton University Press, 1984) vol. two; Benson, supra, note 9; Coleman, *Risks and Wrongs*, supra, note 7, chs. 16–19; *PCJ*, supra, note 12; and his *PoP*, lectures four and five; Perry, supra, note 2 and his 'The Moral Foundations of Tort Law' (1991–1992) 77 *Iowa LR* 449–514; Weinrib, supra, note 7, chs 3, 4 and 5.

[16] For Perry, supra, note 2, corrective justice is certainly a moral principle: see p. 237. For Weinrib private law liability is a 'special morality' and this, of course, must be understood by recourse to corrective justice (supra, note 7, p. 2). For Coleman corrective justice is a pre-political (and thus presumably moral) principle whose content is affected by legal and

power of corrective justice comes under investigation. Suppose, for example, it is claimed that corrective justice is a moral principle. As such, it must therefore have some normative weight in our non-legal deliberations: it must have some plausibility whether or not it is embodied in or provides a foundation for private law. Furthermore, if it does have some independent normative power, it can quite easily be cast in the role of normative foundation of private law: although that foundation exists outwith the law, it can exert a powerful gravitational pull over both the law's structure and content. Such a normative foundation must therefore be evaluated from two different directions: its plausibility must be examined from both the terrain of its 'home ground', namely, morality, and from the perspective of private law. It must be a natural, *bona fide* member of our moral system and provide a satisfactory justification and explanation of private law. If, by contrast, corrective justice is regarded as a political principle only, then it needs be evaluated only from the terrain of those principles. A number of such principles already presumably inform the law, insofar as any actual legal system embodies the rule of law ideal and its cognate principles about, for example, retrospective laws and like cases being treated alike. The principal question about corrective justice when conceived as a political principle is how well or badly it relates to other important political principles and whether or not it provides justificatory or explanatory insight into the law itself.

DISTRIBUTIVE JUSTICE

For John Rawls, one of the most important political philosophers of the last half-century, social or distributive justice is the pre-eminent and most uncompromising social virtue.[17] For Rawls, the general idea or concept of social justice entails a concern with the proper balance between competing claims over the benefits and burdens of social life, whereas specific conceptions of social or distributive justice offer competing sets of principles which determine this balance.[18] Different accounts of distributive

political practices (*PCJ*, supra note 12, pp. 69–70). Yet Coleman also holds that corrective justice does not rest upon a pre-political account of basic (or even outcome) responsibility; the latter must be legal-cum-political (*PoP*, pp. 50–53). On this view, then, corrective justice is a moral-cum-political principle dependent upon a legal-cum-political (but certainly not moral) account of basic and outcome responsibility.

[17] *A Theory of Justice* (Oxford: Clarendon Press, revised edn, 1999), pp. 3–4 (hereinafter referred to as '*TJ*' in notes).

[18] *TJ*, p. 9. Henceforth, we will speak only of distributive justice in order to drop the clumsy 'social or distributive' locution.

justice thus 'provide a way of assigning rights and duties in the basic institutions of society and they define the appropriate distribution of the benefits and burdens of social cooperation'.[19] The fact that some political philosophers reject these three claims – that distributive justice is the primary social virtue, that accounts of distributive justice offer sets of principles to determine *inter alia* the distribution of the benefits of social co-operation, and that the concept/conception distinction is a useful way of thinking about distributive justice – cannot concern us here.[20] The history of thought about distributive justice, although long, rich and fascinating, must for present purposes be ignored.[21] Taking Rawls's three claims as the parameters within which the idea of distributive justice will presently be considered risks simplification but provides a clear focus for discussion. Furthermore, when conceived in accord with Rawls's three claims, it is clear that accounts of distributive justice are first and foremost political principles for dealing with the benefits and burdens of collective life. They therefore have a far more specific role than many principles of (non-political) morality.

To ensure greater clarity two additional issues must also be addressed. One is the content of different conceptions of distributive justice, the other their subject matter. Rawls's conception of distributive justice has two principles:

> First: each person is to have an equal right to the most extensive scheme of equal basic liberties compatible with a similar scheme of liberties for others.
> Second: social and economic inequalities are to be arranged so that they are both (a) reasonably expected to be to everyone's advantage, and (b) attached to positions and offices open to all.[22]

These principles are lexically ordered, the first taking priority over the second. Furthermore, the two principles govern both major aspects of life in a political community conceived as a grouping for mutual advantage, namely (i) the assignment and distribution of fundamental liberties; and (ii) the burdens and products of collective endeavour. The latter products

[19] *TJ*, p. 4.

[20] For some doubts about both the primacy of justice and the concept/conception distinction, see T. Campbell, *Justice* (London: Macmillan, 1988), pp. 3–8; for doubts about Rawls's view of the content of distributive justice, see D. Miller, *Social Justice* (Oxford: Clarendon Press, 1976), pp. 40–51.

[21] For an engaging account of this history, accompanied by the argument that thinking about distributive justice has a shorter lineage than often assumed, see S. Flieschacker, *A Short History of Distributive Justice* (Cambridge, Mass.: Harvard University Press, 2004).

[22] *TJ*, p. 53.

include those economic, social and cultural resources – like a standard of living far above bare subsistence, employment, public security, health and safety – that can either only be created by co-operative group activity or only achieved to a satisfactory degree by such activity. Acting together, says Rawls, we achieve benefits otherwise beyond our solitary endeavours.

Not all conceptions of distributive justice include something like Rawls's two principles. Some conceptions deal only with the distribution of the social, economic and cultural burdens and benefits of co-operation, offering accounts of how these should be distributed. One such conception holds, for example, that these benefits and burdens should be distributed according to the moral merit of recipients, another that distribution be according to recipients' needs. The distribution and assignment of the basic liberties is, on such conceptions, dealt with by principles beyond the range of distributive justice. Still other conceptions of distributive justice combine principles of desert and need with yet other principles of distribution, holding that different distributive principles apply in different contexts.[23] So, for example, while the principle of merit is appropriate, on such complex conceptions of distributive justice, for the distribution of some advantages like remuneration for labour, it is inappropriate for the distribution of health care. Finally, the historical entitlement account of distributive justice holds that the distribution of social and economic benefits or 'holdings' is just when such holdings accord with either a principle of justice in acquisition, a principle of justice in transfer or a principle of justice in rectification. In what even its author recognizes as one of the worst rallying slogans ever offered, distributive justice on this view is a matter of '[f]rom each according to what he chooses to do, to each according to what he makes for himself . . . and what others choose to do for him and choose to give him of what they've been given previously (under this maxim) and haven't yet expended or transferred'.[24]

For Robert Nozick, an important advantage of his historical entitlement account of distributive justice is that it allows consenting capitalist acts between adults.[25] That is to say, once citizens' entitlements are established as just in accord with one or other of the principles of acquisition,

[23] For two broadly similar accounts along these lines, see M. Walzer, *Spheres of Justice* (Oxford: Martin Robertson, 1983) and D. Miller, *Principles of Social Justice* (Cambridge, Mass.: Harvard University Press, 1999).

[24] R. Nozick, *Anarchy, State, and Utopia* (Oxford: Blackwell, 1974), p. 160. The three principles are discussed at pp. 150–153. Note that Nozick would not be keen for the historical entitlement theory of justice to be labelled 'distributive' since he has worries about that term: pp. 149–150.

[25] *Anarchy, State and Utopia*, supra, pp. 160–164.

transfer or rectification, they are free to do what they like with their holdings consistent with the fundamental moral and political rights of others. By contrast, 'patterned' conceptions of distributive justice may have to prohibit such consensual capitalist acts since they insist that the distribution of benefits and burdens must correspond to some principle or other like, for example, strict equality. They must, therefore, uphold the pattern and prevent disturbances. This might mean either preventing citizens in a political community in which the distribution of benefits and burdens corresponds with some preferred pattern acting so as to disturb it by, for example, giving some of their holdings to others in a process of exchange. Or it might simply require re-distribution in accord with the pattern after such disturbances.

In distinguishing between patterned and historic principles of distributive justice, Nozick highlights an important point about what may be called the *structure* of such principles as opposed to their *content*. Indeed, his specific point about the potential conflict between patterned principles and freedom spurred many philosophers and jurists to address the issue. The way in which many chose to tackle it was by developing 'dynamic' conceptions of distributive justice. In such conceptions, the distribution of benefits and burdens (but usually not basic liberties) accords with the preferred principles of justice, yet is also responsive to citizens' choices.[26] Thus departures from distributive justice that are the result of uncoerced individual choices are not baleful, while departures that flow from other sources are *prima facie* illegitimate. In examining the ways in which various accounts of distributive justice may function as normative foundations for private law, these various distinctions must not be overlooked.

This, however, throws into relief the second point about distributive justice: what is its subject matter? Put another way, this is the issue of the range of an account of distributive justice, the aspects of individual and communal life to which its principles, if it has more than one, apply. It might be thought that if distributive justice is, as Rawls maintains, the pre-eminent social virtue, then it should extend to every aspect of life. Distributive justice should therefore govern not only the general distribution of the benefits and burdens of social co-operation but also every particular instance in which such benefits and burdens might be in play. Thus arrangements between family members that involve such benefits

[26] The most notable and ambitious recent account of this type is R. Dworkin, *Sovereign Virtue* (Cambridge, Mass.: Harvard University Press, 2000).

and burdens, those of informal social groups such as, for example, amateur football or games clubs, as well as the relations between nations, could well be within its ambit.[27] For his part, Rawls confines the subject matter of distributive justice to the basic structure of a society, by which he means

> the way in which the major social institutions distribute fundamental rights and duties and determine the division of advantages from social cooperation. By major institutions I understand the political constitution and the principal economic and social arrangements. Thus the legal protection of freedom of thought and liberty of conscience, competitive markets, private property in the means of production, and the monogamous family are examples of major social institutions.[28]

It is not immediately clear from this characterization of the basic structure that private law should be regarded as one of its components. If it is not, then this poses a major problem for those philosophers and jurists who argue that some conception of distributive justice does indeed provide a normative foundation for private law. Of course, it may be argued that Rawls's account of the basic structure is either mistaken or can be plausibly interpreted so as to include private law. Either way, the issue must be taken seriously. It cannot simply be assumed that private law is obviously grist for the mill of distributive justice.

MIXED ACCOUNTS

Unsurprisingly, mixed accounts of the normative foundations of private law combine a number of values or principles, sometimes moral, sometimes political and – perhaps most common – sometimes both. The most obvious combination includes only corrective and distributive justice but mixed accounts can embrace a much wider range of values. It is not therefore inconceivable to imagine a mixed account including a range of moral and political values in conjunction with ostensible non-moral, non-political 'pragmatic' values like efficiency, cost reduction and wealth maximization. Such wide-ranging, mixed accounts are not considered in what follows, partly because they raise difficult questions about the true

[27] For an account of justice between nations see J. Rawls, *The Law of Peoples* (Cambridge, Mass.: Harvard University Press, 1999); for justice and the family see S. M. Okin, *Justice, Gender, and the Family* (New York: Basic Books, 1989).

[28] *TJ*, p. 6. Rawls has tackled the issue of the basic structure on other occasions: besides *TJ* at pp. 6–10 see also J. Rawls, *Political Liberalism* (New York: Columbia University Press, 1996), pp. 257–288 and his *Justice as Fairness: A Restatement* (Cambridge, Mass.: Harvard University Press, 2001), pp. 10–12.

status of the allegedly non-political or non-moral values they invoke: for example, can the value of wealth maximization really be plausibly understood without reference to some wider consideration of justice?[29] They are also set aside because they manifest in its most obvious form one general problem such types of account generate, namely, the problem of (in)coherence or (in)stability. The problem arises if, as seems plausible, the more inclusive a mixed account of the normative foundations of private law is, the greater is the likelihood that it will be riven by tensions between its constitutive elements. The converse assumption is that the fewer elements contained in a mixed account the more likely it is to be stable and coherent. While both assumptions underpin the discussion in Chapter 10, the hunch in play there is that 'parsimonious' mixed accounts, by which is meant those that combine few rather than many values, are most likely to succeed.

In addition to the problem of incoherence, mixed accounts might be threatened by a lack of generality, a specific manifestation of the general requirement that accounts of the normative foundations of an institution and its constitutive practices must 'fit' that institution and practices. This problem arises from the fact that private law doctrine is, obviously, diverse. The various kinds of private law wrongs seem quite different one from another and it is not always obvious that they share underpinning principles and values which explain their development and differences. Of course, this is no great surprise given what we know about how private law developed in the common law jurisdictions: it is the work of many judicial minds deciding particular cases over many centuries. A degree of entropy is therefore built-in to the very process of private law's development and this can make the job of providing a normative foundation, particularly one sensitive to the features of legal doctrine, tricky. Since private law doctrine can look a little incoherent and *ad hoc*, then so, too, can the theory that is its normative foundation. Or, at least, that is the potential problem a mixed theory faces. Such a theory lacks generality if the normative foundation it provides either does not get beyond holding that the many doctrines of private law have many different normative foundations or is applicable to only one or a few aspects of private law. While few mixed normative theories display such a complete lack of generality, many are threatened by milder versions of the problem.

The problems of incoherence and generality are not the only ones with

[29] For one who thinks not, see R. Dworkin, *A Matter of Principle* (Oxford: Clarendon Press, 1985), chs. 12 and 13.

which mixed accounts must grapple. There is at least one other problem, of intelligibility, that must be faced. This is the difficulty of ensuring that the normative foundation in play not only fits the institution and its constitutive practices in the broad sense of being *consistent with* its principal features and some of its details, but also *makes good normative sense* of those features and details. This difficulty also ensnares corrective and distributive justice accounts of the normative foundations of private law and, as is clear from aspects of the discussion in Chapters 8 and 9, those accounts are not always successful in grappling with it. Whether or not the same must be said for mixed accounts of the normative foundation of private law will be established in Chapter 10. Finally, it must be noted that the discussion of mixed theories in Chapter 10 is slightly different in emphasis from the treatments of corrective and distributive justice in Chapters 8 and 9. Those chapters principally examine particular arguments about the role of corrective and distributive justice in relation to private law. As a result they focus in considerable detail upon particular exemplary works. The tenor of the discussion in Chapter 10 is a little different, since the discussion initially focuses upon the general problems faced by any conceivable mixed theory (which is not to say that the problems facing particular examples of such theories are ignored).[30] In part, this change in emphasis is a result of there being fewer dominant exemplary works in this area as compared with, for example, the domain of distributive justice. It is also in part a result of the view that mixed theories of the normative foundations of private law represent the future. At the risk of offering yet another unsubstantiated generalization, mixed theories are where the (intellectual) action is (and that's a good thing, too). That being so, it is important to ensure that the discussion beings on the correct footing, with a clear appreciation of both snags and opportunities.

The structure of what follows should now be clear. Each of the next three chapters addresses a different account of the normative foundations of private law, evaluating each account both in general terms and in light of the three issues identified at the beginning of this chapter (hereinafter dubbed 'the key issues or questions'). The key issues are easily characterized in the form of three questions: (i) what is the nature of obligation to make recompense?; (ii) what is the general normative basis of private

[30] The mixed account examined in most depth belongs to T. Honoré, *Responsibility and Fault* (Oxford: Hart Publishing, 1999), ch. 4.

law?; and (iii) why is the obligation an obligation to make financial recompense rather than an obligation to right the wrong and the losses that flow from it in some other way? These three substantive chapters are followed by a fourth, Chapter 11, which is the conclusion to the whole book. It highlights some of the themes and loose ends that have emerged in both Parts I and II and tries, where possible, either to trim or tie up the latter.

8

Corrective Justice

Corrective justice is the idea that liability rectifies the injustice inflicted by one person on another.

E. Weinrib, 'Corrective Justice in a Nutshell' (2002) LII *University of Toronto Law Journal* 349–356, p. 349.

Over the last 30 or so years, the topic of corrective justice and its relationship with private law has preoccupied many jurists. This might seem odd, especially as some of these jurists draw their inspiration from Aristotle's account of corrective justice, first written approximately 2,500 years ago. Yet, once the rise of law and economics in the North American legal academy is borne in mind, the preoccupation with corrective justice makes more sense. For, in the hands of its proponents corrective justice allegedly provides a principled account of the general bilateral structure of private law and a promising account of private law's normative content.[1] It therefore does what economic analysis of private law patently fails to do, according to many of its critics (who are also often proponents of corrective justice). The state of the debate between economic analysis of private law and proponents of corrective justice is not, however, the principal topic on our agenda. Our aim is much more limited: to elucidate and evaluate the answers corrective justice theorists give to the key questions identified in the previous chapter.

But even this already limited task is itself further restricted. Since there has been an explosion of scholarship in this area, it is impossible in this book to provide anything like a thorough analysis of all the corrective justice literature.[2] Instead, the focus is upon the two exemplary accounts of corrective justice provided by Ernest Weinrib and Jules Coleman.[3] An

[1] A 'principled' account of private law's bilateralism is one which lacks the *ad hoc* features of, for example, the accounts offered by Economic Analysis of Law. For a reminder of the issues here see Chapter 1, pp. 33–38.

[2] The scale of which is confirmed by, for example, a Westlaw or equivalent internet search.

[3] Their most recent book-length contributions are E. Weinrib, *The Idea of Private Law* (Cambridge, Mass.: Harvard University Press, 1995); J. Coleman, *The Practice of Principle* (Oxford: Clarendon Press, 2001).

additional restriction on the discussion that follows is that these two jurists are in the main concerned only with the relationship between tort law and corrective justice. This narrowness of focus is not a problem, if it is reasonable to think that the accounts of corrective justice offered by Weinrib and Coleman have application over and beyond tort law. That thought is certainly entertained by one of these jurists and it seems well founded insofar as corrective justice promises to illuminate the general issue of what it is that makes private law private.[4] Furthermore, the narrowness of focus is in one sense very helpful, for if these accounts of corrective justice do not perform well as normative foundations for tort law – their chosen object of explanation – then it is reasonable to think they will not perform well with regard to other segments of private law.

There are a number of factors that combine to make the accounts of corrective justice offered by Weinrib and Coleman exemplary. One is that both thinkers have explored and developed the issue for a number of years, albeit from slightly different directions. Coleman's work on corrective justice and private law has clearly developed from his critical evaluation of some of the key works of Economic Analysis of Law (hereinafter '*EAL*'). Weinrib, by contrast, does not often directly engage with the details of *EAL*; his critique of it derives from a more general critique of 'functionalism' in contemporary legal thought and his account of corrective justice arises from an engagement with the thought of ancient Greece.[5] Another factor that makes both jurists' work exemplary is its originality. Although they approach the topic of corrective justice from

[4] Coleman, of course, is not sure corrective justice can extend to either contract law or the law of products liability: see *Risks and Wrongs* (Cambridge: Cambridge University Press, 1992) part I and ch. 20. In *The Idea of Private Law*, supra, Weinrib's focus is wider than tort even though he concentrates in the main upon it (see pp. 114–118, 133–134, 140–142 and 197–199 for some thoughts on restitution; for contract, see pp. 50–53, 104, 128–129 and 136–140). For a sustained foray beyond tort law see his 'Restitutionary Damages as Corrective Justice' (2000) 1 *Theoretical Inquiries in Law* (Online Edition), Article 2. For a corrective justice approach to contract law see P. Benson, 'Abstract Right and the Possibility of a Nondistributive Conception of Contract: Hegel and Contemporary Contract Theory' (1989) 10 *Cardozo LR* 1079–1198. The relation between corrective justice and the law of restitution is explored by many of the contributors to *Symposium: Restitution and Unjust Enrichment* (2000–2001) 79 *Texas LR* 1763–2197 and by H. Dagan in *The Law and Ethics of Restitution* (Cambridge: Cambridge University Press, 2004).

[5] For Coleman's engagement with *EAL* see his collection *Markets, Morals and the Law* (Cambridge: Cambridge University Press, 1988); Weinrib's most direct engagement with *EAL* is probably 'Understanding Tort Law' (1989) 23 *Valparaiso University LR* 485–526 at pp. 486–489 and 498–510.

rather different directions, their contributions are each path-breaking in their own right: it is no great exaggeration to say that their work is the universally acknowledged starting point for thinking in the field. In addition to being tremendously influential, Weinrib's and Coleman's work is also marked by the highest standards of clarity and argumentative transparency, even when the issues are abstract and difficult. These considerations, then, ensure that from among the many discussions of corrective justice, the efforts of Weinrib and Coleman have particular salience.

This, of course, is not to say that their accounts of corrective justice are identical. In quantitative terms the two probably differ over as many issues as they agree about. The analysis that follows is therefore a little awkward, since we must be careful not overlook differences while appreciating similarities. That being so, it is worthwhile to restate briefly some of the features both accounts have in common.[6] There are at least four. First, corrective justice is the duty to correct specific wrongs one has done (caused or occasioned) to another. Second, the victim must seek redress from the wrongdoer rather than anyone else – such as one who might be better placed financially than the wrongdoer to correct the wrong – for the harm the wrong caused or threatened. Third, if the author of a specific type of wrong has indeed thereby harmed the victim, then she must correct that wrong or the loss that flows from it or both. The wrongdoer cannot shift the costs of correcting the wrong she has done from herself to strangers who might be better placed, in terms of wealth or efficiency, to put it right.[7] Finally, the obligation to correct that corrective justice generates is agent-relative: it is an obligation a specific agent owes to another agent by virtue of something that has occurred between them. Corrective justice duties are not therefore duties owed by every agent (or human being) to every other agent (or human being) regardless of any interaction between them.

With these similarities in mind, we can turn to three matters that any corrective justice account of the normative foundation of private law must address. The first two matters raise the key issues identified in the last chapter, since they concern the adequacy with which each account plays the role of normative foundation (tackled in the first section below)

[6] This is a paraphrase of Chapter 7, pp. 256–259.

[7] Although it can be shifted to those related to the wrongdoer by insurance contract. This practical possibility might be thought to cause a conceptual problem for proponents of corrective justice but it does not seem to. For some interesting observations on insurance (and other procedures) as a means of burden-shifting, see M. Reiff, *Punishment, Compensation, and the Law* (Cambridge: Cambridge University Press, 2005), pp. 215–221.

and the nature of the obligation to correct (tackled section two on p.289). The third matter (also tackled in that section) is, however, more specific. It examines what both Weinrib and Coleman have to say about the relationship between corrective and distributive justice. The difference between Weinrib and Coleman on this matter is but one of a number that come to light in the following two sections.

FOUNDATIONS

To assess whether or not the accounts of corrective justice provided by Weinrib and Coleman function as normative foundations and, if they do so, to analyse their exact role, we must begin by considering how these jurists understand the enterprise upon which they are engaged. Only when we know that will we understand and be able to evaluate the method they employ. And only then will we be able to determine exactly the role corrective justice plays in their theories of private law. The subsection below, sketches some similarities between Weinrib's and Coleman's method, while the subsection on p.276 highlights a problem their method faces. The third subsection (p.283) examines Coleman's more recent reflections on method. For Coleman the issue of the method to be employed when doing philosophy of private law is a far more interesting and pressing issue than it is for Weinrib. Or, perhaps more accurately, Coleman has been far more preoccupied with the issue in print than has Weinrib. The final subsection (p.286) returns to the varieties of 'foundation talk' elucidated in Chapter 7.

INTERNAL STRUCTURE AND MIDDLE-LEVEL THEORY

There is a fairly broad and clear consensus among what may be labelled 'orthodox' jurists about the method to be employed in order to provide an adequate understanding and explanation of law.[8] Variations on this method are employed by jurists concerned with the most abstract questions of legal philosophy, such as those about the nature of law and adjudication, and by those philosophers of private law that eschew both

[8] As a matter of general jurisprudence, I spell out what I mean by 'orthodoxy' in my *Understanding and Explaining Adjudication* (Oxford: Clarendon Press, 1999), pp. 1–17. How this view manifests itself in some philosophy of private law scholarship is incompletely explored in W. Lucy, 'The Crises of Private Law', ch. 7 of T. Wilhelmsson and S. Hurri (eds.), *From Dissonance to Sense: Welfare State Expectations, Privatisation and Private Law* (Aldershot: Ashgate Publishing, 1999).

EAL and the many versions of Critical Legal Studies.[9] The key tenet of this method is: any adequate theoretical account (or explanation or understanding)[10] of any social action, practice or institution must, in the first instance, capture the way in which that action, practice or institution is understood by those whose patterns of behaviour and thought constitute that action, practice or institution. (Hereinafter this tenet is labelled 'the methodological injunction'.) In Herbert Hart's hands, the methodological injunction was translated into the language of 'the internal point of view', which held that an adequate account of legal rules and a legal system had to illuminate how those who accepted those rules and that system understood the rules and the system.[11] Although the substance of his account of law and adjudication is quite different from Hart's, Ronald Dworkin also embraces the internal or participant's point of view as a fundamental methodological injunction.[12] So, too, albeit in slightly different language, do Weinrib and Coleman,[13] although for current purposes their concern is only with what is involved in giving an adequate account of private law or some dimension thereof and not the more general issues that preoccupied Hart and Dworkin.[14]

The assumption that gives the methodological injunction its initial plausibility – and which requires that theorists attempting to understand and explain some aspect of social action or of practices and institutions take up the viewpoint of authors of those actions and participants in those practices and institutions – is hard to deny. It holds that social action is purposive and rule-governed and that, therefore, we can only fully understand and explain it in light of the purposes, goals and values it is

[9] For an account of some themes of North American critical legal studies see my *Understanding and Explaining Adjudication*, supra, part II.

[10] In what follows, the terms 'theory', 'account', 'explanation', 'understanding' and their cognates or admixtures are regarded as synonyms, all referring to the effort to interpret an institution and its constitutive practices at a level of generality greater than that common among participants. Such laxity is not always excusable: see *Understanding and Explaining Adjudication*, supra, note 8, ch. 2 for general discussion of the some of the issues in play here (albeit as they arise within 'accounts' of adjudication).

[11] *The Concept of Law* (Oxford: Clarendon Press, 2nd edn, 1994) at, for example, pp. 88–91.

[12] See *Law's Empire* (Oxford: Hart Publishing, 1998), pp. 11–15.

[13] It is a mistake to assume that Weinrib and Coleman are the only philosophers of private law to subscribe to this methodological injunction. For another particularly interesting instance see A. Brudner, *The Unity of the Common Law* (Berkeley: University of California Press, 1995), ch. 1.

[14] Coleman's interests always have ranged far beyond philosophy of private law and into exactly the territory explored by Dworkin and Hart: see, for example, *The Practice of Principle*, supra, note 3, part two. This aspect of his work is not considered here.

supposed to serve. It seemingly follows that access to those purposes, goals and values is best provided by determining what those whose behaviour, patterns of thought and expectations constitute the action (or practice or institution) think are its purposes, values and goals. That reference to the goals of an action is indispensable for a proper understanding of the action is obvious from many simple, low-level examples. Consider, for instance, someone raising their arm. To understand this in anything more than purely physiological and neural terms, an account is needed of the social context in which it occurred and the agent's own view of both that context and their action. Only then will it be known whether the arm-raising event was: (i) an action the agent took themselves to be doing as opposed to a reflex or other event that happened to them; and (ii) what the meaning (or point, or purpose or goal) of the action was (it could be *inter alia* a vote in a ballot, an indication that danger threatens, or part of a dance routine). It seems reasonable to extrapolate from the apparent indispensability of reference to the internal point of view in such instances to its being indispensable for an understanding and explanation of *all* social practices and institutions. Such practices and institutions are, after all, not much more than amalgams of many particular actions. On this basis, then, rests the appeal of the methodological injunction. We now need to determine how Weinrib's and Coleman's commitment to it arises. Of the two, Coleman's commitment is, in the first instance, most obvious and unambiguous.

Coleman's commitment to the internal point of view as a fundamental methodological injunction arises from his endorsement in *Risks and Wrongs* (*RW*)[15] of both 'top-down' and 'middle-level' theory. The distinction between the two seems important for Coleman, even though he offers both, his account of tort law being an instance of the latter while his account of contract law is an example of the former (*RW*, p. 9).

> In top-down explanations, the theorist begins with what she takes to be the set of norms that would gain our reflective acceptance, *at least among those practitioners who adopt the internal point of view*. Then she looks at the body of law . . . and tries to reconstruct it plausibly as exemplifying those norms. Parts of the law . . . [may] fail to be plausibly reconstructed . . . [and] identified as mistakes. (*RW*, p. 8; emphasis mine)

By contrast, the theorist engaged in middle-level theory will '*immerse . . . herself in the practice itself* and ask . . . if it can be usefully organized in

[15] Supra, note 4.

ways that reflect a commitment to one or more plausible principles' (*RW*, ibid; emphasis mine). From these statements, it seems that the primary difference between the two approaches is their starting point. Middle-level theory begins with an attitude of some deference towards the action, practice or institution under examination and the trajectory of its account or explanation moves from within the action, practice or institution as participants understand it to an assessment of its nature, function and content. By contrast, the starting point of top-down theory seems to a set of norms that might account for the nature, function and content of an action, practice or institution. The action, practice or institution is then 'read in light of' such norms, the principal constraint on this process being the participants' own views of the action, practice or institution.

Whether or not the distinction between top-down and middle-level approaches is ultimately defensible is, for present purposes, unimportant. Far more significant is what both approaches have in common: each, albeit with differing degrees of stringency, embraces the internal point of view. That much is obvious from the italicized sections of the statements just quoted. Lest there be any lingering doubt about this, consider one more of Coleman's statements about method: he 'is concerned to understand the law *from the standpoint of practitioners* who ask not only, "How may we carry on this practice in a way that is faithful to its inherent norms?", but rather, "How may we carry on this practice in a way that is faithful to norms that are both inherent in it and reflectively acceptable to us?" ' (*RW*, p. 7; emphasis mine). If this is not an unambiguous endorsement of the methodological injunction, then it is hard to envisage what such an endorsement might look like.

Two closely related steps taken by Weinrib in *The Idea of Private Law* (*IPL*)[16] illustrate his commitment to the methodological injunction but, as will be seen in the following subsection, this commitment seems at one point to be fairly shallow. The first consists of Weinrib's arguments against functional understandings of law; the second is his effort to offer an account of private law that captures its 'internal structure', or 'self-understanding', or, in a cognate phrase, that is 'immanent' within the law. Functionalist accounts of law, for Weinrib, are a diverse family of views united in the belief that any adequate account of law must understand it in light of its goals. Weinrib's principal indictment against this belief is that, in seeking to understand law in terms of goals external to it – in the

[16] See note 3, supra.

sense that they are not obviously and explicitly marked in legal doctrine – functionalist accounts either cannot represent or actually misrepresent how law is understood by those whose actions and beliefs in part constitute it.[17] As a result, the accounts of law embodied in functionalist theories are remote from 'juristic experience' (*IPL*, p. 3). Furthermore, such theories are guided by the questionable assumption that the law cannot be understood in its own terms, that it must, to be intelligible, be explained in light of something external. In this respect, functionalist theories embody a common sense assumption about explanations, namely, that an adequate explanation of something – Y, for example – must be in terms of something other than Y. But even in common sense this assumption does not always obtain. As Weinrib observes, there are many things, such as love and friendship, that we think need not (perhaps even should not) be understood in terms of objects external to them. Private law, Weinrib suggests, may be of this type, its only 'function', if that word must be used, is to be private law (*IPL*, p. 5).

We have yet to find a particularly sturdy peg on which to hang Weinrib's commitment to the methodological injunction: a one-off invocation of 'juristic experience' is a slender reed incapable of bearing much weight. More evidence of a more dependable kind is found in Weinrib's views as to what an adequate account of private law should look like. Such an account must 'treat[.] private law as an internally intelligible phenomenon by drawing on *what is salient in juristic experience* and by trying to make sense of legal thinking and discourse *in their own terms*' (*IPL*, pp. 2–3; emphasis mine). Treating private law in this way, reflecting juristic experience, 'directs us to our experience of the law, *especially the*

[17] There are two ways in which this aspect of Weinrib's indictment of functionalism could be understood. One is that he regards all reference to functions (and related cognates like purposes, goals or values) as being references to something outside the practice or institution in question. Another is that he regards the particular functions functionalists ascribe to private law as being external to it. There seems no reason to accept the first view, since it is simply implausible to think that all talk of function is in some sense external to the thing in question (what, exactly, is 'external' in giving the function of a knife or a particular dance and why should that be thought problematic?). If Weinrib's true view is the second, then his anti-functionalism is not incompatible with the methodological injunction's invocation of the point, purpose, value or goal of an action, practice or institution. His argument, as against functionalists, is what participants accept as the purposes, values or goals of an action, practice or institution are internal to that action, practice or institution. At least, he thinks this is true in the case of the practices and institution of private law and of other ideas like love and friendship. For more on Weinrib's sometimes puzzling anti-functionalism, see J. Raz, 'Formalism and the Rule of Law', ch. 11 of R. George (ed.), *Natural Law Theory* (Oxford: Clarendon Press, 1992) and M. Stone, 'On the Idea of Private Law' (1996) IX *Canadian Journal of Law and Jurisprudence* 235–277 at pp. 242–243.

experience of those who are lawyers. This experience allows us to recognize issues of private law and to participate in its characteristic discourse and reasoning' (*IPL*, p. 9; emphasis mine). It does not seem unreasonable to regard these statements as bespeaking commitment to the methodological injunction, or something very similar. If they do not illustrate a concern with the understandings of participants in the practices and institution of private law, then how is the emphasis upon 'juristic experience', 'the experience of lawyers' and 'internal intelligibility' to be understood? If the experience of lawyers is not the experience of participants in the practice, and if juristic experience is not the experience of participants, then the participants in the practices and institution of private law are utterly mysterious. But, read naturally and charitably, statements such as

> [a]n internal account deals with private law on the basis of the juristic understandings *that shape it from within. Jurists share, if only implicitly, assumptions* about the institutional and conceptual features that their activity presupposes, about the function these features play in their reasoning, and about the significance of coherence for the elaboration of a legal order. (*IPL*, p. 13; emphasis mine)

and those already quoted suggest, at the very least, a *prima facie* commitment to the methodological injunction. Whether or not they warrant more than this, and whether or not this makes a difference, is explored next.

A PROBLEM SHARED IS STILL A PROBLEM

Weinrib and Coleman's commitment to the methodological injunction raises a pressing problem. To see precisely how it arises, we should reiterate the nature and appeal of this method in their hands. Both want to give an account of private law; in order to do so, both think that the correct approach is one that takes up the participants' or internal point of view. Both argue that only when this approach is taken do we get an account of private law that (i) captures those features that participants in that institution-cum-set-of-practices regard as significant; and that (ii) understands the value, or the point or the purpose of that institution-cum-set-of-practices. According to Weinrib and Coleman, one feature of private law – or more precisely the tort law segment thereof – that participants regard as significant is its bilateral structure. Weinrib and Coleman also claim that that this feature, as well as other features of tort law, are a manifestation of, or best understood in light of, corrective justice. They might also make an additional claim here which, given the tenor of their arguments, is not the least bit surprising. The claim is *that participants* in this institution-cum-set-of-practices also hold that this and other features of it are best understood by reference to, or in light of, corrective justice. As against proponents of *EAL*, Weinrib and Coleman can therefore claim two things. First, that their accounts of private law take seriously a feature of the institution that participants regard as important and which *EAL* struggles to accommodate (bilateralism). Second, that they give an account of the normative value of the institution (corrective justice) which participants would either offer themselves or accept, this being something that *EAL* cannot achieve.

The difficulty Weinrib and Coleman face as a result of their commitment to the methodological injunction is 'the fit problem'. The difficulty is this: what to do if, in offering a theoretical account of private law that supposedly captures what the participants regard as significant in the institution and its constitutive practices, that account does not reflect the views of all participants? This is best characterized as a problem of fit by virtue of the dissonance between some aspects of the theory and the views of some participants. Suppose, for example, that, as against Coleman, there are some participants in tort law that understand it in the way that either Richard Epstein, George Fletcher or proponents of *EAL* do;[18] and that, as against Weinrib, some participants do not understand tort law in terms of either Aristotle's account of corrective justice or Kant's notion of abstract right (see *IPL*, chs. 3 and 4). These or similar suppositions are not implausible in light of the fact that some judges – undeniably lawyers, certainly participants in the institution of private law and surely sources of juristic experience – have displayed a taste for characterizing law in terms antithetical to those used by Weinrib and Coleman. The American judge Learned Hand's formula for negligence liability is but one, albeit a most noteworthy, example.[19] Moreover, these suppositions are clearly plausible if the interpretative attitude has taken

[18] R. Epstein, 'A Theory of Strict Liability' (1973) 2 *Journal of Legal Studies* 151–204; G. Fletcher, 'Fairness and Utility in Tort Theory' (1972) 85 *Harvard LR* 537–573; and, for example, S. Shavell, *Economic Analysis of Accident Law* (Cambridge, Mass.: Harvard University Press, 1987).

[19] *United States v Carroll Towing Co*, 159 F 2d 169, 173 (2nd Cir 1947). Also antithetical to corrective justice accounts of tort law is the dicta of Justice Traynor in *Escola v Coca Cola Bottling Co* 24 Cal 2nd 453 (1944), on which see E. Weinrib, 'The Insurance Justification and Private Law' (1985) XIV *Journal of Legal Studies* 681–687. For some of Judge Posner's thoughts about *EAL* in the court room see *In re High Fructose Corn Syrup* 295 F 3d 651 (7th Cir 2003). A sustained argument that economic concepts such as these actually do very little genuine work in judicial decisions is provided by R. Wright, 'Hand, Posner, and the Myth of the "Hand Formula" ' (2003) 4 *Theoretical Inquiries in Law* (online edn), Article 8.

hold in a community. In that case, citizens come to regard their institutions and practices not simply as existing but as having value, taking them to serve some interest or purpose or enforce some principle. The requirements of their institutions and practices are not taken to be 'necessarily and exclusively what they have always been taken to be but are instead sensitive to . . . [their] point'.[20] In such a context, it is not surprising to find more than one account of the point, value or purpose of an institution like tort law in circulation; and this, of course, is exactly the kind of context in which the fit problem would loom large.

There are at least two conceivable responses to the fit problem. One is to insist that a theoretical account of any social practice or institution need accommodate the views or language of the participants at the outset only. The substantive theoretical language of the account offered need not explicitly reflect the language and views of the participants but must be connected to them only in the sense of being an explication thereof. On this view, the theoretical account of the institution and its cognate practices makes explicit what is implicit, articulating the commitments participants incur by virtue of their involvement. Another response is to maintain that explanations and understandings of social practices and institutions based upon the methodological injunction need only accommodate or be consistent with *some* views of *some* participants. Those attracted by this response must then offer a justification for the limitation invoked: why, for example, is it permissible for a theoretical account of private law to accord only with the views of participants of a certain class or type, or with the views of only 60% (or more or less) and not the other 40% (or more or less) of participants?

It is clear that Weinrib adopts the first response to the fit problem:

> [a]n internal understanding of private law reaches corrective justice and the Kantian concept of right by reflecting on the juristic experience of private law and on the presuppositions of that experience. . . .
>
> The relationship between private law and its theory can be formulated as a difference between what is explicit and what is implicit. In one sense, the theory is implicit in the functioning of private law. Because they are categories of legal theory rather than ingredients of positive law, corrective justice and Kantian right are not themselves on the lips of judges. But even though these theoretical categories do not figure explicitly in the discourse of private law, they are implicit in it as a coherent justificatory enterprize in that they provide its unifying structure and its normative idea. They are as present

[20] R. Dworkin, *Law's Empire* (Oxford: Hart Publishing, 1998), p. 47.

to private law as the principles of logic are to intelligible speech. (*IPL*, pp. 19–20)

Thus the fact that features of Weinrib's account of the normative basis of private law are absent from, or simply do not fit with, the language and understandings of some participants is not on this view an embarrassment. At least, not at first glance. It does, however, suggest that Weinrib's commitment to the methodological injunction is not as deep-rooted as might be assumed, since participants views inform his account only at the outset, having no great impact on its theoretical outputs. Furthermore, a second and more discriminating glance shows that this response to the fit problem generates grounds for some embarrassment. It arises in this way. One of the most famous proponents of *EAL* holds that that approach unearths '[t]he [i]mplicit [e]conomic [l]ogic of the [c]ommon [l]aw'.[21] *EAL* does so by examining the material at the forefront of juristic experience – legal doctrine – in light of the ukases of economic efficiency or wealth maximization. And, while such accounts allegedly offer only *ad hoc* explanations or understandings of some features of the institution and practices of private law, like its bilateral structure, they undoubtedly offer interesting and intelligible accounts of some of its other features and doctrines. In this respect the balance of advantage cannot be said to rest decisively in favour of Weinrib's account for that, too, cannot plausibly accommodate some entrenched features of private law like, for example, strict liability.[22] Nor can it be said, as against *EAL*, that economic accounts of the institution and practices of private law are completely alien to participants: some, at least, do offer accounts of some aspects of private law that utilize concepts familiar to *EAL*. If, by contrast, it is argued against *EAL* that the majority of participants in the practices constitutive of private law do not speak the language of economic analysis, then the reply is equally plain. *EAL* aims to capture what is implicit in the practice, what participants take for granted, and to make explicit what holds various features of the institution and its practices together.

Here, then, is the reason why Weinrib should be embarrassed. For, despite the many declarations that his account of the normative foundation of private law is 'internal' or 'immanent', that it captures 'juristic experience', its methodological structure (as opposed to its substantive content) seems no different from that of *EAL*. In giving an account of private law, both approaches take seriously some aspects of what some

[21] R. Posner, *Economic Analysis of Law* (New York: Aspan Publishing, 6th edn, 2003, p. 249).
[22] *IPL*, ch. 7.

participants think, say and do, albeit each approach takes different aspects seriously. Both approaches also provide something by way of justification for what they ignore: the fact that some participants speak neither the language of corrective justice nor that of *EAL* is insignificant because the theories of private law offered by Weinrib and *EAL* aim to articulate what is implicit as opposed to what is explicit. One of the primary advantages of Weinrib's account of the normative basis of private law thus seems to have evaporated. The impression gained from his attacks on functionalism and his arguments in favour of 'internal' accounts of law is that the latter are in some way more consistent with or closer to the views of participants. The implication is that this proximity is a significant virtue, since the closer to the participants' views a theory is, the more accurate or fruitful or illuminating it is likely to be. But the substance of Weinrib's account is not obviously closer to the views of participants than the accounts offered by proponents of *EAL*: the two are, if anything, the same in terms of methodological structure. The embarrassment for Weinrib, then, is that of methodological parity with *EAL*.

A final point before turning to Coleman's response to the fit problem. It is that Weinrib's claim, in the statement quoted above, that corrective justice and Kantian right are present to private law in the same sense that the principles of standard logic are present to intelligible speech, does not establish much distance between his account and *EAL* accounts. This is because the intelligibility claim is an exaggeration, if taken to imply that those accounts of private law that do not invoke corrective justice and Kantian right are unintelligible. Discourse that ignores the rules of standard logic yields contradictions and is often unintelligible in other ways. But economic accounts of private law that eschew Kantian right and corrective justice, although they might be objectionable for other reasons, are plainly neither unintelligible nor contradictory. We might not like what *EAL* says, but we can undoubtedly understand what it says.

There are textual hints to suggest that Coleman favours the second response to the fit problem.[23] In *RW* he criticizes the accounts of tort law offered by Fletcher, Epstein and proponents of *EAL* because they fail to fit the 'core' of tort law. That core consists of

> two features, one structural, one substantive. The structural feature is that in the typical case decisions about who should bear a loss are rendered within a framework restricted to victims and those they identify as their injurers . . .

[23] I ignore textual evidence to suggest that Coleman also adopts the first response on the ground that, if he does, he faces something like the embarrassment that threatens Weinrib.

> The substantive feature is that if a victim can show that her loss is wrongful in the appropriate sense, the burden of making good her loss falls to the individual responsible for it. (*RW*, p. 198)

If it is plausible to regard professors of tort law as participants in that institution and its constitutive practices or, if that is implausible,[24] it is nevertheless plausible to think that their theoretical views have adherents among participants in the practice, then Coleman's response to those views, and to the fit problem in general, is unambiguous. To participants in the institution who view it in the ways suggested by either Fletcher or Epstein or *EAL*, Coleman says: you have misunderstood the core of your own institution. Only those participants whose views of the institution and its practices capture its core are, then, to be taken seriously in any theoretical account of the institution and its constitutive practices. But on what grounds can this limitation be justified?

The limitation initially seems suspiciously convenient for Coleman, since his corrective justice account of the normative foundation of tort law clearly does capture the core. Furthermore, suspicion toward this solution to the fit problem increases once two issues are considered. These issues do not form a coherent package; rather, they undermine each other. But that does not mean Coleman need not address them.

The first issue consists of a denial of the basis of Coleman's limitation: it denies that the alternative accounts of the normative basis of tort law provided by Epstein, Fletcher and some proponents of *EAL* (which are also shared by some participants in the institution) fail to accommodate the core. Furthermore, this denial can be accompanied by an assertion: these alternative accounts simply accommodate the core in a way that is different to that adopted by Coleman's corrective justice account and, further, throw additional light on other, closely related issues.[25] So, for example, proponents of *EAL* could concede that their account of the bilateral structure of tort law is not 'principled' in the way Coleman's account is: they can concede that their explanation of why only claimants can sue defendants regards that relationship as less fundamental than does Coleman's account. But why must it be regarded as fundamental,

[24] Just about every invocation of the methodological injunction, be it within philosophy of private law or jurisprudence in general, is marked by a failure ever to specify exactly who 'participants' in an institution or practice (or complex thereof) might be.

[25] They therefore have the virtue of unifying previously discrete issues (J. Coleman, 'Second Thoughts and Other First Impressions', ch. 13 of B. Bix (ed.), *Analysing Law* (Oxford: Clarendon Press, 1998), p. 299) or 'consilience', as Coleman subsequently calls it (*PoP, supra*, note 3, pp. 41–53).

if it is not so regarded by each and every participant in the practice? It is surely not inconceivable that some participants will regard this feature of tort law as simply an historical accident and, since there are many such in our law, this view cannot be dismissed as eccentric. Moreover, the argument that the accounts in competition with Coleman's can fit the core of tort law, but in a slightly different way than his account, seems even more plausible when the theories of Epstein and Fletcher are borne in mind. For the substance of these accounts, in some respects at least, is much nearer to some participants' views than is the substance of various aspects of the economic analysis of tort law. If it is true that all these competitor accounts of the normative basis of tort law fit the core, then Coleman must find another basis, consistent with the methodological injunction, on which to recommend his account.[26]

The second issue is that of the significance of the core. Why must the core of tort law be regarded as dominant in this way, such that a theory that does not accommodate it must be classed a failure? Two arguments are clearly unavailable to Coleman in response to this question. He cannot, first, maintain that participants in the practice regard the core as crucial, since *ex hypothesi* not all do (we are assuming that some participants echo the views of Epstein, or Fletcher or *EAL*).

Nor can Coleman argue that the views of those participants who take the core seriously are more important than the views of other participants. At least, he cannot argue in this way on the basis of his account of corrective justice, since the explanatory theory or justification of the institution and its constitutive practices is then determining the contours, or at least the core, of that institution. This seems circular if we expect Coleman's account of tort law, including his argument that corrective justice is its normative foundation, to illuminate features of the institution that must in the first instance be identifiable without course to Coleman's theory. Expecting some features of the institution to be independently identifiable in this way leaves room for different accounts of it to offer competing explanations and understandings of those features. It is on the basis of their fit with such features that the relative success and failure of different theoretical accounts can be judged.[27] But if the features of an institution that a theoretical account of it must accommodate are

[26] I examined some of Coleman's possible responses to this issue in 'Rethinking the Common Law' 14 (1994) *Oxford Journal of Legal Studies* 539–564 at pp. 558–564.

[27] Coleman does think that some features of the institution are theory-independent: see *RW*, supra, note 15, pp. 383 and 480; also 'Second Thoughts . . .', supra, note 25 at p. 301.

determined exclusively by the theoretical account itself, then this indicator of success or failure is otiose. If it is the case that Coleman's corrective justice theory of tort law determines that the core is the most significant feature of tort law, and his account accommodates the core, this cannot be used to discredit alternative accounts. This is because, if alternative theoretical accounts of the institution function in the same way as we are imagining Coleman's to function, then those accounts themselves determine which features of the institution should be regarded as significant. And clearly there is no guarantee that these accounts will regard as significant the same features that Coleman's account takes to be important.

The general difficulty for Coleman here is that of the 'distance' between his theoretical, corrective justice account of the institution and the significant features of the institution that any theoretical account must fit in order to be plausible. If his theory determines what features of the institution are significant, then his theory presumably cannot fail to fit those features. Judged solely on the basis of the arguments in *RW*, Coleman lacks a satisfactory way of tackling this difficulty.[28] That he recognizes it, however, is plain from his subsequent work. Our judgment upon his treatment of the issue must therefore be postponed until the end of the following subsection.

HOLISM AND CONCEPTUAL EXPLANATION

In *The Practice of Principle* (*PoP*)[29] Coleman summarizes his view of the relationship between tort law and corrective justice thus:

> [s]tarting at . . . the ground level, we have practices of corrective justice – a system of practical inferences that purports to determine when the imposition of a liability is justified. The structure of these inferences in tort law gives determinate content to its [tort law's? corrective justice's?] key concepts, and thereby makes explicit the requirements of the principle of corrective justice; while at the same time the principle of corrective justice organizes the concepts of tort law, explains the nature and structure of the inferences those concepts license, and in doing so, guides the practice of tort law. The principle of corrective justice, in turn, occupies a mid-level between the practices of tort law and an upper-level principle of fairness in allocating the costs of life's misfortunes. Here again the higher principle is said to be given determinate content by the practices subordinate to it, while at the same time guiding and constraining them. (*PoP*, pp. 54–55)

[28] See the arguments outlined in 'Rethinking the Common Law', supra, note 26.

[29] Supra, note 3.

This statement is important for it directly tackles the difficulty posed at the end of the last subsection. The difficulty is resolved, on the view stated here, by Coleman's deployment of an holistic approach to explanation and justification which derives from a more general semantic and epistemic philosophical position he calls pragmatism. For current purposes, the key feature of an holistic approach is the claim that 'the content of every concept depends to a greater or lesser degree on the content of every other' (*PoP*, p. 55). Thus, the content of corrective justice is in part provided by the institution of tort law and its constitutive practices, itself a manifestation of corrective justice. Corrective justice both informs and is informed by a more abstract notion of fairness which also exercises some normative force upon the practices of tort law, the latter being a detailed manifestation of the notion of fairness as applied to the distribution of human misfortunes. Coleman's statement of the precise way in which corrective justice explains tort law – 'when we see the inferential practices of tort law in the light of the principle of corrective justice, they hang together in a way that makes the best sense of those practices. Add to this the fact that tort law is plainly a normative practice, and the way corrective justice makes sense of it is by expressing the norm that governs it' (*PoP*, ibid) – must be read in light of his commitment to holism. Thus, the direction of the explanation cannot be simply one way, from corrective justice to tort law; each must to some extent illuminate the other.

What are we to make of Coleman's holism: does it calm our fears about the lack of distance between his corrective justice account of the institution of tort law and the institution itself? Not completely, for the simple reason that this worry about distance has two dimensions, only one of which Coleman tackles. One dimension is the distance from institution to theoretical explanation or understanding, in the sense that features of the former must surely be independent of the latter. The other is that a good explanation or understanding must have some effectiveness within the institution, must do some discernible work in determining at least some of the moves participants make within the institution. Coleman only addresses the latter dimension, and then in a not entirely satisfactory way.

The weakness in Coleman's demonstration of the way in which moves within the institution can be illegitimate from the perspective of corrective justice is that it is vague. For the attempt to show that his corrective justice account of tort law rules out some moves within the institution, thereby also showing that corrective justice is to some extent independent of that which it seeks to explain, eliminates moves participants are never likely to have to make. Coleman shows, for example, that fairness, 'mediated by corrective justice' (*PoP*, p. 57), requires that no person be permitted to unilaterally set the terms of interaction with other individuals. And this, he says, rules out any move in tort law to adopt a subjective standard of fault or negligence. Any such move would, from the perspective of corrective justice and fairness, be a mistake. So far as it goes, this is unexceptionable. But notice how odd a move this would be within the practices of tort law. First, its very language is unlike that which would be used by participants. When faced with doctrinal choices, participants frame those choices in terms of the specific doctrine in question: they ask, for example, what is the nature of the duty owed by one who is alleged to have created a private nuisance or what is the standard of care of one who professes a special skill or expertise? It is doubtful participants ever ask: what is the standard of liability here? Which makes salient the second point. Questions such as the latter are almost never asked in general terms because they already have answers: in the tort systems of the common law world, there is now no question of the standard of negligence being subjective. That question has not been a live one for a very long time. So, showing that one's explanatory-cum-normative theory of tort law rules out a question which, if asked by participants, would be otiose, is not to demonstrate anything particularly interesting or illuminating. The judgment would surely be different if, for example, the theory in play answered the question of the precise range of the duty of a surveyor or property valuer.[30]

As to the first dimension of the distance problem, Coleman adds little to the thoughts offered in *RW*, save for the fact that there is an interesting absence in his later thinking. He still maintains that any account of tort law must explain the core, but lacks a legitimate argument as to why the core should be considered important. Such an argument must, remember, rest neither upon unanimity among participants in the institution nor derive the core's importance from the theoretical account that seeks to explain or understand the core. One might therefore expect to find in *PoP* an argument seeking to justify the significance of the core either by reference to some views of some participants in the institution or in some other way. This expectation is, however, disappointed. Indeed, there is no explicit recourse to the methodological injunction in that part of *PoP*

[30] The judgement would also surely be tinged with amazement if the theory generated an answer to a case like *South Australia Asset Management Corporation v York Montague Ltd* [1997] AC 191.

which develops Coleman's own view of tort law and corrective justice. The internal point of view certainly appears in Coleman's discussion of matters of general jurisprudence, such as Hart's account of rule following, but is not in play anywhere else. Thus, since Coleman does not invoke the methodological injunction, he cannot provide an argument justifying the significance of the core by reference to the views of some participants.

This might, however, be thought an exaggeration. For, although Coleman does not explicitly invoke the methodological injunction in *PoP*, he might do so *implicitly*. The vehicle of this implicit commitment, it could be argued, is Coleman's account of the type of analysis of tort law that he offers in *PoP*: it is a 'conceptual analysis'. Providing a 'conceptual analysis of a social institution is to identify the central concepts that figure in it, and to explicate their content and their relationships with one another: we identify the criteria for the proper application of each key concept in the domain and . . . show what these . . . criteria have in common' (*PoP*, p. 13). And how are such central concepts and criteria of tort law to be identified, if not by recourse to the views of participants? When taken in conjunction with Coleman's criticism of some versions of *EAL* for explaining tort law without reference to the 'inferential practices of participants' (*PoP*, p. 25), this is suggestive evidence that the methodological injunction is in play, albeit in a background role. But to state this argumentative line is to show its very obvious limitation. For, even if Coleman is implicitly committed, by virtue of doing conceptual analysis, to the methodological injunction, restating that commitment does not answer the questions already raised about it. We require some justification of the significance of the core and showing that Coleman does, despite initial appearances, espouse the methodological injunction in *PoP* is certainly not to provide such a justification. It is, rather, to arrive at the point of such a justification being required, if it is assumed that the participants are not univocal on either what counts as the core or on why it is significant.[31] Thus the difficulty that besets Coleman's methodological position in *RW* also ensnares his position in *PoP*.

FOUNDATIONS: HOW?

Our discovery, if it can be called such, is that these two accounts of the normative foundation of private law are ensnared by the fit problem and

[31] He maintains that '[a]ny conception of the core of tort law is bound to be controversial' ('Second Thoughts . . .', supra, note 25, p. 297) but the reasons for this view are not stated: the thought is offered *en passant*.

its ramifications. The problem arises from Weinrib's and Coleman's apparent commitment to the methodological injunction and its implication that an account of the normative foundation of private law must in some sense be consistent with the views of participants in that institution. Neither jurist has a satisfactory response to the possibility of participants not sharing the theoretical language and concepts that they use in their accounts of the institution. Weinrib seems, despite first impressions, to take the language and views of participants no more seriously than proponents of *EAL*. This is particularly surprising in light of Weinrib's objections to functionalism and his effort to provide an 'internal' account of the special morality of private law. Coleman's response to the fit problem is unsatisfactory in another way: he has no argument as to why a subset of participants' views – the subset that takes the core seriously in the way Coleman's theory does – dominates or should be regarded as more salient than another.

The fit problem is not so severe as to completely undermine these two accounts. It illuminates a tension that both accounts suffer from and must, at some stage, resolve, particularly if there is to be some genuine methodological distance between these accounts and *EAL*. But this tension should not blind us to other aspects of Weinrib's and Coleman's accounts of tort law. One, which is noted here, is the precise way in which corrective justice features in each account as a normative foundation. Another, which is taken up in the next section, is the exact basis of the duty to correct that corrective justice supposedly generates.

Chapter 7 noted two broadly different ways in which some or other consideration or group of considerations can fulfil the role of normative foundation. The first way was captured by the architectural understanding of foundation talk. One branch of this family of views would hold that corrective justice is the distinct and separable basis upon which private law arises and on which it depends for normative support. All but one version of the architectural reading holds that the relationship between foundation and superstructure is one way: the latter is in some sense determined by the former. Another branch of this family of views is more subtle in that the architectural image becomes an epistemic image: here corrective justice is the notion that in some way 'makes sense' of the institution and practices of private law. The second way in which foundation talk could be understood is unrelated to the architectural metaphor and is probably better characterised without recourse to the idea of foundations. On this view, the normative basis or foundation of private law is actually better understood as something immanent within the law rather than as a distinct or separable foundation. Which role, of these three, do Coleman and Weinrib ascribe to corrective justice?

It seems that for Weinrib corrective justice and Kantian right are normative foundations in something like an epistemic sense: they are the presuppositions of the practice, conferring meaning on it over and beyond the meaning participants give it. This seems entirely appropriate when we bear in mind the limited role that participants' views actually have in Weinrib's account: they are the starting point of his theory and certainly not its end point. However, it seems also to be true of Weinrib's account that corrective justice and Kantian right are immanent within the institution of private law, so that talk of them acting as 'foundations' might be inappropriate. If corrective justice and Kantian right are genuinely presupposed by private law, then there is a sense in which they are clearly not separable from it in the way foundations are distinct from the building that arises upon them. This, of course, follows from the strongest interpretation of the idea of 'presupposition' but, on that view, there cannot be room for any other competing account of the presuppositions of private law.[32] It seems Weinrib has this strong sense of presupposition in mind when, for example, he says that corrective justice and Kantian right are present to private law in the same way as the rules of standard logic are present to intelligible speech or writing. But, as already noted, this would imply that other accounts of the normative foundation of private law are unintelligible and this is clearly not so. If, then, Weinrib must espouse a weaker account of presupposition, his account of the normativity of private law must distinguish itself from its competitors in another way. What that other way might be is not our current concern. More important is this: the way in which corrective justice and Kantian right function as an account of either the normative foundation or simply the normativity of private law obviously determines the way in which Weinrib's account must be evaluated. And, as things currently stand, that process of evaluation must proceed along two paths, for Weinrib's account of private law is ambitious: it must be examined both as giving sense to, and as being immanent within, the institution and its constitutive practices.

For Coleman, corrective justice is a normative foundation in something like the architectural sense: at least, this is the best account of Coleman's view in *RW*. His view in *PoP*, however, is quite different, since he there

[32] There are semantic and pragmatic types of presupposition both of which can vary in strength. An apparently additional type was also sketched by P. Strawson, *Introduction to Logical Theory* (London: Methuen, 1963), pp. 173–179.

conceives the role of corrective justice in relation to tort law as being either an epistemic one, in which it makes sense of tort law, and/or as being immanent within or embodied by the law. This combination of roles is, of course, a consequence of Coleman's holism. From Coleman's holistic perspective it makes little sense to distinguish the normative foundation of private law from the law itself because they inform, refine and exemplify one another. They are in no sense as distinct as foundation is from superstructure. Rather, private law and corrective justice are mutually supportive elements on this view, their relationship being entirely different from the one-way process of influence in which superstructures depend on foundations.

THE OBLIGATION TO CORRECT

Weinrib and Coleman seldom, if ever, speak of 'the obligation to correct'. For them, corrective justice creates an obligation of repair or recompense, a duty to make good the wrong and/or the losses it creates. The 'recompense' usage, however, is probably best avoided for the simple reason that it is natural for lawyers to read 'obligation of recompense' as 'obligation to make *monetary* recompense'. There is, of course, no necessity to this reading: nothing in the term 'recompense' entails that it must involve the transfer of money by way of correction.[33] Rather, this is simply a matter of association; in order to avoid the association we eschew the term that causes it. That done, we can examine the nature of the obligation to correct that corrective justice supposedly generates. This can best be done by posing three questions. First, why must we correct the wrongs we do to others that fall within the ambit of corrective justice? Why, in other words, should we regard this as an *obligation*? Second, what is the precise content of the obligation to correct? And, third, how does this putative obligation relate to the other moral, political and related obligations we have?

Why do we have an obligation to correct the wrongs we do to others? This question is posed not as means of investigating philosophically the rational power either political morality or morality *simpliciter* has over us. Nor is it intended as an examination of the conditions of moral imbecility. What follows is addressed only to those who can understand

[33] None of the senses given in *The Shorter Oxford English Dictionary* mention money; interestingly, some mention 'atonement'.

and recognize the various claims morality makes upon us. Furthermore, what follows is premised upon a large assumption. It is that, even though the areas of law with which we are primarily concerned – tort and contract – undoubtedly impose a legal obligation to correct the contractual and tortious wrongs we do, it nevertheless makes sense to try to determine whether this obligation is more than 'merely' legal. The 'merely' remark is from one perspective a massive understatement, since the consequences of breaching some of one's legal obligations could not be more serious. But another perspective, adopted here, asks if and how far our undoubtedly very serious legal obligations either *reflect* some of the moral, political and other obligations we have or are *simultaneously* both legal and moral (or political or other) obligations.[34] So, as agents of reasonably good moral standing, why, if at all, do we think there is an obligation to put right the wrongs we do to others over and beyond the fact that the law imposes such an obligation?

First, a word about the general notion of 'obligation'. Is an obligation just one consideration among many – just one reason, of the same status as all the others that might incline our conduct one way or the other – or is it a special kind of consideration? A common thought in response to this question is that obligations surely play a distinctive role in our deliberations because they are a particularly weighty type of consideration or reason. One way of putting this is to say that obligations always have greater presumptive weight in our deliberations than other (non-obligatory) considerations. So, for example, in deliberating whether to do A or B, the fact that A is an obligation means that we always initially have stronger or better reason to do A than B. Much weight is borne by the term 'initially' here and the motivation for using it is clear: on this view of obligation it remains a possibility that obligations can be outweighed by other considerations. Of course, if these other considerations turn out to be obligations in disguise, then the point is trivial. It is obvious that we can have some obligations that are weightier than others: my obligation to the person next to me who will die without the most minimal aid is surely weightier than my obligation to meet you on time. On the presumptive view of obligation, obligations, while generating considerations for acting one way rather than another that are generally weightier than other kinds of consideration, can nevertheless be outweighed in some circumstances

[34] This clumsy formulation results from trying to capture a difference between Coleman and Weinrib which will be examined soon.

by non-obligatory considerations.[35] What these considerations might be need not concern us here.

Another way of unpacking the idea that obligations play a distinctive role in our deliberations is to hold that they are in fact compelling considerations. To be under an obligation, on this view, is be compelled to do that which one is obliged to do, unless that obligation is itself overridden by another weightier obligation. It is not just that obligations are *generally* weightier considerations than the others that might incline us to act one way or another: they are *always* weightier than such other considerations. We might say that on this view obligations occupy a higher category of weightiness than most other, if not absolutely all, considerations. Obligations are thus some of the most important considerations in our lives. Fortunately, we do not have to decide between these two different accounts of the nature of obligation for current purposes. The point of introducing them is, rather, to highlight the distinct nature of the considerations that must inform the obligation to correct. They must be particularly weighty: either presumptively weighty, in the sense that they generally dominate other non-obligatory considerations or compellingly weighty, in that they always dominate almost all other considerations.[36]

We can now return to our question: what are the grounds of the obligation to correct the wrongs we do to others? One immediate common sense thought here is that the obligation to correct surely arises from the wrong we have done: if there is no wrong, then how can an obligation to correct arise? What, indeed, is there to correct in the absence of a wrong and/or wrongdoing?[37] Of course, this thought remains valid whether or not the wrong in question is of the very worst or of the most minimal kind. My accidentally jostling you in a crowd can be corrected by an apology: such, indeed, would be expected, whether or not contact was a result of my clumsiness or the sheer weight of numbers. In this instance, my conduct is wrong and stands in need of correction even though it has

[35] This view of obligation is an obvious echo of W. D. Ross's treatment of *prima facie* duties (and obligations) in his *The Right and the Good* (Oxford: Clarendon Press, 1930), ch. II. For a critical treatment see J. Searle, '*Prima Facie* Obligations', ch. V of J. Raz (ed.), *Practical Reasoning* (Oxford: Clarendon Press, 1978).

[36] For a more detailed characterization of a view similar to this, see L. Green, 'Law and Obligations', ch. 13 of J. Coleman and S. Shapiro (eds.), *The Oxford Handbook of Jurisprudence and Philosophy of Law* (Oxford: Clarendon Press, 2002) at pp. 518–519.

[37] The distinction between wrongs and wrongdoing that makes the use of both terms necessary is that the former can be specified without reference to any properties of the perpetrator. Wrongdoing, by contrast, is a combination of wrongs and some general properties of the perpetrator like, for example, agency, or more specific properties such as, for instance, intention.

not significantly harmed you. Where my wrongdoing occasions you serious harm much more than an apology might be expected by way of correction. But, here again, it is the wrong I have done you, conjoined with the harm it has brought about, that seemingly drives the obligation to correct. Whether my conduct is a relatively harmless wrong, as in the case of jostling, or an extremely harmful wrong, as where I hit you with my car, it is the wrongdoing itself that seemingly animates the *obligation* to correct. A presumptively or even compellingly powerful reason to act in a certain way must have at its basis some particularly important human interest and there are few such interests more important than that of being free from the wrongful and harmful interventions of others. Indeed, since harming and thus wronging others has long been accepted as a good ground for the criminalization of some conduct, there seems no reason why it should not be a good ground for liability in private law.

One important implication of the common sense thought that wrongdoing drives the obligation to correct is that theories of corrective justice must provide an *independent, substantive* but also fairly *limited* account of wrongs and wrongdoing. Saying that a theory of corrective justice's account of wrongs and wrongdoing must be independent means that it cannot simply take for granted the account of wrongs and wrongdoing already embodied in the law itself. At least, it cannot do this if it is to exercise normative force over the law, providing a basis upon which the law can be evaluated. That such an account of wrongs and wrongdoing must be substantive means no more than that its content must include a list of protected human interests and an elucidation of how they are to be protected and valued if undermined. That an account of wrongs and wrongdoing must be limited is obvious once we recognize that there are many harms we can inflict upon one another without any suggestion of legal liability or an obligation to correct arising. Losses that arise from commercial and sporting competitions, for example, or those involving matters of the heart, are usually regarded as legitimate in the sense that 'victims' have to bear them. So an account of corrective justice must say which losses fall within its ambit and which do not or, in other words, which are wrongs from the perspective of corrective justice and which are not. We need to know why Romeo's absconding and living happily ever after with my beloved Juliet is not a breach of corrective justice, whereas Romeo negligently driving his car into mine during the hasty elopement is.

Do Weinrib and Coleman see things in this way, that is, regard the notion of wrongdoing as fundamental to their theories because a primary element of any obligation to correct? Their answers to this question are examined separately. In the course of that examination other arguments Weinrib and Coleman offer to show the basis of the obligation to correct are also analysed. Some attention is also paid to the precise content of this obligation and its relation with the other obligations we have.

WEINRIB'S ANSWER

It is not clear that Weinrib provides an answer to our question about wrongs and wrongdoing. The principal reason for this is that the Aristotelian components of his theory of corrective justice allow little room for a substantive and independent account of wrongs and wrongdoing.[38] To see why this is so, we examine three of those components: rectification, correlativity and the distinction between corrective and distributive justice.

Rectification, correlativity and the two forms of justice

The first component is neither problematic nor difficult: it holds that 'corrective justice has a rectificatory function . . . correcting the injustice that the defendant has inflicted on the plaintiff' (*CJN*, p. 350).[39] What is interesting about this component is an absence: corrective justice's rectificatory function is not accompanied by a catalogue of wrongs and wrongdoing constitutive of injustice. It is natural to assume, in the presence of talk about rectification, that there must be a clear account of what it is that needs be rectified, some specific mistake or list of errors or prohibited conduct which, if they occur, must be put right. Yet no account of such wrongs is forthcoming from Weinrib, except the account of wrongs recognized in legal doctrine: 'the concepts and principles of tort liability set out the conditions under which the defendant's conduct counts as a wrongful infringement of the plaintiff's right' (*CJN*, p. 353). But what, if anything, is problematic in this response? Surely it is

[38] The exegetical issue of the accuracy and plausibility of Weinrib's interpretation of Aristotle is side-stepped in what follows as are many general questions about Aristotle's own treatment of corrective justice. For Aristotle's own discussion, see *Nicomachean Ethics*, Book V in J. Barnes (ed.) *The Complete Works of Aristotle* (Princeton, New Jersey: Princeton University Press, 1984) Vol. II. For a treatment of some of the latter questions see: J. Neyers, 'The Inconsistencies of Aristotle's Theory of Corrective Justice' (1998) XI *Canadian Journal of Law and Jurisprudence* 311–328.

[39] Henceforth, in text and notes, '*CJN*' refers to E. Weinrib, 'Corrective Justice in a Nutshell' (2002) LII *University of Toronto LJ* 349–356. Each of the components sketched in this wonderfully brisk and economical essay are examined at greater length in chs. 3–5 of *IPL*, supra, note 3. Note that this chapter alternates between use of 'plaintiff' and 'claimant' because, although the latter is now the norm in England and Wales, the former is the norm in Canada (where Weinrib received his legal education) and the US (where Coleman received his).

perfectly legitimate for Weinrib to eschew any effort to develop a catalogue of wrongs and wrongdoing from scratch and simply point instead to the catalogue already available in legal doctrine?

The answer to this question takes us back to how we expect corrective justice to function when cast in the role of normative foundation of private law. We already know that for Weinrib corrective justice operates epistemically as a normative foundation, since it makes sense of the institution and practices of tort law, and is also immanent within, or a weak presupposition of, the institution and its constitutive practices. But, even when cast in these roles, is it legitimate for Weinrib's account of corrective justice simply to take tort law's catalogue of wrongdoing for granted? Some, including Hans Kelsen and Richard Posner, have thought this move illegitimate.[40] For the problem here is that as a normative foundation corrective justice is open to the charge of emptiness or redundancy if large swathes of the institution and practices it supposedly animates fall beyond its influence. If corrective justice has nothing to say about wrongs and wrongdoing that is independent of what legal doctrine tells us about those matters, then its normative power seems very limited. Since on Weinrib's view corrective justice apparently lacks the wherewithal to act as a basis upon which to take the moral or normative measure of some aspects of the law, then it seems miscast in the role of normative foundation. How are we to make sense of this? One possibly helpful factor is this: Weinrib's unwillingness to provide a substantive account of wrongs and wrongdoing may be traced to the second and third Aristotelian components of corrective justice.

As articulated by Weinrib and Aristotle, the idea of correlativity in corrective justice and private law is in at least one respect neither intuitively obvious nor straightforward. In another respect, however, it is both. At a common sense level, our thinking about the nature of a correlative exchange or transaction is uncomplicated: it implies the notion that whatever X does or gives to Y he receives either the same or an equivalent back from Y. It does no violence to our ordinary thought and language to regard this as a correlative transaction. And when Weinrib and Aristotle

[40] When made by Aristotle rather than Weinrib. See H. Kelsen, *What is Justice?* (Berkeley: University of California Press, 1960) 110–136 at pp. 133–134; R. Posner, *The Problems of Jurisprudence* (Cambridge, Mass.: Harvard University Press, 1990) pp. 321–322. A penetrating discussion of this issue is Stone, supra, note 17, pp. 253–262. For a defence of something very close to the Aristotelian view as characterized in the text see D. Klimchuk, 'On the Autonomy of Corrective Justice' (2003) 23 *Oxford Journal of Legal Studies* 49–64, pp. 60–64. The case is somewhat weakened by failure to show that what is alleged to be wrong with the 'foundational asymmetry view' he impugns is genuinely troublesome.

explain the correlativity of gains and losses in corrective justice, it is just this meaning they have in mind – corrective justice operates so as to remove the gain the defendant has obtained from the plaintiff by returning it, or its value, to the plaintiff. The defendant's gain is the plaintiff's loss and it is this that corrective justice addresses: '[t]he remedy consists in simultaneously taking away the defendant's excess and making good the plaintiff's deficiency' (*CJN*, p. 350). The notion of correlativity of gains and losses in corrective justice is supplemented with the notion of correlativity in rectification:

> [a] correlatively structured remedy responds to and undoes an injustice only if that injustice is itself correlatively structured. In bringing an action against the defendant, the plaintiff is asserting that the two are connected as doer and sufferer of the same injustice. What the defendant has done and what the plaintiff has suffered are not independent events. Rather, they are the active and passive poles of the same injustice, so that what the defendant has done counts as an injustice only because of what the defendant [sic; plaintiff, surely] has suffered, and vice versa. The law then rectifies this injustice by reversing its active and passive poles, so that the doer of injustice becomes the sufferer of the law's remedy. (*CJN*, ibid)

The idea of correlativity in play here is the same as that involved in the correlativity of gains and losses; it is, therefore, perfectly intelligible. So when does this notion become counterintuitive and problematic? As soon as we imagine implementing both correlativity in gains and losses and in rectification within the context of an actual legal dispute.

Think, for example, of a dispute arising from Y taking 10 of Z's sheep. The notions of correlativity of gains and losses, and correlativity in rectification, seem perfectly realizable here: on the assumption that Y's taking Z's sheep was wrong, then a corrective justice remedy that returns the 10 sheep from Y to Z is correlative in the relevant respects. The remedy recognizes the correlativity or equality of gain and loss between Y and Z and rectifies it as between Y and Z. But how do we ensure that a remedy is correlative in rectification, and thus tracks the correlativity of gains and losses, if Y has simply killed Z's sheep? Or, perhaps more difficult: suppose Y has seriously injured Z by either negligently driving into her or by negligent surgery.[41] What, exactly, is Y's gain here and in what sense

[41] See S. Perry, 'The Moral Foundations of Tort Law' (1991–1992) 77 *Iowa LR* 449–514, pp. 456–458. For an interesting attempt to analyse the gains in such cases see M. Kramer, 'Of Aristotle and Ice Cream Cones: Reflections on Jules Coleman's Theory of Corrective Justice', ch. 8 of B. Bix, supra, note 25, at pp. 170–176.

is it correlative or equal to Z's loss? Weinrib's response to questions of this kind is clear: they are misguided because they

> assume[..] that gain and loss refer to the difference in the parties wealth before and after the injustice. But since, in Aristotle's account, the baseline for the parties' gain and loss is their initial equality, this assumption would imply that corrective justice presupposes – absurdly – an initial equality in the parties' wealth. In fact, however, equality is merely Aristotle's way of referring to the entitlement of each of the interacting parties to have what is rightfully theirs. (*CJN*, p. 354)

The way in which the correlative gains and losses to the parties are to be determined, then, is by reference to 'a notional equality' (*CJN*, p. 349) in which each has what is rightfully theirs. Corrective justice takes no interest in the actual quantity of the parties holdings *vis-à-vis* one another or with regard to any external standard. The standard of equality that constitutes the baseline for corrective justice is thus not substantial or, it could be said, 'actual' in any of these ways. Rather, it is 'notional' because so remote from actual or genuine equality. The standard in play, being that of the parties legitimate entitlements, is a standard of equality in the very thin sense that the parties entitlements are given equal respect by being taken for granted. The actual value, worth or quantity of their entitlements is irrelevant.

Correlativity and the notional equality upon which it depends impede the development of a substantive account of wrongs and wrongdoing in a very obvious way. A substantive account of wrongs and wrongdoing is an account of actual harms to the interests of human beings and a specification of the ways those interests are protected and valued. And there is no *a priori* ground to think that correlativity, of either gain and loss or in rectification, will be possible on such an account. Furthermore, when incorporated in the law such an account must commit itself, not just to the evaluation of the worth of abstract legal rights, but to an evaluation of their value to actual people placed in specific economic and other circumstances. The brutal materiality of private law's assessment of the value of losses – it tells us, for example, the value of various limbs[42] – might seem shocking to those who see it as redressing a notional inequality. But if it is doing that, it is also undoubtedly making good the actual losses to real

[42] See H. McGregor, *McGregor on Damages* (London: Sweet and Maxwell, 17th edn, 2003) Vol. II, ch. 35, esp. pp. 1299–1302 and The Judicial Studies Board, *Guidelines for the Assessment of General Damages in Personal Injury Cases* (Oxford: Clarendon Press, 7th edn, 2004).

human beings placed in specific circumstances. And there is surely an obvious problem here. For it is *prima facie* difficult to envision how corrective justice's correction of a notional equality is at the same time exactly coextensive with the award of monetary damages to real people to reflect their actual losses. It seems puzzling to regard a sum of, for example, £100,000 awarded to compensate the relatives of a claimant for his death and associated losses as a result of his employers' negligence as at the same time the restoration of notional equality. Or, perhaps more accurately, it is a puzzle why that award is *better understood* as the restoration of notional equality rather than as an effort to right the wrong done.

The questions raised by Weinrib's and Aristotle's recourse to a baseline of notional equality – a move motivated, remember, by the effort to make sense of the correlativity of gains and losses – are neither answered nor dissipated by invoking the notion of Kantian right. This notion is the means Weinrib used in *IPL* to unpack the idea of equality upon which corrective justice rests; it is not obviously identical with the notional equality invoked in *CJN*.[43] Kantian right is, in effect, an account of the nature of the agents whose conduct is governed by private law. It envisages them not as actual here and now beings with all their constitutive particularities, projects and commitments, but as abstract self-determining agents. 'The fundamental feature of this agency is the agent's capacity to abstract from – and thus not to be determined by – the particular circumstances of his or her situation. Inasmuch as this capacity is a defining feature of self-determining agency, all self-determining agents are equal with respect to it' (*IPL*, pp. 81–82). This conception of agency not only resonates well with the notional equality that provides the baseline upon which corrective justice operates; it also illuminates two other issues.

First, Kantian right can actually provide a formal account of wrongs and wrongdoing, since it holds that 'the free choice of . . . one must be capable of coexisting with the freedom of the other in accordance with a universal law' (*IPL*, p. 104). Free choices manifest in one's external conduct that are not so capable can thus be deemed wrong. Second, Kantian right and its constitutive conception of agency makes sense of one of Aristotle's apparently un-Aristotelian observations. It is that corrective justice ignores both the moral assessment of the character of those subject

[43] The possible tension between the notional equality of *CJN* and the equality of Kantian right in *IPL* is resolved by Weinrib's remarks in 'Correlativity, Personality, and the Emerging Consensus on Corrective Justice' (2001) 2 *Theoretical Inquires in Law* (online edition), Article 5 at p. 37, note 14. In this essay Kantian right is unpacked as a conception of juridical personality.

to it, and the moral quality of their conduct, while also being blind to differences in wealth between them.[44] Thus if correlativity is indeed a fundamental feature of corrective justice, then the abstract conception of agency in Kantian right is a helpful means of realizing it.

But this conception of agency compounds the questions raised of notional equality. If corrective justice and the law of tort are informed by Kantian right and its constitutive conception of agency, we are still left with the same series of puzzles already noted, although they are somewhat amplified. It is, for example, *prima facie* very difficult to see how to plausibly move from a judgment like 'X's conduct is based upon a free choice incapable of coexisting with the freedom of another under a universal law' to a decision like 'Y is entitled to damages in the amount of £20,000'. We might also wonder how to go about compensating Y, envisaged as an abstract agent, for injuries Y suffered as a real flesh and blood agent in all her particularity and with all her existing commitments and projects. Do *abstract* agents need *real* compensation? It is one thing to hold that abstract agents can only realize themselves in the 'external sphere' (*IPL*, p. 129), and thus must be entitled to control over some aspects of that sphere, but quite another to claim that tort law's award of real money to actual people for wrongs suffered is simply an implication of this. For, if it is said that tort law's remedying of wrongs is indeed a true implication of respect for abstract agency, abstract agency itself appears less important than it initially seemed. This notion, remember, supports the baseline of notional equality and informs the correlativity of gains and losses. Abstract agents are all equal in the sense that all have the capacity for self-determining agency; and the gains of one abstract agent can easily correlate with the losses of another if and when the deeds of one undermine the self-determining agency of the other. But '[i]t seems that to bestow normative significance on the concrete quality of the plaintiff's holdings' – which is what the law actually does – 'would be precisely to abandon this picture of equality. It would make the defendant's obligations turn not on the plaintiff's equal status as a person [or, more accurately, an abstract agent], but on the unequal value of her possessions'.[45]

The problem for Weinrib, then, is to square the actuality of the

[44] On the irrelevance of the moral standing of the parties see Aristotle, supra, note 38, Book V, 4, p. 1786.

[45] Stone, supra, note 17, p. 267. For an extensive treatment of the issue see Perry, supra, note 41, pp. 483–488. As is evident, the discussion in the text owes a good deal to these two classic essays.

law with the abstract and notional nature of some aspects of his (and Aristotle's) account of corrective justice. Although an undoubtedly interesting issue, this problem is not our current concern. The point in issue is, rather, the absence of a substantive account of wrongs and wrongdoing in Weinrib's theory of corrective justice. The notion of correlativity and, in particular, the ideas of notional equality and the abstract conception of agents on which correlativity depends, obviously impede the development of such an account. It makes as little sense to offer an account of real wrongs and real wrongdoing for abstract beings as it does to try and unpack a notional equality in substantive terms. This is not, however, the last impediment to the provision of such an account of wrongs and wrongdoings. That is found in the third Aristotelian component of Weinrib's theory of corrective justice.

This third component consists of the relation between corrective and distributive justice. Weinrib's (and Aristotle's) view of this relation has already been labelled, in Chapter 7, as 'the separation thesis'.[46] At the very least this holds that corrective and distributive justice are different and quite distinctive forms of justice and that the two represent categorically different 'modes of ordering' (*IPL*, p. 72). Furthermore, '[b]ecause corrective and distributive justice are . . . categorically different and mutually irreducible patterns of justificatory coherence, it follows that a single external relationship cannot partake of both' (*IPL*, p. 73). Or, at least, this follows *if* we subscribe to Weinrib's somewhat curious understanding of what it is for a justification to be coherent.[47] Whether or not we should so subscribe is not currently relevant; rather, the key point is that the effort to hold an impermeable line between the two forms of justice makes it almost impossible to offer a substantive account of wrongs and wrongdoing. Why? Because such an account, being a catalogue of genuine protected interests and the ways in which they can be undermined, sails too close to the wind of distributive justice. Developing an account of the interests of human beings that the law should protect quite naturally brings in its wake other, apparently distributive questions. It is clearly legitimate, when faced with such an account of protected interests, to ask questions like, for example: how are such protected interests distributed among a group? Do all who allegedly have such protected

[46] Not to be confused with what some call the separation thesis in general jurisprudence, which is supposedly constitutive of some varieties of legal positivism. For a helpful discussion see N. MacCormick, 'Natural Law and the Separation of Law and Morals' in George (ed.), supra, note 17.

[47] On which, see Stone, supra, note 17, pp. 243–245.

interests genuinely have them? And, if all do, how are the means of protecting such interests distributed? These questions, obviously, take us into the terrain of distributive justice. For both Weinrib and Aristotle that terrain raises issues allegedly qualitatively different from those in play in the domain of corrective justice.

The basis of the obligation to correct

Since it is clear that Weinrib's account of corrective justice does not invoke an independent and substantive account of wrongs and wrongdoing, it is also evident that we are no nearer to answering the question about the basis of the obligation to correct. The common sense thought on this issue was, remember, that the obligation to correct surely derives much of its power from the fact a wrong has been done and/or harm caused. Weinrib's unwillingness to provide a specification of wrongs and wrongdoing independent of the law means not only that his account of corrective justice is open to the charge of emptiness, but that it is also incompatible with this common sense thought. Yet it might be unduly hasty to conclude that things do not, therefore, look promising for this account of corrective justice. For it might it be the case that, in holding Weinrib's theory answerable to both the emptiness charge and the common sense thought, we are holding it to a standard by which it should not be judged. To understand this, we need return to and rethink the idea, important in the discussion in the first section of this chapter, of what it is to provide an 'internal' or 'immanent' account of an institution and its constitutive practices.

Consider this view of a 'properly' Aristotelian account of an institution or social practice:

> [s]uppose Aristotle were endeavouring not to give a recipe but only to make us aware of the contours of a practice in which a certain kind of case (a transaction) is central. The practice is thought to be of ethical interest because a distinctive sort of reason is in play in it; and it is through our grasping just this sort of reason that we can understand the contours of the practice.[48]

Applied to the institution of tort law, this view holds that corrective justice simply is the 'characteristic sort of reason *already* captured in the ongoing activity of argument and judgment directed towards the situation to which modern liability rules are a judicially evolved response'.[49] It holds, in other words, that the institution and its practices 'can be

[48] Stone, supra, note 17, p. 258.

[49] Ibid, p. 259 (emphasis in original).

understood to have, simply as such, an ethical significance, i.e., . . . without the mediation of a theory concerning the appropriate social allocation of resources [or, we may add, concerning wrongs and wrongdoing]'.[50] On this view, then, an internal account of an institution need have little if anything to do with participants' views: the referent of 'internal' is not the views of those whose conduct and beliefs constitute the institution and its practices but the kind of reason immanent or implicit within the institution.[51] While this seems to compound the problem of methodological parity with *EAL*, it has another implication apparently helpful to Weinrib. It is that to require this theory of corrective justice to provide a substantive and independent account of wrongs and wrongdoing, and to require it to be answerable to the common sense thought, is to look outwith the institution of tort law for an understanding of the theory. This is to miss the distinctive type of reason for action, founded in corrective justice, that the institution itself embodies. It might also be to venture into the prohibited realm of deliberation about the appropriate social allocation of resources.

This view of the nature of a properly Aristotelian, internal account of an institution can also be invoked to defend Weinrib's theory of corrective justice against another version of the emptiness charge. This version holds not that the account is normatively empty because it takes for granted the normative status of the catalogue of wrongs and wrongdoing provided in the law, but that it is empty because it assumes the remedies the law provides are normatively required. In particular, this account of corrective justice simply takes it for granted that rectification of wrongs requires, first and foremost, monetary compensation (damages). While this is undoubtedly a surprisingly laconic and disappointingly unimaginative account of the content of the obligation to correct, it also faces more severe difficulties. Prime among these is a lacuna: no argument is provided to show that, of the range of conceivable ways in which wrongs could be and actually are rectified, the damages remedy is either normatively necessary or normatively respectable.[52] Nor can the damages

[50] Ibid.

[51] See Weinrib, supra, note 43 at, for example, pp. 1 and 35 for remarks to this effect.

[52] Which is not to imply that Weinrib pays no attention to other legal remedies (see *IPL*, p. 195 (injunctions in nuisance) and 'Restitutionary Damages as Corrective Justice', supra, note 4). The problem, though, is the same as with his discussion of the damages remedy, namely, that no argument is offered to show the normative salience of this particular remedy over and beyond other conceivable options. B. Zipursky, 'Civil Recourse, Not Corrective Justice' (2003) 91 *Georgetown LR* 695–756 at pp. 709–724 is particularly acute on the problems theories of corrective justice have in accommodating private law remedies.

remedy be assumed to be normatively necessary. The danger in this manoeuvre is obvious, if it is the case that a number of legal doctrinal rules are a matter of convention (or *determinatio*).[53] This means that the content of many specific legal rules is not normatively necessary. What is necessary is that there be a rule on the matter in question (for example, which side of the road to drive upon) and that everyone abide by it; the actual content of the rule adopted (drive right, drive left or drive middle) is, however, normatively insignificant. Now this could well be true of those doctrinal rules that specify many or some legal remedies; it seems very likely true of, for example, the choice various legal systems have made between the options for the default remedy for breach of contract (either damages or specific performance/implement). As to damages for tortious wrongdoing, it might equally be the case that it does not matter, normatively speaking, what the actual remedy is – monetary compensation, apology, replacement of damaged goods, specific performance or repair – so long as the same general remedy is available. If private law remedies are thus a matter of convention, it seems dangerous to assume that any particular remedy has pre-eminent normative salience.

The reply to this version of the emptiness charge is clear: to look for a normative justification for the remedy tort law normally gives is to look outwith the institution for an understanding of it. If we are properly Aristotelian, and if we truly see the ethical significance of the institution and of the reasons for action embodied within it, then we see that this version of the emptiness charge is misplaced. The remedies tort law offers are simply embodiments of corrective justice. Whether or not this reply is compelling is not pursued here, except in terms of a broad argument about this general line of thought explored at the end of the next subsection. For now, we must note how the considerations that inform this reply can also provide a reply to our question about the basis of the obligation to correct.

Asking for the basis of this obligation in the manner we have, as if an argument could be provided that was independent of the institution to such a degree as to provide a normative basis against which to judge the institution, is to misrepresent the nature of this account of tort law and corrective justice. On a properly Aristotelian account, to see the characteristic sort of reason embodied in the institution is to see an obligation to correct: if we do not see the latter, we must have misunderstood the

[53] See J. Finnis, *Natural Law and Natural Rights* (Oxford: Clarendon Press, 1980) pp. 284–289 for *determinatio*; N. MacCormick *Legal Reasoning and Legal Theory* (Oxford: Clarendon Press, 1978), p. 1 for convention. Although closely related, the two ideas are not identical.

former. This resonates well both with Aristotle's general observations about the nature and content of ethical thought and some of Weinrib's statements about tort law and corrective justice.

As to the former, one particularly compelling interpretation of Aristotle's thought is that, for him, understanding the nature of particular ethical precepts and of ethical matters in general comes principally through application. 'Doing' ethics, in various life contexts, is the path to knowledge. And the effort to state in advance the nature and basis of the obligation to correct is, it might be said, completely contrary to this way of thinking, to emphasize 'theoretical' over 'practical' knowledge.[54] For Weinrib, corrective justice is the 'special' or 'inner' morality of tort law. One Aristotelian implication that can be drawn from this is obvious: to see this special morality is to see that it generates an obligation to correct. Showing the morality of private law is, for Weinrib, to show that it creates obligations: they are in fact one and the same thing. To then ask 'what is the basis of the obligation to correct?' is to make a moral mistake, to misunderstand the fact that this morality is a morality of obligation. To look beyond the law for an account of the basis of the obligations it imposes upon us is to ignore the law's own distinctive moral and normative structure, to overlook its internal normativity. On this view, then, the obligation to correct arises from the special morality of the law and that, of course, is a matter of corrective justice. It does not therefore make sense, on this view, to speak as we did at the beginning of this section of private law obligations being 'merely' legal, as if it were a further question whether or not these obligations were morally binding. For Weinrib, it seems likely that these particular legal obligations – and possibly all legal obligations – are also moral obligations.

As to the general question of the relation between the obligation to correct and other moral, political and normative obligations, two points can be made. First, the obligation to correct is on Weinrib's view qualitatively quite different from any obligations that arise from distributive justice. This much must be so if corrective and distributive justice are indeed incompatible forms of ordering (*IPL*, pp. 68–75). Second, the obligation to correct must be a fairly distinctive member of the family of obligations that we have in our lives. This is because it is unusual for many of our obligations to be moral because legal as opposed to being

[54] Stone, supra, note 17, p. 260 drawing on, in particular, J. McDowell, 'Eudaimonism and Realism in Aristotle's Ethics' in R. Heinamen (ed.), *Aristotle and Moral Realism* (Boulder: Westview Press, 1995), pp. 201–218.

simultaneously moral and legal. The latter scenario is not unusual if it is possible to have moral obligations that are also given legal form: think, for example, of parents' obligation to nurture their children. Nor is it inconceivable that the law holds steady or gives detail to either vague or general moral obligations, so that what is a non-specific general moral obligation (to support one's community, say) becomes a precise legal obligation (to pay local taxes). What is unusual, however, is to have a legal obligation that is by virtue of being such an obligation also 'therefore' a moral obligation. At least, this is unusual in a context in which few accept that there is a general obligation to obey the law simply because it is the law.[55] But Weinrib's view of the obligation to correct, because it does not look beyond the law for its basis, seems structurally very similar to an argument that holds a legal obligation is also a moral obligation *by virtue of being a legal obligation.* If this is indeed the structure of Weinrib's argument, then is generates an obvious snag: is the fact that the obligation to correct is a legal obligation enough to give it sufficient weight to count as a presumptive or compelling obligation? In a world in which the authority of law is never taken for granted, this question will always be asked.

The authenticity argument

Many more quibbles and doubts might be raised of each element of the argument just considered. So as to distinguish it from the three Aristotelian components of Weinrib's account of corrective justice, it is labelled 'the authenticity argument'. The argument holds that a genuine, properly Aristotelian understanding of corrective justice provides a distinctive (possibly unique) understanding of the principal features of tort law such as, for example, its account of wrongs and wrongdoing and the obligation to correct. As against the three related difficulties so far raised for the Weinrib/Aristotle account of corrective justice – two versions of the emptiness charge and the absence of an argument supporting the obligation to correct – the authenticity argument's response is clear. It claims those alleged difficulties actually arise from a misunderstanding of the nature, aims and ambitions of this theory of corrective justice. What follows takes issue with some of the details of the authenticity argument

[55] The dominant view of both the obligation to obey the law and of political authority in general is now 'philosophical anarchism'. One of its key tenets is that there is no general obligation to obey the law, although there certainly are particular obligations to obey particular laws. Good general discussion is provided by S. Shapiro, 'Authority', ch. 10 of Coleman and Shapiro, supra, note 36 and Green, supra, note 36.

and notes a general problem that also appears to undermine it. If the argument is undermined in these ways, then the solutions it offers to the problems in Weinrib's account of corrective justice are themselves undermined. We are thus left with an account of corrective justice, cast in the role of normative foundation of private law, subject to charges of emptiness and opacity.

The first problem with the authenticity argument is that Weinrib does not offer it in defence of his theory of corrective justice. It is Martin Stone's suggested solution to both versions of the emptiness charge.[56] This, of course, does not undermine the cogency of the argument itself, but it does raise doubt about the possibility of invoking it to defend Weinrib's account of corrective justice. As Stone notes, the argument is incompatible with one strand of Weinrib's defence of his theory of corrective justice, namely, the invocation of Kantian right. For Weinrib, Kantian right is, in *IPL* at least, the means of understanding the idea of equality upon which corrective justice rests. For Stone, by contrast, the invocation of such an account of equality is to ground this account of corrective justice in an external standard. And that, according to Stone, is not something either Aristotle, or those who have 'the perspective of someone who already accepts that tort law expresses genuine reasons', would regard as necessary.[57] It seems, then, that Weinrib faces a dilemma: either adopt the properly Aristotelian approach Stone recommends and jettison Kantian right; or persevere with Kantian right and attempt to resolve the difficulties, particularly that manifest in the first version of the emptiness charge, which his theory faces as a result.

Even if Weinrib were inclined to invoke the authenticity argument – a conclusion that could be based upon the fact that Kantian right makes no appearance in *CJN* – it is unclear he would be wise to do so. For, if he does, a second problem looms. Although the authenticity argument's account of what it is to offer an internal, non-functional understanding of an institution and its constitutive practices obviously has some resonance with what Weinrib says, and particularly with some exemplary instances of such internal accounts (love and friendship), it can also be said to rest on weak foundations. And two such foundations are the exemplary instances just noted: because, suggest Stone and Weinrib, friendship and love cannot be understood in anything but an internal or immanent way, that gives good reason to understand private law in the same way. But why should we accept these two exemplars as being closely analogous to

[56] Supra, note 17, pp. 258–262. [57] Supra, note 17, p. 263.

private law? Contesting the propriety of the analogy does not obviously commit us to an objectionable functionalism, so the move cannot be ruled out by Weinrib in advance. Nor is it motivated by simple wilfulness: it is not merely idle obscurantism to worry about the obvious and large differences between private law as we know it here and now and either love or friendship.

The seriousness of the law, the fact that it is a potentially brutal power in our lives, was made vivid by Robert Cover's remark that 'legal interpretation takes place within a field of pain and death'.[58] We do well to remember this, however far from the sharp point of the law's implementation our thinking may carry us. Remembering it also throws into relief just how unlike law is from either love or friendship: true, both are and should be important forces in our lives. True, both can be a cause of much personal misery and pain. But neither surely have anything like the potential for harm law has and neither raise anything like the distinctly political worries that legal power and force do. We might, in moments of whimsy, imagine campaigning against the harm love does; yet campaigning, as many do, against the harm unfair or unjust laws do is far from whimsical. Furthermore, while both love and friendship should be forces in our lives, they do not, except for the most romantic or lovesick, claim pre-eminence over all other considerations. Modern law does claim this pre-eminence and we ignore it at our peril. If these features of law do indeed serve to distinguish it as qualitatively different from love and friendship, then we may wonder about the propriety of understanding it in the way those qualitatively different phenomena should be understood.

This second difficulty touches upon a larger issue. It can be formulated with a question: is a properly Aristotelian approach to understanding law, ethics and morality currently possible? This is the third problem that the authenticity argument faces. Suppose that everything about the authenticity argument is unimpeachable or, at least, that it rests upon compelling analogies and could be unproblematically adopted by Weinrib. Even then the argument might not succeed, despite its internal coherence and plausibility. Why? Because what the argument requires of us is currently very hard to achieve. It requires we accept a way of understanding institutions and practices such that their ethical or moral significance is sufficiently elucidated simply by our seeing the distinctive kind of reason

[58] And 'legal interpretative acts signal and occasion the imposition of violence upon others'. Both statements are from R. Cover, 'Violence and the Word' (1986) 95 *Yale LJ* 1601–1629, p. 1601.

those institutions and practices embody. But this may no longer be enough for us. Suppose our world is indeed one in which ethical, moral and normative reflection in general is geared around 'administrative ideas of rationality' wherein considerations pro and con must always be transparent, clearly stateable and subject to an impartial decision procedure.[59] Being told that an institution and its constitutive practices embody a distinctive reason is not, on this view, enough to validate either institution or practices, on the one hand, or to legitimize that reason, on the other. It might be sufficient for those already committed to the institution and the reason it supposedly embodies, but such pre-commitment is itself suspect on the view we are considering: all such pre-commitments themselves stand in need of justification. Another way of putting this is to say that we ask more by way of justification than the authenticity argument can provide because, in terms already used, we are children of the interpretative attitude.[60] This attitude is one in which social institutions are never or rarely assumed always simply to embody and track right reason, or the politically required or the morally right. Greater rational transparency is required than the demonstration that some institutions or practices simply have ethical or moral significance 'as such'.

This argument is broader than that offered by Bernard Williams and others about the impossibility of an Aristotelian morality.[61] That more specific argument holds that some of the assumptions, principally those about human nature, upon which Aristotle's account of morality depends are simply not available to us: they have been undermined and discredited by scientific knowledge. Nor, thinks Williams, are intellectually respectable surrogates available for these assumptions. The difficulty just posed for the authenticity argument is by no means the same as this argument from Williams, nor could it be, without some justification for the extrapolation from Aristotle's general thought about morality to his ideas about private law and corrective justice. The difficulty we have highlighted with the authenticity argument persists whether or not the assumptions about human nature that support Aristotle's account of morality are defensible.

[59] The phrase belongs to B. Williams, *Ethics and Limits of Philosophy* (London: Fontana Press, 1985), p. 197. The argument (if it actually deserves that label) of this paragraph owes a great deal to Williams.

[60] See R. Dworkin, supra, note 20.

[61] Williams, supra, note 59, ch. 3; see also his *Shame and Necessity* (Berkeley: University of California Press, 1993), ch. 6 and M. Nussbaum, 'Aristotle on human nature and the foundations of ethics', ch. 6 of J. Altham and R. Harrison (eds.), *World, Mind, and Ethics* (Cambridge: Cambridge University Press, 1995). For a somewhat different but undoubtedly related argument, see A. MacIntyre, *After Virtue* (London: Duckworth, 1981), chs. 9–18.

Some will, no doubt, note that *EAL* looks like a manifestation of 'administrative rationality' in the context of philosophy of private law. This observation may well be accurate. But this ought not to be an embarrassment, since the fact that there can be extreme manifestations of this kind of approach cannot, without more, undermine the whole approach. There are bad instances of almost everything – terrible poems and awful music, for example – but these do not make all poetry and all music bad. We can therefore hope for a theory of corrective justice that fits our current highly and perhaps in some ways undesirably rationalistic temper. It must offer a normative basis for private law that is independent of the institution, because it takes few or none of its features for granted, and transparent, the justification it offers being plausible to both those already committed to the institution and to those who are not. Whether or not Coleman's account of corrective justice fits this bill is one of the issues now due for examination.

COLEMAN'S ANSWER

The first order of business, though, is to determine if Coleman, unlike Weinrib, does indeed offer a substantive and independent account of wrongs and wrongdoing as the basis of the obligation to correct. He does. An account of wrongs and wrongdoing is an important part of his 'mixed conception' of corrective justice which 'imposes on wrongdoers the duty to repair their wrongs and the wrongful losses their wrongdoing occasions' (*RW*, p. 324). In addition to examining the account of wrongs and wrongdoing that Coleman's mixed conception relies upon, we must also keep in mind two other matters. One is the content of the obligation to correct that the mixed conception generates, while the other involves the exact relation between that obligation and other possible sources of obligation such as, for example, distributive justice.

The obligation to correct

For Coleman, two components combine to trigger an obligation to correct under corrective justice. One, ignored in what follows but obviously related to the components of legal liability-responsibility discussed in Part I, is responsibility. Y only incurs an obligation in corrective justice to Z if he is, in the appropriate senses, responsible for harming Z.[62] The

[62] 'Senses' because, as became clear in Chapter 3, responsibility is, *inter alia*, a matter of being 'a responsible being' as well falling within the ambit of our practices of legal and moral liability-responsibility.

second component is that the harm Y has done Z must either be a wrong or an instance of wrongdoing. These two types of harm, and the wrongful losses they create, are the only ones that fall within the range of corrective justice. Wrongs, according to Coleman, 'are actions contrary to rights' (*RW*, p. 331) and can be justifiable or not; either way, '[i]nvasions of rights give rise to claims in justice to repair whether or not the injurer's conduct is justifiable' (ibid). By contrast, 'wrongdoing consists in the unjustifiable or otherwise impermissible injury of others' legitimate interests. Wrongdoing is unjustifiable harming' (ibid).[63]

Although this is a promising start, it must also be established that the account of wrongs and wrongdoing Coleman's theory of corrective justice utilizes is both substantive and independent. It is already obvious that the account of wrongs and wrongdoing is narrow in scope, since only two types of harm give rise to a duty to correct. To be substantive, an account of wrongs and wrongdoing must either invoke or presuppose both a catalogue of protected interests and an outline of the ways in which they are upheld and valued. These interests must also be interests of real human beings rather than abstract agents. An independent account of wrongs and wrongdoings is one that does not simply take for granted the catalogue of wrongs in the law: it provides a means of evaluating the law and must therefore be separable from the law. As to the substantive and independent nature of Coleman's account of wrongs and wrongdoing, one thing is certain: the interests protected by rights and those upheld by a duty to correct wrongdoing are not the interests of merely abstract agents, nor do they uncritically incorporate those interests protected by the law. Taking the notion of wrongs first, Coleman is clear that the rights infringed by wrongs are of the kind and content that many normative moral and political theories either attempt to justify or simply assume (*RW*, pp. 340–345). Furthermore, a normative theory of rights is required, says Coleman, to specify the kinds of protection – of the three available in the Calabresi-Melamed schema[64] – conferred upon particular rights (*RW*, pp. 338–341).

It is a mistake to infer from this that the mixed conception of corrective justice is tied to a particular normative theory. Coleman's view seems rather to be that the mixed conception rests upon or is compatible with one or more or even a combination of such theories (*RW*, p. 433). There

[63] This account of wrongs and wrongdoing is, of course, out of kilter with that offered in Chapter 6. The reason for rejecting Coleman's account was stated at pp. 218–219.

[64] G. Calabresi and A. D. Melamed, 'Property Rules, Liability Rules and Inalienability: One View of the Cathedral' (1972) 85 *Harvard LR* 1089–1128.

is nevertheless a relation of intelligibility here, since both the idea of corrective justice and its institutional embodiment must, in order to be respectable, make normative sense. That sense is in part derived from a more general moral or political theory or some combination of such. The particular normative theory of rights that Coleman champions, but which does not entail the mixed conception, is a version of liberalism in which 'equality, respect for persons, and their well-being' (*RW*, ibid) are crucial. A liberalism of this stripe therefore justifies, or assumes, a catalogue of civil, political and private law rights familiar in the Western democracies (*RW*, ch. 21). Of course, such a theory rarely specifies exactly what the content of our private law rights should be, over and beyond recognizing the importance of rights to holdings and their protection (property and tort) as well as rights to alienate holdings (contract). This lack of detail may well be based on the good ground that the content of particular contract, tort, property and other private law rights is often a matter of convention or *determinatio*. The question of whether we have such rights is, by contrast, a matter of fundamental importance.

The duty to correct the losses that result from wrongdoing arises not from an invasion of rights but from unreasonably harming or putting at risk the legitimate interests of others. This, of course, raises two related questions: how are we to determine what conduct or

> which risks are unreasonable? My idea is that informal conventions typically arise within communities of individuals as ways of giving local expression and content to the prohibition of unreasonable risk taking. These conventions govern the behavior of local communities; members of the communities develop expectations about the behavior of others and internalize constraints regarding their own behavior. These conventions are local, not global. It is failure to comply with them that typically grounds duties in corrective justice.
>
> Central to the idea of *wrongdoing in corrective justice* is this conventionalist notion of local norms. (*RW*, pp. 357–358; emphasis mine)

While these conventional, local norms are invoked by Coleman solely to determine which *risks* it is unreasonable to take with others' interests, there is no reason why this same move cannot determine when *conduct* is unreasonable, assuming such a judgment can be made without recourse to the notion of risk.

For Coleman wrongdoing, like a wrong that invades a right, does not require any culpability on the part of the wrongdoer. What is wrong here is not (or not necessarily) the agent whose conduct is an instance of wrongdoing but the conduct itself:

> [t]he failure to abide by the relevant norms of conduct is enough to render the action a form of wrongdoing (in the same way that failure to abide by the constraints imposed by rights renders conduct a wrong) and the losses that result wrongful (in both cases) even if it is inadequate to render the agent a culpable wrongdoer, someone who would be worthy of blame. (*RW*, p. 334)

This view is in accord with the notion of outcome responsibility which, as was argued in Chapter 2, is the general conception of responsibility embodied in private law. This particular point is but one illustration of Coleman's constant effort not to lose sight of private law's many distinctive features.

Wrongs and wrongdoing

What are we to make of this account of wrongs and wrongdoing? Although it appears to have some distinct advantages over Weinrib's account, and while it gives a reasonably clear response to the common sense thought, are there reasons why it should nevertheless be rejected? At least two gripes could be made about the account as so far stated, although they are not overwhelmingly powerful. The difficulties with the substance of the mixed conception of corrective justice might therefore lie not here but in contiguous terrain.

One gripe challenges both the independent and substantive dimensions of this account, holding that these are little more than gestures.[65] Thus, it is no exaggeration to claim that Coleman says very little, beyond the invocation of the Calabresi-Melamed schema, about the various ways in which the interests protected by private law should be protected. Nor does he specify how, when invaded, they are to be valued. Moreover, although his account of wrongs and wrongdoing implicates some or other normative theory of rights, it says little of substance about the content of such a theory. So, for example, Coleman offers no specification of the precise private law rights that such a theory will or must guarantee nor does he illuminate the relation between these rights and other civil rights. A related complaint could be made about his account of the interests protected by the duty to repair wrongdoing: these arise from apparently vague, conventional norms, the range of which seems unclear prior to a particular determination of what is and is not reasonable. Furthermore, it might seem that these conventional norms, insofar as they are found in

[65] In *PoP* Coleman partially accepts and deflects this criticism, holding that an account of wrongs, wrongdoing and the duties they generate is a 'first-order' enterprise which is not strictly the domain of corrective justice; it is nevertheless the ground upon which the 'second-order' duty to repair arises: pp. 32–36.

the law itself, provide no independent basis upon which to evaluate the law. But, since Coleman does not say that they exist only in legal form, and as his description of them suggests they come into being in a far less formal way that does much law (*RW*, pp. 358–359), this specific point may be an exaggeration. And, while there might be something in the general complaint that Coleman's account of wrongs and wrongdoing lacks specificity, the charge also seems uncharitable, since it asks too much. For an account of wrongs and wrongdoing, and the associated catalogue of interests and their means of protection, although an important part of any theory of corrective justice responsive to the common sense thought, is nevertheless a *subsidiary* part of such a theory. This gripe seemingly expects of Coleman a complete defence of a full-blown normative theory of rights, a catalogue of protected interests, an outline of the ways in which those interests are upheld and valued, as well as a complete theory of corrective justice and its relation with tort law. This may well be to expect too much. Coleman has gestured in the right direction and that, given his other tasks, is perhaps enough.

This point about the lack of specificity of Coleman's account of wrongs and wrongdoing gives rise to a second, more limited complaint. It is that the obligation to correct wrongdoing, arising as it does only after a determination of which risks or what conduct is unreasonable, clearly does not protect rights. This might be troubling for many, particularly those who hold that adjudication is a process of weighing the competing legal and moral rights of disputants.[66] On Coleman's view, it seems that a substantial part of private law adjudication is devoted not to the weighing of competing rights but to conferring protection on various interests *ex post*. This also implies that many of the interests protected by private law are not knowable in advance of particular judicial decisions. Of course, Coleman might respond by holding that rights are in play in the determination of the duty to correct wrongdoing. While this would require some changes to his distinction between wrongs and wrongdoing, the benefit would be to capture the intuition that rights are surely in play in adjudication. However, there are at least two ways in which they can be in play. In one, disputants' rights are announced by the courts *after* a determination of the reasonableness of defendants' conduct; in another, the process of adjudication is a matter of weighing *pre-existing* rights rather than creating them *de novo*. Again, some would object to the first view, since for them rights, as opposed to other interests agents may have,

[66] Such as Ronald Dworkin: see *Taking Rights Seriously* (London: Duckworth, 1977), ch. 4.

are protected interests or spheres of choice (i) the contours of which are knowable in advance of any particular decision about whether or not they have been breached; and (ii) which operate so as to pre-empt all or most other considerations that might be in play.[67] On this view, *ex post* determinations of rights are a contradiction in terms, while *ex post* weighing of rights is not.

This large issue cannot be resolved here. As a criticism of Coleman's account of wrongdoing, it certainly shows that there is a case to answer, captured by the oddity, for some at least, of much of private law adjudication being a rights-free zone. However, rather than consider the possible answers Coleman might have, we must instead look at two other principal aspects of this theory of corrective justice. One of these is the content of the obligation to correct (or repair); the other is the relationship between this and other obligations.

The content of the obligation to correct

Coleman is clear that the obligation to correct is agent-relative (or specific).[68] It is an obligation owed by one agent to another as a result of what that agent has done to the other. He is also sometimes unambiguous as to the precise content of this agent-specific obligation. For he occasionally assumes it can be discharged in only one way, namely, by payment of monetary compensation from the wrongdoer to the person she has wronged equal to the amount of the wrongful losses suffered. Now while this is often the default remedy in some areas of tort law, it is certainly not the only remedy. It is also far from clear why corrective justice requires this specific remedy. The point here is thus the same as that pressed against Weinrib. Given that there are numerous conceivable ways in which wrongs could be corrected, why is it that corrective justice makes salient the award of financial compensation for loss that is common in the law of torts? The suspicion is that jurists who offer theories of corrective justice simply assume the normative necessity of the remedy with which they are most familiar. Should we suspect Coleman of doing this or does he actually do it?

It is not absolutely certain Coleman actually does this. Or, more accurately, it is not certain that he consistently does this. One instance in which

[67] Ibid.

[68] Coleman uses both terms interchangeably: see *RW*, p. 319 and 'The Practice of Corrective Justice' in D. Owen (ed.), *Philosophical Foundations of Tort Law* (Oxford: Clarendon Press, 1995) at p. 55.

he seems to make this assumption is when he claims that '[b]ecause wrongdoers have a duty to repair in corrective justice, the proper mode of rectification is one that imposes liability for those costs on them' (*RW*, p. 327). Here we have a move from 'repair' to 'costs' that is made without remark, as if they were one and the same thing, although they are plainly not. There are often many ways in which I can repair a wrong I have done, just as there may be a number of ways to repair a fault in my central heating system. If it is the case that no one response is pre-eminently salient, then I must try the various alternatives. But why is it that the duty to repair a corrective justice wrong *can only* be satisfied by the payment of monetary compensation, by taking upon myself the costs the wrong has caused to my victim? Is Coleman's theory of corrective justice, understood as a normative principle or set of such principles creating an obligation to correct wrongs and wrongdoing, so detailed and precise that it dictates only one way of correction which, somewhat surprisingly, corresponds almost exactly with the default remedy in many systems of tort law?

It might be objected that we have misinterpreted Coleman's reference to 'costs' here by taking it to refer only to monetary losses. While it is true that 'costs' could indeed refer to much in addition to such losses and that these additional losses could be repaired in a variety of ways over and beyond the payment of compensation, this view is not one Coleman seriously entertains. This much is clear from his claim that '[t]he particular duty . . . [corrective justice] imposes is to repair the loss. There may be other agent-relative reasons for acting that arise as a consequence of wrongfully injuring another, for example, the duty to apologize or to forbear from future harming, but these do not arise from corrective justice' (*RW*, p. 329). In ruling out that these other ways of correcting the loss are required by corrective justice, Coleman thereby implies that corrective justice is concerned with only one way (or a very restricted number of ways) of repairing the loss. That way is, of course, monetary compensation and its cognates. But why is it that these other duties do not or cannot arise from corrective justice? If corrective justice insists only that wrongs and wrongful losses should be corrected, then we would expect it to leave open the specific question of how those wrongs and associated losses are to be repaired. And, of course, apology, promise of forbearance and monetary compensation are three possible ways in which this could be done. Are there any reasons to think that corrective justice singles out only the latter as morally necessary and rejects the former?

One possible argument in *RW* derives a duty to repair the financial losses of one's victims from the way in which the victim's rights are protected. According to the Calabresi and Melamed schema, one way in which rights can be protected is by liability rules: 'these protect rights by conferring a right to compensation on right holders in the event that someone takes that to which the right holder is entitled' (*RW*, p. 336). Since corrective justice imposes a duty to repair rights violations, and since some rights may be protected by liability rules, then the duty to repair must in some instances be a duty to compensate the victim. It then seems a small step from the duty to compensate the victim to a duty to repair the financial losses of one's victim. This argument does not, however, succeed in showing that the duty to repair *must in all instances* be one to financially compensate one's victim. First, and as we well know, the range of corrective justice extends beyond rights invasion: it also protects victims from wrongdoing and that, of course, is a matter of protecting their legitimate interests rather than just their rights. Liability rules, by definition, do not protect legitimate interests unless they are also rights. A second consideration that undermines this argument is equally obvious. The duty to financially compensate the victim, if it does indeed flow from a liability rule, is not a duty at all until such time as we have a justification for that duty. The justification for one or other of the three means of protecting rights available in the Calabresi and Melamed schema must, according to Coleman, flow from a normative theory of rights (*RW*, pp. 338–343). It would also seem to be the case that the justification of the duty that arises from one of those means of protecting rights must flow from the same source. And, as we have already noted, Coleman – not unreasonably – takes few steps toward providing such a theory.

There is also a third consideration that undermines this argument. It consists of some of Coleman's own observations, thus confirming that his position on the normative necessity of the obligation to financially compensate one's victims in corrective justice is uncertain. Think, for example, of the observation that with rights protected by property rules 'failure to comply with those rules is a wrong, but in the absence of a liability rule, the right that is wronged provides no grounds for compensation' (*RW*, p. 484). For those inclined to accept the Calabresi and Melamed schema, this observation is unimpeachable but, for current purposes, its significance is different. Coleman accepts that in this instance the obligation to correct generated by corrective justice is *not* an obligation to pay financial compensation. This thought is congenial to the idea that corrective justice is 'blunt' with regard to the means by which wrongs and wrongdoing should be corrected.[69] There is no way to be sure that this idea lies behind Coleman's apparent uncertainty about the precise content of the obligation to correct that corrective justice licenses but, if it does, then that is well and good. But we should not simply take it for granted that all general normative notions like corrective justice are blunt: whether they are or not will depend on the range of arguments such notions generate in relation to particular features of the institution and practices in question. That the notion of corrective justice lacks an unambiguous answer to the question of the content of the obligation to correct suggests that in this respect at least it is blunt. Yet, as a general matter, it is often helpful to assume, until a demonstration to the contrary is forthcoming, that general normative notions are blunt. Why?

Primarily because of the cautionary role the assumption performs. Whether it is used of the notion of corrective justice, or of other general normative notions, the idea of bluntness is invaluable because it puts theorists on their mettle to provide specific arguments supporting particular features of the institution and practices in question. If, for example, corrective justice is indeed blunt, then specific arguments for particular means of correcting wrongs, including those currently embodied in the law itself, must be provided. In the face of the spectre of bluntness one such means cannot be assumed to be any more salient, from the perspective of corrective justice, than any other. Furthermore, if corrective justice or any other general normative notion is blunt in this way, it serves as a prophylactic against the whiggish assumption that features of existing institutions and practices are *prima facie* normatively respectable. An appreciation of the possibility of bluntness brings an awareness of the distance that must be travelled from a normatively appealing general notion (like corrective justice) to a precise normative justification for particular aspects of some or other institution and its constitutive practices (like the default remedy in tort law). This type of gap should neither be ignored nor assumed out of existence.

The context of the obligation to correct

Coleman's understanding of the relation of the obligation to correct with other obligations we have is complex, requiring evaluation along two dimensions. One concerns the proper description of the obligation to

[69] I am here stealing and expanding the idea of bluntness as elucidated in N. E. Simmonds, 'Bluntness and Bricolage', ch. 1 of H. Gross and R. Harrison (eds.), *Jurisprudence: Cambridge Essays* (Oxford: Clarendon Press, 1992).

correct: is it a moral obligation, a political obligation or a 'merely' legal obligation? The other raises the relation between corrective justice obligations, on the one hand, and those that might flow from distributive justice, on the other. The view Coleman offers in *RW* is that the obligation to correct is best described as a moral duty: corrective justice primarily expresses the demands of a private morality (*RW*, p. 362). This moral obligation can, however, take legal form for Coleman thinks that there can be good reasons for a liberal state to give it legal effect. Coleman's argument is not, however, that the state *must* implement corrective justice: '[t]he state has the moral authority, but not the duty to implement corrective justice' (*RW*, p. 367). A system of tort law and corrective justice is therefore morally acceptable but a state that does not have such is not guilty of a moral mistake. So, for example, an accident compensation scheme along the lines of that in New Zealand cannot, therefore, be ruled illegitimate on corrective justice grounds. This is because those grounds are not, for the state at least, normatively overriding and can be outweighed by countervailing considerations.

The claim that the obligation to correct is primarily a moral obligation capable of transformation into a legal obligation seems unproblematic. That being so, was it a mistake to express doubts, as we did in Chapter 7, about Coleman's view of the nature of the obligation to correct? Not necessarily. This is because a tension arises between the unambiguous view just stated and some of Coleman's thoughts about, for example, responsibility. For instance, he rejects what he takes to be Stephen Perry's position that there is an 'abstract, prepolitical conception of outcome responsibility that provides a single set of constraints affecting the justice of tort institutions' (*PoP*, p. 52). Coleman's view is that the notion of responsibility is informed by and embedded in our practices, such as tort law, and that judgments of attribution (who did this?) are inseparable from judgments of allocation (who pays for this?). The substance of Coleman's view of this matter, and the question of whether or not there is indeed a genuine dispute between him and Perry, is not relevant here. The significance of Coleman's thinking on this issue is, rather, that it blurs the clear line drawn in *RW* between the moral obligation to correct, on the one hand, and its enactment in law, on the other. For, if the obligation to correct arises upon, *inter alia*, a conception of responsibility neither pre-political nor non-legal (because responsibility is embodied in and given sense by institutions and practices some of which are undoubtedly legal), then it seems odd to regard the obligation as primarily or purely moral. How can one of the bases of this obligation, namely, a political and/or legal conception of responsibility, give rise to a non-legal, non-political moral obligation?

Whatever the resolution of this puzzle, it seems clear that Coleman regards the moral obligation to correct as a weighty one (*RW*, pp. 359–360). Since it is morally wrong not to discharge the obligation, then the obligation must be more than merely one consideration among others inclining us to act one way or another. On the assumption that moral requirements are generally more demanding than other considerations, Coleman's view of the obligation to correct must therefore be that it is either a compelling or *prima facie* compelling consideration in our practical reasoning. As is clear, however, this view of the moral obligation does not for Coleman serve to transform it, directly and immediately, into a legal obligation.

Coleman's account of the relation between corrective and distributive justice is best described as the co-existence thesis, well characterized by his talk of 'the fundamental unity of distributive and corrective justice' (*PoP*, p. 53). This unity is not, however, a matter of distributive and corrective justice being identical in content or in the claims they make upon us. Rather, '[p]art of the connection between redistributive institutions and tort law [the domain of corrective justice] is that together . . . [they] embody the requirements of fairness with regard to how we allocate the costs of life's misfortunes' (*PoP*, p. 44). Yet corrective justice and distributive justice institutions differ because the latter pursues fairness with regard to those misfortunes that are no one's responsibility, while the former pursues fairness with regard to misfortunes owing to human agency (*PoP*, ibid). They also differ, for Coleman, in that corrective justice obligations are agent-specific, while distributive justice obligations are agent-general.

Although the first difference appears plausible, it is not as unproblematic as it may seem at first glance. This is primarily because the boundary between misfortunes that are and those that are not attributable to human agency is not in any sense a matter of brute of fact.[70] It might seem so if, for example, we think of the harm caused by natural events like earthquakes and hurricanes and compare them with the harm caused by reckless driving or by faulty hospital operations. Human agency seems far more obviously implicated in the latter instances than in the former;

[70] This point and the others in this paragraph draw upon the discussion in the second section of Chapter 5.

indeed, it seems odd to accord such agency any role in the former – after all, no human agent initiated either the earthquake or hurricane. But in a world in which weather patterns and seismic changes are monitored with a view to assessing their effects on human populations, it is both possible and common to attribute some of the effects of such natural events to human agency. Many of our common sense causal judgments are made against a background of expectations about appropriate conduct; when those expectations are upheld, and everyone has acted appropriately, the occurrence of a bad outcome is unlikely to be attributed to human agency. When those expectations are not upheld, it is not uncommon to regard the departure from normal standards as causally salient. With regard to natural events like hurricanes and earthquakes, such expectations will almost never lead us to view human conduct as the cause of those events, but they could well inform the judgment that some human conduct was causally salient in bringing about situations in the aftermath of those events. One such situation could be the scale of human suffering. If the circumstances were right we would, for example, have no trouble in saying that the failure to give warning of an earthquake, or a failure to stockpile medical supplies in advance of such an event, was causally significant in determining some of its consequences. It is also the case that events that once were regarded as no one's responsibility – famines, for example – are now usually regarded as being the product of human conduct and thus as someone's responsibility.

The crucial point is that Coleman's attribution of different roles to corrective and distributive justice rests on a far from simple distinction which is richly normatively significant. Furthermore, the distinction itself, since it is not a matter of brute fact – of looking and seeing – assuredly stands in need of justification on each occasion it is invoked. Before seismic monitoring it might well have been right to conclude that the human carnage resulting from earthquakes was indeed no one's responsibility; in an age in which such monitoring is the norm, that conclusion is untenable. Since our judgments on what is and is not attributable to human conduct can change, that distinction itself cannot be taken for granted. It might not therefore be a reliable basis on which to determine the realms of both corrective and distributive justice.

The second difference Coleman highlights between corrective and distributive justice consists of the distinction between agent-specific and agent-general duties. He is by no means the only jurist to think that corrective justice creates agent-specific duties and that distributive justice does not.[71] But this distinction, too, seems contestable. For why should we accept that distributive justice cannot create agent-specific reasons for action, that is, give Z a reason for doing C because of something Z has done to Y? Suppose, for example, that the best possible theory of distributive justice was strictly egalitarian and thus demanded that everyone have precisely the same amount of resources and other determinants of human welfare. If I crash my car into Y and injure him or his holdings, I have undoubtedly undermined the pattern of resources that distributive justice requires. Surely it makes perfect sense to hold that my duty in this case is to correct the misdistribution and thus return Y to the situation she was in prior to my intervention? And surely this duty is agent-specific: it is a duty I owe to Y as a result of my conduct toward Y. It is not also natural to regard this as a distributive justice duty? If it is, then it is not an obviously dubious extrapolation to suggest that this particular theory of distributive justice is by no means unique in generating such an agent-specific duty and reason for action. If a strictly egalitarian account of distributive justice can generate such a duty, why can not Rawls's second principle of justice, or any other account of distributive justice for that matter, do likewise?[72] Of course, maintaining in this way that distributive justice generates agent-specific reasons is not to deny that is also generates agent-general reasons.

The point about distributive justice generating agent-specific reasons could be met in two very different ways, neither of which provides succour for Coleman. It could be maintained, for example, that distributive justice cannot create agent-specific duties because it is 'done' at a single, temporal point of origin which is thereafter superseded by the consensual acts and choices of those once bound by the original compact. If distributive justice is 'done' in this way, presumably by analogy with 'equal starts' accounts of equality, then its demands need not trouble us thereafter.[73] The duties to correct wrongs that arise after the justice compact cannot, then, be duties of distributive justice. It seems just as difficult to see how events in the ancient past can generate agent-specific duties for humans here and now, as it is to see how the moment of justice can constrain us now. To state this point is, however, to appreciate it's multiple weaknesses. One is that it conceives of distributive justice as a static rather than dynamic set of standards, yet there is no *a priori* reason to accept this

[71] See Chapter 7, p. 258.

[72] J. Rawls, *A Theory of Justice* (Oxford: Clarendon Press, revised edn, 1999), pp. 52–65.

[73] A good discussion of equal starts is: H. Steiner, 'Capitalism, Justice, and Equal Starts' (1987) 5 *Social Philosophy and Policy* 49–71.

view. Another is that it assumes agent-specific duties cannot arise from events long ago, yet we all accept that we have duties that do indeed arise from historically distant events. My duties to my children or to my parents are obvious examples; less obvious, perhaps, are 'our' duties to make reparation to the victims and their successors of our atrocities or injustices.[74]

Another response to the argument that distributive justice generates agent-specific duties is equally problematic. What might be said of the example that the argument invokes is this: it simply shows corrective justice at work. That is, the agent-specific obligation I owe to Y as a result of harming Y's interests and thus disturbing the pattern of strict equality arises from corrective and not distributive justice. It could be maintained that the distributive requirement of strict equality generates only agent-general duties and reasons for action, whereas the obligation to correct my own disturbances of that pattern are agent-specific and arise from corrective justice. Yet there are at least two difficulties with this response. First, the distinction between corrective and distributive justice has become very slippery here; so much so, indeed, that the suspicion arises that the formal agent-specific/agent-general distinction is determining the substantive corrective/distributive distinction. This seems *prima facie* odd because there are no obvious grounds on which to believe that a formal distinction between the type of reasons we can have must determine the range of substantive moral or political views. The oddity is akin to holding that the rules of grammar determine the content of what we say as opposed to the way it should be said. A second and oft-noted difficulty with this response is that it casts corrective justice in an entirely subservient role with regard to distributive justice.[75] The role of

[74] The idea of reparation – surely a near cousin of corrective justice – is no longer only invoked in the contexts of criminal justice and post-war settlements between nation states. It is now spoken of as a possibly appropriate response to atrocity, exploitation and state lawlessness towards citizens. Three very different but equally fascinating discussions are B. Bittker, *The Case for Black Reparations* (Boston: Beacon Press, 2003 (originally 1973)); J. Feagin, *Racist America* (London: Routledge, 2000), ch. 8; and J. Borneman, *Settling Accounts: Violence, Justice and Accountability in Post-Socialist Europe* (Princeton, New Jersey: Princeton University Press, 1997).

[75] This is sometimes called the 'distributive' reading of corrective justice, two examples of which are: W. Waluchow, 'Professor Weinrib on Corrective Justice' in S. Panagiotou (ed.), *Justice, Law and Method in Plato and Aristotle* (Edmonton: Academic Printing and Publishing, 1987) 153–157; and J. Gordley, 'Contract Law in the Aristotelian Tradition', ch. 6 of P. Benson (ed.), *The Theory of Contract Law: New Essays* (Cambridge: Cambridge University Press, 2001) at pp. 307–310. L. Alexander, 'Causation and Corrective Justice: Does Tort Law Make Sense?' (1987) 6 *Law and Philosophy* 1–23 is also helpful on this issue,

corrective justice, on this view, is that of general factotum, tidying up disturbances of a distribution that must be maintained. The moral or normative power of the obligation to correct therefore derives entirely from the demands of distributive justice. It follows that were the requirements of distributive justice shunned in a particular community, then corrective justice would lack a *raison d'être* there. This 'distributive' reading of corrective justice is not, however, espoused by Coleman.

Coleman's view of the way distributive and corrective justice interact becomes evident in his account of the normative context in which corrective justice obligations will have weight. He holds that

> [w]hile the set of holdings that can be secured by a practice of corrective justice need not coincide exactly with the holdings that should exist according to the best theory of distributive justice, holdings must nevertheless satisfy certain minimum conditions of moral legitimacy in order for us to speak of protecting them by a practice of corrective justice. (*PoP*, p. 33)

This statement, in conjunction with other remarks, shows that Coleman thinks there is some relation between distributive and corrective justice but that it is not as close as proponents of the distributive reading maintain. Perhaps the relation he has in mind is this. The minimum moral legitimacy a distribution of holdings must have, if it is to generate a morally weighty obligation to correct disturbances of that distribution, must accord with the substance of a second-, third- (or worse) best conception of distributive justice. Clearly, a distribution of holdings appalling from the viewpoint of all non-ideal conceptions of distributive justice would completely undermine the weight of the obligation to correct, but it is not obvious how far beyond this Coleman would go. Perry has argued that Coleman must, by virtue of some arguments he uses, go considerably beyond this and embrace something like the distributive reading of corrective justice.[76] While Coleman has resisted this, he is nevertheless in an uncomfortable position. For the wisdom of resisting the collapse into the distributive reading, while maintaining that there is a significant relation between corrective and distributive justice, is questionable in light of two related worries. One doubts the utility of this argument because Coleman struggles to carve out a clearly delineated

especially pp. 6–11, as is S. Perry, 'On the Relationship Between Corrective and Distributive Justice' in J. Horder (ed.), *Oxford Essays on Jurisprudence: Fourth Series* (Oxford: Clarendon Press, 2000), 237–263.

[76] See 'The Distributive Turn: Mischief, Misfortune and Tort Law', ch. 7 of Bix (ed.), supra, note 25 and Coleman's reply, in the same volume, at pp. 310–316.

middle ground here, while the other doubts the existence of logical space between the distributive reading and the separation thesis. This line is therefore difficult to hold by virtue of being hard to see.

Finally, we must return to the point with which the discussion of Weinrib concluded, namely, our current rationalistic temper. A properly Aristotelian approach to understanding tort law and corrective justice seemingly runs up against this temper. Does Coleman's account of tort law and corrective justice do likewise? Apparently not. Coleman offers a normative basis for private law that is in many respects independent of the institution, taking few of its features for granted. His account is also rationally transparent, in the sense that the normative argument it develops does not depend for its power upon a pre-commitment, among those to whom it is addressed, to the institution of tort law. The argument takes little or nothing on trust and constantly attempts to be explicit about, and question most of, its assumptions and starting points. Coleman's account of the normative foundation of tort law is therefore philosophy for those caught in the interpretative attitude and all that flows from it, both good and bad.

RECAP AND LOOSE ENDS

We have noted some methodological and substantive problems with Weinrib's and Coleman's attempt to show that some conception of corrective justice constitutes the normative foundation of private law. The methodological snags arose from an apparent commitment to offer an account of the normative foundation of tort law that captured the participants' point of view. The specific difficulty for Weinrib was that his commitment to the methodological injunction appears every bit as slight as that of some proponents of economic analysis of law. While the substance of Weinrib's account of tort law and corrective justice is radically different from that of any *EAL* account, there is little methodological distance between them: both aim to make explicit what is implicit in participants' understanding of the institution. And what both approaches regard as implicit in the institution and its constitutive practices is, of course, far indeed from what many participants explicitly say. For Coleman the methodological problem is slightly different. His commitment to the methodological injunction seems reasonably secure, although it is not as evident in some recent work. The problem it generates for him is that of providing an explanatory fulcrum upon which his account of corrective justice must be brought to bear. That fulcrum is, for Coleman, the core of tort law and his difficulty lies in offering an account of the core that is accepted by all participants in the institution and which is not determined by any theoretical considerations.

The substantive problems faced by Weinrib and Coleman are quite different. The principal problems faced by Weinrib's theory of corrective justice arise from its copious Aristotelian baggage. The apparent emptiness of the theory's account of wrongs and wrongdoing, its seemingly uncritical embrace of the details of much legal doctrine and its generally counter-intuitive nature mean that it is difficult to accept. That, of course, does not entail that we must succumb to functionalism; it means only that we need not – perhaps now cannot – take up Weinrib's particular alternative to functionalism. Coleman provides another apparent alternative to functionalism.[77] One benefit this alternative has is that the substantive difficulties it faces are more modest than those ensnaring Weinrib's account. The primary difficulties for Coleman do not arise from the account of wrongs and wrongdoing that his theory of corrective justice invokes. Rather, difficulties arise with his view of the content of the obligation to correct and from his attempt to defend the co-existence thesis as an account of the relation between corrective and distributive justice. His account of the content of the obligation to correct is somewhat uncertain. At some points he comes close to assuming the moral necessity of the damages remedy in tort, whereas at other points he seems attuned to the possibility that corrective justice may be blunt on such matters of doctrinal detail. His defence of the coexistence thesis is, by contrast, far from uncertain. It is simply problematic because committed to drawing a line it may be impossible to draw.

Finally, three loose ends must be noted, one of which is taken up again in the final chapter. Two of these loose ends involve related lacunae in Weinrib's and Coleman's accounts of private law and corrective justice. The first is that they pay insufficient attention to the relation between corrective justice and public law. While both are primarily concerned to explore the relation between corrective justice and tort law, they assume that in so doing they also draw a significant line between private and public law. Indeed, Weinrib in particular comes close to espousing the view that to offer a non-functionalist account of private law is of necessity to meaningfully distinguish private law from public law (*IPL*, pp. 7 and 48). But

[77] It is not clear that Coleman would escape being tarred with Weinrib's anti-functionalist brush; this, however, is as much an indictment of the over-wide brush as of any particular feature of Coleman's account.

the difficulty is that neither Coleman nor Weinrib give any independent reason for thinking that many or all of the components of corrective justice are inapplicable to public law.[78] The notions of wrongs and wrongdoing surely have some echo in the public law context, as does the idea of correcting such wrongs, although as a matter of legal doctrine both the methods of correction, and the means of wronging and wrongdoing, differ from private law. Of course, it might be argued in response that corrective justice concerns only 'transactions', as Aristotle indicated,[79] and that these fall within the realm of private but not public law. Yet this looks altogether too stipulative and too glib: the fact that Aristotle made this assumption is not in itself reason for us to follow him.

The second loose end notes another gap: neither Weinrib nor Coleman does much to show that bilateralism – what they regard as one of the most important structural features of private law – is not also a feature of public law. One reason for this may be that both think bilateralism is a feature of public law provided, of course, that the notion can be amended in some respects. One such change is that the payment of compensation from wrongdoer to their victim need not be necessary: in public law this method of correcting a wrong is not always appropriate. What is sometimes required instead is that the public body or servant involved is simply required to do what they are legally empowered to do in a competent and /or reasonable way. It seems Coleman and Weinrib could not resist this extension insofar as both accept that the compensation remedy is not the only one in play in private law and, therefore, that it is not the only remedy licensed by corrective justice.[80] If other remedies are available in private law, why not also in public law?

These two gaps give added salience to the final loose end. Recall that in Chapter 1 we thought one question philosophical accounts of private law should address was that of the significant differences, if any, between private and public law. While there are clearly many, many contingent differences between the two, significant differences – those, for example, that might indicate a qualitative distinction between public and private law – are harder to find. It seems that the two theories of corrective justice examined here provide little help with this task. Indeed, by paying scant

[78] Weinrib has engaged in a debate more general than but to some degree resonant with this: see O. Fiss, 'Coda' (1988) 38 *University of Toronto LJ* 229–244 and Weinrib's response 'Adjudication and Public Values: Fiss' Critique of Corrective Justice' (1989) 39 *University of Toronto LJ* 1–18.

[79] Supra, note 38, p. 1784.

[80] See, for example, *RW*, p. 484 and the references to Weinrib at note 4, supra.

attention to the two issues just noted, they provide no help at all. Now it is clearly unfair to criticize Weinrib and Coleman for failing to address an issue they did not intend to tackle but that is not the compliant here. The charge is, instead, slightly less unfair: that this matter is undoubtedly worthy of serious attention from philosophers and jurists yet it gets little. This is surely a puzzle since, if we should not expect the issue to be addressed in accounts of the normative foundation of private law such as those supplied by Coleman and Weinrib, where shall we hope to find it tackled? The issue is clearly unfashionable while the reasons for this are far from clear. Perhaps our mistake is to expect fashions and fads to be determined by reasons.

9

Distributive Justice

> Justice is the first virtue of social institutions, as truth is of systems of thought.
>
> John Rawls, *A Theory of Justice* (Oxford: Clarendon Press, rev. edn, 1999), p. 3

The idea of corrective justice has indeed preoccupied many philosophers and jurists. To say this of the notion of distributive justice is, however, to understate matters. Since the first publication of John Rawls's tremendously influential *A Theory of Justice* in 1971[1] moral and political philosophers, jurists, economists and social choice theorists have created a massive and detailed literature exploring almost every single aspect of the topic in depth. Their concern with distributive justice has thus gone beyond preoccupation and neared the realm of obsession. While many contributions have been commentaries upon and evaluations of *A Theory of Justice* itself, some of the most influential have also developed theories of distributive justice both independent of and in opposition to that offered by Rawls.[2]

Although it is true that the theories of distributive justice offered by Rawls and his competitors have influenced and been taken up by jurists in general terms, it is nevertheless relatively rare for jurists to deploy a particular account of distributive justice as a normative foundation for private law. By contrast, it is not at all rare for jurists to speak about private law being concerned with matters of distributive justice, but this is usually done in a slightly oblique way. Rather than directly deploy a particular

[1] Oxford: Clarendon Press, 1971.

[2] A short list of the most influential works since Rawls would have to include, *inter multos alios*, R. Nozick, *Anarchy, State and Utopia* (Oxford: Basil Blackwell, 1974); M. Walzer *Spheres of Justice* (Oxford: Martin Robertson, 1983); B. Ackerman, *Social Justice in the Liberal State* (New Haven: Yale University Press, 1980); B. Barry, *Theories of Justice* (Berkeley: University of California Press, 1989) and *Justice as Impartiality* (Oxford: Clarendon Press, 1995); G. A. Cohen, *Self-Ownership, Freedom and Equality* (Cambridge: Cambridge University Press, 1995) and *If You're an Egalitarian, How Come You're So Rich?* (Cambridge, Mass.: Harvard University Press, 2000); R. Dworkin, *Sovereign Virtue* (Cambridge, Mass.: Harvard University Press, 2000); and, by no means least, D. Miller, *Principles of Social Justice* (Cambridge, Mass.: Harvard University Press, 1999).

account of distributive justice to throw light upon some aspect of the law, jurists and philosophers of private law instead often content themselves with noting either one or all of the following three points.

First, that private law is in part a system of rights and duties and, as such, it is in the first instance a means of distributing such rights and duties and, thereafter, a way of maintaining a particular distribution of such rights and duties. This will be labelled the 'simple argument' about private law and distributive justice. Second, some jurists and philosophers note that, as they currently stand and as they are applied by the courts in particular cases, the doctrines of private law undoubtedly have distributive effects both within and beyond the legal world. From this they infer that private law must 'therefore' be a matter of distributive justice. This can be called the 'external argument' about private law and distributive justice. Since this and the simple argument are in substance the same, differing only because the focus of the latter (private law *in toto* or some large chunk thereof) is much wider than the former, the two are treated together in what follows. The third point jurists and philosophers of private law often make is that some doctrines of private law seemingly manifest a concern for fairness, or equality or loss distribution. It is then inferred from this that private law must embody some conception of distributive justice. Let us call this the 'internal argument' about private law and distributive justice. What simple, external and internal arguments have in common is that they are *indirect*. This becomes obvious when we note what a *direct* argument about the relation between private law and distributive justice might look like.

Direct arguments about the relationship between private law and distributive justice have the structure already envisaged and regarded as obvious: some or other detailed account of distributive justice is invoked to explain and justify both the structure and content of private law or some segment thereof. Although an obvious strategy for jurists interested in the relationship between private law and distributive justice, this approach is far from common and that is puzzling. While it is possible to unearth legion examples of jurists deploying one or other indirect argument, only two examples of the direct argument are considered in this chapter. The examples are drawn from a short list.[3] There might, of course, be good

[3] They belong to Ackerman, supra, note 2 and R. Dworkin, *Law's Empire* (Oxford: Hart Publishing, 1998). There are almost no other notable works invoking direct arguments, not even among representatives of American critical legal studies. For current purposes, work of the latter kind is overlooked because it raises diverse, broad and challenging issues that

reasons why relatively few jurists and philosophers argue that private law in general, or particular segments thereof, does or should embody a specific account of distributive justice. One such reason raises the issue of the extent of distributive justice and is examined in detail below. This issue is surely an obvious one, even to those who regard distributive justice as a sovereign social virtue, the most important of all of our fundamental political commitments.[4] For, however important distributive justice is, there are surely limits to its scope, assuming it cannot and should not dominate each and every aspect of human life. If there are indeed realms in which the writ of distributive justice does not run, then it is important to be clear about where they are and the basis of the restriction. It could turn out that private law is a realm either completely or *prima facie* immune to the injunctions of distributive justice and, were that so, the task of constructing a direct argument would then look very dubious indeed.

The first step in what follows is to introduce some distinctions that will structure our thinking about distributive justice. Although not all of the distinctions will be to the forefront of all that follows in this chapter, all are in play at some point (one has already been used). These preliminary matters are tackled briskly in the first section (p.330). The first substantive step is taken in the second section (p.334). This consists of an analysis of three indirect arguments about the relation between private law and distributive justice and culminates with some speculation about why such arguments are more common than direct arguments. That speculation leads directly to our second substantive step, the fulcrum of the third section (p.350). It examines an argument which, if successful, pre-empts all talk about a relation between distributive justice and private law. The fourth section analyses two examples of the direct argument and *inter alia* assesses how well they deal with this pre-emptive objection. Of the three key issues highlighted in Chapter 7, only the first issue, about the foundational role of distributive justice, and the second, about the nature of the obligation created, are fleetingly present in what follows. This is because the arguments about the relationship between private law and distributive justice are so problematic that the key issues hardly have occasion to arise.

distract from our main purposes. For an excellent example of the genre, see D. Kennedy, 'Paternalist and Distributive Motives in Contract and Tort Law, with Special Reference to Compulsory Terms and Unequal Bargaining Power' (1982) 41 *Maryland LR* 563–658.

[4] As Rawls and Dworkin do. For a refreshingly unorthodox view of this matter, see T. Campbell, *Justice* (London: Macmillan, 1988), pp. 6–8.

PRELIMINARIES

Theories of distributive justice can most usefully be distinguished by reference to their content. Such theories are, however, usually complex and so, obviously, is their content. In speaking of their content, we may have in mind all or any of at least three different but related features: their constitutive principles, the range of application of those principles or the extent of those principles.

The *constitutive principles* of theories of distributive justice are the means by which they tell us how that which is ripe for distribution should be distributed. Thus, there is a remarkable difference between Rawls's two principles of justice and the three constitutive principles of Robert Nozick's historical entitlement theory of justice.[5] There is also an equally significant difference between the constitutive principles of these two theories, on the one hand, and those more 'pluralistic' theories offered by, for example, Michael Walzer and David Miller.[6] One important reason why the constitutive principles of various theories of distributive justice differ so much is that those theories often begin from very different starting points. Consider just two examples. Nozick's guiding assumption is that '[i]ndividuals have rights and there are some things that no person or group may do to them (without violating their rights)'.[7] It is thus no surprise that the three principles of his historical entitlement account of justice protect something like a natural right to self-ownership and rights to various holdings that legitimately flow from it. By contrast, one of Rawls's principal aims in *A Theory of Justice* is to construct a choice situation in which individuals decide, without partiality or self-interest, upon the principles that will govern their collective life. While individuals in that choice situation are all equally free, the principles which they would accept embody much more, thinks Rawls, than a right to self-ownership and some of its implications. Since different theories of justice often also differ both in their assumptions about human nature and the appropriate method for reflecting about justice, it comes as no surprise that their respective constitutive principles are frequently incompatible.

Because they differ in their content, the constitutive principles of theories of distributive justice also often differ in the structure of the

[5] See Nozick, supra, note 2, pp. 150–153 and compare J. Rawls, *A Theory of Justice* (Oxford: Clarendon Press, revised edn, 1999), pp. 52–56.

[6] Supra, note 2.

[7] Nozick, supra, note 2, p. ix.

distributive outcome they require or license. Nozick helpfully distinguished between theories of distributive justice in this way, dividing them into two broadly different kinds: those that require end-state or patterned distributions, on the one hand, and those that do not, on the other. On an end-state or patterned (hereinafter 'patterned') principle 'the justice of a distribution is determined by how things are distributed (who has what) as judged by some *structural* principle(s) of just distribution'.[8] Such principles can be temporally limited, in the sense that the justice of a distribution is determined at one particular time and regardless of how it came about. Alternatively, the principles can operate over a series of different time-slices, so that a cumulative picture of the justice or injustice of a distribution is provided. The significant overarching feature of all such principles is that

> all that needs to be looked at, in judging the justice of a distribution, is who ends up with what; in comparing any two distributions one need only look at the matrix presenting the distributions. It is a consequence of such principles . . . that any two structurally identical distributions are equally just. (Two distributions are structurally identical if they present the same profile, but perhaps have different persons occupying different slots. My having ten and your having five, and my having five and your having ten are structurally identical distributions.)[9]

Historical principles of justice are, by contrast, certainly not patterned principles, holding 'that past circumstances or actions of people can create differential entitlements or differential deserts to things. An injustice can be worked by moving from one distribution to another structurally identical one, for the second, in profile the same, may violate people's entitlements or deserts.'[10] The overall profile or pattern of holdings is not the key issue for historical principles of justice: the way in which the profile came about is all that matters.

The importance of the distinction between patterned and historical principles of justice, according to Nozick, is that the latter protect liberty whereas the former undermine it. Suppose some particular pattern required by a patterned principle of justice is made actual: everyone in our community each has two units of welfare or utility or resources or goods (or whatever). If citizens are allowed to trade their units of welfare

[8] Nozick, supra, note 2, p. 153; emphasis his. What he has in mind by the term 'structural' becomes apparent below. That he regards end-state and patterned principles as substantively the same is clear from p. 156.

[9] Ibid, p. 154. [10] Ibid, p. 155.

– everyone, for example, willingly giving the best opera singer among us 0.25 units of our holdings in order to hear her sing – then we will end up with less than what the principle requires and she with more.[11] The implication is that, if the patterned principle of justice is taken seriously, these capitalist acts between consenting adults should either be prohibited or their distributive consequences redressed. By contrast, such acts would be perfectly permissible on historical principles, if it was established that everyone who has units to trade legitimately holds them; that is, those units are rightfully theirs in light of some historical principle of justice.

Nozick's distinction between patterned and historical principles of distributive justice remains important, even though many theories of distributive justice after (but also including) Rawls strive to reconcile a patterned distribution with freedom of choice.[12] So, for example, Ronald Dworkin's account of distributive justice – what he calls equality of resources – demands an initial equal distribution of resources which citizens are thereafter able to consume, invest or trade in whatever legitimate way they wish.[13] The fact that an initially equal pattern of distribution can subsequently become radically unequal is of little concern to Dworkin, provided the inequality is a result of citizens' choices. A theory of distributive justice that is neither historical (like Nozick's) nor dynamic (like Dworkin's) must either satisfy or circumvent the challenge Nozick lays down.

That the usual aim of the constitutive principles of theories of distributive justice is to state how to distribute what is ripe for distribution is obvious. Equally obvious is that those principles must presuppose or invoke an account of what it is that must or can be distributed. This is the issue to which we refer when speaking of *the range of application of principles of distributive justice*. Many theories of distributive justice are very general, holding that their principles distribute most or all of the significant determinants of human flourishing. The material resources necessary to a basic or higher level of human flourishing are almost always included in such theories; they also often include the significant political

[11] Nozick's example (ibid, pp. 161–164) uses Wilt Chamberlain, a famous American basketball player.

[12] Rawls thinks allocative conceptions of distributive justice, which are obviously patterned, implausible: supra, note 5, p. 77; see also J. Rawls, *Political Liberalism* (New York: Columbia University Press, extended edn, 1996), pp. 282–283.

[13] Dworkin, supra, note 2, ch. 2.

and civil liberties covered by Rawls's first principle of justice.[14] Material resources and political and civil liberties can, of course, be regarded as independently significant determinants of human flourishing and thus supplemented with a more general notion of human welfare. Alternatively, the notion of human welfare, however vague it might sound, can be regarded as the foundation of those other 'things' distributed by principles of justice. However understood, human welfare is often regarded as something ripe for distribution.

The things ripe for distribution mentioned so far can all be plausibly regarded as benefits, but there is no reason to assume that principles of distributive justice do not or should not also distribute burdens. Collective social life imposes burdens in the very minimal sense that some contribution to the common weal is necessary in order to live beneficially, safely and healthy together. In complex societies the minimum form that contribution usually takes is the payment of taxes; in simple communities it may take the form of the contribution of labour power to, for example, protect the group against the elements or other human groups. Although thus far stated in a very abstract way, the range of benefits and burdens that can be distributed by principles of justice can be made much more specific. It is therefore fairly common to find contemporary jurists and proponents of various theories of distributive justice concentrating on particular cases like, for example, the distribution of health care, job opportunities and legal liability.[15]

The issue of the *extent of principles of distributive justice* differs from that of their range of application in this way: the question is not 'what is distributed by such principles?' but rather a jurisdictional question. It is: 'into which aspects of human life do such principles extend?' This latter question becomes indistinguishable from the former if it is held that everything of significance to a valuable human life, wherever and whenever it exists, is distributed by principles of distributive justice. And this thought seems to derive from the idea of simply taking distributive justice seriously – if it is an important value then it should surely extend to all aspects of human life, shouldn't it? A moment's reflection suggests that

[14] The tentative statement of the two principles reads: 'First: each person is to have an equal right to the most extensive equal basic liberties compatible with a similar scheme of liberties for others. Second: social and economic liberties are to be arranged so that they are both (a) reasonably expected to be to everyone's advantage, and (b) attached to positions and offices open to all': Rawls, supra, note 5, p. 53.

[15] Three instances are: Miller, supra, note 2, ch. 8; Dworkin, supra, note 2, ch. 8; P. Cane, 'Distributive Justice and Tort Law' (2001) *New Zealand Law Review* 401–420.

both thoughts are problematic. Suppose I am playing chess with a friend and am close to winning the game: should I refrain from doing so if (by some presumably far-fetched concatenation of circumstances) that would increase his welfare or that of others, such an increase being in accord with what distributive justice requires? Or suppose I am about to wash the dishes after dinner. Before I do so, should I undertake a rigorous assessment of the distribution of household burdens in light of some or other principle(s) of distributive justice and see whether or not my washing the dishes is required by justice? Or should I just get on with it? It seems *prima facie* odd and also a little worrying to regard principles of distributive justice as extending so far into human lives, if only because some areas of life will be misunderstood and perhaps even undermined if subject to distributive concerns. It seems that values other than distributive justice are in play in many areas of life and, even when distributive justice is undoubtedly in play, it is surely not the only relevant value. Clearly, then, the jurisdictional question of the extent of principles of distributive justice is neither insignificant nor does it lend itself to easy common sense resolution. Its significance arises from the effort to take distributive justice seriously; to do this we must know not only how it relates to the other moral and political values we hold dear but also the specific demands it makes upon us. The question of the extent of those demands cannot be resolved by common sense if common sense resolutions are themselves often sources of glaring injustice (an obvious example being the conventional distribution of household and family burdens).[16]

THREE INDIRECT ARGUMENTS

One of the three indirect arguments examined hereinafter belongs to Anthony Kronman; another belongs to Peter Cane. The former, although published almost three decades ago, is still recognized as a classic of philosophy of private law and has received a great deal of attention. No apology is needed for examining it again because, as will be shown, it attempts all the steps any plausible indirect *internal* argument about the relation between private law and distributive justice must take. It also suffers from the principal problem that ensnares such arguments. Kronman's focus is upon some of the main doctrines of contract law. By

[16] The classic political philosophy treatment of the general issue is S. M. Okin, *Justice, Gender, and the Family* (New York: Basic Books, 1989); a classic general treatment is A. Oakley, *Sociology of Housework* (Oxford: Martin Robertson, 1974).

contrast, Cane concentrates upon the law of tort. His essay, although more much more recent than Kronman's, is important and worthy of attention because, like Kronman's, it also attempts all the steps any plausible argument of that type about the relation between private law and distributive justice must take. The key difference is that Cane's argument is an indirect *external* argument about this relation. As such, its substance but not its scope is all but indistinguishable from another slightly different indirect argument about private law and distributive justice that we will label 'simple'. Indirect external and indirect simple arguments are henceforth regarded as identical. Thus, there are only two rather than three indirect arguments for consideration, although the simple argument will not disappear from view entirely.

Before turning to the detail of the specific internal and external arguments offered by Kronman and Cane, it is sensible to clarify a little more the broad differences between these two argumentative types. The similarity they share is obvious: both hold that some or other feature of private law establishes an unimpeachable connection between the law and distributive justice, although the contours of the conception of distributive justice allegedly implicated is not delineated in detail. Of course, this latter step is not necessary if Kronman and Cane take their task to be the restricted one of showing, contrary to those who would deny it, that there is indeed a link between private law and distributive justice. Questions about the content and coherence of the conception of distributive justice allegedly in play need not therefore arise, although they ought not to be postponed indefinitely. And, when eventually addressed, the burden of indirect arguments about private law and distributive justice becomes indistinguishable from that of direct arguments. Indirect arguments must show that all, most or some aspects of private law accord with the content of a particular conception (or family of conceptions) of distributive justice.

Indirect *internal* arguments about the relation between private law and distributive justice move from some feature or doctrine of private law to a conclusion of this kind: the feature or doctrine in question can only be plausibly understood in light of a conception of distributive justice or in light of a worry about distributive injustice. What makes these arguments internal is that they begin within legal doctrine and work out towards the allegedly distributive consequences or implications of doctrine. Moreover, the implications in question are said to flow from the best interpretation or understanding of the doctrine itself and are not a matter of the effects of an interpretation of the doctrine upon the world beyond the law. So it might be argued, for example, that the notion of improper pressure in contract law, and its various doctrinal manifestations, is best understood as being a matter of distributive justice; and that this is so regardless of the distributive effects a particular judicial decision about improper pressure might have in the wider world. Indirect internal arguments are also, almost by definition, limited in scope. Their case for a connection between private law and distributive justice is incremental, working from particular segments of doctrine to distributive implications. This is exactly as we would expect, since it is practically impossible to start an indirect argument with every doctrine of private law. Furthermore, that would assuredly be a mistake in light of two considerations. First, it seems certain that some such doctrines have no obvious distributive implications (s. 25 of the Law of Property Act 1925 might be an example). Second, insofar as some such legal doctrines are matters of convention or *determinatio*, it is folly to attempt to show that they implicate one or other conception of distributive justice.[17] Since the doctrine in question is not directly derivable from such a conception, it is therefore unlikely that it implicates such a conception.

Indirect *external* arguments rarely begin with analysis of the details of particular legal doctrines. They are, by contrast, concerned to chart the distributive effects of either particular legal doctrines or large swathes thereof upon the world. They differ from indirect *simple* arguments only in that the latter are usually much broader, holding that since private law distributes and maintains a system of rights or entitlements and duties it is therefore unavoidably 'distributive'.[18] The thought is that any system of duties and entitlements constrains freedom, therefore having some impact upon what can and cannot be done. If under system of entitlements$_1$ this land is mine in something approaching the private property sense, then there are some things you cannot do with or upon it without my permission. Your freedom is thus in some sense constrained.[19] System of entitlements$_2$ might, by contrast, have no room for private property in

[17] On *determinatio* see Chapter 8, note 53.

[18] See P. Cane, *Responsibility in Law and Morality* (Oxford: Hart Publishing, 2002), p. 190 for an example.

[19] Clearly the sense of freedom in play in a claim like this is unlikely to be the negative one noted in ch. 3, pp. 105–106. This is because, while the law prohibits many actions and courses of conduct, it rarely makes them physically impossible. An exemplary instance of the full force of the simple argument, which relies on a strained conception of negative freedom, is J. Waldron, 'Homelessness and the Issue of Freedom' (1991) 39 *UCLA Law Review* 295–324. The simple argument is also assuredly in play in the work of Robert Hale: see, for example, 'Bargaining, Duress, and Economic Liberty' (1943) 43 *Columbia LR* 603–628.

land in which case I lack the entitlement previously had and you are no longer under the same constraint. The principal interest of both simple and external indirect arguments is in the distributive *effect* of particular legal doctrines, or large chunks of thereof, or of legal systems as a whole.

It is tempting to say that simple and external arguments are interested only in distributive effects upon the world beyond the law. This, however, is a mistake. For, while external arguments can be interested in that, they are often in addition interested in effects upon the existing and future legal world. External arguments can thus be more or less 'local' in the sense that their focus can range from the distributive effects of a decision upon the litigants to the dispute in question, to its effects upon other actual and future litigants and, finally, to its effects upon the wider world both now and in the future. The crucial point about such arguments is that, rather than argue that some legal doctrine cannot be properly understood without reference to an account of distributive justice, they hold instead that *regardless of how particular legal doctrines are understood or interpreted*, judicial decisions about them have distributive effects in the world. Since the focus of indirect external arguments is not with the detail of particular legal doctrines but with the effect of such doctrines, they can be much more general than indirect internal arguments. Indeed, it is not inconceivable to find an indirect external argument taking as its point of departure a very large segment of the law like, for example, contract or tort and examining its distributive effects. It is the effect of that general body of rules rather than of any particular interpretation of one or other of those rules that is often regarded as grist to the mill of a conception of distributive justice.

Having separated these *two* different arguments – the simple and external arguments are, remember, substantively indistinguishable – it must be noted that their boundaries are often blurred in discussions of private law and distributive justice. It is also the case, obviously, that the arguments can be used in conjunction, a consequence being that it is sometimes difficult to separate the two different claims.[20] That the two claims are very different, and the consequences of this, will soon become apparent. In highlighting the purest form of the two different claims made by these two arguments we are to some extent artificially manipulating – principally by straightening and separating – some of the moves

[20] Kronman in particular combines (or perhaps simply fails to separate) internal and external indirect arguments at some points: 'Contract Law and Distributive Justice' (1980) 89 *Yale Law Journal* 472–511, pp. 472–473.

made by Kronman and Cane. Hopefully, this process of straightening and separating is not also a matter of traducing.

DISTRIBUTIVE JUSTICE AND TORT LAW

Cane characterizes his position in *Distributive Justice and Tort Law* (hereinafter '*DJTL*')[21] thus:

> [m]y basic argument will be that tort liability is, from the defendant's perspective, a burden and from the claimant's perspective, a resource and benefit. When courts make rules about the circumstances in which tort liability to repair harm will arise . . ., they contribute to the establishment of a pattern of distribution of that resource and burden within society. (*DJTL*, p. 404)[22]

As we might expect from an indirect external argument, the detail of the particular legal doctrines in play when the courts make liability decisions in tort is not Cane's principal concern. His interest is, rather, in the effects such decisions have whatever the doctrine in play and however interpreted. The effects in which Cane is interested in *DJTL* are those upon the particular claimant and defendant to the legal action in question, but this focus could easily be extended. For example, it would be interesting to examine the distributive effects a decision in a case like *Reynolds*, with which Cane begins his discussion, had on similarly placed litigants. More generally, an analysis of the distributive effects of such a decision on the general area of activity in question (the duty of gambling establishments to their clients) and on related actors in similar fields, would be equally interesting and informative. It seems that the scope of indirect external arguments is limited only by the time available to their proponents.

We might also expect from an indirect external argument a caveat such as this:

> [m]y concern . . . is not whether the distribution of legal liability that tort generates is just according to any particular substantive theory of distributive justice, but merely with the fact that tort law *has distributive effects* that need to be justified if tort law is to be judged an acceptable legal and social institution. (*DJTL*, pp. 404–405; emphasis mine)

This restriction, after all, serves to distinguish indirect from direct arguments about private law and distributive justice.

Cane clearly thinks that his argument has two particularly significant features. One is that it offers a distinctive and plausible understanding

[21] Supra, note 15.
[22] For similar observations see Cane, supra, note 18, pp. 53, 68 and 186–190.

of the relation between tort law, on the one hand, and corrective and distributive justice, on the other. The second is that this understanding constitutes a serious challenge not just to Ernest Weinrib's separation thesis but to any other attempt to defend that thesis. For current purposes only the first feature of Cane's argument is significant; the second, although the point seems well made, is neither unpacked nor evaluated here.

With regard to the first feature Cane's claim is that to appreciate properly the way in which tort law adjudication actually functions, it must be understood as an amalgam of both corrective (or, as he argues, 'transactional') and distributive justice.[23] Cane holds that judicial decisions about who is liable to whom in tort law are obviously and unavoidably matters of distributive justice: they are decisions about who of claimant and defendant is to receive a benefit (a legal right protected) and who a burden (a liability incurred). Once it is accepted that such legal benefits and burdens fall within the range of application of principles of distributive justice, this conclusion seems undeniable. Such decisions are distributive and therefore have distributive consequences in the same way as does my decision to divide up a cake and distribute it in a certain way. For Cane, the significance of corrective or transactional justice here is that it provides the best way to understand the judicial process of applying particular liability rules in specific cases. '[M]aking rules that define the grounds and bounds of tort liability is a distributive task, while applying such rules . . . is a corrective task' (*DJTL*, p. 412). He also adds that corrective justice provides the structure of tort law in which distributive justice operates (*DJTL*, p. 413). His point is presumably that although the bilateral structure of tort law – the fact, *inter alia*, of claimant having to sue defendant and defendant, if liable, having to compensate claimant – derives from corrective justice, decisions about who does and does not incur liability are not constrained by that structure. Rather, within that structure decisions can and are made on purely distributive grounds.

The reason why the first feature of Cane's argument is so significant for current purposes is that it is in one sense undeniable. That is, there seems no plausible way in which to reject the claim that liability decisions in tort law, or in any other area of private law for that matter, have the kind of distributive consequences Cane highlights. Equally, it surely cannot be

[23] For the idea of transactional justice see *DJTL*, p. 409; in other work he also claims that either tort law in general or some of its specific doctrines function in a distributive way: see supra, note 18, p. 79 and p. 137 for two examples.

denied that private law's creation and maintenance of a system of rights and duties has distributive consequences, among which must be included the fact that that system enables some and disables others from either acting in specific ways or using resources in particular ways. For the same reason, it cannot be denied that my dividing up a cake in a particular way and distributing the portions in a specific manner has distributive consequences. The undeniable truth of both simple and external indirect arguments about private law and distributive justice is, then, this: liability decisions in particular, and private law in general, both have distributive consequences. Particular liability decisions distribute specific benefits and burdens – a right to correction or a liability to correct – while private law in general creates and upholds a broad pattern of such benefits and burdens.

It might be thought that we have accepted this alleged 'truth' too quickly. One ground for this is an obvious and significant disanalogy between the legal examples just used and the cake example. While it might be undeniable that both a legal system *tout court* and particular liability decisions within such a system have distributive effects, it could well be maintained that neither are *intended* to have such effects. So, while undoubtedly distributive in outcome, both legal systems and particular liability decisions within them are not distributive in intent: legal systems are not designed, nor are liability decisions made, with a particular distributive pattern in mind. Lotteries that distribute prizes randomly to those that enter operate in an analogous way. They are undeniably distributive in outcome, yet almost never distributive in intent simply because they do not aim to bring about a particular patterned distribution of prizes. By contrast, cakes are divided and distributed with exactly such a distributive pattern in mind: this process is distributive in intent and distributive in outcome. So, too, are systems of income tax designed to bring about a redistribution of wealth from the best off in a community to the worst-off. In order to know what levels of tax to set in such a scheme there must be some idea of the pattern – the relative distribution of wealth between rich and poor – aimed at; without such an aim the scheme has no point. This is not to say that schemes or decisions distributive in intent are always distributive in outcome in the sense intended: there can, of course, be a mismatch between intentions and outcomes. Our scheme to achieve distribution Y may, as a result of oversight or factors beyond our control, bring about distribution Z instead and that may be far indeed from the outcome wanted.

But what is the significance of the distinction between decisions and systems distributive in intent and distributive in outcome? Even if it is accepted that neither particular liability decisions (despite the comments of some judges: see *DJTL*, pp. 410–412) nor legal systems as a whole are distributive in intent, why should this matter to proponents of external arguments? Since such decisions and systems are undoubtedly distributive in outcome, what more needs be said? Perhaps this: it needs be established that the undeniable truth in indirect external (and simple) arguments is not trivial.

The triviality charge arises from this thought: that almost all instances of social conduct have distributive effects and, by analogy, most institutions and practices will have such effects also (because they are in part made up of patterns of conduct). My giving a donation to charity has distributive effects in just the same way as does my purchase of coffee; some or other resource has moved from me to the charity and the cafe in question. Moreover, each transaction could have additional distributive effects: the resource that has moved from me to them could have gone to another charity or to another coffee shop. If I always buy my morning coffee from Mega-corp Coffee rather than Small Café that could have an obvious longer-term distributive outcome: Mega-corp Coffee flourishes and Small Café goes out of business. Since my coffee purchasing decisions are never governed by an intention to bring about a particular distributive outcome, this aspect of my conduct is distributive in outcome only. It could, of course, become distributive in intent also – I might decide that it is a good thing that retailers like Small Café continue to exist and therefore take my trade there (even though the coffee is not as good). I might also decide against buying coffee from Mega-corp because, for example, they exploit coffee growers in the developing world. In these instances, an aspect of my conduct that was never viewed as intentionally distributive now becomes so and I aim at a match between the distributive outcomes of my conduct and my distributive intentions.

So, is the undeniable truth of external arguments trivial? Probably only if it is indeed true that almost every instance of human conduct is actually or potentially distributive in outcome. Establishing this would be difficult but far from impossible. At a bare minimum it requires, first, the identification of an appropriately distributive outcome, however immediate or long-term, that is legitimately causally traced to a specific instance of conduct.[24] In addition, a second hurdle must be overcome: the kind of link

[24] Tracing such long-term causal connections is usually done by reference to the but-for or *NESS* tests and little else; common sense causal principles do not often stretch so far. See Chapter 6 for a reminder of the issues in play.

just specified must be true of almost every thing we do, by which is meant every instance of conduct in the social world. Finally, it must be the case that much of the conduct said to be distributive in outcome in this sense cannot also be plausibly understood as distributive in intent. If these conditions are satisfied then the indirect external argument, while true, is nevertheless trivial because it highlights a feature of the law and of particular liability decisions that is shared by almost every instance of human conduct. It states the obvious; and that, of course, should not be news.

While the triviality charge holds that the fact that almost all conduct, institutions and practices have distributive outcomes is not particularly informative, it need not hold that all talk of distributive outcomes is uninteresting. An instance in which talk of distributive outcomes is almost invariably very interesting is when they are compared with the distributive intentions, if any, which the outcomes supposedly track. The interest here lies in how well or badly our distributive intentions are realized in the world and in discovering the range of factors, over and beyond good intentions, which determine the outcomes that actually come about. Although this question is plainly not one that occupies Cane in *DJTL*, this does not make it any the less interesting for those preoccupied with distributive effects.

A final quibble about indirect external arguments such as Cane's must be noted. Even if the trivial but undeniable truth in these arguments is accepted, another interesting question still arises: is noting the distributive effects of various institutions, practices and other instances of human conduct itself the best way to begin thinking about principles of distributive justice? That the answer may be negative is suggested by the realization that noting such effects does nothing, in and of itself, to show that they *must* fall within the compass of principles of distributive justice. Furthermore, since such effects are legion, the issue arises of whether all are equally significant. Which such effects are particularly significant, and should thus fall within the ambit of distributive justice, is surely not a question that can be answered by simply noting those effects. That question can and should be answered by a theory of distributive justice itself: such a theory should at the outset provide guidance as to which distributive effects are and are not significant. At least, this would be so if it is accepted that distributive justice is not the only value in a community's political morality. If, by contrast, distributive justice is regarded as the sovereign and singular virtue of political morality, then its jurisdiction may well be unlimited and the distributive effects of every institution, practice and instance of conduct simply grist to its mill.

CONTRACT LAW AND DISTRIBUTIVE JUSTICE

In *Contract Law and Distributive Justice* (*CLDJ*) one of Kronman's principal arguments is that the notion of voluntary exchange animating contract law must be understood as a distributive concept.[25] This is because, he argues, the questions asked when determining the voluntariness of a particular exchange are equivalent to the questions posed when deciding 'which of the many forms of advantage-taking possible in exchange relationships are compatible with the libertarian conception of individual freedom' (*CLDJ*, p. 480). It is not just the libertarian conception of freedom or voluntariness in which Kronman is interested, however. His examination of the limits of that conception extends to the liberal conception because he believes that they share a common understanding of the nature and basis of contractual obligations (*CLDJ*, p. 474). When a promisor claims she entered into an exchange only because she was coerced by the other party to do so, or because the other party took advantage of her parlous misfortune; or that she entered the transaction as a result of certain cognitive or volitional impairments, or because of being misled or exploitative sharp practice by the other party, she is, for Kronman, raising the same issue. 'In each of these cases, the fundamental question is whether the promisee should be permitted to exploit his advantage to the detriment of the other party, or whether permitting him to do so will deprive the other party of the freedom that is necessary to make . . . [her] promise truly voluntary and therefore binding' (*CLDJ*, p. 480).

Kronman claims that the contract cases on voluntariness – those dealing with, *inter alia*, duress, undue influence, fraud and misrepresentation – disclose no 'principled basis for determining which forms of advantage-taking ought to be allowed' (*CLDJ*, p. 484). That being so, he considers three principles that might provide plausible answers to this question, concluding that only one is satisfactory. This is the Paretian principle.[26] It allows only those types of advantage-taking which ensure that the person

[25] Supra, note 20. For English contract lawyers there appear to be more obvious doctrinal candidates for such a distributive role: see, for example, Unfair Contract Terms Act 1977 and Unfair Terms in Consumer Contract Regulations 1999.

[26] So called because derived from Vilfredo Pareto's principles of Pareto-optimality (resources are distributed in such a fashion if and only if any further allocation can make one person better off only at the expense of another) and Pareto-superiority (one allocation of resources, A1, is superior to another, A2, if no one is made worse off in the transition from A2 to A1, and the welfare of at least one person is enhanced). For further discussion of the role of the paretian principle in Kronman's argument see my 'Contract as a Mechanism of Distributive Justice' (1989) 9 *Oxford Journal of Legal Studies* 132–147, pp. 142–147.

prejudiced by them will be better off in the long term if those kinds of advantage-taking are allowed than she would be were they prohibited. Kronman rules out one natural interpretation of this principle, namely, that when judges must decide whether or not a particular promisee's conduct should be prohibited, they should take as determinative to enforcement the long-term advantage of *all* those disadvantaged by the transaction. Moreover, for a genuine Pareto justification to be forthcoming, everyone affected by the transaction must ultimately benefit since, in a Paretian world, there are no losers. This illustrates the appeal of Paretianism as a method of social choice since it guarantees complete unanimity on distributional and other issues. If no one loses by the adoption of a particular social policy or course of action, how can anyone object to it? This reading of the Paretian principle is not, however, favoured by Kronman. His preferred version is restricted in this way: it 'requires only that the welfare of most people who are taken advantage of in a particular way be increased by the kind of advantage-taking in question' (*CLDJ*, p. 487). Although this principle therefore lacks the main advantage of a genuine Paretian principle, Kronman nevertheless thinks it has some advantages. One of them is its alleged dependence upon an appealing account of equality, while another is claimed to be its egalitarian conception of the way in which we hold advantages, both natural (like physical capacities) and social (like talents developed in light of such physical capacities).[27]

Neither the particular claims Kronman makes in the course of supporting the Paretian principle, nor his other principal argument – that taxation is not always the best way in which to pursue distributive justice – are of concern here.[28] Our focus is instead upon the connection Kronman purports to establish between the particular doctrinal questions judges ask when deciding cases of duress, undue influence, misrepresentation and mistake, on the one hand, and the Paretian principle, on the

[27] See supra, note 20 at pp. 498–510 and A. Kronman, 'Talent Pooling' in J. Roland Pennock and J. Chapman (eds.), *Nomos XXIII: Human Rights* (New York: New York University Press, 1981).

[28] These and Kronman's other claims have received a good deal of attention. See L. Alexander and W. Wang, 'Natural Advantages and Contractual Justice' (1984) 3 *Law and Philosophy* 281–297; M. Richardson, 'Contract Law and Distributive Justice Revisited' (1990) 10 *Legal Studies* 258–270; T. Dare, 'Kronman on Contract: A Study in the Relation Between Substance and Procedure in Normative and Legal Theory' (1994) 7 *Canadian Journal of Law and Jurisprudence* 331–348; M. Kramer and N. Simmonds, 'Getting the Rabbit Out of the Hat: A Critique of Anthony Kronman's Theory of Contracts' (1996) 55 *Cambridge LJ* 358–371; R. Bigwood, *Exploitative Contracts* (Oxford: Clarendon Press, 2003), pp. 105–111.

other. It is this connection, after all, that makes the argument an internal indirect argument: 'internal' because the starting point is a collection of legal doctrines which supposedly manifest a concern with distributive justice or implicate a particular account of distributive justice; 'indirect' because, whatever the alleged advantages the Paretian principle has, it is clearly not a complete theory of distributive justice. The principle would, at most, be a component of such a theory. So how does it fare as an indirect argument? The answer is: not very well.

The primary difficulty is that insufficient work is done to show that the case law in question is as inadequate as Kronman claims. There is thus a great deal of doubt as to whether or not the space he purports to clear for the Paretian principle, attributing it an explanatory and justificatory role in relation to a number of legal doctrines, is actually available. If the Paretian principle is to explain and justify these areas of doctrine it must be established that they stand in need of explanation and justification. And that is to claim, obviously, that the explanations and justifications offered by the participants (judges, practitioners, commentators)[29] in this particular area of the institution of private law are inadequate. Once that is established, it is perfectly permissible to offer an explanation-cum-justification that, like the Paretian principle, pays no heed to participants' understandings. But are participants' understandings of the basis of the doctrines of duress, undue influence, misrepresentation and mistake obviously inadequate?

We will concern ourselves only with the doctrine of duress. In its non-economic version, this doctrine has been part of Anglo-American and Commonwealth contract law for a long time. Thus, if its basis is still not well understood by those charged with applying it, then there must be a presumption in favour of Kronman. If, however, contract lawyers have a reasonably plausible, albeit not very theoretically refined understanding of the doctrine, then this undermines Kronman's case. This is because the doctrine of duress is, if Kronman's very wide conception of advantage-taking is accepted, surely a central instance of advantage-taking. If a 'normal' contractual duress scenario[30] – one in which a party enters into a

[29] There is, as we noted in Chapter 8, an unresolved question about who is included in the category of 'participant' but, if the institution and practice in question is legal, then those mentioned must at the very least be regarded as participants. If they are not, then who is?

[30] Normal in terms of judicial and textbook reflection rather than normal in terms of incidence. Indeed, in English law relatively few of these 'normal' cases appear in the law reports: the usual examples are *Kesarmal v Valliappa Chettia* [1954] 1 WLR 380 and *Barton v Armstrong* [1976] AC 104.

contract as a result of violence or threats from the other party – is not an example of advantage-taking, then that notion must be understood in a particularly odd or eccentric way.

In the English cases, the language judges most frequently use when tackling duress cases covers two distinct sets of considerations. One set takes as central the conduct of the victim of pressure: the judges are here most interested in whether or not the victim's entering into the contract was 'voluntary', or 'free' or 'intentional' (variations of each idea are also often invoked).[31] Of course, judicial attention is also given, during this process, to the supposed salience of the threat or pressure used and the fortitude of the victim. The other set of considerations concern the conduct of the threatenor: here judges most often raise questions about the relatively legitimacy of the pressure brought to bear on the other party. *Prima facie*, it seems that that pressure must be 'wrong' and this is not mainly, or perhaps not even, a moral judgment. It is, rather, principally a legal judgment: the threat must usually be legally wrong in order for a duress claim to arise.[32]

In light of this, it is no surprise that one of the best available analyses of the doctrine of duress explains it in terms of two principles: the wrongdoing principle and the autonomy (or consent) principle.[33] While each principle is embedded in the case law, in the sense that each captures the considerations upon which judges actually base their decisions, each principle is also an extrapolation from the cases. This latter process means that the two principles, while generally taking at face value the considerations judges invoke when deciding duress cases, also to some extent extend, or clarify and tidy, those considerations. This is perfectly legitimate, if it is possible that judicial statements are occasionally oblique or inconsistent; that these possibilities are actual surely explains the existence of a tradition of commentary upon and evaluation of judicial decisions in both legal education and legal practice. That the deliberations of judges are not always and ever immediately transparent, even to other participants in the institution, does not, of course, generate a presumption against taking those deliberations seriously. It is simply too

[31] Two examples from the many: *Pau On v Lau Yiu Long* [1980] AC 614 at p. 636 and *The Universe Sentinel* [1983] AC 366 at p. 383 and p. 400.

[32] See *The Universe Sentinel*, supra, at p. 385 and p. 400; and *CNT Cash and Carry Ltd. v Gallagher* [1994] 4 All ER 714.

[33] S. Smith, 'Contracting under Pressure: A Theory of Duress' (1997) 56 *Cambridge LJ* 343–373 and his *Contract Theory* (Oxford: Clarendon Press, 2004), pp. 316–340. Smith's view has changed a little between essay and book but the changes are of no concern here. An alternative account of duress is provided by Bigwood, supra, note 28, ch. 7.

hasty to move from the judgment that an action, utterance or text stands in need of 'interpretation', its meaning not being immediately obvious, to the conclusion that that action, utterance or text should therefore be ignored. It is equally hasty to move from the judgment that an utterance, action or text stands in need of interpretation to the conclusion that it is 'therefore' unnecessary to attempt to interpret the utterance, action or text in light of its author's aim, purpose or goal. Other utterances, texts or actions of the author might, of course, disclose the latter.

It seems clear that Kronman makes one or other of these false moves simply because he gives such short shrift to the cases and the deliberations therein. It is as though he is already convinced that the reasons judges have offered for their decisions in these cases are not worth either stating or elucidating in any depth. They are not, that is, worthy of an effort at interpretation in their own terms. Part of the reason for Kronman's apparent hastiness on this issue might well be his reclassification of the question that is in play in duress and other closely related kinds of case – this, remember, is for Kronman the question of what kinds of advantage-taking should be allowed. That is clearly unlikely to be a question that judges themselves will explicitly raise, since it is not a question that the doctrines in play in these cases explicitly raise. While Kronman might regard this as a mistake, it is not in any sense a legal mistake. It might be an intellectual mistake because not asking this question generates confusion and unclarity in the law, but the vital point here is that it is just this claim that Kronman has not established. That is, he does not show that the law is in chaos and cannot be properly understood *except* by reference to the paretian principle. Furthermore, we have just invoked an account of the doctrine of duress in contract that (i) portrays it as intelligible and coherent; and (ii), in so doing, accommodates most of those considerations that the judges themselves say are important in their deliberations. There is, then, at least one other account of the law that claims it is not chaotic and that it can be understood without reference to the Paretian principle.

There is no assurance that this alternative account of contractual duress does not implicate, either directly or indirectly, some or other theory of distributive justice. That is not the point of invoking it here. Rather, the intention is to illustrate a general problem that internal indirect arguments face: the difficulty of establishing that some or other legal doctrine, *understood in its own terms*, unequivocally embodies a particular principle of distributive justice or leads to such a principle. But why insist on the 'understood in its own terms' restriction? Because only then is it certain that we are faced with an internal rather than external argument about the relation between private law and distributive justice. Surely the claim that some or other legal doctrine embodies or leads to a distributive principle is only interesting, and distinct from an external argument, if that embodiment arises from *a natural and normal reading* of the doctrine. If, in order for the embodiment claim to be made out, the doctrine has to be translated into a set of concepts and vocabulary that those who apply it do not use and may not even understand, then that seems suspicious. For in this case the embodiment seems to have been forced upon rather than emerge from the doctrine.

Of course, this problem of 'fit' is far from insurmountable and certainly does not show that indirect internal arguments are impossible or unintelligible.[34] The account of duress that has been offered as an alternative to Kronman's could well function as preamble to a compelling indirect internal argument, rooted as it is in the views of participants. If it could be shown that those views lead ineluctably to some or other plausible principle of distributive justice, then that would indeed be a powerful and pregnant claim. It has not been necessary, in order for the fit problem to be salient, to show that this alternative account of the basis of duress is superior in every respect to Kronman's account. The only significant area of superiority for current purposes – the assessment of Kronman's Paretian principle as an internal argument – is that the competitor account fits legal doctrine better. And the issue of fit, while hardly significant for external arguments like that offered by Cane, is of the first importance for internal arguments since it is, in part, what makes them internal rather than external.

At this stage it might be said in Kronman's defence that his argument is misinterpreted if regarded as an internal argument. There is some weight in this, since Kronman sometimes makes claims that look better suited to an external argument – he speaks more than once of the 'distributive effects' of contract law.[35] Yet the ground on which this alternative reading flounders is that it cannot do justice to Kronman's effort to show that the Paretian principle underpins the law. Undertaking that task makes no sense if one's aim is solely to highlight the distributive effects of the legal doctrines in question. Moreover, this argument in defence of Kronman is of little help: if, after all, his analysis should be read as an external rather

[34] This particular manifestation of the fit problem is clearly a family relative of that discussed in Chapter 8.

[35] See note 20.

than internal argument, then it is open to the triviality charge levelled against Cane.

TWO POINTS

Before leaving indirect arguments about the relation between private law and distributive justice, two loose ends must be tied. The first raises one of the key questions appropriate for any effort to offer a normative foundation for private law: from the perspective of indirect arguments, in what sense, if any, is distributive justice a 'foundation' of private law? Almost as soon as the question is posed it becomes obvious that it is all but irrelevant. This is because indirect arguments do not, almost by definition, invoke substantive accounts of distributive justice. The most they do is gesture to such accounts, since the burden of such arguments is simply to highlight either the distributive effects of private law or the fact that it makes use of ostensibly distributive concepts. Indirect arguments can, of course, serve as a useful preamble to direct arguments and only when the latter kind of argument is made does the foundational question arise. Also, it is only when a particular normative theory is invoked in a foundational role that it makes sense to ask either or both of the remaining key questions about such theories. Hence, there is little point in considering, for example, the specific nature of the obligation to correct created by one or other of the indirect arguments so far considered.

The second loose end concerns the relative prevalence of indirect arguments about private law and distributive justice as opposed to direct arguments. Why is this? One factor that might constitute part of an explanation is that traditional (possibly unreflective) lawyers' wisdom regards distributive justice as irrelevant to the realm of private law. The considerations in play in private law disputes deal only with the disputants' conduct towards one another and how this should be understood in light of relevant legal doctrines. Additional 'broader' considerations are sometimes also invoked by the courts, but these are usually only concerned with what might be called the efficient or proper administration of justice and its effect on the wider world.[36] There is, it is thought, no sensible way in which either these considerations or those that inform a legal judgment about the disputants' behaviour towards one another can be regarded as related to or invoking an account of distributive justice. If

[36] Sometimes captured by English judges in the terminology of 'floodgate' arguments. A helpful analysis of the various kinds of consequentialist arguments in adjudication is N. MacCormick, *Legal Reasoning and Legal Theory* (Oxford: Clarendon Press, revised edn, 1993), ch. VI.

this view is indeed deeply entrenched, then the popularity of indirect arguments is understandable: the deeper this view is embedded, the greater must be the efforts to destabilize it. Another factor that could explain the popularity of indirect arguments as against direct arguments is a worry about the jurisdictional limits of principles of distributive justice. This factor, if apposite, will actually be very troubling for proponents of both direct and indirect arguments, but since it provides a very obvious bar to the former it could also explain the popularity of the latter. If there are areas of social life over which principles of distributive justice have no jurisdiction, this should give distributive justice zealots pause. Suggesting that there are such jurisdictional limits does not, of course, commit one to any form of scepticism about distributive justice. Rather, it bespeaks a view of a community's political morality which accepts that it may consist of a range of different values, rather than of one single value, and that the range of these values may have to be restricted so as to realize them all to some degree. That a deep concern with the just distribution of welfare and resources need not collapse into zealotry, but can instead coexist with an appreciation of the limits of principles of distributive justice, is borne out by the example of Rawls's work.

PRIVATE LAW AND THE BASIC STRUCTURE

Rawls's idea of the basic structure limits the extent of his two principles of justice: those principles apply first and foremost to that structure. Whether or not those principles apply beyond that realm is, for Rawls, best decided on a case by case basis.[37] The idea of the basic structure is significant for at least two reasons. First, it constitutes one of the few explicit attempts by a theorist of distributive justice to chart the jurisdictional limits of distributive justice. While some proponents of theories of distributive justice accept that there must be some such limits, few actually attempt to elucidate them. Second, and more significantly for present purposes, it is not immediately obvious that private law falls within the basic structure. If it does not, then proponents of direct

[37] This, at least, is what I take him to mean when he says 'a theory must develop principles [of justice] for the relevant subjects step by step in some appropriate sequence': *Political Liberalism*, supra, note 12, p. 258. The principles that govern the basic structure have 'a certain regulative primacy' (ibid, p. 257) over the principles applicable to other domains; those domains can still, however, 'act from their own principles designed to fit their particular nature' (p. 262).

arguments about the relation between private law and distributive justice face an obstacle. Of course, in order for the obstacle to be difficult to surmount it needs be shown that it is not unique to only one theory of distributive justice. That is to say, it needs be shown that Rawls's thoughts about the significance of the basic structure can be generalized beyond the contours of his own theory of distributive justice, that the issue the idea highlights is applicable to most or many theories of distributive justice. Thus the first step in what follows must be to elucidate the idea of the basic structure as Rawls understands it and to consider whether the issue it raises is of general application. The second step is to consider whether or not private law falls within the basic structure.

According to Rawls

> [t]he basic structure is understood as the way in which the major social institutions fit together into one system, and how they assign fundamental rights and duties and shape the division of advantages that arises through social cooperation. Thus the political constitution, the legally recognized forms of property, and the organization of the economy, and the nature of the family, all belong to the basic structure. (*PL*, p. 258)[38]

This narrow view of the basic structure regards it as the means by which distributive justice is brought about and maintained in a just society.[39] It is the determinant of what Rawls calls 'background justice' (*PL*, pp. 265–269), the context within which free and fair transactions between individuals and groups take place. Furthermore, it is also the context within which the various social groupings – clubs, religious and leisure collectives, for example – come into being and in which individuals have to live. It therefore determines both the make-up of the social groups and the life chances of individuals in a society. It is, for these reasons, the primary target for principles of distributive justice.

Now some of Rawls's reasons for regarding the basic structure as the first subject of justice derive purely from his own Kantian version of the social contract. The way in which that contract is constructed, through a choice situation he calls the original position, and the way in which those

[38] '*PL*' in both text and references refers to *Political Liberalism*, supra, note 12. For other similar statements by Rawls see supra, note 5, p. 6 and his *Justice as Fairness: A Restatement* (Cambridge, Mass.: Harvard University Press, 2001), pp. 10–12. Rawls's comments on the basic structure in *PL* represent his most sustained treatment of the issue and are thus given pre-eminence in the discussion that follows.

[39] According to Thomas Pogge, a wider conception of the basic structure is at work in *A Theory of Justice*: see his *Realizing Rawls* (Ithaca: Cornell University Press, 1989), pp. 21–25. Whether the wider or narrower conception is in play makes little practical difference to the arguments offered in this section.

choosing principles of justice are conceived in that situation of choice, each give reason to regard the basic structure as particularly important (*PL*, pp. 271–281). But these reasons are not, of course, generally applicable; they lack salience for theories of distributive justice without Rawls's Kantian baggage. Furthermore, reasons that spell out the significance of the basic structure do not show that there are realms beyond that structure to which principles of distributive justice do not apply. Does Rawls provide any reasons of the latter kind which, moreover, are generally applicable, having weight beyond the confines of his own theory of justice? This may seem unlikely, especially in view of Rawls's thought that his theory of justice is one of the few for which the basic structure is particularly significant (*PL*, pp. 259–265).

The outlook may not, however, be quite so bleak. Some of the considerations that Rawls invokes to show the especial significance of the basic structure can do dual service, since they are certainly salient not only for his theory of justice. Think, for example, of his observation about the way in which free and fair agreements between groups and/or individuals can undermine background justice. Even in a society which embodies 'the initially attractive idea that social circumstances and people's relationships to one another should develop over time in accordance with free agreements fairly arrived at and fully honored' (*PL*, p. 265), problems of distributive injustice can arise. This is because there is simply no guarantee that the overall outcome of many, many free and fair transactions between individuals and groups will track the requirements of distributive justice. Rather than leading towards distributive justice, there is just as much likelihood that 'the invisible hand guides things in the wrong direction and favors an oligopolistic configuration of accumulations that succeeds in maintaining unjustified inequalities and restrictions on fair opportunity' (*PL*, p. 267). There are at least two ways in which to protect against this unwanted eventuality: by re-writing (or other kinds of interference in) individuals' free and fair transactions so as to maintain distributive justice, or by addressing whatever distributive injustice arises from many free and fair transactions through the basic structure. Rawls prefers the latter approach to the former; his reasons, both implicit and explicit, are informative.

One reason Rawls explicitly articulates against addressing background distributive injustice through individuals transactions is that

> there are no feasible and practicable rules that it is sensible to impose on individuals that can prevent the erosion of background justice. This is because

> the rules governing agreements and individual transactions cannot be too complex, or require too much information to be correctly applied; nor should they enjoin individuals to engage in bargaining with many widely scattered third parties, since this would impose excessive transaction costs. (*PL*, p. 267)

The point is well made but also a little flimsy: would, for example, Rawls change his mind if there were technological means for coping with the complexity and time-consuming nature of such rules? Imagine a palm-held 'distributive consequence computer' which, holding all the available data on the current distribution of welfare, resources and opportunities in our community, could determine how far the particular transaction into which I am about to enter will move the distribution towards or away from what Rawlsian principles of justice require.[40] Assuming there are no epistemological or related hurdles to the development of such a device, would Rawls require its use?[41] We could also imagine a closely related 'transaction cost elimination device' which delivered data about those with whom we should transact in order to either maintain or move towards a more just distribution of welfare, resources and opportunities. Again, would Rawls require its use?

It seems likely that his answer would be 'no'. For, underlying the 'logistical' considerations just noted, there appears to be a deeper concern with individual liberty. This reason for regarding adjustments to the basic structure as the most appropriate response to injustice is not, however, explicitly articulated by Rawls. It seems to operate instead at the level of an assumption underpinning some of his observations. Consider, for example, his claim that there is a beneficial division of labour between the social rules that constitute the basic structure and those rules the basic structure

> enforces through the legal system . . . that govern the transactions and agreements between individuals and associations (the law of contract, and so on). The rules relating to fraud and duress, and the like, belong to these rules,

[40] This device is a close relative to those imagined by Ackerman, supra, note 2, pp. 174–177. Technological advances in mobile telephony and computing, as well as the development of the internet, have made Ackerman's 1980 technological fantasy seem a lot less fantastic today.

[41] Two alleged (and closely related) epistemological impediments might be (i) that it is impossible to collate the information required to know the overall pattern of distribution; and (ii) that it is impossible to know or predict with confidence the consequences of individual transactions on the overall pattern. Both problems are near relatives of those in play in the 'socialist calculation debate'. For an introduction see L. Von Mises, 'Economic Calculation in the Socialist Commonwealth' ch. III of F. Hayek (ed.), *Collectivist Economic Planning* (London: Routledge, 1935).

> and satisfy the requirements of simplicity and practicality. They are framed to leave individuals and associations *free to act effectively* in pursuit of their ends and *without excessive constraints*. (*PL*, p. 268; emphasis mine)

The obvious benefit, it seems, is greater individual freedom or liberty. Maintaining justice or redressing injustice through the basic structure apparently ensures individuals greater freedom to pursue their aims through free and fair transactions than the alternative. This preference for one means of pursing distributive justice over another is quite in accord with the lexical ranking of the two principles of justice. Since that confers precedence upon the basic liberties, it is no surprise to find this precedence extended into the process by which justice is achieved and maintained in a society. The desire to uphold the greatest possible liberty for citizens surely also underpins Rawls's view of the role of the difference principle, part of his second principle of justice:

> It applies to the announced system of public law and statutes and not to particular transactions or distributions, nor to the decisions of individuals and associations, but rather to the institutional background against which these transactions and decisions take place. *There are no unannounced and unpredictable interferences with citizens' expectations and acquisitions*. (*PL*, p. 283; emphasis mine)

Such interferences would, no doubt, be destructive of the liberties the first principle seeks to uphold.

Rawls thus has at least two general arguments that provide a presumptive case against distributive principles being applied beyond the basic structure. The arguments are general, in the sense that they are of relevance to all non-utilitarian, non-libertarian theories of justice, provided they share Rawls's concern with liberty.[42] Taking liberty seriously thus provides good reason to restrict the extent of distributive principles.

This brings us to the second step, most conveniently approached by addressing this question: is private law part of the basic structure? An obvious argument that it should be draws upon one or other indirect argument: since private law is a very important institution in terms of its distributive effects, it must be regarded as part of the basic structure and

[42] The double limitation is necessary in light of Rawls's argument at pp. 259–265 of *PL*. The classic libertarian critique of Rawls's effort to single out the basic structure for special treatment is Nozick's; see supra, note 2, pp. 204–213. Pogge, supra, note 39, pp. 25–36 thinks Nozick's objections misplaced.

thus subject to principles of distributive justice.[43] Here, then, we have one or other indirect argument used as preamble to a direct argument. The obvious problem, however, is that pointing to the distributive effects of some institution, practice or instance of conduct does not in and of itself show that that institution, practice or conduct *should* or *must* be subject to principles of distributive justice. This, of course, is the point behind Rawls's observation about the way in which a series of free and fair exchanges can undermine background justice. The fact that these exchanges do this does not require that they be directly subject to principles of distributive justice. The distributive effects of these exchanges can be addressed in other ways or completely ignored. Furthermore, some versions of the indirect argument that might be invoked here face their own difficulties. So, for example, it would be a mistake to use either the indirect external or indirect simple argument as preamble to a direct argument without first responding to the triviality objection that both face.

Although this first argument appears unpromising, it is not the only one available. It might, for example, be argued that if the legally recognized forms of property are included in the basic structure by Rawls then so, too, must be the rest of private law. For what are the legally recognized forms of property if not the law of real and personal property? And what protects and allows us to alienate our property holdings, in addition to the law of real and personal property, but contract and tort law? Furthermore, do not these areas of private law contribute to the organization of the economy? If that is part of the basic structure, then surely those aspects of private law that maintain it should also be included? This move from the elements that Rawls includes in the basic structure to the principal areas of private law is not, however, inevitable. For one can speak quite intelligibly of both the legally recognized forms of property and the organization of the economy without thereby referring to any particular legal scheme of property or a specific legal arrangement of the economy. Moreover, one can also say that the economic structure is a key determinant of the distribution of resources in a society (and thus should be regarded as part of the basic structure), without being committed to regarding private law as a key determinant of the economic structure (and thus part of the basic structure). True, private law undoubtedly upholds

[43] Some often just assume that private law must be part of the basic structure: see G. Keating, 'The Idea of Fairness in the Law of Enterprise Liability' (1996–1997) 95 *Michigan LR* 1266–1380, pp. 1302–1304. The assumption is retracted in subsequent work: see Keating, note 47, below, at p. 65, note 5.

particular schemes of property and aids in organizing the economy in a particular way: but if both economy and schemes of property can exist *de facto* before becoming *de jure*, then private law is not necessary to bring them into being.[44] It is, of course, quite consistent with this claim to maintain that private law is an important means of holding a specific scheme of relations of production and property steady once it has come into being. Yet if it is the case that law *follows* rather than *determines* economic relations of production, then there is good reason for principles of distributive justice to focus on latter rather than the former.

This riposte can be conjoined with another argument that private law should not be regarded as part of the basic structure. This argument is directly derived from the reasons Rawls offers for a division of labour between basic structure and other areas of social life. The initial claim would be that it is inefficient to use the doctrines of private law as a means, and the contingent disputes which call for their application as occasions, for the direct invocation of principles of distributive justice. This inefficiency is twofold. First, it arises from the time-consuming and piecemeal nature of this process: using courts and private law to pursue distributive justice is much more hit and miss, and takes much longer (since it must await the occurrence of suitable legal disputes to make their way through the court structure) than, for example, a change in the taxation system. The latter might just require a single amendment of a single legal rule that changes the situation for all citizens (for example, charging an extra penny of income tax from all taxpayers which is directed to education trust funds for all children under the age of six). By contrast, redistribution through private law adjudication might take decades or more to bring about an equivalent redistributive gain. Second, on the double assumption that a doctrine of precedent is in play and that legal doctrines and decisions provide guidance for the actions of citizens, inefficiency will arise in the form of transaction costs. For citizens charged with the task of ensuring that their transactions either do not undermine or actually advance the requirements of distributive justice have to invest far more time and energy in the process of transacting than they otherwise would. And certainly far more than would be required if they could simply ignore the distributive consequences of fair and free

[44] The kind of argument necessary to support this claim is particularly salient in discussions of the distinction between economic base and non-economic superstructure in the thought of Karl Marx. For an exemplary example see: G. A. Cohen, *Karl Marx's Theory of History: A Defence* (Oxford: Clarendon Press, 1978), ch. VIII.

exchanges, those being tackled by appropriate changes to the basic structure.

Of course, these considerations in favour of a division of labour between basic structure and other aspects of social life are primarily logistical: we could imagine technological changes by which they could be overcome. The suggestion that they should not be overcome, even if they could be, must therefore rest on some deeper value or concern that these logistical problems happen to track. For Rawls, that deeper concern is liberty. So, even if it were logistically possible to efficiently track distributive justice through private law doctrine and adjudication, on the one hand, and individuals' transactions, on the other, it is not desirable because doing so reduces the liberty (or undermines the basic liberties) of citizens.[45] We thus return to the priority Rawls assigns to liberty and/or the basic liberties in his theory of justice. This is surely the most important argument that can be made for limiting the extent of principles of justice and, while it cannot be properly considered and evaluated here, its role should not be misunderstood. Its power depends upon acceptance of the idea that justice in the distribution of welfare, resources and other determinants of a valuable life can be constrained to protect other values or to uphold justice in the distribution of other goods (like the basic liberties, for example). If this possibility is rejected, and if justice in the distribution of resources and welfare is regarded as the most important value for a political community, then Rawls's argument from liberty is irrelevant. One may doubt the plausibility or wisdom of such a monotone view of a community's political morality, and even regard a community that embodied such a morality as undesirable,[46] but this does not provide any actual argument to limit the extent of principles of justice. Rawls has such an argument and we have attempted to reconstruct it for general use here. That process has not, however, yielded anything particularly compelling: it has at most generated what lawyers would call a *prima facie* or rebuttable presumption against extending principles of justice to each and every corner of human life. Private law may well reside in one such corner.

[45] The qualification is necessary because Rawls wavers between liberty and the basic liberties as the subject of the first principle of justice: for clear and enlightening discussion see H. L. A. Hart, 'Rawls on Liberty and its Priority', ch. 10 of his *Essays in Jurisprudence and Philosophy* (Oxford: Clarendon Press, 1983). Rawls's response is 'The Basic Liberties and Their Priority' pp. 1–87 of S. McMurrin (ed.), *Liberty, Equality, and the Law* (Cambridge: Cambridge University Press, 1987).

[46] For some pertinent although fictional reflections see S. Lukes, *The Curious Enlightenment of Professor Caritat* (London: Verso, 1995).

TWO DIRECT ARGUMENTS

Suppose private law embodies a legitimate and compelling principle of distributive justice. Suppose also that Croesus and Diogenes are involved in an accident: as a result of his negligence, Diogenes has badly damaged Croesus's Bentley. One last supposition: accept that all the usual requirements for negligence liability have been established. Thus Diogenes owed a duty of care to Croesus, he breached that duty, his breach was a cause of the damage and that damage was not too remote. Must Diogenes compensate Croesus for the damage to his car? Not necessarily. If it is established that Croesus is as wealthy as a King, his immense wealth incompatible with the accepted principle of distributive justice, and that Diogenes is so poor he lives like a feral dog, his lack of resources also contrary to the demands of distributive justice, then surely no duty to compensate arises. For what else can it mean to say that private law (including this segment of tort law) embodies a legitimate and compelling principle of distributive justice, if not that no duty arises if its imposition is contrary to what distributive justice requires? If, by contrast, the holdings of Diogenes and Croesus are in accord with the demands of distributive justice, then the duty to compensate appears *prima facie* valid. That is to say no more than that any grounds for not imposing the duty must be unrelated to distributive justice. Whether such non-distributive considerations can outweigh distributive considerations depends in the main upon one's view of the extent and weight of principles of distributive justice.

A genuine and simple direct argument about private law and distributive justice would require judges to approach cases in the same way as Diogenes's case: first, apply the law; second, test for accordance with distributive justice. A slightly less simple direct argument could also be imagined: it might hold, for example, that since the doctrines of private law are already in accord with what distributive justice demands, then the question of what distributive justice requires does not arise in particular private law cases. A more complex but nevertheless genuine direct argument holds that the doctrines of private law are already informed by principles of distributive justice so that, once those doctrines and their underpinning theory of justice are properly understood, adjudication is a simply a matter of doing justice. Given its structure, this more complex direct argument straddles the boundary between the class of direct arguments and the external subclass of indirect arguments.

The significant feature direct arguments have in common is the invocation of a substantive theory of distributive justice to justify and/or explain some or all of the significant features and doctrines of private law. They therefore do much more than arguments which, for example, by invoking the key concepts but not the substantive principles of some theories of distributive justice, seek to show that tort law is in accord with some conception of fairness or reasonableness.[47] Arguments of this latter kind are, furthermore, often pluralistic in the sense that they regard the principles which provide a normative justification for private law as embodying both distributive and non-distributive considerations. One such argument is briefly touched upon in the next chapter.

The two direct arguments considered here are treated, first and foremost, as either simple or complex direct arguments. The less simple type of direct argument is more or less ignored in what follows because it has little actual impact upon private law – if this particular direct argument is currently true then some or other conception of distributive justice is already the foundation of private law. If the argument is currently false, then it offers only an aspirational picture of what private law will look like in a just society. It should be noted that simple and complex direct arguments are usually intended as foundational in the most obvious sense. That is to say, they provide private law, via some or other conception of distributive justice, with a normative foundation that informs all or at least most of the features and practices of that institution. For reasons that will become apparent, distributive justice is a foundation that determines the shape and content of the superstructure that arises upon it in the most direct and unmediated way: rarely is allowance made for any degree of autonomy between normative base and legal superstructure.

The remainder of this section outlines, in a brief and breezy way, what the two direct arguments entail and notes a general problem both face, in addition to some difficulties unique to each. The general problem does not arise from the content of the particular principles of distributive justice espoused; rather it highlights a difficulty with the idea of applying some or other principle of distributive justice directly to an institution and set of practices like private law. The bright and breezy treatment, and the failure to engage directly with the content of the distributive

[47] Two examples: G. Keating, 'A Social Contract Conception of the Tort Law of Accidents' in G. Postema (ed.), *Philosophy and the Law of Torts* (Cambridge: Cambridge University Press, 2001) and A. Ripstein, *Equality, Responsibility and the Law* (Cambridge: Cambridge University Press, 1999).

principles in play, is in part excused by the fact that both theories are relatively familiar and have received much attention.

Social justice in the liberal state

The first direct argument belongs to Bruce Ackerman. His book *Social Justice in the Liberal State* (*SJLS*) provides an unusual and stimulating account of a version of political liberalism, the substance of which generated much comment.[48] Ackerman's principal goal in *SJLS* is to develop a method he called 'Neutral dialogue' (or constrained conversation) by which all disputes about the distribution and exercise of power and the distribution of resources in a community could be resolved. This method also happens to uphold and justify some of the substantive principles – like anti-paternalism and individual rights – central to most versions of liberal political morality. Ackerman holds that Neutral dialogue consists of three principles. The first is the rationality principle and its two sub-principles, which require that all power relations and distributions of resources be rationally defended (*SJLS*, p. 4). Second is the consistency principle, which demands that the 'reason advanced by a power wielder on one occasion must not be inconsistent with the reasons he advances to justify his other claims to power' (*SJLS*, p. 7). And, thirdly, there is the principle of neutrality which holds that

> [n]o reason is a good reason if it requires the power holder to assert:
>
> (a) that his conception of the good is better than that asserted by any of his fellows, *or*
>
> (b) that, regardless of his conception of the good, he is intrinsically superior to one or more of his fellow citizens. (*SJLS*, p. 11)

These principles, while undoubtedly interesting, are not evaluated here; neither is the general structure of Ackerman's argument nor are all the specific results that the principles yield. The three principles make it obvious, though, that Ackerman is not primarily interested in offering an account of distributive justice; such an account, rather, simply arises from the application of the principles of Neutral dialogue. It is what the principles tell us about distribution and, in particular, the implications Ackerman draws from their application to the context of free exchange (*SJLS*, ch. 6) that is of current concern.

Ackerman's view of the importance of free exchange has interesting

[48] Supra, note 2. Good discussions are Campbell, supra, note 4, ch. 4 and the essays in *Symposium on Social Justice in the Liberal State* (1983) 93 *Ethics* 328–390.

implications for the private law of contract, even though the relationship between distributive justice and private law is not one of his primary concerns. At no point does he address private law in any detail – he is content to highlight some implications Neutral dialogue and its account of distributive justice have for the practice of voluntary transacting. From that, we can imagine the effects his account of distributive justice might have on the law of contract. Finding a direct argument in Ackerman's work is therefore principally an inferential task, a matter of teasing out some of the implications of his more general claims. As against the claim that, in even regarding Ackerman as offering a direct argument about the relation between private law and distributive justice we are misrepresenting his aims and intentions, there is a partial and twofold defence. First, we are not the first to do this.[49] Second, Ackerman's work is one of the very few possible instances of a direct argument being invoked. This defence might, of course, merely add insult to injury.

At the level of ideal theory, Neutral dialogue requires an equal distribution of 'manna', the resource that makes life possible for the imaginary members of Ackerman's spaceship assembly. It also requires on equal distribution of the usual liberal rights which, as a package, guarantee what Ackerman terms '*undominated* equality' (*SJLS*, p. 18; emphasis in original). The assembly, of course, is simply a thought experiment intended to throw light on the nature of Neutral dialogue, its conditions and constitutive principles, as well as its alleged outcomes. In addition to ensuring an equal distribution of the most important resource and promoting undominated equality, Neutral dialogue at the ideal level also mandates completely unconstrained transacting in just circumstances, provided technology ensures that transaction costs are zero. Just circumstances are those in which there is no genetic domination, in which all citizens have received a liberal education and in which the demands of liberal trusteeship have been fulfilled in individual lives (*SJLS*, p. 28). The technological development necessary to guarantee zero transaction costs is Ackerman's imaginary 'transmitter shield'. This device allows each potential transactor to find whoever else in their community may wish to transact with them for a particular purpose. The shields are themselves supposedly costless to operate and direct information only to those actually interested; they serve also to protect their holders from

[49] We are, as will be obvious to anyone familiar with his discussion, following in Campbell's tracks, ibid. Ackerman's work features less prominently in the second edition of Campbell's book (London: Palgrave Macmillan, 2000).

exit costs that might be imposed by transacting with others (*SJLS*, pp. 174–177).

What implications does Ackerman's ideal theory have for the real world of contract law? One implausible implication is this: if the real world embodied just circumstances (equality of resources, liberal education, no genetic domination and compliance with trusteeship), and technology ensured zero transaction costs, then contract law might be unnecessary. This is because whatever assurance contract law provides real world transactors may not be needed in this situation. Alternatively, contract law might exist and continue to fulfil a minimal assurance role, presumably in circumstances where either transaction shields or other citizens are unreliable. In these circumstances, contract would function as surrogate for transmitter shields, limiting exit costs and protecting against non-performance. In a world of this kind, contract law would look very different to the law we know. More interesting and, from the point of view of Ackerman's theory, much more problematic, is the scenario of contracting in a non-ideal world. What will be the shape of contract law, in Ackerman's view, in a world in which neither just circumstances nor complete transactional flexibility obtain?[50]

Such a world will likely be one in which the consequences of injustice upon particular individuals and social groups are felt across generations: it embodies exploitation and its effects (*SJLS*, ch. 8). It is, for Ackerman, the job of non-ideal second- or third-best theory to attempt to implement the outcomes of Neutral dialogue in such a world. And it seems that, when this job is carried out within the confines of transacting and the law of contract, almost every transaction must be vetted for consistency with just circumstances and transactional flexibility, as well as examined for the impact of exploitation. Before any system of transacting can be legitimate, 'the polity must [among other things] correct the systematic biases costly negotiation and imperfect shielding impose upon the citizenry' (*SJLS*, p. 189). Thus, 'government' can be called upon to set aside particular transactions where the outcomes are inconsistent with those that would result in an ideal transactional framework (*SJLS*, ibid). Furthermore, even if there is an ideal system of transactional flexibility in play in our non-ideal world, there is still no guarantee that particular transactions will be allowed to stand if they are in any way tainted by genetic domination, or the maldistribution of liberal education or initial

[50] 'Transactional flexibility' is Ackerman's term for the situation resulting from the use of transmitter shields: supra, note 2, p. 170.

holdings. For Ackerman, 'the claims of free contract must always be appraised against a background of the power relationships established by the transactional framework and the distribution of wealth, education and ability' (*SJLS*, p. 199). As Tom Campbell rightly notes, '[a]ll these qualifications on [free exchange] . . . in effect place so many conditions on it as to render it, after endless corrective interferences, no more than a vestigial residue'.[51]

Were Ackerman's account of justice taken as the normative foundation of existing contract law, then there is no doubt that the law would have to change. Existing contract doctrines that display a concern with contractual unfairness and exploitation would need to be supplemented. For, while these doctrines could plausibly be regarded as manifesting a concern with the consequences of injustice, there are no obvious existing doctrinal candidates, with the possible exception of mistake and misrepresentation, for the role of correcting transactional imperfections. The problem that arises with this normative foundation is, then, obvious: it seems not to be a foundation for private law as we know it but for the private law of a better, more just world. The effort of striving for a more just world is not, of course, an ignoble aim but one can question whether or not the law of contract or other areas of private law are the best or most efficient way of bringing that goal about. The substance and structure of private law seems *prima facie* designed with other concerns in mind and the process of restructuring them so as to better achieve distributive justice either leads, as in Kronman's case, to the misrepresentation of the nature of key doctrines or, in Ackerman's case, to the conversion of the law to a purpose for which it seems very badly designed. The general thought here is surely that Ackerman's efforts yield a normative foundation for a law of contract quite different from that with which we are familiar. Whether or not we regard this as problematic in part turns upon our view of the range and extent of principles of distributive justice; Ackerman seems to view such principles as being maximal in both dimensions.

Equality of resources

The principal claim of Dworkin's theory of distributive justice – equality of resources – has already been noted. It requires an initial equal distribution of resources which citizens are thereafter free to use in whatever

[51] Supra, note 4, p. 118.

legitimate ways they wish.[52] This brief statement does not do justice to the complexities of Dworkin's theory but it is neither possible nor necessary to offer a general evaluation of one of the most impressive and intellectually acute accounts of distributive justice since Rawls's *A Theory of Justice*. Our current interest is very specific: what, if anything, does Dworkin tell us about the way in which his theory of distributive justice relates to private law? Fortunately, we need not construct an answer from scratch. Dworkin provides a ready made answer in *Law's Empire* where he attempts to put his theory of justice to work upon mundane tort law disputes (*LE*, pp. 295–312).[53] Suppose two neighbours – A and B – have incompatible uses for their property: A wishes to quietly study algebra while B wishes to practise his trumpet playing. While both activities are in one sense physically possible, A cannot study algebra properly while B plays trumpet and B cannot play trumpet if A is to study properly. How is this dispute to be resolved? Although Dworkin sometimes takes up the perspective of a law-maker rather than adjudicator, it seems clear that he regards the considerations apposite for the former equally apposite for the latter. These considerations are also apposite for citizens themselves.

The first step toward resolving the dispute between A and B is this. Dworkin says the law-maker or adjudicator or citizen must distinguish between abstract and concrete rights. The former include the general legal rights citizens in most liberal polities have, the latter being the specification of what these general rights entail in specific situations:

> I have an abstract right to use my apartment as I wish and therefore to play my trumpet, as you have to use yours as you wish and therefore to be free to study algebra in peace. We call these rights prima facie or abstract because we know they can conflict: my exercise of my right may invade or restrict yours, in which case the question arises which of us has an actual or concrete right to do as he wishes. (*LE*, p. 293)

When abstract rights conflict, says Dworkin, the decision-maker – judge, law-maker or citizen – must determine what concrete rights the parties have in such a way as to accord equal respect to each parties' interests. The second step is the recognition that market-simulating behaviour is

[52] Do not assume that the job of engineering an initial equal distribution of resources is a simple one. It is not, primarily because it must, for Dworkin, be responsive to certain kinds of luck as well as other factors: see Dworkin, supra, note 2, pp. 73–83. Sustained analysis of Dworkin's theory of distributive justice is provided in *Symposium on Ronald Dworkin's Sovereign Virtue* (2002) 113 *Ethics* 5–143 and the essays in Parts I–III of J. Burley (ed.), *Dworkin and his Critics* (Oxford: Blackwell, 2004).

[53] Hereinafter '*LE*' in text and notes refers to *Law's Empire*, supra, note 3.

often a good way in which to accord equal respect to the parties' interests when their abstract rights conflict, since one who 'abstains from some act on the ground that it would cost his neighbor more than it would benefit him takes his neighbor's welfare into account on equal terms with his own' (*LE*, p. 295). Hence, for Dworkin it seems 'intuitively correct' (*LE*, p. 302) that calculation of relative cost to each disputant is an important means of resolving a conflict between abstract rights.

The third step in resolving the dispute is to assume, apparently in accord with the demands of equality of resources, that both A and B currently have roughly equal resources and that neither is disadvantaged by handicaps or special needs. Against that background, law-maker, judge or citizen must imagine that the concrete rights in dispute have not yet been distributed between A and B and 'act so as to minimize the inequality of the distribution [chosen] . . ., and that means so that the loser loses less' (*LE*, p. 303). And an obvious way in which to determine who loses the least in any particular situation is to compare 'financial costs, not because money is more important than anything else but because it is the most abstract and therefore the best standard to use in deciding . . . [who] will lose more by each of the decisions' (ibid) that might be made. Of course, this financial calculation does not always seem obviously appropriate: what, for example, are the precise financial losses to B if he is not allowed to play the trumpet? Dworkin's suggestion in cases such as these is that judge, law-maker or citizen calculate the damage or losses to B's overall life plan if prevented from playing, and compare it with the same losses to A, if unable to do algebra. But how, exactly, are these loses calculated? By reference to how much both A and B might be willing to pay in order to carry on with their favoured activity: if both have roughly equal resources, this 'willingness to pay' test is a good manifestation of the value each places on his favoured activity (*LE*, pp. 303–304). When the interests of other citizens are affected by a decision about either A's or B's abstract rights, the willingness to pay test is still useful, thinks Dworkin, since it can be generalized to include what those affected by either A's or B's conduct might be willing to pay to prevent it.

Finally, judges, law-makers and citizens must recognize the limits to the 'willingness to pay' or market-simulating test for liability. The test should only be used, says Dworkin, when rough equality of resources obtains between the parties and when the interests embodied in conflicting abstract rights are of a particular type. This type is probably easiest elucidated by showing what it is not: the interests protected by abstract rights that can be subject to the market-simulation test must not be 'fundamental interests . . . [or those] securing each person's independence from other people's prejudices and dislikes' (*LE*, p. 307). What resolution to the case of A and B do these steps suggest? No obvious answer is provided, simply because we do not know enough of the circumstances of A and B to determine what should be done. But the general test is clear: if A and B are roughly equal in resources, and if the interests protected by the abstract rights in play are of the appropriate kind, then the dispute must be resolved in favour of whoever would pay more to carry on with the conduct in question. This is the way in which, in a Dworkinian world, distributive justice determines the resolution of private law disputes and, therefore, supposedly provides the normative foundation of private law.

Much weight rests on the word 'supposedly' in that sentence. For on closer examination it seems that Dworkin does not so much provide a normative foundation for private law as simply assume one. Consider again the third step that those charged with resolving the dispute between A and B must take. This is the assumption that A and B each hold a roughly equal amount of resources. That being so, the willingness to pay or market-simulation test seems quite plausible. But why assume an equality of holdings? The assumption is not warranted by equality of resources, Dworkin's own account of distributive justice, since it allows any amount of inequality of holdings to arise from an initially equal distribution, provided the moves are legitimate. Inequality arising from the different choices citizens make – yours to work hard and invest, mine to spend and surf – is both perfectly possible and, in the right circumstances, perfectly legitimate on Dworkin's account. Nor is the assumption of rough equality of holdings supported by anything we know about the current distribution of welfare and resources in most societies. Of course, making the assumption allows us to envisage how private law adjudication could be conducted in a Dworkinian world; the key point, though, is that our world is not one in which equality of resources has been achieved. It is interesting to imagine what such a world might look like and, further, to speculate how private law doctrine and adjudication might appear in such a world. Yet that task is assuredly not the same as providing a normative foundation for private law as we currently know it.

It may be that we have misunderstood Dworkin's intentions. Perhaps his aim is not to provide a normative foundation for private law as it exists but to generate a foundation for the private law of a truly just society. If, in such a society, rough equality of resources is achieved, then the sketch he provides of how private law adjudication might go does not seem wildly implausible. Yet we must note how different some of the features of private law will be in the Dworkinian world as compared to our own. First, as Stephen Perry notes, private law adjudication in a Dworkinian world 'does not adequately take account of our strong pre-theoretical conviction that, absent special circumstances . . . a moral duty of repair should make the victim whole and not just provide partial compensation'.[54] This point arises from Dworkin's admission that all or nothing decisions in cases such as that of A and B are required only by 'practical circumstances' (*LE*, p. 311) and seemingly not a demand of justice. The implication is surely that if practical circumstances change then the way in which private law traditionally resolves disputes should also change. In a Dworkinian world, private law resolutions will take on the flavour of or actually be compromises. Noting this is, of course, neither to criticize nor to commend: it serves rather to highlight a very significant difference.

Another significant difference between private law in a Dworkinian world and private law as we know it is also noted by Perry.[55] It is that private law in a Dworkinian world will draw a very sharp distinction between injuries to property and injuries to person. The distinction consists of the way in which the relative losses for each type of damage are determined. We have seen that Dworkin thinks the market-simulating mechanism is in general perfectly adequate for injuries to property or its use. That mechanism is not, however, suitable for injuries to the person because those injuries are presumably protected by rights upholding fundamental interests. And the concrete specification of abstract rights which uphold fundamental interests should not, says Dworkin, be carried out through the market-simulation test because that could well undermine those interests: 'suppose I am black and that my neighbours would together pay more for me not to burn leaves in my yard than I could or would pay to burn them, simply because they hate the sight of me' (*LE*, p. 307). Racist neighbours ought not, thinks Dworkin, to be allowed to outbid their victim for the exercise of his rights, since there can be no legitimate legal license for their prejudice. Nor should citizens be allowed – for the same general reason – to outbid others for a concrete right to bodily integrity (*LE*, p. 309). But if the concrete specification of the right

[54] S. Perry, 'On the Relationship Between Corrective and Distributive Justice' in J. Horder (ed.), *Oxford Essays in Jurisprudence: Fourth Series* (Oxford: Clarendon Press, 2000), pp. 237–263, p. 249.

[55] Ibid, p. 252; pp. 247–253 of this essay provide a brisk but penetrating evaluation of Dworkin's discussion of private law and equality of resources that makes an number of points in addition to the two noted here.

to bodily integrity is not to be determined by the market-simulation test, how is it to be determined? While Dworkin does not specify, it clearly must be the case that something other than the market-simulation test be used. 'The question that then arises is whether a . . . theory that views rights and duties of repair as based on two distinct principles, one of which applies to the interest in life and bodily security and the other of which applies to interests in property, is . . . satisfactory.'[56] Whatever the answer to that question, it is clear that our current systems of private law certainly do not invoke two such different principles. In this respect, those systems, whatever their faults, at least have parsimony on their side.

Finally, consider the situation if we refuse to grant Dworkin the assumption of rough equality of holdings in the third step. This completely undermines his effort to establish a connection between private law and distributive justice either in the world as we know it or in a Dworkinian world. For if there is not rough equality of holdings the market-simulation test immediately becomes suspect: willingness to pay does not illustrate the value of some or other activity to a disputant but rather the relative strength or weakness of his holdings as compared to the other. The added complexity here arises from the difficulty Dworkin has in being suspicious of such inequalities of holdings if equality of resources has at some prior point been achieved. Such inequality is both perfectly predictable and perfectly understandable under a theory of justice in which every distribution of resources after the initial distribution is responsive to agents' legitimate choices. There seems little unfairness in refusing to grant Dworkin an assumption to which, under his theory of justice, he is clearly not entitled.

A general difficulty

The general difficulty faced by the direct arguments offered by both Ackerman and Dworkin can seem rather vague. Stated bluntly, it holds simply that distributive justice considerations appear to overwhelm all non-distributive considerations: once admitted to the deliberative agenda distributive justice takes on the role of a cuckoo in the nest, squeezing out all other concerns. This is regrettable insofar as some deliberative agendas – some set of considerations pertinent within a particular institution or one or other of its practices – are not genuinely distributive. The effect of admitting distributive concerns here is not just to add an extra factor to the agenda but to trump all other considerations on the agenda.

[56] Ibid.

That, at least, is how distributive justice considerations seem to operate. Furthermore, this is the case whether or not the deliberative considerations in play are agent-specific or agent-general. It seems, in some cases at least, normal to regard agent-specific duties as generally more important than agent-general duties: as a phenomenological matter the duties we have to perform as a result of our deeds or commitments often seem much more pressing than those we incur simply by virtue of, for example, being members of humankind. Thus my duty to look after my neighbour's children, because I have promised to do so, seems much more powerful and is more immediate than the duty I have towards those many, many children in the world without adequate food and shelter.

To state this is, of course, to morally rebuke oneself, for it seems a mistake always to let agent-specific duties displace agent-general ones. That is not to say that I should ignore the agent-specific duties I owe my neighbour and her children. Rather, it is to highlight the lesser importance of those duties as compared to some agent-general duties. And it seems that when distributive justice grounds agent-general duties those duties are assumed to trump any agent-specific concerns. In part, the moral rebuke just imagined is often informed by considerations of justice: their very generality appears to give them greater power than the much more specific agent-specific duties I might have. The rebuke also seems motivated by the thought that considerations of justice and injustice are simply more pressing and urgent than other considerations. The latter thought is also often in play when distributive justice considerations ground agent-specific duties for here, too, the fact that the duty is grounded in justice seems to give it special urgency and power.

Within private law adjudication distributive justice's cuckoo in the nest tendency is manifest in the way in which it displaces familiar features of the institution. In the pictures provided by Ackerman and Dworkin of distributive justice's role in relation to private law, many of the latter's familiar features and doctrines are lost, simply crowded out by the insistent and supposedly more important demands of justice. This is more evident in Dworkin's case than in Ackerman's, probably because only he turns his mind to the process of adjudication. For Ackerman what is lost or overwhelmed in the face of distributive considerations are the consequences private law usually attaches to individuals' conduct and choices. It seems that on Ackerman's view we are bound only by the voluntary transactions we enter into in something like a perfectly just world. This brings in its wake at least two acute problems. In an imperfectly just world the significance of agency and its link to identity would seem to be systematically undermined by belief in Ackerman's theory of justice: our choices are simply not as significant, in indicating what or who we are, if their validity or authenticity is almost always impugned by distributive considerations. Close on the heels of this comes a problem of moral hazard. For if, in an imperfectly just world, many or all voluntary transactions are undermined in the way just noted, it follows that this risk could be exploited opportunistically. That is, the constant possibility of our voluntary transactions being impugned on justice grounds could well give an incentive, in the right circumstances, to enter into improvident transactions for gain in the hope that they will be set aside. Of course, this could only occur in a limited and precise set of circumstances but that does not eradicate the hazard.

Considerations such as these suggest there is little point in examining the nature and basis of the obligation to correct generated by Dworkin's and Ackerman's accounts of private law and distributive justice. This is because these two views portray the obligation to correct in private law as simply an echo of the broad duty created by distributive justice.[57] At its most abstract that is simply a duty upon both citizens and agents of the justice system to bring about or uphold a just distribution and, although the requirements of that duty may change in particular contexts like, for example, private law, its general nature remains unchanged. There is no reason to think that the broad duty is, in Dworkin's or Ackerman's hands, either solely an agent-specific or purely an agent-general duty. While in their treatment of private law neither jurist addresses this issue explicitly – probably because nothing in their arguments seems to turn on the distinction – it seems fairly safe to suppose that in some circumstances the broad duty is both. And even if conceived as creating only an agent-general duty, there is no additional reason to think that the broad duty cannot give rise to an agent-specific duty in particular contexts. The nature and basis of the duty to correct in private law is, then, the same as the broad duty created by distributive justice. It might differ slightly from the broad obligation in some ways: it might, for example, be an agent-specific manifestation of an agent-general duty, or an agent-general duty responsive to some of the non-justice considerations relevant within a

[57] It might be better to dub as 'general' the duty created by distributive justice, but this term may breed confusion when the issue of agent-general duties arises (leading, for example, to the erroneous assumption that a general duty must be agent-general). It is also tempting to label the broad duty as abstract in Dworkinian terms, but this creates the difficulty of determining whether abstract duties are agent-specific, agent-general, both or neither. I have therefore adopted what seems to be the least unsatisfactory label.

particular context like private law. But, in essence, to know the nature and basis of the broad duty is to know the nature and basis of the duty to correct in private law. The problem with this conception of the duty to correct in private law is the same general difficulty as has already been sketched: there is no guarantee that the distributive duty can be sensitive to non-distributive considerations. Indeed, given what we know of the way distributive considerations operate in our deliberations, it seems likely that it will simply overwhelm those other considerations.

It is important to appreciate that there is no necessity in this. That is, there is no immediately obvious conceptual or normative reason to believe that distributive justice is our most important moral or political value, thus outranking all others. Nor is there such a reason to believe that the duties distributive justice generates, whether agent-general or agent-specific, outweigh all other duties. If there were reasons to this effect, then the 'cuckoo in the nest' process is perfectly understandable; if there are not, then the process requires explanation on other grounds. One version of the conceptual or normative reason necessary to show distributive justice and the duties it generates sovereign over all other moral and political values must be of a particularly impressive kind. Unless it is the result of a monotone account of our moral and political values in which, despite appearances, all the latter are simply manifestations of a single overarching value, it must provide a map of our apparently diverse values and how they relate one to another. In addition, it must also show why distributive justice trumps these other values in some or all contexts. There is no doubt that such an argument could be constructed and that its construction would be an improvement upon the currently common assumption that distributive justice simply dominates or pre-empts all other considerations. One need not be sceptical about distributive justice to resist or interrogate this assumption nor to be interested in distributive justice's precise role within the scheme of our moral and political values.

There is, furthermore, a roughly Dworkinian argument which might fit the bill that is not obviously reliant upon a monotone view of our political and moral values.[58] It holds that, since the state has a duty to treat its citizens with equal concern and respect, and since private law is

[58] Whether or not Dworkin's view of our political values is monotone depends, for example, on his general view of value conflicts and the relationship between liberty and equality. For a brief statement on the former, see R. Dworkin *et al.* (eds.), *The Legacy of Isaiah Berlin* (New York: NYRB Press, 2001), Part II; for his treatment of the latter see *Sovereign Virtue*, supra, note 2, ch. 3.

part of the state, then private law must embody the theory of distributive justice that best upholds equal concern and respect.[59] And that, in Dworkin's view, is equality of resources. Private law must be founded upon equality of resources which itself is a means of guaranteeing equal respect and concern. This response also plays another role, namely, that of a reply to the basic structure objection. It does not, of course, undermine the very idea of the basic structure so much as provide an argument as to why private law should be included within it. We can imagine Ackerman making a substantively similar riposte to the argument from the basic structure, holding that the requirements of Neutral dialogue are simply too important to be constrained by the concerns that restrict the range and application of principles of distributive justice. When judged against the demands of justice arising from Neutral dialogue, the loss of some freedom that Rawls thinks will result from extending the influence of principles of justice into the legitimate private transactions of individuals is simply unimportant (or considerably less important than achieving justice).

While we cannot offer a fully developed reply to these two points here, even if one were available, two things are worth noting. First, the roughly Dworkinian argument contains two potential elisions. These should be highlighted even though Dworkin's actual view of the manifold links between law and distributive justice is undoubtedly much more sophisticated and complex than suggested here, involving as it must a synthesis of the various arguments of *Law's Empire* and *Sovereign Virtue*.[60] The two interesting elisions can occupy us until such time as a thorough synthesis is available.[61] The first concerns the move from the undeniable claim that private law, like all law in modern societies, is in some sense an outcropping of the state, to the claim that private law must 'therefore' embody the account of distributive justice the state upholds in its relation with citizens.[62] That private law is an outcropping of the state is obvious. It is undeniable that the justice system of modern societies is a state enterprise, funded by taxes through either or both central and local governments; that citizens are often allowed to access legal services and claim

[59] See R. Dworkin, *A Matter of Principle* (Oxford: Clarendon Press, 1985), ch. 8.

[60] Supra, notes 2 and 3.

[61] On the evidence of the collections of commentary on Dworkin's work noted supra, note 51, the task seems (probably because of its daunting nature) somewhat unappealing.

[62] The idea of the 'state' in contemporary social and political thought is often vague. I have in mind the possibly somewhat dated but nevertheless compelling conception sketched in G. Poggi, *The Development of the Modern State* (London: Hutchinson, 1978), chs. V and VI.

legal costs from government sponsored funds; and that judges, clerks and almost all other personnel of the justice system are paid from central or local government funds. These facts need not of themselves compromise any commitment to the separation of powers, nor do they automatically suggest that the state, when a representative in legal action in the justice system it itself funds, is in any sense advantaged.

Yet, while access to and the funding of the justice system is surely in some ways a matter of distributive justice, it does not immediately follow from this that all the rules constitutive of the justice system, including for example those that make up the principal doctrines of private law, must themselves be matters of, or even be primarily concerned with, distributive justice. It might be the case that in our society only local and central government fund recreational facilities like neighbourhood and national parks, play and wilderness areas. While provision and funding of such areas, as well as access to them, is in some respects undoubtedly a matter of distributive justice, that surely does that mean that what is done in such areas must always be in accord with the requirements of distributive justice. Am I bound by requirements of distributive justice when canoeing down a river or climbing a hill? Furthermore, will I only be allowed to indulge in such activities if that is a requirement of distributive justice? It might be objected that this analogy is trivial, but that comes close simply to assuming the priority of distributive justice rather than showing it. And, while it must be conceded that there are many detailed differences between state provision and funding of the justice system, on the one hand, and its provision and funding of recreational resources, on the other, the underlying issue nevertheless looks very similar. It is this: why does the existence of state funding *require* that the practice, institution or conduct funded be either a matter of, or be concerned with, distributive justice?[63]

The second potential elision concerns the move from the claim that the citizen's right to equal concern and respect demands equality of resources to the claim that the same right requires that private law uphold or embody equality of resources. The snag here is similar to that just noted: why assume that, just because distributive justice is a requirement in sphere X, its influence must also extend to sphere Y? The assumption would, of course, be warranted were X and Y identical or if they shared features that serve to make them indistinguishable for these purposes. But one principal aim of our discussion of the direct arguments offered by Dworkin and Ackerman has been to cast doubt on this apparently

[63] See Dworkin, supra, note 59, ch. 11 for some pertinent reflections on a related issue.

hasty assimilation, without being able to show that it is demonstrably wrong or mistaken.

This brings the second point into play. It is an observation about the reply we imagined Ackerman making to the argument from the basic structure, but it also highlights a broader issue. This is perhaps the foundational issue that divides those for whom distributive justice is always sovereign over other values from those who regard it as an important but not pre-eminent value among other important values. We imagined Ackerman holding that nothing is more important than the requirements of Neutral dialogue and, where these are translated into an account of distributive justice, that account is more important than any other moral or political value. While we have cast Ackerman (and perhaps to a lesser degree Dworkin) as being unable to envisage other values being more or as important as distributive justice, we ourselves may be prone to the opposite inability, namely, an incapacity to imagine distributive justice as a truly sovereign virtue. If this is indeed so, then the dispute here is deadlocked, a straightforward clash of opposites. The onus is thus on participants to conceive of ways in which the argument can be resolved or, at the very least, advanced. This task cannot be undertaken here.

CONCLUSION

It might by now appear that the treatment of the relation between private law and distributive justice in this chapter has been somewhat disjointed, lacking any overarching or unifying themes. This is both true and regrettable. It is also in some degree unavoidable for the simple reason that the arguments about the relation between private law and distributive justice that have been examined are quite different one from another. They do not therefore raise anything like the same issues nor generate the same difficulties. Two principal difficulties were identified. One was that indirect arguments either run the risk of the triviality charge (if they are external) or ignore the content of legal doctrine (if they are internal). The other was that direct arguments struggle to provide a foundation for anything like our current systems of private law. Indeed it seems that the two sample direct arguments considered here serve, contrary to their proponents' intention, to show that private law as we know it and distributive justice as they understand it are actually incompatible. While these problems are in no sense insurmountable, it does nevertheless seem that distributive justice lags behind corrective justice in the race to provide private law with a normative foundation. The problems that face the best theory of corrective justice appear far more manageable and tractable than those that envelop all efforts to found private law upon some or other principle of distributive justice. If that is so, then it is right to examine one remaining possible strategy in the effort to provide a normative foundation for private law. That is the task of the following chapter.

10

Mixed Foundations

It would be strange if the results of a coherent, richly developed normative theory were to coincide with a major portion of any extended branch of law.

R. M. Unger, *The Critical Legal Studies Movement* (Cambridge, Mass.: Harvard University Press, 1986), p. 9.

This final substantive chapter is necessary because of the arguments of Chapters 8 and 9. Those chapters found wanting the efforts of some accounts of corrective and distributive justice to provide a normative foundation for private law. The limitations of these efforts, some of which are explicitly recognized by their authors, thus leave room for analysis of one remaining possibility in the search for private law's normative foundation. This possibility consists of what are labelled, for lack of a better term, mixed accounts of the normative foundation of private law. In what follows the features and problems of such mixed accounts or theories are examined, first, in their most general terms and then, second, as they arise within one particular mixed account. This emphasis, in which the general issues facing all mixed accounts are highlighted first, and then a specific mixed account is tackled second, does not arise from a judgment that all efforts to provide a mixed normative foundation for private law are either uninteresting or fatally flawed. Just the opposite is true. The slight change of emphasis, at least as compared with our treatment of arguments from corrective and distributive justice, is in part justified because the enterprise of providing mixed accounts of the normative foundation of private law is a relatively open and interesting field. Certainly, this domain is neither already dominated by exemplary accounts nor crowded with a mass of existing work. It is therefore important to ensure that the discussion begins on the right foot, by which is meant that it should be informed by an appreciation of the general issues and difficulties. Only then can we hope that progress will be made.

The first section below briefly sketches the limitations of corrective and distributive justice accounts which make consideration of mixed accounts necessary. It also outlines some of the requirements that any successful mixed theory must satisfy. The second section examines in detail one mixed account in light of those requirements and also considers how it responds to the key questions noted in Chapter 7. This section also briefly notes how other ostensibly mixed accounts fare in relation to one of these conditions, thus highlighting that the problems faced by the first account are not unique to it. The third section offers, among other things, a brief prospectus for the future development of mixed accounts.

THE NEED FOR MIXED ACCOUNTS

Mixed accounts of the normative foundation of private law are on our agenda because of the weaknesses and limitations of corrective and distributive justice accounts. The limitations and weaknesses of the former depend upon the specific theory of corrective justice in play. Of the two examined, both were beset by related methodological snags, while Ernest Weinrib's theory was in addition unable to give a plausible account of private law wrongs and Jules Coleman's struggled to accommodate distributive and corrective justice in a stable relation. This particular problem for Coleman is examined more thoroughly below. It is important not to exaggerate the scale of the problems faced by these two corrective justice theories. There is no implication in the arguments of Chapter 8 that these problems are insurmountable, although addressing them will surely bring about significant changes to the theories in question (particularly Weinrib's). Furthermore, these are only two specific theories of corrective justice. The fact that they are in some respects problematic does not, of course, undermine the very idea of corrective justice; other, less problematic accounts of corrective justice could still emerge. Nevertheless, the problems faced by these two accounts of corrective justice certainly make it sensible to consider other accounts of the normative basis of private law and, as will be seen, one problem corrective justice theories attempt to address actually makes mixed accounts salient.

The problems that beset distributive justice accounts of the normative foundation of private law are diverse, depending on the specific type of argument employed. Two principal types of argument about the relation between private law and distributive justice were considered: indirect (of which there are three varieties: simple, external or internal) and direct. In general terms, however, both types generate one broad difficulty, namely, that the account of distributive justice invoked 'overwhelms' both the structure and content of private law, turning it into something quite unfamiliar. Standard features of the institution and its constitutive practices are lost; 'seeing things their way' is no longer an option.[1] This is not just a methodological worry; it also attests to distributive justice's 'imperialist tendency' to dominate all other deliberative considerations. Again, nothing in the arguments offered in Chapter 9 suggests that the task of developing a distributive justice account of the normative foundation of private law is impossible and should be abandoned forthwith; compelling, successful accounts could still be developed. Yet the problems noted in Chapter 9 serve to create space in which other, different accounts of the normative foundation of private law can be considered.

The remainder of this section does two things. It examines, first, how mixed accounts arise from a concern some corrective justice theories have. The attempt to address this concern is, however, often inadequate and this failure can be taken in two ways. It can be regarded as showing that corrective justice theories should remain 'pure', free from distributive concerns; or as showing that such 'purity' comes at too great a cost, namely, the sacrifice of normative concerns we accept as important. If the latter implication is accepted, then mixed accounts are the only salient option. The second issue addressed is a general one that faces all mixed accounts: they must provide a plausible elucidation of how the various values said to provide the normative foundation for private law interrelate. Some obvious traps that must be avoided are briefly delineated and evaluated.

A FALSE START

One interpretation of Coleman's account of corrective justice is that it is, despite appearances, a mixed account of the normative foundation of private law. He is not unique in offering such an account, since a feature of some of the most interesting efforts to provide a normative foundation for private law is their willingness of accommodate various values or, at least, to specify the relation between a range of values and private law.[2] Current scholarship in this area therefore seems on the cusp of what might be called monism (the belief that only one value can provide private law's normative foundation) and pluralism (the belief that many values have a role in the normative foundation of private law). Generally speaking,

[1] The phrase belongs to Q. Skinner, *Visions of Politics, Vol. I: Regarding Method* (Cambridge: Cambridge University Press, 2002), p. 1.

[2] Two interesting examples are S. Perry, 'On the Relationship Between Corrective and Distributive Justice', pp. 237–263 of J. Horder (ed.), *Oxford Essays in Jurisprudence: Fourth Series* (Oxford: Clarendon Press, 2000); and A. Ripstein, *Equality, Responsibility and the Law* (Cambridge: Cambridge University Press, 1999).

pluralism is politically and morally attractive to liberal democrats, although this should not determine its power to generate normative explanations of the structure and substance of private law.

The thought that Coleman actually offers a mixed account of the normative foundation of private law arises in part from his view of the nature of the relationship between corrective and distributive justice. His view is an instance of the co-existence thesis which holds that, at the very least, corrective and distributive justice are not incompatible and, perhaps, that they can overlap and even operate together in some contexts.[3] What corrective and distributive justice have in common, for Coleman, is that they 'embody the requirements of fairness with regard to how we allocate the costs of life's misfortunes'.[4] They differ because corrective justice pursues fairness with regard to misfortunes owing to human agency, whereas distributive justice aims for fairness in relation to losses that are no one's responsibility.[5] Clearly this is not intended as a mixed account of the normative foundation of private law, primarily because only corrective justice is explicitly in play in private law. But it might nevertheless end up being a mixed account, on the basis of the following argument.[6]

It begins by highlighting Coleman's division of labour between corrective and distributive justice. That division rests upon a distinction between misfortunes that result from human agency, which are matters of corrective justice, and those that do not, which are matters of distributive justice. Yet in many cases the distinction is far from being as obvious and as incontestable as Coleman assumes. Think, for example, of the outcomes of the natural lottery which include our initial physical and mental endowments such as, for example, whether we are born healthy or ill, strong or weak, as well as pre-nurture levels of intelligence (if such exist) and aptitude. Now an immediate reaction to these outcomes is that they are in no sense deserved and, what might seem to follow from this, that they are not the result of human agency (except in the minimal sense that human agency is required to bring other humans into being). Does Coleman's division thus require that the justice of the outcomes of the natural lottery fall to be determined by principles of distributive justice?

[3] See Chapter 8, pp. 318–323 for a reminder.

[4] J. Coleman, *The Practice of Principle* (Oxford: Clarendon Press, 2001), p. 44.

[5] Ibid.

[6] Another might arise from his effort to show that the normative basis of corrective justice duties in part depends upon the overall 'moral legitimacy' of the system of holdings in play in a particular community: Coleman, supra, note 4, p. 33. And yet another could begin from his treatment of contract and products liability law in *Risks and Wrongs* (Cambridge: Cambridge University Press, 1992), part I and ch. 20.

It seems so and, if it does, then Coleman's view is among illustrious company, although many who think the natural lottery presents a problem of distributive justice do not think it is a problem because human agency is not in play.[7] Indeed, the thought that human agency is not in play, except in the most minimal sense, in the natural lottery appears an obvious step too far. For the outcomes of the natural lottery, good or bad, in some sense certainly result from human conduct over and beyond that required to create human life. A mother's ability and choice to live healthily or unhealthily during pregnancy, her choice to refrain from or take up smoking or to use or avoid other drugs that significantly effect the health of unborn children, undoubtedly in part determine the state of her child's health and other natural endowments at birth. It therefore seems that the results of the natural lottery must be a matter of corrective rather than distributive justice on Coleman's view.

The point is that Coleman's view of the division of labour between corrective and distributive justice does not generate clear judgments about when which form of justice is in play. This becomes even clearer when misfortune that results from supposedly obvious instances of non-human agency, like deaths resulting from famine, earthquakes and tidal waves are considered. Some of us – including insurance sellers – characterize these events and their outcomes as 'Acts of God' or something similar, the intention being to mark them out as supposedly unavoidable or uncontrollable. But, while human kind obviously cannot prevent the occurrence of these events, we can predict them and thus have a good deal of power over their outcomes. Buildings can be constructed to withstand earthquakes; food can be stored in anticipation of famine and both seismic and climatic events monitored. The doing or non-doing of these things will certainly have an effect upon the outcome of 'natural' events. Since the doing or non-doing of these things is a matter of human agency, it seems that they must be governed by corrective justice. But the triggers for these instances of agency are, of course, natural events and the misfortunes these generate fall, on Coleman's view, within the maw of distributive justice. Which dominates?

It is eminently possible for Coleman to maintain that in cases such as these and the natural lottery, both corrective and distributive justice are in play. And this is the point at which the argument that Coleman's corrective justice account is actually a mixed account comes to fruition. It is

[7] See, for example, J. Rawls, *A Theory of Justice* (Oxford: Clarendon Press, revised edn, 1999), pp. 62–64 and 86–93.

sometimes unclear when each form of justice is in play on Coleman's account, but it is clear that one or other form usually is in play. It is also clearly possible, on Coleman's view, that both can be simultaneously in play. Thus, we have a mixed account of the normative foundation of private law. It holds that this foundation is part corrective and part distributive justice. The judgment that the account is mixed is premised both on the fact that it contains two values or forms of justice and that it is often difficult to separate them. What, if anything, is wrong with this conclusion?

It seems unimpeachable insofar as it emphasizes a concern Coleman and some other corrective justice theorists share. This is a worry about the way in which corrective justice relates to other values, principally but not exclusively distributive justice. That this is indeed a matter which Coleman thinks should be addressed is obvious and it is right and proper that he tackle it: the very least we should expect from jurists and moral and political philosophers is a map of our values. But there are nevertheless two pressing difficulties with this conclusion. One is that the argument supporting it rests upon a hasty extrapolation from the judgment that it is difficult, in some general cases, to establish which misfortunes flow from human agency and which do not, to the assertion that this distinction cannot be sustained in private law. If that distinction cannot be sustained there, then it is impossible to say private law is the realm of corrective and not distributive justice. But anyone familiar with private law will claim that it is reasonably good at determining which misfortunes flow from human agency and which do not: that, indeed, is one of the principal functions of its many doctrines. So although there may be difficulty with this distinction in some general cases, it does not follow that the distinction cannot do useful work in particular contexts, especially formal, rule-governed contexts like private law.

The second difficulty is that the conclusion arrived at rests upon an uncharitable reading of Coleman's argument. This is because even the strategy deployed here, of setting aside the argument's details,[8] cannot disguise the fact that casting the argument in the role of a mixed account of the normative basis of private law makes it a very bad mixed account. This becomes especially obvious in light of the factors outlined in the following subsection (p.382). The only thing Coleman's account has in its favour as a mixed account is its apparent invocation of more than one value (or form

[8] The principal statements of the argument are (with A. Ripstein), 'Mischief and Misfortune' (1995) 41 *McGill LJ* 91–130 and *The Practice of Principle*, supra, note 4, pp. 44–63.

of justice) at the basis of private law. It contains no explicit treatment of how those values relate to one another nor any indication as to which value dominates and when. It therefore falls a long way short of completing the principal hurdle mixed accounts must overcome. Coleman's account must, then, be interpreted as originally intended: it is a corrective justice account of the normative foundation of private law, albeit one ensnared by the serious difficulty of distinguishing corrective and distributive justice.[9] It is now time to attend to the conditions that any mixed account must satisfy if it is to pass muster. These conditions are of two broadly different types. The first concerns what can be called the generic conditions mixed accounts must satisfy, addressed below as the issues of mixing, ranking and commensurability. The second type consists of those requirements or conditions that any account of the normative foundation of private law must satisfy: fit, intelligibility and the key questions.

MIXING, RANKING AND COMMENSURABILITY

How do the elements of mixed accounts of the normative foundation of private law fit together? It is surely the case that these elements are not mixed in anything like the central sense, in which we mix the ingredients of a cake or constituents of concrete. In both cake and concrete the ingredients are combined in such a way that they cannot subsequently be separated or even identified. This seems entirely inappropriate for any account of the normative foundation of any institution or practice, principally because we treat the 'ingredients' as discrete entities. Thus a normative foundation is mixed only in an extended sense: 'mixed' because the foundation consists of different values rather than just one value. Nor are mixed foundations 'mixed' because, when combined, those values create something different than the sum of their parts; the constituents of a mixed account remain different and maintain their own features even when combined. It might therefore be better to speak of mixed accounts of the normative foundation of private law as 'plural' and 'composite'. 'Plural' to reflect the fact that they contain more than one value, and 'composite' as in the architectural sense of that term, in which one style (Ionic, for example) is added on to another (Corinthian), elements of each remaining visible.[10]

One problem with this suggestion is that it requires two words where

[9] For helpful analysis of this aspect of Coleman's work, see S. Perry, 'The Distributive Turn: Mischief, Misfortune and Tort Law', ch. 7 of B. Bix (ed.), *Analyzing Law* (Oxford: Clarendon Press, 1998).

[10] The example is from *The Shorter OED*.

one, 'mixed' – although used stipulatively – might do. Another difficulty is that unlike architectural styles, values are not easily added on to or otherwise combined with one another. More common and more intuitive is the notion that values, while remaining distinct from one another, can be ranked in relation to one another. It seems especially important that mixed accounts contain a ranking of their constituent values insofar as some or all of those values are moral or political. This is because such values do not come to us bearing clear and ineluctable directions for their application. For example, the claim that distributive and corrective justice together constitute the normative foundation of private law says nothing about which of these two forms of justice operates in which circumstances, assuming both remain discrete. As a general matter, it is rarely certain that moral value 1 applies only in contexts of type X, while political value 2 applies only in situations of type Z. Nor is it often unambiguously certain that, for example, moral value 3 trumps both values 1 and 2 in all situations. Since it seems that moral values sometimes compete with one another for our attention in particular cases, and that political values do the same, and also that there can be inter-systemic competition between moral and political values, some ranking principles are clearly desirable.

Some would, however, deny that ranking principles are available. In moral philosophy those who make this denial are often called intuitionists, their view about the way in which different moral values relate to one another being well characterized by J. O. Urmston. Intuitionists hold, first, that there is 'a plurality of first principles [or values] which may conflict to give contrary directives in particular types of cases; and second, . . . [that there is] no explicit method, no priority rules, for weighing these principles [or values] against one another'.[11] Assuming that this is a good statement of intuitionism, then that doctrine clearly undermines the effort to propound 'ranked' mixed accounts of the normative foundation of private law. At least, it does so on the additional assumption that intuitionism is true not only of first principles of morality but also true of those (second-level?) principles that operate, like corrective justice for example, only in specific contexts. If we grant these two assumptions, what can proponents of mixed accounts say to the intuitionist?

[11] J. O. Urmson, 'A Defence of Intuitionism' (1975) lxxv *Aristotelian Society Proceedings* 111–119, pp. 111. For our purposes intuitionism is regarded only as a claim about how moral values and principles relate to one another; the doctrine also traditionally made claims about the nature of moral knowledge, but these are ignored here. For an excellent brief but general treatment see J. Dancy, 'Intuitionism', ch. 36 of P. Singer (ed.), *A Companion to Ethics* (Oxford: Blackwell, 1993).

Although not wrong, it is insufficient to observe that intuitionism is not now popular among moral philosophers. For, besides being slightly contestable, this observation is worthless without articulating the reasons underpinning this lack of popularity.[12] One such reason may be that intuitionism is simply untrue to moral experience because we do not deliberate in the way it says we do: moral deliberation is both more structured and precise than intuitionism suggests. Recourse to moral experience on matters such as this is, however, a doubled-edged strategy since, for every area of moral experience where deliberation seems more structured and precise than intuitionism would suggest, there are also domains where moral deliberation appears entirely in accord with the intuitionist picture. If moral experience were univocal on this issue, then either intuitionism or its competitors would never even have achieved a toehold in our thinking. A refutation of intuitionism which, it has plausibly been suggested, 'consists in presenting the sort of constructive [ranking] criteria that are said not to exist', is not attempted here.[13] The path taken in the face of its brooding presence is, rather, to assume ranking is possible. The justification for this is that the idea of ranking – like intuitionism itself – has some foundation in ordinary moral experience.

A point passed over too glibly in the discussion so far must now be addressed. The falsity of intuitionism is not the only condition necessary for mixed accounts of the normative foundation of private law to be possible. Another is that value pluralism must be true. By value pluralism we mean that the normative world contains significantly distinct and different values that are neither reducible to a single master value nor just different aspects of that master value. While value pluralism might seem to be so obviously true as to need no argument, it is salutary to note that some accounts of the nature of morality and moral philosophy have either denied it or come very close to denying it. Some versions of utilitarianism are obvious examples. On this point, however, an appeal to moral experience does some helpful work, for not even utilitarians hold that when we deliberate we regard the apparently different moral values in play as all being fundamentally the same. Since our moral experience and intuitions on this matter are univocal, much is required to loosen their grip upon us and the monistic claim thus needs considerable support. Since almost all

[12] The claim is contestable because there is at least one current account of moral deliberation – moral particularism – that looks like a relative of intuitionism. For an overview see the essays in B. Hooker (ed.), *Moral Particularism* (Oxford: Clarendon Press, 2000) and J. Dancy, *Ethics Without Principles* (Oxford: Clarendon Press, 2004).

[13] Rawls, supra, note 7, p. 35.

philosophical accounts of morality and political morality are pluralistic, it seems that such support has not so far been forthcoming. Our ordinary moral experience, which in large measure confirms value pluralism, is regarded as sound in what follows.

If intuitionism is false and value pluralism true, then it is possible that values can be ranked in some kind of rational order. And it is just this possibility that mixed accounts of the normative foundation of private law are surely committed to; 'mixed', from this point on, is regarded as a synonym for 'plural and ranked'. So what are the ranking possibilities open to proponents of mixed accounts? The two most common rankings used by economists and social choice theorists are ordinal and cardinal rankings. A ranking of the former kind is one in which the variables are listed as simply better or worse or more or less important. So, for example, an ordinal ranking of importance of the variables A, B and C could rank A as more important than B and B as more important than C. Because transitivity is usually assumed of the variables in such rankings we can also conclude that A is more important than C. The difference between a cardinal and an ordinal ranking is that the former uses a scale by which, sticking with the example of an importance ranking of variables A, B and C, degrees of importance (or whatever else is being assessed) are determined. A cardinal ranking of A, B and C will therefore tell us not just that A is more important than B and B more important than C, but how much more important A is than B and B than C. Another possible scale ranking worth noting here is that adopted by John Rawls for his two principles of justice. He called it a 'lexical' ordering, 'which requires us to satisfy the first principle in the ordering before we can move on to the second, the second before we consider the third, and so on. A principle does not come into play until those previous to it are either fully met or do not apply'.[14] This ordering principle is a little more informative than an ordinal ranking but clearly not as informative as a normal cardinal ordering.

There is very little at stake in the choice of ranking made by proponents of mixed theories. The important point is that, unless such proponents are intuitionists or otherwise sceptical about ranking, they must at the very least offer some ordering of the values they think constitute the normative foundation of private law. If two of those values are corrective and distributive justice then we need to know which dominates. Moreover,

[14] Rawls, ibid, p. 38. Rawls also notes the correct term should be 'lexicographical' but, rightly, he rejects it because too cumbersome.

the ranking may need to be a little more complicated than this if it is the case, as it surely often will be, that the ranking of these two values varies according to the context. It might, for example, be that corrective justice dominates in some contexts and distributive justice in others. The ranking scale must therefore be given more depth by the specification of these contextual factors. As a general matter, the *prima facie* easiest ranking for proponents of mixed theories to adopt would be an ordinal one, but this initial appeal might be deceptive if there are situations in which it is necessary to know how much more important value X is than value Y. Imagine, for example, that cost/benefit analysis of moral choices is both possible and desirable. That being so, the analysis would work best if it were possible not only to say choice Y were morally better than choice X, but also how much better Y is than X. And that, of course, assumes the possibility of valuing the losses or disadvantages of Y as compared with those of X. Thus, costs and benefits must not only be reasonably precisely specifiable, they must also be commensurable.

Not every ranking of values must be cardinal and facilitate cost/benefit analysis. But every genuine ranking must embody both commensurability and transitivity. The former requires that the weight of value Y can be compared with that of X and a judgment made that Y is either weightier than, less than or the same as X. This possibility assumes a single metric or scale by which the weight of Y and X is determined. Transitivity holds between variables when, in a judgment which holds A to be weightier than B and B weightier than C, the conclusion that A is weightier than C is warranted. Some moral and political philosophers hold that some values are incommensurable and for one – Joseph Raz – incommensurability is marked by a failure of transitivity.[15] Thus, where one faces a choice between three or more incommensurable values, a ranking which holds A more valuable than B and B more valuable than C does not warrant the conclusion that A is more valuable than C. This is a fairly narrow analysis of the nature of incommensurability and that is certainly one of its advantages. Whether or not it is the best analysis of incommensurability is not the important point for current purposes. The key issue is, rather, that the existence of widespread incommensurability among our moral and political values threatens ranking; it thus indirectly imperils ranked (mixed) accounts of the normative foundation of private law.

[15] J. Raz, *The Morality of Freedom* (Oxford: Clarendon Press, 1986), pp. 322–325. The essays in R. Chang (ed.), *Incommensurability, Incomparability, and Practical Reason* (Cambridge, Mass.: Harvard University Press, 1997) provide a good overview of the debate about incommensurability and some alternatives to Raz's account.

How serious is this threat? It depends entirely on our view of the range of incommensurability. The primary advantage of Raz's narrow account of incommensurability is that it lays down a clear and unambiguous test: a failure of transitivity is relatively easy to determine. Furthermore, since this test gives us something definite to look for on the trail of incommensurability, there is little risk of mistaking it for something else such as a tied ranking or a plain old hard choice.[16] Since on this view incommensurability occupies distinct conceptual space, there is also little or no risk of exaggerating the number of incommensurable values and thus the general range of incommensurability. Whether or not we are faced by incommensurability must therefore be determined on a case by case basis: general assertions of widespread incommensurability should be treated with suspicion because too glib, rarely being supported by argument.[17] Whether or not mixed theories are effected by incommensurability thus depends on the values in play. A judgment on this matter must await consideration of particular mixed accounts, one of which is examined in depth in the next section. Before that, a few more general hurdles that face mixed theories are elucidated.

FIT, INTELLIGIBILITY AND THE KEY QUESTIONS

Mixed accounts must not only satisfy the conditions just outlined, which are unique to them; they must also meet the normal conditions of adequacy for any account of the normative basis of private law. There are at least three such conditions. An account of the normative basis of private law must to some extent fit the institution and its constitutive practices, guiding moves within them and making sense, whenever possible, of its structure and substance. In addition to the fit and intelligibility conditions, such an account must address the key questions or issues identified in Chapter 7. These require that an account of the normative basis of private law specify not only the normative basis of the institution in general terms, but also address two more specific questions: what is the normative basis of the obligation to correct? And: is that an obligation to make monetary compensation or simply an obligation to correct?

There is not a great deal that can be fruitfully said about the general conditions mixed accounts must satisfy in advance of actually examining some such accounts and seeing how well or badly they perform. One

[16] Raz, ibid, pp. 323–324.

[17] Although it should be noted that Raz himself often asserts that incommensurability is widespread: see his *Value, Respect, and Attachment* (Cambridge: Cambridge University Press, 2001), p. 5 and *The Practice of Value* (Oxford: Clarendon Press, 2003), p. 140.

obvious point might, however, be worth emphasizing. It is that mixed accounts will be rather more complex and seem less neat than non-mixed accounts. While this is to be expected, it means that the answers such accounts generate to issues like, for example, the key questions, might be tricky to piece together, being neither as obvious nor as transparent as the answers that non-mixed accounts generate. Yet this clearly cannot be taken as a criticism of mixed accounts: to complain about their relative complexity is akin to complaining that a complex matter is indeed complex. Of course, were mixed accounts guilty of portraying a simple matter as unnecessarily complex, then that would be a serious charge. Proponents of mixed accounts are probably only certain of one thing here: that private law, and the task of illuminating its normative foundation, is more complex than proponents of non-mixed accounts assume. The arguments of Chapters 8 and 9 suggest that this assumption is not implausible.

THE NORMATIVE FOUNDATION OF TORT LAW: A MIXED THEORY

The theory examined here belongs to Tony Honoré, although occasional reference will also be made to other ostensibly mixed theories. Honoré focuses mainly upon tort law and his account thus deserves the label 'narrow' because it offers a normative foundation for only one segment of private law. It therefore seems immediately clear that, of the three general requirements – of fit, intelligibility and the key questions – any adequate account of the normative foundation of private law must satisfy, narrow accounts such as Honoré's will have particular difficulty with the first. For how can an account of the normative basis of tort law fit private law as a whole, assuming that different areas of private law embody different values? Although an effort is made in what follows to show that Honoré's account might be extended to include contract law, that process is not exactly comfortable; nor is it a process that other mixed accounts can easily undergo. Nevertheless, even narrow accounts can provide some general insight into the structure and problems of 'wide' mixed accounts of the normative foundation of private law as a whole. Even though the values in play in narrow accounts might differ from the schema of values in play in wide accounts, the former still face the generic problem of ranking and relating their component values confronted by all mixed theories. How well or badly our sample mixed account grapples with the generic problems and the general requirements is thus a reasonably reliable guide to the prospects of mixed accounts in general, whether narrow or wide. Should our sample mixed account prove inadequate in its treatment of tort law, then that bodes ill for the simple reason that it fails to provide a normative foundation for its theoretical 'heartland'. If it fails there, then it seems unlikely to provide useful guidance as to how to proceed elsewhere.

An overview of Honore's account is offered in the subsection below, while two general problems which beset it are tackled in the second subsection (p.393). These problems have nothing to do with either the conditions that mixed theories must satisfy to be plausible, which are tackled in the third subsection (p.401), or the conditions that any account of the normative foundation of private law must satisfy, which are examined in the final subsection (p.403). The last section (p.415) examines the prospects for mixed accounts of the normative basis of private law.

RISK-DISTRIBUTIVE, CORRECTIVE AND RETRIBUTIVE JUSTICE: AN OUTLINE

Corrective justice, for Honoré, is the principle of justice that ties wrongdoer and her victim together:

> [o]n a wide view [corrective justice] . . . requires those who have without justification harmed others by their conduct to put the matter right. [. . .] This they must do on the basis that harm-doer and harm-sufferer are to be treated as equals, neither more deserving than the other. The one is therefore not entitled to become relatively better off by harming the other. The balance must be restored. (*RF*, pp. 73–74)[18]

This is a standard and uncontroversial statement of what corrective justice looks like, save that some think corrective justice requires something more specific – such as monetary damages, for example – than that the wrong 'be put right'. Hence Honoré's view of corrective justice is wide in two senses: first, because it includes a range of possible methods of 'correction' or repair and, second, because the duty to correct can be triggered in the absence of 'fault' (*RF*, p. 78, fn 31). Furthermore, Honoré is not of the view that corrective justice can of itself provide a complete account of the normative basis of tort law. This is because corrective justice alone does not determine the limits of our responsibility: such limits as exist are not determined by any obligation to correct but by the two things such an obligation presupposes, namely, a conception of

[18] The references in brackets in both text and notes to '*RF*' with accompanying page numbers refer to T. Honoré, *Responsibility and Fault* (Oxford: Hart Publishing, 1999).

causation and of responsibility. For without evidence that Y brought about harm to Z, and that Y was also an agent in the basic responsibility sense when she did so, talk of her having an obligation to correct the wrong done to Z is *prima facie* misplaced. The conception of causation in play in private law was outlined in Chapter 5 and the relevant conception of responsibility – outcome responsibility – was elucidated in Chapter 2.

Outcome responsibility, remember, is but one of a range of conceptions of responsibility. It holds that 'if [we are] of full capacity and hence in a position to control our behaviour, [we are] responsible for the outcome of our conduct, whether act or omission' (*RF*, p. 76). Although it is clear that a conception of responsibility must be presupposed by corrective justice, it is uncertain outcome responsibility is that conception. Honoré's general argument in favour of outcome responsibility leads him to conclude that it is and whether or not he is right about this is important for the structure of his mixed account. For he argues that *both* corrective justice and outcome responsibility depend upon a conception of distributive justice he labels 'risk-distributive justice' (*RF*, p. 79) or the risk principle.

The first step to this end aims to establish a justificatory link between outcome responsibility and risk-distributive justice: 'the justification for imposing outcome responsibility on those who cause harm to others rests . . . on distributive justice' (*RF*, p. 78). Specifically,

> [t]he argument for holding people responsible to others for harmful outcomes is that it is fair to make the person to whom the advantages will flow from a [sic] uncertain situation over which he has some control (or which he has chosen to enter into) bear the losses that may equally flow from that situation. . . . This argument . . . tries to spell out what justice requires in situations of uncertainty. (*RF*, p. 79)[19]

This is not a standard principle of distributive justice because it is not concerned with the distribution of general benefits and burdens, most often the incidents of a good or adequate life. Rather, the risk principle distributes only a subset of such benefits and burdens, apparently in ignorance of how all other remaining benefits and burdens are themselves

[19] I have deleted the sentence from this passage that states the betting metaphor subsequently retracted by Honoré: see P. Cane and J. Gardner (eds.), *Relating to Responsibility* (Oxford: Hart Publishing, 2001), ch. 9, pp. 225–226. In an otherwise reliable account of Honoré's argument on this point, Stephen Perry at one point regards the risk principle as being just a 'characterization' of outcome responsibility when, of course, it is a justification of it: see his 'Honoré on Responsibility for Outcomes', ch. 4 of Cane and Gardner, ibid, p. 66; he is nearer the mark at p. 68 (outcome responsibility 'resting on' the risk principle).

distributed. The risk principle is, however, like most principles of distributive justice in that it is entirely general. It places 'on every member of the community the burden of bearing the risk that his conduct may turn out to be harmful to others, in return for the benefit that will accrue should his conduct turn out as he plans' (*RF*, p. 80).

The second step attempts to show a justificatory link between corrective justice and risk-distributive justice. Honoré claims that corrective justice is both distinct from and dependent upon distributive justice.

> It is distinct in the sense that the interests (holdings) that corrective justice protects need not be just from a distributive point of view. The filthy rich can appeal to corrective justice if their holdings are filched by the grinding poor. But to justify corrective justice involves appealing at a certain stage to the *just distribution of risk* in a society. In that respect corrective justice depends on distributive justice. Corrective justice is a genuine form of justice only because the just distribution of risks requires people of full capacity to bear the risk of being held responsible for harming others by their conduct even when they are not at fault in doing so. (*RF*, p. 80; emphasis in original)

The risk principle provides corrective justice with 'a moral basis' (*RF*, ibid).

Were corrective justice and risk-distributive justice the only elements of Honoré's account of the normative foundation of tort law, then it might be thought that there has been a serious misrepresentation. For in order to be a genuine mixed theory, Honoré's account must hold that the normative foundation of private law consists of a plurality of discrete values in some kind of ranking or order. Since it was held that Coleman's account of the normative foundation of private law could not be regarded as genuinely mixed because, *inter alia*, it deployed only two values very similar to those invoked by Honoré, then the same judgment must apply to Honoré's account. But this conclusion is premature, for Honoré holds that at least one other value, that of retributive justice, is also in play in tort law and, furthermore, that it is joined by a bundle of concerns that can be subsumed under the label of 'systemic values'.

Retributive justice has two dimensions: '[o]ne *requires* that a sanction be imposed that is roughly proportionate to the moral gravity of the conduct. The other *forbids* that a sanction be imposed that is out of proportion to the gravity of the conduct' (*RF*, p. 83). While retributive justice clearly has an important role within criminal law, Honoré also shows that the notion is applicable in tort law and he argues that this is perfectly correct. The principal difference between the two domains from the perspective of retributive justice is this: retributive justice's support for fault or *mens rea* concepts in the criminal law does not extend into tort law. One of the usual reasons for requiring *mens rea* in the criminal law but not in private law is reiterated by Honoré, namely, that the seriousness of criminal sanctions means they should be directed only at the morally most heinous conduct (*RF*, pp. 82–83). And such conduct is surely well to the fore in the catalogue of prohibited intentional or reckless wrongdoing provided by large parts of the criminal law.

The systemic values in play in tort law include three quite different considerations related by the fact that they are 'internal' to the process of interpreting and applying propositions of law. These considerations, moreover, are not unique to tort law. Honoré holds that of this trio, only two considerations are genuine, the other, although often thought to be independent, actually being nothing more than a reiteration of one of the dimensions of retributive justice. This 'phoney' systemic consideration is the judicial sensitivity to questions about the foreseeability of the harm brought about. In tort law it is manifest in the requirement that the harm brought about be foreseeable not just in general terms – such as, for example, that some harm is clearly foreseeable from a crane cable breaking and cargo thus falling into the hold of a ship – but in specific terms such as, in this instance, harm by impact. If the harm that actually resulted here is from fire, then the courts could well regard that as unforeseeable. But this sensitivity to foreseeability is simply one way of ensuring that the defendant's compensatory burden is not excessive and thus overlaps with one dimension of retributive justice. Indeed, it is surely best subsumed under that heading rather than regarded as an independent consideration.

The first genuine systemic consideration is that legal rules have a limited scope and, in particular situations, the question may be raised as to whether or not that scope should be extended. Legal rule X, for example, may generate a cause of action for victims of dangerous driving. It may be thought that the rule functions to deter careless driving and as an incentive to careful driving. But what of victims of dangerous driving that results not from the fault of the driver, but from a fault with his vehicle? Does the rule apply here or not? This, of course, is a question about the scope of the rule in question and it is apposite on the assumption that it is undesirable, because too burdensome on defendants, '[t]o require compensation for every type of harm in the context of every rule of . . . law' (*RF*, p. 88). If each and every tort law rule is not intended to generate a right of recovery for every conceivable harm that may fall under it, then those who must apply and interpret those rules must always keep their scope or range in mind. The second genuine systemic value is that the conduct and fault of the claimant serves to reduce the liability of the defendant. While this often seems to be but a requirement of both retributive and corrective justice, it may also have independent standing.

TWO PROBLEMS

The sketch just provided suggests that Honoré's argument faces some difficulties long before the general plausibility conditions for accounts of the normative foundation of private law are even introduced. While it is right to eschew the notion that jurisprudential and philosophical arguments such as Honoré's can reach a state of argumentative perfection entirely free of blemishes and problems, some difficulties are nevertheless so significant that they cannot be overlooked as merely momentary snags.[20] It might be thought that two problems of this stature engulf Honoré's idea of risk-distributive justice. The first questions the nature of the justification the idea provides for corrective justice; this, it is argued, is a red herring. The second questions, albeit in a number of different ways, the plausibility of the risk principle and, in particular, the notion of fairness upon which it relies. This difficulty is not so much one single problem as a series of related problems and is therefore more complex than the first alleged problem. It is also less obviously misguided than the first but, it is argued, it is still nevertheless misguided. The conclusion is that neither of the two alleged problems is as awkward as appearances suggest.

Justification

The worry about the justification that risk-distributive justice provides for corrective justice is primarily a worry about its weight or power. It is clear that Honoré does little more than show how the risk principle supports – in the sense of providing reasons for – corrective justice; he neither rules out other conceivable justifications nor argues that the reasons the risk principle provides are the most compelling possible reasons available. It might therefore be concluded that the justification provided is feeble. This objection throws into relief the question of what

[20] The task of offering legal philosophical arguments is just the same as that of offering general philosophical arguments and was accurately and amusingly characterized by R. Nozick in *Anarchy, State, and Utopia* (Oxford: Blackwell, 1974), pp. xii–xiv.

we expect of a justification, be it for some or other aspect of someone's conduct or for some institution, practice or aspect thereof. One obvious answer to this question is that a 'justification' is simply the reasons for the conduct, institution or practice in question. My 'justification' for visiting the coffee shop and buying coffee is my reason for doing so, presumably the fact that I wanted to drink some coffee. Similarly, the 'justification' for coffee shops is in part to satisfy a demand for this particular kind of beverage in this particular type of environment. It seems clear that risk-distributive justice justifies corrective justice in a similar way, since it articulates the reasons that make sense of the latter. In the absence of something like the considerations embodied in the risk principle the practice of corrective justice appears suspect or morally troublesome, since without a just background distribution of risk it seems unfair to hold agents liability-responsible for both the good and bad consequences of their conduct. That worry about unfairness in part dissipates when the risk principle is satisfied.

It might be objected that this 'weak' conception of justification takes no account of an expectation about the variability in the weight of justifications. The expectation holds that the more 'serious' the conduct or institution or practice in question, the weightier must be the reasons adduced in its favour. One indicator of seriousness is surely the effect the conduct, institution or practice has upon the interests of other agents and, of course, it is hard to imagine an institution that has more potential to adversely effect the interests of agents than the law. Private law is not, perhaps, the most intrusive form of law but its judgments are still ultimately enforced by the coercive apparatus of the state. Thus, it might be said, private law and its various components requires more by way of justification than the argument Honoré offers. Providing reasons that make the practice of corrective justice normatively acceptable or, perhaps, less normatively troubling than it would otherwise seem, falls far short of the kind of justification required for the coercive power structure that arises upon that practice.

There is an undeniable truth in this objection, for it is surely correct that the greater the effect some conduct, institution or practice has upon other agents, then the more compelling must be the reasons supporting it. Not any old reason will justify a decision to go to war, nor will any old reason operate as a justification for the use of potentially fatal physical force upon another individual. The defences available to the charge of murder in most systems of criminal law are, remember, few and limited in their availability; this, we assume, is perfectly appropriate. In democratic societies elected leaders cannot usually commit their countries' armed forces to war with another nation without either a special vote or procedure being followed, the point being to reinforce both the seriousness of the decision and the reasons supporting it. Surely the institutions and practices that can unleash the coercive apparatus of the state, while not exactly the same as these other instances, fall into a similarly serious category and thus require special – by which is meant particularly compelling – justification. And clearly the risk principle does not, in providing reasons for the practice of corrective justice, generate such a justification.

This conception of justification can be described as a 'strong' conception but it is probably more accurate to label it as a 'political' conception. For, while we usually accept that the greater the effect some conduct, institution or practice has upon agents, then the stronger must be the reasons for it, the prime worry in most such instances is that the conduct, institution or practice in question is a manifestation of political power. Thus the operation of the civil and criminal justice systems of most if not all democracies are subject to particular scrutiny because they are in part the locus of state power. So, too, are the various non-criminal, non-civil law regulatory structures employed within modern states at both the local and central government level. Now, if the worry about the justification Honoré provides for corrective justice and, by extension, for tort law, is that it is insufficiently robust because it takes no particular account of the 'political dimension' of the law, then the point can be accepted. The justification the risk principle provides for corrective justice is simply this: it illuminates the reasons that make moral sense of the latter. Those reasons certainly do not address the additional complexities that result from the fact that corrective justice, as embodied in tort law, presents a particular manifestation of 'the' general political problem, namely, the problem of justifying political power and authority.[21] But Honoré is not unique in this. Few if any philosophers and jurists of private law take this extra task on board, being content to articulate the particular reasons and values that the institution and practices of private law might and should

[21] The debate on this issue is as old as Western philosophy itself. For some recent instalments see R. P. Wolff, *In Defense of Anarchism* (New York: Harper and Row, 1970); Raz, supra, note 15, part I; A. J. Simmons, *Moral Principles and Political Obligation* (Princeton: Princeton University Press, 1979) and his *Justification and Legitimacy* (Cambridge: Cambridge University Press, 2001). A good overview is provided in S. Shapiro, 'Authority', ch. 10 of J. Coleman and S. Shapiro (eds.), *The Oxford Handbook of Jurisprudence and Philosophy of Law* (Oxford: Clarendon Press, 2002).

embody.[22] There is no doubt that such reasons and values must in addition satisfy whatever extra demands are made upon attempts to justify political power, but it is uncharitable to chastise Honoré for not taking up the cudgels on this issue. His failing here, if it be judged as such, is a failing shared with most philosophers of private law whose work has featured so far in this book.

The risk principle

The second problem that faces Honoré's account arises from the fundamental justificatory role the risk principle plays in relation to both outcome responsibility and corrective justice. It is no exaggeration to regard the principle as the keystone of Honoré's mixed theory; the problem it faces consists of a family of arguments purporting to show that the principle cannot bear the weight placed upon it. One such argument is immediately and rightly scotched by Honoré: it is the suggestion that the risk principle cannot be a principle of distributive justice because it distributes burdens as well as benefits (*RF*, p. 79). The idea that distributive justice has nothing to do with the distribution of burdens is absurdly utopian, seemingly implying that the advantages of collective life have no concomitant disadvantages, be they conflicts between individuals or contributions to the commonweal. Nor can it be said that the risk principle is flawed because the range of the notion of 'risk' is limitless, the principle therefore requiring the distribution of something that cannot be distributed because its contours are indeterminate. Although there are some general difficulties with the notion of risk, these are not such as to make it unintelligible.[23] Those difficulties provide no reason to think that the range of risk cannot be constrained in the way the outcomes and consequences of conduct are usually limited, namely, by reference to the NESS and common sense causal principles.[24]

A possibly more serious criticism of the risk principle highlights its odd relationship with distributive justice in general. The risk principle is

[22] Which is not to say that philosophers and jurists of private law do not see the issue: see, for instance, J. Coleman, supra, note 6, pp. 362–367 and Ripstein, supra, note 2, pp. 12–15.

[23] A good introductory account is provided by J. Steele, *Risks and Legal Theory* (Oxford: Hart Publishing, 2004), chs. 1 and 2.

[24] Perry, supra, note 19, pp. 69–70 alleges that Honoré's account might suffer from the same causal indeterminacy as he thinks besets 'libertarian' accounts of liability-responsibility. The allegation is, however, undermined by the existence and plausibility of the NESS and common sense causal principles, with which Perry does not engage.

limited, concerned only with the fair distribution of the good and bad outcomes of conduct, the idea of fairness in play being this: if one takes the benefits of one's risky conduct (the good outcomes), then one must also take the burdens (the bad outcomes). But the fairness of this could well be undermined by factors extraneous to the particular segment of conduct in question. Think again of Creosus and Diogenes. Diogenes is, in Honoré's phrase, one of the grinding poor, his holdings clearly illegitimate on any principle of distributive justice. Creosus is the richest of the filthy rich, his holdings also illegitimate on any principle of distributive justice. In what sense, then, does fairness require Diogenes to correct or make right the damage he has done to Creosus's Bentley? True, Diogenes conduct had this unfortunate outcome but many times it has not: he has, let us suppose, often juggled burning torches in the street for money without damaging parked cars. He has undoubtedly taken the benefits of that risky conduct on those previous occasions, but must he, as a matter of *fairness*, put right the bad outcome that has resulted on this particular occasion?

Honoré's reply will surely be 'yes', its basis the claim that risk-distributive justice is just that: it is about the distribution of risks, nothing more. The substance of the criticism just imagined is familiar, having been touched upon in Chapter 9. It was noted that distributive justice has an 'imperialist' tendency to overwhelm all other deliberative considerations, the claims of justice appearing more urgent and compelling than all others. The criticism of the risk principle envisaged embodies exactly this imperialist tendency, overwhelming the line Honoré seeks to draw between the distribution of risks and other things. How, the criticism asks, can we take the distribution of risk seriously in light of the misdistribution of everything else? Why, in other words, does distributive justice in general not dominate all other considerations?

The line between risk-distributive justice and distributive justice in general is clearly not an easy one for Honoré to hold, especially because he allows that general distributive considerations can sometimes outweigh arguments supporting the tort system (*RF*, pp. 90–91). But he is not unique in seeking to mark a border between distributive justice and other considerations, the difficulty he has here being the same as that faced by all who think there are limits upon the range and extent of principles of distributive justice. While this problematic issue cannot be resolved here, we can at least note that Honoré does have some arguments to show that risk-distributive justice might be a special case, insulated from the insistent demands of distributive justice. Risk-distributive justice might be special because of its close connection to outcome responsibility and that, remember, is fundamental to our identities. Replacing risk-distributive justice with – or subjecting its operation to – general principles of distributive justice might undermine both outcome responsibility and our identities. We might cease to regard ourselves as agents in anything like the current sense under such a regime.[25]

A slightly different attack upon the risk principle attempts to directly undermine the notion of fairness upon which it depends, rather than trying to collapse that notion into general considerations of distributive justice. There is a problem here, however, because Honoré invokes two different notions of fairness in his discussions of outcome responsibility. One is in play in the essay that has been our main focus so far, 'The Morality of Tort Law: Questions and Answers' (*RF*, ch. 4). The other plays a role in the arguments of 'Responsibility and Luck' and is regarded as particularly problematic (*RF*, ch. 2).[26] Each is considered in turn, the aim being twofold: to show that the notion of fairness in the first essay is relatively unproblematic and that the problems faced by the idea of fairness in the second have been exaggerated. The conclusion is that whatever notion of fairness Honoré's argument depends upon, whether one or the other or both, does not matter, since each is relatively robust.

The notion of fairness underpinning risk-distributive justice seems clear. On the basis of the statements like those we have already quoted from Honoré's 'Morality of Tort Law' essay, Stephen Perry offers an accurate characterization. The notion of fairness in play holds that 'it is fair to make a person who stands to benefit from his actions also bear the losses that might equally flow from those actions. There is no requirement that all such persons must stand to gain more than they stand to lose from this arrangement'.[27] (The latter observation becomes salient once we turn to the notion of fairness in play in 'Responsibility and Luck'.) If the effort to collapse this notion of fairness into distributive justice is eschewed, what other objections might it face? It seems to have a good deal of immediate, intuitive appeal. As a common sense matter, we often think it 'only fair' that if one takes the benefits of one's conduct then one should also shoulder the burdens it brings. The basic and immediate nature of this idea suggests that it is an intuition 'that one cannot go behind' (*RF*, p. 80), but this, of course, cannot simply be assumed. The

[25] We noted that a similar possibility arises under B. Ackerman's account of justice in transactions: Chapter 9, pp. 369–370.

[26] The two notions are also noted by Perry, supra, note 19, p. 67.

[27] Supra, note 19, p. 67.

basis of the notion might prove to be something even more fundamental, as Honoré concedes. Of course, were it shown that the notion's intuitive appeal was entirely spurious because, for example, it is ideological in the false consciousness sense, or that it lacked a plausible basis, then that would be a powerful indictment. But, as matters currently stand, it is surely the case that this notion and the intuition it embodies are well entrenched in our ordinary thought and not obviously misleading. That being so, the onus of proof must rest upon those that seek to dislodge the notion, for if it is resistant to the type of distributive considerations illuminated by the tale of Creosus and Diogenes, then it seems *prima facie* robust

This appearance might be undermined if this notion of fairness depends upon another which is far less robust. The two difficulties that face proponents of this criticism are, however, fairly daunting. The first can be easily stated: there is no particularly compelling textual evidence in Honoré's work to suggest any link between the two notions of fairness. Such a link cannot be assumed; it must be demonstrated. And such a demonstration is particularly difficult in light of the fact that Honoré's thinking on these matters is still evolving. The second difficulty is that, even if a link between both notions of fairness can be made out, this is of little help to critics. This is because the second notion of fairness is, as will be seen, far less troublesome than some of Honoré's critics assume. It is to this issue that we now turn.

The notion of fairness in Honoré's 'Responsibility and Luck' arises from this thought. It is appropriate to hold those of full capacity liability-responsible for the outcomes of their conduct because, even though they lacked the particular capacity (can particular) to do otherwise on this particular occasion, they nevertheless had the general capacity (can general) to do other than they did. This is proper because agents of full capacity receive the benefits that flow from their conduct when the outcomes are good. Being liability-responsible on those occasions when their conduct yields bad outcomes is not unfair, says Honoré, because overall they benefit more from the system of outcome responsibility than they are disadvantaged. In addition to being fair over the period of a life or some segment thereof, the system of outcome responsibility must also be both impartial and reciprocal (*RF*, pp. 26–27).

Some have questioned the claim that outcome responsibility can be fair over a period of a life or some segment thereof on the basis that there is no empirical foundation for it. Yet while the evidence for such a foundation would, of course, be very hard to gather it is certainly not impossible.[28] For it is in principle possible to collate every instance in an individual's life in which the system of outcome responsibility brings about benefits that redound in some way to that individual's advantage. These would have to include almost every aspect of that individual's conduct, including, for example, all the golf games won as a result of fortuitous putts, being in the precise place at the exact time to meet her life partner and the lucrative results of having bought shares in a particular company. The same could also be done, of course, with regard to the instances in an individual's life in which outcome responsibility redounded to their disadvantage. These instances could include, of course, some of the events just mentioned but which happen to turn out badly rather than well: the marriage or relationship was a disaster, the company went bankrupt. Thus, while the objection is right in that it shows Honoré's claim here is an assumption rather than a well-founded empirical generalization, that assumption is no less dubious than its opposite, namely, that those of full capacity are never overall winners under the system of outcome responsibility. Indeed, it seems that Honoré's more optimistic assumption has greater resonance in our intuitions, experience and common sense than its opposite. For, while the agent whose luck is chronically bad – the movie producer who backs silent films over 'talkies', or the military man whose last words are 'we are surely out of range of the enemy . . .' – is a staple of much humour, he is not a common feature of daily life.[29]

A related complaint about this notion of fairness highlights a feature of some bad outcomes that redound to our disadvantage under a system of outcome responsibility. It is that they sometimes seem hugely disproportionate to the advantages accrued under that system. Now, as we know, Honoré thinks that a principle of proportionality between defendant's conduct and levels of compensation is in play in the realm of legal liability and this might mitigate the worse results of some of the cases imagined. But this will not always be so. Further, it might often seem, when put dramatically, that some bad outcomes outweigh all the good

[28] Steele, supra, note 23, p. 96; Perry, supra, note 19, p. 67.

[29] My intuitions, experience and exposure to common sense clearly differ from Perry's, ibid, where he claims we all know ('or know of' (!)) people of full capacity who are nevertheless 'life's perennial losers'. I don't know anyone who is a perennial loser purely as a result of the operation of the system of outcome responsibility; I do, however, know of perennial losers who are such as a result, for example, of various addictions, ailments and other circumstances far beyond their control. For an in equal measure harrowing and amusing account of one such life see A. Masters, *Stuart: A Life Backwards* (London: Harper, 2006). For Honoré's view on this matter, see his 'Appreciations and Responses', ch. 9 of Cane and Gardner, supra, note 19 at p. 226.

outcomes put together: '[a]n accomplished surgeon who makes a fatal misjudgment may find all their life-saving work overshadowed by this one event, such is the response to losses as opposed to gains'.[30] But a fatal misjudgment, while it can undoubtedly have terrible consequences, surely cannot cancel out each and every advantage our imaginary surgeon has gained from outcome responsibility. It seems both crass and callous to say so, but the surgeon will most likely retain all the advantages accrued from the system of outcome responsibility up to this point and continue to live with those benefits, and accrue more, thereafter. Her career might change, but we do not expect her to sacrifice her life, nor her family nor her way of life as a result of this misjudgment. A terrible outcome that results from one's conduct does not often as a matter of fact eradicate all the life benefits and advantages gained up until that point. Of course, as a phenomenological matter the wrong-doer in such a case might well feel their life has 'ended', might and should feel regret and guilt. But these are things we expect one another to 'get over' eventually and they do not, in most instances, actually reduce the life of the wrongdoer to nothing, to destitution or complete meaninglessness and ruin. While outcome responsibility does indeed lumber us with the horrible outcomes of some of our conduct, it does not and should not, in so doing, eradicate the good outcomes also accrued.

It is for these reasons, then, that this notion of fairness should not be regarded as infirm. It is certainly not as flimsy as some have thought and, indeed, seems as robust as the other notion of fairness Honoré invokes. That being so, and the justification Honoré offers being *prima facie* sound, we can turn to two remaining tasks. The first is to examine how well Honoré's account performs in relation to the plausibility conditions for mixed theories in particular; the second involves assessing whether or not it satisfies the general conditions for any plausible account of the normative foundations of private law.

RANKING AND COMMENSURABILITY

Honoré's mixed account of the normative basis of tort law contains four obvious values: corrective justice, risk-distributive justice, retributive justice and the class of systemic values. In addition, it contains a particular conception of responsibility – outcome responsibility – which is not appropriately regarded as a value because, on Honoré's account at least, it is a constituent of agency and identity. Regarding it as a value might

[30] Steele, supra, note 23, p. 96.

suggest that the notion could be abandoned or reconstructed if of less value than originally thought, but Honoré seemingly regards it as more fundamental than that (*RF*, pp. 29–30). Whether or not he is right about that is not of current concern. The question that demands immediate attention is this: how do the elements of this mixed account fit together and how, if at all, are they ranked in relation to one another?

The answer is reasonably clear. There is a ranking between the components of this mixed theory, although probably only an ordinal one. It is clear that the most fundamental value, given its justificatory role supporting both outcome responsibility and corrective justice, is risk-distributive justice. It is pre-eminent, for without it the latter two notions lack justificatory normative support. Both the value of corrective justice and the notion of outcome responsibility are nevertheless important and, it seems, more important for Honoré than either retributive justice or the class of systemic values. This much seems clear from the fact that Honoré says corrective justice is 'tempered by' (*RF*, p. 92) systemic values and retributive justice, which surely casts them in a subsidiary role. Indeed, it seems that systemic values and retributive justice are subsidiary in a double sense for, not only does 'tempering' suggest the priority of that which is tempered, it is also likely as a practical matter that these two are not always in play in tort law. Thus tort cases are quite conceivable in which, for example, questions about the range of the applicable legal rule, or about the proportionality of the costs as compared to the wrong done, simply do not arise. By contrast, corrective and risk-distributive justice, as well as outcome responsibility, are surely in play in every tort case.

While it is clear from Honoré's presentation that corrective justice is more important than either retributive justice and systemic values, it is not certain which of the latter two dominate when a conflict arises between them. Conflict is perfectly conceivable in the right circumstances: it is not impossible to imagine a plausible scenario in which some damage or loss is foreseeable but entirely out of proportion with the agent's conduct. Indeed, such instances need not be the work of the imagination, as an examination of cases like *The Wagon Mound (No. 1)* and *(No. 2)*[31] shows. So, which dominates: the value of retributive justice or the systemic values? The fact that Honoré treats the former first is a very slender reed upon which to rest an argument that he gives it substantive priority. That reed may receive a little support from the observation that the systemic values are far more specific (and thus less important)

[31] No. 1 is reported at [1961] AC 388; No. 2 at [1967] 1 AC 617.

than retributive justice, but this, too, is far from compelling. Why, for instance, should we assume that greater specificity implies a lower level of importance? Furthermore, it could be the case that, as a matter of everyday practice, judges will regard a more specific consideration as more important than a general consideration, for the simple reason that the latter are less tractable. Thus the more vague or general a consideration is, the more difficult it may be to work with; it is thus disadvantaged in any conflict with more specific considerations.

Perhaps the only tenable judgment about the relationship between retributive justice and systemic values is this: they are less important than risk-distributive and corrective justice, but cannot themselves be ranked as against one another. Whether this is a deliberate ploy by Honoré or simply an oversight cannot be decided by reference to the text alone. The failure to rank these two values, or to even address the issue of their possible parity, is clearly a weakness in a mixed account but far from fatal. It is rather a point on which further guidance is needed and could easily be provided. Since this failure does not obscure the general structure of the ranking offered in Honoré's theory, it can simply be highlighted and then set aside. Nor can it be taken as a sign that some of the values in play in Honoré's mixed account are incommensurable. Since there is an obvious ranking in the account, and since the issue of incommensurability is never explicitly addressed, there is no plausible basis for the claim that Honoré is a proponent of incommensurability.

FIT, INTELLIGIBILITY AND THE KEY QUESTIONS

How does Honoré's argument perform in relation to the general conditions that any acceptable account of the normative foundation of private law must satisfy? That his argument satisfies the specific plausibility conditions for mixed accounts provides no guidance on this question. Moreover, since the account Honoré provides is narrow, and because we must allow the possibility that the account would include even more components were it generalized across the whole of private law, the question of its performance in relation to the general conditions might seem a false one. If it is not a general account, why hold it to the general conditions? The mistake in this question resides in the assumption that those *general* conditions – of fit, intelligibility and the key questions – apply only to *general* (or wide) accounts of the normative foundation of private law which are, of course, those that encompass the whole of private law. But the general conditions are not general in that sense; they are general because applicable to *any* effort to provide a normative foundation for all or part of private law. And there is one such condition in particular that Honoré's account, like all narrow accounts, struggles to satisfy, namely, the fit condition. This condition and the intelligibility condition, with which it overlaps, are tackled in the following subsection.

Fit and intelligibility

It might be thought that Honoré's account performs particularly well in relation to this condition because it fits reasonably well one aspect of the institution and practices of private law, namely, tort law. There are no obvious inconsistencies between the account and either the broad substance or structure of that aspect of private law. Furthermore, although Honoré does not spend much time discussing substantive tort law doctrine, he nevertheless successfully shows that his mixed account fits one feature of doctrine that has puzzled many, namely, vicarious liability (*RF*, p. 81). In doing so, he also shows that his account has some normative purchase on the institution since it can guide deliberation within this admittedly very limited but tricky aspect of it. If Honoré's account does that here, then it bodes well for other areas of doctrine. Yet our judgment on this issue must be tentative for the simple reason that doctrine does not feature in any great depth in Honoré's discussion.

That Honoré's account fits the structure of tort law reasonably well should come as no surprise since corrective justice is a key component of the account; that idea not only fits private and tort law's bipolar structure, it also makes normative sense of it. The latter is, of course, a manifestation of the intelligibility question in the normative context. What corrective justice does here is to provide a normative basis for the range of common sense and juristic assumptions manifest in the thought that it is 'obvious' why claimants can sue only 'defendants' who have harmed them and why defendants must correct the wrong they have done to claimants. Moreover, the theory of corrective justice in play in Honoré's mixed account is perfectly compatible with, indeed actually requires, an account of private law wrongdoing of the kind sketched in Chapter 6. It therefore avoids a problem that besets Ernest Weinrib's theory of corrective justice.

So far, so good. But there is a fly in the ointment: Honoré's account may not satisfy the fit requirement because it is narrow, throwing no light upon the normative foundation of other aspects of private law, particularly contract law. Contract is, after all, one of the key areas of private law with which we are concerned and can be accommodated, either directly or indirectly, by most corrective and distributive justice accounts of the normative foundation of private law. Can Honoré's account also be extended in this direction? Yes. Insofar as corrective justice makes sense of the structure and substance of contract law, then it can work in this way for Honoré just as it does for most corrective justice theorists. Corrective justice, though, must be justified by the risk principle and it is here that dissonance may be thought to arise, for what conceivable role can that principle have in contract law? Perhaps this. The principle that one takes the benefits of one's conduct when it turns out well and its disadvantages when it turns out badly is in play in contract law because promisors of full capacity, whose conduct has not been manipulated by the wrongful conduct of promisees, are normally bound by their contracts whether they turn out well or badly. Furthermore, in one light contract law is simply a means, albeit constrained by the values of individual liberty and fairness, of allocating the risks generated by particular transactions. While corrective justice obligations depend upon a fair background distribution of risk, on Honoré's view, it is surely also the case that it is perfectly legitimate in some instances for agents to re-allocate that distribution, or to allocate new risks, between themselves. This, at least, would seem legitimate if the parties were of roughly similar bargaining power and had behaved in a non-exploitative way toward one another.

Extending Honoré's account in this way clearly introduces additional values such as individual freedom and fairness but this is hardly likely to be a problem.[32] A mixed account of the normative foundation of private law is, obviously, *mixed*: it contains a range of values in some kind of relation or ranking. Unless the ranking is obviously suspect, or the values in play undeniably in conflict, the complaint that a mixed account contains a range of values is otiose. It seems, then, that in general terms at least, Honoré's account can be extended to reach beyond tort law; the fact that little or nothing is actually said about contract law is clearly a problem for him but it is not an insurmountable difficulty. While Honoré's account is assuredly narrow, it perhaps has the makings of a wide (or at least wider) account of the normative basis of private law. It seems in this way capable of being generalised.

Honoré's account is not the only mixed theory ensnared by this specific manifestation of the fit problem. It seems, in fact, that all mixed

[32] That these two values in particular fit well with the substance of contract law has been emphasized by many jurists: see, for a good discussion, C. Fried, *Contract as Promise* (Cambridge, Mass.: Harvard University Press, 1981). See also J. Kraus, 'Philosophy of Contract Law', ch. 18 of Coleman and Kraus, supra, note 21 and D. Kimel, *From Promise to Contract* (Oxford: Hart Publishing, 2003), ch. 3.

accounts invite this problem insofar as all are in one way or another narrow. Two examples will suffice. The first is an account of the normative foundation of tort law provided by Arthur Ripstein in his book *Equality, Responsibility, and the Law* (*ERL*),[33] while the second example consists of an account of the normative basis of contract law. Ripstein's account is narrow in the same way as is Honoré's, dealing with only one segment of private law, and might be thought to face even greater difficulty resolving the fit problem. Indeed, it might be held that Ripstein's theory vividly illustrates the troubling tendency in mixed accounts towards ever greater specificity at the cost of generality. The result is that such accounts fit well the detail of only one segment (part thereof) of private law but lack any general application. The situation is rather like having a perfectly tailored half-suit: the jacket fits brilliantly well but the trousers are not even close to being acceptable.

The central claim Ripstein makes about tort law is that it is a means of upholding fair terms of interaction between citizens, such terms being reciprocal in the sense that no one citizen can impose specific terms of interaction upon another (*ERL*, p. 2). Furthermore, Ripstein holds that citizens *qua* agents have at least two fundamental and different interests in liberty and security. These interests are embodied in '[f]air terms of interaction [which] must allow people freedom to do as they please, but also make sure that they secure from the activities of others' (*ERL*, p. 6). Within tort law, the way in which a balance is struck between these two abstract and fundamental interests in particular cases is through the mechanism of the reasonable person: '[t]he reasonable person is . . . the person who moderates his or her actions in light of the legitimate claims of others. Applied to circumstances of risk, the reasonable person does not expose others to more risk than is reasonable in light of fair terms of cooperation' (*ERL*, p. 56). Translated into an actual decision process, this requires that

> [w]e look to the liberty and security interests of representative persons – the reasonable person – and protect all equally with respect to those interests. To protect all equally requires weighing liberty against security, but any weighing is done within the representative reasonable person, rather than across persons. The point of weighing interests within a representative person is to avoid allowing the particularities of one person to set the limits of another's liberty or security. (*ERL*, ibid)

[33] Supra, note 2. Roughly half of Ripstein's book tackles the criminal law and is ignored here.

In addition to the values represented in the interests in security and liberty that all agents have, those of corrective and distributive justice are also part of the normative foundation of tort law on Ripstein's view. Thus there is no doubt that his account is genuinely mixed, although some questions can be raised about the specific ranking between these values. That, however, is not our current concern. Rather, the question before us is this: does Ripstein's account fit the law? The answer is: yes. Which is to say: most of the principal arguments and concepts deployed by Ripstein fit the structure and main contours of the substance of tort law, although some have cast doubt upon this both in general terms and, more particularly, with regard to Ripstein's understanding of the reasonable person.[34] So what is the problem?

It is that Ripstein's account fits the contours of tort law so well that it is not easily generalizable across private law as a whole. It seems to be a narrow account in the most restrictive sense, offering only an outline of the normative basis of tort law or, more accurately, some aspects thereof, and *nothing else*.[35] Think again of two of the values in play in tort law according to Ripstein: those embodied in agents' interests in security and liberty. While the latter may have some resonance in contract law, it seems unlikely that the former does. Indeed, the interest to be free from the activities of others runs contrary to contract law understood as a facilitative body of rules that allows agents to create legally binding obligations. In this respect, contract law is a means of co-opting one's own activities and interests with those of another and, furthermore, this liberty is neither morally nor politically insignificant. Clearly, then, contract law is not a means of protecting oneself against the activities of others and thus cannot be incorporated within Ripstein's schema. But this is surely an exaggeration.

For the components Ripstein has provided can, with a little extension, generate a normative basis for contract law. First, the interest in liberty that Ripstein says is in play in tort law can, as we have already noted, underpin contract law. The interest in liberty need not be envisaged solely as freedom from the interferences of others; nothing in Ripstein's

[34] See J. Gardner, 'The Mysterious Case of the Reasonable Person' (2001) 51 *University of Toronto Law Journal* 273–308.

[35] Except the criminal law, as already noted. In confining itself only to that tort segment of private law, it has much in common with the account of tort, again ostensibly mixed, developed by G. Keating. See his 'A Social Contract Conception of the Tort Law of Accidents', ch. 2 of G. Postema (ed.), *Philosophy and the Law of Torts* (Cambridge: Cambridge University Press, 2001).

account forbids conceiving the interest in liberty as including 'freedom to' as well as 'freedom from'. And, of course, contract law is a body of facilitative legal rules embodying a general freedom to create specific legal obligations in certain circumstances. Furthermore, contract law can be a means of protecting oneself against the activities of others in myriad ways, from insurance contracts protecting one against damage to contracts for the provision of private security. Moreover, contracting with another for the provision of goods or services is often a good means of protecting oneself from the predations of others: it is always preferable, if possible, to enter into a contractual agreement for a loan with a legitimate bank than with a loan shark. It thus seems that some of the values constitutive of the normative basis of tort law which, at first glance, seem unable to cast any normative light upon contract law, are not actually so limited. And some of the other values in play in Ripstein's account – corrective justice, for example – obviously have as much normative purchase upon contract as tort law. Although much depends upon the detail of the account of corrective justice invoked, its seems generally true that if the notion works (in the sense of making intelligible and illuminating moral significance) in one private law context it also works in others.

We can now turn, albeit very briefly, to the second example. The question is clear: how far can any or all of that family of accounts of the normative basis of contract law be generalized so as to illuminate the normative foundation of tort law? This is the opposite task to that undertaken in relation to Ripstein's and Honoré's accounts of the normative basis of tort law. Of course, not every member of this class of work can be examined here, but we can focus upon one for illustrative purposes: Charles Fried's *Contract as Promise* (*CP*).[36] This might seem the narrowest of narrow accounts of the normative basis of some aspect of private law, since it is apparently exclusively concerned with contract law and its underpinning values. There thus seems no chance whatsoever of Fried's argument casting any light upon the normative basis of other areas of private law. But, just as was the case with regard to Honoré and Ripstein, so too here: we are in the midst of an exaggeration. Without examining each and every account of the normative basis of contract law, the possibility cannot be ruled out that one or more such account is so narrow as to be inapplicable to any other branch of private law. Yet this possibility seems unlikely because the values usually thought to be in play in private

[36] Supra, note 32.

law are drawn from a pretty short list which almost always includes distributive, corrective and possibly retributive justice as well as fairness (insofar as it is distinct from notions of justice), liberty and security. Furthermore, in some circumstances these values do a great deal of work underpinning (or cutting across) a range of doctrinal boundaries. So, for example, it is no surprise whatsoever to find corrective justice in play in both contract and tort law. If these considerations are correct, then it seems dubious to expect Fried's or any other theorists' account of the normative foundation of contract to be incompatible with all other aspects of private law and their respective normative foundations.

Even the most perfunctory reading of Fried's argument shows a concern not just with delineating the range of contractual obligations and their underpinning values, but also with the admittedly different values and obligations found in other branches of private law (*CP*, pp. 21–27). Indeed, although he focuses in the main upon contract law, Fried's general task in doing so is to take steps toward clarifying the way in which the various branches of private law fit together. His aim is to illuminate what is valid in an old picture of the way in which the branches of private law relate (*CP*, p. 2). This is a particularly significant point, since it illuminates a potential tension in our aspirations for or expectations of mixed accounts of the normative foundation of private law. For, while it is assumed that such accounts must be general and thus applicable to private law as a whole, it is also the case that such accounts are expected to fit particular segments of private law. But an account of the normative basis of private law that fits the whole or large chunks of private law might, as a result of such generality, be unable to accommodate significant features of some of those chunks. The aspiration and drive towards generality must therefore be mediated by an appreciation of difference and particularity. This can be achieved by articulating both what is different and what is similar between the various segments of private law, in the manner that Fried hints at but does not explore in depth. It could, for example, be accepted that the respective normative foundations of contract and tort law are significantly different, while maintaining that the two areas are discernibly the same because both are in some sense branches of private rather than public law. That, of course, raises the somewhat unfashionable and neglected question noted in Chapter 1. It is re-examined in Chapter 11.

Another dimension of the fit problem as it manifests itself in Honoré's account highlights a source of dissonance rather than the problem of generalizability. The structure of Honoré's mixed account requires that risk-distributive justice justify both corrective justice and outcome responsibility. Were this requirement incorporated into private law adjudication then dissonance might well arise between one obvious feature of tort law and this account of its normative foundation. For it is clear that considerations of risk-distributive justice, just like considerations of equality of resources or those apposite in any other theory of distributive justice, play hardly any role at all in day to day tort law adjudication. Yet is one of the implications of Honoré's account that such considerations should play a role here? And, if it is, then the complaint against the two direct arguments about private law and distributive justice elucidated in Chapter 9 must also apply here. Thus, Honoré's mixed account does not fit the practice of tort law because it introduces considerations to that practice that are not salient within it; it turns the practice into something other than what it actually is.

It is not, however, obvious that Honoré must accept this implication. Upholding risk-distributive justice as a legitimacy condition of both corrective justice and outcome responsibility is not necessarily to insist that it become a salient factor within private law adjudication, the practice which by extension it also justifies. A legitimacy condition may function as a test for an institution in a wholesale one-off way, in a sense analogous, for example, to the way in which structures might be judged safe or habitable. Surely both the Humber and Golden Gate suspension bridges were, during their construction, at the time of their completion and at numerous times since, subject to tests determining their structural integrity and safety. But once these tests are satisfied at some point the bridges are regarded as safe for use for long periods thereafter, subject perhaps to periodic inspections. Risk-distributive justice might function in a similar way with regard to any particular legal system or segment thereof. If the condition is satisfied by that legal system at some specific time, then the condition need not be in play thereafter either in general or in particular instances of adjudication. Similarly, the structural integrity of Humber and Golden Gate bridges is not tested each and every time a vehicle or person seeks to use them, if at some point each structure has been declared safe. That risk-distributive justice might function as a condition in something like this sense for Honoré is made even more likely by the fact that he, unlike Ronald Dworkin, makes no effort to show that this principle will or could operate in particular cases.[37] Clearly, those who

[37] See the discussion in Chapter 9 at pp. 363–368 for a reminder of Dworkin's position.

offer direct arguments about the relation between private law and distributive justice are not prohibited from regarding distributive justice as a condition in this sense. But, as is evident from Chapter 9, direct arguments are few and far between and the two considered there do not cast distributive justice in that role.

The key questions

Honoré's mixed account provides reasonably satisfactory answers to the three key questions. In the order stated in Chapter 7, those questions demand that an account of the normative foundation of private law specify: (i) the nature of the obligation to make recompense; (ii) the general normative basis of private law; and (iii) why the obligation to make recompense is an obligation to make financial recompense rather than simply to correct the wrong done. Taking the second and most general question first, Honoré's answer is clear, assuming it is legitimate to extrapolate from his narrow account of the normative foundation of tort law to an account of the normative foundation of private law in general. Honoré's view is that the normative foundation of private law is made up of risk-distributive, corrective and retributive justice and the systemic values, these being bound together by a particular conception of responsibility, namely, outcome responsibility. While quibbles and complaints can undoubtedly be raised of the components in this package, there can be no doubt that it gestures towards a reasonably comprehensive mixed account of the normative foundation of private law.

Turning to the first key question, which is not quite the most specific of the three, Honoré's answer is again clear. The nature of the obligation to make recompense is first and foremost a moral-cum-political and then a legal obligation owed by agents of full capacity to correct the wrongs they have caused or occasioned to their victims. Of course, the elements of this obligation must be specified in more detail: an account is required of 'full capacity', 'caused or occasioned' as well as an indication of what 'wrongs' are before it can be accepted wholesale. Some steps have been taken in each of these directions in the chapters in part I of this book and, as is evident from them, Honoré has been in the forefront of this enterprise. But rather than reiterate the discussions found there, it will be more worthwhile to specify the precise moral-cum-political basis of this obligation to correct. Clearly it is a binding moral obligation only if ultimately justified by the risk principle, operating in the role of legitimacy condition as sketched above. Since this principle justifies corrective justice, any obligation that arises from the latter must presumably derive its force from the former. At least, this must surely be the case in normal instances. There might, for example, be exceptional cases in which corrective justice generates an obligation to repair when it is not certain that the risk principle is satisfied. In such a case, morality could well favour victim over wrongdoer. Yet as a general matter, Honoré's position is unambiguous: risk-distributive justice justifies corrective justice; it must therefore justify most or all of the obligations that arise under the latter.

The *legal* obligation that arises under corrective justice is not, for Honoré, 'rigid'. That is, it does not follow from the fact that someone of full capacity has wronged another that the stringency of their duty to repair is always and ever the same. This is because it can be 'tempered' by two classes of consideration, namely, those arising from retributive justice and those subsumed under the heading of systemic values. Thus it is one thing to justify a duty to correct on Honoré's mixed account and quite another to determine the exact stringency of that duty. Furthermore, even though the values that temper corrective justice are *prima facie* juristic or legal values, there is no obvious reason why those that arise from retributive justice should not have application in the moral sphere. Indeed, on one view of morality in general and of our moral duties in particular, these duties should be far more sensitive to the particularities of both our character and circumstances. Moral duties are, then, quite unlike the allegedly inflexible and impartial duties the law places upon us. On this view considerations of retributive justice which, after all, do little more than limit the duty to correct in light of an assessment of the wrongdoer's conduct and character, should apply *a fortiori* to the determination of the moral duty to correct.

The precise weight of the obligation to correct is not easy to determine on Honoré's account. It seems plain that as a legal obligation it has the ostensibly heavy weight that all such obligations have: as a factor in practical deliberation the law purports to outweigh all other considerations. Thus, our legal obligations, viewed from the perspective of the law, are not 'all things considered' obligations to do as the law requires if and when we think that requirement ultimately correct. Legal obligations portray themselves as obligations to do what the law requires *regardless* of other considerations. As a matter of both morality and individual autonomy, we may resist the law's view of the power of the obligations it creates but, even when assessed as only a moral obligation, it seems that Honoré views the duty to correct as reasonably weighty. For, although he does not aim to present a map of all our values and an assessment of the nature of the various duties they generate, the tenor of his treatment of the obligation to correct is one of the utmost seriousness. And this is to be expected, since the obligation to correct often arises in cases when serious harm has occurred. Thus, while Honoré does not tell us the precise weight of the obligation to correct, he undoubtedly regards it as weighty.

A final and important point to note about Honoré's view of the obligation to correct is this: he specifies it in very broad terms. This is significant because it functions as an answer to the third and most specific key question, namely, why is it that the obligation to correct is assumed to be an obligation to make financial recompense? On Honoré's view this assumption should not be made: '[n]othing in the idea of corrective justice requires . . . compensation to be in money. Though in tort law it nearly always takes that form, outside of tort law various forms of substitute provision in kind or in services are treated as proper ways of making good the harm to the sufferer' (*RF*, p. 74). Corrective justice, then, imposes a duty to 'make good the harm' and that, of course, can be discharged in many different ways. Tort law's emphasis upon financial compensation is not a necessary implication of corrective justice for Honoré but, perhaps, simply a historical contingency. Certainly, he offers no argument to show that the emphasis upon financial compensation in tort law is a moral or political necessity. There are two plausible responses to this. It might be regarded as a failing, since the lack of an account of the damages remedy ignores an undeniably significant aspect of both tort and private law. Alternatively, it could be seen as a strength, since it shows a broader understanding of the nature of corrective justice than that displayed by those of its proponents who attempt to tailor it to the exact contours of private law. There are reasons against the former and in favour of the latter view.

As against the former, it should not be assumed without argument that all normative accounts of the basis of private law must fit each and every feature of the institution. While some aspects must be regarded as central, some will undoubtedly be categorized as peripheral. Failure to give a corrective justice-based rationale for the damages remedy seems particularly problematic only if that remedy is focused upon to the exclusion of others. While this tendency is common among corrective justice theorists, there is no good reason to follow them. Indeed, an appreciation of the variety of remedies in private law undermines the plausibility of many corrective justice theories.[38] Moreover, that the idea of corrective justice provides no immediate normative justification for some particular legal remedy will come as no surprise to one who locates that notion in a wider moral-cum-political context. Once freed from the narrow context of tort or private law, corrective justice can be seen as having much in common with many other obligations that we owe to others and with notions like reparation.[39] Conceived broadly, there is no reason to expect our values to do a great deal of detailed normative work such as, for example, determining which of the range of legal remedies is normatively required. Rather, such values may often do nothing more than set the moral and political constraints within which we operate. And precisely how we operate – how we individually conduct ourselves and the detailed social institutions and practices we adopt – within such constrains may be normatively indeterminate. Thus, while corrective justice may morally require that individual agents (and perhaps even the state) do something about the wrongs they do to others, it need not specify precisely what should be done. To demand more than this may be to expect too much of our values.

It seems, then, that Honoré's mixed account performs reasonably well, both in relation to the specific conditions for such accounts and with regard to the more general conditions, including the provision of answers to the key questions, that any theory of the normative basis of private law must satisfy. For present purposes, we can be satisfied that Honoré sketches the broad contours of a *prima facie* plausible mixed theory of the normative foundation of private law.

PROSPECTS

What are the prospects for mixed accounts of the normative foundation of private law? Do they perform any better than the accounts considered in Chapters 8 and 9 whose weaknesses made mixed accounts seem a salient alternative? These questions admit of no easy answer. Perhaps the best way of approaching them is to begin with the fit problem,

[38] See B. Zipursky, 'Civil Recourse, Not Corrective Justice' (2003) 91 *Georgetown L J* 695–756 at pp. 710–714.

[39] When placed in such a context it also raises questions much broader than those traditionally raised by discussions of corrective justice in private law such as: how far back in time does the obligation to correct go? And: why is it a duty only to correct the harm caused rather than that aspect of wrongdoer's conduct or character that led to it?

the snag that causes greatest difficulty for the mixed accounts discussed here.

Generalizability is the particular dimension of the fit problem that causes the difficulty: the mixed accounts which featured in our discussion were all narrow and thus doubt arose about whether they could be extended to other areas of private law (and contract law in particular). This gives rise to at least two interesting and problematic issues. The first can be put in the form of a question: is it a mistake to think the narrow mixed accounts that have featured in the discussion should be generalizable? The thought underlying this question is well founded, it being undeniably true that neither Honoré, Ripstein nor Fried intends to give an account of the normative foundation of private law. Yet even though they do not attempt anything more general than the task of illuminating the normative foundation of either tort law or contract, can they nevertheless be called to account for this 'failure'?

This is only a failure, of course, if there is a broader intelligible question about the nature of private law and that question, clearly, assumes there is something discernible that falls within the parameters of the concept 'private law'. The question about the nature of private law is unfashionable but that does not mean it should be ignored. And it is implausible to think that for Honoré, Ripstein and Fried there is no such thing as private law. This is too bold a claim to accept in the absence of detailed and explicit supporting argument and that, of course, is not provided by any of these jurists.[40] It is therefore not unreasonable to suppose that these jurists accept that the concept of private law is meaningful. They are certainly not alone if they do think that. The idea that the concept of private law is in some sense unitary and refers to a distinctive body of law is very deeply entrenched in legal thinking, although perhaps more deeply embedded in civilian than in common law legal thought. That being so, it is not wildly inappropriate to attempt to extend the mixed accounts considered here beyond their narrow and self-imposed confines. It is also the case that mixed accounts ought to be capable of some degree of generality if only in order to compete with most corrective and distributive justice accounts of the normative foundation

[40] Public law hardly features at all in either Honoré's *RF* or Ripstein's *ERL* and features in Fried's *Contract as Promise* (supra, note 32) only as a point of contrast. *RF* occasionally addresses aspects of the criminal law, but usually only *en passant*; it features far more significantly in *ERL*, but neither Honoré nor Ripstein would accept that the criminal law is in any significant sense the same as private law. For these two, and for Fried, contract, tort, unjust enrichment and property law have more in common with one another than does any member of this list and public law.

of private law. These competitor accounts, remember, usually focus on only one segment of private law yet all promise a greater degree of generality.

The generalizability dimension of the fit problem raises a second issue. It concerns the weight accorded to generality considered as a virtue of accounts of the normative foundation of private law. It does not seem that generality is a pre-eminent virtue in such accounts, the reason being that these accounts should be sensitive to differences between the various branches of private law. There is no *a priori* reason to think that the different branches of private law should have exactly the same normative basis. It is neither impossible nor implausible to maintain that these branches differ in this respect but are still sufficiently similar in other respects to be subsumed under the private law label. Yet when the generalizability dimension of the fit problem is mediated by a requirement to illuminate difference and particularity, we face a complex judgment which is likely to be to the fore in any choice made between competing mixed accounts. For it is probable that more than one mixed account can satisfy most of the particular and general plausibility conditions, thus leaving open the issue of how to choose between them. While this choice could be made solely on moral or political grounds, this way of choosing risks overlooking features of the institution that do not match the moral and political grounds upon which the choice is made. An appreciation of these potentially dissonant features is, of course, encouraged by sensitivity to particularity and difference.

The capacity of mixed accounts to mediate generality and particularity is in one light their key advantage. Unlike accounts that invoke either distributive or corrective justice, which seem committed to the view found strange by Roberto Unger in the statement at the head of this chapter, mixed accounts are neutral on the degree to which private law or some aspect thereof coheres with some or other value or normative theory. Unger additionally claimed that the belief that some or other richly developed normative theory coincides with or matches the requirements of the law is a 'daring and implausible sanctification of the actual'.[41] The point is a good one for, even though he makes it in relation to statute law, it is also surely true of the process of doctrinal development in the common law. Anyone with even a passing familiarity with the history of that process could not plausibly maintain either that the common law followed

[41] R. Unger, *The Critical Legal Studies Movement* (Cambridge, Mass.: Harvard University Press, 1986), p. 9.

some preordained normative blueprint or that it serendipitously happened to match such a blueprint. And the existence of some all-embracing, single normative blueprint which provides the normative foundation of private law is just what mixed theories doubt. In starting with this assumption, mixed theories surely have the balance of advantage over their competitors at the outset. Whether or not that initial advantage is maintained or even increased depends upon how well particular mixed theories satisfy the general plausibility conditions.

The mediation of generality and particularity highlights another feature that philosophical accounts of private law should have. This feature has emerged somewhat haltingly in the treatment of both intelligibility and normative questions and has not until now been explicitly labelled. It is that philosophical accounts of private law, be they normative, conceptual or a combination of the two, should be 'made-to-measure' rather than 'off-the-peg'. Mixed accounts of the normative basis of private law are closer to being made-to-measure because they have the capacity to fit the particularities of the various branches of private law. The fact that they are mixed, that they begin with the assumption that it is unlikely that a single normative blueprint coincides with the law, allows sensitivity to difference, just as a made-to-measure suit is cut to fit the contours of particular person for whom it is made. An off-the-peg suit is, of course, designed to fit the generality of people in a particular size range and, as a result, may fit no one particularly well. Non-mixed accounts of the normative foundation of private law may well operate in this way, fitting some aspects of private law but not others, or covering all areas but fitting none very well. The preference for made-to-measure philosophical accounts of private law over off-the-peg is in part driven by the desire to take the institution and its constitutive practices seriously, in their own terms or at face value. This does not mean that the institution must be regarded in advance as conceptually or normatively respectable, but rather that it be approached with an open mind: the chances of it being conceptually and normatively respectable are surely the same as it being conceptually and normatively disreputable.

Finally, the most difficult question: do mixed accounts of the normative foundation of private law have a promising future, or are they every bit as problematic as the accounts offered by proponents of corrective and distributive justice? In absence of an exhaustive examination of all the available mixed theories (almost all of which are narrow) and all their competitors, this question cannot be answered. What can be said is that the mixed theory examined in detail here shows in broad outline the form a promising mixed account must take, while illuminating the ways in which the plausibility conditions for such accounts might be satisfied. When married to the advantage mixed accounts gain from including corrective justice as one of their components – thus in part stealing whatever thunder corrective justice accounts might claim to have – the implication is that such accounts present an intellectually enticing project. This much is reaffirmed if the capacity of mixed accounts to accommodate generality and difference is regarded as a virtue. That, of course, is far from being a ringing endorsement; it is, however, marginally more positive than the judgments reached in relation to corrective and distributive justice accounts. Thus, in the domain of philosophy of private law at least, the (intellectual) prospects for the future seem to be mixed.

11

Conclusion

The structure and arguments of this book are, in broad terms at least, easily recapped. Part I claimed that private law embodies a particular conception of responsibility, namely, outcome responsibility. It is within the context of this conception of responsibility that the components of liability-responsibility – the conditions that have to be satisfied for many forms of liability in private law – must be understood. It was argued that liability-responsibility in private law has three genuine components: basic responsibility, conduct and causation, and wrongfulness. In Chapter 3 an attempt was made to show the significance and nature of the notion of basic responsibility in private law, it being shown that this notion has at least three related sub-components, namely, intention, rationality and general capacity. Chapter 5 argued that the conduct often required to trigger particular forms of liability in private law includes both acts and omissions and a causal link between such conduct and some particular harm suffered by the claimant. It was claimed that the act/omission distinction is not particularly problematic in private law and a defence and partial retrenchment of one particularly powerful account of causation was also attempted. An agent who is responsible in the basic sense and whose conduct harms another will face private law liability only if, in addition, the harm caused falls within the catalogue of wrongs recognized by the law. Chapter 6 examined the nature and possible normative bases of this catalogue, arguing that wrongfulness in private law has two distinct dimensions which must not be overlooked. One alleged component of private law liability-responsibility – that captured by the principle of alternate possibilities – was discussed in Chapter 4. It was argued that this is not a genuine component, being better regarded as an extension or elaboration of some aspects of basic responsibility.

Part II of the book tackled one question: what is the normative foundation of private law and how should such a foundation function and be understood? Some of the different possibilities here were sketched in Chapter 7, while the remaining chapters examined three particular efforts to provide private law with a normative foundation. Chapter 8 tackled the idea of corrective justice as articulated by two of its most important recent proponents. In the course of considering how well corrective justice functioned as a normative foundation, the conclusion reached was that, of the two versions of corrective justice considered, one was slightly less problematic than the other, although both threw into relief some awkward questions of method. The notion of distributive justice and a variety of arguments about its relation to private law were examined in Chapter 9. The variety of arguments about distributive justice's allegedly foundational role in relation to private law meant generalizations were hard to come by. Perhaps the only generalization that emerged from the discussion in Chapter 9 was that distributive justice is incompatible with some features of private law. Because neither corrective nor distributive justice promised a completely unproblematic account of the normative foundation of private law, a final possibility was examined in Chapter 10. One mixed account of the normative foundation of private law was examined in some detail, the tentative conclusion being that this type of account could well incorporate the advantages and avoid the problems of its competitors.

The arguments of Parts I and II are far from complete and give rise to a number of questions. Three such questions are flagged up in the remainder of this chapter, but not until one other feature of the book's arguments is noted: they are in the main *ad hominem*. The arguments of particular jurists and philosophers have been to the fore in almost every chapter, with relatively little attention given over to generalities. This might seem a petty-fogging approach, submerged in detail and blind to broad movements of thought. Yet while there is some truth in this accusation, there is also a partial defence: in this context, broad movements of thought and grandiose intellectual visions only become available to us through particular texts. It is therefore not a mistake to take those texts and their arguments seriously, subjecting them to close study. Of course, devoting attention to particular arguments leaves little space to tackle broader issues and ensures that there is a near permanent 'extrapolation gap'. This arises because the general inferences drawn in this book about, for example, the limits of corrective or distributive justice accounts of the normative foundations of private law are based upon analysis of particular examples of such accounts, there being no guarantee that all corrective or distributive justice accounts display the limitations of the particular examples. Thus it may well be that some of the arguments offered in Parts I and II succeed in relation to the particular jurists' work against which they are aimed but fail at a general level. This gap has to be endured as the cost of beginning the analysis with a clear grasp of particular issues and arguments; these, after all, are the only guides we have to the shape of broad movements of thought. Only with such a grasp can one be sure of either advancing the discussion or of perceiving its limits. We can now turn to three of the questions left open by the arguments of Parts I and II.

JOINING TOGETHER WHAT WAS SPLIT ASUNDER

The main burden of the analysis of the components of legal liability-responsibility in Part I was to show which components are in play in private law and to make sense of them. The primary task was to attempt to make those components intelligible. Part II tackled three broadly different accounts of the normative basis of private law. These accounts in principle function so as to provide a normative basis for both the core substantive and structural concepts of private law. Thus components of liability-responsibility as well as doctrines like, for example, duress in contract, might ostensibly depend upon a normative foundation. Is it therefore sensible to separate intelligibility questions from normative questions in the way that has been attempted here? Since the components of liability-responsibility we have attempted to make intelligible can clearly be subject to moral, political or other kinds of normative evaluation, why bother separating the two types of question?

It is appropriate at this point to recall what the discussion of these two types of question in Chapters 1, 2 and 6 made clear, namely, that the distinction is not absolute. So, for example, it was accepted that there can be a good deal of fruitful traffic across the border between these two types of question and that answers to one can influence answers to the other. Furthermore, the normative underpinnings of specific understandings of some components of legal liability-responsibility were also highlighted at numerous points in Part I. Yet these underpinnings do not represent the limit of private law's normativity. For it can quite plausibly be maintained that the components of liability-responsibility in private law, or in any other area of law for that matter, are normative in this obvious and fundamental way: they add up to a body of standards by which the conduct of agents is judged. This is undeniable if it is a feature of law's nature that it is a means of subjecting human conduct to the governance of rules and, in so doing, judging human conduct and its authors by reference to those rules.[1] If law is a body of rules and standards by which human conduct is judged, then law is normative in the same way as any other body of conduct-guiding rules (like the rules of grammar, for instance). It is because they are normative in this sense that the conduct-guiding rules of any legal system give rise to two distinct moral-cum-political worries. One is about the coercive power the application of those rules can unleash, while another concerns the link, if any, between the content of those rules and the content of morality.

These worries, and the normative issues that precede them, have featured at numerous points in the preceding chapters. Distinguishing intelligibility questions from normative questions has not therefore impeded our perception of the issues. Nor has illuminating intelligibility and normative questions, the issues they raise and the ways in which they intersect, made it obvious that questions of the former kind are always strictly reducible to questions of the latter type. Only if that were so would the distinction be imperilled. One strategy that might seem to imperil the distinction consists of insisting that the notion of responsibility in play in private law and, presumably, the components of liability-responsibility discussed in Part I are 'political'. Arthur Ripstein is one proponent of this claim, but it is uncertain exactly what it entails.[2] In holding that the conception of responsibility in play in tort and criminal law is political, Ripstein intends to distinguish it from a metaphysical or moral conception of responsibility. The primary advantage of so distinguishing is that a political conception is supposedly free a number of philosophical snags, like that about the individuation of conduct, which dog moral and metaphysical conceptions.

Yet it is unclear why calling a conception of responsibility political rather than moral or metaphysical should have this remarkable insulating effect: the issue of whether Ripstein's conception is subject to the difficulties that ensnare other conceptions is surely not a matter of terminology but of substance. It would, in other words, actually have to be shown that this conception is indeed free from these difficulties. Furthermore, it was noted in Chapter 3 that the basic responsibility component of private law legal liability-responsibility is not immune to these general philosophical problems, although it was also noted that the courts resolve particular manifestations of these difficulties in a

[1] See L. L. Fuller, *The Morality of Law* (New Haven: Yale University Press, revised edn, 1969), p. 46.

[2] *Equality, Responsibility, and the Law* (Cambridge: Cambridge University Press, 1999), pp. 12–15.

pragmatic manner. This, however, is not a result of the conception of responsibility – outcome responsibility – being political rather than moral or metaphysical. It is simply an observation that the imperative to decide actual cases short-circuits philosophical disputes and that the law's philosophical commitments are often blunt between competing theories. That the conception of responsibility in play in private law is thus to some extent free from the problems that beset moral and metaphysical conceptions is true, but this is true because of contingent institutional features of the law itself and not as a result of labelling or categorization.

Whether or not the conception of responsibility outlined in Part I should be regarded as political on Ripstein's view is also unclear – much would depend on the consequences of deploying this label over and beyond its alleged capacity to avoid philosophical snags. Of what additional significance is it to claim that the conception of responsibility embodied in private law is political? Jules Coleman has offered an argument to show that the conception of responsibility in private law is not independent of the practice of holding agents responsible and this might also amount to an argument showing that that conception is political. At the very least, the argument that private law's conception of responsibility is not independent is made in conjunction with an argument that there is no 'pre-political' conception of responsibility against which the legal conception must be judged.[3] Coleman might thus be making the claim that if there are no pre-political conceptions of responsibility then there are only political conceptions. On this view, any conception of responsibility embodied in a set of practices and, presumably, an institution like private law, must be political and not pre-political. What are we to make of this?

The components of legal liability-responsibility examined in Part I are undoubtedly bound up in an institution and set of practices. That, after all, is what makes them components of *private law* liability-responsibility rather than another form of responsibility. On Coleman's view those components are therefore presumably political, one implication of this being that they are not pre-political, which, it seems, means they are *not* 'independent of our institutions of responsibility'.[4] But why must we accept that conceptions of responsibility are either embedded in

[3] *The Practice of Principle* (Oxford: Clarendon Press, 2001), pp. 46–53.

[4] Ibid, p. 50.

practices and institutions or completely free of them? Is it impossible for conceptions of responsibility to exceed the boundaries of the institutions and practices in which they originated or are often found? Furthermore, is it certain that a general account of responsibility cannot be formulated from the various particular conceptions embedded in practices and institutions? Surely we can talk in general terms – free from reference to specific practices and institutions – of what it is to be a responsible being, or of the limits and bearers of responsibility? And it is surely this kind of generality to which many philosophical accounts of responsibility aspire.

It is difficult to see the precise basis of Coleman's objection to such general responsibility talk, although it is clear that he is opposed to it. Furthermore, his apparent denial that there is a general practice- and institution-independent notion of responsibility – 'there is no single sense of responsibility that underlies all or our practices and institutions of responsibility' – seems ripe for refutation in the same way as are practice-based accounts of the morality of promising.[5] But whether or not a general notion of responsibility is possible and, if it is, what might be its relation to the conceptions of responsibility found in various institutions and practices, is not particularly relevant to the point in issue here. For although the discussion in Part I often compares the components of private law legal liability-responsibility with other, supposedly more general and usually moral or common sense, conceptions of responsibility, there is no implication that the latter must be independent of various practices and institutions. This part of Coleman's argument need not therefore cause us much concern. Nor, in the end, need the other aspect of his argument. For we have already accepted that the components of legal liability-responsibility discussed in Part I are normative and embodied in an institution and its constitutive practices. In Coleman's language they might therefore be dubbed both political and practice-based. Does this in any way imperil the distinction between normative and intelligibility questions? Not unless the attempt to make the components of normative systems (like legal liability-responsibility in private law) intelligible is also a process of moral-cum-political evaluation. But why should it be? In what sense is every effort to understand *necessarily* a process of moral-cum-political evaluation? While it may be both impossible and

[5] The statement belongs to Coleman, ibid. For an attempted refutation of practice-based accounts of promising see T. Scanlon, 'Promises and Practices' 19 (1990) *Philosophy and Public Affairs* 199–226.

undesirable to separate these two aspects of thought in each and every instance, it is surely eminently possible to do this in many cases. It seems that both historians and anthropologists can understand conduct, practices and institutions very different from our own without necessarily judging them in moral or political terms. And, if that is so, it is also surely possible that philosophers and jurists can do the same when examining the institutions and practices of their own legal systems.

A final point about the distinction between intelligibility questions and evaluative questions. This distinction has been stressed on the following ground: it helps to avoid confusion and makes some matters clearer. There is no grander and more dubious claim in play here about, for example, the rationally suspect nature of moral or political evaluation or disputation. One can be the most rational or realist of moral rationalists or realists, or the most sceptical of moral non-cognitivists or emotivists, and still find this a useful distinction to draw. The distinction in itself is hardly ever a reliable guide to broader views of the nature of morality.

MADE-TO-MEASURE PHILOSOPHY

> A person who is trying to understand is exposed to distraction from fore-meanings that are not borne out by the things themselves
>
> H-G Gadamer, *Truth and Method* (London: Sheed and Ward, 1975), p. 236

The second question that remains open is this: what is and what should be the relation between a 'theory', 'account' or 'philosophy' of private law and its object? It was claimed at numerous points in the preceding chapters that accounts of private law should fit some of the principal structural and substantive features of the law and, where possible, make those features both intelligible and normatively respectable. There are, of course, no guarantees in this process. It cannot therefore be assumed that some or all of the principal substantive and structural features of private law will prove to be both intelligible and normatively respectable. This assumption seems particularly dubious when private law's history and complexity in the common law world is borne in mind: it is the work of many, many minds over a long period of time and has developed without the guidance that might be provided by a pre-existing blueprint. Given this, and the other entropic forces that shape the common law, it would be a surprise if private law doctrine contained no mistakes or wrong turnings.

The requirement that non-sceptical accounts of private law – or of any other institution or set of practices for that matter – must fit the institution and attempt to make it intelligible is always likely to be problematic.[6] One reason for this is that some accounts might fit some features of the institution while other features are accommodated by other accounts; different accounts may also make different sense (normative and other) of one and the same feature or set of features. That being so, how are we to judge which of these competing accounts better satisfies the requirements of fit and intelligibility? Insofar as the answer to this question is a matter of judgment, then the possibility arises that there might be more than one reasonable judgment. Thus while undoubtedly demanding, the fit and intelligibility requirements may not always generate clear answers to questions about the success or failure of particular accounts of private law or any other institution. Furthermore, the more complex the institution and set of practices in question, the greater is the space for differences to arise along the dimensions of fit and intelligibility. Yet it should not be assumed, in light of the variability between accounts of the nature of private law that this possibility permits, that the fit and intelligibility requirements do no genuine work in discriminating between competing accounts. Taken together, these requirements provide a caution to those who would offer an account of private law or any other institution which, at its most general, demands that the institution be taken seriously in its particularity and detail.[7]

It is easy to caricature this demand with an attempted *reductio*: taking private law seriously in its particularity and detail is, of course, what our textbooks do and they, obviously, are not *philosophical* accounts of private law. Yet this point can be accepted to some extent, although with the caveat that some legal textbooks are undoubtedly philosophically significant, without conceding the *reductio*. For while it is obvious that philosophical or jurisprudential accounts of private law should not simply replicate our textbooks, it is equally clear that such accounts do not have *carte blanche* to disregard significant features of private law. Without implying that

[6] Some of the most interesting recent sceptical accounts of private law belong to American Critical Legal Studies. Their scepticism derives from a number of claims such as, for example, that private law is 'ideological', 'political' and 'contradictory'. A classic example is D. Kennedy, 'Form and Substance in Private Law Adjudication' (1976) 89 *Harvard LR* 1685–1778.

[7] One of the best treatments of this issue and, indeed, of all the general issues that face philosophical accounts of private law is N. E. Simmonds, 'The Possibility of Private Law', ch. 6 of J. Tasioulas (ed.), *Law, Values and Social Practices* (Aldershot: Dartmouth Publishing, 1997).

the process is wilful, it is clear that a number of the accounts of private law considered here do indeed overlook very significant features of the institution. Some accounts of the components of legal liability-responsibility in private law, for example, either deny the existence of strict liability or assume its impropriety. This is often done on the basis of a commitment to a conception of responsibility clearly not embodied in private law. Liability-responsibility in private law often arises regardless of one's intentions and desert: philosophers and jurists who object to this are thus unable to account for a significant feature of the institution, never mind appreciate the conception of responsibility – outcome responsibility – it embodies. Similarly, those who offer normative accounts of the basis of private law that invoke either corrective or distributive justice are often unable to account for significant features of the institution. In the case of some theories of corrective justice, for instance, this manifests itself as an unwillingness to tackle the issue of wrongfulness in private law. In the case of some arguments from distributive justice the issue often arises as an inability to accommodate obvious features of the adjudicative process. On such arguments private law adjudication becomes a process quite different to that with which we are familiar.

The problem here might be this: these accounts of private law approach their object with some philosophical pre-commitments to the fore. One such pre-commitment is attitudinal. It is probably hardly ever explicitly articulated and ascribing it is thus a hazardous business. But it seems clear that an assumption which informs much of the philosophical and jurisprudential literature is that private law is in need of philosophical attention, that its ailments – the principal one being the forces of entropy that seem to shape it – can be cured by a dose of philosophical rigour. That pre-commitment is often joined by some or other substantive commitment like, for example, the belief that corrective justice (or some other normative notion) is the key to understanding the nature of private law. Only in light of some such notion will the underlying coherence of private law be disclosed; only some such notion as this keeps the forces of entropy at bay. One baleful consequence of substantive pre-commitments such as these is that the object of the account is shaped in the image of the pre-commitment, often with results that Procustes would be proud of.

This can perhaps be avoided by according the institution and its constitutive practices a proper respect. That term, along with cognates like 'taking it seriously' and 'appreciating its particularity', can sound alarmingly vague and in one sense they are: for it is not possible, in advance, to specify in detail what it is to give an institution or practice or even some segment of social conduct 'proper respect'. That is only genuinely disclosed by engaging with, by trying to understand and account for, the institution, practice or conduct in question. But in general and again quite vague terms, the matter might be put thus: taking the institution, practice or conduct seriously, or in its own terms, is to approach it with as few substantive philosophical pre-commitments as possible. This, of course, is to deny neither that some loosely theoretical pre-commitments make it possible for theorists or philosophers to perceive the institution, practice or conduct in question nor that some such pre-commitments must generate the theorist's or philosopher's interest in the first instance.

In order for theorists and philosophers to be able even to perceive the institution, practice or conduct that is of interest to them they must, of course, share the language of those whose institution, practice or conduct is in question. This point seems most obvious when undertaking anthropological or historical study, since groups distant from us in time, beliefs, complexity and social structure are most difficult to 'know'. When it is said that knowledge cannot be obtained of such groups without learning their language that is often literally true. But even groups with which we share a language are not immediately transparent to us simply by virtue of that fact: think, for example, of English-speaking societies and their legal systems. Significant knowledge of the latter is not obtained by virtue of learning English; far from it, as any first year law student will testify. Sharing a language simply makes the move towards 'thinking like a lawyer' easier. But without an appreciation of the specific meaning of the concepts this group employ no adequate understanding – an understanding they themselves would find intelligible – of their conduct, practices and institutions is possible. 'Thinking like a lawyer', just like 'thinking like an Zande tribesperson', is first and foremost a matter of mastering the language and concepts of that group.

That language, like any natural language, is an inter-linked system of discriminations, assumptions and preconceptions about the social and natural worlds. It will also be in part a language of self-description and evaluation, containing concepts and values specifying what a good lawyer or tribesperson is, as well as concepts illuminating what is in general good and bad. It is thus in no sense a value-free or perfectly 'neutral' method of representing the world beyond language, lacking theoretical constructs; it is rather, in some sense, a means of both organizing and having knowledge of the world.[8] On this broadly hermeneutic view, it makes no sense to think of language as a non-purposive, non-theoretical means of appropriating the world; and it is equally senseless to attempt to understand some social group's institutions, practices or conduct without learning their language.[9] But in learning the language of those whose conduct, institutions or practices one seeks to explain and understand, one must take up the roughly theoretical pre-commitments latent in that group's language. These pre-commitments are initially unavoidable, although they can at some point be interrogated and can perhaps be set aside.

Similarly, the theorist or philosopher must have some roughly theoretical pre-commitments in order for an area of study to become salient.[10] These determine the nature of the research questions on the agenda of a particular disciplinary group: thus sociologists' questions may well differ from those of the historian, economist, philosopher or jurist, but all are conditioned by some assumptions about why particular questions are worth asking. No contemporary social or political scientist would, for example, even think of developing a theory of holes in response to the question 'why are there holes and does their incidence vary between different political systems?'[11] That question is simply not on the agenda of political or social science because neither those disciplines nor the cultures in which they exist regard it as in any sense interesting. And all research questions are formed within a particular disciplinary and wider social context, so that the research questions salient for all theorists are in some sense the questions of the epoch, being influenced by ideas,

[8] A picture supposedly in opposition to this (usually associated with non-specified unreflective empiricists) is that a language is possible which reflects 'reality' immediately, without the use of theoretical constructs and evaluative terms. The former are taken to exceed the limits of empirical perception and thus regarded as somewhat dubious; the latter are taken to be irredeemably suspect because beyond the limits of cognition. Whether or not any social scientist or philosopher ever held such a crude view is a moot point, but it is sometimes associated with John Locke (see R. Rorty, *Philosophy and the Mirror of Nature* (Oxford: Blackwell, 1980), part two).

[9] The classic recent statement of the hermeneutic approach is H.-G. Gadamer, *Truth and Method* (London: Sheed and Ward, 1975). For his view of the importance and awkwardness of pre-commitments (which he calls 'fore-meanings') to understanding and interpretation, see pp. 235–274.

[10] The starting points here are: M. Weber, 'Value Judgements in Social Science', ch. 4 of W. G. Runciman (ed.), *Weber: Selections in Translation* (Cambridge: Cambridge University Press, 1978); 'The Logic of Historical Explanation', ibid, ch. 6; and his ' "Objectivity" in Social Science and Social Policy' in E. Shils and H. Finch (eds.), *The Methodology of the Social Sciences* (New York: Free Press, 1949).

[11] A closely related question was posed (tongue-in-cheek of course) by A. MacIntyre in his *Against the Self-Images of the Age* (Notre Dame: Notre Dame University Press, 1978), ch. 22, p. 260.

assumptions and theories influential in the wider culture. Without such questions, theorists lack a starting point for their studies, will have no reason not to develop, for example, a political or social (as opposed to a cosmological) theory of holes. That research questions are conditioned in this way certainly does not imply that the processes by which starting points and the ways in which certain research agendas or 'questions of the epoch' become salient cannot be subject to sociological, philosophical, historical or economic study.

Since in these two instances it seems that some broadly theoretical pre-commitments are unavoidable, the claim that theorists and philosophers of private law ought to approach their object of study without pre-commitments is clearly dubious. But the pre-commitments had in mind by proponents of this claim need not be those just elucidated. While those pre-commitments are indispensable, other more substantive pre-commitments might not be. And it might be such substantive pre-commitments that undermine some philosophical accounts of private law in the sense that they impede appreciation of important features of the institution. A particular conception of corrective or distributive justice, or a conception of responsibility, surely count as substantive theoretical pre-commitments in the sense that they are not essential to either apprehend private law nor vital in order to make a theoretical interest in that object either salient or possible. Notions such as these should not, then, be to the fore at the *beginning* of an examination of private law but may well be the *outcome* of such an examination. Yet if a particular conception of responsibility or of corrective or distributive justice is to be such an outcome it must, of course, be consistent in most respects with the object in question: it must fit private law and make it intelligible. If, by contrast, such conceptions are genuine pre-commitments they will impede an account of that institution in the sense of making only some aspects of it visible: the substantive theoretical pre-commitment picks out in advance and regards as significant only those features of the institution upon which it confers salience. And it does this regardless of the view of the participants whose conduct in part constitutes the institution and its constitutive practices.

If some conceptions of responsibility or of corrective or distributive justice, or other notions, do indeed function as pre-commitments in many philosophical accounts of private law, then it is no surprise that such accounts miss some significant features of the institution. Such pre-commitments function rather like an ideal conception of the human body in tailoring clothes: the clothes produced will undoubtedly fit everyone in some respects but fit almost no one very well. If the ideal person of my stature has arms of a certain length then clothes designed on that basis may fit me but they may not: it depends how closely I approximate the ideal. This, of course, is a general problem with off-the-peg tailoring. By contrast, made-to-measure or bespoke clothing is designed to fit me, not some ideal conception of a person of my age or height. Such clothing is made on the basis of a template – a series of measurements – of me, in all my particularity. I'm measured first and then the clothing is made to fit. Philosophical accounts of private law could be constructed in a similar way, but only if the institution is in the first instance treated in such a way as to appreciate all its particularities and significant features. Once that is done, it might well be 'accounted for' in philosophical terms, the theory or account or explanation or understanding being designed to fit that particular institution. Of course, the case for tailor-made philosophies of private law is a long way indeed from being made out by these reflections; the charge that some existing accounts are off-the-peg is also a long way from being conclusively made out. But we now nevertheless have an admittedly inchoate answer, or the makings of an answer, to the question with which this section began: the relation between private law (the institution and its constitutive practices) and philosophical accounts of it should be made-to-measure not off-the-peg. This should not be taken to imply either that a theoretical (or philosophical) understanding of private law is impossible or that particular kinds of philosophical approach are unworthy.[12]

WHAT'S PRIVATE ABOUT PRIVATE LAW?

> The rough intuitive distinction between the distributive or "social" justice of the basic structure, and the more procedural (or "civil") justice of transactions within that structure cannot be expected to precisely map the conventional distinction between public and private law.
>
> N. E. Simmonds, 'Justice, Causation and Private Law' in M. Passerin d'Entreves and U. Vogel, *Public and Private* (London: Routledge, 2000), p. 163

It does not take a great deal of scepticism to think that this question, posed initially in the first chapter and touched upon intermittently in subsequent chapters, is still unanswered. Indeed, for a moderate sceptic

[12] For an argument that comes close to making the first claim, see S. Waddams, *Dimensions of Private Law* (Cambridge: Cambridge University Press, 2003); and for an instance of the second, see R. Posner, *The Problematics of Moral and Legal Theory* (Cambridge, Mass.: Harvard University Press, 1999).

this much might be expected, since the question about the distinctive nature of private law is simply a red herring. Attempting to answer it is like nailing jelly to a wall. This moderate sceptic might also point out that a number of hints about the dubious nature of this question appear in the chapters of this book but, somewhat balefully, they have been ignored.

One such hint was ignored in the first chapter: it was noted there that the question about the nature of private law is not fashionable and, our moderate sceptic can now add, it is obvious why. Since there is no such thing as private law, then no sane jurist or philosopher will waste time tackling questions about its nature. Furthermore, none of the work that has featured in the discussions in Parts I and II has been concerned with some abstract notion of private law and its alleged distinctiveness. All the work featured here has, rather, been concerned only with particular branches of law, principally contract and tort. Again, this is surely a hint ignored: if there is an interesting question about 'private law', why is it ignored by these scholars? A hint was also provided by the occurrence of two common problems in the works discussed here. These are the problems of fit and generalizability. In both Part I and II it was noted that some accounts of some features of private law, be it one or other of its components of legal liability-responsibility or an argument about its normative foundation, struggled to fit other features. It was also noted, principally in Part II, that some accounts of the normative foundation of private law were actually only accounts of the normative foundation of one segment of private law. A problem with such normative accounts was that of generalizing them. But it now seems obvious why the fit and generalizability problems loom so large in the preceding chapters. The misguided idea that there is something usefully and discernibly categorized as 'private law' has led us to stretch and mangle arguments that were in no sense intended to address that (chimerical) subject, either directly or indirectly.[13]

Is there nothing in the works analysed and the arguments offered in Parts I and II that illuminates the nature of private law? The two most obvious candidates for this role are, of course, the argument from private law's bilateral structure and the notion of corrective justice. It might thus be maintained that what makes private law distinctive is the nature of the

[13] Of course, one of the texts discussed in Chapter 8 promises an account of 'private law' (E. Weinrib, *The Idea of Private Law* (Cambridge, Mass.: Harvard University Press, 1995)) and it is not alone in using that term, as is clear from two recent texts that do not feature in this book: Waddams, supra, note 12; J. Gordley, *Foundations of Private Law* (Oxford: Clarendon Press, 2006).

relationship between claimant and defendant. The principal features of this relationship are: (i) claimant alleges that the defendant has wronged him and thus seeks a remedy from defendant; (ii) the remedy consists of defendant having to do something to correct the wrong: for example, defendant may be required to pay an amount of money to claimant commensurate with the loss defendant's wrong caused the claimant; (iii) claimant must sue defendant – the person who has allegedly caused his wrong – rather than a wealthier third party or the state; and (iv) defendant, if liable, must compensate claimant rather than direct claimant to a wealthier third party or the state. The notion of corrective justice is invoked to give normative substance to these features that define the bilateral structure of private law. Thus corrective justice allegedly provides a normative explanation of why claimants sue defendants (rather than third parties); why defendants adjudged liable must compensate claimants and, in some cases – although much depends on the particular theory of corrective justice in play – why the remedy must take the form it often does in private law.

The answer to the unanswered question is, then, neither as difficult nor mysterious as the moderate sceptic implies: private law is distinctive because it embodies a bilateral relation based upon corrective justice. But if this is what makes private law 'private', then there is indeed a large difficulty. For surely legal action in public law – in some jurisdictions, at least – has this bilateral structure and can thus be said to embody corrective justice? There are, of course, different procedural rules (about *locus standi*, for example) and different remedies available in public law as compared to private law, but the relationship is structured in the same way. A claimant must take action against a specific defendant and allege that a wrong has been done that stands in need of correction; if the court agrees then it is the defendant who must correct the wrong done. Of course, the defendant may be a government department or other representative of local or central government or of some other quasi-government body, but why is this significant? In a private law action either claimant or defendant (or both) could be representatives of one or other form of government.

It is usually the case that the wrong alleged in a public law dispute is unlike those alleged in private law disputes. Public law wrongs often involve the failure of a public or quasi-public body to do something or to act properly; thus they seem rather different from run of the mill private law disputes about, for example, road traffic accidents or failures to deliver goods. But are these differences so significant as to justify the claim that the two legal domains must be regarded as categorically different? The different rules of standing and different remedies in private law and public law could become significant if a sufficiently detailed theory of corrective justice required a specific set of remedies and rules of standing, the required set coinciding with existing private law and not public law. Yet in light of our discussion of corrective justice this possibility must be regarded as remote; certainly no such specific and plausible theory of corrective justice is currently available.

The attempt to articulate what is distinctive about private law has not generated much interesting comment from public lawyers.[14] The principal effort of public law jurists has been aimed at articulating the normative foundation of public law with little attention devoted to how that may differ from private law. One of the most interesting British scholars to work this seam is Trevor Allan. Yet for all the interest of his substantive analysis of public law, his thoughts on how private and public law differ are clearly formulated *en passant*. So, for example, he is content to note some far from compelling technical distinctions some judges have offered and affirm that private law is the general framework within which public law and public powers operate.[15] He also notes that some have affirmed the constitutional pre-eminence of private law over public law, but this claim depends upon a far from secure conception of two allegedly different types of social and legal order.[16] Overall, his view of the distinction between private and public law is that it is somewhat vague and troublesome, his suspicion being that there might be more than one such distinction at work in public law itself.[17] There is no reason to doubt Allan's judgment on this matter. Indeed, from one so reflective and deeply immersed in both the case law and the jurisprudential literature of public law, the judgment must be taken seriously. Taking it thus serves

[14] 'Not much' does not mean 'none'. To the interesting efforts noted in Chapter 1 we must also add P. Cane, 'Public Law and Private Law: A Study of the Analysis and Use of a Legal Concept', ch. 3 of J. Eekelaar and J. Bell (eds.), *Oxford Essays in Jurisprudence: Third Series* (Oxford: Clarendon Press, 1987) and B. Zipursky, 'Philosophy of Private Law', ch.16 of J. Coleman and S. Shapiro (eds.), *The Oxford Handbook of Jurisprudence and Philosophy of Law* (Oxford: Clarendon Press, 2002).

[15] *Law, Liberty and Justice* (Oxford: Clarendon Press, 1993), pp. 127–130; the unpersuasive technical distinction is that public law remedies, unlike private law remedies, are 'inherently discretionary', a claim unencumbered by any specification of what either 'discretionary' or 'inherently' might mean.

[16] *Constitutional Justice* (Oxford: Clarendon Press, 2001), p. 33 (commenting upon the view of F. A. Hayek).

[17] Ibid, pp. 10–11.

to reinforce, although such reinforcement is plainly unnecessary, the difficulty of distinguishing private and public law.

The apparently intractable nature of this difficulty can give rise to a sceptical question: why bother? Although laziness might motivate this question, it can also have respectable intellectual grounds. For it might be thought that it is so difficult to distinguish private and public law because they are actually indistinguishable. Dawn Oliver has offered an argument to this effect.[18] It holds that, since private and public law have a similar function (they are concerned to regulate the exercise of power), and both have a number of values in common (such as respect for the interests of individuals), they should be regarded as being or becoming one and the same.[19] For Oliver the two bodies of law are in the process of becoming integrated: it is therefore no longer possible or valuable to attempt to draw a significant distinction between them.[20] This argument is worked out in detail with respect to a number of areas of public and private law doctrine.

There is, however, room to question what the argument actually shows. For it is surely no great surprise that the law – be it public, private or criminal – is animated by a limited set of values, some of which, when sketched at a suitably abstract level, are seemingly in play everywhere. Given the myriad links that exist between almost all areas of any actual legal system and the positive morality of the society of which that system is a part, this much can be expected. Furthermore, the broad similarity in terms of both function and values between private and public law does not in any way block an argument that the two are nevertheless significantly different. Noting the obvious similarity between a domestic tabby cat and a tiger clearly provides no rationale for regarding them as exactly the same in all contexts. Physiological similarities might, of course, justify the same treatment of both tabbies and tigers by veterinarians. But such similarities clearly do not require that we react in the same way when faced with a tabby and a tiger. In this context the significant difference between these two roughly similar creatures is, of course, that one can kill and eat humans while the other cannot (or not without a great deal of additional help). As a general point, then, it seems that there can be significant differences even in the midst of similarities; showing the similarities between public and private law is not therefore an unimpeachable way of denying differences.

[18] *Common Values and the Public-Private Divide* (London: Butterworths, 1999).

[19] Ibid, chs 1–3.

[20] Ibid, pp. 248–250.

Is there any plausible answer to the question 'what makes private law private?' There might well be, but nothing like a fully-fledged answer has emerged in this book to either this question or to its close relative, 'what makes public law public?' All but one of the answers canvassed here and in Chapter 1 are unsatisfactory and that remaining answer hardly deserves that unambiguous label. To call it an 'answer' implies something far more definite and much better worked out than the very tentative suggestion actually provided. The suggestion, remember, was that the distinction between public and private law might become fundamentally important only in light of a normative argument showing both: (i) the moral and political significance of a realm of private project pursuit; and (ii) the importance of giving that realm legal protection, the most obvious legal domain for that end being private law. An argument such as this need not, of course, be committed to the wildly implausible view that there is one and only one distinction between 'the public' and 'the private'.[21] Nor must it be ignorant of the purpose of the distinction it draws: there is thus no pretence or assumption that the distinction defended is in some sense part of the natural fabric of the world reflecting neither particular moral and political interests nor a more general political world view.[22] The principal problem with this argument, for present purposes, is that it awaits proper formulation; it has not, in other words, been unpacked in anything close to an acceptable manner. Ultimately it must be completely unpacked and defended, but that task is one of many not undertaken here. This question, then, remains unanswered.

[21] If a reminder of the implausibility of this view is needed, see the essays in M. Passerin d'Entreves and U. Vogel (eds.), *Public and Private* (London: Routledge, 2000).

[22] A point well brought out in R. Geuss, *Public Goods, Private Goods* (Princeton: Princeton University Press, 2001).

Index